The New Testament: The History of the Investigation of Its Problems

The New Testament

The History of the Investigation of Its Problems

Werner Georg Kümmel

SCM PRESS LTD

Translated by S. McLean Gilmour and Howard C. Kee
from the German
Das neue Testament: Geschichte der Erforschung seiner Probleme
(Copyright © 1970, Verlag Karl Alber)

334 01130 2

First British edition 1973
published by SCM Press Ltd.
56 Bloomsbury Street London

Translation © Abingdon Press 1972

Typeset in the United States of America
Printed in Great Britain by
Redwood Press Limited
Trowbridge, Wiltshire

CONTENTS

Preface to the First Edition

A problem-oriented history of research has the task of exhibiting the basic lines of inquiry which have arisen during the course of change in investigating a body of subject matter. In accordance with the goal of the series [ORBIS ACADEMICUS] of which this study is a part, the history of New Testament research problems which is here set forth therefore does not present the entire history of New Testament study, but limits itself deliberately to the delineation of the lines of inquiry and the methods which have proved to be of permanent significance or to anticipate future developments. Such a limitation requires a selection which must ignore many researchers and much research because, while they certainly made contributions to our knowledge in matters of detail, they did not further the major lines of inquiry.

The task of such a problem-oriented history of problems, however, makes still another limitation necessary. Whether a new line of inquiry was permanently important and was later to prove fruitful cannot easily be determined for the period of research to which we ourselves belong. Consequently, with the consent of the editor of this series I have traced the new lines of inquiry only into the first decade of the period after World War I, lines of inquiry in pursuit of which we are still engaged today. And I have made detailed citation only of scholars who have already exceeded the biblical span of years and whose lifework therefore is already largely a matter of record. Nevertheless, references in the notes will offer the reader the possibility of orienting himself to further work on individual problems.

The excerpts are reproduced in the original form and spelling or are translated as literally as possible. Explanatory matter on my part has been included in the text within square brackets*; all other additions to the text of the excerpts come from the several authors.

* Translator's note: Square brackets in this translation are also used to set off material translated from some other edition than that which a given translator on occasion has used. In each instance reference is made in the respective note to this departure from the English source.

For help in securing access to material which was at times difficult to obtain—a good part of the older holdings of the University Library at Marburg was lost or destroyed during the course of World War II—I am indebted, in addition to the officials of the University Library and of the West German State Library at Marburg, above all to my assistant, Pastor Dr. Erich Graesser, and to cand. theol. et. phil. Renate Zinkhan. My colleague Friedrich Müller gave me friendly assistance in identifying the numerous citations from classical antiquity; information for the biographical appendix came to me from several quarters; and in the readying of the manuscript for the printer I was aided by my sons, stud. phil. Werner Kümmel and stud. phil. Hans Kümmel. A special expression of thanks is due my former pupil, Pastor Erich Arbenz, of Schiers (Graubünden), who undertook the burdensome task of preparing the indexes of names and subjects.

Marburg/Lahn, I May, 1958   Werner Georg Kümmel

Preface to the Second Edition

The text part of this second edition has remained in essentially unaltered form, although it has been checked through and improved where mistakes or inaccuracies appeared. On the whole however, it agrees with the first edition, even to the numbering of the pages of the text. On the other hand, the notes, the bibliography, and the biographical summaries have been completely revised and brought up to date in the present state of research. In spite of many requests, I have decided to abide by the limitation indicated in the preface to the first edition—that is, to describe research only up to 1930—since the reasons given there seem to me to be valid still. An extension of the history of New Testament problems in a somewhat different form may be found in my essay, "Die exegetische Erforschung des Neuen Testaments in diesem Jahrhundert," in the composite work, *Bilanz der Theologie im 20. Jahrhundert,* Vol. II, 1969, pp. 279 ff.

I have received notice of mistakes and omissions from different sources. Special thanks are due to Prof. Dr. S. M. Gilmour, Andover-Newton Theological School, Newton Center (Mass.), who in the course of translating the text proposed many improvements; and to my assistant, Dr. O. Merk, who stood by me tirelessly to avoid inaccuracies and to provide information; and to my colleagues, Dr. Karlhans Abel and Dr. Ernest-Wilhelm Kohls, who offered me valuable information.

Marburg/Lahn, November 17, 1969   Werner Georg Kümmel

Translator's Preface

When the late Professor S. McLean Gilmour died in 1969, he left a nearly complete typescript of his translation of W. G. Kümmel's history of New Testament research. The manuscript represented hundreds of hours of painstaking work, not only in the translating performed by Gilmour himself, but also in arranging for permission to reproduce existing translations of German works quoted by Dr. Kümmel. When premature death prevented him from seeing this task through to completion, the publisher, at the suggestion of the author, asked me to complete the translation. I agreed to do so with the understanding that all that remained to be done were the notes and the biographical material. On reading through the main body of the translation, however, it seemed necessary to make numerous modifications, both in the material that had been freshly translated and in the translations utilized by Professor Gilmour. Most of the changes were stylistic in nature; many were checked at first hand with Professor Kümmel, who encouraged me to carry out these revisions. The basic translation remains that of Dr. Gilmour, while the rendering of the elliptical and compressed language of the notes and appendix is my own. I am obligated for assistance on church historical matters to Professor Edward Dowey of Princeton Seminary and to Provost Gerhard Spiegler of Haverford College. On translation questions, my Bryn Mawr colleagues, Professors Nancy Dorian and James Scott, have offered welcome advice.

I have followed the pattern set by Gilmour of translating the titles of all non-English-language works mentioned in the text and in the notes, except where the correspondence between the two languages is so close as to make the meaning self-evident. For the most part, an attempt has been made to offer in the translation idiomatic equivalents, but for technical terms for which English offers no precise counterpart a literal rendering has been employed. Thus "history-of-religions" translates both the nominal *Religionsgeschichte* and the adjectival *religionsgeschichtlich*, except where ambiguity would result, in which case the awkward "religio-historical" has been allowed to stand. Explanations concerning the academic titles used in Germany are offered in the introductory paragraph preceding the biographical appendix.

References to the pages in the second edition of the German original have not been included, on the assumption that (1) a non-German reader would not find them helpful, and (2) that the index of names, which includes references to both pages of the text and to the notes, corresponds so closely to the index in the German original that the equivalent passages can be easily located. My student assistants at Bryn Mawr, Miss Vicky Scott and Miss Carolyne Tordiglione, have prepared the index for this edition.

It is to be hoped that the value of this compendious survey for all who are interested in tracing the history of New Testament interpretation, especially in the period since the rise of critical historical methods, will fully justify the protracted and arduous labor that has gone into making Professor Kümmel's monumental work available for English readers.

Thomas Library   Howard Clark Kee
Bryn Mawr College
Bryn Mawr, Pennsylvania

Part I
The Prehistory

1.
Ancient and Medieval

It is impossible to speak of a scientific view of the New Testament until the New Testament became the object of investigation as an independent body of literature with historical interest, as a collection of writings that could be considered apart from the Old Testament and without dogmatic or creedal bias. Since such a view began to prevail only during the course of the eighteenth century, earlier discussion of the New Testament can only be referred to as the prehistory of New Testament scholarship. It is true, of course, that the writings of the New Testament were expounded in countless commentaries from the time of the earliest church fathers and that thereby much historical knowledge and also many a relevant insight were handed on or discovered. But even where a special effort was made in such exposition to be true to the literal sense of the text, as, for instance, by the School of Antioch during the fourth and fifth centuries; such exegesis was not undertaken with any conscious historical purpose and was also preserved only within the framework of ecclesiastical tradition. Consequently, it is improper to speak of scientific study of the New Testament or of a historical approach to primitive Christianity prior to the Enlightenment.

Only in one respect did the ancient church begin to raise historical questions concerning the New Testament writings. When it began to place early Christian writings as authoritative documents alongside the Holy Scripture it had taken over from the Jews and in the course of so doing began to inquire by what standard those that were to be acknowledged as authoritative were to be separated from those that were to be rejected, the question of the authorship of a defined group of early Christian writings took over the center of theological interest. However, even before it had begun to pursue such investigations, the great "heretic" **Marcion,** about the middle of the second century, had given his splinter church a closed canon—one that consisted of a severely altered Gospel of Luke and of ten equally severely reworked letters of Paul. Furthermore, brief explanatory notes were prefixed to this collection of Paul's letters which gave an account of the origin of these ten Pauline documents. Later, the notes also passed over into the Latin ecclesiastical manuscripts of Paul's letters. In these "prologues" not only was an answer given to the question that Marcion regarded as most important, viz., the polemical purpose of the letters, but also to purely historical questions concerning the places of composition and the addresses of these letters. The medieval church was made familiar with this kind of historical issue by means of manuscripts of the Vulgate. Not all statements so transmitted are taken from Paul's letters themselves. Some are based either on independent tradition or on deduction. Accordingly, in this respect this very ancient text anticipates a historical concern that was not to reemerge until much later.[1]

The Romans live in Italian territory. They were deceived by false prophets and under the name of our Lord Jesus Christ had been led astray to the Law and the Prophets. Writing to them from Corinth, the apostle recalls them to the true evangelical faith.

The Corinthians are Achaeans. And they too in like manner listened to the word of truth from the apostles and in many respects were corrupted by false prophets, some deceived by the wordy rhetoric of philosophy, others by the sects of the Jewish Law. Writing to them from Ephesus by Timothy, the apostle recalls them to the true and evangelical wisdom.

The Colossians, like the Laodiceans, are also residents of Asia Minor. And, although they also had been led astray by false apostles, the apostle did not personally come to them, but also corrects them by a letter. They on their part had heard the word from Archippus, who also had accepted the ministry to them. Consequently the apostle, already a prisoner, writes to them from Ephesus.

The Thessalonians are Macedonians in Christ Jesus who, having accepted the word of truth, persevered in the faith, even when persecuted by their fellow-citizens; moreover, they did not accept what was said by the false apostles. Writing to them from Athens, the apostle praises them.

Though these "prologues" raised questions about matters of fact, they were only concerned with facts that lent themselves to unequivocal corroboration. However, when the orthodox church on its part set about making up its mind concerning the question of which early Christian writings were to be included in the new canon, the decisive criterion it employed was whether a writing had an "apostolic" author or not.[2] Now, not all the writings that were later given final canonical status in the New Testament make a clear statement of authorship, or even clearly designate their authors as "apostles." Moreover, in the case of some writings the problem arises in connection with the matter of authorship whether, in view of their style or content, they can come from the writer, known to us from other writings, to whom tradition attributes them. This accounts for the fact that, in connection with this peculiarly ecclesiastical difficulty of defining the canon, the historical question about the author of an early Christian writing had to be enlarged to include that of the correctness of a traditional ascription of authorship. The first to raise this question was the great exegete and textual critic Origen (ca. 185-254), and he did so concerning the Letter to the Hebrews, in so doing making special use of style criticism.[3]

> That the character of the diction of the epistle entitled To the Hebrews has not the apostle's rudeness in speech, who confessed himself rude in speech [II Cor. 11:6], that is, in style, but that the epistle is better Greek in the framing of its diction, will be admitted by everyone who is able to discern differences of style. But again, on the other hand, that the thoughts of the epistle are admirable, and not inferior to the acknowledged writings of the apostle, to this also everyone will consent as true who has given attention to reading the apostle. . . .
> But as for myself, if I were to state my own opinion, I should say that the thoughts are the apostle's, but that the style and composition belong to one who called to mind the apostle's teaching and, as it were, paraphrases what his master said. If any church, therefore, holds this epistle as Paul's, let it be commended for this also. For not without reason have the men of old time handed it down as Paul's. But who wrote the epistle, in truth God knows. Yet the account which has reached us [is twofold], some saying that Clement, who was bishop of the Romans, wrote the epistle, others, that it was Luke, he who wrote the Gospel and the Acts.

As the passage quoted above makes evident, Origen clearly recognizes the impossibility on stylistic grounds of ascribing the Epistle to the Hebrews to Paul. Nevertheless, since many churches hold a contrary opinion, he does not draw any unequivocal conclusions and thereby indicates that he does not believe that historical criticism can deliver a final judgment.

It was otherwise with his student, **Dionysius of Alexandria** (bishop, ca. 247-65). Both by stressing the linguistic and stylistic differences between the Revelation and the other Johannine writings and by demonstrating the altogether different manner by which their respective authors characterize themselves, Dionysius furnished completely convincing proof that the Revelation to John could not have been written by the author of the Gospel and the Letters of John and consequently that, unlike these latter, it is not "apostolic" in origin. It is true that in advancing this proof Dionysius was motivated by considerations of church politics. By excluding Revelation from the Canon he hoped to undermine the biblical support for an apocalyptic heresy (chiliasm). Nonetheless, the fact remains that he advanced a genuinely historical argument and, in so doing, asserted more clearly than his teacher Origen the validity of historical criticism.[4]

Some indeed of those before our time rejected and altogether impugned the book, picking it to pieces chapter by chapter and declaring it to be unintelligible and illogical, and its title false. For they say that it is not John's, no, nor yet an apocalypse (unveiling), since it is veiled by its heavy, thick curtain of unintelligibility; and that the author of this book was not only not one of the apostles, nor even one of the saints or those belonging to the Church, but Cerinthus, the same who created the sect called "Cerinthian" after him, since he desired to affix to his own forgery a name worthy of credit. . . .

But for my part I should not dare to reject the book, since many brethren hold it in estimation; but, reckoning that my perception is inadequate to form an opinion concerning it, I hold that the interpretation of each several passage is in some way hidden and more wonderful [than appears on the surface]. For even although I do not understand it, yet I suspect that some deeper meaning underlies the words. For I do not measure and judge these things by my own reasoning, but, assigning to faith the greater value, I have come to the conclusion that they are too high for my comprehension, and I do not reject what I have not understood, but I rather wonder that I did not indeed see them. . . .

After completing the whole, one might say, of his prophecy, the prophet calls those blessed who observe it, and indeed himself also; for he says: "Blessed is he that keepeth the words of the prophecy of this book, and I John, he that saw and heard these things" [Rev. 22:7-8]. That, then, he was certainly named John and that this book is by one John, I will not gainsay; for I fully allow that it is the work of some holy and inspired person. But I should not readily agree that he was the apostle, the son of Zebedee, the brother of James, whose are the Gospel entitled According to John and the Catholic Epistle. For I form my judgment from the character of each and from the nature of the language and from what is known as the general construction of the book, that [the John therein mentioned] is not the same. For the evangelist nowhere adds his name, nor yet proclaims himself, throughout either the Gospel or the Epistles. . . .

John nowhere [mentions his own name], either in the first or the third person. But he who wrote the Apocalypse at the very beginning puts himself forward: "The Revelation of Jesus Christ, which he gave him to show unto his servants quickly, and he sent and signified it by sending his angel to his servant John; who bore witness of the word of God and his testimony, even of all things that he saw." . . . "John to the seven churches which are in Asia; Grace to you and peace" [Rev. 1:1-2, 4]. But the evangelist did not write his name even at the beginning of the Catholic Epistle, but without anything superfluous began with the mystery itself of the divine revelation: "That which was from the beginning, that which we have heard, that which we have seen with our eyes." . . . Nay, not even in the second and third extant epistles of John, although they are short, is John set forth by name; but he has written "the elder," without giving his name. But this writer did not even consider it sufficient, having once mentioned his name to narrate what follows, but he takes up his name again: "I John, your brother and partaker with you in the tribulation and kingdom and in the patience of Jesus, was in the isle that is called Patmos, for the word of God and the testimony of Jesus" [Rev. 1:9]. Moreover at the close he speaks thus: "Blessed is he that keepeth the words of the prophecy of this book, and I John, he that saw and heard these things" [Rev. 22:7-8].

16

That the writer of these words, therefore, was John, one must believe, since he says it. But what John, is not clear. For he did not say that he was, as is frequently said in the Gospel, the disciple loved by the Lord, nor he which leaned back on His breast, nor the brother of James, nor the eye-witness and hearer of the Lord. For he would have mentioned some one of these aforesaid epithets, had he wished to make himself clearly known. Yet he makes use of none of them, but speaks of himself as our brother and partaker with us, and a witness of Jesus, and blessed in seeing and hearing the revelations. I hold that there have been many persons of the same name as John the apostle, who for the love they bore him, and because they admired and esteemed him and wished to be loved, as he was, of the Lord, were glad to take also the same name after him; just as Paul, and for that matter Peter too, is a common name among boys of believing parents. So then, there is also another John in the Acts of the Apostles, whose surname was Mark, whom Barnabas and Paul took with themselves [Acts 12:25], concerning whom also the Scripture says again: "And they had also John as their attendant" [Acts 13:5]. But as to whether it were he who was the writer, I should say No. For it is written that he did not arrive in Asia along with them, but "having set sail," the Scripture says, "from Paphos Paul and his company came to Perga in Pamphylia; and John departed from them and returned to Jerusalem" [Acts 13:13]. But I think there was a certain other [John] among those that were in Asia, since it is said both that there were two tombs at Ephesus, and that each of the two is said to be John's.

And from the conceptions too, and from the ideas and the word order, one might naturally assume that this writer was a different person from the other. For there is indeed a mutual agreement between the Gospel and the Epistle, and they begin alike. The one says: "In the beginning was the Word"; the other: "That which was from the beginning." The one says: "And the Word became flesh, and dwelt among us (and we beheld his glory, glory as of the only-begotten from the father)" [John 1:14]; the other, the same words slightly changed: "That which we have heard, that which we have seen with our eyes, that which we beheld, and our hands handled, concerning the Word of life; and the life was manifested" [I John 1:1]. For these words he employs as a prelude, since he is aiming, as he shows in what follows, at those who were asserting that the Lord has not come in the flesh. Therefore he was careful also to add: "And that which we have seen, we bear witness, and declare unto you the life, the eternal life, which was with the Father, and was manifested unto us; that which we have seen and heard, declare we unto you also" [I John 1:2-3]. He is consistent with himself and does not depart from what he has proposed, but proceeds throughout under the same main ideas and expressions, certain of which we shall mention concisely. But the attentive reader will find frequently in one and the other "the life," "the light," "turning from darkness"; continually "the truth," "the grace," "the joy," "the flesh and blood of the Lord," "the judgment," "the forgiveness of sins," "the love of God toward us," the "commandment" that we should "love one another," that we should "keep all the commandments"; the "conviction" of "the world," of "the devil," of "the antichrist"; "the promise of the Holy Spirit"; "the adoption of the sons of God"; the "faith" that is demanded of us throughout; "the Father" and "the Son": these are to be found everywhere. In a word, it is obvious that those who observe their character throughout will see at a glance that the Gospel and Epistle are inseparably in complete agreement. But the Apocalypse is utterly different from, and foreign to, these writings; it has no connexion, no affinity, in any way with them; it scarcely, so to speak, has even a syllable in common with them. Nay more, neither does the Epistle (not to speak of the Gospel) contain any mention or reference to the Apocalypse, nor the Apocalypse of the Epistle, whereas Paul in his epistles gave us a little light also on his revelations, which he did not record in a separate document.

And further, by means of the style one can estimate the difference between the Gospel and Epistle and the Apocalypse. For the former are not only written in faultless Greek, but also show the greatest literary skill in their diction, their reasonings, and the constructions in which they are expressed. There is a complete absence of any barbarous word, or solecism, or any vulgarism whatever. For their author had, as it seems, both kinds of word by the free gift of the Lord, the word of knowledge and the word of speech. But I will not deny that the other writer had seen revelations and received knowledge and prophecy; nevertheless I observe his style and that his use of the Greek language is not accurate, but that he employs uncultivated idioms, in some places committing downright solecisms. These there is no necessity to single out now. For I have not said these things in mockery (let no one think it), but merely to establish the dissimilarity of these writings.

The question of the "apostolic" authorship of a few New Testament writings that were finally canonized continued to be discussed in the ancient church until the beginning of the fifth century, but was nowhere treated again with the methodical clarity of Origen and Dionysius. Furthermore, the ancient church—and the medieval church, for that matter—ceased to pursue such historical inquiry. Nevertheless, **Eusebius** (who died in 339), the "Father of Church History," in addition to the remarks of Origen and Dionysius that have already been quoted, preserved numerous other accounts of disputes about the authorship of a few New Testament writings, accounts that become familiar to the medieval church by way of the Latin translation of his *Ecclesiastical History*. And, somewhat later, **Jerome** *(ca. 340-420)*, the great compiler of the Latin Church, in his list of authors entitled "Lives of Illustrious Men," an essay heavily indebted to Eusebius, noted in his catalog of the several "apostles," which of the writings credited to them had been disputed by many Christians. The great authority of Jerome was such that at least the fact was known into the Middle Ages that the question of the authorship of a few New Testament writings had once been debated.[5]

Simon Peter . . . wrote two epistles which are called catholic, the second of which, on account of its difference from the first in style, is considered by many not to be by him. Then too the Gospel according to Mark, who was his disciple and interpreter, is ascribed to him.

James . . . wrote a single epistle, which is reckoned among the seven Catholic Epistles and even this is claimed by some to have been issued by someone else under his name, and gradually, as time went on, to have gained authority.

Jude the brother of James, left a short epistle which is reckoned among the seven Catholic Epistles, and because in it he quotes from the apocryphal Book of Enoch it is rejected by many. Nevertheless by age and use it has gained authority and is reckoned among the Holy Scriptures.

The epistle which is called the Epistle to the Hebrews is not considered [Paul's], on account of its difference from the others in style and language, but it is reckoned, either according to Tertullian to be the work of Barnabas, or according to others, to be by Luke the Evangelist or Clement (afterwards bishop of the church at Rome) who, they say, arranged and adorned the ideas of Paul in his own language, though to be sure, since Paul was writing to Hebrews and was in disrepute among them he may have omitted his name from the salutation on this account. He being a Hebrew wrote Hebrew—that is, in his own tongue and most fluently—while the things which were written well in Hebrew were even more eloquently turned into Greek and this is the reason why it seems to differ from other epistles of Paul.

John, the apostle whom Jesus loved . . . wrote also one *epistle* which begins as follows, "That which was from the beginning, that which we have heard, that which we have seen with our eyes and our hands handled concerning the word of life" which is esteemed by all men who are interested in the church or in learning. The other two of which the first is, "The elder to the elect lady and her children," and the other, "The elder unto Gaius the beloved whom I love in truth," are said to be the work of John the presbyter to the memory of whom another sepulchre is shown at Ephesus to the present day.

As we have noted above, the Middle Ages had some knowledge of a historical questioning of the New Testament writings on the part of the ancient church, and the prologues to Bible manuscripts also handed on some information about the conditions under which the writings came into being. However, because the New Testament, like the Bible as a whole, was regarded only as part of the ecclesiastical tradition, the question of the conditions of origin and of the historical peculiarity of the individual writings of the New Testament could not come under scrutiny until the end of the Middle Ages. And in this respect humanism made no essential change. It is true, of course, that the Vulgate, the ecclesiastically sanctioned Latin translation of the New Testament, was subjected to criticism by such humanists as Laurentius Valla and Desiderius Erasmus.[6] And not only Erasmus, but also Cardinal Cajetan, the man who as papal legate tried to compel Luther to recant at the Diet of Augsburg (1518), were stimulated by Jerome to renew the ancient church's criticial assessment of the writings that were disputed in antiquity.[7] Nevertheless, the interest in sources that was manifested in all this, and the greater emphasis laid by the ancient church on criticism as compared with that of the Middle Ages, were insufficient to lead to a consistently historical inquiry. In the end Erasmus declared himself ready to submit to the judgment of the Church if it were to contradict his own;[8] and in its fourth decree the Council of Trent (1546) expressly condemned Cajetan's critical views, with the consequence that they could no longer be represented within the confines of the Catholic Church.[9]

2.

The Period of the Reformation

As we have seen, humanism was unable to call a genuinely historical criticism of the New Testament into being within the framework of the Catholic Church. However, in connection with the theology of the Reformation three fundamental observations were made, though to be sure their revolutionary consequences for New Testament research did not at first become apparent.

In the first place we draw attention to the basic recognition of the Reformers that it is not the Church and not the pope who can determine the sense of Holy Scripture, but that Holy Scripture is the only and final source of revelation for Christians; and that consequently Scripture is to be explained by Scripture itself. During the altercation with Cajetan and Eck (1518-19) at the Diet of Augsburg and at the debate at Leipzig Martin Luther, in the course of disputing the authority of the councils, reached the conviction that only Scripture could impart the truth of God. Then, in a form that was to have worldwide historical consequences, he articulated this insight at the end of his address in defense of himself to the Diet of Worms (1521), and repeated it still later in his confession published in 1538 (the so-called Smalcald Articles.) [10]

The Holy Scriptures must needs be clearer, easier of interpretation, and more certain than any other scriptures, for all teachers prove their statements by them, as by clearer and more stable writings, and wish their own writings to be established and explained by them. But no one can ever prove a dark saying by one that is still darker: therefore, necessity compels us to run to the Bible with all the writings of the doctors, and thence to get our verdict and judgment upon them; for Scripture alone is the true over-lord and master of all writings and doctrines on earth. If not, what are the Scriptures good for? Let us reject them and be satisfied with the human books and teachers.

Here I answered:

"Since then your serene majesty and your lordships seeks a simple answer, I will give it in this manner, neither horned nor toothed: Unless I am convinced by the testimony of the Scriptures or by clear reason (for I do not trust either in the pope or in councils alone, since it is well known that they have often erred and contradicted themselves), I am bound by the Scriptures I have quoted and my conscience is captive to the Word of God. I cannot and will not retract anything, since it is neither safe nor right to go against conscience.

"I cannot do otherwise, here I stand, may God help me, Amen."

A deed or word of the Holy Fathers cannot be made an article of faith. Otherwise whatever of food, clothes, houses, etc. they had would have to become an article of faith, as has happened with their relics. It is the Word of God that is to determine an article of faith—nothing else, not even an angel.

And about the same time (1520) for **Huldreich Zwingli** the Word of God had become the only vehicle—and a vehicle effective in its own right—of the renewal of world and Church.[11]

Now if we have found that the inward man is as stated, and that it delights in the law of God because it is created in the divine image in order to have fellowship with him, it follows necessarily that there is no law or word which will give greater delight to the inward man than the Word of God. For according to the saying of Isaiah 28, "the bed is shorter than that the adulterer can stretch himself on it, and the covering narrower than that he can wrap himself in it." That is, God is the bridegroom and husband of the soul. He wills that it should remain inviolate, for he cannot allow any other to be loved—that is, to be as highly esteemed and precious—as he is. Nor does he will that the soul should seek comfort anywhere but in him, or allow any other word to minister comfort but his Word. For in the same way it is the husband's will that the wife should cleave only to him, lavishing all her care upon him and seeking no other comfort but that which he can give.

When the children of Israel were at their worst, in the days of Sodom and Nineveh, and the whole world in the days of Noah, [God] sent prophets and his Word to them, and those who changed their ways survived, while those who despised his Word were miserably exterminated or imprisoned. In our time do we not see the world in all lands and stations so evil that we shudder at the sight? But, since the Word of God now appears in the midst of all the evil, do we not see that this is the act of God, who does not will that his creatures, whom he had purchased and paid for with his own blood, should be lost miserably and en masse?

In this way the Bible, which had hitherto been tacitly understood as an expression of the teaching of the Church, was suddenly set apart and the religious interest so directed to its proper understanding that biblical exegesis came to occupy the center of attention as the most important task of all theological activity. And, since the Bible could no longer have its assured meaning imposed on it from without, it had to be explained wholly from within, and even as early as 1519 Luther had given this recognition its classic formulation, viz., that the Bible must be its own interpreter.[12]

Furthermore, since we believe that the Holy Catholic Church has the same Spirit of faith that it received at its beginning, why should it not be permitted

21

today to study the Holy Scripture, either alone or above all else, as the early church was permitted so to do? For early Christians had not read Augustine or Thomas. Or tell me, if you can, what judge can decide the question, whether the statements of the church fathers have contradicted themselves. As a matter of fact, a judgment must be pronounced by making Scripture the judge, something that is impossible if we do not accord primacy to Scripture in all questions that are referred to the church fathers. This means that [Scripture] itself by itself is the most unequivocal, the most accessible [facillima], the most comprehensible authority, itself its own interpreter [sui ipsius interpres], attesting, judging, and illuminating all things, as Psalm 119 [vs. 130] affirms: "The explanation," or to render it more exactly in accordance with the Hebrew, "the opening or the door of thy words gives light and imparts understanding to the simple." Here the Spirit clearly grants illumination and teaches that insight is given only by the Word of God, as by a door or opening, or (to use a current phrase) as the first stage with which one must begin on the way to light and insight. Further: "The beginning and the head of thy words is truth" [Ps. 119:160]. You see that here also truth is imparted only to the "head" of the words of God; that is, if in the first instance you learn the words of God and use them as the point of departure in pronouncing judgment on all words.

This insight, fundamental in similar fashion to the thinking of all the Refomers, when consistently pursued, has to lead to a strictly historical exegesis of the Bible, and that particularly so since by Luther it was bound up with a second, no less significant, insight. From the medieval tradition Luther had been familiar with the method by which the early church had found in every biblical text a fourfold scriptural sense (literal, allegorical, moral, anagogical—having a spiritual meaning with reference to last things),[13] but as early as 1517 he had completely broken with it. More important, however, is the fact that Luther also more and more abandoned an allegorical explanation of Scripture and emphasized that the Word of God has but one meaning, a simple, unequivocal one, even though occasionally he still resorted to allegorical interpretations for devotional ends. And in the very placing of value on the single, literal sense of the text, Luther stood opposed to the humanistic tradition; this insight was a discovery peculiarly his own; he defended his practice both against his papist opponents and against Erasmus; and at the end of his life he expressly reiterated the hermeneutical principle.[14]

The Holy Spirit is the plainest writer and speaker in heaven and earth, and therefore His words cannot have more than one, and that the very simplest, sense, which we call the literal, ordinary, natural, sense. That the things indicated by the simple sense of His simple words should signify something further and different, and therefore one thing should always signify another, is more than a question of words or of language. For the same is true of all other things outside of the Scriptures, since all God's works and creatures are living signs and words of God, as St. Augustine and all the teachers declare. But we

22

are not on that account to say that the Scriptures or the Word of God have more than one meaning.

Now, is this matter of the free will to remain forever uncertain and undecided, as one that cannot be proven or refuted by any simple text, but only, with fabricated inferences and figures of speech, to be introduced, belabored, and driven hither and yon, like a reed in the wind, by people who are completely at odds with one another?

Consequently we may justly maintain that we are not to introduce any extraneous inferences or metaphorical, figurative sayings into any text of Scripture, unless the particulars of the words compel us to do so; unless the mind refuses to accept the simple words, e.g., if the text runs counter to other important passages of Scripture and its natural thrust and meaning, which the alphabetical symbol or the grammar and natural usage, as God created language among men, brings to utterance. For if anyone at all were to have power to depart from the pure, simple words and to make inferences and figures of speech wherever he wished, what else then would Scripture be but a reed that the wind tosses and blows about, or an unstable Proteus and Vertumnus which now would be this and then would be something else. If anyone at all were to have power to do this, no one could reach any certain conclusions about, or prove anything of, any article of faith which could not in this fashion (what I am saying is a *tropos* or biblical word that is not easy to comprehend) be contested . . . .

I have paid especial attention to the fact that all heresies and error in Scripture have not arisen out of the simple words of Scripture (although the Sophists have spread the byword throughout the whole world that the Bible is a heretical book), but that all error arises out of paying no regard to the plain words and, by fabricated inferences and figures of speech, concocting arbitrary interpretations in one's own brain.

The Doctor said: When I was young I was learned and, strange to say, before I became a theologian I busied myself with allegory, tropology, and analogy and did all sorts of silly juggler's tricks; if anyone had such a skill today he would consider it an amazing gift. I know that sort of thing is utter nonsense, and now I have given it up. This is the method I now employ, the final and best one: I convey the literal sense of Scripture, for in the literal sense there is life, comfort, strength, learning, and art. Other interpretations, however appealing, are the work of fools.

These two observations of Luther's inevitably pointed the way to a scientific approach that would with full seriousness deal with the New Testament in its historical peculiarity. But still more significant than this basic reevaluation of the position of the Bible within the whole field of theology—a reevaluation Luther shared with all the Reformers—was Luther's own discovery, which must have been made in course of translating the New Testament at Wartburg and which he articulated in the prefaces to this translation when it was published in September, 1522. From the writings of Eusebius and Jerome, Luther had learned, as had the humanists and Cajetan, that the early church had disputed over the admission of some writings into the canon because there was uncertainty as to their authorship by an "apostle." This questioning, which by itself can lead only to a literary judgment about the author and in this way gave occasion for doubting the canonical status of nonapostolic writings, Luther, with a hitherto unknown power of discernment, now sharpened into a tool of theological criticism. He pointed out that the statements of the Epistle to the Hebrews that a second repentance is impossible were incompatible with the demand for repentance in the Gospels and in Paul's letters; he noted that the teaching about justification in the Epistle of James is wholly incompatible with Pauline teaching (an observation he made again at a much later date in a Table Talk); he noted, further, the unquestionable facts that the Epistle of James lacks any real coherence and reflects an essentially Jewish framework of thought; and, on the basis of the prosaic nature of the rest of the New Testament, he criticized the fantastic character of the Revelation to John and the fact that it wholly ignores the central Christian message.[15]

Hitherto we have had the really certain chief books of the New Testament. But the four following [Hebrews, James, Jude, and Revelation] had, in ancient times, a different reputation. In the first place, that this Epistle [to the Hebrews] is not St. Paul's, nor any other apostle's is proved by the fact that it says, in chapter 2 [vs. 3], that this doctrine has come to us and remains among us through those who themselves heard it from the Lord. Thus it is clear that he speaks of the apostles as a disciple to whom this doctrine has come from the apostles, perhaps long after them. For St. Paul, in Galatians 1 [vs. 1], testifies mightily that he has his Gospel from no man, neither through men, but from God Himself.

Again, there is a hard knot to untie in the fact that in chapters 6 [vss. 4-6] and 10 [vs. 26] it flatly denies and forbids sinners repentance after baptism, and in chapter 12 [vs. 17], it says that Esau sought repentance and did not find it. This seems, as it stands, to be against all the Gospels and St. Paul's Epistles; and although one might make a gloss on it, the words are so clear that I do not know whether that would be sufficient. My opinion is that it is an epistle of many pieces put together, and it does not deal with any one subject in an orderly way. . . .

Who wrote it is not known, and will not be known for a while; it makes no difference. We should be satisfied with the doctrine that he bases so constantly on the Scriptures, showing a right fine grasp upon the reading of the Scriptures and the proper way to deal with them.

Preface to the Epistles of Saint James and Saint Jude

Though this Epistle of St. James was rejected by the ancients, I praise it and hold it a good book, because it sets up no doctrine of men and lays great stress upon God's law. But to state my own opinion about it, though without injury to anyone, I consider that it is not the writing of any apostle. My reasons are as follows.

First: Flatly against St. Paul and all the rest of Scripture, it ascribes righteousness to works, and says that Abraham was justified by his works, in that he offered his son Isaac [Jas. 2:21], though St. Paul, on the contrary, teaches, in Romans 4 [vss. 2-3], that Abraham was justified without works, by faith alone, before he offered his son, and proves it by Moses in Genesis 15 [vs. 6].

Now although this Epistle might be helped and a gloss be found for this works-righteousness, it cannot be defended against applying to works the saying of Moses of Genesis 15, which speaks only of Abraham's faith, and not of his works, as St. Paul shows in Romans 4. This fault, therefore, leads to the conclusion that it is not the work of any apostle.

Second: Its purpose is to teach Christians, and in all this long teaching it does not once mention the Passion, the Resurrection, or the Spirit of Christ. [The author] names Christ several times, but he teaches nothing about Him, and only speaks of common faith in God. For it is the duty of a true apostle to preach of the Passion and Resurrection and work of Christ, and thus lay the foundation of faith, as He himself says, in John 15 [vs. 27], "Ye shall bear witness of me." All the genuine sacred books agree in this, that all of them preach Christ and deal with Him. That is the true test, by which to judge all books, when we see whether they deal with Christ or not, since all the Scriptures show us Christ (Romans 3 [vss. 21 ff.]) and St. Paul will know nothing but Christ (I Corinthians 2 [vs. 2]). What does not teach Christ is not apostolic, even though St. Peter or Paul taught it; again, what preaches Christ would be apostolic, even though Judas, Annas, Pilate and Herod did it.

But this James does nothing more than impel [the reader] to the law and its works; and he mixes the two up in such disorderly fashion that it seems to me he must have been some good, pious man, who took some sayings of the apostles' disciples and threw them thus on paper; or perhaps they were written down by someone else from his preaching. He calls the law a "law of liberty" [1:25], though St. Paul calls it a law of slavery, of wrath, of death and of sin (Galatians 3 [vss. 23-24]; Romans 7 [vss. 11, 23]).

Moreover, in chapter 5, he quotes the sayings of St. Peter, "Love covereth the multitude of sins" (I Peter 4 [vs. 8] . . . and of St. Paul (Galatians 5 [vs. 17]), "The Spirit lusteth against hatred [against the flesh]"; and yet, in point of time, St. James was put to death by Herod, in Jerusalem, before St. Peter. So it seems that he came long after Sts. Peter and Paul.

In a word, he wants to guard against those who relied on faith without works, and is unequal to the task in spirit, thought, and words, and rends the Scriptures and thereby resists Paul and all Scripture, and would accomplish by insisting on the Law what the apostles accomplish by inciting men to love. Therefore, I cannot put him among the chief books, though I would not thereby prevent anyone from putting him where he pleases and estimating him as he pleases; for there are many good sayings in him. [One man alone is no man in worldly things. How, then, should this single individual avail against Paul and all the other Scriptures?]

Concerning the Epistle of St. Jude, no one can deny that it is an extract or copy from St. Peter's second epistle, so very like it are all the words. He also speaks of the apostles as a disciple coming long after them [vs. 17], and quotes sayings and stories that are found nowhere in the Scriptures. This moved the ancient Fathers to throw this Epistle out of the main body of the Scriptures. Moreover, Jude, the Apostle, did not go to Greek-speaking lands, but to Persia, as it is said, so that he did not write Greek. Therefore, although I praise the book, it is an epistle that need not be counted among the chief books, which are to lay the foundation of faith.

Preface to the Revelation of Saint John

About this book of the Revelation of John, I leave everyone free to hold his own ideas, and would bind no man to my opinion or judgment: I say what I feel. I miss more than one thing in this book, and this makes me hold it to be neither apostolic nor prophetic. First and foremost, the Apostles do not deal with visions, but prophesy in clear, plain words, as do Peter and Paul and Christ in the Gospel. For it befits the apostolic office to speak of Christ and His deeds without figures and visions but there is no prophet in the Old Testament, to say nothing of the New, who deals so out and out with visions and figures. And so I think of it almost as I do of the Fourth Book of Esdras, and I can in nothing detect that it was provided by the Holy Spirit.

Moreover, he seems to me to be going much too far when he commends his own book so highly,—more than any other of the sacred books do, though they are much more important,—and threatens that if anyone takes away anything from it, God will deal likewise with him, etc. [22:18-19]. Again, they are to be blessed who keep what is written therein; and yet no one knows what that is, to say nothing of keeping it. It is just the same as if we had it not, and there are many far better books for us to keep. Many of the fathers, too, rejected this book of old, though St. Jerome, to be sure, praises it highly and says that it is above all praise and that there are as many mysteries in it as words; though he cannot prove this at all, and his praise is, at many points, too mild.

Finally, let everyone think of it as his own spirit gives him to think. My spirit cannot fit itself into this book. There is one sufficient reason for me not to think highly of it,—Christ is not taught or known in it; but to teach Christ is the thing which an apostle above all else is bound, to do, as He says in Acts 1 [vs. 8], "Ye shall be my witnesses." Therefore I stick to the books which give me Christ, clearly and purely.

Many sweat hard at reconciling James with Paul, as, indeed, does Philip [Melanchthon] in the Apology, but unsuccessfully. "Faith justifies" stands in flat contradiction to "Faith does not justify." If anyone can harmonize these sayings, I'll put my doctor's cap on him and let him call me a fool.

From the beginning, Luther took these judgments so very seriously that, in contrast to the traditional arrangement, he put the four writings he had subjected to theological and historical attack (Hebrews, James, Jude, and Revelation) at the end of the New Testament (where they have remained in all editions of the Luther Bible) and did not enumerate them in the table of contents. And though in later editions he deleted or toned down the sharpest judgments on James and Revelation, he never altered this order of these four writings or listed them in his table of all the books of the Old and New Testaments.[16] In this way attention was drawn for the first time to the fact that within the New Testament there are material differences between the books of instruction—differences that cannot be reconciled—and as a consequence it became possible to observe the multiplicity of the ways of thinking and the historical genesis of the world of thought of the New Testament. But all this stood in marked tension with the presupposition of the Reformation that Scripture, explained by and of itself, is the sole and unambiguous medium of revelation. Consequently, Luther's personal discovery was virtually still-born and was quickly forgotten again.

But even the basic views of Holy Scripture that were common to all

Reformation theology, that Scripture is the only source of all revelation and that it has one, unambiguous meaning, could not at first exert any influence in the direction of a genuinely historical approach to the New Testament. To be sure, the Catholic Church at the Council of Trent (1546) had opposed to the Protestant view of Holy Scripture as the only source of revelation the dogmatic decree that the divine truth is contained "in the written books and the unwritten traditions which have come down to us" received by the apostles from the mouth of Christ himself or passed on as it were from hand to hand by the apostles at the dictation of the Holy Spirit, and that the writings of the Old and New Testaments and the oral tradition are "accepted and reverenced by the Church with the same pious emotion and respect (*pari pietatis affectu ac reverentia*) ." [17] Thereby the Catholic Church asserted that no contradiction could or should exist between Scripture and church doctrine and that, accordingly, Scripture could in no case be the only and sufficient source of revelation. Over against this the Protestants had to prove that Scripture alone is sufficient as a source of revelation and is wholly explicable by and of itself. And so, in opposition to the teaching of the Council of Trent, the first methodical examination of the proper interpretation of Scripture was undertaken, the *Key to the Scriptures* of **Matthaeus Flacius Illyricus** [18] that was published in 1567. This comprehensive work, which undertakes a methodical discussion of the problem of scriptural interpretation only in part two, therefore owes its origin to the attack of Catholic theology on the basic contention of the churches of the Reformation. But this investigation which goes far beyond this concrete occasion, represents the real beginning of scholarly hermeneutics, something that, despite all tentative beginnings within the orb of humanism, was only able to come into being within Protestantism.[19] The crucial contribution to this development was made by Flacius' first treatise, "On the Proper Way to Understand Holy Scripture," while the other treatises deal with style, parts of speech, and individual theological questions. But this first "hermeneutics," quite consciously taking its departure from Luther, actually shows why the basic views of the Reformers concerning the meaning of Holy Scripture and the method of understanding it were not yet able to bring about a really historical approach to the New Testament. As a student of humanism and in accord with Luther's views, Flacius not only lays down the rule that the grammatical sense must be expounded first and foremost, but he also admits a symbolic interpretation of a text only when the literal interpretation would be meaningless. And then, if all other possibilities are excluded, he accepts it as the only meaning. Consequently he wholly rejects the teaching of a multiple sense of Scripture, in the conviction that only so does exegesis maintain solid ground under its feet. And accordingly he quite rightly emphasizes that the individual text can confidently be explained only out of its special context and in light of the purpose indicated thereby, a conclusion that he admirably supports with the example of the various possible interpretations of Luke 7:47.[20]

Let the reader exert himself to comprehend the simple and original sense of the sacred writings, and, in particular, of the passage he happens to be reading. He is neither to pursue any shadows nor follow the phantoms of allegories or eschatological exposition [*anagoges*], unless the passage is manifestly an allegory and the literal sense in general is useless, or even absurd.

And therefore the literal sense, which others also call the historical or grammatical, must always be set forth first of all, as the noblest; for it alone leads to sure and clear meanings. It alone is suited to provide the arguments with which the dogmas of religion are supported. It alone provides the necessary proofs, whereas from allegorical or anagogical [interpretation] only probable and superficially serviceable [proofs] are produced. And one must never relinquish the simple and true sense of the words, except when a figurative [tropological] meaning is inherent in the words, or the saying, grammatically explained, signifies something absurd, so that one must have recourse to the allegorical interpretation. . . . Therefore I am very anxious that he who exercises diligence in working out the literal or grammatical sense be convinced that he is acting properly and wisely.

Already above I have reminded the reader that the purpose [*scopus*] both of Scripture as a whole and of its separate parts and passages must be most diligently noted; for thereby a marvelous light is cast for us on the meaning of the individual sayings. Let me cite an illuminating example of this: In the instance of the passage in Luke 7:47, "for she loved much," it is disputed whether the forgiveness of sins that is spoken of there is the cause or the effect of love. The Papists hold that it is the effect; we, the cause. This dispute could easily be settled in the following way, viz., by examining whether Christ, after the fashion of a teacher who instructs a docile disciple, there explains a few things and brings their causes or consequences to the attention of the Pharisee; or better, whether he asserts something assured in order to disprove the false opinion of the Pharisee, who regarded that woman as wholly unjust and, puffed up with his own righteousness, was amazed that Christ would have anything at all to do with such an unjust person. If he is only teaching an apt pupil, then naturally this saying, "for she loved much," shows that love is the cause of the forgiveness of sins. However, if the passage confutes the false opinion or reflection of the Pharisee and [the little sentence] is simply an assertion, then that little sentence contains the explanation or proof of the forgiveness or justification that has already taken place. But it is obvious that we have to do with an assertion, or a confutation of the Pharisee. It is one thing, however, to assert or to demonstrate something to a gainsaying adversary; it is quite another thing to teach an obedient and docile pupil and to explain to him the causes and effects of a matter.

It is clear that Flacius was quite aware that if the literal meaning of a biblical text is to be grasped it is necessary to understand the text in the sense that it conveyed to its original readers, and furthermore, to recognize the purpose that the biblical writer had in mind; in other words, to listen to what the text has to say. Accordingly, he combined the valid insights of the humanists with the attitude of the Reformers to the biblical text in a most pertinent fashion and pointed the way to a really historical approach to a study of the biblical texts.[21]

Further, since the true and literal sense properly has preeminence, one must be aware of what is required if one is to obtain it. For effort and study by themselves cannot grasp it completely or fully draw it out. Therefore it is my judgment that those who wish to concern themselves usefully with Holy Scripture must have a fourfold understanding of it.

The first [understanding seeks to ascertain] how the readers understood the individual words. This demands the best possible command of the sacred languages, above all of Hebrew, and then also of Greek. Without that, O Reader, you are necessarily dependent on the judgment of others, or you must guess at the meaning. Along with that you can easily mistake the interpreter's meaning if you do not at once take notice of what he had in mind or of how in the passage in question he has used or misused his words. — *① Verbal*

The second [understanding seeks to ascertain] how [the readers] understand the sense of the passage that is imparted by the words of the individual sentences. This is necessary, not only that the individual words may be understood, but also that what belongs together may be properly combined and what is to be separated may be separated. Only so [can one avoid] getting a false meaning from badly constructed sentences because of a mistaken combination or separation. These two methods of understanding the text can be assigned to grammar so that there is, as it were, a grammatical understanding of Scripture. *② Grammatical*

The third [understanding seeks to ascertain] how the hearers understand the spirit of him who speaks—be it the spirit of God, of a prophet, or an apostle, or of an evangelist. But I call spirit the reason, the understanding, the judgment, and the purpose of the speaker. In this way not only what is spoken becomes known, but also why and to what purpose it is spoken. Without this knowledge even he who understands the words and the meaning of the language still understands too little in Scripture. In this respect many are quite deficient, especially among the blind Jews, who so cling to the outer shell of the writing that they are quite incapable of comprehending the spirit of the most important passages of Scripture. This and the following understandings of Scripture can be summed up under one name, viz., the theological treatment of Scripture. *③ Theological*

The fourth [understanding seeks to ascertain] how the application of any given passage of Scripture is to be understood. For Scripture divinely inspired is useful for teaching, for clarification, for correction, and for instruction in righteousness, that the man of God may be perfect and equipped for every good work, II Tim. 3:16, 17. This understanding is assisted usually by assiduous and devout reading and especially by meditation. And in my judgment this method constitutes the most important function of reading Scripture. *④ Devotional*

Although this basic insight was correct, it was blurred and consequently deprived of real effect by two presuppositions which made a historical approach to the New Testament actually impossible. Because Scripture is the sole source of divine revelation and is to be explained from and by itself, it must be understood as a unity; it can exhibit no contradictions. Where such contradictions appear to be present, they rest on a false understanding of the texts.[22]

Nowhere is there a real contradiction in Scripture (as Quintilian points out concerning the laws [*Inst. orat.* VII. 7. 2]), but where there appears to be one, we are to assume that we and our great ignorance are to blame for the impression, either because we do not understand the matter or the discourse, or because we have not taken the circumstances sufficiently into consideration. Consequently, what appears in Scripture to contradict something else, when one fails to consider the causes, persons, times, and motives, actually is not contradictory when one gives due weight to the tacit or express difference of causes, motives, places, times, or persons.

This view is an inevitable consequence of faith in Scripture as the self-sufficient norm of belief. At the same time, however, it betrays the fact that the historical peculiarity of the New Testament as distinct from the Old is no more appreciated than the historical peculiarity of individual writings or authors within the New Testament. And "the limitations of this exegesis, which are rooted in the unhistorical and abstractly logical understanding of the principle of the whole body or canon of Scripture, come clearly to light."[23] Furthermore, it is at once apparent that this presupposition requires the application of a standard by which the correctness of the interpretation of every separate text within the framework of Scripture can be tested, and Flacius expressly declares that this standard is "agreement with the faith" (*analogia fidei*).[24]

Every understanding and exposition of Scripture is to be in agreement with the faith. Such [agreement] is, so to speak, the norm or limit of a sound faith, that we may not be thrust over the fence into the abyss by anything, either by a storm from without or by an attack from within (Rom. 12:6). For everything that is said concerning Scripture or on the basis of Scripture must be in agreement with all that the catechism declares or that is taught by the articles of faith.

Paul had said that even the early Christian prophet in his inspired utterance should speak only as a believer and had characterized such conduct as "agreement with the faith" (Rom. 12:6, "in proportion to our faith").[25] The Reformed theology had taken up this Pauline concept but had reinterpreted it to mean agreement with the traditional body of belief. Flacius, to be sure, omitted any more exact definition of the extent or the essence of these articles of faith because he saw in them nothing but the harmonious interpretation of self-explanatory Scripture.[26] Nevertheless, the demand that an understanding of a biblical text must conform to "the analogy of faith" actually robs the study of the content of Scripture of any real freedom to understand the meaning of Scripture in light of its historical setting and independently of traditional patterns of thought. The new insight of the Reformers that the Bible must be understood in a literal sense and that it is to be explained by itself could not lead to a strictly historical view of the New Testament so long as interpreters failed to recognize the historical character of the New Testament and the consequent necessity of investigating it historically and without prejudice.

For the time being, then, no really historical approach to the New Testament was possible. Nevertheless, in connection with the new attitude of Reformed theology towards the Bible some essential steps in the direction of a historical understanding of the New Testament still were taken. That this was done is above all to the credit of the evangelical humanist and great classical philologist **Joachim Camerarius**, who in 1572 published a commentary on selected passages from the New Testament. In this he refrained from ascribing any great importance to the traditional interpretation of the text by the church fathers, on the ground that the writers of the New Testament must be explained in light of their own times. As a matter of fact, in the introduction to this commentary he expressly declares that he wishes only to make the language of the New Testament author intelligible by observation of the language of the classical writers.[27]

Since in an effort to understand these writings [the New Testament] I have carefully reflected on the meaning of the words and the explanation of the sentences and in the course of reading authors of both languages [Greek and Latin] have endeavored to determine and observe what of importance they have to contribute to this understanding, I have been requested in past years to gather and publish what I have noted of this sort, not after the example of Erasmus or of anyone else, but in accordance with the method and manner of my profession, which is the study of grammar. The meanings of words and the explanations of forms of speech that I have noted in the Epistles of the Apostle Paul and the other canonical epistles I have therefore assembled in a book and have handed over for printing by us that they might be available to those who would like to get acquainted with them.

And Camerarius applied this principle to the extent that he wrote explanations of only those New Testament texts to whose explication he believed he could make some contribution. In the course of this exegesis, in addition to employing Greek and Latin classics, he paid special attention to the grammatical sense of the words and the relationship between the separate texts. In the case of I Pet. 3:19, an important and much disputed passage, he even refrained from making any comment, on the ground that it seemed to him that the text admitted of no certain explanation.[28]

"In those days" [Matt. 3:11]. Not in those days in which Joseph migrated to Nazareth, but a long time afterwards. Matthew's account actually passes over some twenty-five years, if it was actually at the beginning of the thirtieth year of his life that Jesus was baptized by John. "In those days," therefore, in which Jesus was still a resident of the town of Nazareth.

"To repent," however, has the meaning, "to change in heart and mind." That, of course, is a turning round from an earlier way of thinking and from things which now displease. If these things must now appear to him perverse and evil, he naturally repents of his former life. In his *Electra* [V. 570] Sophocles says of "repentance": "Do not yourself be the cause of calamity and of anything of which you must repent." In an epigram Ausonius says [*Epigr.* 33. 12, ed. by R. Peiper—the speaker is a goddess of that name] that not even Cicero gave "repentance" a Latin name. "That one may experience repentance," she says, "I am called *Metanoea* [the Greek word for 'repentance']." Using ecclesiastical terminology, however, translators have rendered the Greek into Latin by the Latin word for "repentance" [*poenitentia*]. But it is the doctrine of the Christian Church that explains what is the character and consequence of Christian change or repentance. "For the kingdom of heaven is at hand" is appended as the reason for this summons. Now ἤγγικε [has drawn near] is actually a past tense of the verb, but one that has a present meaning [is at hand], a phenomenon of the Greek language that can be observed in the instance of numerous Greek verbs.

"Born from above" [John 3:3]. In the writings of this evangelist as well as other authors the adverb ἄνωθεν means "from above," as a bit further on, "He who comes from above" [John 3:31]. And once again, "unless it had been given you from above" [John 19:11]. And in the *Melpomene*, Herodotus says [IV. 105] of serpents: "A host from above fell upon them out of the desert." And Theocritus says of a pipe that is skilfully constructed on all sides of wax of the same sort [Idyls VII. 19]: "the same beneath, the same from above." Nevertheless, the Greeks use this adverb also in a temporal sense, which the Latin translator renders "born anew [*denuo*]." Now, I readily admit that this latter interpretation is supported by the words in the letter of the apostle Peter: "Who by his great mercy has begotten us anew to a living hope through the resurrection of Jesus Christ from the dead" [I Pet. 1:3]. And further: "born anew, not of mortal and perishable but of immortal and imperishable seed" [I Pet. 1:23]. However, the meaning [of John 3:3] amounts to the same by either interpretation. Since man's origin is earthly, those namely who are born "from above," that is, divinely, are those who are born again, or born anew.

"To those in prison" [I Pet. 3:19]. Doubtless there is here an ellipsis for "to those who are in prison." But what sort of diction this is, or what it means in this citation, is wholly beyond my comprehension. Some Greeks have understood it to signify that Christ had already been a herald of the gospel before the deluge, though [only] in his spirit, that no disobedience might at any time be condemned by God except that against Christ. Consequently these [exegetes] interpret "to the spirits in prison" as a reference to the souls of those who at that time did not believe and who therefore now lie in prison or in a dungeon until Christ comes for judgment. However, Clement of Alexandria in his *Stromateis*, Book VI [45. 1-4, ed. Stählin]—followed in this respect by other Greeks—understood this proclamation of the gospel to be one Christ delivered after his death to those in the underworld on earth. This, accordingly, is one of those passages in Holy Writ concerning which scrupulous piety can make full enquiry and be uncertain as to what is said, without incurring censure, and concerning which, it would also appear, diverse meanings can be admitted, as long as there is no breach of the rule, "one must be of the same mind," that is, a pious agreement with respect to the faith [must be maintained], and as long as there is no departure "from the agreement with the faith" [ἀπὸ τῆς ἀναλογίας τῆς πίστεως—Rom. 12:6].

This incisive interpretation of the New Testament from the vantage point of classical authors, begun by Camerarius, was carried much further by **Hugo Grotius.** In his early youth Grotius had acquired a comprehensive knowledge of Greek and Latin literature (he was a pupil of the great philologist of the latter part of the sixteenth century, Joseph Scaliger) and in theological matters leaned in the direction of the Arminians, who were freer than the Reformed churchmen and critical of their dogmatics. From this standpoint Grotius, toward the end of his life, wrote his *Notes on the New Testament* (1641 pp.) , which, by abundant citation not only of classical but also of Hellenistic-Jewish literature and of the church fathers, was instrumental in preparing the way for an interpretation of the language and religious ideas of the New Testament in terms of their setting in the history of their own times. Furthermore, even when Grotius is unable to make any contribution to exegesis by means of such parallels, he occasionally succeeds, by careful examination of the textual history of a New Testament passage, or by nothing but contextual exegesis of it, in finding an interpretation that is still recognized as valid.[29]

The fact that the following words, "for thine is the kingdom and the power and the glory, forever," are not found in the oldest Greek manuscripts (though they are in the Syriac, the Latin, and the Arabic) provides us with the proof from which we learn that not only the Arabic and the Latin version, but also the Syriac were made after the liturgy of the churches had taken on a fixed form. For the doxology, according to the custom of the Greeks, began more and more to be appended in writing to the prayer, a fact that was unknown to all Latins. Furthermore, the "amen" appears also not to have been added by Christ, but is accounted for by the custom of the ancient church of using this word to give assent to a public recitation.

"And in Hades" [Luke 16:23]: This, if I am not mistaken, is the only passage in Holy Writ that lends any support to the belief of most people that the "place of torture" in a proper sense is called "Hades." But, as we have elsewhere pointed out [note on Matt. 16:18], the truth is that Hades is the place that is withdrawn from our sight: so far as the body is concerned, indeed, when it receives a grave in which the body lies without a soul, but so far as the soul is concerned, that whole sphere or condition in which the soul is without a body. The Rich Man, then, was in "Hades," but Lazarus also was in "Hades," for Hades is divided into various regions. For both Paradise and Hell, or, as the Greeks said, Elysium and Tartarus, are in "Hades." It is quite certain that the Greeks spoke in this way, and in the sixth book of the

Aeneid [vss. 637 ff.] Vergil conforms to this Greek practice.

> Diphylus says: "For two ways, we believe, lead to Hades, the one the way of the just, the other the way of the ungodly." [This passage cannot be located among the fragments of Diphylus' poetry that have been preserved.]

> The passage in Sophocles [Frag. 753] is also familiar: "Thrice fortunate are those of mortals who go to Hades after they have viewed these sacred rites; there for them alone is life, and there for all others, evil."

In like manner also Diodorus Siculus [I. 96. 4] explains "the mythical invention of Hades" as "the punishments of the ungodly" and "the flower gardens of the pious." Plato [Phaed. 69c] says: "Those who have handed down the sacred rites have said: Whoever goes to Hades unconsecrated and uninitiated will lie in filth; on the other hand, whoever arrives there purified will dwell with the gods."

Iamblichus also uses the word in this sense. And Plutarch speaks of Lucullus [Lucullus 44. 2] as "an old man in Hades." And Iamblichus, of whom we have just spoken, says the same [Protrepticus 9. 53, ed. Pistelli]. "As the wise among the poets say, we shall receive rewards for righteousness in Hades." That no one may be in any doubt about the Jews, I cite Josephus as surety, who declares that Samuel had been summoned "from Hades" [Antiq. VI. 332. 14, 2]. Similarly, where he speaks of the Sadducees he says (Bell. Jud. II. 165. 8, 14) : "They reject [the idea of] rewards and punishments in Hades." Where he describes the view of the Pharisees, the same [author says] [Antiq. XVIII. 14. 1, 3]: "They also believe in the immortality of souls and that they receive punishments and rewards under the earth, according as they have lived virtuously or evilly in this life; and that the latter are to be detained in an everlasting prison, while the former shall have power to revive and live again." It is clear that he [Josephus] locates both the punishments and the rewards of the soul in Hades, which same he speaks of as "under the earth," since the Greeks were accustomed to call those things in Hades "things under the earth." In like manner Zonoras [Epit. his. 6. 3c Dind.], in the course of explaining the view of the Pharisees, speaks of punishments under the earth, whether it be that Hades is thought of as actually under the earth, or whether, as is more probable, that it [Hades] be regarded as no less out of sight than that which the earth conceals in its remotest recesses. For this reason Plutarch says [De primo frigido 953. A] that "the inner core of the earth is called Chaos and Hades." Iamblichus speaks of "judgment under the earth" [the reference has not been located]. So also Pindar speaks of the Eleusinian Mysteries as follows: "Blessed is he who has viewed them and [then] goes under the earth; he knows the end of life, but [also] knows its god-given beginning" [Frag. 137, ed. Snell = Clement of Alexandria Strom. 3. 518]. Plutarch says with respect to the quotation from Homer [Iliad 16. 856], "His soul fled from his mouth [the precise meaning of the Greek word in this context is uncertain] and went down to Hades": "To an invisible and unseen spot, whether it be located in the air or under the earth." In Concerning the First Cold [De primo frigido 948. E] the same Plutarch [says]: "That which is invisible in the air bears the name Hades." In like manner, in Concerning the Proper Way of Living [De diaeta I. 4; VI. 474 Littré], Hippocrates contrasts "light" and "Hades." Even Josephus speaks in another passage, where he describes the opinions of the Essenes, as follows [Bell. Jud. II. 155. 8, 11]: "And their opinion is like that of [the latter-day?] Greeks, that good [souls] have their habitation beyond the ocean, in a region that is neither oppressed with storms of rain or snow, or with intense heat, but that this place is such as is refreshed by the gentle breathing of a west wind that is perpetually blowing from the ocean; while they allot to bad souls a dark and tempestuous den, full of never-ceasing punishments." Here he localizes Hades beyond the ocean. Again, in another passage [*Bell. Jud.* III. 374. 8, 5], Josephus, in line with the same way of thinking, allots the pious man a seat in "the holiest place of heaven." But it is [quite] certain that these ways of speaking—under the earth, in the air, beyond the ocean, and what according to Tertullian is beyond the fiery zone—designate nothing else than the "invisible," which to us is inaccessible. Likewise, in his *Concerning the Soul* [chap. 58], Tertullian locates [the place of] torment and [the place of] refreshment in the underworld: "During the interim let the soul be punished or refreshed in the same place, in the underworld, in expectation of judgment, whether of acquittal or of condemnation, and to some extent in the putting into effect and in the anticipation of this [judgment]." He expresses similar sentiments in his *Against Marcion* IV [chap. 24]. To this we add a passage from Ambrosius' *Concerning the Blessing of Death* (chap. 10 = Corp. Script. Eccles. Latin. 32. 1. 2. 741 ff.]: "It would be enough if one were to say to them [the philosophers] that the souls freed from their bodies long to reach Hades, that is, an invisible place that in Latin we call the underworld. Finally, also, Scripture has called those dwelling-places storehouses of the souls."

"[The kingdom of God] is in the midst of you" [Luke 17:21]: Already in your midst, that is, the kingdom of God begins to extend its powers among this very Jewish people, without becoming apparent to you. The mighty works are an evident sign of this state of affairs, above all, the driving out of demons. In Matt. 12:28 Christ speaks as follows to the same Pharisees: "But if it is by the Spirit of God that I cast out demons, then the kingdom of God has come upon you." Here, likewise, by the word "you" the whole people of the Jews is meant. The phrase "between you" is properly interpreted "in your midst." Cf. Matt. 21:43.

This rigorous exegesis of various passages in the New Testament in terms of their historical setting helped to prepare the way for a genuinely historical interpretation of the New Testament as a whole. However, the bold conjectures concerning the historical situation of some New Testament letters that Grotius advanced in the prefaces to his annotations were almost more significant. For what Grotius undertakes in these prefaces is to explain the inherent difficulties of a text on the assumptions that the text in the form in which it has been handed down does not correspond to the original, or that the traditional view concerning the time of composition or the authorship of a letter must be abandoned. To be specific, Grotius clearly noted the indisputable fact that Paul expected that the judgment of the world and the end of the present age would take place during his own lifetime. What is important in this connection is not whether Grotius' hypotheses are convincing (they are hardly that!), but that Grotius makes any use at all of historical conjecture as a tool of New Testament interpretation, and does so because he believes that only so can the historical setting of a New Testament document be clearly understood.[30]

Preface to the Second Letter to the Thessalonians

In my previously published discussion [in Vol. I] of a part of this letter ["On chap. 2 of the so-called Second Letter to the Thessalonians"] I said that it seemed to me probable that this was the earliest of the Pauline letters that have come down to us. There is a strong argument for this conjecture at the end of the letter [3:17], where the apostle expresses the hope that those to whom the letter is written will pay attention to what is a mark of his hand in signatures to letters, something he would hardly have done if this letter had already been preceded by another letter to Thessalonica. Furthermore, I said that this letter had not been written to those whom Paul had converted from among the Gentiles after he himself had come to Thessalonica, but to certain Jews who were among the first to join themselves to Christ and then, after the outbreak of the persecution after Stephen's death, made their way first to Syria (Acts 8:4; 11:19), and then to Cyprus and other places, among these latter Macedonia, the ancient fertile territory for Jewish trade. That this is the case is made apparent by chap. 2:13: "because God chose you from the beginning to be saved." For the phrase "from the beginning" obviously refers to the Jews, who in Eph. 1:12 are called "those who were the first to hope." Preeminent among these Jews to embrace the Christian religion was Jason, that is, Jesus (for the name Jason is the same as Jesus, just as Silas is the same as Silvanus), a relative of Silas and Timothy who later extended hospitality to Paul, Silas, and Timothy when they came to Thessalonica [Acts 17:5-6]. It seems, however, that Timothy's ancestors had [already] lived in Thessalonica in past times and that this is why in Acts 20:4 Timothy is reckoned among the Thessalonians. And since this church, drawn from among the Jews, constituted [only] a small proportion of the population of Thessalonica, it had consequently no presbytery and therefore orders were issued that any of them who did not live in accordance with the rules of Christ were to be shunned by the others [II Thess. 3:6, 14]. If a presbytery had been there at that time the offenders would have been excommunicated, as was the case with those at Corinth [I Cor. 5]. Since this was the state of affairs and the prophecies of Paul which are in the second chapter of this letter must relate to events that could happen within the space of a lifetime—in connection with three passages (cf. Grotius on I Thess. 4:15; I Cor. 15:52; II Cor. 5:3] we have already observed that Paul believed he could experience that last and universal judgment during the course of his own lifetime—I have concluded, having compared history with the prophecies, that the reference here is to none else than the emperor Caius [Caligula] and Simon Magus, whose acts correspond precisely to the words of the prophecy. According to the most exact chronologies, among which I reckon as best that of Dionysius Petavius, a man of true learning and piety, Saul, surnamed Paul, was converted to Christ in the thirty-sixth year of the reign of Tiberius. Thereafter Tiberius presided over Roman affairs for another three years. If the events that are here reported of Caius really took place (that is, partly in the third and partly in the fourth year of his imperial rule), and if it is reported that Caius had already secretly considered those plans that later came to light, then I am led to deduce that this letter was written in the second year of Caius' reign. However, it should cause us no surprise that this letter was so long kept secret from those to whom it had been written. The fact is that it could not be published without great danger as long as the house of this Caesar reigned. For after that attempt to set up Caius' statue in the temple of the Most High God no one could any longer doubt that [Caius] himself was designated by those obscure names, "the man of sin," "the son of perdition," [II Thess. 2:3] and what follows. And there can also be no doubt that Claudius, the uncle of Caius, and Nero, who had been adopted into Claudius' family, would have been greatly vexed by it. When finally Vespasian became emperor and the nation of the Jews had been destroyed, this letter could be made public safely and usefully for all and attract due attention, since all events from first to last correspond to the predictions. And as we have said, that was the reason why among those letters that were written to the churches (for those that were addressed to individuals hold a special place) this letter is the last—last, not in order of composition, but in terms of distribution. Consequently, it is commonly called the Second Letter to the Thessalonians, just as that book of Maccabees is called the third that in order of composition was the first.

Preface to the So-called Second Letter of Peter

Even in times long past many of the ancient interpreters believed that this epistle is not from the apostle Peter, both because its diction differs greatly from that of the first letters—a fact that Eusebius and Jerome acknowledge—and because many churches did not recognize it. Let me add another argument why this letter seems not to be from Peter. Peter died during the reign of Nero. On the other hand, this letter, or the letter which, as it seems to us consisted of the third chapter, and was attached to it, was written after the overthrow of Jerusalem. The fact is that no Christian believed that the last day of the world would arrive until the ruin of the nation of the Jews had taken place. However, many expected that within a short time thereafter the destruction of the world would come about, as we have pointed out in connection with II Thess. 2 and still other passages. This author, however, wishes Christians to remain patient in expectation of that day, in case it should come more slowly than was anticipated: this [patience] was to be a sign of the great patience of God, who still wishes many from among Jews and Gentiles to be converted to him. For my own part, I think that the author of this letter was Simeon or Simon, the Bishop of Jerusalem after James's death, the successor and imitator of that James whose letter we possess. For the name of this bishop is written by Eusebius [*Ecclesiastical History* III. 32. 1-3] and others both as Simeon and as Simon. From the same source it is also known that he lived after the destruction of Jerusalem to the time of Trajan and at that time was crucified for the name of Christ.

It is my guess that the title of the letter once read: "Simeon, a servant of Jesus Christ," just as also James and Jude address their letters [James 1:1; Jude, vs. 1], but that those who wished to make this letter more impressive and more popular added "Peter" and "apostle," and to Paul's name in 3:15, "our beloved brother." I believe this supposition will be confirmed if anyone discovers older copies of our letter than we presently possess. This letter is missing from the older books of the Syrians. Tertullian never cites a proof text from this letter.

Preface to the So-called Second Letter of John

The conviction that this letter and the one that follows do not come from the apostle John was already held by many of the ancients, from whom

Eusebius and Jerome [in this respect] did not differ. There are many arguments in support of this position. In the first place, that there were two Johns in Ephesus, the apostle and his disciple, the presbyter, is a fact that has always been attested by the tombs, of which one was in one spot and the other in another; Jerome saw these tombs. Furthermore, this writer does not call himself apostle, but presbyter, whereas the apostles, even when they write to private individuals, do not customarily omit the title by which their writings are usually commended. For when Peter, exhorting presbyters, affably refers to himself as their "fellow elder" [I Pet. 5:1], this occurs outside the salutation, out of a certain cordiality, just as similarly the emperors call themselves "fellow-soldiers." Moreover, these letters were not accepted by many nations and consequently were not translated into their languages, notably the so-called Second Epistle of Peter and the Epistle of Jude, since they were not regarded as apostolic letters. Finally, it passes belief that one who wished to be called a Christian would have had the audacity to set himself in opposition to an apostle.

In his interpretation of the New Testament Grotius was fructified above all else by the blossoming classical philology of the sixteenth and seventeenth centuries in France, England, and Holland, with its research into the meanings of words and its discovery of Hellenistic-Jewish writings.[31] In like manner the study of postbiblical Judaism, carried on mainly in connection with research in the field of biblical Hebrew, bore its fruit for the historical understanding of the New Testament. The Anglican priest **John Lightfoot** had reached the correct conclusion that the language of the New Testament, written by and for Jews, could only be understood if one were familiar with the language of the Jews at that time. Since he was convinced that the rabbinical literature contained the language and concepts of the Jews of the New Testament era, he applied himself to the study of this literature and during the years 1658-78 published his voluminous notes on the Gospels, in the preface of which he discussed the leading ideas that determined his exegesis.[32]

In the first place, since all books of the New Testament are written by and among and to Jews, and since all speeches contained in it likewise are by and to and concerning Jews: for these most indubitable reasons I have always been persuaded that this Testament must be familiar with and must retain the style, idiom, and form and norm of Jewish speech.

And in view of this, in the second place, I have come to the equally compelling conclusion that in the more obscure passages of this Testament (of which there are many) the best and on the whole the most reliable way of eliciting the sense is this: to inquire carefully into what way and in what sense these modes of expression and phrases were understood, in terms of the ordinary and common dialect and ways of thinking of that people, both of those who made use of them, and also of those who heard them. For the point is not what we can forge on the anvil of our own thought concerning these modes of expression, but [only] what meaning they had for those who used and heard them in their ordinary sense and in their ordinary speech. Inquiry can be made in no other way than by consulting the Talmudic authors, who spoke the ordinary dialect of the Jews and discussed and explained all that was Jewish. For these reasons I was induced to apply myself especially to the reading of those books.

In addition to a wealth of information about Palestinian geography, the book is notable especially for its numerous quotations from the Talmud and Midrash (including medieval commentaries) relating to all New Testament passages that stand in need of explanation in terms of archaeology, history, or the history of religions. In this way Lightfoot undertakes the task of explaining the historical conditions in the environment of primitive Christianity, not in accordance with the later assertions of the church fathers, but primarily in light of contemporary Jewish sources, and with these aids he is able to make numerous correct observations (the baptism of John the Baptist and that of the primitive church was baptism by immersion [note on Matt. 3:6]; the reference to those who sound trumpets before them as they give alms can only be meant metaphorically [note on Matt. 6:2]; the name "Abba" with which Jesus addresses God is used by the Jews only for a "natural" father [note on Mark 14:36], etc.). So it was that Grotius and Lightfoot set in motion the efforts of students of the history of religions to view the New Testament in the setting furnished by its historical environment. However, though their accomplishments were notable and though they greatly increased the knowledge of the history of New Testament times, by and large they were unable to break through the wholly unhistorical position of the rigidly orthodox Protestant and also Catholic theologians with respect to the New Testament. New basic points of view were needed to make possible a breakthrough in this direction.

Part II
The Decisive Stimuli

1.
Textual Criticism

About the turn of the seventeenth to the eighteenth century ideas fundamental to a consideration of the New Testament emerged in two areas—ideas that prepared the way for the first attempts at a strictly historical view of the New Testament—in the field of textual criticism and in the critical attitude toward religion by English Deism.

The Greek text of the New Testament was first published in 1514 in Spain in a polyglot edition of the University of Complutum (Alcalà) and in 1516 in Basel by Erasmus.[33] However, of these editions it was only that of Erasmus, carelessly prepared from poor manuscripts, that found wide distribution. From the middle of the sixteenth century on, it was repeatedly reprinted through the medium of the presses of the Parisian bookseller R. Estienne (Stephanus), and this text, unchanged after 1633, came to be known as the *Textus receptus* ("received text"). It was regarded by Protestant theologians as inspired and held to be inviolate. To be sure, occasional editions presented variants derived from manuscripts discovered by chance, but no one ventured to make the slightest change in this received text since no critical account was taken of the circumstances of its genesis.

In this situation a theologian, for the first time, set himself the task of investigating as a historical problem the historical facts encountered in the New Testament. As early as 1678 the French priest **Richard Simon** had published *A Critical History of the Old Testament,* a book that even before its appearance was largely destroyed at the instigation of Bossuet. Simon, however, refused to be intimidated and in 1689 issued his *Critical History of the Text of the New Testament,* which was followed at brief intervals by the *Critical History of the Translations of the New Testament* (1690) and the *Critical History of the Chief Interpreters of the New Testament* (1693). With the publication of these books the study of the New Testament was divorced for the first time from the study carried on by the ancients. More than that, by extensive employment of the critical observations of the church fathers and by the use of all manuscripts available to him, Simon was the first to employ critical methods in a historical study of the origin of the traditional form of the text of the New Testament and of the question of the proper understanding of it. There is, therefore, good reason to call Simon "the founder of the science of New Testament introduction." [34] However, it must not be overlooked that many of the motives of Simon's critical work were quite other than historical. To be sure, Simon expressly declared that he wished only to serve the truth, but he also carried on his work in order that it might prove useful to the Catholic Church; [35] and he believed that he would be able to achieve that goal by demonstrating that in opposition to the Protestant doctrine of the Bible as the only source of revelation, this Bible was so unreliably transmitted and so incapable of being clearly understood by itself alone that the tradition of the Catholic Church was needed if the Bible were to yield reliable teaching for faith. [36]

In all my work I have undertaken to side only with the truth and above all not to attach myself to any master. A true Christian who professes to follow the Catholic faith must no more call himself a disciple of St. Augustine than of St. Jerome or of any other church father, for his faith is founded on the word of Jesus Christ, contained in the writings of the apostles as well as in the firm tradition of the Catholic Church. Would that it had pleased God that all theologians of our century had been of this opinion! We should not then have seen so many useless disputes, which only could cause disorder in the state and in religion. Since I have no special interest that puts me under an obligation to what is called a party—the very name "party" is obnoxious to me—I avow that in composing this work I had no other intention than to be useful to the Church by establishing what it holds most sacred and most divine.

The great changes that have taken place in the manuscripts of the Bible—as we have shown in the first book of this work—since the first originals were lost, completely destroy the principle of the Protestants and the Socinians, who only consult these same manuscripts of the Bible in the form they are today. If the truth of religion had not lived on in the Church, it would not be safe to look for it now in books that have been subjected to so many changes and that in so many matters were dependent on the will of the copyists. It is certain that the Jews who copied these books took the liberty of adding certain letters here, and cutting out certain letters there, according as they judged it suitable; and yet the meaning of the text is often dependent on these letters.

Furthermore, the critical study that has been made of the principal versions of the Bible has proved beyond all question that it is almost impossible to translate Scripture. . . . There is no doubt that in spirit the Protestants, who pretend that Scripture is clear of itself, are ignorant or prejudiced. Since they have rejected the tradition of the Church and have wished to recognize no other principle of religion than this very same Scripture, they have had to make the supposition that it [the Scripture] is clear of itself and alone sufficient to establish the truth of the faith, and that independently of the tradition. But when one reflects on the conclusions that the Protestants and the Socinians draw from one and the same principle, one is convinced that

41

their principle is by no means so clear as they imagine, since these conclusions are very different, and the one set absolutely denies what the other affirms.

Far from having to believe with the Protestants that the quickest, most natural, and surest way of deciding questions of faith is that of consulting Holy Scripture, the reader will find in this work, on the contrary, that, if the rule of law is separated from that of fact, that is, if tradition is not joined to Scripture, there is hardly anything in religion that one can confidently affirm. The association with it of the tradition of the Church does not mean that we abandon concern for the Word of God; for he who refers us to Holy Writ has referred us also to the Church, to which he has entrusted the sacred deposit [*dépost*].

All Simon's respect for Catholic principles did not prevent him from pointing out that the Protestant concern for the literal sense of Scripture should prod Catholics also to study the content of the Bible more carefully, and in his great *History of the Interpretation of the New Testament* he chose to emphasize the contribution of those interpreters who applied themselves to literal exegesis. (Among those who were his recent predecessors he referred especially to the Jesuit Maldonat and the Protestants Camerarius and Grotius.) And he also subjected a church father such as Origen to criticism because of an ill-founded alteration of the text.[37]

It must be admitted that interpreters since the beginning of the last century have been much more exact. As a consequence of the studies of the Greek and Hebrew languages that have been pursued, great discoveries have been made, especially with respect to the literal sense of Scripture. Furthermore, as the Arians once gave the orthodox occasion to study the letter of the Sacred Books with greater care, so the Protestants have also provided the Catholics with the motive to examine the text of the Bible with greater application. In the long run, however, religion does not consist by any means in the subtleties of grammar and of criticism, and consequently that in no way has prevented the Catholics from seeking in the ancient fathers certain meanings [of the text] which we can call theological, for our faith is founded in the main on such explanations and not on the new meanings that have been found in recent times. . . .

These reflections and many others of a similar sort that I could add should on no account divert Catholics from applying themselves to a study of the literal and grammatical sense of Scripture. A Gregory, a Basil, a Chrysostom, who shared the opinions we have just noted, [nonetheless] did not neglect to meet the most subtle objections of the Arians and other heretics without recourse to the tradition. They explained the exact meaning [*la force*] of the words without neglecting the subtleties of grammar and criticism. As a matter of fact, since the Sacred Text is the very cornerstone of our religion, it cannot contain anything by which religion itself could be destroyed. Accordingly, in this work an attempt is made to familiarize the reader with those commentators who have shown the greatest concern for the literal sense [*sens literal*].

He [Camerarius] blames the indiscreet zeal of a few Protestants* who believe

---

* "Among theologians of the past there are a few who deny indications of ambiguity in Holy Writ, as if in some way or other they would disparage the teaching of the Holy Spirit, which is never false or dubious" (Camerarius, *Commentary on the Acts of the Apostles 3:21*).

that everything in Scripture is clear and that there is nothing at all in it that is obscure or equivocal; because God gave it to men that it might serve them as a guide, and there is no indication that he wished to deceive them. But his whole work, in which his main concern is to illuminate a large number of equivocal terms, proves the very contrary. These equivocations and ambiguities are common to all languages, and there is no reason to exempt the sacred writers therefrom; furthermore, it is ridiculous to deny a truth that stares one right in the face. This commentator almost never loses sight of what he calls the letter, and he knew how to draw out of a teaching whatever anyone was able to extract from its grammatical or literal sense. "The interpretation of Scripture, viz., of the letter, is one thing, and what is deduced from Scripture is something else again" (*Commentary on I Cor. 6:13*). This is the cornerstone around which one must build if one wishes to have an exact knowledge of what is contained in the books of the New Testament. For whatever skill in theology a man may have, it is impossible to solve a large number of difficulties that are scattered throughout these books without recourse to grammar.

He [Origen] often presses his criticism so far that, on the strength of simple conjectures, he dares to strike words from the text of St. Matthew. For instance, without any manuscript support for doing so, he conjectures that the words in Matt. 19:19, "Thou shalt love thy neighbor as thyself," in this particular setting do not come from Jesus Christ himself (Origen on Matt. 19:19 [*Matthäuserklärung*, ed. E. Klostermann, in *Griechische christliche Schriftsteller, Origenes*, Vol. X, 1935, pp. 385, 27 ff.]), but that they were added at this point by someone else who had read the following discourse inaccurately. Nevertheless, he supports his conjecture on the fact that St. Mark and St. Luke, who report the same event, make no mention of this love of one's neighbor. But this is no more conclusive than the other reasons he advances to demonstrate that these words were inserted at a later date into the text of St. Matthew: for there is no positive [proof] among them. He says only quite generally that it is an established fact that the Greek manuscripts of the New Testament have been altered in many places and that there is convincing evidence of that. However, it is quite impossible to generalize that they have been corrupted in the passage in question.

From this basic point of view, then, Simon, above all in his first work on the New Testament, his *Critical History of the Text*, established indisputable historical facts by a wholly dispassionate observation of the history of the transmission of the New Testament text. By this means he demonstrates that the superscriptions of the Gospels, with their specifications of authorship, do not come from the Evangelists; that "the spurious ending of Mark" (Mark 16:9-20) and the pericope about the adulteress (John 7:53 ff.) are missing from many manuscripts (the latter missing also from a few eastern versions); that the trinitarian insertion in I John 5:7-8 is not included in the original text of Jerome's Vulgate; etc. And in his *Critical History of the Translations* he drew attention for the first time to the fact that there was an Old Latin translation that was earlier than and differed from Jerome's Vulgate.[38] The care with which Simon undertakes the demonstration of such facts is exemplified by his comments on the superscriptions of the Gospels and on the ending of Mark: but these very examples also betray the fact that Simon was prevented by his dogmatic presuppositions from drawing the historical conclusions that his observations demanded.[39]

We have no certain proof in ancient times that would enable us to see that the names that are found at the beginning of each Gospel were put there by those who were the authors of these Gospels. In his *Homilies*, St. John Chrysostom expressly asserts the contrary. Moses, says this learned bishop, did not add his name to the five Books of the Law that he wrote (Homily I on the Epistle to the Romans [= Migne, *Patrologia*, Greek Series, Vol. LX, col. 395]).

Similarly, those who after him gathered the facts did not put their names at the beginning of their histories. This was the case with Matthew, Mark, Luke, and John. In the instance of St. Paul, [to be sure,] he always put his name at the beginning of his letters, except [in the case of] the one that is addressed to the Hebrews. And the reason that St. John Chrysostom gives for this is that the earlier [authors] had written to persons who were present, while St. Paul, on the other hand, had written his letters to persons who were at a distance. If we appeal to the testimony of this church father, we cannot prove with certainty, solely on the basis of the titles that stand at the beginning of each Gospel, that these Gospels were written by those whose names they bear, unless we join hereto the authority of the primitive church, which added these titles. It was on this principle that Tannerus and some other Jesuits depended, at a conference with some Protestants that took place at Regensburg in order to demonstrate that, with only the help of the title of St. Matthew and without the testimony of the ancient ecclesiastical authors, one could not prove with certainty that this Gospel comes from him whose name it bears. They maintained that one can give no other proofs for this truth than those that rest on the authority of men, and not on [that of] Scripture itself, for they have been added: "solely on the testimony of men, though not of all, but [only] of those who constitute the body of the Church." A Protestant theologian who had taken part in this conference wrote a book expressly on this question in order to prove the contrary thesis to that maintained by the Jesuits [Davidus Schramus, *Quaestio . . . quibus probationum generibus possit demonstrari: primum de quatuor SS. Evangeliis esse Matthaei Apostoli*, Giessen, 1617, esp. p. 8].

But, to tell the truth, there is more subtlety than substance in this sort of disputes. For, even if it were true that St. Matthew is the author of the title of his Gospel, one would, [nevertheless] have always to appeal to the authority of the ancient ecclesiastical writers to demonstrate that the title is from him and that this Gospel actually comes from him whose name it bears; unless one wishes to have recourse to a particular spirit of which we have spoken above and which very intelligent persons cannot sanction. . . .

In conclusion, it is in order to remark that, although the apostles are not the authors of the titles that stand at the head of their Gospels, we, nevertheless, must regard them [the titles] in the same way as if they [the apostles] themselves had attached them there, because they have been there from the first beginnings of Christianity and because they have the best of authorization by a constant tradition of all the churches of the world. Erasmus, who had great difficulties with respect to the author of the Epistle to the Hebrews, which does not bear the name of St. Paul, testifies that, if the Church issued a pronouncement about it, he would willingly submit to its decision, which he would prefer to all reasons that one could bring to his attention. "The judgment of the Church counts far more with me than all human considerations," say this critic (Declar[ationes] ad[versus censuras] Theol[ogorum] Paris [iensium] [Opera omnia studio et opera Jo. Clerici, 1703-6, Vol. X, p. 864]).

We have still to examine the last twelve verses of this Gospel [Mark], verses that are not found in several Greek manuscripts. St. Jerome, who had seen a large number of these manuscripts, asserts in his Letter to Hedibia that at his time there were very few Greek manuscripts in which one could read them: "since almost all Greek books lack this chapter" (Hieron[ymus] Epist. ad Hedib[iam] qu. 3 [2= Corp. Script. Eccles. Lat. 55.481. 14-15]). By this word "chapter" St. Jerome is not to be understood as meaning the entire last chapter of St. Mark, as most commentators have concluded, but only [as making a reference] to those words from vs. 9 ("Now when he had arisen" etc.) to the end, as is apparent in those manuscripts that I have consulted on this subject. And in the course of this work it will be [my concern] to show that the ancient ecclesiastical writers meant to convey something quite other by this word capitulum, chapter, than we today understand by the chapters of the New Testament and, for that matter, of the whole Bible.

It must be assumed, then, that reference is not to the entire last chapter of St. Mark—as I have already observed—but only to the last twelve verses. To this [section], then, which contains the story of the Resurrection, St. Jerome has given the name capitulum, chapter. After the words, "For they were afraid," the oldest Greek manuscript of the Gospels in the Royal Library [Bibliotheque Nationale] contains the remarks, written like the rest of the text and from the same hand: φερετέ [= φέρται] που καὶ ταῦτα ("somewhere we read the following"). "Now, all that they were bidden they quickly told Peter and his companions. But afterwards Jesus himself by means of their ministry made known from east to west the holy and immortal message of eternal salvation" (from Codex no. 2861 in the Royal Library [= Codex L of the Gospels]).

Later on in this manuscript the following observation occurs, written in the body of the book and by the same hand as the text: "After the words 'For they were afraid,' the following is also found: 'Now when he had arisen,'" etc., to the end of the Gospel [Mark 16:9 ff.]. One can easily conclude from this, that those who read this ancient Greek manuscript believed that the Gospel of St. Mark ended with the words, "For they were afraid." Nevertheless, they added the rest, written by the same hand, but only in the form of a note, because it was not read in their church. This, then, agrees entirely with the testimony of St. Jerome in his Letter to Hedibia. . . .

Euthymius, who made learned and judicious comments on the New Testament, confirms all that we have reported, and at the same time he justifies the observation of St. Jerome in his Letter to Hedibia. This is what he says about these words of St. Mark, "For they were afraid" (chap. 16:8): "A few interpreters say that the Gospel of St. Mark ends here and that what follows is a later addition. Nevertheless, we must expound it also, because it contains nothing contrary to the truth" (Euthymius, Commentary on Mark, chap. 16, from Ms. no. 2401 in the Royal Library [= Migne, Patrologia, Greek Series, Vol. CXXIX, col. 845]).

There is another manuscript copy of the Gospels in the Royal Library, rather ancient and written with great care, where we read this observation on the same passage, "For they were afraid" [Mark 16:8]: "In a few copies the Gospel ends here; but the following words, 'Now when he had risen,' and so on to the end of the Gospel, are found in many [manuscripts]" (from Ms. no. 2868 in the Royal Library [Gregory, no. 15]). In this manuscript comments are made on the small sections as well as on the last verses, just as in all the rest of the Gospel. This proves that there were read in the church, for whose use this [manuscript] was employed. And the Synaxarion, which contains the Gospel for the whole year in sequence, likewise refers to the day on which this Gospel is read. I have also read a copy in the library of Monsieur Colbert, one that is written most carefully, where, after the words, "For they were afraid," the same note is found and is expressed in the same terms (from Ms. no. 2467 of Monsieur Colbert's Library [Gregory, no. 22]).

It seems to me that these observations, which are based on good Greek manuscripts, are more than sufficient to justify the critical comment of St. Jerome in his *Letter to Hedibia* concerning the last twelve verses of St. Mark. In his time [these verses] cannot have been read thus in most Greek churches. Nevertheless, this church father did not believe that they had to be rejected out of hand; for he endeavored in this letter to reconcile St. Mark with St. Matthew, much as Euthymius does; and, after having noted that some interpreters of the New Testament believed that these words were added, he does not for this reason fail to expound them, whether or not they belong to the Gospel of St. Mark.

But, in spite of all these considerations, we can have no doubts at all about the truth of this chapter, which is just as ancient as the Gospel of St. Mark. This is why the Greeks quite generally read it today in their churches, as can be proved by [reference to] their lectionaries. There happens to be one of these lectionaries in manuscript form in the Royal Library. This manuscript is actually not ancient, but it is excellent and has served some church in Constantinople. One can hardly find a more ancient testimony than that of St. Irenaeus, who lived before there was any discussion about the difference between Greek manuscripts. This church father explicitly refers to the end of the Gospel of St. Mark (*Adv. Haer.* III. 11 [6; ed. Harvey, II. 39]). "At the end of the Gospel, however, " he says, "Mark declares: And the Lord Jesus, then, after he had spoken to them, was received up into heaven and sits at the right of God." By this passage he means the 19th verse of the last chapter of this Gospel; and the entire chapter contains only twenty verses.

Finally, on this matter there is no diversity, either in the oldest Latin manuscripts or in the Syriac. By them it can be proved that this chapter was read in those Greek manuscripts on which these very ancient manuscripts, above all the Latin, depended. It is also found in the manuscript at Cambridge [Codex D, *Cantabrigiensis*] and in the so-called Alexandrian Manuscript [Codex A, *Alexandrinus*], which are the two most ancient manuscripts we have in Europe.

Simon's empirico-critical method, with its resort to so many unfamiliar facts, encountered stiff resistance, particularly on the part of Protestants, but also from Catholics, and had no immediate results.[40] However, although an entirely new spiritual climate was needed to give impetus to Simon's basic conviction that exegesis is to be concerned only with the truth, nevertheless, as we have already noted, Simon contributed in one respect to the rise of a genuinely historical attitude toward the New Testament, viz., in the field of textual criticism.

Here the Anglican theologian **John Mill** had already been working for years, to increase the number of variants beyond the few known from earlier editions of the Greek New Testament by reference to the manuscripts and translations available to him. He had already had his edition printed as far as II Corinthians when Simon's critical histories of the text and the translations of the New Testament came into his hands. "When I had read this history through with the avidest eyes, I felt myself, with a delight that can scarcely be described, transported so to speak into a new world in which this man, singularly learned and extremely discerning in this branch of biblical scholarship, taught us countless things about our New Testament books, about the apocryphal gospels and other sectarian writings of this sort, about the manuscripts written in the West and the East, about the Italian, Syriac, Armenian, Ethiopic, Coptic, and still other versions, and finally about the variant readings of the Greek manuscripts and the versions, of which I had previously known nothing at all." [41] Mill's book appeared in 1707 in Oxford, after about thirty years of labor, and was republished three years later by the Westphalian L. Küster in Amsterdam in an edition that was somewhat enlarged and considerably improved in form. This beautifully printed folio, "the first truly great edition of the Greek New Testament," [42] reproduced unaltered the "received text" of the Greek New Testament and, in an apparatus below, that occupied much more space than the text itself, offered a list of parallel passages and cited readings of all available manuscripts, translations, and printed editions. Furthermore, it included an extensive introduction that presented all facts then known of the origin of the separate books of the New Testament and of the canon and that also gave a history of the New Testament text from its beginnings among the church fathers to the middle of the seventeenth century, as well as a description of all manuscripts and translations of the New Testament known to be extant. Although Mill did not yet dare to alter anything in the "received text," he did discuss critically the material he had so abundantly gathered and occasionally even rendered a decision in favor of a change in the traditional text (for instance, he believed that John 5:4 should be omitted) though, to be sure, he usually came to the support of the "received" reading (for instance, with respect to John 7:53 ff.).

However, this edition stimulated an unprejudiced examination of the textual transmission of the New Testament, and the Swabian pietist **Johann Albrecht Bengel** soon took a step beyond Mill, with whose book he had early become acquainted. Bengel was shaken in his confidence in the New Testament as the Word of God by the abundance of variants he found in Mill's edition, and he then sought by his own textual studies to regain that confidence. His edition of the Greek New Testament,[43] which appeared in 1734 after several advance notices, offered after the text an extensive "critical apparatus," which contained an "introduction to illuminate all variant readings" and a discussion of all variants that he had taken under consideration. His text differed in countless—but in most cases materially unimportant—places from the "received text," wherever he had been able to find a printed predecessor for it. (For instance, an insertion that Erasmus had made in Acts 9:6 of the Greek text from the Latin Bible was removed.[44]) More significant still was the fact that Bengel presented below the text a few materially important variants, which he arranged in five groups in order of their importance: (1) such variants as had already been printed that are to be regarded as original; (2) such variants in manuscripts as are superior to the reading in the text; (3) readings of value equal to the reading in the text; (4) less certain readings; and (5) readings that are to be rejected, although accepted by many. This evaluation of readings very often agrees with the critical judgment of the present day. (I Cor 6:20, where the addition at the end of the verse is deleted, belongs to the first group and Rom. 6:11, where there is a corresponding deletion, to the second; Bengel, on the other hand, regards Mark 16:9 ff. and John 7:53 ff. as original.) It was made, furthermore, on the strength of well-considered critical principles. Bengel recognized that "the [number of manuscripts supporting a reading] by itself was a matter of little importance," and that it was possible to group manuscripts in families and thereby evaluate their worth more adequately. More than this, in the course of evaluating a reading he demanded above all that the question be raised, "Which reading is more likely to have arisen out of the others?" and, as the gauge by which this question is to be answered, he formulated the classical precept: "The more difficult reading is to be preferred to the easier" (*Proclivi scriptioni praestat ardua*).[45] The articulation of this procedure and principle marked a decisive breakthrough for an editing of the New Testament text that would really go back to sources. It is only too easy to understand why Bengel, to begin with, was violently attacked from all sides.[46] Bengel himself regarded this work of textual criticism only as the prolegomenon to his brief exposition of the New Testament, which appeared in 1742, the *Gnomon* (Rule of Life),[47] which has remained permanently helpful because, by means of an exegesis oriented especially to context and grammar, it opened up the possibility of independent thinking on the part of the interpreter, without, to be sure, making conscious use of historical principles of interpretation.

Then, however, a further step, and a long one, was taken in the direction of a really historical investigation of the New Testament by

Johann Jakob Wettstein of Basel, a contemporary of Bengel. In contrast to Bengel, an orthodox pietist, Wettstein grew up in the atmosphere of a "rational orthodoxy" that was espoused at the time by the faculty of the University of Basel.[48] Even in his student days he took up the study of the manuscripts and translations of the New Testament and investigated the holdings of many libraries that he visited on his travels. Then, as pastor, he began the preliminary work on his own edition of the New Testament. When it became known that, following the so-called "Alexandrian" manuscript of the New Testament in London (Codex A), he intended to render the text of I Tim. 3:16 "He was manifested in the flesh," instead of "God was manifested in the flesh," and when sample sheets of the first pages of the new edition of the New Testament that he had in mind showed that Wettstein had included in the text itself the variants to the "received text" that he accepted, legal action was taken against him, and he was dismissed from the pastorate. He went to Amsterdam, and it was there in 1751-52 that the new edition[49] appeared in two large folio volumes. Since Wettstein now no longer dared to change anything in the "received text," he attached references to the text that clearly drew attention to the variants that he regarded as the original readings—variants that were printed immediately below the text itself—so that the reader can recognize the improved text at a glance.[50] Also under the text Wettstein offers a critical text apparatus—selective, to be sure, but in his list much more inclusive than any predecessor—which employs for the first time the letters and numbers for manuscripts that are still in use to our own day and which even records contemporary conjectures (e.g., re: Col. 2:17-18 and James 4:2). Finally, a second, much more extensive apparatus under the text offers a collection of parallel passages from classical and Jewish literature, unsurpassed to this day, that is intended to make possible an understanding of the New Testament text against the background of its time. In addition, Wettstein not only added to his edition an extremely careful description of the whole manuscript tradition of the New Testament, but also attached a brief essay, "On the Interpretation of the New Testament," which openly demanded that the New Testament, like any other writing, be read out of its time and with the eyes of its original readers.[51]

Two things, above all else, are required of a good interpreter: first, that, so far as possible, he establish the text of the ancient writer with whom he is engaged, and, second, that he bring out the meaning of the words as well as possible. In both respects many of those who have undertaken to make observations on the New Covenant have so conducted themselves as to satisfy too little the expectation of their readers. So far as the discovery of the true reading among so many and so great variants is concerned, too litte care was taken, with the consequence that the interpreters either turned at once to interpretation, confident of the reliability of the typographer and satisfied with the edition that chanced to come to hand, or they proceeded to suppress by far the greater part of the variant readings which they had available. The former of the two [procedures] can be absolved only with difficulty of the charge of negligence; the latter, however, encourages the suspicion that, because of bias or envy, the interpreter has been afraid to expose his wares openly and straightforwardly to critical judgment. To clarify the meaning of the Scriptures all [previous editors] have brought together the conjectures and opinions of everyone and have done so either with such brevity that they remain incomprehensible or with such overabundance of matter and words that they overwhelm the spirit of the reader and leave him much more uncertain than before. On both counts, accordingly, I have tried to avoid error. So for my part I have collected the various readings from every available source more carefully than heretofore had been the case, and have determined so to express my judgment concerning them that I might nevertheless leave it to every man to form his own free and unbiased judgment on the matter; on the other hand [I set myself the task] of choosing out of all possible interpretations only that which seemed to me to be the only true one, or the most probable. . . .

Since we read with the same eyes the sacred books and the laws given by decrees of the princes, as well as all ancient and modern books, so also the same rules are to be applied in the interpretation of the former as we use for an understanding of the latter. . . .

We get to know the meaning of the words and sentences in the first instance from other passages by the same author, then from the rest of the sacred writings, as well as from the version of the seventy translators, then from the authors who lived about the same time and in the same region, and finally from common usage. What I said first of all is obvious and is also recommended by Paul in Col. 4:16; cf. also I Cor. 5:9, 11; II Thess. 2:5. Since it is certain, furthermore, that all the writers of the New Testament studied the Greek version of the Old Testament by day and by night, and since it is agreed, on the basis of the testimony of the ancients and on that of the matter itself, that the Gospel of Matthew was avidly read by Mark and the Gospels of Matthew and Mark, together with the letters of Paul, by Luke, who then can doubt that the one can be illuminated by the other? And, since the sacred writers invented no new language, but made use of the one they had learned from their contemporaries, the same judgment is also required of their writings. By "common usage" I understand the common speech of the apostolic age, but not the usage of medieval writers, and much less that of the scholastic and modern theologians. . . .

Another rule is much more useful and more easily comprehended: If you wish to get a thorough and complete understanding of the books of the New Testament, put yourself in the place of those to whom they were first delivered by the apostles as a legacy. Transfer yourself in thought to that time and that area where they first were read. Endeavor, so far as possible, to acquaint yourself with the customs, practices, habits, opinions, accepted ways of thought, proverbs, symbolic language, and everyday expressions of these men, and with the ways and means by which they attempt to persuade others or to furnish a foundation for faith. Above all, keep in mind, when you turn to a passage, that you can make no progress by means of any modern system, whether of theology or of logic, or by means of opinions current today.

2.

English Deism and Its
Early Consequences

Accordingly, both in the presuppositions of Wettstein's text criticism and in his exegesis a move in the direction of a fundamentally historical examination of the New Testament began to manifest itself. Nevertheless, all these impulses toward a comprehensive historical consideration of the New Testament could only come into effective play when men had learned to look at the New Testament entirely free of all dogmatic bias and, in consequence, as a witness out of the past to the process of historical development. This attitude emerged for the first time during the course of the critical study of religion by English Deism.[52] As a result of the confluence of humanistic thought, of the freer theological points of view of the Dutch Arminians, and of the English Latitudinarians, together with the latitudinarian debate against the orthodoxy of the English state church, a theological school of thought came into being. It was fostered by the inherently rational mode of thought of English theology, by the English Revolution of 1688, and by the Toleration Act of 1689, which tried to unify the various theological and ecclesiastical schools by a return to "natural religion" and which declared war on all supernaturalism, even that involved in a consideration of the New Testament. Inspired by many predecessors, **John Locke** entered the lists in 1695 with his book, *The Reasonableness of Christianity, as Delivered in the Scriptures*. To find the true Christianity that lies back of the multiplicity of confessions, Locke here examines the New Testament, emphasizing on the one hand that the New Testament demands nothing but faith in Jesus' messiahship and resurrection, and on the other that this faith remained pure only in the Gospels and in the Acts of the Apostles, whereas the Epistles, with their doctrines that were devised to meet special situations, dilute this truth with alien ideas and pervert the simple gospel. The quest of "rational Christianity," then, leads Locke to make a distinction within the New Testament. Further, it impels him in the same book, but even more expressly in his annotated paraphrases of Paul's letters, published ten years later, to demand that the texts be understood within their respective contexts and in the sense that their authors understood them, and not as scattered sentences detached from their context.[53]

And that *Jesus was the Messiah* was the great truth of which he took pains to convince his disciples and apostles, appearing to them after his resurrection: as may be seen Luke xxiv . . . . There we read what gospel our Saviour preached to his disciples and apostles; and *that* too, as soon as he was risen from the dead; (twice, the very day of his resurrection.)

And, if we may gather what was to be *believed* by all nations, from what was *preached* unto them; so we may certainly know what they were commanded to teach all nations, by what they actually *did teach* all nations. We may observe, that the preaching of the apostles everywhere in the *Acts* tended to this one point: to prove that Jesus was the Messiah.

Indeed, now after his death, his *resurrection* was also commonly required to be believed as a necessary article; and sometimes solely insisted on: It being a mark and undoubted *evidence* of his being the Messiah; and necessary now to be believed by those who would receive him as the Messiah. For since the Messiah was to be a saviour and a king, and to give *life* and a kingdom to those who received him, . . . there could have been no pretence to have given him out for the Messiah, and to require men to believe him to be so, while they thought him under the power of death and of the corruption of the grave. —And therefore those who believed him to be the Messiah, must believe that he was risen from the dead:—And *those who believed him to be risen from the dead,* could not doubt of his being the Messiah. . . .

There remains yet something to be said to those who will be ready to object, —If the belief of Jesus of Nazareth to be the Messiah; together with those concomitant articles of his resurrection, rule, and coming again to judge the world; be *all the faith* required as necessary to justification;—to what purpose were the *Epistles* written; I say, if the belief of those many doctrines contained in *them,* be not also necessary to salvation;—and if what is *there* delivered, a christian may believe or disbelieve, and *yet* nevertheless be a member of Christ's church and one of the faithful?

To this I answer, that the epistles were written upon several occasions; and he that will read them as he ought, must observe what is in them that is *principally aimed at;* and must find what is the argument in hand, and how managed; if he will understand them right, and profit by them.—The observing of this will best help us to the true *meaning and mind of the writer;* for that is the truth which is to be received and believed; and not *scattered sentences* (in a scripture language) accommodated to our notions and prejudices. We must look into the *drift* of the discourse; observe the coherence and connection of the parts. . . .

The epistles, most of them, carry on a *thread of argument,* which (in the style they are writ) cannot every where be observed without great attention. [Yet] to consider the texts, as they stand and bear a part in *that thread,* is to view them in their due light: and the way to get the true sense of them. . . .

The [epistles moreover] were writ *upon particular occasions;* and, without those occasions, had not been writ; and so cannot be thought necessary to salvation; though they, resolving doubts and reforming mistakes, are of great advantage to our knowledge and practice.

I do not deny, but the great doctrines of the christian faith are dropt *here and there,* and scattered up and down in *most* of them.—But it is not in the epistles we are to learn what are the *fundamental* articles of faith; where they are promiscuously and without distinction mixed with other truths, in discourses that were (though for edification indeed) yet only *occasional.*— We shall find and discern those great and necessary points best in the preaching of our *Saviour and the apostles,* to those who were yet *strangers,* and ignorant of the faith; [in order] to bring *them* in and convert them to it.— And what that was, we have seen already out of the history of the Evangelists, and the Acts; where they are plainly laid down; so that nobody can mistake them. . . .

That the *poor* had the gospel preached to them, Christ makes a [sign,] as well as the *business,* of his mission (Matt. xi. 5). And if the poor had the gospel preached to them, it was, without doubt, such a gospel as the *poor could understand;* plain and intelligible.

And so it was (as we have seen) *in the preachings of* CHRIST AND HIS APOSTLES.

If the holy Scriptures were but laid before the eyes of Christians, in its connexion and consistency, it would not then be so easy to snatch out a few words, as if they were separate from the rest, to serve a purpose, to which they do not at all belong, and with which they have nothing to do. But as the matter now stands, he that has a mind to it, may at a cheap rate be a notable champion for the truth, that is, for the doctrines of the sect that chance or interest has cast him into. He need but be furnished with verses of sacred Scripture, containing words and expressions that are but flexible (as all general obscure and doubtful ones are), and his system, that has appropriated them to the orthodoxy of his church, makes them immediately strong and irrefragable arguments for his opinion. This is the benefit of loose sentences, and Scripture crumbled into verses, which quickly turn into independent aphorisms. But if the quotation in the verse produced were considered as a part of a continued coherent discourse, and so its sense were limited by the tenour of the context, most of these forward and warm disputants would be quite stripped of those, which they doubt not now to call spiritual weapons. . . .

But his epistles not being so circumstantiated [as are the speeches of the Acts of the Apostles]; there being no concurring history, that plainly declares the disposition St. Paul was in; that the actions, expectations, or demands of those to whom he writ required him to speak to, we are nowhere told. All this, and a great deal more, necessary to guide us into the true meaning of the epistles, is to be had only from the epistles themselves, and to be gathered from thence with stubborn attention, and more than common application.

This being the only safe guide (under the Spirit of God, that dictated these sacred writings) that can be relied on, I hope I may be excused, if I venture to say that the utmost ought to be done to observe and trace out St. Paul's reasonings; to follow the thread of his discourse in each of his epistles; to show how it goes on, still directed with the same view, and pertinently drawing the several incidents towards the same point. To understand him right, his inferences should be strictly observed; and it should be carefully examined, from what they are drawn, and what they tend to. He is certainly a coherent, argumentative, pertinent writer; and care, I think, should be taken, in expounding of him, to show that he is so. . . .

He that would understand St. Paul right, must understand his terms, in the sense he uses them, and not as they are appropriated, by each man's particular philosophy, to conceptions that never entered the mind of the apostle. . . .

That is what we should aim at, in reading him, or any other author; and until we, from his words, paint his very ideas and thoughts in our minds, we do not understand him.

Without actually pursuing historical aims, Locke, as a consequence of his basically open attitude with respect to the texts, came not only to demand an exegesis that actually took the text alone into consideration, and therefore was tailored to this task, but also to recognize that the New Testament was anything but a unity in content. Later Deists now trod further along this path. The Irishman **John Toland,** who in his main work, *Christianity Not Mysterious* (written under the influence of Locke), had limited revelation entirely to rational truths, noted in his (otherwise very confused) book, *Nazarenus: or Jewish, Gentile and Mahometan Christianity* (1718), the distinction between a Jewish Christianity that held fast to the Jewish Law and Pauline Gentile Christianity, which rejected the authority of the Law for Gentiles.[54] A few years later **Matthew Tindal** published the book that soon came to be known as "the Bible of all deistic readers," [55] viz., *Christianity as Old as Creation: or the Gospel a Republication of the Religion of Nature* (1730). Because Christianity for him was only a new proclamation of natural religion, and consequently reason must distinguish between truth and error in Scripture, Tindal undertook to make such a distinction and discovered in the course of so doing that primitive Christianity expected the return of Christ during the lifetime of the apostles and in this was mistaken. From this the conclusion had to be drawn that the apostles could have deceived themselves also in other respects.[56]

And as those Prophecies, if they may be so call'd, in the New Testament, relating to the *Second Coming of Christ,* and *the End of the World,* the best Interpreters and Commentators own, the Apostles themselves were grossly mistaken; there scarce being an Epistle, but where they foretell that those Times they wrote in, were *Tempora novissima* [last times]; and the then Age the last Age, and those Days the last Days; and that the *End of the World* was nigh, and *the Coming of Christ at hand;* as is plain, among other Texts, from I *Cor.* 10. 11. *Rom.* 13. 11, 12. *Heb.* 9. 26. *Jam.* 5. 7, 8. I *John* 2. 18. II *Pet.* 3. 12, 13. And they do not assert this as a meer Matter of Speculation, but build Motives and Arguments upon it, to excite People to the Practice of Piety, and all good Works. . . . And tho' they do not pretend to tell the very Day and Hour, when these Things must happen; yet they thought it wou'd be during their Time, and continually expected it. . . . And I think, 'tis plain, *Paul* himself expected to be alive at the Coming of the Lord, and that he had the Word of God for it. . . . If most of the Apostles, upon what Motives soever, were mistaken in a Matter of this Consequence, how can we be certain, that any One of them may not be mistaken in any other Matter? If they were not inspir'd in what they said in their Writings concerning the then Coming of

Christ; how cou'd they be inspir'd in those Arguments they build on a Foundation far from being so? And if they thought their Times were the last, no Direction they gave, cou'd be intended to reach further than their own Times.

Toland's discovery of the central importance for primitive Christianity of the imminent end of the present age was made without any genuine historical interest. Similarly, the craftsman **Thomas Chubb** (1738), with the intention of demonstrating that true Christianity is simple and agrees with natural religion, distinguished the teaching of Jesus as the true religion from the unauthoritative private opinions of the New Testament writers, who had falsified this true religion. And in so doing he discovered the difference between the eschatological proclamation of Jesus and the Pauline and Johannine theology of the saving acts of God.[57]

First, the Gospel of Jesus Christ is not *an historical account of matters of fact.* As thus. Christ suffered, died, rose from the dead, ascended into heaven, &c. These are *historical facts* the *credibility* of which arises from the strength of those evidences which are, or can be offered in their favour: but then those facts are not the *gospel of Jesus Christ,* neither in whole, nor in part. *Luke* vii. 22. *Go your way, and tell John what things ye have seen and heard, how that the blind see, the lame walk, the lepers are cleansed, the deaf hear, the dead are raised, to the poor the gospel is preached,* &c. Here we see that the gospel was preached to the poor by Christ himself, *antecedent* to the transactions I now refer to; and therefore those facts, or any doctrines founded upon them, (such as that of Christ's *satisfaction,* or that of his *intercession,* or the like,) cannot be any part of the gospel. . . .

Secondly, the gospel of Jesus Christ is not any *particular private opinion* of any, or of all the writers of the history of his life and ministry; nor any *private opinion* of any, or of all those whom he sent out to publish his gospel to the world; nor is any of their *reasonings,* or *conclusions* founded on, or drawn from such opinions in any part of that gospel. Thus St *John* begins his history, *John* i. 1, 2, 3. *In the beginning was the word, and the word was with God, and the word was God. The same was in the beginning with God. All things were made by him, and without him was not any thing made that was made.* These propositions, for any thing that appears to the contrary, are only the *private opinion* of St. *John,* who wrote the history of Christ's life and ministry, and they are no part of Christ's gospel; *viz.* that gospel which he preached to the poor, and which he gave in charge to his Apostles to publish to the world. And therefore whether Christ was the *Logos* or Word, whether he was with God, and was God, or whether he made all things in the sense in which St. *John* uses those terms, or not, is of no consequence to us; because these points are no part of Christ's gospel, and they are what the salvation of mankind is not in the least concerned with. Whether Christ pre-existed, or not; or whether he was the agent employed by God in making this visible world, or not; are points which do not affect the saving of mens souls at all; it being sufficient for us to know, that he was the sent of God, and that *the word of the Lord in his mouth was truth.* This I say, is sufficient for us to know, with regard to our salvation; and therefore whether the forementioned propositions are truths or not; is of no consequence to us in that respect. . . .

To this I may add, that the *private opinions* of those who wrote Christ's history, and of those who were appointed and sent out to preach his gospel to the world, were in many instances very *abstruse,* and much above the capacities of the common people. Whereas, the gospel which Christ preached the poor, and which he gave in charge to his Apostles to publish to the world, was *plain* and *intelligible,* and level to the *lowest understanding,* as indeed it *ought,* and *must needs be. . . .*

The doctrines of the *imputed righteousness,* the *meritorious sufferings,* and the *prevailing intercession of Christ* being either separately, or conjunctly the *grounds* of mens acceptance with God, and of sinners obtaining divine mercy, these doctrines do naturally tend to *weaken* and *take off* the persuasive influence of the gospel, and to render it of *none effect;* as by them is pointed out to men *another* way to God's favour and mercy, and *another* way to life eternal than the *gospel* has pointed out unto them; and consequently, the aforesaid doctrines render the doctrine of the gospel useless and an insignificant thing.

What Toland had said of the contrast between Jewish and Gentile Christianity and Chubb, of the misrepresentation of Jesus' teaching by the apostles, the Quaker **Thomas Morgan** set forth in terms of the inner development of the Christian religion in an anonymously published work, *The Moral Philosopher* (1737-40). To undergird the thesis that Jesus had brought true, natural religion, diametrically opposed to the hidebound religion of the Jews, Morgan on the one hand establishes a radical difference between Paul and Peter, and on the other portrays Paul as the true follower of Jesus, in contrast to the Jewish Christians, who perverted the Gospel into a separatist political religion.[58]

St. *Paul* then, it seems, preach'd another and quite different Gospel from what was preach'd by *Peter* and the other Apostles. Nay, as you will have it, they differed about the most essential and concerning Points, as they must have been at that Time, the fundamental Terms of Communion, and the Method of propagating and settling the Gospel at first. But this being supposed, it is impossible they should have been all inspired, or under the infallible Direction of the Holy Ghost. . . .

And this was the vast Difference between the *Jewish* and *Gentile* Christians at first, and in the Apostolical Age itself. That one believ'd in and receiv'd Christ, as the Hope and Salvation of *Israel* only, or as the Restorer of their Kingdom; and the other as the Hope and Salvation of all Men alike, without Regard to any such fifth Monarchy, or temporal *Jewish* Kingdom.

This was a very wide Difference indeed; and at this Rate the *Jewish* and *Gentile* Christianity, or *Peter's* Religion and *Paul's,* were as opposite and inconsistent as Light and Darkness, Truth and Falsehood. . . .

As soon as these *Nazarene Jews,* or Messiah-Men, understood that Jesus was crucified and dead, they gave up all their Hopes in him, and Expectations from him. *We trusted this was the Man who should have saved Israel;* but now it was all over. They had learned nothing from him as a Prophet or Preacher of Righteousness, they knew no better than before how to obtain an heavenly Inheritance, but all their worldly Hopes were vanished, the Kingdom was lost, and nothing else could be worth saving. And hence, when the Women who went first to the Sepulchre, came and told them that Jesus was risen from the Dead and alive again, they looked upon it at first as a mere Imagination or idle Tale, and could not believe it. But as soon as they came to be convinced, they assumed their old Hopes and Prejudices again, and now he was the Messiah and Restorer of the Kingdom as before. But this does not well agree with the many plain, express Declarations which Jesus had made to them while he was living, and conversing among them, that he must die and should arise again on the third Day. . . .

It may therefore be farther observed, that Christ's own Apostles and Disciples grossly misunderstood and misapply'd all that he spoke to them in Parables and Allegories, about the Nature and Extent of his Kingdom, and Design of his Mission. What he intended of a spiritual Kingdom, and the Deliverance of Mankind in general from the Power and Captivity of Sin and Satan, they understood of a temporal Kingdom to be set up and established at *Jerusalem,* under his own Administration, and of the Deliverance of that Nation from their Captivity to the *Romans.* And this Mistake and Delusion they continued in, even after they had received the Holy Ghost, that was to lead them into *all Truth;* and when they came to believe him risen from the Dead, and preached him as such, it was as the *Jewish* Messiah, the Christ, King, and Saviour of *Israel;* and they expected his second Coming very speedily, to set up his Kingdom, and that they should live and reign with him in that very Generation, and before the Decease of some who were then living. This is so very plain in all the Gospels, that it would be but wasting Time, and abusing the Reader's Patience, to quote the particular Passages for it. From this gross Mistake of theirs, the Disciples, or Evangelists themselves, represent Jesus as acting an inconsistent Part, and talking of himself in a prevaricating Way. Sometimes they represent him as owning himself as the Messiah, or as that Prince and national Deliverer who was to restore the Kingdom, according to the Prophets; and at other Times, they make him disclaim and disown any such Character and Pretension. He sharply rebuked the Devil, whom he cast out, for declaring him as the Messiah, or *King of Israel;* and he strictly charged all the Diseased, the Blind, Sick and Lame, whom he cured, and who were restored by the Power and Virtue of this Faith in him, not to speak of, or mention him under his Name and Character; and did all he could to prevent the Spreading of such a Notion and Report of him. The Truth of the Matter, therefore, seems to be this, that our Saviour all along, from first to last, disclaim'd the Messiahship among them. But his own Disciples and Followers could never be convinced to the contrary, but that he must be the Person. They thought, that he might not yet find it seasonable, or a proper Time, to declare for the Messiahship openly; but they did not doubt but Things would soon take another Turn; and, therefore, when he had been actually crucified, his Disciples absolutely gave up all Hope in him, or farther Expectations from him. We hoped *this was the Man who should have saved* Israel; but now their Hopes were all dash'd, and the Thing was come to nothing. And is it credible then, that Jesus should, while he lived, have plainly and expressly told them, that he must be crucified, and should rise again from the Dead on the third Day? Could they be so perfectly stupid or forgetful, as to have no Hope or Expectation at all from such plain and repeated Declarations of his?

All these ideas of the Deists were the result, not of a historical approach to the New Testament, but of a rationalistic critique of traditional Christianity. However, the freedom with which the biblical text was treated—a characteristic of that critique—strengthened tendencies in the direction of a genuinely historical investigation of the Church's Scriptures that were already latent in the theological interpretation of the New Testament. The deistic ideas rapidly became known in France and from this bastion exerted an influence on continental theology.[59] J. J. Wettstein's axioms of interpretation that we have already noted can be shown to be inexplicable apart from this deistic influence. But as early as two decades before Wettstein, **Jean Alphonse Turretini,** a Genevan theologian who belonged to the school of "rational orthodoxy" and who undoubtedly was familiar with the earliest deistic ideas, already demanded an interpretation of Holy Scripture that explains the Bible just as all other human writings are explained and that declares reason to be the sole criterion by which the validity of all exegesis is determined. In 1728 a booklet appeared, based on Turretini's lectures but published by others, that was entitled *Concerning the Methods of Interpeting the Holy Scriptures*—a booklet that Turretini characteristically maintained was a misrepresentation of his views. In it he first rejected as untenable several principles of interpretation that had hitherto been followed, in order to demand in their stead an interpretation grounded on reason and taking into consideration the special character of each book of the Bible.[60]

To begin with, let us keep the fact firmly in view that the [Holy] Scriptures are to be explained in no other way than other books; one must keep in mind the sense of the words and the customs of speech, the purpose [*scopus*] of the author, what goes before and what follows, and whatever else there may be of this sort. That is clearly the way in which all books, as well as all discourses, are understood; since God wished to teach us by means of books and discourses, though not in a different way, it is therefore clearly evident thereby that the Holy Scripture is not to be understood otherwise than are other books. . . .

The Holy Scripture presupposes that those whom it addresses are men, i.e., that they make use of their reason and are endowed with it: furthermore, [it presupposes] general concepts, or concepts peculiar to [read *proprias*] reason, i.e., metaphysical truths, mathematical [truths], as well as all others that are perceived by the natural light. At the same time [Scripture presupposes] the ability to draw conclusions, by means of which we deduce conclusions from certain principles. Otherwise, Scripture would not lead us to draw conclusions and would not make an assertion on the basis of the light of the natural reason, which, however, it always does. Since, therefore, the Scripture presupposes general conceptions, it follows inevitably that it transmits nothing in contradiction to them. And since God, as we have already often noted, is quite certainly the author both of reason and of revelation, it is therefore impossible that these should be in mutual opposition. On the contrary, if it were not so, we should lose our way in the labyrinth of the sceptics, and neither the divinity of Scripture itself nor its sense could be perceived. As a matter of fact, it will never be so clear that Scripture is the Word of God, or teaches this or that, as it is clear that a matter that stands in opposition to general conceptions cannot exist. For instance, if someone declares that Scripture says that there is a distance without length, that two and two make five, he thereby takes away all certainty from human relationships. Actually, if it were not certain that every distance has length, nothing could be certain, and likewise the divinity and sense of Scripture could not be perceived. Consequently, if a sense that clearly contradicts all conceptions seems to be conveyed by certain passages, everything must be attempted or imputed, rather than that this dogma should be accepted. Therefore those passages are to be explained otherwise, or, if that be not possible, as spurious, or the book is not to be adjudged divine. An example of this is [the dogma of] transubstantiation. . . .

No judgment on the basis of the axioms and systems of our day is to be passed on the meaning of the sacred writers, but one must put oneself into the times and into the surroundings in which they wrote, and one must see what [concepts] could arise in the souls of those who lived at that time. This rule is of the greatest importance for the understanding of Scripture; and, despite it, theologians and interpreters commonly proceed quite contrariwise. For, when they impose their meaning on the interpretation of Scripture, they have already in mind a definite system of doctrine that they seek [to discover] in Scripture and [proceed to] relate all passages of Scripture to it. And so they do not so much test their dogmas by the norm of Scripture, as assimilate Scripture to their dogmas. That is certainly the most perverse kind of interpretation and the one least suited to the discovery of the truth. And what actually takes place thereby? Naturally every one, be he Papist, Lutheran, or Reformed, finds his dogmas in Scripture, and there is no one who, on the basis of a reading of Scripture, would divest himself of these preconceived opinions. If, however, we lay aside the ideas of all the opinions and systems of our day and put ourselves into those times and surroundings in which the prophets and apostles wrote, that would certainly be the true way of entering into and recognizing their meaning and [of perceiving] which Christian dogmas are true and which are false. Consequently, in the reading of Scripture one must keep this rule carefully in mind. An empty head, if I may so express myself, must be brought to Scripture; one's head must be, as it were, a *tabula rasa* ["a blank slate"] if it is to comprehend the true and original meaning of Scripture.

The dogmatic books of Scripture, the letters of the apostles, for example, must not be read in part, or in separate sections that are considered by themselves, but in their entirety, just as the letters of Cicero, Pliny, and others are read. And they are not to be read only once this way, but repeatedly, until a certain familiarity with them is achieved. If, on the contrary, individual pericopes are taken from those books and are considered in the light of concepts of systems of our day, then that is often sought in them that is utterly other than the purpose [*scopus*] of the book as a whole and the sense of the author, since the purpose of a book can be discovered in no other way than in the actual context of the discourse. . . .

If interpretations of specific passages, especially of the most important, are accepted by all or most scholars or interpreters, this fact accords them no little authority, but none so great that they may be preferred to [others that are supported by] the most convincing reasons.

Whenever ancient and modern interpreters obviously had no more light than we with respect to certain interpretations and actually advance only hypotheses, then their explanations are to be subjected to an investigation; if their reasons for them prove to be valid, they are to be accepted; if they [are seen to be] bad and wrong, they are to be rejected; if they [show themselves to be] doubtful, one must refrain from agreement.

However powerful these ideas of Turrentini's about methodology were later to prove, they had a very limited influence in their own day. They had first to await the further spread of the content of deistic thought which, forty years later, assured the basically similar ideas of the Leipzig philologist and theologian **Johann August Ernesti** the widespread attention aroused by his little book, *Instruction for the Interpreter of the New Testament* (1761).[61] For the first time Ernesti related his hermeneutical instruction to the New Testament alone, and thereby revealed an insight into the historical difference between the Old Testament and the New and the necessity of their separate examination—an insight that was to have important consequences. Furthermore, his insistence that only the grammatical explanation can do justice to the written word challenged the validity of an understanding of New Testament ideas derived from the "thing," i.e., from ecclesiastical dogma, and thereby prepared the way for a recognition of the essentially historical character of the New Testament texts. Ernesti, however, was basically a conservative and failed to see this latter consequence of his thought. Because of this he denied that it was possible for Scripture to err, and supported this denial by an appeal to the inspiration of the biblical writers. Therefore, not even a well-founded suspicion of the traditional ascriptions of authorship could be entertained. It follows, then, that, when contradictions or difficulties arise, the interpreter is advised to take a different attitude to the inspired biblical texts than he would assume when confronting other texts.[62]

Since the connection that exists between words and ideas arises out of human custom and is determined by practice, it is readily apparent that the sense of words is dependent on the usage of language; and if one knows the latter, one knows also the former. The usage of language, however, is the result of many things: of the time, of religion, of schools of thought and instruction, of a shared life, and, finally, of the constitution of the state. All these have a far-reaching effect on the character of the speech which any writer uses at any given time. For word usage is derived from, or varies according to, all these things, and the same word is often employed one way in everyday life, another way in religion, and still another way by the philosophical schools, which on their part are far from agreeing with each other.

Consequently, the observation of word usage is the special task of the grammarians, whose art is directed for the most part and chiefly to careful determination of what meaning a definite word had at a definite time, the usage of the word by a definite author, and, finally, the relation of the word to a definite form of speech. Therefore the literal sense is also called the grammatical, for the word *literalis* is the Latin translation of *grammaticus* [Greek, "knowing one's letters"]. No less properly it is also called the historical [sense], for it is contained, as other [historical] facts, in testimonies and authoritative records.

Therefore, apart from the grammatical sense there is none other, and this the grammarians transmit. For those who, on the one hand, assume a grammatical, and, on the other, a logical, sense, have not comprehended the role of the grammatical sense; and [this] sense, [furthermore,] is not changed by any use whatever of any discipline, or in the investigation of the sense of things. Otherwise, it would be no less manifold than the things themselves.

And since all these things are common to divine and human books, it is evident that the sense of the words in the sacred books cannot be sought or found in any other way, so far as human effort is involved, than that which is customary or necessary in [the study of] human [books].

It is an altogether perilous and treacherous method to determine the sense of words from things, since, if investigations are to be pursued in the right and proper way, the things must rather be recognized by words and their sense. For instance, something can be true that, nevertheless, is not contained in the words: and it is evident that what is to be established concerning the things must be perceived and judged by means of the words of the Holy Spirit.

Therefore, the sense which, according to grammatical laws, is to be assigned to words, must not be rejected on account of reasons which are derived from things, for otherwise an uncertain interpretation would result. If in human books, however, the thing is obviously inconsistent with reason, one infers either a mistake in the writing or an error on the part of the writer. If in divine books [on the other hand] the sense does not conform to general human ideas, one infers a weakness of human insight and reasoning power. And if [in divine books] the sense clearly contradicts the [content of] the narrative, one must seek to reconcile the two and must not lightly, without good manuscript support, attempt an emendation.

Since, however, the sacred writings are the work of inspired men, it can easily be perceived that there cannot possibly be a real incompatibility of statements in them. For God neither sees what follows as a logical consequence or is consistent with itself, nor so forgets [what he has said] that he is not sufficiently mindful of what he has previously said. If, therefore, the appearance of such a contradiction presents itself, one must look for a method of appropriate reconciliation.

With respect to most [of the books], we hold that the fact that the books of the New Testament have as their authors those whose names they bear is so certainly transmitted by ancient and unanimous authority that nothing more certain may be established concerning any author of any ancient book. And they offer no grounds for any justifiable suspicion that they were written at any other time than we believe, or by other people, or even by men who were not inspired.

Ernesti, therefore, failed to take the final step to a basically historical view of the New Testament. Nevertheless, as Wettstein had already done in connection with New Testament textual criticism, he had now reached the point in the course of reflection on the proper understanding of the New Testament—a reflection that owed its stimulus to Deism—at which truly scientific New Testament research could come into being.

Part III
The Beginnings of the Major Disciplines of New Testament Research

1.
J. S. Semler and J. D. Michaelis

Scientific study of the New Testament is indebted to two men, Johann Salomo Semler and Johann David Michaelis for the first evidences of a consciously historical approach to the New Testament as a historical entity distinct from the Old Testament. In terms of their basic orientation, these scholars have to be characterized as more nearly conservative, rather than revolutionary. Both men had been influenced by the textual criticism of Bengel and Wettstein; both were directly dependent for the questions they asked, as well as for many of the answers they gave, on the writings of the English Deists; both adopted R. Simon's attitude of critical inquiry.[63] It was **Johann Salomo Semler,** however, who gave the scientific study of the New Testament the more vigorous impetus to further development. Although Semler was the son of a pastor concerned with religious education, he early immersed himself in classical and Oriental languages and authors. But further, due to an inner struggle with the "pietistic sanctimoniousness, bereft of both spirit and soul" [64] that he found repugnant, he learned to plunge into the testimonies of the past and to acquire a comprehensive knowledge of sources drawn from the most varied periods and fields. Under the influence of his teacher at Halle, Sigismund Jacob Baumgarten, he developed a conservative rationalism and a historical interest open to deistic stimuli, in order to become—after his teacher's death (1757), to be sure—"bolder, more ready to advance, and freer in argumentation." [65] The historical interest which Semler had taken over from Baumgarten led him to interrogate from a rigorously historical point of view all religious traditon, including the New Testament. His research embraced the whole domain of theology: shortly after Semler's death, Eichhorn published a "List of Semler's Writings" that included 171 separate publications! [66] At no point, however, was he able to give a well-constructed, logically progressive presentation of the content of any matter, and his collections of material and reflections are clothed in a prolix and often obscure language that, for good reason, has been called "probably the worst German that a German intellectual has ever written." [67] This formlessness also characterizes the work by which Semler most influenced the development of scientific New Testament study, namely, his *Treatise on the Free Investigation of the Canon* (1771-75).[68] In this four-volume work a coherent presentation of the subject matter is given only in the first half of the first and second volumes, while the more extensive remainder is given over to debates with Semler's critics—debates, however, that lead again and again to basic arguments. It is in this work that Semler formulates the two theses that were to prepare the way for a "free investigation" of the New Testament. On the one hand, Semler declares that the Word of God and Holy Scripture are not identical, for Holy Scripture also contains books that had importance only for the remote times in which they were written and that cannot contribute to the "moral improvement" of the man of today. Consequently, by no means all parts of the Canon can be inspired, nor can they be accepted by Christians as authoritative. All this, however, leads to Semler's second thesis, namely, that the question of whether a book belongs to the Canon is a purely historical one, for the Canon, as Semler viewed it, represents only the agreement of the regions of the Church as to the books from which lections were to be taken, and every Christian is fully entitled to undertake a "free investigation" of the historical circumstances under which every book of the Canon was written and of its permanent worth for further religious development.[69]

Holy Scripture and the Word of God are clearly to be distinguished, for we know the difference. If one has not previously been aware of this, that is no prohibition that keeps us from making the distinction. To Holy Scripture (using the particular historical expression that originated among the Jews) belong Ruth, Esther, the Song of Songs, etc., but not all these books that are called holy belong to the Word of God, which at all times makes all men wise unto salvation. . . .

The problem of inspiration, therefore, is not nearly so important as it is still the custom to regard it. Let us suppose, for instance, that the whole story of the woman taken in adultery in John 8 were lacking, as it is lacking in many ancient copies and translations of large parts of the Church: a piece of so-called Holy Scripture would then be lacking, but the Word of God would be lacking in nothing whatever, for it is and remains unchangeable, despite all these accidental and continuous changes in a document whose copyists, it must be admitted, enjoyed no divine aid. . . .

If a reader is already familiar with the moral truths and their inherent value, to the extent that they are of use to him, and if he is already engaged in the practice of such principles; if he is already so humane that he is glad to help all men to that inner orderliness that he, to his own true happiness, has begun to experience; if he finds the tone of the Apocalypse unpleasant and repulsive when it speaks of the extermination of the heathen, and so forth;

how can such a one find in this book nothing but divine, all-inclusive love and charity for the restoration of men, without which he cannot regard it as in a special, peculiar way the work of God, who is sheer love in all his relationships with men? It must remain open to many people, then, who have begun to experience the salutary power of truth, to pass judgment in light of their own knowledge both on individual books and on certain parts of many books, with reference to their moral and generally beneficial value, just as it is open to other readers, in accordance with their real or assumed insight, unreservedly to represent and declare all books of the whole Old and New Testament, as they have been written or printed together, to be divine, without such a special distinction of content. . . .

Far be it from me, then, utterly to hate all so-called naturalists because of the freedom they exercise in refusing to accept the ancient, familiar assertions of the general and indistinguishable sanctity of the so-called whole Bible. Every intelligent person, if he is fortunate enough to take his own mental powers seriously, is free—yes, it is his very duty—to pass judgment on these matters without any fear of men. Wherever he can discover nothing divine or worthy of the highest being, nothing that in its intention has the divine quality and character of contributing more and more easily to his own inner betterment, there he cannot and must not conceive of such writings in their entirety and without distinction as being, in defiance of his own understanding, quite certainly and very greatly useful to his own edification, just for the sake of others who in this matter follow a custom of regarding them in due course as of great merit and conducive to growth in inner excellence. . . .

What Bengel said on those occasions when he found it very difficult in his consideration of many passages in the New Testament to decide between the variant readings: "No one needs the whole; another passage leads another person to salvation" (a remark, by the way, that few understand), is preeminently true also of this investigation. Several scholars have already said that, so far as we and our own needs are concerned, the whole Christian scheme of salvation can be assembled and employed just as well, just as correctly and fully, from a single book, from a few small passages of many books, as from all together; for much in such books had necessarily to relate to the circumstances of the first readers in the times when they were written and imparted, and all that is now useless for the purpose we set before ourselves. So far as it is a list of so and so many books no one has made the Canon an article of faith; rather, men have distinguished the content of the books which is in fact permanently useful from the range of their parts which is quite often only accidental. . . .

The only proof that completely satisfies an upright reader is the inner conviction brought about by the truths that confront him in this Holy Scripture (but not in all parts and individual books). This has been called elsewhere, in a brief and biblical but somewhat obscure phrase, the witness of the Holy Spirit in the soul of the reader. From this comes divine faith (*fides divina*): this I have also chosen above all to recommend as the more certain and easier proof. I have acted so frankly in all this, however, that at the same time I have added to it the subsumption: books, or parts of books, where this argument cannot possibly apply, but in which the final aim of all alleged inspiration still lingers on, whether in large or in small writings, can be left unread and unused without personal anxiety or concern for this final aim. . . .

In light of these very clear circumstances it is certain that the common idea of the constant uniformity and homogeneity of the Canon, or of the list of sacred writings publicly acknowledged by Christians, is without ground or historical justification, whenever anything more is meant by it than that it was an agreement for the public and for the public practice of religion: an agreement to which some thoughtful Christians did not commit themselves. In this respect the church either had a different custom in the use of such writings for public reading, or for the ordering of religion, a custom that distinguished them in reality from other churches, or they had gradually reached an agreement and made common cause with many or few others. Both these elements must be kept in mind: the public reading and the variety of books used for this purpose, until gradually a common agreement was reached with respect to these matters. Canonicity, then, is established by the opinion of the clergy that no other books could be used as public lections and for compulsory instruction than those that were reckoned by this church among the canonical books. . . .

It is, therefore, correct and historically true that, since the fourth and fifth centuries, the Canon or list of public documents of the Christians has not been subjected to any further objection or doubt by Catholics. The primary reason for this, however, is the common agreement of the bishops who, especially in the Occident, fixed and ordered for all time, by express church laws, what books of the so-called Old and New Testament were to stand in the official list or canon and were now to be read in public. However, this brief, but basically true, account of this matter at the same time carries with it the following: all thoughtful readers are free to undertake the special investigation of these books, so far as their private use of them is concerned, and this right cannot be abrogated by a canon that was introduced for public use. . . .

In particular, the entire common idea of the Canon and of the equally divine origin and value of all books and parts hitherto included in it is absolutely not an essential part of the Christian religion. One can be a righteous Christian without ascribing one and the same origin of divine inspiration to all books that are included in the Old and New Testament, or regarding them on the same level, and therefore also without crediting them with the same general utility. And there can be no universal, unchangeable certainty with respect to them, as there always is, however, a general and unchangeable certainty and character of the Christian religion and of its actual basic doctrines and principles.

From this assumption that the books of the Bible have to be viewed from a rigorously historical perspective, Semler now actually draws the inevitable consequences. Above all, going beyond Ernesti, he demands an interpretation that not only attempts to understand the text in terms of its own grammatical structure, and therefore without the intrusion of one's own ideas, but also puts it quite deliberately into its ancient setting and explains it as a witness to its own time, and not primarily as intended for today's reader.[70]

A head that is already full of ideas and thoughts; however they may have been determined, about moral precepts that concern God, or the world of spirits, or our condition; on undertaking an interpretation of a biblical book has actually explained it no more than has one who is called a simple Christian, who uses the Bible in a way that is useful to him.

An interpreter ought not to interject anything of his own ideas into the writing he wishes to interpret, but to make all he gets from it part of his current thinking and make himself sufficiently certain concerning it solely on the basis of its content and meaning. Nevertheless, it is obvious that the very opposite appears on the pages of most interpretations, and consequently an attitude and intention is assumed that makes the application of that fundamental rule actually and really no longer possible.

Edification by Scripture, because of its very nature, is only a secondary concern in general. Correct understanding of Scripture is the primary concern, or the second intermediate goal to the final goal of edification. But knowledge necessarily comprehends also general truths, which must first be recognized and used before any special application and subsumption is possible. The dogmas which concern God and his intentions, actions, and behavior towards us must first be known exactly and correctly, in and for themselves. A man must first know what conversion, faith, justification, grace, and so forth are, before he becomes a convert, or can become, or wish to become, a believer. A man must first know the actual reason for such changes, that such and such things ought to and can happen by means of the biblical witnesses. As a result of and in connection with this knowledge, which has the nature of a history and becomes effective historically and by means of testimonies, the action of God now comes into play, in accordance with the needs of particular persons, to their varying edification. It is no more possible for all people to achieve one and the same level of edification than it is for them to acquire knowledge of one sort. It is therefore false to assume that Holy Scripture always, and in the first instance, brings about men's edification and must also be directly employed to that end. It is absolutely necessary that the proper historical knowledge first be acquired, and only later the saving knowledge awaited.

In brief, the most important factor in hermeneutical skill is that one both know the linguistic usage of the Bible quite surely and exactly, and also distinguish the historical circumstances of a biblical discourse and be able to reconstruct them. And therefore it is now possible for one to speak of these matters in such a way as is demanded by the different times and other circumstances of our contemporaries, or as will make the composition of its interpretation comprehensible to them. One can sum up all the rest of hermeneutics in these two propositions. The former, however, is comparatively the more important, and one furthers or hinders the other to the extent that one has really learned the linguistic usage properly, or not.

Once interpretation has been deliberately divorced in this way from edifying concerns and the text considered as a historical record, the way is opened for a recognition of the differences between the Old Testament and the New, and within the New Testament itself, as well as for the employment of literary hypotheses to assist in the explanation of obscure historical facts. Building on Bengel's differentiation of families within extant New Testament manuscripts, Semler distinguishes two recensions of the Greek text of the New Testament, an "Eastern," and a "Western, Egyptian, Palestinian, Origenian," recension, and thereby reveals the first inkling of the difference between the large mass of later manuscripts (which he called the "Eastern" recension) and the smaller group of more valuable witnesses. Furthermore, the observation, for instance, that the two final chapters of the Epistle to the Romans were missing from Marcion's text leads him to the hypothesis that both these chapters are Pauline essays that were attached to the Roman epistle at some later date.[71] In this way he explains a difficulty in understanding the transmission of the text by assuming a secondary emendation of it, i.e., by means of literary hypothesis. Since his time, this has become commonplace procedure with respect to the text of the New Testament. Or, to take another instance, because the Apocalypse provides Semler with no "food for the soul" and because this book is Jewish rather than Christian, Semler is unable to ascribe it to the author of the Gospel of John. Consequently, he employs the observation of factual differences between the writings to discover, by such biblical-historical comparison, the historical setting (and therewith also the religious orientation) of a text.[72] More particularly, however, on the assumption that there were different original forms of the Canon, he concludes that there was a sharp contrast in the primitive Christian community between the Jewish-Christian and the Gentile-Christian wings, and seeks to allocate the individual documents of the New Testament to one or the other of these. In so doing he not only recognizes a difference of categories within the New Testament, but for the first time as a conscious act, sets the New Testament books into the historical context of primitive Christianity and makes the individual biblical authors the object of investigation.[73]

In the course of the investigation of the Canon, which actually belongs to the Church of Christ (*ecclesiasticus*), or of the books which the very first Christians accepted and introduced as authoritative apostolic writings for the purpose of public instruction, I am now able also to say something more about the letters and writings of the apostles to assist in understanding the very ancient dissimilarity and disunity of the Christian teachers. It can be demonstrated from the oldest of the extant writings that there was for long a party of Christians that belonged to the Diocese of Palestine and that consequently accepted the writings of those apostles who actually carried on their ministry among the circumcized; that Paul did not direct his letters to these Christians, who belonged to the diocese of James and Peter; and that they, therefore, also did not have the Pauline letters among their authoritative writings. On the other hand, the party of Christians that belonged to Paul's diocese was quite aware that James, Peter, and Jude had not sent it any letters; and it, consequently, was also not able to exhibit and introduce those writings among its congregations. Both parties are Christians and have separated themselves from the Jews; but the way of thinking of the Palestinian Jewish-Christians is still too simply and too much accustomed to all sorts of local ideas and insignificant concepts, for other Christians who do not dwell among these natives to be able to accept this kind of teaching for themselves as though it were for their advantage. On the basis of the most ancient residue of a history, the aversion of the supporters of Peter for the followers of Paul is undeniable. . . .

If one were to deny the very real distinctiveness of Jewish teaching or of teaching oriented to Jewish-Christians, he would deliberately have to speak, as it were, against the very clear light of the sun in wishing to regard all the ideas and ways of speaking presented in these very different books as equally good and equally suitable instruction for all men of all times.

With all these ideas, Semler is the founder of the historical study of the New Testament. For him the Bible as a book is no longer inspired and can therefore be viewed impartially with the eyes of the historical investigator, without endangering the Word of God, which he wishes at all costs to guard. To be sure, because of his splintered syntax and unsystematic method of research, Semler's major contribution was to furnish stimuli and to indicate tasks, for "he did not break a new path for his age, but tried to formulate critical ideas that were beginning to dawn in every direction and to create a firm basis for them." [74] Only by the actual undertaking of the individual historical tasks by his contemporaries and successors could his stimuli take effect. If all this manifested a very personal limitation in the great instigator, it is also true that his uncompromising transformation of theology into a historical science and his consistent view of the Canon as an exclusively historical entity concealed a danger that he himself did not envisage—a danger that later F. C. Baur in his day was able correctly to formulate: "As soon as one determines the idea of canonicity only in accordance with the moral content of a document, everything at once becomes relative." [75] And consequently the science of New Testament studies from its very beginnings was brought up against a problem that it did not at first recognize, viz., how the pressing and unavoidable historical task was to be reconciled with the theological object of that task, namely, the New Testament. The vigorous criticism of Semler that broke out at once[76] was directed in large part against his denial of the inspiration of the Bible as a whole and against his subjective definition of what as the "Word of God" has permanent worth, on the ground that Semler's criticism undercut every sure basis of faith. And it is quite understandable that Semler, accused of destroying the Christian religion by his investigations, defended himself with the claim that his inquiries were basically historical and were not concerned in any way with true religion.[77]

Readers who themselves have actually read through all three of my investigations and were not already prejudiced by anger and indignation against me, will undoubtedly judge quite differently than a few reviewers have judged. What virulent poison are these studies of mine, and with what pestilential contagion they threaten all theology! Such violent and utterly unfounded condemnation that their own spleen has directed at me will once more lose all effect to the degree that unprejudiced readers have passed judgment on these investigations themselves, in accordance with their utterly blameless and for the most part historically incontrovertible content.

I am therefore convinced that I do not impede true Christian religion in any way by these serious investigations of the Canon, or really interfere with its power and spiritually beneficial efficacy.

The way of posing questions that Semler demanded and put into practice was able to become a genuinely scientific study of the New Testament only when the New Testament and its individual writings were subjected to a rigorously historical investigation. This step was taken by **Johann David Michaelis.** He took over a title, "Introduction to Holy Scripture," [78] already often used for works of a different sort, and as early as 1750 published his *Introduction to the Divine Scriptures of the New Covenant.* To begin with, this work was to a large extent an elaboration of R. Simon's critical textual studies,[79] but in its bulky, two-volume fourth edition of 1788 it was expanded into a comprehensive discussion of the historical problems of the New Testament and its individual books, and thereby inaugurated the science of New Testament introduction. In this work, after an extensive and critical account of previous studies, Michaelis treats for the first time, and wholly independently, the question of the language, textual criticism, and origin of the individual writings. In so doing he presents a variant form of the text-critical thesis of different text recensions, first put forward by Semler; admits the basic possibility and necessity of conjectures; and denies any mutual literary dependence of the Synoptics, while tracing their relationship to the common use of "other apocryphal gospels" (II, 930) and consequently presenting for the first time the hypothesis of an *Urevangelium* ["original, lost gospel"]. He even notes the anti-gnostic polemic in the Gospel of John and hazards the guess that John had taken "the Word" as an expression for a divine person "from the Gnostics" (II, 1137) and had written "against the disciples of John the Baptist, the Sabians [Mandaeans]" (II, 1140) —the first, therefore, to recognize the relationship of the Fourth Gospel to the gnostic world of thought. He also questions the apostolic origin of a few New Testament writings. It is doubtless true that Michaelis "laid the foundation for the structure of a wholly critical introduction to the New Testament in a most fortunate way." [80] Nevertheless, it is not actually in these countless individual observations that the enduring significance of Michaelis' *Introduction* is to be found. The reader is struck at once by the fact that Michaelis completely ignores the historical problem of the formation of the Canon, as well as Semler's *Treatise on the Free Investigation of the Canon,* and is content simply to assert the great age of the Canon in terms of its main constituents.[81] The problem of the historical origin of the Canon is overlooked, however, because Michaelis makes the presupposition that only those writings of the New Testament that stem from apostles are canonical, and consequently inspired; that this question of apostolic origin, however, is to be clarified by historical research. Accordingly, he recognizes no grounds whatever for counting Mark, Luke, and the Acts of the Apostles among the canonical books; he argues for the exclusion of the Greek text of Matthew, which represents a translation, as well as of James and Jude; and leaves open the question of the canonicity of Hebrews and the Book of Revelation.[82]

Before we proceed to examine the various grounds for the authenticity of the New Testament, it may not be improper to premise a few observations on the importance of this inquiry, and its influence in determining the divinity of the Christian religion. And we shall find its influence to be such, as to make it a matter of surprise that the adversaries of Christianity have not constantly made their first attacks upon this quarter. For, if they admit these writings to be as ancient as we pretend, and really composed by the persons to whom they are ascribed, though we cannot from these premises alone immediately conclude them to be divinely inspired, yet an undeniable consequence is the truth and divinity of the religion itself. The apostles allude frequently in their epistles to the gift of miracles, which they had communicated to the Christian converts by the imposition of hands in confirmation of the doctrine delivered in their speeches and writings, and sometimes to miracles which they themselves had performed. Now if these epistles are really genuine, it is hardly possible to deny those miracles to be true. The case is here entirely different from that of an historian, who relates extraordinary events in the course of his narrative, since their credulity or an actual intention to deceive may induce him to describe as true a series of falsehoods respecting a different land or a different time. An adversary of the Christian religion might make this objection even to the evangelists: but to write to persons with whom we stand in the nearest connection, "I have not only performed miracles in your presence, but have likewise communicated to you the same extraordinary endowments," to write in this manner, if nothing of the kind had ever happened, would require such an incredible degree of effrontery, that he who possessed it would not only expose himself to the utmost ridicule, but giving his adversaries the fairest opportunity to detect his imposture would ruin the cause, which he attempted to support.

The question of whether the books of the New Testament have been inspired by God is clearly more theological than the prior question of whether they are genuine. Therefore it does not wholly belong within the limits I have to accept in writing an introduction to the New Testament, if I am to avoid an incursion into the field of dogmatic theology. Nevertheless, there are some things that have to be said about it.

The question, whether the books of the New Testament are inspired, is not so important as the question whether they are genuine. The truth of our religion depends upon the latter, not absolutely on the former. Had the Deity inspired not a single book of the New Testament, but left the apostles and evangelists without any other aid, than that of natural abilities to commit what they knew to writing, admitting their works to be authentic, and possessed of a sufficient degree of credibility, the Christian religion would still remain the true one. The miracles, by which it is confirmed, would equally demonstrate its truth, even if the persons, who attested them were not inspired, but simply human witness and their divine authority is never presupposed, when we discuss the question of miracles, but merely their credibility as human evidence. If the miracles which the evangelists relate are true, the doctrines of Christ recorded in the Gospels are proved to be the infallible oracles of God . . . even if we admit the apostles to be mistaken in certain nonessential circumstances. . . .

The inference then to be deduced from what has been advanced in this section is as follows: Inspiration is not absolutely necessary to constitute the truth of the Christian religion, but it is necessary in order to promote its beneficial effects. If the parts of the New Testament are inspired, they make collectively a single entire work, in which the doubts arising in one passage are fully explained by another: but if the several parts of the New Testament are not inspired, the chain by which they hang together is destroyed, and the contradictory passages must occasion anxiety and distrust. . . .

Yet, after weighing with all that care and caution, which so important a subject requires, the arguments which may be advanced on both sides, it is perhaps advisable to divide the question. To the epistles inspiration is of real consequence, but with respect to the historical books, viz. the Gospels and the Acts of the Apostles, we should really be no losers if we abandoned the system of inspiration, and in some respects have a real advantage.

I will now proceed to a more satisfactory proof, and for that purpose shall divide the books of the New Testament, which we receive as canonical, into two separate classes, which we must take care not to confuse. The greater number bear the names of apostles, namely, Matthew, John, James, Peter, and Jude: others again were not written by apostles, but by their companions and assistants, viz. the Gospels of Mark and Luke, and the Acts of the Apostles.

With respect to the writings belonging to the first of these classes, their inspiration depends on their authenticity. If they are written by the apostles, to whom they are ascribed, we consider them as divinely inspired; if not written by apostles, they can make no pretension to inspiration.

Beside those books of the New Testament, which we have shewn to be inspired as having been written by apostles, there are three which were written by their assistants, viz. the Gospels of Mark and of Luke and the Acts of the Apostles. The question is, what are the grounds for placing these likewise in the Canon?

I must confess, that I am unable to find a satisfactory proof of their inspiration, and the more I investigate the subject, and the oftener I compare their writings with those of Matthew and John, the greater are my doubts. . . .

Taking all this into consideration, I can regard the writings of Mark and Luke as approved, to be sure, by eyewitnesses and apostles; Peter and John, not as inspired, but as written with supernatural help and infallibility. They, or I should say their readers, lose nothing on this account. It is enough for us if only, like other good historical documents, they are trustworthy.

If it can be shewn, that real contradictions, such as are wholly incapable of a reconciliation, exist in the four Gospels, the only inference to be deduced is, that the writers were not infallible, or in other words, not inspired by the Deity; but we are by no means warranted to conclude, because the historians vary in their accounts, that the history itself is a forgery . . . .

If the Greek Gospel of Matthew is not the original, which was penned by the evangelist, we cannot ascribe it to a verbal inspiration, and it is moreover not impossible that the translator in some few instances mistook the sense of his author. We have no reason however to be alarmed on this account, because the most material parts, or those in which we are chiefly interested, are recorded likewise by one or more of the other evangelists.

The arguments therefore on both sides of the question [of the authorship of Hebrews] are nearly of equal weight: but if there is any preponderance, it is in favor of the opinion, that Paul was not the author. For the intention to revisit Jerusalem, which the author of this epistle expresses, would hardly have been formed by St. Paul on his release from imprisonment. And if Paul was really the author, it is difficult to account for the omission of his name at the opening of the epistle, since the omission cannot well be ascribed to a translator, who would not have neglected to retain a name which gave authority to the epistle. . . .

I now come to the very important inquiry, whether the Epistle to the Hebrews, under these circumstances, ought to be received as an infallible rule of faith, and placed among the canonical books of the New Testament. . . . If then the epistle . . . was written by the apostle Paul, it is canonical. But if it was not written by an apostle, it is not canonical: for, however excellent its contents may be, they alone will not oblige us to receive it, as a work inspired by the Deity.

Under the circumstances, however highly I value the epistle (to the Hebrews), I know nothing certain to say of its divine inspiration. This stands or falls with the question of whether Paul or someone else wrote it—a question whose answer continues to remain in doubt.

If the James who wrote this epistle [James], was either the elder apostle James, the son of Zebedee, or the younger apostle James, the son of Alphaeus, it is canonical. But if it was written by the James, who was a half brother of Christ, and not an apostle, we can have no proof of its inspiration and infallibility. And inspiration and infallibility are not just everyday matters that one can accept without proof. Therefore, if is not by a James who was an apostle, I cannot accept the inspiration of the letter—the letter, furthermore, about which the ancient church was so divided.

From the account, which has already been given, it appears, that we have very little reason for placing the Epistle of St. Jude among the sacred writings.

But before the question in debate can be brought to a final issue, we must return to the inquiry instituted in the first section of this chapter, relative to the person and character of the author. If the Jude, who wrote this epistle, was the apostle Jude, the brother of the younger apostle James, we must place it without further hesitation among the apostolic writings, and pronounce it canonical. And in this case, we must either believe in the story of the dispute between Michael and the devil, and in the prophecies of Enoch, or admit that the arguments, which have been alleged against the two quotations in the Epistle of Jude, affect the infallibility of the apostles themselves. On the other hand, if the author of this epistle was not Jude, the apostle, but Jude the half brother of Jesus, I can see no reason why we should account it as of divine origin. . . .

I cannot therefore acknowledge that this epistle is canonical. And I have really some doubts whether it be not even a forgery, made in the name of Jude, by some person, who borrowed the chief part of his material from the Second Epistle of Peter, and added some few of his own.

Michaelis, to be sure, now seeks in a purely historical way to demonstrate the trustworthiness of the writings that in this fashion have been shown to be not inspired. Therefore he concerns himself in detail, for instance, with a "harmony" of the Gospels, or of the agreement between Paul and James, in order by such means to be able to maintain the dogmatic reliability of the noncanonical Gospels of Mark and Luke and of the Epistle of James. Nevertheless, he sees himself constrained to admit that the New Testament is no longer a whole that can be explained by its several parts, and must leave the question of divine origin open wherever he cannot definitely assert the apostolic composition of a document. The reasons for this hesitant attitude on his part are easy to discern: it is due, on the one hand, to the resumption of the principle of the ancient church—a resumption already evident in the writings of the humanists and of Luther—that only apostolic documents can be canonical; on the other hand, to an awareness of the impossibility of basing the inspiration of New Testament writings on the inner witness of the Holy Spirit, or on demonstrated moral values.[83]

Neither an inward sensation of the witness of the Holy Ghost nor the consciousness and experience of the utility of these writings in improving the heart, can decide these issues. With respect to that inward sensation, I must confess that I have never experienced it in the whole course of my life; nor are those persons who have felt it, either deserving of envy, or nearer the truth, since the Muhammedan feels it, as well as the Christian. And, as this internal divine sensation is the whole proof, on which Muhammed grounded his religion, which so many millions have adopted, we must naturally conclude it to be self-deceit. The other test is likewise insufficient, since pious sentiments may be excited by works, that are simply human, by the writings of philosophers, or even by doctrines founded on error; and if it were possible to draw a conclusion from these premises, the premises themselves are uncertain, since there are instances of men of the most despicable character, who have fancied they had attained the highest pitch of holiness.

But all this introduces a fateful and perverse factor into the situation. At the very moment that the New Testament texts are recognized as historical entities that must be subjected to rigorous historical investigation, this historical investigation is declared to be the criterion by which the inspiration of the New Testament writings is established. Accordingly, not only is it quite improper to undertake this in order to solve a dogmatic question, but also the investigation is so severely subordinated to dogmatic interests that a really historical investigation must be severely hindered. The consequence of this false formulation of the problem was and is "that questions of introduction become dogmatically important" [84] and that the free investigation demanded by Semler on the basis of his historical criticism of the Canon appears in fact to be no longer possible.

2.
The Literary Problems

The strictly historical study of the New Testament that had its beginning in the breakthrough by Semler and Michaelis resulted first of
all, in a serious consideration of the literary problems and, along with
that, an analysis of the history of primitive Christianity and of the primitive Christian world of thought. Semler's pupil, **Johann Jakob Griesbach,**
who in his travels had broadened the base of the text-critical material
for the New Testament that had been assembled by Mill and Wettstein,
published in 1774-75 an edition of the Greek New Testament which
printed his own recension instead of the "received text," and which was
equipped with an extensive critical apparatus. Although Griesbach in
this edition was very cautious about his text emendations,[85] nevertheless
his new recension marked the end of the undisputed reign of the "received text." This was achieved by virtue of a severely methodical criticism. Building on the hypotheses of Bengel and Semler, Griesbach assigned the text witnesses to three recensions, which he designated Alexandrian, Western, and Constantinopolitan, and of which he recognized
only the first two as valuable,[86] thereby laying the foundation for textual
criticism and for the study of the history of the text that has stood from
his day to ours. Moreover, in the second edition of his Greek New Testament Griesbach declared it to be the task of the critical examination of
the text of the New Testament to combine the judgment on the value
of the individual witnesses to the text and the internal criticism of a
reading on the basis of the linguistic peculiarities of the author and of
the context, and in this way to reach a decision as to the original text
that would be methodologically sound.[87] Having prepared the ground
for a truly new presentation of the text of the New Testament, Griesbach
now also undertook the task of the literary investigations of the New
Testament writers beginning with the Gospels. Even Michaelis had tried
in his *Introduction* to provide a harmony of the four Gospels. Griesbach,
on the other hand, by separating the Fourth Gospel from the first three
and printing the latter together in parallel columns under the title,

>

"A Synopsis of the Gospels of Matthew, Mark, and Luke," laid the foundation for a truly historical investigation of the literary interrelationships of the Gospels. In so doing his specific intention was to furnish an indispensable tool for a comparison of the three Gospels that were henceforth to be known as the "Synoptics," for he held that, since the three evangelists offer an unreliable chronological arrangement of their subject matter, a harmonization is impossible.[88]

I frankly acknowledge and wish my readers to keep in mind that under no circumstances will one find a so-called "harmony" in this little book. Although I am quite aware of all the trouble learned men have taken to prepare a harmony in accordance with the rules they have laid down, I believe, nevertheless, that not just a little but almost no profit at all can be derived [from their harmonies] that my synopsis—despite its inexactitude—does not offer. Furthermore, I doubt very much whether a harmonistic account can be composed from the books of the evangelists that with respect to chronological sequence agrees sufficiently with reality and is built on sure foundations. How could that be done? When none of the evangelists anywhere exactly follows the temporal sequence? And when there does not exist sufficient evidence from which to deduce who deviates from the chronological order and at what point he does so? And to this heresy I confess.

The freedom in the investigation of the relationship of the Gospels to one another that he had won in this way Griesbach demonstrated by opposing the traditional view that Matthew had been used by Mark, and both by Luke.[89] Griesbach supported this hypothesis by advancing (not very convincingly, it must be admitted) the reasons that had caused Mark, who normally chose to take his material from Matthew, now and then to follow Luke, and very occasionally to substitute for the reports of both his sources a narrative known to him from the oral tradition. In the course of so doing he was the first to make the suggestion that has been repeated again and again since his time, viz., that the original ending of Mark's Gospel, "in which doubtless the journey of Jesus to Galilee was recounted, has been accidentally lost." And Mark's method of composition, as he envisaged it, by which the evangelist simply made a choice of his material from the other Synoptists, causes Griesbach to make the concluding comment: "Whoever assumes that Mark wrote as an inspired author must think of him as having been very meagerly informed (*satis exilem informent necesse est*)." [90]

In the course of the initial literary investigation of the "synoptic question," a question that had become a "problem," several other attempts at a solution were independently advanced. The Tübingen theologian **Gottlob Christian Storr**, although primarily concerned as a biblical supernaturalist with demonstrating the truth of the New Testament documents, nevertheless was the first to employ a strictly historical argumentation to establish the dependence of Matthew and Luke on Mark, arguing convincingly that on the common assumption it would be impossible to account for Mark's omission of so much of Matthew and Luke.[91] And there were also others to whom it no longer seemed obvious that the relationship of the first three Gospels to one another could be explained only by the hypothesis of a mutual use of these Gospels, however this hypothesis might be phrased. Here also recourse was had to the aid of a literary hypothesis.

In 1776 **Gotthold Ephraim Lessing,** in an article entitled "Theses aus der Kirchengeschichte" [Theses from the history of the Church] (a posthumously published document), made the suggestion that the three synoptic evangelists had gone back independently of each other to an Aramaic gospel of the Nazarenes and that "this [assumption] alone explains the agreement which exists in the words used by these evangelists." [92] A couple of years later, in an essay entitled "Neue Hypothese über die Evangelisten als bloss menschliche Geschichtschreiber betrachtet" [New hypothesis concerning the evangelists regarded as merely human historians] [93] (also a posthumous publication), Lessing developed this idea, and the very title clearly shows the presuppositions on which his hypothesis was based. In connection with the controversy over the publication of the Reimarus' fragments (to which reference is later to be made) Lessing wished to clarify his thinking concerning the value of the Gospels as sources and consequently examined the relationship of the Gospels to one another as a purely literary problem. In so doing he combined the references of the church fathers to a gospel of the heretical Jewish Christians (Nazarenes) with the supposition, based wholly on deduction, of a Hebrew _Urevangelium_ ["original, lost gospel"] which lies back of all three Synoptics. In the course of developing this hypothesis he was characteristically led to infer from the briefer content of Mark's Gospel that a shorter version of this primal document served as Mark's basic source.[94]

Thus there was a narrative of Christ written earlier than Matthew's. And during the thirty years it remained in that language in which alone its compilers could have written it. Or to put the matter less definitely and yet more accurately: it remained in the Hebrew language or in the Syriac-Chaldaean dialect of Hebrew as long as Christianity was for the most part still confined to Palestine and to the Jews in Palestine.

Only when Christianity was extended among the Gentiles, and so many who understood neither Hebrew nor a more modern dialect of it were curious to have better information about the person of Christ (which, however, may not have been during the first years of the Gentile mission, since all the first Gentile converts were content with the oral accounts which the apostles gave to each one), was it found necessary and useful to satisfy a pious curiosity by turning to that Nazarene source, and to make extracts or translations from it in a language which was the language of virtually the entire civilized world. The first of these extracts, the first of these translations, was made, I think, by Matthew. . . .

Indeed, the original of Matthew was certainly Hebrew, but Matthew himself was not the actual author of this original. From him, as an apostle, many narratives in the Hebrew original may well derive. But he himself did not commit these narratives to writing. At his dictation others wrote them down in Hebrew and combined them with stories from the other apostles; and from this human collection he in his time made merely a connected selection in Greek. . . .

If he made this selection in a better known language with all the diligence, with all the caution, of which such an enterprise is worthy, then indeed, to speak only humanly, a good spirit must have assisted him. And no one can object if one calls this good spirit the Holy Spirit. . . .

It is enough that so much is certain, that Luke himself had before him the Hebrew document, the Gospel of the Nazarenes, and transferred, if not everything, at least most of the contents to his Gospel, only in rather different order and in rather better language.

It is still more obvious that Mark, who is commonly held to be only an abbreviator of Matthew, appears to be so only because he drew upon the same Hebrew document, but probably had before him a less complete copy.

In short, Matthew, Mark, and Luke are simply different and not different translations of the so-called Hebrew document of Matthew which everyone interpreted as well as he could. . . .

And John? It is quite certain that John knew and read that Hebrew document, and used it in his Gospel. Nevertheless, his Gospel is not to be reckoned with the others, it does not belong to the Nazarene class. It belongs to a class all its own.

If therefore Christianity was not to fall asleep and to disappear among the Jews again as a mere Jewish sect, and if it was to endure among the Gentiles as a separate, independent religion, John must come forward and write his Gospel.

It was only his Gospel which gave the Christian religion its true consistency. We have only his Gospel to thank if the Christian religion, despite all attacks, [continues] in this consistency and will probably survive as long as there are men who think they need a mediator between themselves and the Deity: that is, for ever.

Although Lessing did not develop this hypothesis in detail, it was nevertheless of great significance as the first attempt to trace the development of the gospel tradition by a purely literary examination of it, without the presupposition of inspiration; and the hypothesis of a lost Aramaic original Gospel necessarily robbed the canonical Gospels of the unconditional trustworthiness with which they had hitherto been credited. On the other hand, although Lessing recognized the basic difference between the Synoptics and John, yet he gave John a higher rank as a Gospel more valuable than the Synoptics, without raising the historical question of the value of John as a witness.

But the assumption of a lost Hebrew or Aramaic Primal Gospel that Lessing had made became really discussable only when **Johann Gottfried**

Eichhorn, a pupil of J. D. Michaelis, gave it a defensible form in his comprehensive study, "Über die drey ersten Evangelien" [Concerning the first three Gospels] (1794). Eichhorn holds that a mutual use of one Synoptic Gospel by the other two is impossible because none of the Gospels consistently offers the better text and context when compared with the others. Consequently, all he believes to be left is "the hypothesis of a common source from which all three must have drawn." The verbal variations of the evangelists from one another lead, according to Eichhorn, to the conclusion that this lost Primal Gospel was composed in Hebrew or Aramaic, but Eichhorn not only assumes that there were different translations by the canonical evangelists, but also suggests that each evangelist had used a different form of the Primal Gospel, enlarged and altered by additions and changes, and had also enlarged it on his own part. Going still further, he suggests that Matthew and Luke took the material common only to them "from other literary sources upon which they . . . drew in addition to the original document, variously reworked and enriched, which has been described above." [95] However complicated this hypothesis—and ten years later, in the first volume of his *Einleitung in das Neue Testament* [Introduction to the New Testament] he advanced a basically still more complicated version of it—it brought to light two problems that require solution: (1) Because the wording of the parallel passages of the evangelists often does not agree, the oldest form of the tradition must be sought behind our canonical texts, and, where possible, actually in the Hebrew-Aramaic language milieu, if one wishes to get back to the original tradition of the words of Jesus; and (2) in addition Eichhorn recognizes that the agreements that only Matthew and Luke exhibit point to a special literary source, whose existence and character, it must be admitted, Eichhorn was not yet really able convincingly to demonstrate. And Eichhorn himself saw that the reduction of the oldest tradition to a lost Primal Gospel that lies back of our Synoptic Gospels is the presupposition for a separation of an ancient, reliable tradition about Jesus from later additions, and he hoped by freeing the apostolic tradition from later embellishments of it to be able better to ward off the attack on the truth of Christendom by representatives of the Enlightenment.[96]

This discovery of the Primal Gospel is of great importance for the explanation of the words used by the evangelists and the proper understanding of their meaning, for the criticism of the New Testament in general and of the evangelists in particular, indeed, for all theology.

To make a beginning with the uses that the last-mentioned [i.e. theology] derives from this theory: by this discovery we are directed to those parts of the life of Jesus which the first teachers of Christendom regarded as alone essential for the establishment of the Christian faith among their Jewish contemporaries.

And this is one of the most important of the preliminary questions for the simplification of Christian dogma, and one on which German theology for forty years has worked so assiduously. . . .

The reconstruction of the Primal Gospel demonstrates that neither that which Matthew nor that which Luke reworked had anything to say of the conception, birth, and youth of Jesus; and it was only later times, from which we cannot expect any reliable information about these matters, that enlarged the Primal Gospel with them: And can they therefore be regarded as anything more than sagas which, to be sure, may have a basis in fact, but a basis which can no longer be distinguished from the embellishments with which tradition has clothed it? . . .

He would be actually a traitor to religion who in his zeal for matters of tradition would wish to oppose the attempt to reduce the Gospels solely to their apostolic content and to free them again from the additions and embellishments that were made at a later time in the course of their reworking. He would oppose the only means by which not only apparent, but also very well-grounded, objections to the life and deeds of Jesus can be removed and their credibility be rescued from attacks of intelligent doubters. . . . What articles of faith would be endangered? What doctrine would the Christian religion have to give up? If thereby a few theological speculations should get into trouble and lose the apparent support on which they have heretofore rested, what harm can come of that? Should the inner credibility and truth of the·gospel story be abandoned, or exposed to the mockery of witty or witless opponents of religion, in order to maintain a few theological speculations? Should a mere nothing, an inherited theological opinion, be bought for so high a price? Far be it from every genuine friend of the religion of Jesus to pay it! By this freeing [of the Primal Gospel from its accretions] countless doubts with which Jesus, his life, and his teaching have been assailed become completely meaningless. . . . By this separation of the apostolic from the nonapostolic which higher criticism—if only its gift be not spurned—recommends for the most important of reasons, the means are found·to establish the credibility and truth of the gospel story on unshakable foundations.

While Eichhorn developed Lessing's idea of a Primal Gospel into a complicated and accordingly problematical literary hypothesis **Johann Gottfried Herder** drew from it another and no less significant consequence. He deals separately with the two elements of Lessing's presupposition that the portrait of Jesus in the first three Gospels ought not to be confused with that in the Fourth and discusses it therefore in two monographs, "Vom Erlöser der Menschen. Nach unseren drei ersten Evangelien" [Of the Redeemer of men; according to our first three gospels], and "Von Gottes Sohn, der Welt Heiland. Nach Johannes Evangelium" [Of the Son of God, the Savior of the world; according to the Gospel of John] (1796-97).[97] But he also goes further. He disputes the right to harmonize the three Synoptics on the grounds that each evangelist should be permitted to make his own contribution: "There are four evangelists, and let each retain his special purpose, complexion, time, and locale."[98] He can oppose every attempt at harmonization because, just as Lessing had done, he regarded all four evangelists as independent elaboraters of a Primal Gospel, but in his view a Primal Gospel that was oral rather than literary. Herder came to this conclusion by reason of a clear insight into the spiritual roots of the process of gospel formation: The oldest Gospel was the oral proclamation of Jesus the Messiah and consequently had no biographical interest; the first evangelists resembled rhapsodists, and an oral Primal Gospel took shape from their testimony to faith and was only then committed to writing when its remoteness from the original witness of the apostles made such a fixation imperative. This oral transmission of the Gospels preserved the actual words of Jesus more exactly than their narrative framework and consisted of separate pericopes. As the most primitive Gospel, Mark best reproduces this oral Primal Gospel, while Matthew offers an expanded version of it that seeks to demonstrate that Jesus is the Messiah of Jewish dogmatic expectation, and Luke, who was aware of Matthew's additions, wished to create "an actual historical account" after a wholly Hellenistic pattern. Some forty years later John, on the other hand, wrote an "echo of the earlier Gospels at a higher pitch" which undertook to set forth Jesus as the Savior of the world, and in this connection Herder clearly recognizes John's familiarity with gnostic language and world outlook.[99]

John (the Baptist's) proclamation (kerygma) was only the voice of a precursor, of a servant who prepared the way; as soon as a Messiah from heaven was declared, the Gospel came into being, the Good News namely that "he who had long been hoped for is come." With it [that Gospel] Jesus came to Galilee (Mark 1:14, 15); he proclaimed it from the roll of scripture (Luke 4:17, 19). This Gospel his disciples preached; the form, the duties, and the hopes of his kingdom Christ set forth in parables and in teachings: He suffered and died for this Gospel, and after his resurrection he entrusted them [his apostles] with the responsibility of spreading it throughout the world. Therefore, before any of our Gospels was written, the Gospel was there in the proclamation of Christ and of the apostles.

When Peter at the first Pentecost spoke of the God-authenticated man who was promised through the prophets, the man anointed with the Spirit of God who had brought the true kingdom of God to earth, had shown himself alive after his crucifixion, and had ascended to heaven in order at his own time to reveal himself together with his kingdom, this was therefore a full Christian Gospel (Acts 2:22-39), and one that we discover again, in other words but with just the same content, in all the discourses of Peter and the [other] apostles. . . .

Consequently Christianity did not begin with the writing of Gospels but with the proclamation of things past and to come (kerygma, revelation), with interpretation, teaching, comfort, exhortation, preaching. . . .

In general the Gospel of John best demonstrates the idea . . . that they (the Gospels) are not in any sense biographies, but were intended to be historical documentation of the Christian confession of faith that Jesus was the Messiah, and after what fashion he was the Messiah. John's Gospel as the latest pursues this purpose in most definite outline, and in the course of so doing an actual biography is wholly lost to view, though it is also true that one ought not to think of biography as the main concern even of the older Gospels. They are what their name implies. . . . When therefore under such circumstances a Gospel was written, it could be recorded in no other sense than this. There was neither purpose nor motive to report anecdotes out of the private life of Jesus, for those who composed it [the Gospel] and those for whom it was composed were not the public interested in writing and reading that is characteristic of our times. . . .

Since therefore we learn nothing of this period, and our Gospels are clearly composed according to the principles determined for them by the earlier oral Gospel, who would fail to recognize this outline in them, and along with it also the purpose, that was all-important to the disciples of Christ? They were written that you may believe that Jesus is the Christ, the Son of God. . . .

Just as it was therefore impossible that Christianity, as it spread at such a time, in this environment, among those peoples, could survive without literary records, that is to say, without Gospels, so it is just as foreign to think of an apostolic Gospel chancellory in Jerusalem that sent tracts with each teacher to each congregation and equipped him with written Gospels. In the Acts of the Apostles, which records the most remarkable development of the first quarter-century of Christianity, we find not a trace of it, but rather an utterly different approach to the founding of congregations. The apostles were sent out to teach, not to distribute evangelical tracts. . . .

The whole idea of our evangelists as scribes (*grammateis, scribae*) assembling, enlarging, improving, collating, and comparing tracts is strange to, and remote from, that of all ancient writings that speak of their activities, and even more foreign to conclusions drawn from observing them themselves, and most of all to their situation, their motivation, and the purpose of their Gospels. . . .

Furthermore, their whole appearance belies the notion that they drew from one so-called Primal Gospel. Neither apostolic nor church history knows of any such Primal Gospel; no church father in combating the false gospels appeals to such a Primal Gospel as to the fount of truth.

However, it was inevitable that in the course of their instruction these oral evangelists should acquire a circle of followers (*cyklus*) within which their message was preserved, and this circle was that which the apostles themselves possessed from the beginning of their proclamation of the Gospel. . . .

In our three Gospels the same parables occur, to cite one example, the same miracles, narratives, and discourses, from which it may be seen that the general tradition of these gospel rhapsodies (if I may be permitted to use the word) was admirably suited to these accounts. Often they are reported with the same words; that is the very nature of an oral saga, especially an apostolic one, retold as it was again and again, as we note in the sermons of Peter and the letters of the apostles. They were fixed, sacred sagas.

In the case of a free, oral narrative, not everything is equally untrammeled. Sentences, long sayings, parables are more likely to retain the same form of expression than minor details of the narrative; transitional material and connecting formulae the narrator himself supplies. This distinction is evident in the case of our Gospels. Positive, in particular vigorous, obscure, parabolic expressions are everywhere identical, even when differently applied, while in detail, in connecting matter, in the ordering of events the accounts diverge most readily. . . .

The common Gospel consisted of individual units, narratives, parables, sayings, pericopes. This is evident from the very appearance of the Gospels and from the different order of this or that parable or saga. . . . The fact that it consists of such parts vouches for the truth of the Gospel, for people such as most of the apostles were, more easily recall a saying, a parable, an apothegm that they had found striking than connected discourses. . . .

When this evangelist [Mark] is regarded as a frugal epitomizer of Matthew or as a comparably cautious compiler of our Matthew and our Luke, and is read after Matthew, as is usually the case, almost all his worth disappears. But why is he read in this way? If Mark's Gospel were to stand by itself (as of course it did when it first was written), it would occupy a high place by reason of the simple principle: "Mark's Gospel is not an abbreviation, but a Gospel in its own right. What others have in a more expanded form and differently has been added by them, not omitted by Mark. Furthermore, Mark is witness to an original, briefer version, to which what the others include over and above what is in it is to be regarded as an addition." Is not this the natural point of view? Is not the briefer, the unadorned, usually the more primitive, to which, then, other occasions later add explanation, embellishment, rounding out?

With these insights into the significance and the forms of the most ancient gospel tradition and the character of all the canonical Gospels as vehicles of witness, Herder was the first to recognize the problems that much later were to concern that branch of gospel research known as form criticism. It may well be that in his conception of the evangelists as narrators of oral "sagas" Herder was influenced by the hypothesis of the philologian F. A. Wolf with respect to the origin of the Homeric poems.[100] However, Herder's insight into the witness-bearing character of the most ancient tradition about Jesus was more significant, an insight that rested on a study of the Acts of the Apostles and on his own poetic empathy with the literary individualities of the evangelists. Furthermore, by his emphasis on the primitive character of the Gospel of Mark and his assumption of a knowledge of additional tradition on the part of both Matthew and Luke, Herder prepared the ground for the recognition of the priority of Mark and the emergence of the two-document hypothesis of gospel origins, although he himself denied any literary connection between our Gospels.

With all that, however, Herder in the last analysis pursued a still more far-reaching goal, historical and at the same time theological: He seeks to lay the basis for reading "the Gospel itself" as mediated in the Gospels by the Primal Gospel common to all evangelists. Thereby the problem of the historical Jesus emerged here also, though it must be admitted that Herder, because he was unable to construct any clear picture of the worth of the sources employed by the several evangelists, never really comes to grips with it. And still another question is raised, namely, whether "the religion about Jesus," that is to say, the primitive Christian faith in Christ, must not be brought back again to "the religion of Jesus," to Jesus' personal relationship to God and his teaching about brotherly love, and this anticipates a problem that was not actually to be settled until the twentieth century.[101]

Consequently, what we must read in the Gospels is the Gospel itself, which concerns the teaching, the character, and the work of Jesus, i.e., the provision he wished to make for the highest good of men. Since all these three belong together, we will treat them in relation to one another.

The teaching of Jesus was simple and comprehensible to all: God is your Father and you are all brothers one of another. . . .

What makes the teaching of Christ, which can be so briefly summarized into an all-dominating conviction, an endless quest, is expressed by the character of Jesus just as fully and just as simply in his two names: He was called Son of God and Son of man. For the beloved of God, the Father's will was the most important rule, the mainspring of everything, even of the most arduous tasks, including the sacrifice of his life. Respect, honor, riches, unmerited ignominy, scorn—he was as indifferent to the one as to the other. There was a work to be done to which he knew himself to be called, the work of God, that is to say, the concrete and eternal design of God's providence to save the human race and assure its blessedness. This work he carried out as Son of man, that is, as a pure duty and in the highest interests of mankind. . . .

And this character was unmistakably demonstrated in his fulfillment of his work, for work it was, not just teaching. To bring a kingdom of God to the nations, in other words, a real order and disposition that would be worthy of both God and men, that was his calling; that was his purpose. . . .

Therefore the so-called religion about Jesus must necessarily change with the passage of time into a religion of Jesus, and do so imperceptibly and irresistibly. His God, our God; his Father, our Father!

Whoever contributes to bringing back the religion of Jesus from a meretricious slavery and from a painfully pious Lord-Lording to that genuine Gospel of friendship and brotherliness, of convinced, spontaneous, free, glad participation in the work and intent of Jesus as they are clearly set forth in the Gospels—he himself has taken part in Christ's work and has advanced it.

Herder's assumption of an oral Primal Gospel was taken up by the church historian **Johann Carl Ludwig Gieseler,** but his systematization of the hypothesis actually succeeded only in making its difficulties apparent.[102] Gieseler assumed that the Aramaic Primal Gospel took form "largely by itself" and that this Primal Gospel in turn was translated orally into Greek. In this latter process, however, two variant Greek forms developed. On these the Synoptic Gospels are dependent, while John, though he also knew these cycles of oral narratives, wished in addition to teach "philosophically trained Christians" a "proper understanding of Christianity." This hypothesis accordingly predicated three closed oral sources; it could not account for the literal agreement between two or three of the Synoptics in their Greek dress; and consequently the assumption of an oral Primal Gospel as the only explanation of the relation of the canonical Gospels to one another became exceedingly problematical. A hypothesis that **Friedrich Schleiermacher** proposed to put in place of that of a Primal Gospel was to prove even less convincing. He undertook to demonstrate by careful analysis of Luke's Gospel [103] that the entire Lucan document was only a composite of reports that had been transmitted either separately or in small, pre-Lucan collections. His observation of the originally independent character of the individual units of the synoptic tradition was acute, but he failed to correlate it with the fact that the Synoptic Gospels exhibit a remarkable agreement both in the sequence of gospel matter and in actual wording. When Schleiermacher in the course of interpreting the most ancient references to the composition of Matthew's Gospel advanced the suggestion that a collection of the sayings of Jesus that goes back to the apostle Matthew had been incorporated into this Gospel as an important component, he touched on a genuine problem.[104] Still more significant, however, was his demonstration that I Timothy cannot come from Paul by reason of its language usage and of the situation it presupposes, which under no circumstances can be fitted into the life of Paul, as well as its lack of homogeneity. It must be admitted, however, that the real difference of the letter's content from that of the genuine Pauline letters was still unobserved. Schleiermacher expressly refuses to defend his appeal to I Timothy's use of language as an argument on the grounds that he "cannot see any reason why the New Testament books should be treated in any respect any differently from others, or what measure one should use to reach a decision concerning a suspicion of their authenticity other than in the case of other ancient writings," and with reference to the question of what happens to the canonicity of the letter if it is proven unauthentic he does not hesitate to answer: "He who . . . pays attention only to the content of the letter, taking the pious deception no more seriously than was intended by the author, could certainly let it keep its place [in the Canon]." [105] This avoids the disastrous equation of apostolic authenticity and canonicity that J. D. Michaelis had made. At a later time, in his posthumously published lectures on *Einleitung in das Neue Testament* [New Testament Introduction], Schleiermacher expressly insists that in apostolic times very probably anyone conscious of being in essential agreement with what an apostle had taught "was able to regard the publication of his writing under the apostle's name as a wholly acceptable fiction" and that Greek literature proves without a shadow of doubt that such pseudepigraphy was customary.[106] This observation made it possible later to discuss the critical issues wholly without prejudice and at the same time to determine the value of the content of the texts without regard to the results of critical examination.

That Schleiermacher historically speaking had stopped halfway with his separation of I Timothy from the two other Pastorals was shown a few years later by **J. G. Eichhorn,** who demonstrated on the one hand that all three Pastoral Letters stand together, but on the other hand also that their very religious language differs from that of Paul.[107] Then, however, in addition to those whose authenticity had already been doubted in the course of the compilation of the Canon, and accordingly also by Michaelis, still other New Testament writings were necessarily subjected to historical interrogation. This was true in the first instance of the Gospel of John, although, as we have seen, the very pioneer of the ground-breaking attempts to give a historical explanation of the origin of the Gospels had regarded John's Gospel as an especially valuable historical work and as apostolic in authorship. After a few voices had been hesitantly raised against the authenticity of John's Gospel as early as the last decade of the eighteenth century, several scholars at the beginning of the nineteenth questioned the Johannine authorship of the Fourth Gospel with less equivocation.[108] The Franconian superintendent **Erhard Friedrich Vogel,** writing anonymously, deliberately left the concept of revelation out of consideration in his study of New Testament writings and attempted to prove [1801-1804] that in view of many indications the Gospel of John could have been written only after the apostle's death. More than that, in a two-volume discussion of recent commentaries he demonstrated not only that the opinions of these commentators were in large part completely arbitrary, but also that the text of the Gospel to a large extent was wholly inexplicable.[109] In 1804 the Hessian pastor **Georg Konrad Horst,** taking his lead from H. Vogel, ventured the opinion as "a mere conjecture" that the christological contradictions in the Gospel of John go back to the author's use of several sources and that both the late attestation of the Gospel and its Alexandrian ideas make it impossible to assume that its author was one of Jesus' disciples.[110] Furthermore, in his presentation of the teachings of the various apostolic writings (1808) **Hermann Heimart Cludius,** Superintendent of Hildesheim, says that the Gospel of John represents a Christianity quite different from that of the Jesus of the Synoptics and cannot have come from the pen of an eyewitness, and especially that the contradictions in the Gospel indicate that it has been worked over by various redactors.[111] But doubts as to the apostolic origin of the Fourth Gospel did not attract much attention until **Karl Gottlieb Bretschneider,** the General Superintendent of Gotha, in an investigation published in 1820, written in Latin to avoid offending the uneducated public, added to the arguments against the possibility that the author of the Gospel of John was an apostle and an eyewitness, the clear proof that this Gospel could not have had its origin on Jewish soil and that it offers a version of Jesus' teaching that is irreconcilable with the simple and Jewish form of it in the Synoptics: "It is accordingly quite impossible that both the Jesus of the [first] three Gospels and that of the Fourth can at the same time be historically true, since there is the greatest difference between them, not only in the manner of discourse but also in the argumentation and the behavior of the two; it is also quite incredible that the first evangelists invented Jesus' practices, teachings, and method of instruction; but it is quite believable that the author of the Fourth Gospel could have created his Jesus." The sharp contours of this argument were blurred, however, by the fact that Bretschneider declares at the outset: "We do not regard the Gospel of John as inauthentic; it only appears to us to be so." [112] And it comes as no surprise to find that as early as four years later, when his book had raised a storm of objections, Bretschneider explained that he had published his hypotheses "not that they should be accepted as valid, but that they might be examined and, if found baseless, refuted. If I erred in that respect it is most fitting that it [my theory] should be abandoned and that the truth should prevail." [113]

However, this kind of denial of the apostolic origin of John raised the question of the agreement of the Synoptics and the Fourth Gospel, and sooner or later a satisfactory answer to it had to be forthcoming. Moreover, the critical question concerning the reliability of the traditional derivations of New Testament writings was necessarily extended to still other hitherto undisputed books: **H. H. Cludius,** who as we have just seen contested the apostolic origin of the Gospel of John, traced I Peter back to a nonapostolic Gentile Christian on the grounds that the distinctiveness of the letter clearly indicates that Peter was not its author; and two decades later **Wilhelm Martin Leberecht de Wette** insists that there is some reason for doubting the Pauline origin of II Thessalonians and of the Epistle to the Ephesians, although he himself does not venture to deny the authenticity of these letters.[114]

This whole questioning attitude, which subjects the New Testament writings individually and as a whole to a strictly historical examination, got its first comprehensive expression in **J. G. Eichhorn's** five-volume *Einleitung in das Neue Testament* [Introduction to the New Testament].[115] Eichhorn deals in succession with the conditions under which the several books had come into being, the history of the collection of these books, and finally, the history of the text, although in so doing he himself is so cautious a critic that, except for the Pastoral Letters, he confidently contests the authenticity only of II Peter, while leaving the question open in the instances of James, Jude, and I Peter. For Eichhorn, to be sure, the question of the authenticity of the Synoptics becomes wholly unimportant because the historical worth of these Gospels actually depends entirely on the different forms of the nonapostolic Primal Gospel which were assumed to lie back of them. It is more significant, however, that Eichhorn now, breaking with J. D. Michaelis, is the first seriously to maintain that the investigation of the conditions under which the New Testament and its writings came into being has completely to disregard the question of inspiration. Consequently he also demonstrates on purely historical grounds that before the middle of the second century there was no New Testament, and even declares that the definition of an orthodox collection of Christian records of religion appears to have been prompted by Marcion's heterodox one, "which had become well-known in the Catholic Church." [116] He is also quite aware that the Canon was closed by church decrees in the fourth century and at that the major condition for admission to the Canon was that the apostolic origin of a book should be recognized by all. And going further, he maintained that we—in contrast to the ancient church—could accept even these books as apostolic that were not written by an apostle, provided they were in agreement with apostolic doctrine. In this way Eichhorn seems to have arrived at the same conclusion reached by Schleiermacher at the same time: namely, that the authority of a New Testament document depends entirely on its content. But he then suddenly ascribes first rank only to the writings of the apostles. This ambivalence indicates that Eichhorn also does not yet consider the literary investigation of the New Testament a wholly historical undertaking, and the theological significance of this literary research still remains unrecognized.[117]

It was the teaching of Jesus contained in the writings of the apostles that wrought the mighty consequences on earth, not its representation in the New Testament; the former came from God, the latter from men.

In every book of the New Testament the author's individuality can be recognized. How else is this to be explained if the material that came from Jesus has not been worked over by each writer in terms of his own peculiar use of language, his own power of imagination, his own capacity for thought? . . . No other rules of criticism need be applied to their writings than are used with reference to other human writers.

Therefore, O holy men, however reverentially I bow myself before you, to whom we are indebted for writings of such immeasurable influence, my reverence, as you yourselves have said, must not pass over into any superstitious idolatry that would fancy itself guilty of a sacrilegious temple robbery if it were to attempt to illuminate your sanctuary by the use of the principles of human criticism. No! The books of the New Testament are to be read as human books and examined as human books. Without fear of giving offence, therefore, one may investigate the nature of their origin, inquire into the constituents of their subject matter, and ask questions as to the sources whence their influential content has flowed. The more exact the criticism and the more rigorous the judgment, the better.

It is criticism alone that can determine the main content of the books that can serve as *regula fidei* ["a rule of faith"]. The Church assuredly was right when it assumed that the purest Christian doctrine was to be expected of the apostles. But to achieve that aim it was not indispensable to have books that had been written by the apostles themselves. Also such books could serve that end for whose agreement with apostolic doctrine there was the requisite certitude. Even the early Christian centuries were aware of this. Otherwise they would have been unable to make any place in their canon for the Gospels of Mark and Luke. In this they made only one mistake, viz., that they limited the guaranty of the agreement with apostolic doctrine to the demand that they must have been written under the supervision of the apostles, a demand that led them to the unhistorical hypothesis that Mark had been written under Peter's supervision and Luke under Paul's. It is enough if it can be shown that the writers as contemporaries and companions of the apostles were able to have precise knowledge of the historical and dogmatic elements of the Christian doctrine and if a careful comparison of their writings with those of the apostles shows that the former are in complete agreement with the latter. In all this, however, there are two ranks that may exist among the documents of religion. Documents, to be sure, from both ranks must be examined, for only such an examination leads to the certitude of their worth as religious documents. It is only from the nature of the examination that the difference between them becomes evident. The apostolic writings need be tested only by themselves and be coherent only with the tradition about them, while the writings of apostolic times, on the other hand, must cohere both with the tradition about them and with the content of the apostolic writings. The former speak as eye and ear witnesses; the latter as reliable reporters. The former are indebted to themselves for the content of their writings; the latter to another incontestable authority. Consequently the former are ranked higher as sources of faith; the latter lower.

3.
The History of Primitive Christianity and Its World of Thought

Although all these literary investigations still fail to show any clear concern to fit the New Testament writings into the history of primitive Christianity, nevertheless, particularly in the investigation of the origin of the Gospels, it becomes apparent that the researchers were desirous of discovering something of the earliest Christian world of thought by the disclosure of the older tradition incorporated in the Gospels. And so the question concerning the history of primitive Christianity emerged first of all in connection with the problem of the historical Jesus. It was Hermann Samuel Reimarus who, quite against his will, took the initiative. Reimarus, a teacher of Oriental languages at Hamburg Preparatory School [Gymnasium], had prepared an extensive critique of Christianity from the point of view of radical English Deism "in order to quiet his conscience," [118] but had kept it strictly to himself. Lessing had heard in Hamburg of this document and had taken a first draft of it with him to Wolfenbüttel, where he published seven fragments in installments, the last a treatment, "Vom Zwecke Jesu und seiner Jünger" [On the purpose of Jesus and his disciples] that contained Reimarus' reconstruction of early Christian history. In this Reimarus tried to show that the great task is "completely to separate what the apostles present in their writings from what Jesus himself actually said and taught during his lifetime." According to Reimarus, Jesus was wholly a Jew, had no intention of setting forth any new articles of faith, and preached the nearness of the messianic kingdom in the secular, Jewish sense. Only when this hope had to be abandoned with the death of Jesus did the apostles "come up with the idea of a suffering spiritual redeemer of the whole human race." The apostles invented this new system in order to be able to maintain their "design on worldly grandeur and privilege," and by means of the theft of Jesus' corpse they made possible the proclamation of Jesus' resurrection.[119] In developing this reconstruction Reimarus expressly points out that, because the disciples had inserted their new system into it, only traces of this history of Jesus are still to be found in the Gospels. Lessing did not betray the identity of the author of the *Fragments* and, although J. G. Hamann suspected it as early as 1777, it did not become common knowledge until Reimarus' son made it public in 1813.[120] Consequently indignation was vented on "the Unknown" and then on Lessing, the publisher, who, however, never associated himself with Reimarus' views.[121] On the other hand, since D. F. Strauss characterized Reimarus as one of "the most honest and most worthy representatives" of the task of the eighteenth century, so far as the Bible and Christianity are concerned, and A. Schweitzer described Reimarus' writings as "a historical performance of no mean order," [122] Reimarus has been described again and again as the initiator of the quest of the historical Jesus. This, however, is unquestionably an overstatement of the importance of Reimarus' criticism, which makes massive use of ideas taken over from the English Deist[123] and spins the two decisive motifs of its historical reconstruction out of whole cloth: namely, the political character of Jesus' preaching and the deception perpetrated by the disciples for materialistic reasons after Jesus' death. The importance of the publication of the *Fragments* lies rather in the fact that for a large circle the historical task of distinguishing between the proclamation of the historical Jesus and the preaching of the early church was made imperative, while at the same time a problem was raised that demanded attention: namely, what role in the emancipation of Christianity from Judaism is to be attributed to Jesus.

But first much time had to pass before the historical problem raised by Reimarus was really attacked. When J. S. Semler objects in his long-winded *Beantwortung der Fragmente eines Ungenannten* [An answer to the fragments of an unknown] that the contradictions alleged by the author [Reimarus] are due to the fact that for him "a description by any evangelist" must be "as true as those of the others," while actually account should be taken of the differences between the authors of the Gospels—in other words, that source criticism should be practiced,[124] he raises the decisive objection to Reimarus' method. To be sure, Semler himself wished to distinguish "a twofold teaching method in the Gospels," the one "sensuous, pictorial," which was to facilitate the understanding of the Jews, and the other that already has "the pure content of the spiritual teaching of Jesus" and can dispense with those pictures, so that "the literal and the figurative or spiritual understanding really took place at one and the same time." [125] But this distinction between the meaning of the letter and its actual spiritual sense overlooks the historical task, which seeks to understand the meaning of the texts by means of their very temporally conditioned forms and consequently must first try to clarify the historical value of the sources.

The Heidelberg theologian **Heinrich Eberhard Gottlob Paulus**, who as a consistent rationalist became known as one who did not hesitate to explain the Gospel accounts of miracles even by the banal and the absurd,[126] takes the matter a step further. In the first volume of his commentary on the first three Gospels, which appeared as early as 1800, Paulus declared his intention to be to prepare the way for "a historical and pragmatic survey of the life of Jesus" and, as the basic task of such an investigation, to get behind the judgments of the narrators to the facts. To be sure, not only did this first attempt at a pragmatic representation of the history of Jesus accept the still unquestioned presupposition that "in the Gospels every word is a veritable and reliable reproduction of what actually happened," [127] but also the further presupposition that this pragmatic connection of what really happened can be made clear by the disclosure of the natural events that the ancients had mistakenly regarded as miraculous.[128]

Because he [the author] is searching for nothing but the historical meaning and thereby wishes to prepare the way for the study of the history of primitive Christianity, he assumes that his readers wish him to treat his subject matter pragmatically and historically. Let us elaborate what is meant by this. In the first place, the interpretation or philosophically critical disclosure of the meaning intended by the narrator is to be regarded as the most important principle of all historical research. In the second place, a clear distinction is to be drawn between what is narrated and what happened. By this means the reader, having been made acquainted with all the circumstances and details of the narrative—in terms generally of the knowledge of the times and specifically of the place, time, way of thinking, customs, preconceived opinions, judgments that were possible or impossible in those days, and so forth—may be encouraged by the most candid account to find out what really happened and to visualize as adequately as possible what is narrated in light of all the circumstances that influenced and affected it. This will enable him to separate everything from the narrative that was not fact but the narrator's own view, interpretation, and opinion and to find out what happened in part more fully than is customarily described in any narrative, in part less adulterated with extraneous matter and more in accordance with its original form. Only something so discussed, be it a discourse, or a deed, or a consequence associated in some other way with human action, can be a genuine historical object and a not imaginary but historical occasion of psychological and historically oriented philosophical inferences. All this is true, of course, only if one in so doing always keeps strictly enough in mind the degree of probability with which one has been able in each instance to determine the philosophical meaning of the narrator, the local color that has been added, and the extent to which what is narrated has been purified of its admixture of opinion. All conclusions naturally can only be as positive as our knowledge of what happened, on which those conclusions are based.

My greatest wish is that my views of the miracle stories should not by any means be regarded as the most important matter. Oh, how vain would be piety or religion if what is true depended on whether one believes or disbelieves in miracles! . . . I implore you never to think that I myself lay any great weight on my researches into the possible relation of effect and cause in connection with those events. I also ask you not to imagine, however, that the main issue is settled if someone can say, "He attempts to give a natural explanation of miracles." The true friend of history will only be concerned not to regard secondary elements as unintelligible and consequently incredible before he has even attempted to discover whether perchance they might be quite intelligible and all the more credible. One may be assured in advance that the main point is that the most inexplicable changes in the course of nature can neither refute nor confirm any spiritual truth, since one cannot deduce from any event of nature what spiritual purpose determines that it should happen in such a way and in no other.

The truth that is to become an active conviction for us through the medium of the primitive church is twofold. It concerns in part the person of Jesus and in part the religious content of his teaching, portrayed also by his life and death. The truth of the latter is self-evident, demonstrated by its inner spirituality, to the extent that it concerns piety or conformity to God's will. The reverent esteem of Jesus' person, however, rests in the first instance on the very fact that Jesus reveals as no other, such a divine doctrine, so different from that current in his day, not in words and ideas only, but also in deeds and sufferings. In addition, however, account must be taken of his other personal qualities, which justify the summary statement: He who had the qualities to show forth a divine life among men was properly accorded the dignity of the messianic name. . . .

With respect both to the person and the teaching, then, the percipient reader recognizes primitive Christianity as self-evidently true. He also recognizes that the miraculous happened and was a prominent feature of Jesus' ministry. He rejoices, however, that he no longer needs those miracles as proof either of the fact of Jesus or of his person, for this way of proof would be very difficult and unsure. On the other hand, the direct approach leads to the goal of considering the matter as it actually was, for everyone who wants to see what God proposes appearing in human form. . . .

Since it is apparent from the narrative that he who fashioned the accounts and those who transmitted them preserved them for us with astonishment as something whose cause they were unable to explain, then the historical method of interpretation, which seeks to put us back so far as possible into the thoughts and circumstances of the eyewitnesses and the narrators, concludes without further ado from the same tradition that the facts at that time were inexplicable in terms of their origin and therefore have been transmitted as wonder stories. With reference to these same historically conditioned wonder stories he who takes the sources as they are has not a scintilla of doubt—and quite properly—that in terms of their origin they were inexplicable to their age and to the authors of the accounts and consequently were objects of wonderment, that is to say, wonders.

Since many events are narrated as astonishing because at that time their deeper causes could not be investigated and were inexplicable in terms of the knowledge and the circumstances of the age, it follows understandably that no boundary stone can be set up that would say: What happened was inexplicable, and consequently no explanation ever will, may, or ought to be attempted. Where the causes can no longer be discovered, the inexplicability obviously remains self-evident. But why disapprove of the attempts, made possible by a later insight into the connection of effects with their causes, to explain facts that have never been disproved? Can a fact then be called inexplicable if one is not even permitted to attempt to understand it in light of possible causes?

On these principles Paulus later published his *Das Leben Jesu als Grundlage einer reinen Geschichte des Urchristentums* [The life of Jesus as the foundation of a purely historical study of primitive Christianity] (4 vols., 1828). In this work he gave an account of Jesus' life on the basis of all four Gospels and in so doing showed that he practiced neither genuine source criticism as the presupposition of historical representation nor historical criticism. However, he did try to give a connected account that was pragmatically based, although on shaky grounds, in which the rationalistic explanation of miracles appears only as a part of this pragmatic reconstruction of history. Paulus' rationalistic presuppositions prevent him from seeing that the faith of the disciples played a decisive role with respect to the historical Jesus and then, to an even greater extent, in connection with the forms or patterns impressed on the account of Jesus by the early Christians. And **D. F. Schleiermacher** began in 1819 as the first to deliver lectures on the life of Jesus, lectures to be sure that were not published until long after his death, and then only on the basis of his own and his students' notes. He has indeed an understanding for the "God-consciousness of Jesus," but uses John's Gospel uncritically as the framework of his account. Consequently he still practices no real source criticism, and by his portrayal of the story of Jesus lays even less ground for the investigation of the history of primitive Christianity than does H. G. E. Paulus; rather, Schleiermacher represents Christ in terms that correspond to his Christian faith.[129]

Therefore it is quite understandable that **Karl Hase,** later a church historian at Jena, felt compelled in 1829 to publish a textbook on the life of Jesus because "our literature still lacked any purely historical and scholarly account of the life of Jesus." And in his little book, equipped with an elaborate series of literary references, Hase unquestionably succeeded in providing the first account of Jesus that at essential points is historical. To be sure, in his explanation of the miraculous he makes extensive use of rationalistic methods (the appearance of a meteor at the baptism of Jesus was mistaken for a voice from heaven; the story of Jesus' temptation "is a true though subjective account, told . . . in Oriental manner as a parable or *haggadah*," the daughter of Jairus was only asleep, and so forth). Accordingly he reinterprets Jesus' promise of the imminent messianic glory as a prediction of the triumph of Christianity because "the suggested allegorical understanding of his prediction is most probable in light of the caution otherwise consistently exercized by Jesus, who, despite the firmest faith in the miracles of the spirit, always respected the tranquil course of history and of providence." Furthermore, that a genuine source criticism is still lacking is evident from the fact that the discourses of Jesus in the Synoptics and in John are viewed as equally historical on the assumption "that the character of Jesus' discourses peculiar to each is due only to a different choice on the part of the writers of history," and even more from the statement that the miracles of the transformation of water into wine at Cana and of the resurrection of Lazarus can be accepted as historical on the simple assumption that John reports them as an eyewitness.

Although in his use of such ideas Hase stands on essentially the same ground as H. E. G. Paulus and Schleiermacher, nevertheless his efforts to give a genuinely historical account of Jesus are clearly apparent in two respects. Where the sources give insufficient information concerning an event, as in the instance of the narrative of the raising from the dead of the widow's son at Nain or in that of the angels at the empty tomb, "[such silence] makes it impossible to reach a sober historical judgment." Consequently, because of the state of the sources Hase occasionally leaves a historical question undecided, and in his preface he admits that many were compelled to regard this attitude, suited to a rigorous historical investigation, as something new and objectionable. Hase anticipates that even more objection would necessarily greet his claim that Jesus by his acceptance of the Jewish hope of a messiah also shared the expectation of a political renewal, but that, because of "the gradual clearing away of erroneous ideas taken over from the general nationalistic ethos," he was then led to reject "the political element in the theocracy" in order "to maintain only its spiritual and moral content." In this connection Hase therefore assumes on Jesus' part an inner development to which the Gospels bear no direct witness, and he himself has to admit that "the apostles do not carefully distinguish between the sayings that come from the first and the second periods" and that consequently we do not know "what inner struggles led to this victory." With this hypothesis, however, he ventured for the first time the conjecture that has since reappeared in the most varied forms: namely, that a change took place in Jesus' way of thinking, and in this way he showed that Jesus as a historical person must be subjected as any other to psychological and genetic analysis. To be sure, not even Hase yet recognized the historical task in its full dimensions because he took as the goal of an account of the life of Jesus the description of "his true stature as the God-man . . . [reached] by means of the genuinely human development of his life." And in all this failed to understand the radical nature of both the historical and the theological tasks.[130]

As regards the fundamental questions concerning the nature and the work of Jesus, I shall probably satisfy neither extreme of the theological parties; but I think my view is that which the best of our contemporaries have either adopted or will adopt. The time has passed in which the president of a consistory could say to a pastor (who excused himself by the example of Jesus for an action which had been found fault with), "Imitate our Master on his good side, and not on his bad side." But neither will that time return in which one could say, as a good old gentleman once said to me, "You must treat of the *human nature* of Jesus in the first part of your history, and of his *divine nature* in the last." The good spirit of our time has rejected the naturalistic history of the great Prophet of Nazareth; but no sickly spirit of the time will succeed in forcing upon us any unnatural history of the God-man.

On the other hand I expect all sorts of objection to the idea, although it is a subordinate one, of the theocratic relationship and living movement of Jesus' plans. Everything here depends on whether a perfectly clear view of the life of Jesus can be had without [assuming] this theocratic relationship. This idea has arisen out of my total perspective [on the life of Jesus], and I regard it as a vital part of the view of the Lord as I have come to see him. Only if it could be demonstrated that a perfectly clear and self-contained concept of his whole being is possible without assuming this relationship and is appropriate to a historical development of his life, would I not only be refuted but in this respect also converted.

It will be seen that I have spoken doubtfully concerning some events in the life of Jesus, and stated the opposite views without deciding between them. I love nothing better than a brief, decisive word. Any one can see, both in my writings and my life, that in regard to my convictions I do not trouble myself whether I shall please or displease. In philosophy we ought to have distinct convictions; for we may find them in our own mind, and be certain about them. But in matters of history, where our judgment is determined by tradition, the imperfections of which we are unable to supply, prudence may often require us to abstain from any conclusion. The only scientific approach then will consist in a thorough knowledge both of our ignorance and of its cause.

It was to be expected that historical research into the early Christian world of thought should begin and at first be predominantly concerned with the person and teaching of Jesus. However, even before the appearance of Hase's *Leben Jesu* [Life of Jesus] the Zürich theologian **Leonhard Usteri** had published the first historical account of the *Entwicklung des Paulinischen Lehrbegriffs* [Development of the Pauline doctrine].[181] Usteri had undertaken "to investigate the inner consistency of the entire Pauline teaching" because "almost nothing at all has been done in this field, although the task was inviting enough." Since the comprehensive accounts of New Testament theology, to which reference will shortly be made, had also treated the teaching of Paul only in accordance with the conventional arrangement of the material by dogmatic theology, Usteri's book actually does represent the first systematic study of Pauline thought. Furthermore, by undertaking with reference to the several groups of ideas a comparison of Pauline teaching with that of the rest of the New Testament, Usteri recognized the decisive historical problem. In fact, even the really theological task of the interpretation of Paul is seen, although again and again the attempt is made to trace Paul's concrete ideas back to general concepts valid for all men of all ages.

But at all these points it is also apparent that in his pioneer attempt at a comprehensive presentation of Pauline theology Usteri failed to give a really historical account. This is evident even in his judgment on the sources. Though it is true that he excludes the Letter to the Hebrews, he nevertheless goes on to say: "All the other thirteen books I felt free to use without qualification, for even if I had perhaps permitted myself to raise not unimportant doubts regarding one, or at most two, this would not have prevented their use in any way whatsoever." Consequently, in spite of the fact that he was aware of Schleiermacher's doubts of I Timothy, Usteri made use of the Pastoral Letters as Pauline almost without hesitation.[132] And when he characterizes "the sharp break between Christianity and pre-Christian times" as "the viewpoint from which my account is written and on which everything depends" and then in Part Two proceeds to deal with "the redemption of the individual" before his account of "the Church of God," the individual's experience of redemption instead of the contrast between the pre-Christian era and that of the fulfillment in Christ is wrongly made the governing principle of the presentation. The hesitancy of Usteri's pioneer attempt at a historical investigation can also be noted in that the comparison of the Pauline ideas with the rest of the New Testament is not enough to accord Pauline thought its historical niche within the development of early Christian thought, but almost without exception such comparison proves to the author's satisfaction that Paul's ideas are in complete agreement with those of the rest of the New Testament. But that Usteri's attempt at historical research was only hesitant is apparent most clearly from the fact that, in dependence on ideas that Schleiermacher had developed in his *Christian Faith*, Usteri reduces the Pauline message of redemption again and again to the element of piety in an individual's self-consciousness (Usteri dedicated his book "to his beloved teacher Mr. Friedrich Schleiermacher . . . as a mark of deepest love and respect"). Of justification he says: "God forgives the man who acknowledges and accepts the love of Christ as revealed especially in his death, because this acceptance (faith) cannot remain without effect, but love must constrain him (II Cor. 5:14) henceforth to live no longer unto himself but unto him who died for him." And the Spirit of God is defined as "the active and triumphant power of the will" that is a gift of God because "no one at all can generate power from himself." It is quite in accord with this minimizing of the objectivity of the divine act of salvation that Usteri, while he does not actually completely deny the Pauline expectation of the imminent second coming of Christ, does reinterpret Paul's confident expectation of living to see the end of the world as the conviction that the second coming "probably could still be experienced by the apostles, as well as by most of his contemporaries," expressly appealing for support of this reinterpretation to Rom. 13:11-12 and I Thess. 4:17. So the problem of the historical presentation of the Pauline proclamation and its integration in the development of early Christian thought is raised by Usteri, but not yet really attacked.

It was actually inevitable that the discussion of the theological views of the Johannine writings was now also undertaken. The approach to this, however, was very hesitant.[133] It was not until 1839 that a comprehensive account of the Johannine theology appeared, written by K. Frommann, the professor at Jena. It can easily be seen from this comprehensive work, which makes use of the whole range of prior research, what it was that basically prevented the taking hold of this task. Though scholars had been aware since Herder's time of the need of distinguishing the Johannine portrait of Christ from that of the Synoptists, they were, however, by no means clear about the historical attitude of the Gospel of John vis-à-vis that of the Synoptics. On the contradictory view that one can distinguish with confidence between the transmitted accounts of Jesus' discourses and the evangelist's own observations, Frommann then attempts, but still very imprecisely, to draw a distinction between reliable and edited reports of Jesus' discourses in John's Gospel. His intention of making only the theological viewpoint of John himself rather than the discourses of Jesus the object of his reconstruction (Frommann excludes the Revelation to John from consideration) then leads to the conclusion that the Gospel's prologue is his most important source, and accordingly his book falls into two major parts: "Of the Logos before He Became Flesh," and "Of the Logos Become Flesh." Furthermore, this representation is basically more systematizing than really decriptive and, despite the fact that at every point a comparison with the rest of the New Testament is undertaken, there is no real attempt to indicate the historical relation of Johannine thought to that of the rest of the New Testament. It is only in his comparison of "the Synoptic and Johannine Christology" that the author can say "that the former is related to the latter as the seed to the blossom." So we are compelled here again to conclude that the task of giving a historical account of the Johannine world of thought was defined by Frommann but not yet accomplished.[134]

4.
Biblical Theology

Taking as their goal a historical view of the New Testament, scholars had begun to investigate on the one hand the literary problems of the individual New Testament writings and on the other the several forms of the New Testament proclamation. In due course it was inevitable that the need to bring into focus the entire content of New Testament thought should emerge as a historical problem. To be sure, as early as the seventeenth and eighteenth centuries biblical proof texts had been assembled for use by dogmatic theology, arranged, however, in accordance with purely dogmatic interests.[135] And beginning with the year 1771 the Göttingen theologian G. T. Zacharia had published a *Biblische Theologie* [Biblical theology] which undertook to present the biblical arguments for theological doctrines as a means of subjecting dogmatic theology to criticism. This presentation, however, not only treated the Old Testament and the New on the same level, but also made no allowance whatever for a historical development and uncritically assumed the complete unity of the whole body of biblical teaching.[136] It was not until Johann Philipp Gabler, a student of J. G. Eichhorn, delivered his inaugural address at Altdorf in 1787 that the fundamental difference between biblical and dogmatic theology was set forth. According to Gabler, biblical theology has a historical character and consequently does not share at all in the changes that overtake dogmatic theology as it accommodates itself to a given time. The task of research into biblical theology is therefore the collection and differentiation of the ideas of the biblical writers, and only on the basis of this collection can the permanently valuable and consequently dogmatically usable content be separated from the categories determined wholly by the historical situation of the time.[137]

Biblical theology bears a historical character in that it hangs on what the sacred writers thought about divine things; dogmatic theology, on the other hand, bears a didactic character in that it teaches what every theologian through use of his reason philosophizes about divine things in accordance with his understanding, with the circumstances of the time, the age, the place, the school [to which he belongs], and similar matters of this sort. Considered by itself the former always remains the same, since its arguments are historical (although represented this way by one person and that way by another), while the latter, on the other hand, as constant and assiduous observation over so many centuries more than demonstrates, is subjected along with other human disciplines to manifold change . . . . The sacred writers, however, are surely not so changeable that they could make use of such a variable manner and form of theological discipline as this. I do not mean by this to say that everything in theology is to be regarded as uncertain and doubtful, or even only that everything is to be permitted to the human will. All that I have said heretofore amounts to this: We are carefully to distinguish the divine from the human and to undertake a separation of biblical and dogmatic theology. And after we have set aside everything in Holy Scripture that is valid only for those times and their people, we are then to make basic to our philosophical consideration of religion those ideas which the divine Providence intended to be valid for all places and times, and so more carefully demarcate divine and human wisdom. . . .

What is of greatest concern in this very important matter is that we carefully assemble the sacred ideas and, if they are not expressed in Holy Writ, reconstruct them out of passages compared with one another. In order that this process may proceed the more happily and not be something done at random or arbitrarily, much care and circumspection is necessary. Above all the following must be kept in mind: These sacred writings do not contain the opinions of one man or of his age and his religion. To be sure, all sacred writers are godly men and are fortified with divine authority; however, not all have the same kind of religion in mind. Some are teachers of the old and actually elementary form of doctrine, which Paul himself designates with the name πτωχὰ στοιχεῖα [weak elemental spirits]; others are teachers of the new and better Christian form of doctrine. Consequently the sacred writers cannot all be valued alike when we consider them in terms of usefulness for dogmatics—however much we must cherish them with equal respect because of the divine authority with which their writings are endowed. Surely I do not need to argue that the Spirit of God most emphatically did not destroy in every holy man that man's own ability to understand and the form of natural insight into things. Finally, if inquiries are directed—as they are at least in this instance—only to the discovery of what each of these men thought concerning divine matters, and if that can be discovered—leaving the question of divine authority out of consideration—only from their writings, then it would seem to me to be quite enough—to avoid treating anything that requires proof as already proven—entirely to overlook the doctrine of divine inspiration in this initial investigation (where with what authority these men wrote is of no consequence, but only what they thought) and only to employ it when the dogmatic use of biblical concepts enters into consideration.

Since this is so we must distinguish between the several periods of the old and new religion—if we do not wish to work in vain—as well as between the several authors, and finally between the several forms of speech that each uses, dependent on time and place, be it the historical, the didactic, or the poetic genus. If we leave this proper path, however difficult and unpleasant it may be, we are certain to lose our way in some treacherous bypath or other. We must therefore carefully assemble all ideas of the several writers and arrange them in their proper sequence: those of the patriarchs, those of Moses, David, and Solomon, those of the prophets—each of the prophets, for that matter: Isaiah, Jeremiah, Ezekiel, Daniel, Hosea, Zechariah, Haggai, Malachi, and the rest. And as we proceed we are for many reasons not to despise the Apocrypha. In similar fashion, from the epochs of the new form of doctrine, the ideas of Jesus, of Paul, Peter, John, and James. Such work in the main falls into two parts: One is concerned with the proper interpretation of the passages relevant to the task at hand; the other with the careful comparison of the ideas of all sacred writers one with another. . . .

Therefore, after these opinions of the godly men have been carefully assembled from Holy Writ, suitably arranged, properly related to general concepts, and carefully compared with one another, we may profitably undertake an investigation of their usefulness to dogmatics and of the proper determination of the limits of biblical and dogmatic theology. In this the main task is to investigate which ideas are of importance to the permanent form of Christian doctrine and consequently apply to us, and which were spoken only for the people of a given age or were intended for a given form of instruction. It is acknowledged, surely, that not all matter in Holy Writ is intended for people of every sort. On the contrary, a large part of it by God's decree is intended rather for a given time, a given place, and a given sort of people. For example, who, I ask, would relate the Mosaic regulations, long since done away with by Christ, to our time, and who would insist on the validity for our time of Paul's exhortations that women should veil themselves in the sacred assembly? The ideas of the Mosaic form of instruction, which are confirmed neither by Jesus and his apostles nor by reason itself, can therefore be of no dogmatic value. By similar ways and means we must zealously examine what is said in the books of the New Testament with reference to the ideas or needs of the early church and what we must regard as belonging to the abiding doctrine of salvation; what in the words of the apostles is truly divine and what is fortuitous and purely human. . . .

Once all this has been properly observed and carefully established, then at last those passages of Holy Scripture will be separated and transparent which —unless their text be doubtful—relate to the Christian religion of all times and express a truly divine form of faith in lucid words, words that can properly be called classical and that can be made basic to a careful dogmatic investigation.

When these comprehensive concepts have been wrought out of those classical words by proper exegesis and—once wrought out, carefully compared to one another and—once compared, arranged suitably in proper sequence, so that in the process an enlightening and acceptable connection and arrangement of the truly divine doctrines emerges, then the consequence in fact is a "biblical theology," a biblical theology that corresponds to the strict meaning of the phrase to which the late Zachariä adhered—as we know—in the composition of his famous work. And when such solid foundations of "biblical theology"— understood in this strict sense—have been laid after the manner we have described up to this point, we shall have no wish to follow uncertain ideas set forth by a dogmatic theology that is conditioned by our own times.

With these programmatic declarations Gabler not only clearly emphasized the historical character of "biblical theology," but also recognized the need of distinguishing the several modes of teaching in accordance with their historical sequence and saw that the normative character of the biblical writings only becomes evident when this historical approach to them is taken seriously. However, Gabler himself did not undertake this presentation of biblical theology that he had desiderated, but he did prepare the way for the accomplishment of this task by a still further insight. His teacher, J. G. Eichhorn, had adopted the observations of Christian Gottlob Heyne (1729-1812), the classical philologist at Göttingen, concerning myth as the conceptual and articulative form of the childhood of the human race and applied it first to the Old Testament myths and then also to those of the New. Gabler in turn took over Eichhorn's ideas and carried them further.[138] According to these scholars, the mythical concepts of the Old Testament writers are the primitive way of interpreting the remarkable, whose actual cause is not yet apparent. This viewpoint was first inevitably applied to the New Testament [139] by Eichhorn and used to explain the miraculous events it records.

Acts 12:3-11. The account of the apostle Peter's escape from prison is so reported that essentially it contains nothing but that Peter himself did not know how the deliverance had actually been effected. Only when he stood alone in the street, left to his own resources, did he "come to himself." He could think of nothing to say to solve the puzzle of how he got out of the prison so quickly and easily except that a so sudden and unexpected turn in his situation could only be the work of divine Providence. . . . Above all, of what had happened to him there remained only the consciousness of the occurrences that had affected him most strongly: the shaking that awoke him, the removal of his fetters, the putting on of his mantle, the easy opening of the outer gate. Beyond that he had no idea of what had happened to him.

From the course of this report it is apparent that in this passage we cannot find any historical account of the real nature of his deliverance, but an explanation of it based on Jewish ideas.

The visible hand of Providence had set him free: this conclusion Peter was compelled to draw from the whole incident. Jewish theology, which always furnishes Providence with a corps of angels to carry out its purpose, could account for the occurrence in no other way than that an angel of the Lord had delivered him from the prison. Once this category was chosen, everything that had happened—the shaking, the speaking, the guidance—must have been the work of an angel of the Lord! Here also a careful distinction must be made between the event and its Jewish embellishments; once this is done the account follows an easy and natural course, uninterrupted by the miraculous. Perhaps in all this many a person raises only the objection that in addition to the angel mention is made also of the light that illuminated the cell (vs. 7: "and a light shone in the cell"), but there is more than one way of explaining this. In my opinion the reference to a light belongs merely to the description of the angel, which a Jew could only think of as clothed in brightly luminous splendor, for it was a heavenly being. No sooner did he think of an angel by night in the dark cell than he had to picture the cell as illuminated by the angel's splendor.

101

Enough has been said. The "angel of the Lord" points by no means yet to anything marvelous. It points to nothing but an unexpected happy deliverance by Providence. But since Peter himself did not know how to explain the true nature of his deliverance, we are still less qualified to do so.

Eichhorn traced back the "mythical" explanation of an event that in itself was natural to the primitive conceptual forms of the day. Gabler went on to give reasons why such an explanation is necessary by showing that the task of the modern exegete is to confirm not simply what is written, but also what historical and factual reality the written text conceals. This appears most impressively in connection with the story of Jesus' temptation. According to Gabler, it is not enough to establish that the evangelists thought of the temptation as actually by the devil. We must also ask how this mythical account could have come into being in order then to illuminate its original factual content. And Gabler expressly emphasizes that it is quite right to speak of myths also in the New Testament, since the primitive history of Christianity also belongs to ancient times and therefore knew only narratives that were orally transmitted and consequently mythically embellished. According to Gabler, it is only by this insight that it is possible to separate true revelation from its temporally conditioned form of presentation. In this way he recognizes with all clarity not only the fact of mythical language in the New Testament, but also the task of interpreting its content.[140]

If exegesis is to be nothing more than giving an account of the meaning of a writer—of what he himself meant by what he said—then no doubt the conventional explanation of the story of Jesus' temptation as an objective appearance and activity of Satan is the only true one, for in their account Matthew and Luke appear to have nothing else in mind. Once this fact has been established, the task of the grammatical exegete is indeed at an end, since he has only to concern himself with the true meaning of his author.

If we know only the grammatical meaning of a biblical passage, we in our day are very little further ahead. It is now the turn of historical and philosophical criticism, which subjects such a biblical passage to its closest examination. This critical analysis functions in the area of explanation of content, just as the discovery of the grammatical meaning functions in the area of the explanation of words. The task of the Bible exegete involves both. In fact, then, we can draw a valid distinction between interpretation and explanation: to the former belongs only the attempt to recover the meaning of the passage; to the latter, on the other hand, the explanation of the matter itself. . . . In our day is anyone satisfied, for example, with the merely grammatical interpretation of the Mosaic cosmogony and of the earliest story of mankind? Agreed that the ancient poet believed that the world really had come into being and been fashioned in this way and that sin in the world really had had the origin he described. But can we still believe it in our time? Since we are now convinced that these events cannot have occurred in this way, do we not rather ask: "How did people in the ancient world arrive at these ideas and sagas (myths) "? . . .

We have to approach the story of Jesus' temptation in the same way. There can be no doubt, I should say, that the evangelists believed they were reporting a true occurrence. The grammatical interpreter has only to concern himself with this, and then his work is finished. But the business of explaining the Bible is by no means over. Indeed his work has only begun, for the fact that the evangelists regarded this as an account of a true occurrence in the world of the senses does not demonstrate by any means that it actually happened in this way. The evangelists, as can be seen from the whole tenor of their narrative, firmly believed in demons and in illnesses caused by demons, but that does not mean that we can regard the insane and epileptic whom Jesus healed as really "possessed." The first question that emerges from a consideration of the story of Jesus' temptation is this: . . . Can Jesus have been tempted in such a personal way—in an assumed form—by the devil? Can Jesus have followed the devil so complacently everywhere he took him? As a matter of fact, the Jewish devil (and this is certainly the devil of the story) is a product of Persian and Babylonian thought, and the Jews first became acquainted with him during the Exile: how then can he be assumed in this instance to have any real existence? . . . Consequently no attempt to explain the story of Jesus' temptation as the evangelists narrate it has any real chance at all of succeeding. But the evangelists believed it. In this instance, then, the explainer of the Bible has the full right and even the duty of investigating further: How did the Evangelists arrive at this belief? Whence did they get this story? And this puts us on the right track: What is it that may really have happened to Jesus to give rise to this story? This is the road the explainer of the Bible must take. And so it is readily apparent that the recent exegetical attempts to answer the question are anything but arbitrary, baseless, and fraudulent. On the contrary, they wholly correspond to the rules and regulations of a sound hermeneutics —not, to be sure, of the conventional hermeneutics that goes no further than the explanation of the words, but of a higher hermeneutics that includes the illumination of the biblical subject matter itself. . . .

Now the task of exegetical criticism involves the careful examination of the grounds for and against a given type of interpretation and on the basis of that decides which is to be preferred to others as the more probable way of conceiving the event. . . . The content of the temptations arose out of individual sensual desires, just as the content of their rejections arose out of special, firm, rational principles. In the case of visions, these products of an excited fantasy, there is, to be sure, no awareness of external things (the soul is wholly turned inward on itself), but unlike dreams, the subjective consciousness is all the more active. Partly because of this visions are more deceptive than dreams and more difficult to distinguish from the waking state, as the example of the apostle Paul in II Cor. 12: 2-3 convincingly demonstrates. The dominant idea of the time that evil comes from the devil lent the vision the more definite form. As soon as the pure soul of Jesus revolted against the ideas that were introduced by sensuousness, then the fantasy submerged the image of the devil, in whose mouth it placed these sensual promptings characteristic of him; but it was reason that triumphed.

Better and more exact natural and religious philosophy and a more thorough study of the historical records of other ancient peoples and of classical literature in general, combined with respect for the records of the Christian religion —records that we did not wish to abandon, but only wanted better to explain by analogy with the cultural spirit of the ancient world, that they might retain their well-earned repute—were consequently the single and sole source of the mythical mode of handling the Bible. These remarks, I hope, have sufficiently justified the mythic method of interpreting the Bible.

The question of whether we may assume myths also in the New Testament appears to be more difficult and more serious. . . . The objections to so doing may be resolved into two: (1) the term is unsuitable and (2) it alienates and excites unnecessarily.

The first objection rests on the following points. "When one speaks of the myths of the New Testament one uses the word in a sense other than its connotation in ordinary, everyday language. By myths we usually mean such pseudo-historical accounts of supernatural objects and such astonishing stories as come down to us from ancient times, when there were still no literary chronicles and when facts were still handed on merely by means of oral saga. Unless it retains this character, the concept of myth becomes far too arbitrary, and one would then have to assume that myths were embedded still more deeply in history." However plausible this argument sounds, it falls far short of convincing us of the unsuitability of the term "myth" as applied to certain New Testament narratives and of the method of treating these narratives as myths. Leaving aside the mistaken assumption that only accounts of supernatural objects may be called myths, it must be admitted, to be sure, that myths must have their origin in ancient times and can deal with only such matters as have been handed down to us orally, rather than by means of literary chronicles. But the fact is that all this is true also of the New Testament accounts which in recent times have been treated as mythical. Why then should we be barred from calling them myths, since the term "myth" suits them perfectly? . . .

But it is said—and this is the second objection—that the term "myth" when applied to New Testament narratives alienates and arouses attention unnecessarily. . . .

To strict supernaturalists and believers in revelation it is true that the use of this term will be offensive, but so also will be the whole way of treating the Bible as mythological, call the method what you will and disguise the new view of the Bible as carefully as you may. If, however, you have already reflected without prejudice on the conditions of a divine revelation and have learned to distinguish between revelation and the documents of revelation, then neither the name, New Testament myth, nor the thing itself causes any shock. If such myths, myths that in part contain or presuppose ideas of God that are most unworthy, were still to be defended as true history, that would be the most direct way of making the whole Bible in our day a laughingstock. However, by means of the method of treating it as mythological the pure fact in it is separated from later embellishments and from mere comment, and the true revelation then appears with greater clarity.

The ideas of Eichhorn and Gabler now become the foundation on which the first really comprehensive account of New Testament theology was built. **Georg Lorenz Bauer,** a professor at Altdorf, taking his departure from Eichhorn and Gabler composed a comprehensive account of all the myths of the Old and New Testaments, an account in which he also employs the myths of other peoples to support the mythical explanation, for instance, of Jesus' supernatural conception, and in each individual case carefully specifies the reasons for assuming a myth.[141] More significantly, following Gabler's injunction he also published a *Biblische Theologie des Neuen Testaments* [Biblical theology of the New Testament] (4 vols., 1800-1802) in which for the first time the following subjects are treated separately and in sequence: "The Christian Theory of Religion according to the First Three Evangelists"; "The Christian Theory of Religion according to the Gospel and Letters of John"; "The Christian Concept of Religion (1) According to the Apocalypse, (2) According to Peter, and (3) According to the Letters of II Peter and Jude"; and finally, "The Doctrine of Paul." Bauer also defines as a strictly historical science the "biblical theology" that he undertakes to present.[142]

Biblical theology is to be a development—pure and purged of all extraneous concepts—of the religious theory of the Jews prior to Christ and of Jesus and his apostles, a development traced from the writings of the sacred authors and presented in terms of the various periods and the various viewpoints and levels of understanding they reflect.

How could we then work towards this separation of truth from error more confidently; how could we endeavor on our part to get closer to an answer to the question that interests many thousands of well-disposed people, the question, namely, whether Christianity is a rational and divine religion which deserves to be respected, believed, and followed by the learned and the unlearned; how better could we do this than, from the records of the Christian religion, the writings of the New Testament, quite impartially, without predilection for them or bias against them, and with the preliminary knowledge necessary to their proper understanding, to seek to present what the Christian theory of religion actually is; how Jesus wishes himself to be regarded; and for what reasons he demands that we believe in him? For only after having honorably carried out such research can one who accepts nothing without first having tested it, but who at the same time also keeps his ear open to the voice of truth, determine whether to accept or reject Christianity.

The goal of strictly historical research is also reached to the extent that the several "doctrines" are compared to one another, and so the peculiarity of each didactic form emerges, and the attempt is made by means of the "mythical" method of interpretation to discover the real meaning, for instance, of Jesus (in using the ideas about demons Jesus was accommodating himself to the inadequate ways of thinking of his contemporaries, while his reference to his return to judge the world was intended to be taken literally), or to prove that "John's manner of teaching and tone, taken as a whole, approach more closely the teaching manner and tone of Jesus; although in other respects the other evangelists may also have reproduced the didactic discourses of Jesus before the multitude with reasonable accuracy." [143] However, three points show that, despite all this, Bauer's procedure is not really historical. (1) The individual "doctrines" are treated according to the same scheme that theology employed to present its dogmas, so that the inner connection of the several didactic forms does not appear and questions are raised concerning the various didactic forms for which the text gives no warrant. (2) Bauer wants to prove that Christianity is "a rational and divine religion," and consequently he reinterprets everything that stands in the way of this purpose (the Johannine message of the Logos become flesh means: "God's power and efficiency, wisdom and holiness, were at work in a special way in the soul of Jesus, as they had not hitherto been at work in any other man, so that God or his Logos was in Christ") , and separates "what in Jesus' doctrine represents ideas of the time, to which he accommodated himself, and what is generally valid truth for all times and places." [144] (3) A historical development of ideas cannot be traced when the several didactic forms are simply placed side by side, and in an arbitrary chronological arrangement at that. However, these inadequacies do not take away from Bauer the honor of being the first to undertake the task of presenting the biblical theology of the New Testament.

In the last mentioned respect only, **W. M. L. de Wette,** who worked in Berlin at that time as a colleague of Schleiermacher's, attempted in his *Biblische Dogmatik* [Biblical dogmatics] to blaze a more strictly historical trail. At first glance the very title of his book, which appeared in 1813, *Biblische Dogmatik Alten und Neuen Testaments* [Biblical dogmatics of the Old and New Testaments], suggests that here also the account of the various doctrines is ordered completely after the analogy of the subjects dealt with by dogmatic theology (Doctrine of God, of Angels and Demons, of Man, and so forth) and consequently not in accordance with the inner laws of the several didactic forms. Furthermore, the task of biblical dogmatics is said to be "to comprehend the religious elements that occur in the Old and New Testaments to the extent that they usually appear in dogmas, but in their precise relation to it, divested of the latter's foreign phraseology. . . . All that in terms of content and form belongs to science and practice we omit and take into consideration as the heart of the matter what only belongs purely to faith." [145] Although in this de Wette stresses as the concern of biblical theology not the historical reality as it emerges but the timeless content of time-bound writings, he was nevertheless the first to distinguish the proclamation of Jesus from the apostolic teaching and to differentiate within the latter various subgroups, thereby pointing at least in the direction of a really historical account and in specific cases, already anticipating those developments.[146]

With respect to their different understanding and treatment of Christianity, the New Testament books can be grouped as follows: (1) Jewish Christian, to which belong the first three Gospels, the Book of Acts, the Letters of Peter,

James, and Jude, and the Apocalypse. They are characterized by an intimate connection of Christianity with Jewish Christology and for this reason demonstrate the dignity of Jesus by predictions and miracles, especially demon exorcisms and the like. Luke shows much influence by Paul. (2) Alexandrian or Hellenistic, to which the Gospel and the Letters of John and the Letter to the Hebrews are to be reckoned. Characteristics: Representation of Jesus as Logos. They are free of Palestinian superstition and treat the Old Testament mystically and pragmatically. (3) Pauline, including the Letters of Paul and, in part, the Book of Acts. Characteristics: Doctrine the divinity of Christ; Pauline universalism; antagonism to Jewish ordinances and doctrine of salvation by works.

These historical arguments give us the following heuristic results: (1) We distinguish the teaching of Jesus from the interpretation of it given by the apostles and evangelists; (2) Even in the teaching of the individual apostles and in the several writings of the New Testament we retain the characteristic differences, with the consequence that we get in the main the following forms of apostolic Christianity: (1) Jewish Christianity; (2) Alexandrian Christianity; (3) Pauline Christianity. The second form is closely related to the third. Individual teachings are common to all three formulations.

With respect to Jesus' predictions of his death, it is certain that he foresaw it, though not as early as John 2:19, 21; 3:14-17. On the other hand, the prediction of his resurrection is probably only a later explanation of earlier allegorical discourses, and for the simple reason that he himself expected his death, while the disciples hoped for nothing less than the Resurrection. . . .

We cannot prove from what Jesus said that he taught a doctrine of the atonement. Jesus' death was credited with this very important significance first by the apostles. . . .

The genuine Christian independence was lost in part by the apostles, due to the fact that, although filled with the Spirit, they could not free themselves entirely from faith in authority. The principle of their religion is consequently revelation faith and Christolatry. To be sure, to the extent that they freely took over and developed Jesus' teaching, their independence had still some elbowroom, but for later Christians this became increasingly restricted. One unhappy consequence of this religious attitude even as early as the times of the apostles was the dogmatic and mythological treatment of religion.

5.
Exegesis and the Laying of Its Hermeneutical Foundation

Obviously exegesis and its methodological basis, hermeneutics, finally discerned the task of the historical examination of the New Testament. It was in this very undertaking, however, that the problematical nature of this insight came most clearly to light. Ernesti had demanded that the grammatical interpretation should concern itself only with the New Testament texts themselves; Semler, going further, had required that the texts should be studied in light of their historical circumstances; and Gabler had added historical and philosophical criticism to the task of exegesis as his predecessors had defined it, in order that it might include also an explanation of the content of the texts. Hermeneutical discussion now got underway with reference to this and in terms of time ran parallel to the first comprehensive presentations of New Testament introduction and theology. As early as 1788 the Leipzig theologian, **Karl August Gottlob Keil,** in a program whose fundamental principles he reiterated in a textbook on hermeneutics of 1810, advanced the thesis that there is but one method of understanding all writings of whatever sort, including therefore the Bible: namely, the grammatico-historical understanding, which attempts to think the author's thoughts after him. In interpreting the New Testament books the fact that they are divinely inspired is to be left out of consideration; the exegete must not ask whether the text he has explained is right or wrong in its assertions.[147]

By the very nature of the matter, to interpret an author means nothing else than to teach what meaning he intended to convey by the several words of his book or by his formulae of speaking, or to assure that another who reads his book thinks the same things that he did when he wrote it. It can easily be recognized, therefore, that every interpretation is historical to the extent that it ascertains and teaches the matter that presents a historical fact and is historically true, that this matter is found, and that it also confirms this by historical arguments, that is by testimonies, authorities, and other [circumstances] that form the basis of the story. For the interpreter is not to concern himself about the nature of what was written by another, whether it is spoken truly or falsely, but he is anxious only to understand what was spoken by him. And when he has taught this to someone else he seems rightly to have discharged his duty in all respects. To know and to teach what someone has thought and put into words, is that not thoroughly to understand a fact as such [rem facti]? The function of the interpreter closely resembles that of the historian and is intimately related to it. For just as the [historian] has undertaken above all to find out what has been done by another, but not, however, how well or how badly it was done or ought to have been done by him, so the [interpreter] also in his study must meditate on some [author] in order that he may know and explain to others what was said and written by someone else. But if that must be done in the case of any given author, so undoubtedly also in the case of the sacred [writers], since it is sufficiently established that they can be understood in no other way than as human [authors]. And also the interpretation of their books will be historical to the extent that in their explication one must ask at any given place what the sacred writers themselves thought and what their readers for whom their books were first destined were intended to think. . . . The former [the theologian] must ask what value is to be ascribed to the several opinions expounded by the sacred writers, what authority is to be attributed to them in our age, and in what way they are to be turned to our use. The office of the latter [of the exegete] . . . however, consists only in making plain what was handed down by those authors. . . .

This one thing I wanted to show, namely, that in the sacred books in most places such matters are handed down as either are themselves historical or at least have something [about them] that can be called historical. This [proposition] is ultimately confirmed by the fact that, just as the mode of saying something and the way ideas are linked must be peculiar to every sacred author, corresponding to the different nature of his temperament and spirit, so also he must have his own way of thinking and of presenting material. This very fact made it necessary that not all formed one and the same idea of the dogmas of religion, but one looked at them from one and another from another direction. For the same reason a further consequence was that even what the individual authors have handed down concerning this or that chapter of the holy doctrine is different to a certain extent from the other, and that something like a system of doctrine peculiar to each author can be put together. If, however, the nature of the sacred writings is such as I have described, then it is apparent that we must necessarily apply the historical interpretation to them . . . if indeed we wish to follow a safe road in interpreting them. Now if this [mode of interpretation], as I have already said, is the only one that leads to the knowledge of the true meaning of an author, and that it can also have its place in connection with these books, then this is due to their historical character. This requires, namely, that a single and definite sense be assigned to the individual words and sentences. If this were not the case, the interpretation of those books would be uncertain and would rest on no secure foundation.

In the case of a sacred no less than a profane author it is the task of the interpreter to bring to light what the author himself thought as he wrote, what meaning is suggested by his own discourse, and what he wished his readers to understand. Since, however, the biblical books have divine authority nnd their authors, just as divine envoys, delight in singular worthiness, it is therefore obvious that no interpreter need be troubled when he gets ready first and foremost to interpret those books. If he were to be, he would necessarily fall back into that error that has long since been exploded, viz., that "the words of the sacred books only mean what they can," and he would open a bubbling spring of different ways of interpreting the sacred books that could be stopped by no human effort of art.

This "historical" method of interpretation, based solely on the establishment of the actual facts and so far as method was concerned paying no attention to the canon as Holy Scripture, not only found numerous practitioners in the field of hermeneutics,[148] but in particular was deliberately adopted in numerous commentaries. **Leopold Immanuel Rückert,** at that time an instructor in the preparatory school [*gymnasium*] at Zittau, wrote a commentary on the Letter to the Romans (1831) that may be cited as one instance. In the preface he expressly demands that the exegete take no account at all of himself and his views and feelings, that he exercise complete "freedom from prejudice," and abstain from every judgment on the truth of the text he has interpreted.[149]

I am convinced that the interpreter of Paul, completely disregarding his own ego, ought on the other hand to have put on, so far as humanly possible, the whole individuality of the apostle. He is not to think with his own head, not to feel with his own heart, not to view from his own standpoint, but to put himself on the same level as the apostle, know nothing but what he knew, have no idea that he did not have, know no feeling that was unknown to him, never ask: How would I think of a matter if I were Paul, how pass judgment on an issue, use what categories of thought, how be affected by something? but always: How did Paul have to look at a matter, how think, how feel— the real, historical person whose character, level of education, system of thought, and disposition are known to us from the Acts of the Apostles, his own letters, and our sources for a study of the theology of his time? In short, so long as he interprets Paul he must strive to identify himself completely with the apostle, must have studied himself into him, to be able to give his reader or hearer, who lacks nothing more than just this knowledge, a completely true picture of the apostle's spirit in the letter he is engaged in interpreting. . . .

In other words, I require of him freedom from prejudice. The exegete of the New Testament as an exegete, because of the significance that the New Testament has for the Christian Church as the source and norm of its theological knowledge, has no system, and must not have one, either a dogmatic or an emotional system. In so far as he is an exegete, he is neither orthodox nor heterodox, neither supernaturalist nor rationalist, nor pantheist, nor any other ist there may be. He is neither pious nor godless, neither moral nor immoral, neither sensitive nor insensible. For he has no other duty but to examine what his author says in order to communicate this as a pure result to the philosopher, the dogmatician, the moralist, the ascetic, or what have you. Therefore, as an exegete he has no interest but one, viz., to understand the apostle correctly and, having comprehended his ideas as purely and as accurately as possible, to lay them before his reader without admixture of alien matter. Every other interest must vanish before this one; most of all, the belief that the apostle speaks the truth; that is to say, that he says what the interpreter regards as the truth. It must be a matter of no consequence to him whether Paul speaks truth or falsehood; whether a moral spirit or an immoral spirit breathes through his letters; whether his teaching is healthy or very unhealthy. He is only to present what Paul says, what spirit gives life to his message, what his teaching is.

And in 1829 **Heinrich August Wihelm Meyer,** later a pastor in Hannover, published the first volume of his *Critical and Exegetical Commentary* on the New Testament—a commentary series that has passed through many editions and has continued to appear to our own day—and declared that its purpose was to establish only the historico-grammatical meaning of the text.[150]

The area of dogmatics and philosophy is to remain off limits for a commentary. For to ascertain the meaning the author intended to convey by his words, impartially and historico-grammatically—that is the duty of the exegete. How the meaning so ascertained stands in relation to the teachings of philosophy, to what extent it agrees with the dogmas of the church or with the views of its theologians, in what way the dogmatician is to make use of it in the interest of his science—to the exegete as an exegete, all that is a matter of no concern.

These representatives of a "purely historical" interpretation not only equated the task of understanding the New Testament wholly with that of the historical understanding of any other writing, but also left the question of its truth wholly out of consideration. In due course, however, two objections were raised. One came from the ranks of the "historical" school of interpretation itself. As we have seen, Gabler had demanded, vis-à-vis the conceptual forms of the New Testament, that not only the content should be ascertained, but also the matter itself should be clarified by historical and philosophical criticism. **G. L. Bauer** took up the task at this point in his *Entwurf einer Hermeneutik des Alten und Neuen Testaments* [Sketch of a hermeneutic of the Old and New Testaments], a book published a year before his *Lehrbuch der Biblischen Theologie* [Textbook of biblical theology]. Bauer takes his departure from the view that appropriate interpretation must be grammatical and historical in order that the author may be understood as he himself wished to be understood. The biblical authors are therefore to be explained just as the profane, without taking the presupposition of divine revelation in Holy Scripture into consideration. To this extent Bauer agrees with K. A. G. Keil and his school. However, to this "general hermeneutics of the Old and New Testaments" he now adds a "special hermeneutics," and in this he demands historical criticism "with respect to Jesus' miracles" and, "with respect to the discourses of Jesus," a differentiation of the view of the evangelists from "what Jesus actually said." Most of all, however, Bauer demands, in the first instance with respect to the Old Testament,[151] that the interpreter acknowledge the presence of myths and undertake to examine these myths in light of their factual basis and

111

their purpose. In this, however, even within the framework of a "grammatico-historical interpretation," an interrogation of the texts with respect to their content of meaning in association with a critical treatment of them is declared to be the task of the interpreter.[152]

The only valid principle of interpretation, whether the author be profane or biblical, is this: Every book must be explained in accordance with the linguistic peculiarities that characterize it; this means grammatical interpretation and results in a literal understanding of the text; and the presentation and clarification of the ideas that appear in it, ideas dependent on the customs and the way of thinking of the author himself and of his age, his nation, sect, religion, and so forth, is the task of what is called historical interpretation. Only when the meaning of the author has been ascertained can the work of the philosopher begin. . . .

But however willingly we may admit that divine revelation is contained in Holy Writ, this revelation must not be presupposed, but must rather emerge as a consequence of its content as this has been properly interpreted. . . . In this connection we must proceed only according to the rules of historical interpretation as already cited, just as with Plato, Aristotle, etc., and attempt to ascertain what kind of ideas the biblical authors expressed. . . .

The characteristics by which a myth is recognized and is distinguished from a true account are the following: (1) When it reports on the origin of the universe and the earth, of which no one was a witness; (2) When everything is ascribed to the activity of gods or of heavenly beings who appear in person and act directly, rather than to natural causes; (3) When everything is represented in terms of the senses, and men speak and act when in fact they only thought; and (4) When the narrative is so constituted that what it relates neither happens now nor can happen in the course of the orderly routine of nature, but surpasses all comprehension.

But the characteristics by which myths are distinguished from one another must be observed from the inner constitution of the myths [themselves]. The myths which explain the causes of things, of the world and of physical events, are philosophical; those in which are narrated—decked out in the miraculous and concerned with the most ancient tribes of men and the founders of people —are historical. Both can be poetically embellished and expanded with all sorts of additions. . . .

Once a narrative has been recognized as mythical it must be so interpreted. In this interpretation the following rules are to be observed: (1) The kind of myth the story represents is to be determined; (2) If it is a philosophical myth its purpose is to be ascertained, e.g., Gen. 1 undertakes to explain the origin of the universe; Gen. 2 and 3 the origin of evil in the world; (3) If it is a historical myth, the actual fact that lies back of it is to be distinguished from the miraculous additions. This can be done by noting the spectacular, the incredible, including the intervention of deity or of angels. For example, in the story of the Deluge there is a basis of fact, viz., that there was a great flood, like the Deucalion; but that it was God's punishment for the corruption of the human race at that time, that God forewarned Noah of its coming and commanded him to build the Ark, that the flood covered the whole earth, and that one pair of all animals was saved in the Ark, that is mythical; (4) If it is a poetical myth the occasion for it and its successive embellishment are to be observed, e.g., the poetical myth of the Cherubim. . . .

With respect to the recorded discourses of Jesus the interpreter has to note: (1) The evangelists do not present them word for word, for none wrote them down on the spot, but that they give an account of their content, each after his own fashion. For Christ, measured in terms of style, speaks one way in Matthew and quite another way in John. It follows from this (a) that at times they can easily have ascribed an idea of their own to Jesus, or have expressed many things more definitely than Jesus had spoken of them, e.g., concerning his passion and death, concerning the destruction of the Jewish state; (b) that at times they can have misunderstood him and consequently have furnished his words incorrectly with glosses, as, it seems, in John 12:32, 33; 2:21.

(2) Accordingly, in the separation of the teachings of Jesus, the judgment of the evangelists must be precisely distinguished from what Jesus said. More frequently than the other evangelists, John interpolates his own observations into the accounts of Jesus' deeds and discourses and uses these accounts as vehicles of his own philosophy. . . .

The evangelists also narrate many miracle stories about Jesus. With respect to these the interpreter has a double responsibility: (1) He must prove their hermeneutical certainty; that is, he must show that according to the words of the author a true miracle is narrated, such as is the resurrection of a dead man, the feeding of several thousand people with a few loaves of bread, the healing of a blind man by a mere word or by simple contact. . . . (2) He must demonstrate its historical certainty; that is, that these marvelous events actually happened as they are narrated; which examination must be undertaken according to the principles of historical criticism. This latter requires that the interpreter be guided by one principle, not by several. No one is permitted to accept some facts in the Gospels as true without further investigation and then give them a natural explanation, while rejecting others as untrue. . . .

While Bauer in this way demanded a deepening of the grammatico-historical interpretation as more suited to its objective, a few years later (1807) in an address delivered at Göttingen on the occasion of his inauguration as rector of the university (and later in a defense of this address), C. F. Stäudlin raised a vigorous protest against the exclusive right of this method of interpretation. The very title of his address, "Dass die geschichtliche Auslegung der Bücher des Neuen Testaments nicht allein wahr ist" [That the historical interpretation of the books of the Old and New Testaments is not the only true one], shows that Stäudlin by no means questioned the need and relevance of the historical interpretation. However, because the teaching of Jesus has to do with unchangeable, divine truths that cannot have merely temporary historical significance, and because the declarations of the apostles convey deep religious perceptions, only he can understand the New Testament who has this sort of impression of Jesus and a similar religious perception. "Moral, religious, philosophical" interpretation, therefore, belongs inseparably to the relevant interpretation of these writings, and without an assured recognition of the inspiration of these documents it is impossible to understand them properly.[158]

It is the almost unanimous opinion of interpreters that only the grammatico-historical meaning of Holy Scripture is the true one and that those who interpret it otherwise present, not the meaning of the writings, but their own, or one different from that of the writings. Although we have never doubted the need and usefulness of he historical interpretation, we have been of the opinion, nevertheless, that this is not the only true and sufficient one, that it has been misused by most, and that Christianity and theology have suffered seriously from its being extended beyond its limits and unjustly used by those with false principles or none at all.

It is preposterous to undertake to explain the sense and the thoughts even of a great and wise man only from historical notices and from the history of the age which preceded him and in which he lived. But it is still more preposterous to attempt to do this with respect to a man who declared himself to be the Son of God and was believed to be such, and who claimed to reveal eternal, unchangeable, heavenly truth, not only for his own but also for all ages. Consequently that rule of historical interpretation is not quite certain and generally applicable, the rule, namely, which demands that one always determine the meaning of the sayings of Jesus as it best suits his first hearers, that one therefore is always to state what these latter thought with regard to his discourses. Jesus did not set out to make himself clearly understood, so that all he delivered to his hearers, and even to his apostles, could not yet be clear to them, and they would better understand, wholly fathom, and more fully know it only after his death, with the help and guidance of the Spirit. . . .

To these belong many sayings about his messianic dignity, his second coming, heaven and hell, and so forth. These teachings can be understood and explained far better by us than they were by many of Jesus' hearers. Furthermore, the merely historical interpreter cannot adequately appreciate and clarify the weight and nature of Jesus' teachings. He sees everywhere only history and historical relationships. But Jesus' teaching is not merely something historical, not merely a part of history, not simply of a historical nature; it also contains eternal, unchangeable, divine truths which one can fully explain to himself and make comprehensible to others, never on the ground of history and grammar alone, but rather by one's own spirit, by meditation, by elevation to ideas of the reason, and from [the truths] themselves.

I know no Jesus who has no knowledge of the plan of Providence for him, who erroneously regards his age as the last, who is under the delusion that he will return visibly to earth after his death and will then inaugurate his kingdom among the generation then alive, and who, having grown doubtful of this after his resurrection, leaves his disciples of the opinion that he would shortly come again visibly from heaven and in the end deceives others just as he does himself. Such a Jesus would have been a fanatic with a mind that, at least with respect to certain fixed ideas, would have been deranged, so that in the sacred records of his teaching and his life this is not the way I see him. He wanted to introduce a religion that would be eternal and for all and was as firmly convinced that this was the plan of Providence as that his religion had a divine origin. . . .

Even the saying of Jesus in Matt. 16:18 proves this, the saying, namely, in which he clearly promises that his Church, and therefore also his teaching, will endure eternal and unshaken. It is not necessary for me to enter here into the question of whether Jesus regarded his age as the last and wanted it to be known that even his own generation expected his visible return. Even if this were the case, his religion was to endure until the end of the world and was to spread during this last world era without distinction among the peoples of the earth. Even in this case we cannot assume that this era would be so short that it would be impossible to distinguish Jesus' own time from future times and to say that he intended to reveal truths not only for his own but also for all times. Moreover, the sayings of Jesus about his coming or his second coming, about his kingdom and the end of the world, can also be explained otherwise and in such a way that he need not be charged with any error. . . . I am aware that this explanation has its difficulties and that many different objections have been leveled against it, but the other explanation has also its great difficulties and I prefer the former because it alone fits the concept that has emerged from my study of the New Testament concerning the spirit, the wisdom, the foresight of Jesus, and the totality of his teaching and enterprise.

No one will deny that the deepest and most profound religious perception is expressed in the sayings and in the writings of the apostles. For this very reason no one who is not inspired by a like perception can understand and fathom the full meaning of all these sayings. He who lacks this perception, who is chained fast to what can be known only by the senses—the rough, the dissolute, the immoral, the godless man—does not understand what the sensitive, the spiritual, the godly man, says as such. It is foolishness to him; he cannot understand it; he perverts it; he laughs at and mocks it. . . .

In view of all I have said, does it not follow that the books of the New Testament are not to be explained just as other books? There are general rules of interpretation that must be applied to every book without distinction, but there are others which accommodate to the special content, the special character and purpose of certain books. With reference to the former, the books of the New Testament must be interpreted just as all other books, but with reference to the latter they must be interpreted as are books of their genus or, at any rate, of similar character and purpose. They contain history and doctrine, both of which are intimately related to each other. They were written in part as records, in part as explanations and applications, of divine revelations in deeds and in teachings. Those who composed these books did not address them to all men to be sure, but they did believe they had comprehended in them a doctrine and a history that were of utmost importance to mankind, that would be proclaimed ever more widely, and that summed up God's decrees for the redemption and happiness of sinful mankind. These books are full of glimpses into the depths of divine and human nature. They are written with profound religious and moral feeling. They have produced an immeasurable effect. . . . This cannot be the result just of accident and good fortune. On the contrary, something must be inherent in these books that creates this effect in them, that has raised them to this dignity. Such books, it should be emphasized, must not be interpreted only grammatically and historically, but also morally, religiously, philosophically. All powers of the spirit, of reflection, of emotion, of religious exaltation, must be brought into play to plumb the depths of their meaning. . . .

To be sure, in interpreting the New Testament much depends on what kind of idea of its divine inspiration [*theopneustie*] one holds. The merely historical interpreters, moreover, take little or no account of this. They are so far in the vanguard that they have left it wholly behind them. Consequently it is impossible [for them] to see how the interpreter could carry his task even a step further.

115

Stäudlin in this way takes the idea seriously that the books of the New Testament are not just historical records but are at the same time constituent parts of the New Testament canon, and by his instructions endeavors to do justice to this fact. But these instructions are not only very general, but also fail utterly to raise the question of how such an "accord" of the interpreter and his assessment of the inspiration of these writings can be combined in terms of method with a genuinely historical exegesis. Nevertheless, he did broach the problem of the interpretation of the New Testament as a theological task and demanded a satisfactory answer.

It must be admitted that the gulf between Keil and Stäudlin with respect to an adequate method of interpreting the New Testament was not bridged even by **Schleiermacher.** Schleiermacher's rigidly systematizing hermeneutics, presented in lectures as early as 1809 but only published after his death, became epoch-making because he complemented the grammatico-historical understanding by the psychological understanding, the latter one that endeavors "to comprehend every given complex of ideas as a moment in the life of a definite individual." [154] That, of course, is a requirement for any adequate understanding of the ideas of anyone other than oneself, but this is due only to the fact that Schleiermacher's hermeneutics in the last analysis does not have a theological but only a psychological goal. According to Schleiermacher, the New Testament Canon, viewed psychologically, cannot be treated any differently than other writings because the interpretation even of "Sacred Scripture" can be nothing but the interpretation of the ideas of the authors of these books, authors who were men as other men. Schleiermacher proposes to tolerate a special hermeneutics for the New Testament only because of the New Testament's peculiar linguistic features.[155]

In this connection we now have to ask ourselves incidentally whether on account of the Holy Spirit the Sacred Writings must be treated in a different fashion. We cannot expect a dogmatic decision about inspiration, because such a decision must actually itself rest on the interpretation. In the first place, we cannot permit a distinction to be made between apostolic speeches and apostolic writings, for the future Church had to be built on the speeches. However, it follows also from this, in the second place, that we cannot believe that the whole of Christianity is the intended audience in these writings, for in fact they are all directed to specific people and could not be properly understood in later times if they had not been properly understood by their first readers. But those readers would want to look for nothing else in them but a specific significance because for them the totality had to emerge from a host of specifics. Consequently we must interpret them in this light and assume as a result that even if the authors had been mere mouthpieces, the Holy Spirit could only have spoken through them as they themselves would have spoken. . . .

The question of whether and to what extent New Testament hermeneutics is a special kind has now been answered. From the linguistic point of view, it does not appear to be special for the New Testament is first of all related to the Greek language. From the psychological point of view, however, the New Testament appears not to be one entity, but a distinction has to be drawn between didactic and historical writings. These are different species which demand, to be sure, different hermeneutical rules. But all this does not constitute a special hermeneutics. It is true, though, that the New Testament hermeneutics is a special type, but only with reference to the composite area or Hebraizing character of its language.

Unlike Keil and his school who seek only to understand historical records as historical documents, the reason for this "flattening out" of New Testament hermeneutics is for Schleiermacher, then, the presupposition that "the knowing of another is only possible because in the last analysis all men are basically alike." [156] From the standpoint of this philosophical presupposition Schleiermacher was not able to understand the problem of how the New Testament in its historical givenness could nevertheless be understood as "the Word of God." [157] Friedrich Lücke, a pupil of Schleiermacher's and later the publisher of his *Hermeneutics*, took up the task at this point. In 1817, while he was a young instructor at Berlin, he published his *Grundriss der neutestamentlichen Hermeneutik und ihrer Geschichte* [An outline of New Testament hermeneutics and its history] in which he takes his departure wholly from Schleiermacher's presupposition that the New Testament can be understood only by reason of the unity of the human spirit; in hermeneutics the theological element is only a modification of and more precise definition of the general philosophical element.[158] But neither Keil nor Stäudlin, according to Lücke, was able to establish the grammatico-historical interpretation as adequate or prove it inadequate because the New Testament, "the record of the early Christian religion," must "be understood as a revelation of religion distinguished from all others by definite characteristics, or, to put it more precisely, as a universal historical fact." Consequently Lücke demanded a "Christian philology" that, on the basis of a "Christian disposition," is able to understand the religious element in the New Testament. And a few years later, in a still more explicit form, Lücke asserted that Holy Scripture must be explained otherwise than any other book and in this connection emphasizes the reality of the New Testament canon and the confirmation of this reality by the Christian theologian as the indispensable presupposition of a relevant exegesis of the New Testament.[159]

Since by the literal sense only individual ideas and conceptual relationships can be fully and directly expressed, never the whole of a discourse or a document, much less religious ideas and feelings, it follows that the grammatical principle of interpretation is not adequate completely to ascertain and present the content of the New Testament records of religion. . . .

Since in the New Testament not only the external historical beginnings but also the inner ideological origin of Christianity is set forth, the historical interpretation, which is concerned only with the former, must be regarded as insufficient. . . .

Not merely the possibility of any understanding of any document but also the necessity of investigating every individual idea in its relation to the idea of the whole by means of the same power of the spirit and mode of knowledge from which it has issued is grounded on the unity of the human spirit and its forms of knowledge. The most perfect understanding of a writing is possible only under the conditions that one is thoroughly acquainted with the language and with all national, temporal, local, and personal relationships of a document and possesses versatility of spirit and affinity of soul in order to reconstruct the act of writing in that element of explaining.

The possibility of understanding the New Testament also rests on the unity of the human spirit and its forms of knowledge. However, the most perfect understanding of the New Testament canon can be opened only to the one who is most intimately acquainted with the language and times of the New Testament in order most clearly to recognize the outer and inner forms and their relationships to one another; who is engaged continuously in perfecting and sanctifying his Christian disposition through the fellowship of the Church in order to separate the religious element more and more purely and fully; who possesses enough versatility of spirit to identify himself easily and certainly with the individuality of all New Testament authors; who is conscious of his affinity of soul with at least one of the New Testament writers in order more perfectly to accomplish the act of reconstruction with respect at least to one; and, finally, who by his historical study has sufficiently achieved the universal historical mind and depth of perception to be able fully to comprehend as such the idea of the whole, the Christian revelation, in contrast to every other. . . .

All . . . rules and regulations of exegetical research as well as of the representation of the content of the New Testament unite in the principle of Christian philology, from which in turn they can be logically deduced. . . .

He in whom the genuinely Christian mind and truly systematic spirit are not so combined as Christian philology's loftiest task requires, can neither . . . recognize nor carry out the idea of New Testament theology.

Side by side with the axiom that Holy Scripture is to be interpreted as any other literature, the older dissimilar canon that it is to be interpreted otherwise still asserts its claim. The history of exegesis shows that neither the one nor the other by itself leads to the goal, but only both in proper combination and mutual limitation. The former axiom leads only to the outer court of the book, the latter to the inner. Whoever only reads it as any other book also only understands that in it which it has in common with every other book. Only he who reads it otherwise understands what is peculiar to it. Only he who has both keys and uses them properly (that is, without confusing them and in proper combination) is fully able to open the book. Therefore the full task of biblical hermeneutics is so to construe the general hermeneutical principles that the peculiar theological element can be combined in a truly organic way by means of them, and likewise so to fashion and fix the theological element that the general principles of interpretation retain their full validity. This result cannot occur, however, by robbing the theological element as fully as possible of its characteristic peculiarity and so dissolving it to the general. . . . The peculiar theological element consists, as we see it, in two things: in the first place, in the fact that the writing (we are speaking here in the first instance of the New Testament document) is a sacred one, the canon of Christian truth, and is this because it contains the pure, primal Word of God in the form of the special, absolutely complete revelation in Christ; in the second place, however, its uniqueness lies in the fact that the interpreter is a Christian theologian, and as such a member of the Christian Church whose existence and continuance rest essentially on the recognition of the first proposition, and that as a theological art and science exegesis is conditioned and determined by the general basis and purpose of all theology as a positive [science], rests on it, and helps achieve it. The possibility of uniting both elements—on the one hand the theological element in the sense specified and on the other hand the generally scientific element, in hermeneutical theory and art—is given along with the possibility of theology in general.

It is evident from the ideas he advanced that Lücke clearly saw the problem of how the strictly historical examination of the New Testament is to be undertaken and carried out at the same time as an avowedly theological task, but the possibility of a satisfactory solution still eluded him, for he based the theological task psychologically, rather than on the essence of the New Testament message. Finally it is also evident at the same time that all these founders of the several disciplines of New Testament science could not yet achieve an adequate conception of the task of New Testament science because neither the historical problem of the New Testament nor the question of understanding it theologically against the background of this historical problematic was recognized with sufficient clarity. And it was first necessary that the historical problem be more radically stated before the two issues could really merge.

Part IV
The Consistently Historical Approach to the New Testament

1.
David Friedrich Strauss and Ferdinand Christian Baur

During the years between 1770 and 1790 two scholars, J. S. Semler and J. D. Michaelis had given the decisive stimuli for a historical investigation of the New Testament. Half a century later, during the decade 1833 to 1842, the decisive works appeared that first presented a consistently historical view of the New Testament, and once again two men contributed the greatest share: D. F. Strauss and F. C. Baur. And once more it was the criticism of the person and history of Jesus that brought this viewpoint to the fore. **David Friedrich Strauss,** at the time still an instructor in the Theological Preparatory School [*proseminar*] at Maulbronn, raised the urgent question, in basic agreement with Hegel's distinction between "form," "notion," and "idea" in religion, whether "the historical constituents of the Bible, especially of the Gospels," *also* belong to the "idea" of religion and are therefore to be held fast, or can fall away as mere form. On a visit to Berlin in 1831-32 Strauss had become acquainted with a transcript of Schleiermacher's "Life of Jesus" lectures but had been "repelled by them at almost every point" because Schleiermacher construed the person of Jesus from the Christian consciousness, preferred the Fourth Gospel, and gave a "natural" explanation of numerous events of Jesus' life.[160] So Strauss, who in the meantime had been called to the seminary at Tübingen as a private tutor, took up the task of shedding light on the historical basis of the Christian faith by a critical treatment of the tradition about Jesus in taking into account all of contemporary research. *Das Leben Jesu, kritisch bearbeitet* [The life of Jesus critically examined] appeared in 1835-36 in two volumes, and even the first aroused such a storm of criticism that Strauss was relieved of his tutorial post as a consequence. Numerous refutations were published.[161] Strauss first answered them with three volumes of *Streitschriften* [Polemical writings] (1837), then moderated his criticism of the Gospel of John in the third edition of his *Life of Jesus* (1838-39), and then finally in the fourth edition (1840) restored the original text. But these developments are primarily of biographical interest. In the history of New Testament research it is only the original *Life of Jesus* that is of importance, and it was of such epoch-making significance that it has been said that "because of it the year 1835 has been properly called the great revolutionary year of modern theology." [162]

What made this comprehensive and strictly historical work so revolutionary? It was first and foremost the radical criticism with which Strauss at every point of the gospel story plays off rationalist over against conservative interpretation in truly absorbing debate, only to show that both interpretations are untenable and to put the "mythical" in their stead. Strauss guarded himself against maintaining that nothing at all had happened. It is quite possible to put together an outline of the historical figure of Jesus from Strauss's suggestions.[163] But these suggestions are scattered hither and yon, and the reader gets the impression on the whole that hardly anything is left of the story of Jesus. Strauss himself insists that he possesses the freedom to exercise his criticism because by philosophical reconstruction he "restores the dogmatic significance" of the eternal verities of the Christian faith, though, to be sure, "instead of an individual an idea, but a real one . . . is set as subject of the predicates which the Church accords to Christ." [164] This, however, does not alter the fact that Strauss regards the bulk of the gospel material as "mythical." He took over this idea from the mythical school of Eichhorn, Gabler, Bauer, and de Wette,[165] but he charges his predecessors with having failed to understand the idea of myth purely as the investiture of primitive Christian ideas or as unintentionally poeticizing sagas, and with failing to extend the idea to all the gospel material.[166] Strauss regards the Old Testament as the main source of saga formation, but also contends that the messianic expectation among the Israelite people was simply transferred to Jesus.[167] In this critical work it is apparent that Strauss not only lacks a clear understanding of the literary relationship of the Synoptics to one another, but also that he extends the bounds of the mythical much too far.[168] At the same time, however, it is also clear that New Testament research was brought once and for all face to face with the task of developing a methodical critical analysis that would include all the material. And it is further notable that throughout all his sharp critical work Strauss holds fast at *one* essential point to the reliability of the tradition. That Jesus knew himself to be Messiah seems to him to be indisputable, although, to be sure, he assumes that Jesus arrived at this idea only gradually, and that Jesus anticipated his return he believes also to be probable.[169] .

It appeared to the author of the work, the first half of which is herewith submitted to the public, that it was time to substitute a new mode of considering the life of Jesus, in the place of the antiquated systems of supernaturalism and naturalism. . . .

The new point of view, which must take the place of the ones indicated above, is the mythical. This theory is not brought to bear on the gospel history for the first time in the present work: It has long been applied to particular parts of that history, and is here only extended to its entire compass. It is not by any means meant that the whole history of Jesus is to be represented as mythical, but only that every part of it is to be subjected to a critical examination, to ascertain whether it have not some admixture of the mythical. The exegesis of the ancient church set out from the double proposition: first, that the Gospels contained a history, and second, that this history was a supernatural one. Rationalism rejected the latter of these presuppositions, but only to cling the more tenaciously to the former, maintaining that these books present unadulterated, though only natural, history. Science cannot rest satisfied with this half-measure: the other presupposition also must be relinquished, and the inquiry must first be made whether in fact, and to what extent, the ground on which we stand in the Gospels is in any way historical. . . .

The majority of the most learned and acute theologians of the present day fail in the main requirement for such a work, a requirement without which no amount of learning will suffice to achieve anything in the domain of criticism, namely, the internal liberation of the feelings and intellect from certain religious and dogmatical presuppositions; and this the author early attained by means of philosophical studies. If theologians regard this absence of presupposition from his work, as unchristian: he regards the believing presuppositions of theirs as unscientific. . . .

The author is aware that the essence of the Christian faith is perfectly independent of his criticism. The supernatural birth of Christ, his miracles, his resurrection and ascension, remain eternal truths, whatever doubts may be cast on their reality as historical facts. The certainty of this can alone give calmness and dignity to our critical work. . . .

If anyone should wish to maintain that the historical times within which the public life of Jesus falls make the formation of myths about it unthinkable, there is a ready answer, viz., that early, even in the most arid historical era, an unhistorical cycle of legendary glorification forms about a great individual, especially when a far-reaching revolution in the life of men is associated with him. Imagine a young Church which reverences its founder all the more enthusiastically, the more unexpectedly and the more tragically his life course was ended; a Church impregnated with a mass of new ideas that were to re-create the world; a Church of Orientals, for the most part uneducated people, which consequently was able to adopt and express those ideas only in concrete ways of fantasy, as pictures and as stories, not in the abstract form of rational understanding or concepts; imagine such a Church and you are driven to conclude that under such circumstances that which emerged had to emerge: a series of sacred narratives by which the whole mass of new ideas aroused by Jesus, as well as of old ideas transferred to him, was brought to light as individual elements of his life story. The simple historical framework of the life of Jesus—that he grew up in Nazareth, was baptized by John, gathered disciples, moved about as a teacher in the land of the Jews, was opposed especially to Pharisaism, and issued a call to the kingdom of God; that in the end, however, he succumbed to the hate and envy of the Pharisaic party and died on the Cross—this framework was elaborated with the most varied and most meaningful skeins of pious reflections and fantasies, and in the process all the ideas which primitive Christianity had concerning its Master who had been torn from it were transformed into facts and woven into the account of his life's course. It was the Old Testament, in which the earliest congregation of Christians, drawn predominantly from Judaism, moved and had its being, that provided the richest material for this mythical embellishment. . . .

Taking all this into consideration, little any longer stands in the way of the assumption of myths in all parts of the gospel narratives. Furthermore, the term "myths" itself will give an intelligent man no more offence than a mere word should give such a person at any time, for everything of double meaning that clings to that word because of the recollection of pagan mythology disappears as a result of the argument to this point, viz., that by New Testament myths nothing else is to be understood than the expression of primitive Christian ideas formulated in unintentionally poeticizing sagas and looking very like history.

The boundary line, however, between the historical and the unhistorical, in records, in which as in our Gospels this latter element is incorporated, will ever remain fluctuating and unsusceptible of precise attainment. Least of all can it be expected that the first comprehensive attempt to treat these records from a critical point of view should be successful in drawing a sharply defined line of demarcation. In the obscurity which criticism has produced, by the extinction of all lights hitherto held historical, the eye must accustom itself by degrees to discriminate objects with precision; and at all events the author of this work, wishes especially to guard himself, in those places where he declares he knows not what happened, from the imputation of asserting that he knows that nothing happened.

Thus here [in connection with the story of the Transfiguration], as in every former instance, after having run through the circle of natural explanations, we are led back to the supernatural; in which however we are precluded from resting by difficulties equally decisive. Since then the text forbids a natural interpretation, while it is impossible to maintain as historical the supernatural interpretation which it sanctions, we must apply ourselves to a critical examination of its statements. . . .

It appears here as in some former cases, that two narratives proceeding from quite different presuppositions, and having arisen also in different times, have been awkwardly enough combined: the passage containing the conversation [Mark 9:9-13] proceeding from the probably earlier opinion, that the prophecy concerning Elias had its fulfillment in John; whereas the narrative of the Transfiguration doubtless originated at a later period, when it was not held sufficient that, in the messianic time of Jesus, Elias should only have appeared figuratively in the person of the Baptist, when it was thought fitting that he should also have shown himself personally and literally, if in no more than a transient appearance before a few witnesses. . . .

According to this, we have here a "mythus," the tendency of which is twofold: first, to exhibit in the life of Jesus an enhanced repetition of the glorification of Moses; and second, to bring Jesus as the Messiah into contact with his two forerunners: by this appearance of the lawgiver and the prophet, of the founder and the reformer of the theocracy, to represent Jesus as the perfecter of the kingdom of God, as the fulfillment of the law and the prophets; and beyond this, to show a confirmation of his messianic dignity by a heavenly voice. Finally, this example may serve to show with peculiar clarity, how the natural system of interpretation, while it seeks to preserve the historical certainty of the narratives, loses their ideal truth—sacrifices the essence to the form: whereas the mythical interpretation, by renouncing the historical body of such narratives, rescues and preserves the idea which resides in them, and which alone constitutes their vitality and spirit. Thus if, as the natural explanation would have it, the splendor around Jesus was an accidental, optical phenomenon, and the two appearances either images of a dream or unknown men, where is the significance of the incident? Where is the motive for preserving in the memory of the Church an anecdote so void of ideas, and so barren of inference, resting on a common delusion and superstition? On the other hand, while according to the mythical interpretation, I do not, it is true, see in the evangelical narrative any actual occurrence—I yet retain a sense and a purpose in the narrative; I know what the first Christian community thought it meant, and why the authors of the Gospels included so important a passage in their memoirs.

The results of the inquiry which we have now brought to a close, have apparently annihilated the greatest and most valuable part of that which the Christian has been wont to believe concerning his Savior Jesus, have uprooted all the animating motives which he has gathered from his faith, and withered all his consolations. The boundless store of truth and life which for eighteen centuries has been the nourishment of humanity, seems irretrievably laid waste the most sublime leveled with the dust, God divested of his grace, man of his dignity, and the tie between heaven and earth broken. Piety turns away with horror from so fearful an act of desecration, and strong in the impregnable self-evidence of its faith, pronounces that, let an audacious criticism attempt what it will, all that the Scriptures declare and the church believes of Christ will still subsist as eternal truth, nor is there need for one iota of it to be renounced. Thus at the conclusion of the criticism of the history of Jesus, there presents itself this problem: to reestablish dogmatically that which has been destroyed critically.

Strauss's judgment on the Fourth Gospel had possibly a still more revolutionary effect than his radical criticism. In their presentations of the life of Jesus even Schleiermacher and Hase had still assumed the historical reliability of the Fourth Gospel. But Strauss not only demonstrated that in the Fourth Gospel the Evangelist has imposed *his* speech on the Baptist and on Jesus, but also showed, with particular effect with reference to the contradiction between the Gethsemane scene and the farewell discourses in John, that in John's Gospel myth formation has been *consciously* at work and that consequently vis-à-vis the Synoptics we have to do with an *advanced* form of the myth. Thereby Strauss became the first to pose research in the traditions about Jesus with the alternative, "Synoptists or John," an alternative that New Testament research from then on could no longer evade.[170]

While ... in John, Jesus remains throughout true to his assertion, and the disciples and his followers among the populace remain true to their conviction,

124

that he is the Messiah; in the Synoptic Gospels there is a vacillation discernible —the previously expressed persuasion on the part of the disciples and the people that Jesus was the Messiah, sometimes vanishes and gives place to a much lower view of him, and even Jesus himself becomes more reserved in his declarations. . . .

Thus, on the point under discussion the synoptic statement is contradictory, not only to that of John, but to itself; it appears therefore that it ought to be unconditionally surrendered before that of John, which is consistent with itself. . . . But here again we must not lose sight of our demonstrated rule, that when analyzing narratives concerned with glorification such as our Gospels, in questionable cases that statement is the least probable which most closely corresponds to the objective of glorification. Now this is the case with John's statement; according to which, from the beginning to the close of the public life of Jesus, his messiahship shines forth in unchanging splendor, while, according to the synoptic writers, it is liable to variation in its light. But though this criterion of probability is in favor of the first three evangelists, it is impossible that the order can be correct in which they make ignorance and concealment follow on plain declarations and recognitions of the messiahship of Jesus, and we must suppose that they have mingled and confounded two separate periods of the life of Jesus, in the latter of which alone he presented himself as the Messiah. . . .

The most natural supposition is that Jesus, first the disciple of the Baptist, and afterwards his successor, in preaching repentance and the approach of the kingdom of heaven, took originally the same position as his former master in relation to the messianic kingdom, notwithstanding the greater sublimity and liberality of his mind, and only gradually rose to the point of thinking himself the Messiah.

Since in the other Gospels Jesus speaks in a thoroughly different tone and style, it would follow, if he really spoke as he is represented to have done by John, that the manner attributed to him by the synoptists is fictitious. Now, that this manner did not originate with the evangelists is plain from the fact that each of them is so little master of his matter. Neither could the bulk of the discourses have been the work of tradition, not only because they have a highly original cast, but because they bear the impress of the alleged time and locality. On the contrary, the Fourth Evangelist, by the ease with which he controls his materials, awakens the suspicion that they are of his own production; and some of his favorite ideas and phrases, such as, "The Father shows the Son all that he himself does [John 5:20]," . . . seem to have sprung from a Hellenistic source, rather than from Palestine. But the chief point in the argument is, that in this Gospel John the Baptist speaks, as we have seen, in precisely the same strain as the author of the Gospels, and his Jesus. It cannot be supposed, that besides the evangelist, the Baptist, whose public career was prior to that of Jesus, and whose character was strongly marked, modeled his expressions with verbal minuteness on those of Jesus. Hence only two cases are possible: either the Baptist determined the style of Jesus and the evangelist (who indeed appears to have been the Baptist's disciple) ; or the evangelist determined the style of the Baptist and Jesus. The former alternative will be rejected by the orthodox, on the ground of the higher nature that dwelt in Christ; and we are equally disinclined to adopt it, for the reason that Jesus, even though he may have been excited to activity by the Baptist, yet appears as a character essentially distinct from him, and original; and for the still more weighty consideration, that the style of the evangelist is much too delicate for the rude Baptist—too mystical for his practical mind. There remains, then, but the latter alternative, namely, that the evangelist has given his own style both to Jesus and to the Baptist: an explanation in itself more natural than the former, and supported by a multitude of examples from all kinds of historical writers.

After the assurance of already achieved victory expressed in the farewell discourses [John 14–17], and especially in the final prayer, for Jesus to sink into such a state of mind as that described by the synoptists [Matt. 26:36 ff.], would have been a very humiliating reverse, which he could not have foreseen, otherwise he would not have expressed himself with so much confidence; and which, therefore, would prove that he was deceived in himself, that he held himself to be stronger than he actually found himself, and that he had given utterance to this too high self-valuation, not without a degree of presumption. Those who regard this as inconsistent with the equally judicious and modest character which Jesus manifests on other occasions, will find themselves driven to the dilemma, that either the farewell discourses in John, at least the final prayer, or else the events in Gethsemane, cannot be historical. . . .

The motive also for heightening the prescience into a real presentiment, and thus for creating the scene in Gethsemane, is easy of discovery. On the one hand, there cannot be a more obvious proof that a foreknowledge of an event or condition has existed, than its having risen to the vividness of a presentiment; on the other hand, the suffering must appear the more awful, if the mere presentiment extorted from him who was destined to that suffering, anguish even to bloody sweat, and prayer for deliverance. Further, the sufferings of Jesus were exhibited in a higher sense, as voluntary, if before they came upon him externally, he had resigned himself to them internally; and lastly, it must have gratified primitive Christian devotion, to withdraw the real crisis of these sufferings from the profane eyes to which he was exposed on the Cross, and to enshrine it as a mystery only witnessed by a narrow circle of the initiated. . . .

Herewith the dilemma above stated falls to the ground, since we must pronounce unhistorical not only one of the two, but both representations of the last hours of Jesus before his arrest. The only gradation of distinction between the historical value of the synoptic account and that of John is, that the former is a mythical product of traditional formation in the first degree, the latter is in the second degree—or more correctly, the one is a product in the second degree, the other in the third. Common to the synoptists and to John is their presentation of Jesus as foreknowing sufferings even to the day and hour of their arrival. Then comes the first modification which the pious legend gave to the real history of Jesus; the statement of the synoptists, that he even had an antecedent experience of his sufferings, is the second step of the mythical; while, that although he foreknew them, and also in one instance had a foretaste of them (John 12:27ff.), he had yet long beforehand completely triumphed over them, and when they stood immediately before him, looked them in the face with imperturbed serenity—this representation of the Fourth Gospel is the third and highest grade of devotional, but unhistorical embellishment.

Though Strauss by his clear and radical criticism compelled New Testament research to undertake the historical examination of the New Testament, whatever its consequence, nevertheless his negatively oriented work lacked on the one hand a basis in source criticism, and on the other the purpose of arriving at a positive presentation of the history of primitive Christianity from the critical study of the gospel narratives.[171] **Ferdinand Christian Baur** deliberately undertook both these tasks, although he was able to reach results that proved of permanent value only with respect to that of presenting a critical history of primitive Christianity. In the seminary at Maulbronn, where D. F. Strauss—as later also at Tübingen—was his pupil, Baur through B. G. Niebuhr's *Römische Geschichte* [Roman history] had already developed enthusiasm for historical scholarship employing critical source analysis,[172] and when in 1826 he accepted the post as professor of the historical branches of theology at Tübingen, in studies in the history of religion, [*Symbolik und Mythologie, oder die Naturreligion des Altertums* [Symbolism and mythology; or the nature religion of antiquity] (1824-25), he had already won through from the supernatural viewpoint of his first publication to an approach that treated Christianity on the same basis as other religions.[173] To begin with Baur took a thoroughly conservative attitude with reference to the primitive Christian sources. In an address on the speech of Stephen in the book of Acts delivered in 1829 there is not a trace of doubt about the historicity of the speeches in Acts or of the book as a whole, though even in this paper Baur observes that there are two kinds of apologetic speeches in Acts, of which the one believes that Christianity is to be reconciled with the Jews (Peter), and the other doubts that the Jews can be converted to Jesus (Stephen).[174] While it is true that J. S. Semler had already indicated that there were these two opposed groups within early Christianity,[175] it is Baur who, in his celebrated article on "Die Christuspartei in der korinthischen Gemeinde" [The Christ party in the Corinthian church] (1831), first made a systematic study of this grouping and, as he himself reports twenty years later, was led from this position step by step to a fundamental view concerning the history of early Christianity.[176]

Long ago, before Strauss's *Life of Jesus* appeared—a book, of course, that was concerned with critical analysis of the Gospels—my own critical investigations of the Pauline letters, the other main point of departure from which a new groundwork for New Testament criticism must be won, were already underway. It was my study of the two Corinthian letters that first caused me to concentrate my attention more directly on the relation of the apostle Paul to the older apostles. I became convinced that enough data are to be found in the letters of the apostle to enable us to see that this relationship was one quite other than is ordinarily assumed; that where it is taken for granted that there existed a complete harmony between all the apostles, there was actually an opposition, one which even went so far that the very authority of the apostle Paul was brought into question by Jewish Christians. Further research in church history made it possible for me to look more deeply into the significance of this opposition during postapostolic times, and it became ever more clear to me that the opposition between the two parties that are to be distinguished more strictly and precisely in apostolic and postapostolic times than has so far been the case, the opposition between the Paulinists and Petrinists, or Judaizers, had a significant influence not only on the different formulations of the Peter legend, but also on the composition of the book of Acts and of such canonical letters as, in particular, the Second Letter of Peter. I presented the first results of my critical research in an essay in the Tübingen *Zeitschrift für Theologie* [Journal of theology] of 1831 . . . entitled, "Die Christuspartei in der korinthischen Gemeinde, der Gegensatz des paulinischen und petrinischen Christentums [in der ältesten Kirche] . . ." [The Christ party in the Corinthian church; the opposition of Pauline and Petrine Christianity (in the ancient church)]. My investigations with respect to Gnosis led me to the Pastoral Letters and resulted in the conclusion that I supported in my book of 1835 concerning these letters, namely, that the Pastorals cannot have been written by the apostle Paul, but that their origin is to be explained by the same party tendencies that in the course of the second century were the moving principle of the Christian churches that were taking form. My continued preoccupation with the Pauline letters and my deeper penetration of the spirit of the apostle Paul and of Pauline Christianity increasingly confirmed me in the conviction that there is a very essential difference between the four main letters of the apostle and the shorter ones in the collection of his letters and that the authenticity of several of the latter, if not of all, can be very seriously doubted. What I summed up in my book on the apostle Paul of the year 1845 and presented in further detail as a unit includes, with the exception of my book on the Pastoral Epistles, all my investigations in the letters of Paul and in the book of Acts, a book which stands in such a close relationship to them. The question of the Gospels, which was raised anew by Strauss's *Life of Jesus,* only aroused my acute interest after I had attained an independent view of the relation of the Johannine Gospel to the Synoptics. The basic difference of this Gospel to the Synoptics impressed me so much that at once the view of its character and origin came to me which I developed in the *Theologischen Jahrbüchern* [Theological yearbooks] of 1844. That view furnished a new standpoint both for New Testament criticism and for the study of the gospel history. If the Gospel of John is not, as the others, a historical account, if it actually is not intended to be a historical account, if it has undoubtedly an ideological tendency, then it can no longer stand vis-à-vis the Synoptics in a historical opposition. It is therefore no longer possible to employ Strauss's tactics and methodology with which he now opposes the Johannine account to the synoptic and now the synoptic to the Johannine, and from which only the conclusion can be drawn that we no longer have any idea of what can be retained of the gospel story. To the degree that the historical value of John sinks, that of the Synoptics rises, since there is now no reason to raise doubts of the latter's reliability because of the Johannine Gospel. Since we are able to acknowledge the clear and evident difference and to do so without reserve, we have the key to its very simple explanation. Not by any means do I intend to say by this that in the Synoptic Gospels we have a purely historical account, but only that a definite point of view now emerges by which this whole relationship can be understood. By this route I was led further in my investigations in the Gospel of Luke and summed them up in the *Theologischen Jahrbüchern* [Theological yearbooks] of 1846 and then expanded this summary in my second main book on the criticism of the New Testament, my *Kritischen Untersuchungen über die kanonischen Evangelien* [Critical investigations of the canonical Gospels] of 1847.

The article on "Die Christuspartei in der korinthischen Gemeinde" [The Christ party in the Corinthian church] maintained, on the basis of both the Corinthian letters, that Paul at Corinth was charged by the Judaizing adherents of Peter with not having been a disciple of the earthly Jesus, and Baur then also discovered the opposition of these Petrine Christians to Paul in other Pauline letters and in the primitive church, but also drew attention to later tendencies to gloss over the differences between the two directions.[177]

Now a large part of the content of both letters consists of an assertion of the apostolic authority that the opponents of the apostle Paul did not wish to recognize to the full extent. Why is this, if not for the reason that they did not wish to recognize him as a genuine and legitimate apostle because he was not one in the same sense as Peter, James, and the other apostles of Christ [I Cor. 1:12], not one who like these had stood in the same immediate relationship to Jesus during his life on earth? Peter himself had no part in the faction at Corinth that bore his name, as indeed we may infer from the fact that Peter himself had not come to Corinth. However, everything points to the conclusion that itinerant pseudoapostles who invoked the name of Peter had also come to Corinth. . . .

The same Judaizing opponents against whom the apostle declares himself in both the letters addressed to the Corinthian congregation meet us also in other letters of the same apostle in several passages in which, partly indirectly and partly directly, he believed himself compelled to take them into account. One of the more certain of the passages of this sort is Phil. 3:1-2, where the apostle attacks false teachers who laid great weight on circumcision and all else that belonged to hereditary Judaism, and in this sense put a confidence in the flesh that stood in conflict with the faith in the death of Christ on the cross. Though, as in II Cor. 12:12, the apostle compared himself with them with the assertion of the same advantages with reference to his person, he did so only because he wished thereby all the more emphatically to express his contempt for these externals in the connection under review. But it is the Letter to the Galatians that offers us the choicest parallel to the polemical tendency of both Letters to the Corinthians and which throws further light on the nature of the attacks against which the apostle had to defend himself. The opponents whom the apostle attacks in the Letter to the Galatians belong wholly in the same class with those with whom he had to do in the Letters to the Corinthians. . . . The attack on these Judaizing false teachers makes up a large part of the Letter to the Galatians, and here there can be no doubt about the matter. However, it is usually less frequently observed that these very false teachers combined with their Judaism attacks on the apostolic authority of the apostle Paul that can have had no other tendency than those against which the apostle had to defend himself vis-à-vis the Corinthian congregation. . . .

After this fashion two opposing parties with a very distinct difference of views had come into being as early as those early times in which Christianity had yet hardly begun to break through the narrow bounds of Judaism and to open up for itself a successful field of work in the pagan world. The party that set itself against the apostle Paul had its beginnings in Jerusalem, where the younger James, the brother of the Lord, stood in high esteem as the leader of the Christian congregation. The party's Jerusalem origin is what we might have expected and is also explicitly noted by the apostle Paul in Gal. 2:12, a passage in which we see the party appear first in Antioch with the tendency that it thereafter pursued assiduously. As they spread their teachings the pseudoapostles of this party appealed above all to the authority of James and of Peter, though we can scarcely believe that the [real] Jewish apostles themselves approved them and could give recognition to sham emissaries of this sort. . . .

If the conflict of the Jewish Christian and Gentile Christian parties affected the relationships of the most ancient church as deeply as I believe I have shown, it is then very natural that . . . attempts at mediation and settlement . . . were also made very early. It cannot be denied that the Letter of James has . . . such a tendency. However, should not both Petrine letters also be viewed in the same light? The observation has already often been made that First Peter has striking points of agreement in language and ideas with the Pauline letters (de Wette). Since this phenomenon does not support any doubt of the letter's authenticity, it can then only be explained on the assumption that the apostle Peter saw himself impelled by means of the whole thrust of his letter to lay his agreement with the apostle Paul before the congregations in Pontus, Galatia, Cappadocia, Asia, and Bithynia, among whom, as might be expected, the conflict of these two parties and directions must have emerged with especial acuteness. Second Peter betrays a mediating tendency of this sort even more strikingly, a tendency which, by making all the more understandable the special purpose of the author in wanting his letter to be regarded as one written by the apostle Peter himself, adds further weight to the already overwhelming suspicion that it is unauthentic. . . . Finally, at the end of his letter (3:15), where he refers to the apostle Paul as his beloved brother, praises the wisdom given to him, appeals to his letters, and warns against the misunderstandings his letters can occasion, as well as against the misinterpretations wrested from them, the author expresses his letter's conciliatory purpose most unambiguously, a purpose that not without reason he puts into the mouth of Peter as he approaches his death (1:13-15), in order to make it, as the apostle's last will and testament, all the more worthy of consideration. How is it possible to overlook the fact that in the whole letter the author's main purpose was to counter every doubt of the complete harmony of the two apostles, in order thereby to remove everything that seemed able to justify the persisting conflict?

Accordingly, by purely exegetical means Baur had demonstrated that the history of primitive Christianity, like all human history, was determined by the interplay of human conflict and actually took place within the nexus of such an interplay. However, in the article from which the above excerpts were taken Baur still betrays no doubt of the authenticity of the letters he was later to attack (Philippians, James, I Peter) and has nothing to say about the place of the book of the Acts within the conflict he describes. A few years later (1835), however, in his book on the Pastoral Epistles, he declares that the criticism of the New Testament canon is not to be terminated "even with reference to the Pauline letters" (though, to be sure, the Letter to the Philippians is here also cited without reservation as a genuine letter of Paul's) , that I Peter by its mediating character betrays its origin in postapostolic times, and that from Paul's speech in Acts 20 "one sees . . . only too clearly that this whole farewell discourse was written *post eventum*." We can see by this judgment how Baur begins to view further books of the New Testament critically in light of his insight into the conflict in the primitive church, but at the same time a basically new point of view emerges in his argumentation. He takes up the objections to the Pauline origin of the Pastoral Letters which had already been raised by Schleiermacher and then more emphatically by Eichhorn, but demands that criticism demonstrate "also positive data which transfer us from the apostle's time into another circle of relationships foreign to him," because only by basing it on such positive data can we clarify the total view of the whole circle of relationships into which a book must be placed. He therefore seeks to show that the false teachers that are attacked in the Pastorals can only be comprehended against the background of the time of the Gnostics of the later postapostolic age and that the church order of widows cannot possibly be placed in apostolic times, and so proceeds to argue on the other hand that the origin of the Pastoral Letters can be explained very satisfactorily by the hypothesis that Paulinists, possibly at Rome, in view of the gnostic misuse of Paul and the attacks of Judaizers on Paul, had to hit upon the idea that "the apostle Paul, for the purpose of confuting the Gnostics, must be made to say . . . indirectly in writings that now first reached the light of day what could not be found with the directness that was desirable in his already extant letters." [178] In this way Baur gained for New Testament research the perception that it can no longer abandon, namely, that the task of the historical criticism of the New Testament writings is only fulfilled when the historical place of origin of a writing within the framework of early Christian history is also established.

This first masterful historical investigation of the New Testament of Baur's, one that sought to be guided only "by the single interest of objective historical truth," hands on at the same time, however, one theological legacy fraught with peril. Despite the critical objections raised by Schleiermacher and his successors, the attempt to ascribe the Pastorals to Paul appeared to Baur as "an effort so far as possible to guarantee for the future that the letter under attack [I Tim.] would also have the place in the Canon that it has already maintained for so long," that is as an effort by which one can regard himself as justified in "placing an ordinary human message alongside the divine apostolic message as one of completely equal worth." [179] In a reassertion of the idea first expressed by

J. D. Michaelis, this requires of historical criticism that it answer the *theological* question of the canonical validity of the New Testament writings as the Word of God, with the consequence that the negative result of such criticism carries with it a denial of the canonical worth of a New Testament book.[180] And over against this, naturally, the defense of the traditional ascriptions of authorship must become at the same time a preservation of the canonical worth of the New Testament books.

If all this shows a rationalistic heritage in Baur, yet during the same years (after 1833) the philosophy of Hegel won predominant influence over him. Hegel's view of history as a dialectic process of the resolution of the "being-in-itself" and the "being-for-itself" in the "being-in-and-for-itself" combined in Baur's thought with the opposition of Petrine and Pauline Christianity which he had observed by historical method and which was settled in postapostolic Christendom, and this triple beat of thesis, antithesis, and synthesis now becomes the clue to the understanding of the history of early Christianity. And history for him becomes the self-unfolding of the spirit in which the particular has to retire behind the general; *"critical* method in positive terms means: *speculative* method, understanding of *history* as the process of the *idea* of history." [181]

These philosophical tendencies now reveal themselves increasingly in Baur's more massive works on the history of primitive Christianity, works that followed one another in rapid succession. To begin with the critical judgments in connection with the question of the place of the individual New Testament writings in the course of the altercation between Jewish Christianity and Gentile Christianity became sharper. The insight that the chronologically earlier First Letter to the Corinthians is a more reliable source for our understanding of the phenomenon of "speaking with tongues" than the later Acts of the Apostles appeared or the first time in an essay on speaking with tongues that was published in 1838,[182] and in a study of the origin of the bishop's office that appeared in the same year it is established that "all Jewish Christians of earliest times exhibit a more or less Ebionite character," i.e., that they correspond to the later heretical Christianity that was opposed to Paul. On the other hand, not only the Pastoral Letters, but also the Epistle to the Philippians and the Epistle to the Hebrews appear as attempts of the Pauline party to overcome the conflict with the Jewish Christians by a *rapprochement,* and the Acts of the Apostles is interpreted as the apologetic effort of a group interested in establishing harmonious relations.[183]

The Paulinists by their very nature and as a consequence of their basic beliefs had to be more tractable and more inclined to establish cordial relations with the opposition party. What other alternative was open to them? On the one hand they saw before them a very determined opposition, one that pursued a fixed direction with utmost consistency, but on the other hand they wanted to have nothing to do with an extreme of Paulinism such as developed from Gnosticism and reached its fruition in Marcionism. This in and by itself is most probable, but documentary historical proof is not lacking if we do not shut our eyes to evidence which in every case can only be perceived by critical insight. This is the place where my investigation of the Pastoral Letters makes its special contribution, for all that I have said that explains the origin of these letters is also a moment in the history of the Christian Church as a catholic institution. However, the Pastorals by themselves are by no means the only phenomenon of this kind in our Canon. Close to them, as it seems ever more probable to me, stands the Letter to the Philippians, in which, in addition to those "bishops" and "deacons" in the letter's salutation, and in addition to so much else into which this is not the place to enter in detail, also Peter's pupil Clement is introduced (4:3) as the foremost of the "fellow-laborers" of the apostle Paul. . . .

Indeed, in terms of its basic idea and most inward predisposition, even the Acts of the Apostles, however in other respects we may estimate its historical reliability, is the apologetic attempt of a Paulinist to facilitate and bring about the *rapprochement* and union of the two opposing parties by representing Paul as Petrine as possible and, on the other hand, Peter as Pauline as possible. Over the differences which, according to the apostle Paul's own unambiguous declaration in the Letter to the Galatians, had undoubtedly really arisen, it seeks so far as possible to throw a reconciling veil, and the hate of Judaism on the part of the Gentile Christians and of paganism on the part of Jewish Christians—a hate that disturbed the relationship of the two parties—is forgotten in the common hate on the part of both of the unbelieving Jews, who made the apostle Paul the constant object of their irreconcilable hate. . . .

Of these irenic writings which form a class of their own and which belong to a definite period, the Letter to the Hebrews is perhaps to be regarded as the first member. In all its peculiarity . . . it appears perhaps to be regarded as the first attempt, though one still made with a certain ambiguity, to pursue the business of bringing both parties into harmony and of establishing peace by this literary means, by letters put into circulation in the name of the apostle.

This understanding of the Acts of the Apostles as governed by an "irenic tendency" was taken up soon thereafter by Baur's pupil **Matthias Schneckenburger,** who tried to demonstrate that the author of the Book of the Acts wished by parallel accounts of Peter and Paul to equate Paul with Peter. "The picture of Paul and his activity that emerges is a onesided one, one that does not conform throughout and in detail with the apostle's own account in his letters, and one that a Paulinist could not sketch without a secondary apologetic purpose." Schnecken-burger, to be sure, wished in spite of this to hold fast to the tradition of Lucan authorship of the book of the Acts and by demonstrating its irenic tendency to protect it "against threatening dangers from the side of criticism." [184] **F. C. Baur** himself, however, reached more critical results in his book on Paul (1845) that summed up all his previous studies. With respect to the history of the apostolic age he regards it as an important task to recognize that *a choice* must be made between the two divergent presentations of the book of the Acts and of Paul and seeks to prove by careful analysis of the book of the Acts that this book exhibits the conscious tendency to set aside the differences between Paul and Peter and in the interests of this tendency has *altered* the history. With special reference to the divergent accounts of the Apostolic Council by Paul and the Acts of the Apostles, he reaches the conclusion that only Paul's account can be regarded as authentic.[185] And, because of its "apologetic and irenic tendency," he dismisses the book of the Acts entirely as a reliable source for the history of the apostolic age. Thereby not only is a clear understanding won of the fact that there are primary and secondary sources for the history of primitive Christianity, but also the proper methodological requirement is raised, namely, that the values of the sources and also the meaning of a document can be properly determined only by taking its purpose into consideration. This "tendency-criticism," while basically fully justified, is, to be sure, misused by Baur, even in connection with the book of the Acts, in that every deviation of the secondary source is traced back to a conscious alteration of the historical facts.[186]

[For Paul], as in the gospel story, historical criticism has before it two divergent accounts that must be evaluated vis-à-vis one another if we are to derive pure history from them, the report of the book of the Acts and the historical data contained in the apostle's own letters. One might think that, in all those cases in which the narrative of the book of the Acts does not wholly agree with the apostle's own statements, the latter have such a decided claim to authentic truth that the contradiction of the book of the Acts can warrant no consideration, but this rule, however evident it must appear from the very nature of the case, has so far not been followed as it deserves to have been. By commencing with the assumption of the thoroughgoing identity of the presentation of the book of the Acts and the apostle's own statements in his letters, the differences that occur, even when they cannot be denied, are regarded as too few and inconsequential to be given any further weight. In fact, interpreters have not infrequently sided with the book of the Acts against the clear assertions of the apostle. Consequently, not only has the historical truth been obscured, but also the fairness and impartiality to which the apostle is entitled in any judgment of his apostolic life and work are imperiled. In order to allow no appearance of a serious difference in his relationship with the other apostles, some have had no hesitation in ascribing to him in many instances a way of acting which, if it were true as represented, would cast serious reflections on his character. An account of this part of the primitive history of Christianity, therefore, if undertaken in accordance with the more rigorous axioms of historical criticism, can only be at the same time an apology for the apostle.

Between the Acts of the Apostles and the Pauline epistles, as far as the historical contents of the latter can be compared with the Acts of the Apostles, there will be found in general the same relation as between the Gospel of John and the Synoptic Gospels. The comparison of both these sources must lead to the conclusion that, considering the great difference between the two statements, historical truth can belong to only one of them. To which it does belong can only be decided by the undisputed historical rule that the statement which has the greatest claim to historical truth is that which appears most unprejudiced and nowhere betrays a desire to subordinate its historical material to any special subjective aim. For the history of the apostolic age the Pauline epistles take precedence over all the other New Testament writings, as an authentic source. On this account the Acts must fill a secondary place; but there is also the further critical point that the same rule which defines the relation of the Synoptic Gospels to the Gospel of John, finds its application in the Acts of the Apostles; while I am at this place, and in order to indicate the standpoint of the following inquiry, I must express this opinion on the Acts of the Apostles, that I can find in it no purely objective statement, but only one which is arranged on subjective grounds: and I must also express a great wish to refer to a critical work [Schneckenburger] which I venture to follow all the more, as it afforded me important results when I devoted myself to a quite different line of work some time ago. . . .

The first two chapters of the Epistle to the Galatians form a historical document of the greatest importance for our investigations into the true standpoint of the apostle and his relations to the elder apostles. But if these chapters are to be of any value in the interest of the truth of the history, we must first of all free ourselves from the common arbitrary suppositions which generally attend this inquiry, by which the most complete harmony is established between the author of the Acts of the Apostles and the apostle Paul, and one narrative is used as a confirmation of the other. It is self-evident that as the apostle appears as an eyewitness and individual actor in his own affairs, his statement alone ought to be held as authentic. Then again an unfavorable light is thus shed on the Acts of the Apostles, the statements in which can only be looked at as intentional deviations from historical truth in the interest of the special tendency which they possess.

Baur now assumes exactly the same critical attitude toward the Pauline letters as to the book of the Acts, and concludes with reference to the former that only the four great letters (Romans, I and II Corinthians, Galatians) can be regarded as genuine letters of the apostle, while all the other letters belong to the time in which the conflict between Jewish Christianity and Gentile Christianity is beginning to be resolved. And it is apparent that the thrust of the dialectical theory of history had to lead to this result, for in fact the smaller letters of Paul cannot be accounted for as products of the conflict of the two parties.[187]

The foregoing inquiry shows what a false picture of the individual character of the apostle Paul we should obtain if we had no other source than the Acts of the Apostles from which to derive our knowledge of it. The epistles of the apostle are then the only authentic documents for the history of his apostolic labors, and of the whole relation in which he stood to his age, and in proportion as the spirit that breathes through them is great and original, so do they present the truest and most faithful mirror of the time. The more we study the epistles the more we perceive that a rich and peculiar life is summed up in them, as the most direct testimony to it. Only in the epistles is that shadow, whose false image the Acts of the Apostles brings forward in the place of the real apostle, placed in direct contrast with him. . . .

What, then, we have still to ask, is the true object of these epistles, if they be not by Paul, and can only be understood in the light of the features of that later age from which they sprang? The central idea around which everything else revolves in them is to be found in their Christology; but it is impossible to assume that the object for which they were written was the purely theoretical one of setting forth those higher views of the person of Christ. The occasion out of which they arose must have been some practical need in the circumstances of the time; and even the idea of the person of Christ is at once brought into a certain definite point of view. Christ, it is manifest, is taken here as the center of the unity of all opposites. These opposites embrace the entire universe; heaven and earth, the visible and the invisible, and everything that exists has in Christ the basis of its existence; in him, therefore, all oppositions and distinctions disappear; even up to the highest spirit-world there is nothing that has not its highest and absolute principle in him. This metaphysical height is sought, however, only in order to descend from it to the immediate present and its practical necessities; for here also there are opposites of which only Christ can be the reconciling and atoning unity. Here, accordingly, we find the standpoint from which the object and the contents of the epistles can be satisfactorily comprehended. It is obvious that they point to the distinction of Gentile and Jew Christians; and thus they clearly belong to a time when these two parties were still, to some extent, opposed to each other, and when the removal of their mutual opposition was the only road to the unity of the Christian Church.

Although this central result of Baur's with respect to the briefer letters of Paul cannot be maintained, yet his demand that every single writing be arranged in a total historical perspective is a permanent legacy of his work. And Baur himself is aware that there "can be unending debate" about detail; "what alone in the final analysis can tip the scales in favor of a view put forward in a wider perspective is, indeed, only the general, on which also the detail is again and again dependent, the consequence of the whole, the convincing inner probability and necessity of the matter which comes to the fore of itself and before which sooner or later the party interests of the day must be struck dumb." [188] This recognition by Baur of the fundamental significance of a total historical perspective, in connection with the influence of Hegelian philosophy has the effect in the concluding account of "The Doctrinal System of the Apostle" that Pauline theology is constrained into a distinction of the doctrine of justification as "the representation of the subjective consciousness" from "the view of the objective relation in which . . . Christianity stands to paganism and Judaism." In this way the significance of Christ is reduced to "the principle . . . of self-consciousness relieved of all finite limitations and freed of all disturbing conventions," and "the doctrine of Christ" emerges in connection with the "special discussion of secondary dogmatic questions." In this account of the Pauline theology as the doctrine of the unity of the subjective and the objective spirit, it is not so much the historian as the disciple of Hegel who has the last word, but in spite of this objection it must be admitted: "It might indeed be easier to dispute the results than the method, and even still easier to dispute the method than to undertake the task in a really better way." [189]

The same methodological interest of Baur's appears in his second main work on the New Testament, one that was published shortly after his book on Paul, his *Kritische Untersuchungen über die kanonische Evangelien* [Critical studies of the canonical Gospels] (1847). Now for the first time Baur opened a debate with Strauss, in order to substitute the "historical" view of Jesus for the "negatively critical" view of Strauss and his opponents. Vis-à-vis the Gospels, also, Baur raises the question of the tendency of the evangelists and demonstrates first of all by a careful analysis of the Gospel of John that in relation to the Synoptics it possesses no special historical tradition, but that probably its historical matter is contrived out of the idea of the divine dignity and glory of Jesus. This shows that John has no desire at all to give a historical report, but wants to express an idea. And the ideal "of a Christian Church consisting equally of Gentiles and Jews" which John supports (John 10:16) points to a time "when Christianity in the course of its development had already left the conflicts of the early period far behind." Consequently the Gospel of John is not only denied the authority of an eyewitness, but is also dismissed as a source of no consequence for the history of Jesus, without thereby ceasing to be the "witness of a genuine evangelical spirit." [190]

Since it is true that everything historical reaches us only through the medium of the writer of the narrative, it follows that also in connection with the gospel story the first question is not, what objective reality this or that narrative has in itself, but rather, in what relation what is narrated stands to the consciousness of the writer of the narrative, by whose mediation it is for us an object of historical knowledge. Historical criticism must take its stand here. Only from this bastion can it hope to arrive at an at least better motivated view of the determination of the boundary line between the historical and the unhistorical, "this most difficult problem in the domain of criticism."

The first question that criticism has to ask of these Gospels can therefore only be: What did each respective author wish and have in mind? and only with this question do we reach the firm ground of concrete historical truth.

Once we have the proof before us, even with respect only to one Gospel, that a Gospel is not merely a simple historical account but can also be a tendency writing, this is then the general point of view from which criticism has to regard the Gospels, and from this the rule formulates itself, viz., that to the degree to which a definite tendential character is revealed in a historical presentation of this sort, to that degree it falls short of being what it is usually held to be, namely, an authentic historical report. But such writings can only be tendency writings to the extent that they are products of their time. The criticism that views them in this light, and can recognize by means of it alone a new moment of the critical consciousness, is properly called historical, because it makes it its essential task to put itself into the whole complex of temporal relationships from which these writings issued. However, unless it wishes to take its departure from an arbitrary presupposition, it must not limit the circle of these relationships just to the time within which its alleged apostolic origin would fall, but must extend it as far as it can be extended on the basis of the actual data about its historical existence.

The very systematic character of the tendency, this thoroughgoing relation of the detail to an idea that governs everything, prevents us from accepting any of the Synoptic Gospels as a different, independent, historical report. Only the tendency differs. If we leave this tendency out of consideration, together with the modifications that derive from it, which necessarily affect the historical account, what content is left to us as something independent of the tradition of the synoptic evangelists? Accordingly, even here the view commends itself to us, the view that alone can enable us to reach a critically historical comprehension of the Johannine Gospel, viz., that the Gospel derives its historical elements from the same evangelical tradition which constitutes the content of our Synoptic Gospels, or from our Synoptic Gospels themselves, but it does not intend to be a strictly historical Gospel. It subordinates its historical content to an overriding idea. In accordance with its basic idea, it has regarded the historical matter it has taken eclectically from the gospel tradition in a different light, brought it into different combinations, and, as could not have happened otherwise, more or less reworked it so that vis-à-vis the Synoptic Gospels it seems to be in part parallel to them, in part divergent from them, but just because of that a new and independent Gospel. The fact is that only its idea and tendency are different. The historical content itself, so far as we know how to analyze it and trace it back to its elements, remains the same.

Even in the investigations that have been undertaken heretofore, the relation of our Gospel to the Synoptics could not remain unobserved, and consequently in the studies that have been made to this point the main data have emerged that go to make up the view that is to be advanced regarding this relationship. It rests on the certainly undisputed rule that when two different reports concerned with the same subject are so related to one another in their difference that only one of the two—not both at the same time and in the same way—can be historically true, it is to be assumed that the overwhelming historical probability lies on the side of that report which least of all betrays any interest, beyond the purpose of purely historical narration, that could have an influence on the historical record. The more apparent it is, then, that such an interest lies at the base of the Johannine Gospel, in that from beginning to end it has no concern for a purely historical account, but for the presentation of an idea which has run its ideal course in the march of events of the gospel story, all the less should it be possible to entertain any doubt about how the two reports are related to each other, if our concern is only for the purely historical question of which of the two is to be regarded as the historically more reliable in all those instances in which the historical difference is not be to denied.

With these observations Baur gained the same insight for the Gospels as for the relationship between Paul and the Acts of the Apostles. And while Strauss posed the alternative for the study of Jesus, "Synoptics or John," but then, despite his insight into the advanced mythical character of John, proceeded to devalue both sources, Baur recognized unequivocally that the Synoptics are superior as historical sources to John, and this recognition belongs to the abiding results of New Testament research. To be sure, Baur now directed toward the Synoptic Gospels the question concerning the tendency of the author and sought to prove that the Gospel of Luke, dependent on Matthew, shows the same irenic tendency as does the Book of the Acts, and that Mark, dependent on Matthew and Luke, likewise betrays the point of view of neutrality. Only Matthew is basically historically reliable and has no tendency, and its account of Jesus as the fulfiller of the Jewish Law enables us to understand the origin of Christianity from within Judaism. Although Baur knew of the proofs recently published of the greater age of Mark's Gospel, he arrived at his evaluation of the relationship of the Synoptic Gospels to one another by way of the method of tendency criticism, since it was only in Matthew that he could recognize a "Judaizing character." It is certain that this judgment about the sources of the gospel story is wrong,[191] but that does not detract in any way from the extremely important fact that Baur basically recognized the greater historical value of the Synoptics and therefore, over against Strauss's criticism, which played John against the Synoptics and the Synoptics against John, won a sure historical footing for research in the tradition about Jesus.

To be sure, even here Baur does not free himself of his rationalistic heritage. Wherever Matthew reports that Jesus anticipates his speedy return Baur denies the Gospel any worth as a historical source, for "Jesus cannot possibly have spoken in this way." [192] And, just as in the investigation of the Pastoral Letters he had intruded the irrelevant question of their canonical status in case of their nonapostolic authorship, so Baur now, in a work on the nature of the science of New Testament introduction, declared that historical criticism of the traditional ascriptions of authorship was concerned with the principle of the canonical authority of these writings. In doing so, however, Baur, by the rationalistic equation of historical-critical and dogmatic judgments, had abandoned his own insight that the Gospel of John is "a witness of a genuinely evangelical spirit," even though it does not come from the apostle John.[193]

Now, if the biblical books are made at all the object of detailed reflection, as the concept of introduction in any case assumes they will be, what other question could have greater importance than whether they considered in their unity as a whole or each separately, they actually are as they are presumed to be according to the traditional idea of the Canon? And if the question as we have raised it also implies the possibility that the investigation of this or that book will lead to a result that must make its canonical authority, to say the least, very doubtful, what importance is accorded to the science of theology, which has to decide in the end which books of the Canon are canonical or not, what right each book of the Canon has to its place in it, and whether all those ideas we are accustomed to associate with the Canon can also be historically justified? The higher and more peculiar the attributes which the books that make up the Canon receive by virtue of their canonical authority, the more important the degree of certainty with which they are properly to be regarded as canonical or not.

The canonical writings are the subject of the science of introduction; not as they are in themselves, but with all those ideas and presuppositions that make them canonical. As canonical writings they are writings with which the concept of a definite dogmatic authority is linked. The dogma that they are divinely inspired writings applies to them, that they are the documentary expression and aggregate of divinely revealed truth which is to be the determining norm of all the theoretical and practical behavior of men. Now, the actual object of criticism is just this dogmatic element associated with them, the principle of their canonical authority. The science of introduction, therefore, has to investigate whether these writings are also by their own right what they are said to be by virtue of the dogmatic idea that is held of them, and, since the first presupposition of such a dogmatic view is that they are actually written by the authors to whom they are ascribed, it follows that the first task is to answer the question, by what right they represent themselves as apostolic writings.

To be sure, Baur did not stop with criticism of the sources, but went on to a history of primitive Christianity, though he was not able to complete a comprehensive account.[194] However, the basic elements of his view can be clearly discerned. In it, on the one hand, the picture of history that had hitherto only been suggested is fully worked out; the conflict between Hebrews and Hellenists marks the life even of the primitive church: after the Apostolic Council the conflict between Jewish and Gentile Christianity reaches the stage of a complete separation; the Judaistic side is represented in ancient times by the "Revelation" that was the work of the apostle John and later by the Clementine Homilies, while the Pauline side is defended by the four main letters of Paul and later by Marcion; a harmonious agreement between both parties is pursued from the Jewish Christian side by the Letter of James and from the Pauline by the briefer letters of Paul, Hebrews, the Pastorals, and I Peter, while the Gospel of John stands on the threshold of the Catholic Church. But in addition to this historical reconstruction that is the outcome of tendency criticism there is also, on the other hand, the description of the New Testament world of thought as of something that had become historical: "If New Testament theology is treated strictly in accordance with historical concepts, it is not enough to distinguish several doctrines and set them . . . side by side, but progress of development must be shown," and consequently New Testament theology is defined as "the history of Christian dogma in its movement through the New Testament.[195] Thus the idea that the New Testament exhibits a development of thought is taken seriously for the first time, and, in addition to this, Baur correctly recognizes that the Pauline view of Christ forms the bridge between the Synoptic and Johannine Christology.[196]

First, we have the Christology of the Synoptic Gospels, and here it cannot be contended on any sufficient grounds that they give us the slightest justification for advancing beyond the idea of a purely human Messiah. The idea of pre-existence lies completely outside the synoptic sphere of view. . . . The synoptic Christology has for its substantial foundation the notion of the Messiah, designated and conceived as the υἱὸς θεοῦ [Son of God]; and all the points in the working out of the notion rest on the same supposition of a nature essentially human . . . . The highest enunciation concerning Christ in the synoptic Christology is, that all power is given unto him in heaven and in earth (Matt. 28: 18) ; or that he sits at the right hand of God—an expression which denotes his immediate share in the divine power and the divine government of the world. He is exalted to this point by his death and resurrection. The connecting link between these two points which join heaven and earth is the Ascension, in which he is even seen to float from earth to heaven in visible form.

It is obvious, that in this Christology the general point of view is the elevation of the human to the divine, and that in the conception of the Messiah the second of these steps always implies the first. In contrast to this point of view stands that of the Johannine Logos-idea. According to this, the substantial conception of the person of Christ is the conception of his essence as divine in itself. Here the thought travels, not from below upwards, but from above downwards, and the human is therefore only a secondary thing, and added afterwards.

Between these two opposing points of view, the Christology of Paul occupies a place of its own, and we cannot fail to see that it gives us the key of the transition from the one to the other. On one side Christ is essentially man, on the other he is more than man; and his humanity is already so enhanced and idealized, that the sense in which he is man is certainly inconsistent with the synoptic mode of view, which stands on the firm basis of his historical and human appearance.

With this insight Baur now combines as well the first attempt to represent the teaching of Jesus as "the basis and presupposition of all that belongs in the history of the development of the Christian consciousness," as "the primal period that still lies outside the sphere of historical development," because the teaching of Jesus is "not theology at all, but religion." The Sermon on the Mount shows, then, that "Christianity as it is represented in its original form as the teaching of Jesus is a religion that breathes the purest moral spirit"; that Jesus wished to be Messiah only in the spiritual sense; and that "in this emphasis on attitude as the only thing in which the absolute moral worth of man consists, Christianity is something essentially new.[197] Now, after this moral teaching of Jesus there comes, in contrast, the theological doctrine of the apostle concerning the person of Jesus that for the first time takes over the center of the stage.[198]

141

When we compare the teaching of Jesus and that of the apostle Paul, we are struck at once with the great difference which here exists between a teaching that is expressed still in the form of a general principle, and a doctrine that has already taken on the definiteness of a dogma. But there lies between much also that is the necessary presupposition without which this progress would not have been possible! Above all, this is the death of Jesus, together with all that belongs with it, the most important moment of the process of development through which Christianity received a character essentially different from that of its original form. By it the person of Jesus first won the great significance that it has for the Christian consciousness. While it is true that, from the standpoint of Jesus' teaching, everything that he teaches receives its particular significance only because it was he who taught it, nevertheless he never makes his person the immediate object of his teaching—at least, not if we take our departure, as here we must, from the representation of the gospel story. It is not so much on the significance of his person that all depends, as on the truth of his teaching. He has only come in order, by the moral demands he made on men, to introduce the "kingship of God," to invite them to enter it, and thereby to open it. The "Gospel" as such, the proclamation of the "kingship of God" as a morally religious community based on the teaching of Jesus, is here all that counts. From the standpoint of the apostle, on the other hand, the actual center of gravity of the Christian consciousness, the basis on which everything rests, is not the teaching of Jesus but his person; everything depends on the absolute significance of his person; the central question does not concern what Jesus taught, in order by his teaching to lead men to blessedness, but what he did and suffered to become their redeemer. In this way, then, the simple moral content of Jesus' teaching first became a doctrine that had been formulated and developed by theology. The main facts of the story of Jesus, his death, his resurrection, his ascension, and his celestial activity, are the content in similar fashion of many dogmas to which, as to the substantial elements, all else has been subjoined.

It was fateful that in this first historical presentation Baur, by reason of his presuppositions in the realm of philosophy of religion, reduced Jesus' proclamation to a "purely moral element" and therefore overlooked the significance of Jesus' person in his proclamation, just as he pushed aside the expectation of the end. Consequently the understanding of the transition from Jesus to the early church was put for long on the wrong track, and the possibility of reaching a really theological understanding of the historical Jesus in this direction was excluded. Nevertheless, whatever objections may be raised to Baur's results—the overly rigorous critical judgments concerning the New Testament writings and the conflict of Jewish and Gentile Christianity, the spiritualization of the proclamation of Jesus and of Paul, the misinterpretation of the critical task vis-à-vis research in the New Testament canon—all this does not alter the fact that Baur recognized two problems to whose clarification New Testament research continues to devote itself: the arrangement of the New Testament writings in a total historical perspective, and the understanding of the sequence and of the historical development of the

New Testament world of ideas. And more than that, Baur recognized the fundamental significance of the historical understanding of the person and proclamation of Jesus and the importance for the historical evaluation of the New Testament writings of the question concerning the object in view ("tendency") of every single book. Since Baur's time, scientific work on the New Testament has been possible only when the fundamental methodological principles he indicated have been followed and his overall historical view has been superseded or improved.

2.
The Dispute with Strauss and Baur in Light of a Basic Solution of the Problem of Sources

By disputing the critical *results* achieved by Strauss and Baur but by continuing their methodological procedures, further research might have undertaken a genuine historical exploration of primitive Christianity in order to reach a solution of the theological task of understanding the New Testament. To begin with, however, traditional theology made a real debate difficult by challenging the right of Baur and his pupils (as D. F. Strauss once was) to a place within the discipline of theology and, accordingly, on the theological faculties. Shortly before his death Baur himself was forced to complain bitterly that the "Tübingen School" that had followed his lead had been dissolved by compelling its main representatives to transfer to other faculties.[199] And the fact only serves to support this complaint that in his memorial address on Baur soon after the latter's death a colleague of his on the same faculty—M. A. Landerer—declared: "Since Baur in his last book called Paul's conversion a miracle whose mystery could not be explained, it follows that Baur's whole conception of primitive Christianity and its history must be reformulated."[200] If the theological legitimacy of Baur's research was utterly denied after this fashion, it has to be admitted that even Baur's most loyal pupils contributed to this unfortuante development by their radical elaboration of Baur's views. In an almost inquisitional examination of the Acts of the Apostles (1854), **Eduard Zeller** sought to prove that this largely unhistorical book had been written with the tendency of "obtaining the recognition of Gentile Christianity in its independence and its freedom from the Law by means of concessions to the Judaistic party." Accordingly, for him the book of the Acts ceases to be "an ostensibly historical report on the apostolic age" and becomes a "primary document of the ecclesiastical situation at the beginning of the second century,"[201] and this also shows how the schema of the conflict of opposing primitive Christian parties compels the researcher to suspect at once a conciliatory tendency on the part of the author of the Acts of the Apostles behind every factual difference in the sources or every historical difficulty and to overlook completely the driving religious motives. In his comprehensive account of the *Nachapostolischen Zeitalters* [Post-apostolic age] (1845), **Albert Schwegler** went still further. Here Baur's reconstruction of history is so far systematized that the conflict between Jewish Christianity and Paulinism is assumed to have continued from the time of the primitive church to the end of the second century, and the postapostolic age is described as "the development of Ebionitism to Catholicism, of Judaism to Christianity." In the course of Schwegler's account primitive Christianity appears as a Jewish sect with which Paul is "everywhere engaged in a courageous and vigorous but unfortunately usually unsuccessful struggle," and "the Jewish element still" prevailed "decisively over the Christian" until the end of the second century. Only the four great letters of Paul and the Revelation to John belong to the apostolic age. All other early Christian literature comes from the second century, and every individual writing belongs to the Jewish Christian or Pauline sequence of development, either in the time of the original conflict of these two antagonists, or in that of their later irenical reconciliation, or, finally, in that of Catholic neutralism.[202] In all this not only is "Baur's view of the original conflict and the gradual reconciliation of the primitive Christian parties . . . exaggerated into a caricature,"[203] but the role of Paul and of Gentile Christianity in the origin of the post-apostolic church is completely underestimated and the variety of primitive Christianity is overlooked. And because no attempt is made to give an account of Jesus, on the grounds that the sources do not permit us "to undertake a completely sure and inclusive characterization of his personality,"[204] there is no longer any discernible path of development from Jesus by way of the primitive church to Paul and into the post-apostolic age, and Baur's attempt to overcome the negative criticism of Strauss is again abandoned.

On the other hand, the countless efforts to counteract this perverse development of the historical method by a simple defense of the traditional New Testament ascriptions of authorship and to save the traditional historical picture by postulating the unity of the primitive Christian world of thought were unsuccessful.[205] Let us give one example. The Teyler Theological Society in Holland asserted: "It is a known fact that the so-called 'Tübingen School' seeks above all to ground its enmity to Christianity on the assumption of an absolute difference between the teaching and thrust of the apostle Paul and the other apostles." In 1848, against this background, **Gotthard Victor Lechler,** one of Baur's former pupils, attempted to give a new overall account of primitive Christianity.[206] However, his insight was valid that the primitive church already stood somewhat apart from Judaism and differed in many respects from the later heretical Jewish Christians, while on the Pauline side as a rule there were not only Gentile Christian but also mixed congregations. But his reconstruction failed in its effect because he regarded all New Testament writings as genuine, accepted the book of the Acts as a historical document, and denied any essential difference between Paul and the early apostles. Any real advance of historical knowledge on the basis of Baur's methodological principles was impossible until a more certain answer could be given to questions of sources and consequently a more reliable historical picture could emerge.

Even before Baur's most important works had appeared, a non-theologian had undertaken from two sides to provide that presupposition of further progress in research. Under the stimulus of Schleiermacher, the philologian **Karl Lachmann**, known for his editions of classical and Old German texts, had set himself the task of defining the presuppositions for the production of a really critical text of the New Testament. Even Griesbach, the first who dared to touch "the received text," still had taken his departure from that text and had improved it with great caution, but Lachmann's edition of the Greek and Latin New Testament, which first appeared in 1831 without detailed argumentation, but then in 1842-50 with an extensive apparatus, was the first text to be based exclusively on the most ancient manuscripts.[207]

In this Lachmann's express intention, as he notes in a "rendering of account" that he published before the appearance of his first edition, was not to offer the *true* reading, but, by a strictly mechanical application of critical principles, to recover the text of the fourth century, and to do this by a purely *objective* method so that subjective interpretation could make use of a text that had been determined objectively.[208]

As soon as I surveyed the field of New Testament criticism it became clear to me that, if I wished to make a significant contribution, Griesbach could not be my guide. Not that I doubt Griesbach's independence and thoroughness, or the great and timely contribution he made. His criticism, however, is too incomplete and, because he wants to be cautious, too incautious. No one knew as well as he how accidentally the common reading, the so-called "received text," had come into being, and yet he made it basic. "Is there reason to depart from the usual reading?" was his question, whereas the natural one can only be, "Is there reason to depart from the best authenticated reading? . . ." Shall we not then preferably regard the reputation of the text that the Church has employed for three hundred years as unfounded, when it is possible to obtain one that is fourteen hundred years old and to approach one that is sixteen hundred years old? Is it not worthier of a critic to assume responsibility both for what he allows to stand, as for what he changes?

The determination of a text according to the tradition is a strictly historical task. . . . On the other hand, the criticism which breaks through the bonds of tradition and affords conjecture its right is unfettered and increases in extent and assurance with growing knowledge and spiritual freedom. It is an invaluable jewel of our Church, but, like the latter, also capable of infinite development.

Therefore, that we may never lose firm historical footing, it seems best to me to determine the text unalterably according to tradition alone, as soon as this will be possible. Such determination will certainly not hinder the progress of criticism. . . . And, as has been said, I have not established the true text, a text that no doubt is often preserved in a single source, though just as often wholly lost, but only the oldest among those that can be proved to have been in circulation.

Since Lachmann therefore took his departure from the manuscripts instead of the printed text, he made it possible for the first time to discover the oldest and consequently the most reliable text of the New Testament, and so all work on the text of the New Testament since his time is built on the foundation he laid. To be sure, the method Lachmann followed could not yet really achieve its goal. On the one hand, the manuscript material at Lachmann's disposal was not yet adequate to achieve, by means of the mechanical method he had chosen, a sure determination of the text that was in circulation everywhere in the fourth century, and this same mechanical method of determining the text compelled Lachmann more than once to adopt, without any notation, a form of the text that he regarded as spurious (e.g., the Marcan ending, 16:9 ff.) .[209] Mainly, however, Lachmann erred when he thought it was possible and necessary to reconstruct a text "without interpretation." [210] for in this way errors in and alterations of the original text in the manuscripts cannot possibly be observed.

However important it was that Lachmann by his edition now gave the impulse to the decisive work on the restoration of the original New Testament text, a restoration that got underway later in the nineteenth century, it is still more important that in this occupation with the New Testament he also reached a conclusion that was to be basic for further gospel research. As early as his report in which he rendered an account of his edition of the text, Lachmann had mentioned that he had not been able to persuade himself that "Mark had used our Matthew and Luke." [211] In an article on "The Order of the Narratives in the Synoptic Gospels" published shortly thereafter (1835) he demonstrated that the agreement of the three Synoptics in the *order* of the narratives extends only so far as Matthew and Luke agree with the order of Mark; where they depart from this order they also depart from one another. In addition, Matthew's deviations from Mark's order can be explained by the Matthaean evangelist's insertion of Marcan material into a collection of Jesus' sayings that lay before him.[212]

I want now to consider only the order: since that is the simplest procedure of all and—so far as I see—has not been attempted by anyone, it must be apparent what success one can achieve from this point of departure.

But the difference in the order of the narratives of the Gospels is not as great as it seems to most; indeed, it is the greatest when all these writings are compared in their entirety, or Luke with Matthew; it is slight when Mark [is compared] with each of these separately.

I understand the Gospel of Matthew just as Schleiermacher did; . . . it was I say put together, first of all from brief and interwoven discourses of the Lord Jesus Christ, into which later others have inserted narratives.

Lachmann thus advanced an irrefutable argument for the priority of Mark vis-à-vis the other two Synoptics and at the same time drew attention to the need of assuming still another source for the other synoptic matter. Shortly thereafter (1838), but independently of Lachmann, the former Saxon pastor **Christian Gottlob Wilke** published a comprehensive and minutely detailed investigation of the relation of the Synoptics to one another, by which he demonstrated that the assumption of an oral primal gospel or of individual original collections of narratives does not explain this relation. Rather, the agreement of the three Synoptics in their presentation and relation of the discourses of Jesus and the presence of almost all the Marcan matter in Matthew and Luke can only be satisfactorily explained on the assumption that Mark is the earliest evangelist and that his work is basic to both other Synoptists. In other words, the connection of Matthew and Luke to one another, so far as it concerns the material they have in common with Mark, makes it necessary to assume that Mark is the common element.[213]

The relation of the narrators to one another is . . . this, namely, that (a) the Marcan text is always involved in the agreement, in that it either harmonizes with both the others at one and the same time, or with one of them—sometimes with the one, sometimes with the other—and that (b) Matthew and Luke only agree with each other in terms of whole sentences when Mark at the same time agrees with both.

We have therefore to assume that the other evangelists have the *entire* work of Mark before them, i.e., all the passages it contains. But in what form? Are we to assume a Gospel of Mark *before* the Gospel of Mark, or, what amounts to the same thing, that Mark only copied another work and expanded his copy only here and there with single words and formulae which he incorporated into secondary clauses?

Mark is the original evangelist. It is his work that forms the basis of both the other Gospels of Matthew and Luke. This work is not a copy of an oral primal gospel, but an artistic composition. Its originator was not one of the immediate followers of Jesus, and this explains why, despite the fact that it has assumed the appearance of a historical narrative, its composition is conditioned less by historical connection than by premeditated general principles.

By these investigations Wilke proved that the oldest preserved tradition about Jesus is to be found in Mark's Gospel, and he also already recognized that this oldest of our gospel writings owes its *structure* not to historical recollection but to theoretical principles. But the total relationship of the Synoptic Gospels to one another was not yet convincingly explained by the proof of the priority of Mark, and it is to the credit of the philosopher **Christian Hermann Weisse** that, in a work that appeared contemporaneously with Wilke's book, he resumed Lachmann's observations of Strauss's *Life of Jesus* "as something to be welcomed, a contribution by no means prejudicial . . . to true Christian knowledge and insight, but rather beneficial," he saw himself driven by the challenge of Strauss's criticism to an attempt at the "reconstruction of the historical picture of Christ." In the course of his work, however, he recognized that for its purpose the relationship of the Synoptic Gospels to one another had first to be explained, and as a consequence of his investigations he achieved a twofold insight. The Gospel of Mark, as the one most primitive in order and in diction, is the oldest of the Synoptics; the Gospel of Matthew and the Gospel of Luke, however, have combined with Mark's Gospel a collection of Jesus' sayings that goes back to the apostle Matthew. Thus not only was the priority of Mark proved from a new angle, but also the need was revealed of assuming a second source, for whose existence Weisse already also treated the double tradition (doublets) in Matthew and Luke as important proof. These observations provided adequate support for the first time to "the two-source hypothesis," and Weisse now drew from it also historical conclusions by attempting a sketch of the historical picture of Jesus on the basis of a criticism of the tradition of Mark and of the second source. Into this, however (as had happened in connection with Baur's picture of Jesus), Weisse's philosophical presuppositions intruded disturbingly. He not only eliminated the realistic expectation of the imminent end on the part of Jesus as unworthy of "a spirit of such stature" and watered down the judgment Jesus preached into an inward, subjective experience, but also, after the "flash of the higher consciousness" that came to Jesus at his baptism, inserted quite arbitrarily a lengthy "period during which the idea . . . implanted in him by the birth from above underwent a fermentation and was finally suppressed." So the image of Jesus that had been erected on a secure historical foundation had from the beginning a patina compounded of a spiritualization of the message and a psychological interpretation of the person of Jesus. Nevertheless, these false conclusions do not undermine the fact that only the firm support that Weisse gave to the differentiation of the oldest sources of the gospel tradition made it possible at all to gain any sure knowledge of the historical Jesus and consequently of the origin of primitive Christianity.[214]

Is is generally agreed that in his Greek style Mark is the most Hebraizing of the evangelists. We scarcely need to remind ourselves how much easier it is to assume a paraphrase from a Hebraizing source into pure Greek than the reverse—the latter, in fact, an accomplishment that might well be the only example of its kind that the history of literature would have to afford. But that remark can be expanded still further so as perhaps to exhaust by its precise and proper phrasing all that can be said from this point of view in support of the probability that the other evangelists made use of Mark and the improbability of the converse proposition. The very Hebraisms of our Gospel are a consequence, if you will, or perhaps more correctly, to some extent a necessary element in a more general and more pervasive characteristic of his manner of composition, one that is a telling indication of his independence and originality. On the one hand it is possible to designate this characteristic as awkwardness and clumsiness, in other words, as one that is due to the author's unfamiliarity with literary expression, partly in general, and partly in his use of this specific subject matter, which had not previously been the object in similar fashion of literary articulation. On the other hand, however, the trait to which we have referred conveys the impression of a fresh naturalness and an unpretentious spontaneity, which distinguish Mark's presentation most markedly from all other gospel accounts.

Vis-à-vis Mark's narratives, the author of the First Gospel acts with few exceptions only as an epitomizer in those sections that are common to both. Where he remains closer to his predecessor's account he endeavors to smooth its roughnesses, to purge it of its idiomatic expressions, and especially to substitute more varied and complicated constructions for Mark's monotonously recurring connection of independent clauses with "and." The third evangelist in as few places is also an epitomizer, but not infrequently he is an explanatory paraphrast who deliberately undertakes to transform Mark's brittle account into a flowing narrative, to round the edges, and to improve the connection in detail with all manner of pragmatic asides.

Still another consideration, in addition to style and representation of detail, is that of the composition and arrangement of the whole. We wish to regard this as decisive for our view of the origin and mutual relation of the Synoptic Gospels.

[A common norm is basic, one which] *is found everywhere and only in those sections that the first and third evangelists have in common with Mark, not, however, in those that are common to them but not to Mark.*

Even in those sections which all three Synoptics have in common, the agreement of the two others is always one accounted for by their common dependence on Mark. In other words, the two other Gospels agree with each other in those sections, both with respect to the arrangement as a whole and to the arrangement of words in individual cases, always and only in so far as they also agree with Mark. However, as often as they deviate from Mark, they also deviate . . . in each instance mutually from one another.

In the First Gospel, especially, it is possible to point to a whole series of doublets, so to speak, of individual sayings of the Lord where the one formulation belongs to that narrative sequence which this Gospel has in common with Mark, while the other proves to be drawn from that other major source from which the Gospel gets its name. . . . Such repetitions are less frequent in Luke, although here too they are not altogether lacking. Indeed, in such instances Luke usually makes it a practice to omit Mark's version and to hand on the apothegm in the form he had found it in Matthew [the Sayings-Source] but in his own free way, either incorporated in a context that appealed to him or recast as an anecdote.

150

This leads us to reflect briefly on the mutual relationship of the two other Synoptics to one another in those places where they are not both dependent on Mark. We have already noted that we regard this relationship as an independent one, independent, that is to say, in the use of the common sources by each of the two, but not in the sense that each of them, throughout or for the most part, had used sources that the other had not used. It is our most certain conviction that not only Mark but also Matthew's collection of sayings is a source common to both.

While the theory of the priority of Mark now gradually won a few supporters, at least outside the Tübingen School,[215] almost two decades after the appearance of his *Evangelischen Geschichte* [Gospel history] (1856) Weisse felt it necessary to complain with justification that no successor to himself "had trodden the path that had been blazed by the investigations of Schleiermacher and Lachmann." [216] A few years later (1863), however, **Heinrich Julius Holtzmann** redressed the balance in his work on *Die Synoptischen Evangelien* [The Synoptic Gospels], a study that summed up all previous research in magnificent fashion. He not only demonstrated most convincingly, by an appeal to the primitive character of its narrative style and diction, that Mark's Gospel was a source of the two other Synoptics, but also showed just as convincingly that we must assume a second source back of Matthew and Luke, one that consisted mainly of discourses. By basing this proof mainly on the linguistic peculiarities of the sources and on the connection of the accounts, Holtzmann grounded the two source hypothesis so carefully that the study of Jesus henceforth could not again dispense with this firm base. In these source investigations Holtzmann differentiated a source back of Mark (that he called "A") and tried to prove that Mark had abbreviated this source by deleting the discourses it contained, but all this was not an essential part of his argument, especially in view of the fact that he himself later discarded this hypothesis of a "primal Mark" [*Urmarkus*].[217] It was actually more important that he refrained from assuming further literary sources of the Synoptics, on the ground that we have to presuppose an oral tradition prior to and contemporaneous with the composition of Mark's Gospel, and with this the task of recovering this oral tradition, a task that was taken up by Herder, was once more envisaged. Most important of all in its consequences, however, was the fact that Holtzmann, following Weisse, regarded the report in Mark, which he had shown to be the earliest, and in like manner the information from the second source, in the order in which Luke gives it, as harmonious and reliable records of the course of history. From this point of view he now drew a picture of the historical Jesus that portrayed a progressive development of the messianic consciousness that first came to Jesus at the time of his baptism, and a progressive revelation of his messianic dignity until the confession of his messiahship at Caesarea Philippi, after which time Jesus marched to meet his tragic end. With this thesis of two stages in Jesus' activity, Holtzmann now combined an absolute denial of the expectation on Jesus' part of a second advent and of a visible manifestation of the rule of God. On the contrary, Jesus wanted to found a kingdom of God in the ideal sense ("to wish to found a theocracy in the midst of the Roman Empire would have been the fantasy of a fanatic"). All this meant, however, that the methodologically incontestable surmounting of the Tübingen tendency criticism by a clarification of the sources for the study of the history of Jesus was encumbered from the beginning with a psychologically oriented understanding of Jesus influenced by idealistic philosophy, and the importance for Jesus, and so for the early church, of the expectation of the end, an importance which D. F. Strauss had stressed, was denied on the strength of this spiritualizing interpretation of history. "The victory, therefore, belonged, not to the Marcan hypothesis pure and simple, but to the Marcan hypothesis as psychologically interpreted by a liberal theology," [218] and this liberal picture of Jesus in one form or another dominated and interfered with research for almost four decades.[219] But that does not detract from the significance of the service Holtzmann rendered by building a firm source foundation for further study of the tradition about Jesus.[220]

We are quite aware that the investigations here presented will impress many a *theological* reader as a project remote from all religious interests, indeed, at more than one point even inimical to them to undertake and complete these investigations apart from being an exercise in ingenuity possessing doubtful worth, has nothing further to contribute. And yet we are convinced that it is only by the way we have taken here that it will be possible to stir up a debate on the historical beginnings of Christianity, a debate that no longer must inevitably lead, as has usually been the case since the publication of Strauss's work, to discussions at the very outset of more general content and to an area that puts almost insurmountable difficulties in the way of understanding the historical object as such.

To be more precise, we are concerned here only with the question, whether it is now possible to recover the historical figure of him to whom Christianity not only traces its name and state, but whose person it has also made central to its special religious outlook, in a way that will satisfy all proper demands of the advanced historico-critical sciences; whether it will be possible, by the use of a conscientious historical criticism which is the only legitimate methodology to recapture what the founder of our religion really was—the genuine and untouched image of his essential being—or whether we have to abandon once and for all the hope of attaining such a goal.

It is the Synoptics' common plan . . . which always will form the main barrier to the direct attribution of all three of them to an oral source, quite apart from the fact that this oral source was certainly in Aramaic, not in Greek, and that the mode of its transition from the Aramaic tradition into a Greek form that is marked by an equally stereotyped character can *never* be made conceivable.

Now that we have shown the untenability of the hypothesis [of a primal (oral) gospel] in the concrete form in which it has won its place and its name, the general truth that lies back of it must be emphasized all the more decidedly. Both facts are established, viz., both that the common content of our Gospels was first handed down orally, and that individual fragments of our Synoptic Gospels derive directly from this source. So then we . . . will be permitted to advance it as at least inherently possible that, if the whole Second Gospel should turn out to rest in the first instance on oral tradition, also a series of peculiarities of Matthew on the one hand, and of Luke on the other, are to be explained by the same source, a source that still flowed fresh, even after its main content had already been fixed in literary form.

There can be no doubt that both Matthew and Luke must have found already in a literary precursor, those parts that their respective discourses have in common, and in a precursor that not merely assembled fragments of speeches, but also narrated facts.

Indeed, not merely in relation to Matthew, but also vis-à-vis Luke, Mark "A" shows itself to be a thoroughly coherent whole, with no interpolation spoiling the arrangement.

But the most striking evidence of all for the credibility of both sources lies in the artless congruence of the material content of Jesus' discourses.

Finally, attention must be drawn to how perfectly homogeneous are the two sources with respect to the material that in general they offer for a more searching attempt to define the moral character of Jesus. In each of them a harmoniously constructed spiritual picture is unfolded, whose basic feature consists in the robustness of the divine consciousness that manifests itself at all times and at all places; a manifold and progressive development of a life whose driving principle is shaped by the religio-moral factor that operates with a power that completely divests itself of all the theological disputations and scholastic opinions of his day; that, avoiding all attempt to achieve knowledge that can be formulated scientifically produces instead eternal moral truth, free from and devoid of historical limitation, to such an extent that no one any more will wish to seek for a second example in history of the progressive consciousness of the divine.

We may perhaps characterize it as the most precious result of our investigations that by them we are enabled to draw a rather definite picture of the historical character of the person of Jesus and of the activity that filled his span of life. At the same time we see in it the most assured advance by which, without having to resort to the blunted weapons of an apologetic that rests on dogmatic presuppositions, we leave behind us, once, and for all, the results of the Tübingen School. *H. J. Holtzmann*

It is undeniable that in "A" and in Mark, respectively, we are noticeably closer to the person of the Lord than in Matthew or Luke. The historically conditioned, the humanly individual, retreats least before the general and divine. On the contrary, so much of more finely applied detail, painted with earthy colors whose texture is determined by temporal and local, even individual conditions, is offered the eye of the research scholar that we can say: Nowhere does what the man Jesus was stand out so clearly as in "A" and in the Gospel of Mark, respectively. . . .

In Mark, on the other hand, the peculiar, the extraordinary, begins with the

153

act of baptism, when the Holy Spirit, with whom, accordingly, Jesus is not thought of as having had originally any relation, "comes upon him" (1:10). While what actually happened can no longer be clearly determined from Mark's account of the marvelous occurrence (1:10) and the divine announcement (1:11), nevertheless this account, which rests perhaps on a report given of it by Jesus himself, is to be regarded as more original than those of the other Synoptics, which more or less objectify the event. In any case it is the view of the source book that an actual heightening of Jesus' self-consciousness took place on that occasion; "a great clarification of his divine calling came to him, that struck the eye of his spirit as a flood of light from heaven, the ear of his spirit as the voice of God." So, from this time on his whole person and being, at least in one specific respect, has something that lies beyond our ken. It makes effective his power, he for whose understanding no comparison of ordinary observations affords us the key. Indeed, according to our reporter, from the moment of the baptism a mightily urgent inworking of the Spirit takes place that leaves the bearer of the Spirit no rest until his work is in full process.

If we now inquire concerning the outlines within which is sketched the external course of Jesus' public ministry, so energetically inaugurated, we find them among all Synoptics only in our Second Gospel. It is almost universally admitted that there is chronological and geographical disorder in the Third Gospel, at least in the great insertion, 9:51–18:14. In this respect the First Gospel also suffers from the . . . . defects that even in the Sermon on the Mount Jesus speaks as Messiah, and yet continues to withhold a declaration of his messiahship; that as early as 14:33 the disciples greet Jesus as Son of God, and yet only in 16:16 does Jesus' messiahship dawn on Peter; and so forth. Furthermore, it is impossible to plot the course of this, as it were, ever-present Messiah on any map, while in the Second Gospel we know almost always at what point we are, for the circles the Lord describes in his journeys are enlarged very gradually and deliberately. The same progress prevails in this external part of the account as in that of the inner development and the gradual emergence of the messianic idea. . . . The public activity, however, . . . is presented in terms of seven ever-expanding circles that can be drawn quite definitely, although the author need not always have been aware of the transition.

If we glance back at these seven stages of the public ministry of Jesus, the result is confirmed for us that it was only gradually, and only at the very end, with clarity that the disciples confidently recognized in Jesus the Messiah, a recognition he did not compel them to make. It is quite compatible with this if a certain minimum of confidence that they had found the Messiah in him was present in their hearts from the beginning. At the same time on the other hand, the mistrust with which the Pharisees followed him who was becoming Messiah is made amply apparent by the fact that even in Galilee, whither they had followed him, they keep a most careful watch over him and seek to restrict his activity (2:6; 3:6, 22). . . . Consequently his opponents quickly reach the decision to bring about his death (3:6).

So the life course of Jesus quickly drew on towards its tragic end, an end that Jesus himself with ever-increasing clarity foresaw as divinely necessary and predicted as the only possible one, but also as the only one worthy of him. From the beginning the hatred of the Pharisees and the indolence of the people permitted no other prospect. The former could not help but be exceedingly provoked by the uncompromising severity with which Jesus uncovered all that they were, their loveless hearts, their morality which in its innermost being was full of holes and tattered, their outward appearance of virtue, their hypocritical pride. A calamitous break had soon to come as a consequence of an inflexible opposition of this sort between one who, by all appearance, was intent on representing himself as the fulfillment of the messianic hopes of the people, on the one hand, and the toughest, most easily offended hierarchy that ever was. But it was easy to foresee that even in Galilee only the minority of the people would dare to face with him the danger of such a break. For only *one* circumstance could have blunted the force of the capital judgment that had early been determined: a series of unmistakable and energetic demonstrations on the part of the people. But to ensure that such should take place, Jesus, though only temporarily, would have had to adopt the popular, potent, quickly kindled messianic idea, or rather, would have had to put himself at its disposal. Judged by all other human political standards, this path would be free of risk, because it alone would have been practicable; but he took not a single step in that direction. His refusal to follow this path in spite of the extraordinary means that were at his disposal is the only adequate basis for explaining his downfall.

So the Second Gospel, in a narrative block cast in a single mold, beginning with 10:1, gives an account of the final destiny, a destiny, as we have seen, that had been prepared in advance. Apart from a few aberrations, the other Synoptics have therefore stayed close here also to the course of events as Mark narrates it. But it is only in Mark that the passion story bears especially clearly that impression of originality that is characteristic of most sections. It is necessary only to compare the reports of the agony of Gethsemane, of the involuntary and painful silence before spiritual and secular judgment, of the fierce struggle on the Cross, to reach the conclusion that the later reports have added more to the completeness than to the intensive lifelikeness of the picture of Jesus.

Eduard Reuss of Strassburg initiated for the rest of the New Testament the same methodological surmounting of the Tübingen tendency criticism by furnishing a more appropriate answer to the question of sources than Holtzmann had accomplished for the Synoptic Gospels. Even before Baur's larger works appeared, Reuss had published the first edition of his *Geschichte der heiligen Schriften Neuen Testaments* [History of the Sacred Scriptures of the New Testament] (1842). This study differed from previous "New Testament introductions" in that the discussion of the various books was set within the framework of the history of the early church, and thus it anticipated Baur's demand that the individual writings should be explained in light of the whole course of early history. As an alternative to Baur's first study of the parties in Corinth, Reuss also immediately suggested the thesis that "the strict Judaizers" should be distinguished from "the moderate Jewish Christians," of whom only the second group could recognize Paul.[221] But it was only in his *History of Christian Theology in the Apostolic Age*, a two-volume work that appeared in French ten years later, and in the editions subsequent to that of his *History of the Sacred Scriptures of the New Testament*, that he raised really far-reaching objections to Baur's total view. He acknowledges that it is proper to emphasize the conflict between Jewish Christianity and Paulinism, but shows that there was also a mediating group within Jewish Christianity, a group to which the original apostles belonged. He draws the right conclusion from this observation, namely, that the different groups and views do not need to be placed after one another in a historical sequence, but that they obviously existed side by side almost from the beginning. And therefore he recognizes the dubiety of the reasons that lead to rejection of the authenticity of the briefer letters f Paul and to the late dating of the other writings of the New Testament. Reuss was correct in his insight that the conflict of radical Jewish Christianity and Paulinism was not the only historically powerful reality of the apostolic age, and that therefore writings that do not reflect this conflict can be sources of this age. But it is still more important that, having fully recognized the historical difference between the Synoptics and John, Reuss now, in opposition to Baur and his pupils and even earlier than Holtzmann, made an account of Jesus' proclamation a prolegomenon to his history of the apostolic age and thereby demonstrated that even the preaching of Jesus reveals the fundamental opposition to contemporary Judaism that Paul later debated in theological terms. And it was also of great significance that Reuss, while fully stressing the strictly historical character of the discipline of New Testament introduction and the understanding of biblical theology as the beginning of the Christian history of dogma, by this very means endeavored to emphasize the *theological* character of this branch of learning and consequently to take into account "the religio-ecclesiastical point of view," thereby restating the vexed problem of New Testament science as a theological undertaking. Reuss's work on the New Testament was of undoubted value, though this fact has not always been adequately recognized, and it detracts little from it that his judgments on the circumstances of origin of the individual New Testament books were largely conservative, or at least wavering, though they became more definite as edition succeeded edition. It was a matter for concern, however, that even Reuss utterly failed to recognize the importance for early Christianity of the expectation of the end. He not only denied that Jesus expected the imminent introduction of the kingdom of God and held that this expectation was due to a misunderstanding on the part of the primitive church, but also made ineffectual the recognition that Paul expected the end in the immediate future by terming it unessential and by holding that Paul took the first steps, though only the first steps, toward a spiritualization of the expectation of the end. In this respect Reuss also was guilty of the same error of spiritualizing the New Testament as was H. J. Holtzmann.[222]

From a methodological and practical point of view our science is connected with theology, and belongs to the circle of theological sciences; in the first place, as one of the sciences auxiliary to biblical exegesis, which to Protestant theologians at least, has ever been the foundation and point of departure for the apprehension and presentation of Christian doctrine. It stands in the same relation to it as do biblical philology, archaeology, and hermeneutics. But it is especially when it does not content itself with treating its material on its purely literary side, but conceives it in close and constant connection with the development of doctrine and life, that it appears also as a special division, distinct in itself, of the history of the Christian Church. In no other sense does it lay claim to a theological character.

The form which we here give the science of introduction is a natural consequence of the historical point of view to which we adhere. Aside from the greater extent of the material, this history is distinguished from the ordinary introductions in that here the facts are arranged immediately as the result of preliminary critical analysis, while elsewhere criticism adapts itself to the ordering of the facts determined by convention. Our work is not intended as an introduction to something else, but as an independent portion of history, ennobled by the dignity of the subject matter, given coherence by a ruling idea, limited by its own aim, and complete, if not in knowledge and judgment, of which indeed none may boast of the highest degree, yet complete with respect to the idea which combines the miscellaneous and which inspires the dry and dead with life and motion.

The idea of such a treatment of the material is doubtless not new, yet the carrying out of it is contrary to the current method.

When, however, from a different point of view, Baur . . . defines "introduction" as the science of the criticism of the Canon, . . . we have only to say that his own numerous writings are the best proof that criticism is everywhere simply the preparatory work for history, not history itself; that a historical science, like criticism, approaches perfection only when it ventures to pass over from the form of inquiry to that of narration; . . . and above all that so long as the conception and form of the science are under discussion the particular views of a single critic on the special questions relating thereto cannot furnish an absolute standard. [In addition, the present account is far too indebted to what it has learned from the famous Tübingen historian to want to dispute about that in which it cannot follow him.]

That the church was by no means purely Pauline after the death of the apostle, indeed even less so than during his lifetime, has been proved incontestably by the school of Baur from the history of the second century and from the later apostolic literature.

We have already seen that at the beginning there were formed in the apostolic church two parties, of which the one, the more numerous, consisted of strict Judaists, who neither could conceive nor would endure the renunciation of the ancestral Law of Israel; the other, much smaller, but spiritually superior, the Pauline, in theory had broken with the Law and in practice ignored it. It has also been intimated that matters were not allowed to rest in this state of simple disagreement, but that an attempt was made to bring about an adjustment, both in doctrine and life, and which should insure peace, and especially should satisfy those who from mere lack of spiritual energy were unwilling to renounce the old, yet in their dawning discernment were unable to reject the new. To this number belonged especially the heads of the church at

Jerusalem. But their formula in reality produced, in the first place, not peace, but a third party, and as respects doctrine only a clearer sense of the necessity of advancing beyond a position which proved itself to be a mere palliative.

The clear light which the researches of Baur have shed upon the history of the early church has more than once been gratefully acknowledged in this book, and oftener still been used in silence. The emphatic dissent which has been or is yet to be expressed from some of his principles or conclusions does not alter this fact. After our declaration that the arguments urged by him against the genuineness of the Pauline epistles seem to us altogether inconclusive, we come here upon a second point in which we differ essentially from him.

We distinguish the strict Judaists, against whom Paul's polemic (especially Galatians) is directed, and who are also condemned in Acts 11; 15; from the moderate Jewish Christians, who wished to lay upon the Gentiles the Noachian precepts, . . . but for the Jews made "observing the customs" (21:21) and "living in observance of the law" (vs. 24) a matter of conscience, because the opposite would have been a formal ἀποστασία ["apostasy"] (vs. 21). Such Christians and Paul could mutually recognize each other (Gal. 2:7), but could not work well together (vs. 9). There existed between them no division or schism, but it was quite necessary that their fields of labor should be distinct, and, to avoid talebearing, even some tension.

This moderate party may have been very few in number and without influence; the Epistle to the Galatians proves indisputably that the στύλοι ["pillars"] at Jerusalem belonged to it.

When once the impulse of an intellectual development has been given and the soil prepared for it, no long time is needed to bring forth the most varied growths of thought. And when have the germs of religious speculation, both true and false, been more abundantly scattered in all lands and amid all classes of the civilized world than in the apostolic age? There is certainly no necessity, then, that we should distribute over a longer period the results of such a development which meet us here at the outset, or regard them as intelligible only in case they belong to some much later generation. Taken as they are, they are still, even on the judgment of the ancient church, which everywhere exaggerated them, imperfect enough to be recognized as their fruits. Therefore, even should the names and personality of the writers remain once and again doubtful or altogether unknown to us, yet the majority of their works ought ever to maintain even their traditional claims as monuments of the primitive days of Christianity.

This is the third and most essential difference between the views of Baur and our own: he eagerly and expressly regards the proved differences as successive, developed one out of another, and adduces later traces of the use or currency of any principle or formula as direct proofs of its later origin. Both conclusions are much too hasty. The manifold, the merely similar, even the derived, may easily be simultaneous; and every century has seen illustrations of the fact that ideas and systems, often immediately upon their entrance into the world, are accepted by some unconditionally, by many are altered, mutilated, extended, developed. Even were we obliged to explain everything in the New Testament literature which Baur regards as polemic or irenic in precisely his sense, there would be no necessity of bringing it down fifty to eighty years. For such a conclusion there have been adduced only very doubtful arguments, not a single conclusive one.

158

Special mention is due here only to the completely altered view of the early history of Christianity and its literature advocated and established by Ferdinand Christian Baur and his followers of the Tübingen School. According to this view the peculiar doctrinal content of each writing gives the key to its origin; so that the idea of the development of the apostolic doctrine appears essentially complete before the investigation of the New Testament documents with respect to the time of their origin has properly begun. Now inasmuch as this system at the same time assumes a much more gradual progress of this development than is usually assumed, on the one side in the direction of higher speculation, on the other toward the fusion of Jewish Christian and Pauline elements, a later date results for the origin of most of the books found in our present canon, the majority of which consequently fall in the postapostolic period, and even in the second century.

The prevailingly negative results of the criticism of Baur and his school are in themselves no proof of error, as apologetics has only too often represented it; but the system has its weak points, in which it must be essentially changed or fall. We have already pointed out in this connection the studiously obscure reserve of judgment respecting Jesus; the gulf between him and Paul; the altogether too harsh intensification of the opposition between the latter and the other apostles; the failure to recognize the germs of organization even in the earliest Jewish Christianity, and their propulsive power; the assumption, never yet justified, of so very late a date for most of the N.T. writings; the rashness of judgment by which the genuineness of many of them is denied— often sacrificed rather to the logic of the system than to sufficient proof; the character of the process of development as it is represented, which is throughout rather eternal and mechanical than internal and dynamic, etc. Not even in the light of the most recent discoveries, by which many things have been altered or modified, should we be able wholly to retract any of these criticisms. But the system will never be effectively combated when it is rejected as a package.

Biblical theology is then essentially a historical science. It does not demonstrate, it narrates. It is the first chapter in the history of Christian doctrine.

Let us only contrast the spirit of the Gospel with the tendency of Jewish teaching, as manifested in two striking phases. The former appeals first of all to the soul of man, to his religious feeling, to the inner yearnings of his heart; it seeks to regenerate and to bring him thus to God, the sole source of all happiness. Now this end and the means which lead to it are the same for all men; all are found in the same condition of estrangement from good, in the same state of misery and peril; the Gospel is then equally needful for and equally within the reach of all. The case is altogether reversed with the theology and philosophy of Judaism. The very terms thus used indicate that we have here a privileged class, claiming to rise to a higher degree of light and knowledge than can be shared by the common world—illuminati who will naturally be prone to look with contempt on the masses. Then this teaching addresses itself preferentially, and often exclusively, to the intellect, to speculative reason, or to remembrance alone, and makes religious knowledge consist either in hollow forms which mould the outer without nourishing the inner life, or in cold, dazzling abstractions, lofty but insubstantial. Thus the Gospel prevailed to establish the Church and change the face of the world, while Jewish theology allowed the synagogue to perish, and produced only the Talmud and the Kabbala—a code for monks, and a philosophy for dreamers or magicians.

159

It was not homogeneous with any aspect of Judaism; new and specific elements kept it radically distinct from all existing Jewish systems and schools. Whatever of truth and goodness these possessed by inheritance through tradition, the Gospel sanctified, spiritualized, raised into a higher sphere; and nothing is a stronger proof of its originality than the powerlessness of Judaism to follow an impulse which could not have failed to lead it on to perfection, if there had not been a radical incongruity between the two.

The Gospel was not to the first disciples a new religion opposed to Judaism; it was the fulfillment of the old. . . .

We may give in a word the substance of Judaeo-Christian theology. In its primitive simplicity it is summed up . . . in the confession, *Jesus is the Messiah.* . . .

At the commencement . . . the hopes of the young Christian community were closely akin to those of the synagogue. The remarks we have made with reference to the messianic beliefs among the Jews, may therefore help us to understand those of the apostles and their disciples, and all we have to do is prove the fact of this identity.

We must bear in mind, however, that the preaching of the apostles, based as it was on experiences peculiar to the disciples, and on convictions derived directly from their individual relations with the Savior, contained a germ of divergence and of progress, the importance of which was felt more and more, and which in the end broke the bond between the Church and the synagogue. The disciples believed and knew that Messiah had already been personally revealed . . . and his resurrection, while it raised their drooping courage, reawakened in new force the hopes of the future, which they had previously fixed on his person. Now this fact of a twofold messianic revelation, this idea of two appearances of the promised Christ—the one in humiliation, the other in glory, the one past, the other future—did not present itself as a mere chronological modification of the theory of the schools, but introduced a radical change into its constituent elements.

It is, in truth, an opinion, very imperfectly justified by history, that Judaeo-Christianity rejected the idea of the divinity of the Savior. . . . The very utmost that can be said is that this idea did not form the basis of the religious convictions of that school in regard to Christ, and that it was content without arriving by reflection at any exact and final conception on the subject. It must even be admitted that many Christians of this class remained complete strangers to any spiritual or speculative development of faith in this direction. But it is equally true of the language used by Paul, that it was adapted to meet the requirements of religious feeling rather than those of speculative thought. . . . We cannot, then, contrast the teaching of Paul with the ideas dominant among the first Christians in Palestine, as though it embodied a perfectly distinct system of doctrine.

It may be said that the difference between Paulinism and Judaeo-Christianity is reduced to one single principle. Both sides recognize salvation by Christ; in both we find faith, hope, and charity; both speak of duty and reward. But in Judaeo-Christianity all this is a matter of knowledge, instruction, understanding, of memory even, of imagination often, and, lastly, of conscience, which is permeated with it, and adopts it on the faith of a teaching supported by tradition, and established by the written word. To Paul, and according to his view, all these facts, all these convictions, are the direct results of the religious feeling. He finds them in himself, not as the creations or inventions of a spontaneous act of his reason, but placed within him by the Holy Spirit of God, and by him vitalized and rendered fruitful. In both schools a knowledge of Christ and his Gospel might have been gained through the preaching of a missionary, or by the study of a book. In the one, however, Jesus would have remained primarily a historical personage, having his place, indeed, not only in the past, but also in the present and the future, and standing always at the summit of the scale of beings, exalted to the right hand of God, having given commandments to his disciples to be observed, and promised blessings by them to be obtained. In the second or Pauline school, Christ reveals himself preeminently in the individual himself; it is in his own spiritual nature that the man feels and finds Christ; his death and resurrection become phases in the life of every Christian; and that life itself is derived purely from the ultimate union of the two personalities, the individual existence being renewed, fashioned, sanctified by and according to the ideal and normal existence of the Savior.

The adversaries of Paul were not content, therefore, with opposing him merely in the arena of word and doctrine. They soon reached open hostilities, and labored ardently to destroy a work which on conviction they detested. While Paul, with a prudent and honorable reserve, carefully avoided encroaching on what he considered to be the ground of his colleagues, ... the opposing party organized a regular countermission, with the avowed object of bringing back those who had received only the Gospel according to Paul, to the Gospel preached by them of Jerusalem.

At a very early time in the history (of the Church), long before there was any question of theological literature, we already see dawning on the horizon a certain spirit of conciliation that, at first almost instinctively, settled in the midst of the parties and controversies, occupied the terrain that had served them as an arena, and endeavored to calm their ardor by covering them with its flag of peace and concord. At the conference in Jerusalem, at this first and solemn theological debate, we already see the need for peace and the practical views carrying off the victory over the principles. Indeed, while on the one hand the maintenance of the Mosaic Law was demanded of all those who wanted to enter the Church, and while on the other hand its abrogation was proclaimed even for those who had hitherto observed it, in view of these two diametrically opposed opinions, which, however, were both based on axioms that permitted no exception, what attitude seized the apostolic assembly? It composed a resolution that was a slap in the face both to the one and to the other axiom; it composed a decree that was not based on any absolute principle, and that consequently ought to have had no chance of success. And yet, for a time at any rate, it was the only practicable expedient, and consequently justified by the circumstances. The Jews were to remain Jews; the Gentiles were not to be compelled to Judaize; all customs were to be respected, all repugnances treated with deference: that is what was proposed and adopted; in the last analysis, that is what had to happen of itself, if it had not been ordered. A naive, inconsequential decision, if you will, but admirably wise, especially because, without being conscious of it, it demonstrated this great truth, that men are not made for theories, but theories ought to be made for men.

3.
The Correction of Baur's Picture of History

By employing Baur's methodological principles, **Albrecht Ritschl** now carried further the necessary correction of the historical picture drawn by the Tübingen School. With respect to individual questions, such as the authenticity of the briefer Pauline letters, he had early differed with his teacher Baur, but he still regarded himself as one of Baur's adherents when he wrote the first edition of his book on *Die Entstehung der altkatholischen Kirche* [The origin of the ancient Catholic Church] (1850). In this work, to be sure, he rejected Schwegler's hypothesis of a conflict of Jewish Christianity and Paulinism that persisted to the end of the second century, but on the whole he still considered this conflict to be the decisive factor in the earliest history of Christianity. In the second edition of this book (1857), however, Ritschl finally parted company with Baur's historical picture shortly after he had broken personally with Baur and his pupils.[223] Like Reuss, but probably independently of him, Ritschl recognized the difference between Jewish Christians and the original apostles, and therefore challenged the hypothesis of a radical conflict between Paul and the original apostles, a theory Baur had built on philosophical presuppositions. But he took still another step. He demonstrated that the extreme Jewish Christianity had no influence at all on the origin of the Ancient Catholic Church. On the contrary, a Gentile Christianity with wide appeal, but little influenced by Paul, was the root of early Catholicism. This correct observation was supported in part by the evidence that the early church followed the lead of Jesus in his opposition to Judaism, but especially by the proof that Paul and the original apostles had a common fund of faith, although in this latter respect Ritschl restricted the conflict between Paul and the original apostles too narrowly to the question of the validity of the Law for Jewish Christians in Gentile Christian territory. Ritschl also overlooked the importance for Jesus of the expectation of the end, and in the question of the authenticity of many writings he is very uncritical (James, I Peter). The important thing, however, is that he understands early

Christian history as the development of various forms of community, rather than as the conflict of doctrines, and therefore also observes the varied development of the constitution of the Church in the church in Jerusalem and in Gentile Christianity. Only from this point of vantage did an overall history of early Christianity become possible.[224]

The investigation would . . . not be further advanced if we were to insist on presupposing the Jewish Christian party and the Pauline party, their conflict and conciliation, as the schema into which the history of apostolic and postapostolic Christianity must fit. It is necessary to distinguish much more, if we are to make proper combinations. Consequently, we point out that not only must the original apostles, who lived as Jews, be distinguished from the Jewish Christians, and various sects of Jewish Christians be distinguished among the latter group, but also that the Gentile Christianity that was in process of becoming Catholic and the group influenced by Paul are not identical. These observations support combinations that become the more probable to the extent that they do not compel us to regard every Christian phenomenon of the spirit during the epoch in question either as Jewish Christian, Pauline, or neutralizing. Furthermore, we do not undertake to show that all the Christian streams that are to be described are equally capable of development and that they all flow into the unity of the Catholic Church. On the contrary, we shall be able to emphasize more strongly than heretofore the lack of capacity for development in Jewish Christianity. If in the course of so doing we insist that Catholic Christianity did not issue from a conciliation of Jewish and Gentile Christians, but is only a stage of Gentile Christianity, we do not thereby claim to prove by this a development independent of external influences and circumstances. We also do not regard it as the criterion of the correctness of an account of this history that we should pay no attention to its external relationships. But the view must be wrong which regards as possible the conciliation of early Christian groups that issue from a double gospel, for a unification even for external reasons always comes about only where the same inner reason is at work. But the fact that breaks through the Old Covenant, the fact that Jesus is the Christ, whose confession, even in the mouth of the original apostles, is nothing less than a wholly inner Jewish idea, forms the identical content of the gospel of all apostles, and faith in it is the hallmark of entrance into the New Covenant, if it is not invalidated by additional conditions. . . .

Jesus acknowledged the Law and the Prophets to the extent that they contain the highest objective of man in the commands of love to God and to men. He fulfilled them in accordance with the idea of righteousness at work in them, in that by those commands he set forth the principle of the Law for the kingdom of God. Accordingly, he invalidated for the kingdom of God all in the Mosaic Law that does not correspond to this highest principle; therefore, not only Sabbath rest, the sacrificial cult, and rites of purification, but also the permitting of divorce, the *jus talionis*, the limitation of the duty of love to love for one's friends, and the taking of oaths. Nevertheless, he neither abrogated circumcision and the place of special privilege of the people of Israel within the kingdom of God, nor actually freed his disciples, who belonged to Israel, from the observation of the Mosaic cultus. On the contrary, he left the weaning of his followers from the worship that had come down to them from their forefathers, just as

163

he left the full perfection of the Christian law, to future development under the leadership of the Holy Spirit. . . .

Therefore, although the original apostles develop Jesus' fundamental moral idea only in the form of its practical application in matters of detail, they did not in any way deny the place that Jesus had given it with respect on the one hand to the kingdom of God, and on the other to the Mosaic Law. And, moreover, the beginnings of a dogmatic conception of the person of Christ in Peter and John are evidence that the original apostles even in this direction do not lag behind Paul, but recognize, just as he does, the absoluteness of the revelation in Christ. . . .

When Paul drew the conclusion from this exclusive importance of faith for righteousness that the Mosaic Law was not binding on Gentiles, it is true that he does not directly concur with a precept that comes from Jesus. However, he does agree indirectly with the abrogation that is contained in the fulfillment of the Law that Jesus intended. And when Jesus left the renewal of the moral duties by means of the principle of love in matters of detail to the further development of his Church, it was necessary in addition that love should be understood, not merely as a task imposed by law, but, as it happened with Paul, as a result of faith, as a necessary subjective and religious motive.

In light of these indications, we are far from presupposing a fundamental conflict between Paul and the original apostles. If such a conflict had existed, they could not have had the common history which, according to the documents that no one questions, was theirs. To be sure, we shall have to acknowledge that a conflict in practical matters did exist between both, but the ground it covers will be so severely limited that the essential agreement in the leading ideas set forth by Jesus will only be the more clearly obvious.

The appearance of conflict between the teaching of Paul and the standpoint of the other apostles is mainly due to the fact that the categories of thought peculiar to Paul have so attracted attention that the circle of religious ideas and basic views common to all the apostles has been largely overlooked. The demonstration of the latter will not detract from the originality of Paul, but will simultaneously certify his connection with the original apostles.

Paul does not differ from the apostles when he entertains the hope, aroused by Christ himself (Mark 13:30), of the imminent return of the Lord (I Thess. 4:16-17; I Cor. 15:32). The eschatological intensification of the concepts of salvation through Christ that is common to all the apostles has its roots in this expectation. But also we can perceive in this a perhaps striking, but probably explicable, departure of all the apostles from the view represented by Christ. Christ relates all the signs of the saving purpose [of God] to his immediate ministry. In him and in his work men become members of that kingdom, and only its evidence in full power and dignity is reserved for the future. By separating believers and unbelievers, by dividing next of kin inwardly as with a sword for the sake of faith or unfaith, he executes judgment in the here and now. The future judgment is only intended for special classes of men: for those heathen who have not heard the Gospel; for the twelve tribes of Israel which, as a whole group, were likewise not witnesses of Jesus' proclamation; for the hypocrites who have slunk into the congregation of believers. Jesus assures believers salvation as a present possession; leads them in the present into eternal life. On the other hand, the apostles are at one in placing the expectation of judgment, the appearance of the kingdom of God, the obtaining of the inheritance, of salvation, and of eternal life in the future, albeit the near future, and relate the ideas concerning all those events and values to the return of the Lord. This change of view is to be understood in light of the fact that everything that comes through Christ and is acquired by faith in him, from the human point of view, always includes what is to be, and that the divine purposes that are bound up with Christ must be reflected in the future, since his work is not yet complete. There are only minor exceptions to this in the apostles, and in Paul, at most Col. 1:13 is to be reckoned as one. On the other hand, the apostles employ other concepts to designate the present relationship of believers, the concept of their holiness, of their new creation of rebirth, and, paticularly in Paul, of their righteousness. But these ideas do not exclude the perspective on the future of salvation to which they are oriented; just because they are moral ideas, they reckon on what is to be. Paul's interest in the second coming of Christ rests on this solidarity of all the apostles. We are therefore not to think of this hope as an indifferent element in his total point of view, but as one that influenced even his individual system of doctrine to an important extent.

Even Paul recognizes . . . a point of identity of the New Covenant with the Old. From his standpoint even Paul can describe Christianity as the true Judaism (Phil. 3:3), just as this was done vis-à-vis the Jews by the group that was in rivalry with him. But the difference is that Paul regards Christianity as in continuity and agreement with the divine promise, but in opposition to the Mosaic Law, while the view opposed to his maintains the continuity and agreement of Christianity with the Law and considers the promise simply as bound up with men's life in accordance with the Law.

The original apostles recognize only faith in Christ as the condition of entrance into the New Covenant, but insist on the view, based on the Old Testament, that their whole people has been called to enter first into the fulfillment of the promise given to it, and therefore seek to maintain its nationality by the full observance of the Law as a religious duty. The strict Jewish Christians, on the other hand, recognize and desire no Christianity except on the basis of their membership in the people Israel, into which Gentile Christians would have to gain entrance by accepting circumcision and the whole body of Mosaic custom. Consequently they deny Paul's apostolic calling, a calling which the original apostles had expressly acknowledged. When the Jewish Christians in Galatia, and probably elsewhere also, now found it impossible to pursue their plans against the freedom of Gentile Christians under the authority of the original apostles, they misused their names, whether by deliberate intention or because of a misunderstanding of the Jewish usage that was a bond between both groups. However astonishing the fact, it would be just as false to conclude that, because the Jewish Christians invoked the original apostles, the latter agreed with them. . . .

With respect to the division of responsibility between the circumcision and the Gentiles (Gal. 2:7) Paul thought only of _geographical_, but James, on the other hand, of _ethnographical_ boundaries. It is clear that agreement was not reached on the matter of whom the Jews of the Dispersion were to follow. The opposing claims of the apostles with respect to the practice of Jewish Christians who lived in Gentile territory were therefore the cause of a conflict, but also the only conflict between Paul and the original apostles that came to the surface of consciousness, and concerning whose solution by them themselves we lack any direct information. On the other hand, the actual Jewish Christianity is divested of apostolic authority and does not constitute the reason for a lasting conflict between the apostle to the Gentiles and the immediate disciples of Jesus.

In the epoch from the apostolic age to the time of the exclusion of Jewish Christians from the Church, the opposite pole to Jewish Christianity is Gentile Christianity, not Paulinism. To a living entity such as Jewish Christianity, another entity, not merely a doctrine, stood at that time in opposition. The studies of this period of the Christian Church have consequently not yet brought an understanding of it, and the question of the origin of the ancient Catholic Church has therefore not yet been answered, because the opposed views have revolved about the basically wrong problem of whether the Catholic Church developed on the foundation of Jewish Christianity or on that of Paulinism. With all that Paul, though neither the first nor the only missionary to the Gentiles, is, nevertheless, the founder of the Christianity of the Gentiles. This, however, does not guarantee that his specific doctrinal system ever dominated the religious connection of Gentile Christians en masse. On the contrary, we must question whether the series of ideas presented in the letters to the Galatians and to the Romans was adopted fully and completely even by Paul's loyal and devoted adherents. . . . So, in that formulation by which the Reformation taught us to understand and adopt Pauline doctrine, it was never the credal conviction of the Gentile Christians of the first and second century. On these grounds alone, Gentile Christianity and Paulinism cannot be equated.

It must further be kept in mind that Paul's missionary activity, however wide it may have extended, still touched only a limited circle of Gentile territory. It never reached Egypt, eastern Syria, and Mesopotamia at all—lands in which Christianity appeared early. The missionaries to those countries, as they are named by legend, also do not belong among Paul's adherents, but to the original church in Jerusalem, and yet from the beginning they planted Gentile Christian congregations in terms of the principles of the original apostles as preserved by the Jerusalem decree. Moreover, it is to be noted that in many districts Paul's initial influence was displaced by the subsequent and permanent impact of other apostles, as in Asia Minor and western Syria. Notwithstanding that, the congregations of these lands, acknowledging John and Peter as their authorities, remained in the independence of pagan custom which Paul had originally implanted in them. For this reason, also, it is incorrect to identify Paulinism and Gentile Christianity and, where no special dependence on Paul can be detected, to presuppose Jewish resistance to him.

In his study (1831) of the Corinthian factions, [Baur] sketched the outlines of his construction of the history of the first two centuries, a construction from which he never again departed. He sketched it without considering the sources in their entirety. Furthermore, for the "Christianity of the first three centuries" he also neglected to use, for example, the writings of the great church teachers at the end of the second and at the beginning of the third century to determine the practical and basic viewpoint of Catholic Christianity. What can be the reason for this incomplete use of the sources for the historical period to whose problems and their solution Baur was aware that a life's work must be devoted? So far as it is possible to peer into the unexpressed workings of the mind of another person, I cannot avoid the conclusion that Baur, in accordance with the absoluteness of the philosophical knowledge that he believed he had obtained, credited his penetrating insight into historical combinations with a greater certainty of correctness than even the most brilliant conception of history can achieve in its first formulation. I may be mistaken in this; but I do not believe that this explanation does an injustice to the scientific honor of this famous man.

Carl Weizsäcker completed what Ritschl had begun. He had been called as a representative of a mediating position to succeed Baur and, in his *Untersuchungen über die evangelische Geschichte* [Research in the history of the Gospels], a book which appeared in 1864, he had accepted the two-source theory but had still ascribed the Fourth Gospel to the apostle John and had maintained that, without the acknowledgment of the "great historical truth of this Gospel . . . the deepest relationships and the great consequences . . . of the story of Jesus remain a puzzle." [225] On the other hand, in his magnum opus, his *Das Apostolische Zeitalter der christlichen Kirche* [The apostolic age of the Christian Church], a book which was published some twenty years later (1886), he came considerably closer to Baur's point of view, not only with respect to the question of the compatibility of the synoptic and the Johannine portraits of Christ, but also in his basic understanding of the history of early Christianity; so close, in fact, that his book appeared to a contemporary as "a return to Baur's ideas." [226] To a certain extent this judgment was a just one. Like Baur, Weizsäcker had a very low estimate of the historical value of the book of the Acts and assumed, for instance, that, despite a familiarity with Paul's Letter to the Galatians, it "sacrifices important facts" in the interest of asserting "the harmony and the unquestioned repute of the leadership of the apostolic Church." Like Baur, Weizsäcker believed that the opponents of Paul in all his letters are the Jerusalem Judaizers. And Weizsäcker also followed his teacher Baur in that he tried to explain the New Testament writings in the light of their historical context within early Christianity and assumed the late origin of many New Testament books. (In addition to the Catholic Letters and the Pastorals, II Thessalonians, Colossians, and Ephesians are also unauthentic.) It is more important, however, that Weizsäcker, like Ritschl, clearly recognized the difference between the original apostles and the extreme Judaizers and emphasized the far-reaching agreement between the original Jerusalem church and Paul. And in this connection Weizsäcker, by drawing on the synoptic tradition, succeeded in discovering a new source for our knowledge of the primitive church and, at the same time, in recognizing different factors involved in the transmission of Jesus' words and deeds, thereby preparing the way for form criticism. Weizsäcker also included the history of Christian worship and of ecclesiastical life in his presentation. But, most important of all, Weizsäcker also recognized that the conflict between the extreme Judaizers and the Pauline mission

167

first erupted as a consequence of the recognition of Paul's mission by the original apostles and reached its high point in the altercation between Paul and Peter at Antioch (Gal. 2:11 ff.), an altercation that "led to a rift that never was healed." An hypothesis related to this, that the "apostolic decree" reported by the Acts (15:28-29) was first drawn up as a consequence of this dispute at Antioch, rounds out the impressive historical picture painted by Weizäcker and has maintained its place to our own time. Although in other matters Weizsäcker also conforms to the practice of isolating primitive Christianity from the religions of its environment and consequently overlooks the motive powers of piety, nevertheless, while always holding fast to a strictly historical methodology, he occasionally returns to the theological problem, declaring, for instance, that Paul's power over the spirits is founded on the fact that "at all times [he] is wholly in accord with the Gospel." In this respect, also, Weizsäcker's classic work points to developments beyond itself.[227]

The conviction that the resurrection of Jesus meant his departure to heaven, until he should return and complete the kingdom, had thus an immeasurable practical effect. But that was not all. The faith in Jesus also underwent a change. In his lifetime his followers had learned to look upon him as the Messiah of God. In this sense he was called not only Son of David, but also Son of man, and Son of God. But this does not imply any conception of his nature inconsistent with his being merely human. What was extraordinary in his actions was throughout ascribed to the agency of the Spirit of God who accompanied him. . . . Nevertheless the person of Jesus was viewed after the Resurrection in a new light. The Jesus, who had been received into heaven and who was living there, was only now completely proved to be the heaven-sent Messiah. And although this did not yet imply his preexistence, still it was impossible to separate the form of the earthly, and that of the present heavenly life in the conception of his Person. The latter reflected back on all the memories of the former. Here we have the starting point for the belief that ended in the doctrine of Christ's superhuman nature. Paul was the first, so far as we know, clearly to follow out this path. But he did not do so in opposition to the original apostles. On this point there was no dispute.

We are not, however, entirely destitute of authorities, when we seek to depict these early times historically. The most important has been preserved for us in the oldest gospel tradition. . . .

The whole delineation which it is possible for us to give of the primitive Jewish-Christian church depends, partly, upon information received from another quarter, partly, on a few indications which we can ascribe to it merely by the aid of conjecture. While recognizing this, we must not overlook another source, which to some extent supplies the want. It exists in the first three Gospels. These books themselves were not indeed composed in their present form in that church before the destruction of Jerusalem, nor were they written by eyewitnesses of the events which they record. The Third Gospel expressly says this in its preface. The author distinguishes the tradition of the eyewitnesses, who were also the first ministers of the Word, the earliest propagators of the

Gospel, from the narratives which later writers formed from it; he ranks himself with the latter, although many others already preceded him in the work. To these the first two Gospels also belonged. It can easily be proved that their authors edited existing material, and that neither of them was at home in, or had a clear conception of, the country and the localities, the individuals and the circumstances, with which he dealt. The case was different, however, with the sources they edited. With regard to them we can state just as positively that they originated in the primitive church; their contents and type of thought, the antagonisms and manifold historical references, and, again, their language, style, and form point to the life of the Christians in the midst of Judaism.

The words of Christ, accordingly, did not circulate in that church in a wholly unrestricted form, but they took the place of a permanent doctrine; they were necessarily renewed from day to day in the recollection of the members, and, simply because they were regarded as binding precepts, they came to be stereotyped and recognized through the concurrence of the witnesses.

We must adopt another point of view in deciding how a knowledge was transmitted of the events in which at least a large number of the first members of the Church had participated—that is, accordingly, how the experiences and deeds of Jesus were remembered. These entered at first only partially into the actual teaching of the Church, i.e. only in so far as they proved the fulfillment of prophecy, and therefore justified belief in Jesus as the Messiah. In this case, however, it was not so much the historical narrative as the text of Scripture, to which the facts were referred, that formed the foundation of a lecture. Whatever else lived in their recollections were certainly made the subject, not of addresses in the Church, but of informal conversation among its members. This was changed whenever the gospel message was transferred to wholly new spheres, and delivered to men who had hitherto been absolutely ignorant of Jesus and his deeds. It was not then enough merely to assert, as in Acts 10:38, "that God anointed Jesus of Nazareth with the Holy Spirit and with power: and that He went about doing good, and healing all who were oppressed by the devil, for God was with Him." Such summaries presuppose a knowledge of the events. But it was above all necessary to offer evidential narratives, pregnant and convincing examples to those who, as yet, knew nothing of this life, this healing and working of Jesus. Then and there, however, the sway of mere personal recollection ceased, and gave place to a definite version, which, as the product of joint effort, acquired a more determinate form through its purpose and its repetition. We need not in this case, any more than in that of the sayings, resort to the thought of a formal agreement and decision on the part of definite agents. But here, as there, authority certainly took root, and produced a certain usage. Nor need this narrative exemplar have come into vogue only when the Gospel passed to the Hellenists; we may assign it to the foreign Jewish-Christian mission of the primitive church. It only followed, however, the arrangement of the Lord's sayings, the rule of life in the Church; that was always first. And, similarly, it is involved in the nature of the case that the form of the sayings was stricter than that of the narratives, and that the latter crystallized more slowly. In the one case we are dealing with precepts, in the other with examples. The former were delivered to the whole Church, the latter were carried beyond its pale by individual missionaries. . . .

We must assume it as a rule that the narratives were first of all independent, and were then combined into such groups. And this can only have been done for didactic purposes. Some sort of activity on the part of Jesus—an aspect of his intercourse with men, a verification of his calling and of his mission—was thus to be indicated. Chronology had, as a rule, nothing to do with it. So far as we can see, the historical writers were the first to attempt a chronology.

The relation in which even the primitive church stood to the Law was not so simple as not to require justification in the form of a doctrine of the Law, which it would naturally assume. Paul said to Peter, according to Gal. 2:16, "because we know that man is not justified by the works of the law, but only by faith in Christ Jesus," and in this he did not merely utter his own opinion, but plainly a principle which, though reported in his own language, had been formerly agreed to with Peter. The extent to which the minds of the early apostles had been occupied by this question is shown most clearly, however, by the emphasis with which, in Matt. 5:17 ff., the words enjoining the preservation of the Law are stated: "Think not that I am come to destroy the law or the prophets; I came not to destroy, but to fulfil—whosoever therefore shall break one of these least commandments, and shall teach men so, shall be called least in the kingdom of heaven." But the upholding of the Law was called for not merely by false accusations, but by their own consciousness, the seat of conflict between liberty and bondage. The primitive apostles could repeat the assurance given by Jesus. Not only was it far from their thoughts to come into collision with the civil authority, but the Law was and remained for them the sacred record of the divine will. The practice of rectifying its precepts, which they followed in imitation of Jesus, did not revoke their principle; the practice could be grounded upon the sacred writings themselves, and their method is significantly indicated by the manner in which Christ's solemn assurance combined the Law and the prophets. The rectification was found in prophecy. There can be no doubt then that they believed in a forgiveness of sin, imparted by the word and afterwards effected by the death of Jesus, and thus we have the doctrine that forgiveness is to be obtained through faith in him. Therefore fidelity in observing the Law regarded as a means of salvation certainly required to be supplemented by this faith. In this we have the conviction which Paul assures us was that of Peter. But it also establishes the whole power exerted by the proclamation of the kingdom. Jesus had spoken of the kingdom both as present and future without any distinction of terms. The expectation of it, an assured hope, was a mighty spiritual force in the life of the Christian. But he had also learned from Jesus to think of the future kingdom of the Messiah as wholly a kingdom of heaven, or of God, as the kingdom of divine righteousness belonging to a new, a spiritual order. . . .

If after all this we may speak of a theology of the primitive church, we are clearly justified in doing so, in so far as certain principles were taught, both with regard to the binding force of the Law, and with regard to the nature of the kingdom and Jesus' messianic character, and since, further, these principles were taught theologically, i.e. were proved by interpreting the sacred writings. But there did not yet exist a Christian theology in the stricter sense of the term, for the categories applied to the contents of the faith still belonged essentially to Jewish thought. The relation to the old religion was quite the same in the world of thought as in the world of fact. The new wine was contained in the old bottles.

The relations which existed between Paul and the church in Jerusalem during the fourteen years that elapsed after his first visit [Gal. 1:18; 2:1] could not well be preserved longer; it is even surprising that it lasted as long as it did. . . . But when this type of Christianity not only spread, but at the same time assumed a fixed form, and gave rise to a church side by side with their own, explanations became almost inevitable between the two parties. We ought not to begin by looking upon these as the result of an actual opposition, or an attempt at arbitration between two hostile parties. If their previous relations had been of such a nature, the apostle could not have spoken as he has done about the fourteen years of peace. We have therefore yet to discover from the further course of the narrative, whether at last opposition to his procedure rose on the side of the Jewish Christians and compelled negotiation. Speaking quite generally, however, the actual circumstances rather support the view that the great conflict known to history did not precede, but arose out of the conference; the Judaistic view, which consisted in the one-sided tendency that opposed Gentile Christianity with its freedom from the Law, arose among the Jewish Christians only after the conference, or at least only thereafter came into effect. . . .

The case is somewhat different with his mention of the false brethren themselves, who came in stealthily, in order to spy out and undermine the freedom of his mission [Gal. 2:4]. But we are still led to look merely to events in Jerusalem. The whole passage about his resistance would have lost its point if he had had any earlier dealings with these people. The significance of the crisis lay just in the fact that he encountered them now, and had to maintain his freedom, that is, the freedom of his gospel against them, for the first time. It was here therefore, and here first of all, that they faced him, and revealed their intentions. But then we must apply to the community in Jerusalem what he says of their "coming in." He regards them as intruders into the Church, false brethren who attached themselves to it. And this throws a new light on the history of the early church itself, of which, since the persecution under Agrippa I., we know little or nothing. For it implies that the church had been increased by the admission of zealots for the Law, who formed a new element in its membership. . . .

Paul's narrative in Galatians does not end with the peace agreement at Jerusalem. He goes on without a break to tell what took place in Antioch (2:11-12).

Paul does not tell us the issue of the conflict in Antioch. . . . Yet we can hardly entertain any doubt as to the extent of his success in Antioch. If Peter had yielded there, if therefore the matter had been adjusted in the direction of Pauline principles, Paul could not have failed to mention it in the Galatian letter. He has recorded with a perfect sense of his triumph the recognition he had obtained in Jerusalem of the rights of his Gentile mission; and he could not have here failed to relate a corresponding triumph in Antioch, where the greater principle was at stake. The aim of his letter demanded as much. But he has nothing to report, except the words in which he proved his spiritual superiority, the convincing power of his thought. Of actual success there is nothing. We cannot doubt, therefore, that at the time the schism was left unhealed. . . .

Into these [Galatian] churches the new Judaism thrust itself. We are entitled to assume that this was the first field on which it tried its strength. . . . It had not been the doctrine of the primitive church and the apostles. They had lived in the free spirit of Jesus, and, thanks to unbelieving Judaism, they had preserved their attitude of spiritual independence to the Law. The key to an explanation of the present principles is to be found in the history of the transactions in Jerusalem and Antioch. It was necessary now to solve the question of Gentile Christianity, and these men tried to cut the knot in their own way. If this principle was to conquer, Paul must be overthrown. Hence the attack upon him, and the invasion of his church.

The Apocalypse shows us, and not in a solitary trait, that as often as the seer beholds Jesus himself, he recognizes him as the Master whom he had followed when his disciple. The Gospel of course tells of his intercourse with Jesus. But the interval between the present conception of the author and the actual intercourse with Jesus of Nazareth is not less than that between the seer and the Lamb, or the dread figure of the Judge in heaven. It is even a greater puzzle that the apostle, the Beloved Disciple of the Gospel, he who reclined at table next to Jesus, should have come to regard and represent his whole former experience as a life with the incarnate Logos of God. It is impossible to imagine any power of faith and philosophy so great as thus to obliterate the recollection of the real life, and to substitute for it this marvellous picture of a divine being. We can understand that Paul who had not known Jesus, who had not come in contact with the *man,* should have opposed to the tradition of the eyewitnesses the idea of the heavenly man, and that he should have substituted the Christ who was the Spirit for his earthly manifestation, pronouncing the latter to be positively a stage above which faith must rise. For a primitive apostle it is inconceivable. The question is decided here, and finally here. Everything else adduced from the contents of the Gospel—the curious style of address; the transparent allegory in the histories, the studied relationship to the synoptic account—is subordinate, though convincing enough. But what cannot have been done by John might be done by a disciple, a man of the Church that esteemed him so highly that it ranked him with Peter. By one writing at secondhand the communications of an apostle could be related to a theology which justified and explained faith in Christ as faith in the Logos of God; by such a writer the whole life, the whole aspect of it, could be transformed into a great haggadic didactic work.

In the second half of the nineteenth century the critical continuation of the radical view of the New Testament pioneered by D. F. Strauss and F. C. Baur had moderated, as we have seen, the extreme critical results of those two scholars, but on the other hand it had governed itself to a very great extent by three of their principles: The New Testament must be explained according to strict historical canons; every early Christian document must be interpreted by giving it its special place in the course of primitive Christian history; the decisive motivating force in the course of the history of early Christianity, however, is the opposition between the teaching of the original apostles, bound up as it was with Judaism, and Gentile Christianity, determined as it was by Paul. Even so conservative a scholar as **Bernhard Weiss,** the New Testament authority at Berlin who exercised a profound influence by means of his com-

mentaries in the Meyer series on numerous books of the New Testament
—even so conservative a scholar as Weiss, despite his emphatic opposition
to the Tübingen School, could not insulate himself against these views.
In the earliest of his textbooks, *Lehrbuch der Biblischen Theologie des
Neuen Testaments* [Textbook of the biblical theology of the New Testa-
ment] (1868)—like his commentaries, widely distributed—he characterizes biblical theology emphatically "as a purely historical discipline"
and asserts that "the two main directions which determine the inner
development [of the apostolic age] are the early apostolic and the
Pauline." Accordingly, he presents first "The Teaching of Jesus according
to the Oldest Tradition," then "The Early Apostolic Doctrine of the
Pre-Pauline Era," and then, flanking the latter, "The Early Apostolic
Doctrine of the Post-Pauline Era." And, although Weiss holds that all
extant Pauline letters are genuine, nevertheless, in his presentation he
separates "the doctrinal system of the four great didactic and polemical
letters" from the teaching of the imprisonment letters and the pastorals.
Then, at the end, outside the framework of this polarity, comes the
Johannine theology, as already in the works of Reuss and Weizsäcker.
In this way Weiss implied that "the Johannine tradition is totally excluded from . . . the sources of this account . . . of the oldest tradition of
Jesus' teaching. According to Weiss, it is "neither possible nor necessary
to make a strict separation in the Gospel of John between the substance
of the discourses of Jesus that stems from true recollection and John's
conception and presentation of them." The Apocalypse, also, "is not to
be interpreted . . . in any way in light of the sources of Johannine theology," although, according to Weiss, all Johannine writings derive from
the same apostolic author.[228] Naturally, then, Weiss also maintains in
his *Lehrbuch der Einleitung in das Neue Testament* [Textbook on
introduction to the New Testament] that Ferdinand Christian von Baur
"deserves the credit of having put the criticism of the New Testament
canon into a fruitful reciprocal interaction with the historical investigation of primitive Christianity" and repeatedly insists that "Baur was the
first . . . to set forth the proper goals of criticism." [229] And in one respect,
at least, Weiss associates himself with the "liberal" research into the life
and teaching of Jesus that Holtzmann had inaugurated, for he assumes a
gradual emergence of the messianic claim on the part of Jesus and a
sequence of a successful and an unsuccessful period in Jesus' ministry.[230]
It is indisputable that Weiss's acceptance of this view of the critical consensus is incompatible with his defense of the authenticity of all New
Testament writings and of the reliability of almost all reported events of
Jesus' life and with his estimate of John's Gospel as a reliable source at
least for Jesus' *life*, but shows all the more clearly how far this consensus
had established itself.

That this agreement extended beyond the German-speaking area becomes readily apparent from the position taken by the English theologian **Joseph Barber Lightfoot**, famous for his careful commentaries on the letters of Paul. Lightfoot appended an excursus on "St Paul and the Three" to his commentary on *Saint Paul's Epistle to the Galatians* in which, expressly appealing to Ritschl, he emphasizes his rejection of F. C. Baur's reconstruction of history. Much as Weiss does, Lightfoot reveals an almost undisturbed confidence in the report of the book of the Acts concerning the most ancient history of primitive Christianity and in the traditional ascriptions of authorship with respect to the New Testament writings. With all that, however, he stands with complete confidence on the ground that the New Testament, as any other book, must be interpreted in accordance with the strict canons of historical investigation,[231] and he also distinguishes the fanatical minority in the earliest Jewish-Christian church from the original apostles, who were ready to compromise, maintains that Paul had to battle throughout his lifetime with the Judaistic opponents and refers to this battle in almost all his letters, and even recognizes that it was a subsidiary aim of the book of the Acts "to show that this growing tendency [of early Christian interests to play Paul and Peter over against each other] was false, and that in their life, as in their death, they were not divided." [232] Consequently, here also essential ideas of the toned-down Tübingen criticism combine with a conservative attitude based on a strictly historical approach.

Adolf Jülicher admirably represents this average opinion of post-Tübingen criticism in his *Einleitung in das Neue Testament* [Introduction to the New Testament], a book that first appeared in 1894. He writes expressly for readers "who regard as justified a *strictly historical* treatment of the study of the New Testament," but for this very reason, in contrast to Baur, he does not consider it the task of the discipline of introduction to criticize the Church's views of the Canon, because by so doing only "suspicion is aroused against the strictly historical character" of the investigation of the New Testament: "Criticism will indeed be applied; not, however, in order to test the value of a dogma, but because, if the truth is to be reached, historical research can never afford to do without criticism in dealing with the legacy of tradition." Furthermore, Jülicher acknowledges the validity of Baur's demand that the books of the New Testament are to be understood within the framework of the history of primitive Christianity. In fact, looking back over his life's scientific work, he explicitly asserts: "The kernel of the Tübingen construction, viz., the conflict between Peter and Paul and the resolution of this conflict, still forms the common presupposition of all scientific work on the New Testament, even of those who do not wish to own up to it." [233] But Jülicher then goes on to maintain that "a great part of the

Tübingen theses" has "proven to be untenable" and to characterize Weizsäcker's *Apostolisches Zeitalter* [Apostolic age] as "a work that accepts and fully develops Baur's basic ideas." Accordingly, Jülicher recognizes the attack of the Judaizers on Paul even in the Letter to the Romans but questions the notions that a permanent division between Peter and Paul resulted from the quarrel at Antioch (Gal. 2:11 ff.) and that this conflict played any role at all in the Catholic Epistles, in the Gospels, and in the Revelation to John. In particular, he denies any party tendency whatever in the book of the Acts. On the contrary, he regards its portrait of history as an idealization of the early Catholic Church. And, while the Gospel of John cannot be used as a source for the history of Jesus, there can be no question of the historical reliability of the synoptic tradition of Jesus. And, quite in line with the harvest of critical investigation from Baur to Weizsäcker, Jülicher also views the New Testament apart from any real connection with its environment and does seriously consider the theological consequences of the insight into the differences within the New Testament proclamation.[234]

The historical system of Baur suffers above all from the mistake, first, of over-rating the importance of Judaism in the early days of Christianity and of ascribing to Paul alone the championship of universalistic tendencies and the building up of Gentile Christian communities, and, secondly, of insisting with rigid one-sidedness that the history of primitive Christianity was dominated till far into the second century by the sole interest of the battle over the Law and the prerogatives of the Jews; whereas in reality this battle was only one factor among many in the formation of its history, and innumerable Christians of the first two generations not only did not understand it, but did not even know anything about it. It is not mainly from ideas and principles that a new religion draws its life: the decisive influences are emotions, feelings, hopes: Baur's picture of the historical development of the Apostolic and post-Apostolic ages is too logical and correct, too deficient in warmth of colour to have probability on its side. Nevertheless the fact remains that Baur inaugurated a new epoch in the study of the New Testament, not only by his numerous flashes of new and unerring insight on questions of Introduction as well as of exegesis and New Testament theology, but principally by the fact that he raised the pursuit of this branch of science to a higher level, and did away with the subjective and detached method of investigation. Since Baur's day the literary history of the New Testament can no longer be dealt with apart from its connection with the history of Christianity as a whole; he has taught us to regard the Books of the New Testament from a truly historical point of view, as the products of and the witnesses to the Christian spirit of a definite age. . . .

Baur's contribution

What the sequel was to this painful dispute we do not learn, but we should have no justification for asserting that it resulted in a definite breach between the parties concerned. Even in the Epistle to the Galatians Paul speaks of Barnabas and Peter in far too friendly a way to leave room for the supposition that a dissolution òf the agreement described in 2: 8, 10 was contemplated on

175

the ground of this one serious difference. Paul does not relate the occurrence for the purpose of prejudicing his readers against Peter or of lowering him in their eyes, but simply to illustrate in the most striking way his own unchanging steadfastness and independence at a critical juncture. . . .

Now, the writer of Luke did not write solely in order to satisfy the thirst of his contemporaries and of posterity for information as to a particular field of history; he wrote to satisfy his own faith, and to increase the convincing power of that faith, convinced himself that this could best be done by making as accurate and complete a description as possible of what had actually occurred. We did not observe any partisan purpose in the Gospel, either in the Pauline direction or in that of endeavouring to reconcile the Pauline and Jewish Christian factions; and this alone makes us somewhat suspicious of the party objects which the Acts are said to have served, no matter whether the book is regarded as a defence of Paul and of his Apostolic rights, or as the programme of the party of union,—a document whose object was to wipe out the memory of the differences between Peter and Paul. And when we find that this school of critics (*Tendenz-Kritiker*) can with equal ease regard Paul as approximated to Peter, and Peter made to show Pauline characteristics, our impression is confirmed that the writer is wrongly credited with *intentions* where in reality all is explained by ignorance, by the incompleteness of his materials, and by his incapacity to carry himself back into the modes of thought even of a just-departed age. It is true that in the Acts the parallelism between Paul and Peter, the representative of Jewish Christianity, is very far-reaching alike in words, deeds and fortunes. . . .

Some of these "parallelisms," however, are undoubtedly founded on fact, while those of the discourses and of the religious points of view represented in them are merely due to the fact that "Luke" himself composed the declarations or discourses in question and put his own thoughts into the mouths of both Apostles; Paul was not Judaised nor Peter Paulinised, but both Paul and Peter were "Lucanised," i.e. Catholicised. . . .

If, then, the sole intention (*Tendenz*) which the history of the Apostles was meant to serve was that of teaching mankind to realise the triumphant advance of the cause of God through the Apostles, we have no right whatever to be surprised at finding certain considerable gaps in the report, for what was alien to that purpose would naturally be passed over in silence. . . . As the writer meant his readers to look upon the Apostolic Age, so he himself had looked upon it all his life. His primary object was, not to mediate between Paul, the founder of the free Gentile Christianity, and the rigidly Catholic Gentile Christianity of about 100; rather he had assumed in all simplicity that in questions of salvation all the Apostles had been quite clear and wholly at one among themselves, and that their faith differed in nothing from the faith by which he had himself received salvation in the Church of his time. . . . This practically accounts for all the preconceptions with which he entered on his task and all the points of view which influenced him in carrying it out; and we thereby understand the reasons which induced the writer to select what was suited to his purpose from materials which may occasionally have been more complete, and even, now consciously and now unconsciously, as in the Gospel, to remodel what he took. According to his own ideas, however, he had acted strictly as an historian throughout. . . .

By far the greater part of this material, the authenticity of which is more than doubtful, was not invented by the Synoptists, but was derived by them from oral or written sources. They themselves were generally responsible only for the form, in the arrangement of which they certainly exhibited considerable freedom, though always in the full belief that they were able to reproduce the traditional material more effectively than anyone else had done before them. It is true that they did not apply historical criticism to the materials they used, but if they had, no Gospels would have been written, and their artificial productions would have fallen into oblivion a few decades after they appeared. Edification was for them the standard of credibility; their task was, not to understand and estimate the historical Jesus, but to believe in him, to love him above all else, to teach men to hope in him: they did not describe the Jesus of real life, but the Christ as he appeared to the hearts of his followers, though of course without dreaming of the possibility of such an antithesis.

Nevertheless the Synoptic Gospels are of priceless value, not only as books of religious edification, but also as authorities for the history of Jesus. Though much of their data may be uncertain, the impression they leave in the reader's mind of the Bearer of Good Tidings is on the whole a faithful one. . . . But, as a rule, there lies in all the Synoptic Logia a kernel of individual character so inimitable and so fresh that their authenticity is raised above all suspicion. Jesus must have spoken just as the Synoptists make him speak, when he roused the people from their torpor, when he comforted them and lovingly stooped to their needs, when he revealed to his disciples his inmost thoughts about his message of the Kingdom, when he guided them and gave them laws, when he contended fiercely with the hostile Pharisees and Sadducees, or worsted them by force of reasoning:—for in no other way can we explain the world-convulsing influence gained by so short a life's work. . . .

Nor should the Synoptic accounts of the deeds and sufferings of Jesus be judged in a less favourable light. . . .

Our confidence is especially won by the sober reserve with which Mark ventured to know nothing of Jesus before his appearance in public, and almost nothing of him after his death. . . . And if the total picture of Jesus which we obtain from the Synoptics displays all the magic of reality, (in Luke just as much as in Matthew and Mark) this is not the result of any literary skill on the part of the Evangelists—which was often indeed defective—nor is it the product of the poetic and creative power of those who passed the tradition on to them; but it is rather owing to the fact that they, while modestly keeping their own personalities in the background, painted Jesus as they found him already existing in the Christian communities, and that this their model corresponded in all essentials to the original.

Justice is done to the Fourth Gospel only when it is regarded as a philosophical prose poem with a religious aim produced in the third Christian generation. As a source for the history of Jesus in the flesh it is, almost valueless, to be sure; on the other hand it stands high above the fantasy Gospels of the post-Synoptic period, to whose ephemeral glitter it offers by its solemn gravity the strongest conceivable contrast. It is historically valuable, nonetheless, as a primary source for the picture of Jesus, to whom, according to the *theology* of the Church (but not according to popular thought), the future was allotted; we learn from it how, soon after A.D. 100, perhaps the greatest thinker of the Christianity of the time regarded the earthly career of the Saviour. Even he has

177

not wholly demolished the actual history, but has only built a new house over it, thereby naïvely identifying truth with reality.

If Jülicher represents the average critical opinion at the end of the nineteenth century with respect to literary matters, **Adolf Harnack** does so with respect to the biblical-theological field.[235] He himself wrote A. Ritschl on the publication of the first volume of his *Dogmengeschichte* [History of dogma] in 1886 that it "would probably never have been written without the foundation you [Ritschl] laid." [236] Ritschl's view that early Catholicism is a development of a popular Gentile Christianity little influenced by Paul is elaborated by Harnack in the familiar thesis: "Dogma is its conception and development is a work of the Greek spirit on the soil of the Gospel," [237] and, accordingly, Harnack radically rejects the view that early Catholic theology arose out of a compromise between opposing "early apostolic doctrines" or that Paul was influenced at all by Greek thought. And in his lectures delivered fourteen years later on *Das Wesen des Christentums* [What is Christianity?], lectures that one of his friends described as "a new edition of the *History of Dogma*, reworked in the interests of practical usefulness," [238] Harnack explicitly denied that Jesus was influenced to any important extent by contemporary Judaism or Hellenism, and even for Paul would admit only to Jewish influence. From this point of view, on the ground of their common dependence on Judaism, Harnack can reject the notions of a conflict between the primitive church and Paul and any essential influence of peculiarly Pauline ideas on the further development of Gentile Christianity (Marcion, who misunderstood Paul, is excepted!), and can even hold that the Gospel of John is derived wholly from Palestinian Judaism. All this indicates that early Christianity stands completely isolated within its environment and is not to have any decisive effect on the subsequent development of the Church. But this assertion is only the negative side of the viewpoint, set forth with greatest warmth, that the essence of Christianity is to be found in the teaching of Jesus, preserved in its authentic form in the Synoptics, about God the Father and the infinite worth of the human soul.[239] And in this respect Harnack associates himself, on the one hand, wholly with the liberal view of Jesus by admitting, indeed, that Jesus expected his imminent return, but by regarding as the real content of Jesus' thought faith alone in the present inwardness of God's kingdom and by assuming that the disciples at a very early time abandoned Jesus' way of thinking in favor of a mere hope for the future. But the other side of this reduction of Christianity to the teaching of the Synoptic Jesus is now the conviction that Jesus "himself [is] Christianity" and "even today [provides] the life of men with meaning and purpose." [240] This emphasis on the central significance of the person of Jesus for his proclamation clearly indicates that an influential representative of the critical consensus recognizes and personally affirms the *theological* importance of the results he had achieved on the grounds of a strictly historical approach to his sources.[241]

The Church doctrine of faith, in the preparatory stage, from the Apologists up to the time of Origen, hardly in any point shows the traces, scarcely even the remembrance of a time in which the Gospel was not detached from Judaism. For that very reason it is impossible to understand this preparation and development solely from the writings that remain to us as monuments of that short earliest period. The attempts at deducing the genesis of the Church's doctrinal system from the theology of Paul, or from compromises between Apostolic doctrinal ideas, will always miscarry; for they fail to note that to the most important premises of the Catholic doctrine of faith belongs an element which we cannot recognise as dominant in the New Testament, viz., the Hellenic spirit.

The Good News which Jesus of Nazareth brought his people consisted in the announcement that the prophetic promises had been fulfilled and the Kingdom of God had now drawn near. This kingdom was depicted by Jesus as future and yet as present, as invisible and yet as visible. In this way—and yet without overturning the Law and the Prophets—he took every opportunity to break through the national, political and sense-gratifying forms in which the people expected the actualization of the Rule of God. But at the same time he turned their attention to a future near at hand, in which believers would be delivered from the oppression of evil and sin, and would enjoy blessedness and dominion. Yet he declared that even now, every individual who is called into the kingdom may call on God as his Father, and be sure of the gracious will of God, the hearing of his prayers, the forgiveness of sin, and the protection of God even in this present life. . . .

In the proclamation and founding of this kingdom, Jesus summoned men to attach themselves to him, because he had recognised himself to be the helper called by God, and therefore also the Messiah who was promised. . . .

Jesus as the Messiah chosen by God has definitely differentiated himself from Moses and all the Prophets: as his preaching and his work are the fulfillment of the prophets' words, so he himself is not a Prophet, but King. He proves this kingship during his earthly ministry in the accomplishment of the mighty deeds given him to do, above all in withstanding the Devil and his kingdom, and—according to the law of the Kingdom of God—for that very reason in the service which he performs. In this service Jesus also included the sacrifice of his life, designating it as a sacrifice which he offered in order to bring forgiveness of sins for his own. But he declared at the same time that his Messianic work was not yet fulfilled in his acceptance of death. On the contrary, the consummation is merely initiated by his acceptance of death; for the completion of the kingdom of God will only appear when he returns in glory in the clouds of heaven. Shortly before his death, Jesus seems to have announced this return in the near future and to have comforted his disciples at his departure, with the assurance that he would immediately enter into a supramundane position with God. . . .

The idea of the inestimable inherent value of every individual human soul

179

. . . stands out plainly in the preaching of Jesus. It is united with the idea of God as Father, and is the complement to the message of the communion of brethren realising itself in love. In this sense the Gospel is at once profoundly individualistic and socialistic.

A community of Christian believers was formed within the Jewish national community. . . . They knew themselves to be the true Israel of the Messianic time . . . and for that very reason lived with all their thoughts and feelings in the future. . . .

The hope of Christ's speedy return was the most important article in the "Christology," inasmuch as his work was regarded as only reaching its conclusion by his return. . . .

Since Jesus had appeared and was believed on as the Messiah promised by the Prophets, the aim and contents of his mission seemed already to be therewith stated with sufficient clearness. Further, as the work of Christ was not yet completed, the view of those contemplating it was, above all, turned to the future. But in virtue of express words of Jesus, and in the consciousness of having received the Spirit of God, one was already certain of the forgiveness of sin dispensed by God, of righteousness before him, of the full knowledge of the Divine will, and of the call to the future Kingdom as a present possession.

Christian communities . . . had arisen in the empire, in Rome for example, which were essentially free from the law without being in any way determined by Paul's preaching. It was Paul's merit that he clearly formulated the great question, established the universalism of Christianity in a peculiar manner, and yet in doing so held fast the character of Christianity as a positive religion, as distinguished from Philosophy and Moralism. But the later development presupposes neither his clear formulation nor his peculiar establishment of universalism, but only the universalism itself.

The dependence of the Pauline Theology on the Old Testament or on Judaism is overlooked in the traditional contrasting of Paulinism and Jewish Christianity, in which Paulinism is made equivalent to Gentile Christianity. This theology, as we might *a priori* suppose, could, apart from individual exceptions, be intelligible as a whole to birthright Jews, if to any, for its doctrinal presuppositions were strictly Pharisaic, and its boldness in criticising the Old Testament, rejecting and asserting the law in its historical sense, could be as little congenial to the Gentile Christians as its piety towards the Jewish people. This judgment is confirmed by a glance at the fate of Pauline theology in the 120 years that followed. Marcion was the only Gentile Christian who understood Paul, and even he misunderstood him: the rest never got beyond the appropriation of particular Pauline sayings, and exhibited no comprehension especially of the theology of the Apostle, so far as in it the universalism of Christianity as a religion is proved, even without recourse to moralism and without putting a new construction on the Old Testament religion. It follows from this, however, that the scheme "Jewish Christianity"—"Gentile Christianity" is insufficient. If there are any Hellenistic influences at all in Paul, they can only be shown to have been transmitted through the medium of Palestinian Jewish theology, in which however, they cannot be confirmed with any real certainty.

The peculiar and lofty conception of Christ and of the Gospel which stands out in the writings of John has directly exercised no demonstrable influence on the succeeding development . . . and indeed partly for the same reason that

180

has prevented the Pauline theology as a whole from having such an influence. What is given in these writings is a criticism of the Old Testament as religion, or the independence of the Christian religion, in virtue of an accurate knowledge of the Old Testament through development of its hidden germs. The Old Testament stage of religion is really transcended and overcome in Johannine Christianity, just as in Paulinism, and in the theology of the Epistle to the Hebrews. . . . But this transcending of the Old Testament religion was the very thing that was unintelligible, because there were few ripe for such a conception. . . . The elements operative in the Johannine theology were not Greek—even the Logos has little more in common with that of Philo than the name, and its mention at the beginning of the book is a mystery, not the solution of one—but the Apostolic testimony concerning Christ has created from the old faith of Psalmists and Prophets, a new faith in a man who lived with the disciples of Jesus among the Greeks. For that very reason, in spite of his abrupt Anti-Judaism, we must without doubt regard the Author as a born Jew.

Besides, critical theology has made it difficult to gain an insight into the great difference that lies between the Pauline and the Catholic theology, by the one-sided prominence it has hitherto given to the antagonism between Paulinism and Judaistic Christianity. . . . That, however, was only very gradually the case and within narrow limits. The deepest and most important writings of the New Testament are incontestably those in which Judaism is understood as religion, but spiritually overcome and the Gospel triumphs over it as a new religion,—the Pauline Epistles, the Epistle to the Hebrews, and the Gospel and Epistle of John. There is set forth in these writings a new and exalted world of religious feelings, views and judgments, into which the Christians of succeeding centuries got only meagre glimpses. Strictly speaking, the opinion that the New Testament in its whole extent comprehends a unique literature is not tenable; but it is correct to say that between its most important constituent parts and the literature of the period immediately following there is a great gulf fixed.

There are only two possibilities here: either the Gospel is in all respects identical with its earliest form, in which case it came with its time and has departed with it; or else it contains something which, under differing historical forms, is of permanent validity. The latter is the true view. The history of the Church shows us in its very commencement that "primitive Christianity" had to disappear in order that "Christianity" might remain; and in the same way in later ages one metamorphosis followed upon another. From the beginning it was a question of getting rid of formulas, correcting expectations, altering ways of feeling, and this is a process to which there is no end.

No doubt it is true that the view of the world and history with which the Gospel is connected is quite different from ours, and that view we cannot recall to life, and would not if we could; but "indissoluble" the connexion is not. I have tried to show what the essential elements in the Gospel are, and these elements are "timeless." Not only are they so; but the man to whom the Gospel addresses itself is also "timeless," that is to say, he is the man who, in spite of all progress and development, never changes in his inmost constitution and in his fundamental relations with the external world. Since this is so, this Gospel remains in force, then, for us too.

Jesus Christ's teaching will at once bring us by steps which, if few, will be great, to a height where its connexion with Judaism is seen to be only a loose one, and most of the threads leading from it into "contemporary history" become of no importance at all. . . .

The picture of Jesus' life and his discourses stand in no relation with the Greek spirit. That is almost a matter for surprise; for Galilee was full of Greeks, and Greek was then spoken in many of its cities, much as Swedish is nowadays in Finland. There were Greek teachers and philosophers there, and it is scarcely conceivable that Jesus should have been entirely unacquainted with their language. But that he was in any way influenced by them, that he was ever in touch with the thoughts of Plato or the Porch, even though it may have been only in some popular redaction, it is absolutely impossible to maintain. . . .

Jesus' message of the kingdom of God runs through all the forms and statements of the prophecy which, taking its colour from the Old Testament, announces the day of judgment and the visible government of God in the future, up to the idea of a kingdom which comes inwardly and which starts from Jesus' message. His message embraces these two poles, with many stages between them that shade off one into another. At the one pole the coming of the kingdom seems to be a purely future event, and the kingdom itself to be the external rule of God; at the other, it appears as something inward, something which is already present and making its entrance at the moment. . . .

There can be no doubt about the fact that the idea of the two kingdoms, of God and of the devil, and their conflicts, and of that last conflict at some future time when the devil, long since cast out of heaven, will be also defeated on earth, was an idea which Jesus simply shared with his contemporaries. He did not start it, but he grew up in it and he retained it. The other view, however, that the kingdom of God "cometh not with observation," that it is already here, was his own.

If anyone wants to know what the kingdom of God and the coming of it meant in Jesus' message, he must read and study his parables. He will then see what it is that is meant. The kingdom of God comes by coming to the individual, by entering into his soul and laying hold of it. True, the kingdom of God is the rule of God; but it is the rule of the holy God in the hearts of individuals; *it is God Himself in His power*. From this point of view everything that is dramatic in the external and historical sense has vanished; and gone, too, are all the external hopes for the future. Take whatever parable you will, the parable of the sower, of the pearl of great price, of the treasure buried in the field—the word of God, God Himself, is the kingdom. It s not a question of angels and devils, thrones and principalities, but of God and the soul, the soul and its God.

At a later period the view of the kingdom, according to which it was already come and still comes in Jesus' saving activity, was not kept up by his disciples: nay, they continued to speak of it as of something that was solely in the future. But the thing itself retained its force; it was only given another title. . . .

The essential elements in the message of the kingdom were preserved. The kingdom has a triple meaning. Firstly, it is something supernatural, a gift from above, not a product of ordinary life. Secondly, it is a purely religious blessing, the inner link with the living God; thirdly, it is the most important experience

182

that a man can have, that on which everything else depends; it permeates and dominates his whole existence, because sin is forgiven and misery banished. . . .

To our modern way of thinking and feeling, Christ's message appears in the clearest and most direct light when grasped in connexion with the idea of God the Father and the infinite value of the human soul. . . . But the fact that the whole of Jesus' message may be reduced to these two heads—God as the Father, and the human soul so ennobled that it can and does unite with him—shows us that the Gospel is in no way a positive religion like the rest; that it contains no statutory or particularistic elements; *that it is, therefore, religion itself.*

Let us first of all consider the designation, "Son of God." Jesus in one of his discourses made it specially clear why and in what sense he gave himself this name. The saying is to be found in Matthew, and not, as might perhaps have been expected, in John: "No man knoweth the Son but the Father; neither knoweth any man the Father, save the Son, and he to whomsoever the Son will reveal him" (Matt. 11:27). It is "knowledge of God" that makes the sphere of the Divine Sonship. It is in this knowledge that he came to know the sacred Being who rules heaven and earth as Father, as *his* Father. The consciousness which he possessed of being *the Son of God* is, therefore, nothing but the practical consequence of knowing God as the Father and as his Father. Rightly understood, the name of Son means nothing but the knowledge of God. Here, however, two observations are to be made: Jesus is convinced that he knows God in a way in which no one ever knew Him before, and he knows that it is his vocation to communicate this knowledge of God to others by word and by deed—and with it the knowledge that men are God's children. In this consciousness he knows himself to be the Son called and instituted of God to be *the* Son of God, and hence he can say: *My* God and *my* Father, and into this invocation he puts something which belongs to no one but himself. How he came to this consciousness of the unique character of his relation to God as a Son; how he came to the consciousness of his power, and to the consciousness of the obligation and the mission which this power carries with it, is his secret, and no psychology will ever fathom it. . . .

Jesus directed men's attention to great questions; he promised them God's grace and mercy; he required them to decide whether they would have God or Mammon, an eternal or an earthly life, the soul or the body, humility or self-righteousness, love or selfishness, the truth or a lie. The sphere which these questions occupy is all-embracing; the individual is called upon to listen to the glad message of mercy and the Fatherhood of God, and to make up his mind whether he will be on God's side and the Eternal's, or on the side of the world and of time. *The Gospel, as Jesus proclaimed it, has to do with the Father only and not with the Son.* This is a paradox, nor, on the other hand, is it "rationalism," but the simple expression of the actual fact as the evangelists give it.

But no one had ever yet known the Father in the way in which Jesus knew Him, and to this knowledge of Him he draws other men's attention, and thereby does "the many" an incomparable service. He leads them to God, not only by what he says, but still more by what he is and does, and ultimately by what he suffers. . . .

It is not as a mere factor that he is connected with the Gospel; *he was its personal realisation and its strength, and this he is felt to be still.*

In this very isolation of primitive Christianity, however, and in this theological presupposition of the historical work on the New Testament, there lay problems that had already loomed for long in the background and now really emerged and thereby compelled New Testament study to confront a completely new set of problems. But before we can discuss this new stage in research we must first refer to a few individual problems that were attacked at the end of the nineteenth century.

4.
Individual Problems

Karl Lachmann had prepared the way for the formulation of a critical text of the New Testament but for lack of sufficient manuscripts and other witnesses of the text from the first five hundred years was unable to produce a convincing edition. Taking his departure from Lachmann's presuppositions, **Constantin von Tischendorf** over a period of decades compared and discovered countless manuscripts in European and Oriental libraries (the most famous of them being Codex Sinaiticus from the fourth century) [242] and, on the basis of all the witnesses at his disposal and of citations from the church fathers, published numerous editions of the Greek New Testament, of which the eighth (1872) offered the critical material for a really methodical formulation of the text in such a superb form that it remains indispensable to our own day. On the basis of this material Tischendorf could claim that he had recovered, not simply the text of the fourth century to which Lachmann had aspired, but that of the second century.[243] Tischendorf's strength, however, lay in collecting, and he failed to formulate clear principles for the construction of his *text.* Consequently the two Cambridge scholars, **Brooke Foss Westcott and Fenton John Anthony Hort**, using material that had come to light in the interim, were the first to create a critical text that was really methodologically sound. In their edition of 1882 [244] they offered a text without apparatus, a text that was constituted "exclusively on the basis of documents, without reference to any printed edition," but they did supply important variants in the margin or below the text wherever in their judgment the text they offered was uncertain or variants existed of equal worth to the readings they had chosen. In this fashion they clearly met Lachmann's requirement. But another fact was still more important. After decades of investigating all the sources, both scholars returned to Griesbach's perception that only by the grouping of witnesses in text families was it possible to reach an assured judgment on the value of manuscripts and, consequently, on their text. By a careful examination of the text of the most ancient of the church fathers they proved finally and beyond all question that the great majority of the later manuscripts (which they called the "Syrian text") belonged to a secondary and therefore worthless recension. Further, they were of the opinion that the original text is almost always to be found in the two great parchment manuscripts of the fourth century (Codices Vaticanus and Sinaiticus), whose text they therefore called "neutral." In all this they demonstrated convincingly that the "received text" derives from the later "Syrian" text and consequently must be abandoned as corrupt; and they likewise showed that the value of the text families can only be determined on the basis of the internal evidence for the originality of their readings. These two observations have retained their validity; and although it was later recognized that the text Westcott and Hort called "neutral" *also* derives from a recension, though a good one, yet their insight into the great worth of this text form has remained basic to all later text editions.[245]

Within the liberal life-of-Jesus research **A. Jülicher** made a fundamental contribution to the solution of a particularly important individual problem. In the first volume of his work on *Die Gleichnisreden Jesu* [The parables of Jesus], which appeared in 1886, Jülicher was able to show that we can only come nearer to the original meaning of the parables that are so important for the understanding of Jesus if we go back of the evangelists' understanding of them to the meaning Jesus himself wished them to convey. That can only be done, however, when we explain the parables, consciously and consistently, as real pictures and not as obscure allegories, by which we admit that the allegorical interpretation imposed on the parables by the evangelists is historically untenable. But Jülicher went still a step further. He ruled out every possibility that the parables are a mixture of genuine pictorial speech and figurative, metaphorical speech and held that no parable contains more than *one* point of comparison, and that point, as a rule, a very general one. With this further step Jülicher no doubt goes too far, but in other respects he succeeded in putting the understanding of Jesus' parables on a methodologically certain basis that is still largely uncontested and so made a very important part of the tradition of the historical Jesus for the first time really intelligible.[246]

The following observations . . . are unassailable. The authenticity of the Gospel parables as we have them cannot simply be assumed. Jesus did not utter them as we now read them. They have been translated, transposed, and inwardly transformed. The reports that two or three evangelists give of the same parable never fully agree. Not only does the expression vary, but also the viewpoint, the arrangement, the occasion, the interpretation, whether it be expressed by means of the context or explicitly; this goes so far that one can speak of a Lucan tune in the parables in contrast to the Matthaean. What one evangelist gives as a parable, another presents in fragmentary form as a comparative statement; traits that are important to one, the other suppresses. What an absurdly uncritical approach in such a state of affairs . . . that takes without question as authentic what two reports agree in giving or what is not contradicted by any parallel account! What Matthew alone tells me about and by means of parables is no more certain than what I find also when Matthew and Luke are in parallel; without careful testing one can never identify the voice of Jesus with the voices of the evangelists.

Thankfully our undertaking to discover Jesus himself in his parables is not hopeless, however. We find no ground for wholesale questioning of the genuineness of the Gospel parables; on the contrary, we see ourselves compelled to ascribe a relative authenticity to them; almost without exception they have a genuine nucleus that goes back to Jesus himself. . . .

Unfortunately there can hardly be any doubt that the evangelists—and their sources before them—have confused the "pictorial speech" [parable] of Hellenistic scribal learning, as we know it from Sirach and which is the twin sister of the "puzzle," with the *mashal* [parable] of Scripture in all its breadth and naturalness. It is the latter that at the same time will have been the *mashal* of Jesus. Or, more carefully put, their idea of parable, so far as they have one at all, is, as we might expect, that of the Hellenistic-Jewish literature. They understand by "parable" not simply *speech that is intended to make something clear by means of comparison*, but on the contrary *speech that is obscure*, that requires interpretation. . . .

So far as I see, we cannot escape explaining the meaning and understanding of the evangelists as a misunderstanding of the essence of Jesus' parables. The difference can be expressed as follows: *According to the theory of the evangelists, the "parables" are allegories, and therefore figurative discourse that to some extent requires translation, while in fact they are—or, we should say, they were, before they came into the hands of zealous redactors—something very different: parables, fables, example paradigmatic stories, but always literal discourse. . . .*

Despite the authority of so many centuries, despite the greater authority of the evangelists, I cannot regard Jesus' parables as allegories. Everything, yes, everything speaks against it. To begin with, we understand the parables by and large without "elucidation." We must only keep in mind that the Synoptists consider them discourses that mean something else than the words imply—something that Christ's disciples, if they could not guess it by themselves, had to ask him about, and he alone solves all the riddles for them. Now, with two exceptions, the evangelists have left us no "solutions of riddles." Does it not then follow that for us the parables, except for the two that were decoded, must be unintelligible? Or are we cleverer, more sensitive, than a Peter, a John? No one will maintain that, and consequently there remains only the choice: either the parables as allegories require a "solution" and, since none has come down to us through tradition, they remain sealed *to us*, or we understand them even without any transmitted interpretation, and in this case an interpretation was never absoluely necessary and the parables are not allegories. . . .

To speak of interpretation in the instance of a parable, interpretation such as an allegory needs, is accordingly a sheer impossibility. The pictorial in the parable, to be of any use, must be understood literally, while the allegory is figurative. This contrast tolerates no mixture of forms. . . . Half allegory and half fable are only mythological entities.

187

The biographer of Jesus cannot overdo immersing himself in and familiarizing himself with these parables. Here, as scarcely anywhere else, he becomes acquainted with extensive, interrelated, coherent lines of thought of his hero, and from these simplest of all discourses he is overwhelmed by an overpowering feeling for the exalted nature of this child of God, wholly unpretentious and so exalted in his simple, hearty truth. Sometimes clearly and joyfully, sometimes softly and movingly, sometimes earnestly and strictly, what he has to say appears to us in the parables; but always he is involved in them with his whole heart and soul; he never thinks of himself, but only of his work, his aim, his people. The essence of the parable and its purpose are as he himself is: to misunderstand either one of these means to misunderstand him. . . .

Let us sum up the results of this investigation. In his parables Jesus has left us "masterpieces of popular eloquence." Here also, in terms of art, he demonstrates himself as Master; so far as we know, nothing higher and more perfect has ever been accomplished in this area.

So far as I see, once we have broken with Origen and his theory of the deeper meaning of parables, we cannot stop . . . half way; either the parables are wholly figurative speech or wholly literal—a mixture of both could be found in individual instances, but in this case would be a sign of clumsiness. The desire in principali scopo ["in the first place"] to have details interpreted can never have been the occasion for parabolic discourse; either everything in them ought to be allegorized, or we ought to take everything in them as it stands and learn something from it, or let it clarify something, in order to utilize it for a higher order. For, though the similarities between the half that illustrates and the half that is illustrated be numerous or limited to a single point: the parable is there only to illuminate that one point, a rule, an idea, an experience that is valid on the spiritual as on the secular level.

In the area of Pauline research the later Bernese dogmatic theologian **Herrmann Lüdemann** made the observation, in his *Die Anthropologie des Apostels Paulus* [The anthropology of the apostle Paul] (1872), that the idea of the "flesh" the central idea of Paul's picture of man, designates partly, in the wider sense, the whole man, and partly, in the narrower sense, the material body as the seat of sin, in contrast to the inner man. In explanation of this observation he pointed to the fact that the one was a concept of Jewish, while the other was one of Hellenistic, origin and tried to show that Paul progressively shoved the Jewish concepts into the background, and consequently also the doctrine of salvation bound up with them (justification by faith), in favor of Hellenistic ideas and of the realistic doctrine of redemption associated with baptism that was involved. In this way Lüdemann not only consistently applied the assumption of a *double* doctrine of redemption, but at the same time attempted an explanation of this state of affairs by deriving both lines of thought respectively from Jewish and Hellenistic premises, and associated with this the thesis that Paul had undergone a development in his thought and that the *actual* Pauline theology is to be sought in the realistic doctrine of redemption which is of Hellenistic derivation. This downgrading of the doctrine of justification by faith, a doctrine regarded by others as central, raised the question, as had the hypothesis of a bifurcated Pauline proclamation, of the inner coherence and the central content of Pauline theology and, at the same time, the question of the relation of this theology to the background of ancient religions, so that Lüdemann's study, which also referred to the importance for Paul of the expectation of Christ's return, raised all the basic problems of further Pauline research.[247]

In Paul, where the "flesh" (sarx) is said to be transient because it is material, we are reminded strongly of the principle of matter, matter for which, in the dualistic way of thinking of the contemporary intellectual world—Platonizing, Hellenistic as well as Greek—transitoriness or even nonbeing was set down as the essential property. What if it were the negativity of the material as such that here comes to light in Paul? What if here not so much an Old Testament as, on the contrary, a Hellenistic element asserts itself?

If it . . . is established that, in addition to the wider concept of the "flesh," a narrower one is to be recognized, . . . that only the former is a Jewish and only the latter a Greek category, it now follows, in light of the opposition of "spirit" and "flesh," that with the former concept, that of a substantial divine spirit partaking of a higher materiality, Paul remains on Jewish ground, but, on the other hand, does not conceive the relationship of the "flesh" to it uniformly, but thinks of it in part, in accordance with Jewish religious thought, as the opposition of the infinite and the finite, and in part as the opposition of the divine spirit to the earthly substance of the human body, and in this latter respect actually takes up a dualistic, Hellenistic element into his circle of ideas. . . .

How does the objective happening that took place in Christ's death and resurrection become effective for the individual subject enslaved by the "flesh"? Everyone will have the answer on the tip of his tongue: "by faith." . . . For the time being we do not wish to decide *against that,* but, on the other hand, we wish also to content ourselves with what the apostle here (Rom. 6:3 ff.) mentions as of primary importance, namely, baptism. . . . In this very passage we see that Paul thinks of baptism as bringing about such an intimate union of the one baptized with Christ that, in the relationship to which it refers, it appears in almost no respect to be less than a realistic identification. The connection is such that what has happened to Christ *eo ipso* is also fulfilled in the one baptized . . . . The old man, the "flesh," which serves "the law of sin" (Rom. 7:25) , is crucified with Christ, and consequently the "body of sin" of the one baptized is abolished, done away with. But when man in this way has died in terms of his "flesh," that is, when his "flesh" has died, he is then set free from sin, that is, from his obligation to serve it as his lord. . . .

If then it is asked how far the "flesh" still has any place at all in the "spiritual man," the answer can only be that Paul thinks of it only in the sense of an intermediate state. And the explanation of such a conviction on his part is to be found in his faith in the nearness of the parousia. During this intervening period the Christian will still partake of the "flesh."

This presentation will have awakened all kinds of doubts in the minds of its readers. Above all, they will have the objection on the tips of their tongues that we have conceived the Pauline circle of ideas so one-sidedly that no one will find in our account what one is accustomed to look for and to discover in Paul. For, although we have been speaking about a redemption of a man by Christ —where, we are asked, are the sublime doctrines of Christ's vicarious sufferings and of righteousness based on faith, doctrines that are so essential to Paul's structure of thought that we seem to have broken loose its finest stones? . . .

The "justification" of Rom. 3:4 is nothing more than a mere judgment of acquittal, the pure *actus forensis* ["judicial act"] that effects no real, objective change in the essential man. As an act of grace, God accepts the believer as he then is, and the nearest thing to a *real* consequence is only a relationship of the justified man to God which, on the part of both, is again of a purely subjective nature: namely, that the believer has "peace with God through our Lord Jesus Christ" (5:1).

But the farther we penetrate from this point into the Letter to the Romans, the more we feel that the apostle begins in his expositions to make a place for and to bring out ever more clearly another style of representation than that previously set forth. . . .

This survey of the first eight chapters of the Letter to the Romans, therefore, discloses a noteworthy fact. . . . We have found that in Paul two lines of thought emerge, lines of thought that are characteristically expressed in different ideas of the "flesh" and which differ from one another from beginning to end.

We must designate these two lines of thought as a religious or subjectively ideal line on the one hand, and on the other as an ethical or objectively real line. And so, then, on the one side we find freedom, responsibility, accountability, culpability, the origin of sin in the free subject himself, objective guilt and subjective consciousness of guilt as the germinating point of the whole development—on the other side a strictly closed causal connection, the natural inevitablity of sin, the origin of sin not so much *in* as *on* the subject, without his knowledge and will. . . .

On the one side a forgiveness of sins and an imputation of an ideal righteousness made possible juridically, in accordance with the "law of faith"—on the other side, redemption of the subject from the "flesh" and bestowal on him of the "Holy Spirit," the principle of a real righteousness by which he is subjected to the "law of the spirit of life" so that, since he walks according to the Spirit, he also fulfills "the righteous demand of the law."

On the one side faith—on the other baptism as the agent of the respective redemption. . . .

We see clearly into the process which led the apostle to lay hold of the dualistic concept of the "flesh" in its full significance and to thrust it into the middle of the dogmatic debate; and once he had brought out its ethical and paraenetic values in the Letter to the Galatians and then had developed its psychic side didactically and dogmatically in the Letters to the Corinthians, he now combined its psychic and ethical elements and gave final dogmatic form to his doctrine of a real redemption of man from "flesh," "sin," and "death." This also finally makes it clear that it was soteriological reflection which drove the apostle to focus on one point all elements of his anthropology such as we find scattered in his earlier statements and so to give full systematic formulation to his doctrine of man and to furnish his soteriology with a broad, sure foundation.

In this teaching, accordingly, we have the apostle's actual, definitive view of man's salvation in Christ before our eyes for the first time. . . .

At the very beginning, in a twofold meaning of the word "flesh," we ran across traces of two levels in the Pauline structure of thought, something which was confirmed by our efforts to establish the place of anthropology within Paul's doctrine of salvation with such a clarity and precision that we had to be concerned about the inner unity of the apostolic doctrine.

Now that we have tried to understand this genetically in all its parts, the relation of its various elements to one another has also become clear to us; we have recognized that in the course of a constant interaction with the development of anthropology a noteworthy transformation has taken place at the very center of Pauline soteriology. The very elements in which we not infrequently see the actual palladium of Paulinism (Christ's vicarious atonement and righ- ~sa feguard~ teousness by means of faith) after having once formed a part of the innermost nucleus of Paul's gospel, have been nevertheless gradually eased out of this central position. In the maturest form of this doctrine they now represent rather only the propylaea through which especially the Christian who comes from Judaism must make his "entrance" if he is to attain those saving gifts, which, however, turn out again to be those real treasures of grace of a new creation and a future glorification of man mediated by Christ.

At the same time, however, we have seen that one of these lines of thought that gradually withdrew from the center goes back to a tradition from which Paul himself comes but which he unmistakably outgrows more and more, until he thinks of it quite objectively and treats it as the object of sacred pedagogy, the Old Testament tradition of legalism. The watchword by which this is always betrayed, we saw to be the wider concept of the "flesh," a concept in which the vaguer anthropology and the looser categories of the Jewish spirit are indicated. On the other hand, we recognized another, narrower, dualistic concept of the "flesh" as the basic constituent of the genuine Pauline circle of thought, a concept that emerges ever more distinctly. The more urgently his developing doctrine of salvation compels him to a fixed dogmatic formulation and usage, the more the apostle is led beyond the horizon of Old Testament consciousness to that of Hellenism, in whose circles this very idea had for long been current as a well-minted coin.

That a homogeneous understanding of Paul is no longer possible when one starts from this divided view of Paul's theology is apparent from the *Lehrbuch der Neutestamentlichen Theologie* [Textbook · on New Testament theology] of **H. J. Holtzmann,** a two-volume work that focuses the whole post-Baur research as though it were a burning-glass. Although Holtzmann basically did not wish to isolate the New Testament from its environment and to take the step "from a New Testament theology to a late Jewish and early Christian history of religion," he falls back nevertheless on the old method of placing the several complexes of ideas and the individual writers side by side, more or less disconnectedly, and only concerning each separate concept is the question asked as to its possible background in the world of the day. In all this the presentation of Jesus' proclamation corresponds to a large extent to the liberal picture

191

of Jesus, to whose creation Holtzmann himself had contributed in his study of *Die synoptischen Evangelien* [The Synoptic Gospels]: the eschatological views were placed at the end, without any clear connection with the proclamation of the kingdom of God: now, as formerly, Jesus' transition to a "passion program" at the time of the confession of his messiahship at Caesarea Philippi is regarded as "an unsolicited result which emerges from every critical analysis of the Gospels that is to be taken seriously." The "messianic element" belongs to "the Jewish foreground" of the gospel history, while the "more human, loftier" element "constitutes its universal spiritual background." In light of this the teaching of the primitive Jerusalem Church appears as a "Pharisaic-Jewish-Christian" misunderstanding of Jesus. More important, however, is Holtzmann's account of Paulinism, for here, in dependence on Lüdemann, there is an almost pervading presentation of the several complexes of ideas in Paul as "a unique summation of ideas which are by definition basically Jewish but Greek in dress," in which "the center of gravity has already shifted to the Hellenistic factor." In spite of this "persuasive disunity in the structure of his thought," Paul the Pharisee and the Hellenist is said to have been "primarily responsible" for the fact "that the Christian history of dogma is actually linked to the message of Jesus," and Paul therefore can even be described as the "secondary," in contrast to "the primary founder of the Christian religion." Thus it is apparent that not only is the inner unity of the New Testament Gospel forfeit, but also no really intelligible development from Jesus to Paul and on into the early Catholic Church can any longer be traced. Nevertheless Holtzmann declares most emphatically that it is the ongoing task of the *historical* study of the Bible to distinguish the permanent element in Christianity from the temporally conditioned. Therefore even Holtzmann, in spite of his atomizing presentation of the New Testament world of thought, holds fast to the presupposition of the incomparable significance of this world of thought and consequently to historical research in the field of biblical theology as *theological* undertaking.[248]

While earlier scholars looked for analogies to Jesus' teachings in the classics and on the ground of these at times even challenged the originality of Jesus, it appears that such a consequence today is more likely to be the outcome of further comparison with the rabbinic literature. . . . Only a consciousness which demonstrably has drawn its nourishment and its strength from the fruitful mother earth of contemporary Judaism will be sure in the long run of conveying a distinct impression of historical reality. Whoever refuses to investigate these matters denies himself a really historical understanding not only of primitive Christianity, but also, if he persists in such behavior, of everything that has come about as a consequence of Jesus' appearance, although by no means exclusively determined by it, viz., of what in terms of general outlook and of sacred as of secular practice is regarded as "Christianity" in the wider sense of the word.

But an even greater loss is that he is not able with any certainty to distinguish the really original and creative element at the heart of Christianity itself from a world of thought that belongs to a contemporary historical milieu. And yet the universal and lasting contribution of biblical-theological studies to scholarship and life can only be this, that we become aware that what Jesus brought as pure fire to the altar, a fire which has not since gone out but, though fed with fuel of the greatest imaginable variety, has continued to glow and in this way has been able to become the enduringly effective principle of a new religious life of peoples, is dependent of the national, local, temporally conditioned elements of the Jewish theology; that is, of the messianic legends and the eschatological perspective. More and more with the passage of time such a separation of the central and the peripheral will be the unavoidable consequence of every treatment of the biblical-theological problems from the historical point of view. . . .

We are the more entitled to distinguish the transitory and the permanent in Paulinism since we are indebted to the apostle himself for full guidance in freeing religious ideas which first appeared in historically and temporally conditioned concepts from their accidental framework and in expressing them in a way that would make them generally intelligible and obligatory. . . .

The more truly the Pauline doctrine is presented as historical, the more surely it becomes evident that, when Pauline passages are read and interpreted in congregational worship, it cannot be this doctrine itself that forms the content of a living and impelling message, but it must be something that stands back of and beyond it. Doctrine is the object of scientific research, of exegetical and historical theology. But it is clear that doctrine cannot be preached, for to make this possible the preacher and the congregation would first have to be artificially indoctrinated with the elements of the Jewish and Hellenistic, or Greek, consciousness that served Paulinism as a presupposition. . . .

However, that Pauline doctrine never wholly shrinks to a scholastic formula, but forms an inexhaustible treasury of motives for a living proclamation of the Gospel, is due to the fact that it is only formally doctrine, but actually an almost direct echo of the first glad message. And so, in the end, we may be permitted to say that the Jewish and the Hellenistic alike are the perishable in Paul, but for Christianity the permanent is what was originally Christian. The former, which are the factors involved in its historical and temporal conditioning, are the concern of our theological and scientific, the latter, which is the resonance of the eternal in the human soul, is concerned with our religious and practical interest.

5.
The Questioning of the Consistently Historical View of the New Testament

Protest was early raised from quite opposite points of view against these methodological presuppositions, as against the results achieved by those who made them. In 1867 **Hermann Cremer** had published the first edition of his *Biblisch-theologisches Wörterbuch der neutestamentlichen Gräcität* [Biblico-theological dictionary of New Testament Greek idioms], a book that treated "the expressions of the spiritual, moral, and religious life" in the New Testament in such a way that New Testament Greek was represented as the transformation of the Greek language into the "organ of the spirit of Christ" and consequently as "the language of the Holy Spirit." By comparing the New Testament with profane Greek and the language of Hellenistic and rabbinical Judaism, he undertook to demonstrate "the differences as well as the kinship of Greek and biblical concepts." [249] Even though these preliminary methodological comments show that Cremer consciously makes the affirmation of the revelatory character of the New Testament a presupposition of his work, nevertheless the individual articles reveal throughout a complete isolation of the New Testament world of thought from that of the profane Greek world and, on the presupposition of the uniformity of the New Testament world of thought, the lack of any evidence of a *development* within the New Testament. The first to take a decisive step in this latter direction was Cremer's later colleague, **Adolf Schlatter**, who at one of the most important points attacked the problem (a problem that Cremer had raised only in general terms) of the understanding of the central New Testament concepts and made a thoroughgoing examination of *Der Glaube im Neuen Testament* [Faith in the New Testament] (1885). In this book, as he himself admits, Schlatter takes his departure both from the conviction that the New Testament testimony is uniform, in spite of all individuation, and that faith on the part of the interpreter himself is necessary if an appropriate presentation of the idea of faith in the New Testament is to be given.[250] But thereafter in numerous later textbooks and commentaries Schlatter distanced himself more and more from acknowledging differences within the New Testament that he had already pointed up in his first work.[251] Schlatter regarded this unity of the New Testament testimony as historically based in that "the environment of Jesus and his disciples was Palestinian Judaism." [252] Therefore he fell back on the use of rabbinic literature for the clarification of the historical background of the New Testament, a procedure John Lightfoot had first employed, and undertook to show why these rabbinical texts, despite their late origin, can really illuminate this background. On these methodological presuppositions Schlatter now seeks to prove that even Jesus gave faith a place of central importance, and he shows most convincingly that, for Paul, faith is throughout the saving reality and that, in particular, even in baptism faith mediates the real salvation. So, in contrast to Lüdemann and Holtzmann, Schlatter attempts to understand Paul's thought as a complete unity by isolating him wholly from Hellenism. Although in this way he unjustly denies Paul's unquestionable contacts with Hellenism, yet he rightly stresses the central importance of faith for Paul and thereby makes it necessary to demonstrate the pervasive unity of Pauline thought in spite of an acknowledgment of the facts denied by Schlatter concerning the religious situation in Paul's time.[253]

Faith is an inward event, and as we undertake a discussion of it we enter the field of history. This concept is all the more applicable in this connection because the New Testament faith, even after its basis was laid by Jesus, does not exist in the Church in a state of rigid inflexibility, but undergoes a lively development, determined individually by each separate apostolic figure. This variety is the direct result of the value of the human personality in the sight of God—the human personality in the individuality of its life. We have no postulates to make concerning faith. We do not maintain that it is a mechanical unity, as though the same concept of faith had to recur everywhere in the New Testament. Nor must we postulate faith's opposite, as that metaphysics must do which, without an opposite, possesses no principle of movement. In fact, we have no postulates to make at all, but we have only to observe what happened. Since in accord with the divine order the spirits lead an individual life, then we shall also find variety in their faith, but, to the extent that their particular life is based on God, their variety will not lack unity. This is the formula: there is a real basis for unity in variety, namely, that the one God is at work in a large number of personalities, of which each has and is to have his own life.

The goal of the following study is history that is wholly objective, for it is objectivity alone that gives an account the character of history. I have not the slightest interest in describing *my own* faith, but only in understanding and recounting what the men of the New Testament experienced, thought of, and described as faith. Nevertheless, I do not wish to hide the fact that what insight I may possess into the role of faith in the New Testament, I have only in the closest connection with what faith I myself have received by the grace of God and Christ. For this reason it is scarcely conceivable to me that the New

195

Testament concept of faith could become transparently clear by way of fantasy alone, fantasy that seeks at second hand to imitate and to experience psychic states of others, without a personal attitude of faith . . . . It would be a groundless and unjustified judgment to complain that this active participation of one's own attitude of faith in itself affects the historical character of the study, as though historical insight is assisted rather than hindered when the events under scrutiny are detached entirely from one's own experience. On the contrary, in one's own experience of faith in Jesus there lies the possibility of, the drive to, and the equipment for, a really historically true understanding of the New Testament. . . .

The chronological and historical confusion in the collected works of the rabbis can be cleared up at least to some extent with the help of Hellenistic literature. The latter proves that the exegetical tradition of the Targums and the Midrash to a considerable extent is pre-Christian. . . .

Such datings demonstrate that the Jewish collections, late as they are and containing as they do such a variety of subject matter, nevertheless undoubtedly are a source of pre-Christian traditions. Since it is admitted that the Gospel was Aramaic and Palestinian before it was Greek and that the New Testament and rabbinical theological idioms go back to a common root, it follows that—using a methodology similar to that employed in comparing Indo-Germanic languages —what the New Testament and rabbinical literature have in common is to be regarded as their linguistic and conceptual possession prior to their separation.

God's gift as Jesus speaks of it has inclusive content. It tenders bread and clothing, and therefore faith has its place also in this sphere. It manifests itself with respect to sin, for God's attitude to it is comprised under the rule: "I forgave thee all that debt, because thou desiredst me." . . . But also the kingdom with its positive values is the gift of God and therefore an object of human petition. . . . In this attitude of Jesus, which promises the divine gift, unlimited, even the highest good, to believing prayer, for its sake alone and only to it, the *sola fide* ["by faith alone"] comes into the world.

Jesus was the hidden one who revealed himself by means of his parables in the man who put the mustard seed in the ground, or in the woman who put the leaven in the dough, and the conception of the synoptists is fully historical, that is to say, it arose out of the view of Jesus himself and the observation of his conduct. But the conception is incomplete. . . . Into the dark earnestness of this portrait of Christ, John brings light by showing that Jesus' only word was not the condemning word, but one that has its presupposition in positive self-witness.

When Paul explained his gospel to the congregation in Rome, he resumed the same line of thought with which he had declared his attitude to Peter at Antioch, according to the Letter to the Galatians. Consequently the individual clauses of Gal. 2:16 provide a summary table of contents of the great argumentative sections of the Letter to the Romans, a remarkable illustration of the value that these convictions had for Paul and of the firmness with which he stated them, convictions that carry his whole message from Antioch to Rome. . . . In Antioch as in Rome, then, Paul's line of thought took its departure from an abandonment of law and works determined by faith. From this point he proceeds to the law of righteousness contained in it, in order to end with an account of its all-sufficiency that makes the whole gift of God the property of man, both for the present and the future.

Do not shove an "as though it were" into the thoughts of the apostle: the believer is to think of himself "as if" he were righteous. This cuts the root of the Pauline concept, for it destroys the act of faith in which it rests. This "as though it were" transposes those impressions that belong to the consciousness of one's own being and conduct to the conduct of God; it is the expression of an inner division, a word of the "doubter." If it is a matter of his own being and doing, then Paul regards himself neither "as it were" just, nor "as it were" unjust, but as unjust in the realest sense, as condemned by God, as handed over to death, and that, eternal death. His being and fate, however, obtain the very opposite character and content by what God has done for him, and the act of faith, which corresponds to the deed of God, consists in the very fact that he knows himself to be just, in the most absolute sense, not merely "as it were" just, and he knows this simply because he knows himself declared just by *God*. . . .

With respect to Christ's resurrection, the believer affirms that God has given him life; his assurance: "I am crucified with Jesus," is carried further in the analogous words: "I was raised from the dead with him," and here also it is nothing else than faith that puts one in possession of life. . . .

By the thoroughgoing dependence of his thought on the turn his life course took as a result of the appearance of Jesus, the Pauline idea of faith proves to be the work of Jesus himself.

In spite of the <u>important reference to the significance of research in the rabbinical literature of late Judaism for the understanding of the New Testament</u> and to the central role of faith in the New Testament, Schlatter's method, built on the presupposition of his own faith, raised a question about the view that had become the prevailing one since Semler, viz., that the New Testament must be studied in accordance with strict historical rules. In his *Geschichte des neutestamentlichen Kanons* [History of the New Testament canon] (1882-92), **Theodor Zahn** led a still more significant attack on the historical view of the New Testament that Semler had pioneered. In this area the view had been widely expressed that it was impossible to speak of a collection of Christian writings as a new "Holy Scripture" before the middle of the second century and that the question of the inclusion of a document in the Canon was one that the *Church* determined. Canonicity, in other words, was a status conferred by the Church.[254] Theodor Zahn, however, the learned connoisseur of ancient church literature, the man whose criticism A. Harnack feared when he published his first writings,[255] and later the author of a strictly conservative *Introduction to the New Testament* as well as of numerous richly informed but very arbitrary commentaries—Theodor Zahn, in the first volume of his (never completed) history of the Canon (the second volume contains only important source studies), attempted to prove that the New Testament "was not brought into being after the middle of the second century by church decree . . . and, on the other hand, was also not the result of a gradual and spontaneous development." On the contrary, "the Catholic Church did not create . . . its New Testament in the second half of the second century but had it transmitted." The collections of the Gospels and of the letters of Paul were, in fact, already in existence before the end of the first century, and the Church had later only passed judgment on the membership in the New Testament of a few other writings.[256]

For more than a hundred years the notion has been abroad among those Protestant theologians who have quarreled with the faith of the Church (and that means with church history) that the Canon of the New Testament came into being after the middle of the second century. The consolidating Catholic Church is said to have equipped itself with this arsenal during the course of its conflict with the gnostic parties, perhaps also in and for the struggle with Montanism. What a few newcomers maintained to begin with, basing their claims on isolated observations, others later attempted to demonstrate more coherently. Today, sometimes with the superior mien of the skilled historian, sometimes in the raucous tone of the demagogue who knows how to impress his rabble, it is made basic to all studies as though it were an assured fact. . . .

It was not a preconceived opinion of the differing character of certain writings or a dogma of the inspiration of the apostolic authors that created the New Testament of the Church and that assured or denied individual books entrance into this collection. On the contrary, it was the actual use of the writings and their authority in the life, and especially in the worship, of the Church, an authority based on tradition, that surrounded them with the nimbus of the holy and that gave rise to the ideas of their supernatural origin and of a value that far outdistanced that of all other literature. Wherever we find these ideas applied to writings of the apostolic age we have sure grounds for believing that a New Testament existed that was esteemed on a level more or less equal to that of the Old Testament. . . .

The doctors of the Church who had occasion to touch on the question [of the origin of the New Testament] express the conviction, without hesitation and without exception, that the New Testament had served the Church from time immemorial as it did in their time. In particular we see the idea expressed in many different ways that the four Gospels, and these alone, had been introduced into church usage from the days of their origin, or from the time of the origin of the several churches that were founded later, a usage that was still basically the ground of their authority. As the oral proclamation of the apostles died out, its place is said to have been taken immediately by the fourfold written Gospel. To be sure, these statements were directed against those who preferred a gospel of another sort, but never in the sense and tone as though such people questioned the fact. It was unquestioned, and only with respect to its significance was it variously assessed. . . . According to the view of the doctors of the Church, what was true of the Gospels was true also of the other major sections of the New Testament. After their composition the letters of Paul were read again and again for edification and instruction in the congregations to which they had been addressed and sometimes were exchanged with each other. The thirteen letters are said to have been known to Marcion as a complete collection when he rejected some of them utterly and arbitrarily abbreviated and otherwise altered the text of others. In like fashion he also rejected the book of the Acts and the Apocalypse, though they had been accepted [by orthodox Christians] long before his time. The Church regarded its New Testament as an inheritance handed down from the beginnings of Christianity. . . .

We found that everywhere about the middle of the second century essentially the same body of apostolic writings that at the end of the century began to be called the New Testament was already in use in church worship and was accorded a place of authority. Even then the Church had one Gospel that was made up of our four Gospels and that included no other. Further, it also had a collection of letters of Paul that included the Pastorals. Luke's book of the Acts had made no less a place for itself in the congregations. The Revelation to John was regarded as a document of divine revelation and as a work of the apostle John. . . .

As its general distribution and recognition already prove, this complex of writings at this time had not attained this status overnight. Marcion no longer had the means at his disposal to undertake a historical criticism of the tradition which enveloped those writings. His own text, which he prepared on the basis of the Church's Bible, proves that those documents already had a text history behind them about 140 and that in particular the Synoptic Gospels had been used in conjunction with each other for a long time. There were two collections which he had before him and made basic to his own new one, a Gospel that consisted of four books, and a collection of thirteen letters of Paul. In addition, several other documents had virtually the same position in the Church, although neither then nor thirty years later was it possible to say that they were joined in one collection or in several.

Zahn was able to defend these theses with the help of a method that A. Harnack could characterize at once in a rejoinder as "a tendency criticism that is worse than that of any Catholic author I have *ever yet* encountered." [257] But the really astounding thing about Zahn's work was not this tendency criticism, but that in his instance the method of historical investigation was used for the purpose of proving that a *well-established* view of the New Testament held by the ancient (and accordingly also the later, conservative) church corresponded to fact. While this put in question the task of New Testament research as a fundamentally and exclusively historical discipline, and thus the legitimacy of all research since Semler and Michaelis, the justification and practicability of such research were now also attacked from an entirely different quarter. In 1870 **Franz Overbeck** came to Basel as professor of New Testament exegesis and ancient church history. In the preface to his new revision of de Wette's commentary on the Acts of the Apostles he had at first acknowledged himself—in spite of material deviations—as a pupil of F. C. Baur with respect to the purely historical consideration of the New Testament text. In his inaugural lecture at Basel he declared that the view of the beginnings of Christianity based on Baur's theories as a purely historical one was fundamentally different from the traditional as well as from the rationalistic, view of Scripture, but that for this very reason it had the task in the present of creating harmony between faith and scientific knowledge.[258]

By the means usually taken by critics until now, I do not believe it possible to give a satisfactory explanation of the fact that the book of the Acts of the Apostles is just as eminently Gentile Christian as it is wretchedly Pauline, and it seems scarcely conceivable to me that a book which assumes toward Judaism and paganism, a stance which is in so general a way characteristic of the ancient church, should be at the same time a product of the simple opposition of parties in the early church. . . .

Furthermore, a book such as the one before us has today to expect the reproach of negativity in the pregnant sense of the word that apologetics has succeeded in naturalizing in linguistic usage and in which it brands as negative everything that vitiates its prejudices. Now, of course, the theological views which my work betrays are not those of apologetics, and that they are anything but indifferent to me as a theologian I do not need to affirm. Nevertheless my commentary is written as little as de Wette's for the sake of a theological thesis. On the contrary, by means of generally accepted methods of exegesis, it seeks only to derive from the text as exactly as possible the historical sense of the book of the Acts which today is the only sense. It may therefore have theological consequences as a byproduct, but not a single line of it was written originally for their sake. . . .

According to custom I am to deliver to you a lecture on this occasion of my inauguration as a professor in the university in this city. As a subject in the field of theology I have chosen the development of and the justification for a purely historical investigation—that is, an investigation that rests on no other presuppositions than those of general historical science—of the origins of Christianity and of its oldest documents. I should like first of all to try to show, by means of a rapid historical survey, that the task of a purely historical understanding of the beginnings of Christianity and of its oldest documents, a task that theology in recent times has pursued so eagerly, is not thrust upon it by the fortuitous skepticism of individuals. Rather, this task has, as it were, been made imperative over the centuries, and theology could do nothing else than take it on, since the solution is just as unavoidable today as it is unattempted in the past. After that I should like at least to try to indicate that the difficulties of the task are inherent in the task itself and that their treatment has brought about a new state of things which no theologian today can ignore. . . .

No weight at all can be given to the general approval with which Baur's individual scientific discoveries were greeted. The main point is that with him theology in general embarked upon a historical treatment of the oldest documents of Christianity. By universally assuming this task, the face of historical theology in general has changed, not just that of a single school. Nowadays the theological criticism that lays claim to the historical foundations of Christianity hitherto taken for granted does not as is frequently maintained, accept the viewpoint of rationalism any more than its theological opponent accepts the viewpoint of the older Protestant orthodoxy. And no more can the one or the other of them think that it has gone back to the point of view of the Reformers. . . .

If then neither the old Protestant orthodoxy nor the earlier rationalism corresponds to the points of view that today oppose each other in the scientific quarrel about early Christianity, are we perhaps to find these viewpoints in Reformation times? Slim chance of that. What today people like to call biblical criticism is not the bold biblical criticism of Luther. And the view of Scripture held by the opponents of that current criticism—to the extent it seeks theological foundation, and that is obviously all we are speaking about here— lacks the coherence of the view of Scripture held by the Reformers. Between the Reformers and all us theologians of the present day who concern ourselves with the beginnings of Christianity and its oldest documents, there is in every instance a most important difference: for us all those beginnings have become a scientific, historical problem in a way that was quite certainly not the case with the Reformers. To say this in other words: the oldest history of Christianity has become "past" to us in a sense that it was not to the Reformers.

It belongs to . . . the nature of theology, which is not a pure science, that from its cluster of problems it does not derive the satisfaction that is so fully experienced by every other science. Serving neither purely religious nor purely scientific interests, it labors at the moral task of bringing about an inner harmony between our faith and our scientific knowledge. . . . So far as the relationship of current biblical criticism to Protestantism is concerned, we do not wish to return to the condition that, whatever results it may finally attain, it only fulfills a task that must have flowed of itself from the Protestant principle of the free investigation of Scripture. We seek an answer only to one question, namely, whether a critical approach which dispenses with the historical presuppositions of earliest Protestantism also necessarily raises the suspicion that it is inimical to Protestantism. . . . It is certain that Protestantism in its youth was happily conscious of being able to call on the freest science of its time for those very presuppositions on which it was founded. A theology that is not always intent on preserving this consciousness for Protestantism would also not be doing justice to its specific Protestant task. . . . Therefore, whatever in other respects its right and necessity may be, i.e., the right and necessity of biblical criticism, whoever works in this discipline will be least in danger of going astray in his work so long as he still retains a moral relationship to Protestantism, so long as he still has a lively memory of the priceless values of purer faith and deeper perception that we owe to criticism and its first valiant champions.

In the second edition of his *Über die Christlichkeit unserer heutigen Theologie* [On the Christianity of our contemporary theology], which first appeared in 1873 and was reissued thirty years later with an introduction and an epilogue, Overbeck denies that a theological view of the New Testament has any justification at all. The expectation of the nearness of the end on the part of early Christians ruled out the possibility of a theological discipline, and even critical theology only pursues the delusion of being able to reanimate Christianity as a religion by theological means. And even more than that, Overbeck insists that "today every theology which . . . restrains the scientific freedom of its teachers abandons its scientific character." [259]

Baur died (Dec. 2, 1860) in the very year that I finished my studies with my examinations for graduation. I was never his personal pupil, and I never even saw him. Consequently I never came into any other than a very "free" relation to his genius that would permit me to call myself in a merely allegorical sense, so-to-speak, "a member of the Tübingen School." Always in this relationship Baur's philosophy of religion, based on Hegel, remained alien to me. What I was able to assimilate from his historical criticism of early Christianity was always limited to what seemed to me the completely victorious battle in behalf of his right to give a purely historical account of early Chrsitianity, that is, an account of it as it actually was, in contrast to the theological apologetics of the time or the pretension of theology to bar him from this right. . . .

Least of all, however, can the fortunes and experiences of Christianity cause us to think of the relationship of faith and knowledge as less filled with conflict. Christianity came into the world with the proclamation of the world's imminent destruction. Its early expectations therefore allowed no more place for a theology than for an earthly history, that is, for virtually none. If Christianity despite this developed a theology more quickly than any other religion, one would nevertheless look in vain in any one of the basic ideas peculiar to it for a special affinity between it and science, since the development can rather be explained fully and easily enough from quite another direction. . . .

The fact is evident enough for calm consideration that Christianity equipped itself with a theology only when it wished to make itself possible in a world that it actually disavowed.

The ancient church, however, was still free of the superstition that the religious perspective concerning a sacred document is to be gained by the use of historical interpretation. In allegorical exegesis it had a sort of surrogate for myth, which was no longer alive. On the other hand, our contemporary theology not only no longer knows anything of another interpretation of the Christian books of religion than the historical, but in general pays homage to the almost incomprehensible delusion that it can again become certain about Christianity by the historical method—an accomplishment, however, which if it were to be achieved would result at most in a religion of scholars, that is to say, in nothing that can seriously be compared with a genuine religion. . . .

If liberal theology believes it must continue the battle it has undertaken and do so in the forms in which it has hitherto been waged; . . . and if it does not wish to destroy the ground under its feet and create a disorder that will prevent any real progress, it will in any case have no other recourse than more unreservedly to embrace the scholarship to which it owes what independent power it possesses and more earnestly to reflect on the extent to which it can still call its efforts Christian. . . .

If the theological teacher has any responsibility whatever in terms of scholarship it can be none other than to make known the new truth he has found and which he is convinced he can demonstrate, while a theology that is generally open to more than the dim suspicion of suppressing the truth under the appearance of its proclamation must soon be overwhelmed by the weight of general contempt.

Let me then without further ado expose the chief damage I have done to the *whole* intercourse between my hearers and myself by saying that it consists in this, that I have stubbornly refused to be the theologian, that is, the counselor, that they especially sought to discover in me. Our community lacked such a theologian, and I was not able to provide him. He was not to be found on my rostrum—on which a teacher stood who attempted to interpret the New Testament and also to give an account of the history of the Church to students who were to be instructed in Christianity *so far as possible without tendentious concerns.*

Overbeck wrote those remarks from the point of view of complete skepticism, a skepticism that, to be sure, only declared in public that it had never experienced any love for theology, but that to unpublished notes confided the confession: "As professor of theology I have kept my basic unbelief to myself, both on the rostrum and in all my relationships with the students committed to my care." [260] But we are not discussing the human problem of why Overbeck in spite of this retains his theological chair until his sixtieth year.[261] We are concerned only with the fact that here, with an ultimate consistency that is still more apparent in the unpublished matter, the right of a theologian to any historical view of the New Testament is put in question on the grounds that only a completely profane interpretation of the New Testament, that is, one that leaves out of consideration every normative meaning, can make any claim to be scholarly. The *theological* task of a *historical* study of the New Testament is in this way denied from the point of view of *radical* unfaith, much as it was denied by Schlatter or Zahn, and thereby the whole development of New Testament scholarship since Semler was characterized as a wrong path.[262]

The interpretation of a text is the main part of his historical adventure. Whoever views a text historically, of whatever sort this text may be—the satires of Petronius or the Fourth Gospel—has above all else to discipline himself. In other words, so far as scientific exegesis is concerned, there is no difference between sacred and profane texts. All stand in need and are worthy of the same protection against the mayhem of the absurd subjectivity of their interpreters. No one forgets this more than theology, whose exegesis rests on the presupposition of the difference that has just been denied, and no theology more than modern theology, whose arbitrariness in the treatment of its sacred texts in the inundation of these texts with worthless hypotheses appears actually as a symptom of the sacredness of these texts. . . .

The cold-blooded contempt with which modern theology has accustomed itself to speak of the allegorical interpretation is better understood when it is observed that this theology nurses the illusion that in the interests of its exegesis it has created a substitute for the allegory it has abandoned. However, allegorical interpretation of Scripture is plainly the same thing as theological interpretation. All theological exegesis (because it assumes that it has words before it in Scripture with which the subjective fantasy of the author has nothing, or at least nothing essential, to do) must make the greatest demands on the fantasy of the interpreter. An exegesis that is to be taken seriously in terms of its theological reference still does that today, even when it no longer intends to be allegorical. The only difference is that the allegorical interpretation does this more unswervingly, more heartily, and more effectively, and therefore represents theological exegesis most perfectly. *All theological exegesis is allegorical,* shamefacedly or unashamedly, or it is no longer theological exegesis at all, but only a means for, in this sense, getting rid of texts that theological exegesis is at pains to retain in their religious authority. In all this it is still a real question who the "freer" are, the ancient, uncritical allegorists, or the modern, covert ones. The former treated their texts with reverence, but asserted *themselves* and their fantasy all the more in a carefree way. The latter pull the texts down off their pedestal, but at the same time are only the more concerned to rein themselves in and hold themselves back. Only the clear critical methods of scholarship make the interpreter really free, even if he thinks he is able to rejoice in his freedom only within the fold of theology.

But the peculiar thing is that Overbeck's fundamental skepticism vis-à-vis the proclamation of the New Testament opened his eyes to two essential facts, to whose safeguarding and clarification New Testament research has repeatedly devoted itself since the end of the nineteenth century. As early as his book, *Uber die Christlichkeit unserer heutigen Theologie* [On the Christianity of our contemporary theology], he pointed on the one hand to "the early Christian expectation of the imminent return of Christ" and its nonfulfillment and therewith recognized the importance of the expectation of the imminence of the end for the whole New Testament world of thought and its development.[263] But on the other hand, and even more importantly, Overbeck also drew attention to the fact that primitive Chrisitan literature down to the time of the Apostolic Fathers, is differentiated on the basis of its own literary form from patristic literature, which modeled itself on Graeco-Roman forms. By this Overbeck not only coined the idea of "early Christian literature," a literature that differed markedly from all later writings, but also saw that this primal literature can be recognized by its literary *forms.* In this way Overbeck anticipated the fundamental observations of "form-critical" study of primitive Christianity, however little (on the basis of his presuppositions) he was able to recognize the connection of the literary forms of the primitive literature with the religious forces of the expectation of the imminent end and with the special nature of the primitive Christian congregations determined by it.[264]

A literature has its history in its forms, and consequently every true history of literature will be a history of form. . . . The Gospels, the Acts of the Apostles, and the Apocalypse are historical forms that disappear at a quite definite point of time in the life of the Christian Church. To be more specific, not only are they actually lacking from this point on in the church's literature, but there is also no possibility at all of their further cultivation. . . .

There was a long time during which the real literary forms that are represented in the New Testament were also living forms, when, for example, in addition to our canonical Gospels many other writings of this sort came into being, among which the four of our Canon may have stood out from early times because of their reputation, but without the claim of exhausting the possibilities of their literary genre or of being basically different from other existing gospels. Looked at in this way, however, the New Testament appears only as the most distinguished remnant of a Christian primitive literature which existed prior to the literature that has alone survived with the Church. . . .

Now that the range of early Christian literature in general is determined as above, we need make only a general observation, suggested by the fragments of this primitive literature we are shortly to survey. It is a literature which Christianity, so to speak, creates out of its own resources, to the extent that it developed exclusively on the ground and on the special inner interests of the Christian Church before its intermixture with the world surrounding it. Not that the forms of this literature would be absolutely new even quite apart from the general method of expression of the language in which it appears, in so far as it is at all possible to speak of forms in it. That can be maintained only of the gospel form, which is really the single original form with which Christianity has enriched literature. The form of the apocalypse, on the other hand, is Jewish. In the area of apocalyptic, as the Christian Sibylline oracles and other writings show, Christianity did not disdain even pagan forms but even here for the most part followed Jewish precedent. All that is worthy of notice here is that, where this primitive literature of Christianity makes use of forms with which it has already been provided, it draws only on the forms of the *religious* literature of earlier times. The forms that it actually wholly avoids, however, are those of the *secular* literature that was in being, and therefore to that extent it can be called, if not purely Christian, yet purely religious. Now, the most important phenomenon of the history of Christian literature in its earliest period is just this, that this breed of Christian literature that is designated as Christian primitive literature and is characterized in general as described above, came to an early end, and did not produce the Christian literature that remained alive with the Church and that in its ancient period is usually called patristic.

The radical objections on the part of biblicists and conservatives, as on the part of skeptics, to the investigation of the New Testament that began with Semler and Michaelis and that works basically according to historical methodology, would necessarily have led, of course, to a rethinking of their presuppositions. But the problems that arose because of the idealistic, liberal interpretation of the New Testament and the consequent isolation of primitive Christianity were at first all too pressing, and consequently the urgently necessary rethinking of New Testament research came about only after a detour that led by way of a still more radical historical consideration of primitive Christianity.

Part V
The History-of-Religions School of New Testament Interpretation

1.
The Pioneers of the History-of-Religions School and Their Opponents

While on the one hand the liberal view of Christianity indicated an almost complete isolation of primitive Christianity within its historical environment (thus for instance, A. Harnack), yet on the other hand there were scholars of liberal persuasion such as Lüdemann and Holtzmann who drew attention to the connection of early Christian thinking with the Judaism and Hellenism of its time and even emphasized the *dominant* importance of Hellenistic influence on Paul. And as early as 1868 the Heidelberg church historian **Adolf Hausrath**, when he wrote his first *Neutestamentliche Zeitgeschichte* [History of New Testament times], had pioneered an effort which was obviously necessary for a strictly historical view: to "incorporate New Testament history once more into the contemporary historical milieu in which it stood while it was still in course; to view it . . . as part of a general historical process." [265] But even though Hausrath in all essentials accepted the Tübingen School's historical reconstruction and that of the liberal interpreters of Jesus and wrote for a wider circle of readers, he failed to bring the living description of New Testament times into a genuine, historical connection with the development of primitive Christianity. It was more important that already another representative of a modified Tübingen picture of history, **Adolf Hilgenfeld,** had drawn attention for the first time (1857) to Jewish apocalyptic as an important element in the prehistory of Christianity and had pointed out that "no connection, or at least no direct connection, [exists] between Old Testament prophecy and Christianity," but that "pre-Christian Judaism itself comprised a preparation for the Christian era." In Jewish apocalyptic Hilgenfeld saw a development toward the inner purification that prepares "for the universalism of the Christian kingdom of God." [266]

The insight into the significance of the Jewish prehistory of primitive Christianity for the historical understanding of the New Testament that is evident here caused **Emil Schürer** to write the first strictly scientific *History of New Testament Times* (1874). Schürer, to be sure, limited himself strangely to Judaism, because paganism could "not count as a historical condition and presupposition of Christianity after the fashion of Judaism." The later, greatly expanded editions of this basic work therefore bear the title, *Geschichte des jüdischen Volkes im Zeitalter Jesu Christi* [A history of the Jewish people in the time of Jesus Christ]. This work not only draws most carefully on all sources and on the whole body of literature to give an account of the political and religious history of the Jewish people from the time of the Maccabees to the destruction of Jerusalem, but also evaluates this history with all fundamental objectivity from the vantage point of its effluence in primitive Christianity. Consequently the dissolution of "ethics and theology . . . into jurisprudence" and the significance of the messianic hope for this very "zeal for the Law" are heavily stressed, because this "fearful load that false legalism had foisted on the shoulders of the people" can then be judged from the standpoint of primitive Christianity as a righteousness that "is not true and well-pleasing to God." [267]

It was **Otto Pfleiderer**, however, one of the last of F. C. Baur's pupils, who was the first to use the findings of the history of religions for the purpose of representing primitive Christianity consistently as the product of a development in connection with the religions of its time, and he therefore "became the father of history-of-religions theology in Germany." [268] The theology of Paul, with which Pfleiderer begins his account of early Christianity,[269] is explained as a combination of Pharisaic-Jewish and Hellenistic-Jewish ideas with primitive Christian faith in Jesus' death and resurrection, so that Paul's thinking can be characterized as "Christianized Pharisaism" and as "Christianized Hellenism." Pfleiderer has to admit that, because of "abrupt juxtaposition of both disparate elements, . . . gaping holes" are evident throughout all of Pauline theology, but he believes that by this assumption he can explain how post-Pauline Christianity came into being as a Christianized Hellenism by purging this Pauline ideological mixture of its Pharisaic-Jewish elements. And in passing Pfleiderer even points out that perhaps also direct influences from the piety of the Hellenistic mystery cults are to be observed in Paul. With this not only the separation of primitive Christianity from its Old Testament-Jewish native soil was accomplished historically, but the history-of-religions method of research in early Christianity that he practiced also serves expressly to explain Christianity as a product of the development of the spirit of classical antiquity and therewith to abandon the *theological* formulation of the question in favor of a purely history-of-religions approach as the only appropriate one for New Testament research.[270]

Because I can . . . no more agree with Ritschl's view of early Christianity than retain Baur's, *still another* possibility seems to me to be open, which is so obvious and simple that it is a matter of amazement that it was not recognized long ago as the only right one. Since the Gentile Christian World Church was planted by the Pauline proclamation of Christ on soil long made ready by pre-Christian Hellenism, this very Hellenism and that very proclamation of Christ were from the outset the two factors from whose combination the peculiarity of Gentile Christianity is naturally explained and from whose mutual relation of penetration or separation, of the predominance or subordination of the one or the other factor, the different forms of development of the early Christian and the ancient Christian method of teaching can be understood without forcing the evidence.

The glib sophistry and dialectic of the Greek philosophers could only repel the strict Pharisee and rabbinical student as a sham wisdom, puffed up with unrealities. But that does not prevent Paul also from coming under the influence of the Greek manner of thought indirectly by way of the Hellenistic-Jewish literature. Indeed, we shall have to make a dominant place especially for the Alexandrian Book of Wisdom among the sources of Pauline theology. One might even go so far as to say that his Christian theology would never have become what it is if he had not also drunk deeply of Greek wisdom as it would reach him through the medium of the Hellenistic Judaism of Alexandria. . . .

The teaching of the Apostle Paul, therefore, had its twofold root in the two historically emergent forms of Jewish theology of his time: it combines both ways of thinking by relating both to the new center, the faith in the death and resurrection of the Messiah Jesus, and by attempting from this central idea to solve the still unsolved problems in an original way. So Paul created a new religious world outlook whose organizing principle consists in the Christian faith in the crucified and exalted Jesus Christ, but whose elements are taken on the one hand from Pharisaic theology and on the other from Hellenistic theosophy. . . .

From Pharisaic theology comes the group of ideas of the state of sleep of the dead, of their simultaneous resurrection, and of a subsequent solemn act of judgment upon which a transformation of earthly conditions is to follow, as well as a metamorphosis of the life of nature, by the freeing of it from enslavement to transitoriness. . . . On the other hand, from Hellenistic theology, drenched through and through with Platonic idealism, comes the idea that the earthly body is a prison house of the soul, which has its true home in the heavenly world into which the pious Christian will enter immediately upon the laying aside of his earthly body (without, therefore, experiencing the intermediate state of sleep) and in which he will be at home with the Lord in untroubled blessedness, no longer subject to the judgment, and clothed with a new body woven of heavenly light, a body that has nothing to do with conditions as we know them on earth. . . .

With this new hope for the future as Christianity's inheritance from Plato, the older Jewish-Christian conceptions now stand in such immediate juxtaposition that it is simply impossible to get a unified picture of Pauline eschatology.

In all this we have found confirmed the expectations to which the Jewish-Greek education of Saul-Paul the Hellenist and Pharisee naturally gave rise: the Pharisaic and the Hellenistic ways of thinking form the two currents which in Paulinism flow through one channel, yet without being really united. The two disparate lines of thought run alongside one another, sometimes mutually complementary, sometimes contradictory or mutually exclusive. This state of matters may, from the logical point of view, appear a defect, and it is certainly a "crux" for such theologians as believe themselves under obligation to construct a Pauline "system of doctrine." The historical investigator, however, will not only find the situation psychologically quite intelligible, but must also recognize that it is precisely this characteristic of the Pauline theology on which its great historical significance was based, and which enabled it to guide Christianity in its expansion beyond the narrow framework of a Jewish-Messianic community into a world-religion. The link of transition could only be a theology which, like the Pauline, shows two faces, and which, to change the metaphor, plants one foot upon the specifically Jewish or Pharisaic system of thought while setting the other well within the circle of thought which was common to both the religiously disposed heathen of the time and to the Jews of the Diaspora who had a Greek education. This circle of thought was Hellenism, which thus united the two highest achievements of the religious spirit of pre-Christian mankind: the Jewish belief in God, and the Platonic belief in immortality. . . . Thus it was that the theology of the Church came into being; not, as is erroneously assumed, by Jewish Christianity having prevailed over Paulinism, but quite the contrary, by the expurgation of the specifically Jewish (Pharisaic) elements from Paulinism and the free further development of his universally intelligible Hellenistic side. But it is also incorrect to regard this as a corruption of Paulinism by introducing foreign pagan elements. The "pagan element" actually means the noble Platonic idealism that was already in Paulinism itself and that actually made it possible for it to win the Graeco-Roman world for Christianity. The faith of the Gentile Christian Church is not a defection or relapse, but the natural further development of the Hellenism that Paul Christianized. Consequently the basic condition for understanding the ancient church is the understanding of Paulinism. But a theology which seeks to explain Paulinism only from the Old Testament is incapable of such an understanding. . . .

It may be recalled in this connection that the reception into the Eleusinian Mysteries was also thought of as a kind of new birth, and that the hierophant especially designated for temple duty had to take a sacramental bath, from which he emerged as a "new man" with a new name and in which "the former was forgotten," that is, the old man together with the old name was laid aside. —May we be permitted to ask whether Paul, when he wrote Rom. 6 from Corinth, was not familiar with this rite of the Eleusinian Mysteries, this "bath of new birth," and described the sacramental significance of the Christian rite after this model? Just as he draws on the analogy of the pagan sacrificial meal to describe the Lord's Supper, so also his mystical conception of baptism could stand in direct relation to that of the Greek mysteries.

I have become more and more strongly convinced in the course of these studies how much that is helpful for the understanding of primitive Christianity is to be learned from the comparison with extra-biblical Jewish, and heathen, religious history and how indispensable, indeed, such comparison is for the elucidation of some of the most important questions. I am well aware that, to many, my practice of drawing parallels from the sphere of heathen religion will appear superfluous, while to some it will even be offensive. In Germany, even more than elsewhere, it is still customary to take up a shy and suspicious attitude towards the application of the scholarly discipline of comparative religion within the field of biblical theology. The few who venture to make use of it draw on themselves, as I know from my own experience, the reproach of "paganizing." That, however, has never made me waver in my conviction, which has remained unshaken ever since I learned under my revered teacher, Ferdinand Christian Baur, that Christianity as a historical phenomenon is to be investigated by the same methods as all other history, and that, in particular, its origin is to be understood by being studied as the normal outcome of the manifold factors in the religious and ethical life of the time. Even though the way in which Baur conceived this development was not, as we all know now, quite accurate in detail, yet the principle of development, which he introduced into the historical study of theology, retains its position by an incontestable right—a position which the temporary reactionary tendency of traditionalism and dogmatic positivism will not ultimately affect in the slightest degree. I believe, moreover, that this tendency is already on the wane, and that the time is not far distant when the application to biblical theology of the historical and comparative methods of the scientific study of religion will be generally welcomed.

When this takes place, people will be able to convince themselves that this scientific investigation of its history in no way endangers the stability of the Christian religion. Quite the contrary. So long as Christianity is conceived of as a miracle, whether unique or repeated, its truth is always more or less problematical for the men of our critical age. But when it is recognized as the necessary outcome of the development of the religious spirit of our race, towards the production of which the whole history of the ancient world was moving onward, in the shaping of which the mental and spiritual acquisitions of the East and West have found their application, their enhancement, and their higher unity—when this is recognized, it becomes, in my opinion, the most solid and imposing apology for Christianity which it is possible to conceive. Of course, the historical investigator ought not to allow himself to be guided in the treatment of particulars by an apologetic purpose, but should seek to discover, with the utmost possible precision, exactly how things were. The more loyally he strives after the attainment of objective truth in his exposition of the manifold concurrent causes, the more certainly will the general result take the form of a defense of essential Christianity.

From various directions this task of understanding primitive Christianity in light of the history of religions was attacked, but without an awareness of the methodological problems involved or of the consequences implicit in Pfleiderer's research. **C. F. Georg Heinrici** is the first to make extensive use of parallels from Hellenism to help in the understanding of Paul's language and of the social forms of the Pauline congregations.

But at the same time he emphasizes that because of Paul's connection with the Old Testament and with the proclamation of the primitive church his thinking is original.[271]

The most ancient social forms of Christianity are wholly original, but are not suspended in midair. Because of the incompleteness of our sources, our knowledge of them is very fragmentary. . . . but these sources can be increased if we methodically take related materials into consideration. . . . To be sure, analogies may not be used as a boy uses any stones whatever to throw at an arbitrarily chosen target. However, where certain layers of social and spiritual life lie in the clear light of history, while in the case of other darker layers a series of indications points to corresponding forms, we are actually compelled to bring the dark into contact with the light, the indistinct with the clear, in order to test the former with *reagents,* that is, to investigate whether the analogies cited do not throw a fuller light on the vital forces and vital forms of the area to be illuminated. Consequently I have compared the symptoms of community life at Corinth with information from Greek and Roman social groups. . . . Investigations of ideas and vocabulary are governed by the same principles. By examining ideas in the light of their sources and vocabulary against the area from which it is drawn, it is possible to reach solid ground for a knowledge of the elements of the Pauline life of the spirit. . . .

The whole doctrinal content of the [Corinthian] letters arises out of the need for an intensive reckoning with the nature and ground of the apostle's missionary proclamation. His training provides him with the forms for this account. These . . . in large part are determined by contacts with Hellenistic culture. . . .

The way he addresses himself to the moral consciousness, advances reasons upon reasons, in order by so doing to win over the judgment of the readers for himself, yes, even the transition formulas and the summaries he employs— all this stands in closest relation to the dialectical method of the Stoic Epictetus, who preached rather than taught. . . .

So the apostle transports us by his theological asseverations, in spite of their historical limitation, to a thoroughly original circle of ideas, by which means he achieved something that Philo and, before him, Plato and the Stoa had struggled for in vain: a vital connection between religion and morality. He owed his ability to do so in the first instance to his Christian insight and then to the Old Testament, while on the other hand he was able to work fruitfully as a teacher of Gentiles because he appropriated for Christianity the truth of ethnic culture. . . .

The linguistic character of the letters, which is not Hebraic, but moves throughout within the framework of Hellenistic Greek, provides the test of the correctness of the results we have so far obtained. It could be demonstrated that actual Hebraisms . . . are scarcely to be found, but that the occasional turns of phrase that indicate Old Testament influence can be explained by an intimate familiarity with the Septuagint and a manifold use of it, based to a large extent on memory. On the other hand, there is such an accumulation of analogies with Polybius, the classicist of Hellenism, with Epictetus, with Plutarch, with Dionysius of Halicarnassus, and others that it can only be explained by a common spiritual sphere of life.

In his reference to the connection of the Pauline congregations with the societies of their religious environment, Heinrici had taken his departure for the investigation of early church order from the presupposition (virtually unchallenged around 1880) that "church" must be a society and "office" must be administrative office.[272] In his lectures on *The Organization of the Early Christian Churches* (1881), the Anglican **Edwin Hatch,** on the basis of the same presuppositions, laid considerably greater stress on the connection of the order of the Christian Church with that of the Greek associations,[273] so that the Christian congregations appeared simply as a special form of the religious associations of their time.[274]

When the truths of Christianity were first preached, especially in the larger towns of the Roman Empire, the aggregation of those who accepted those truths into societies was thus not an isolated phenomenon. Such an aggregation does not appear to have invariably followed belief. There were many who stood apart; and there were many reasons for their doing so. . . . We consequently find that the union of believers in associations had to be preached, if not as an article of the Christian faith, at least as an element of Christian practice. . . . After the sub-apostolic age these exhortations cease. The tendency to association had become a fixed habit. The Christian communities multiplied, and persecution forged for them a stronger bond of unity. But to the eye of the outside observer they were in the same category as the associations which already existed. They had the same names for their meetings, and some of the same names for their officers. The basis of association, in the one case as the other, was the profession of a common religion.

Now in the Christian communities there appears to have been from very early times a body of officers: it must be inferred from the identity of the names which were employed that those officers were in relation to the Christian communities what the senate was in relation to a municipality, and what the committee was in reference to an association. . . . In their general capacity as a governing body they were known by names which were in current use for a governing body; in their special capacity as administrators of Church funds they were known by a name which was in current use for such administrators [= bishops]. . . .

It seems certain upon the evidence that in these Jewish communities, to which in the first instance the Apostles naturally addressed themselves, there existed a governing body of elders whose functions were partly administrative and partly disciplinary. . . .

Consequently, when the majority of the members of a Jewish community were convinced that Jesus was the Christ, there was nothing to interrupt the current of their former life. There was no need for secession, for schism, for a change in the organization. The old form of worship and the old modes of government could still go on. . . .

The origin of the presbyterate in those Christian communities which had been Jewish is thus at once natural and simple: its origin in those communities of which the members or a majority of the members were Gentiles is equally natural, though rather more complex. Two elements have to be accounted for: (1) the fact of government by a council or committee, (2) the fact that the members of such council or committee were known by a name which implies seniority.

(1) In regard to the first of these elements, the evidence shows that government by a council or committee was all but universal in the organizations with which Christianity came into contact. The communal idea which underlay the local government of Palestine had in fact survived in the Graeco-Roman world. Every municipality of the Empire was managed by its curia or senate. Every one of the associations, political or religious, with which the Empire swarmed had its committee of officers. It was therefore antecedently probable, even apart from Jewish influence, that when the Gentiles who had embraced Christianity began to be sufficiently numerous in a city to require some kind of organization, that organization should take the prevailing form. . . .

(2) In regard to the second element, we find the idea of respect for seniority in many places and in many forms. So strong was this idea that the terms which were relative to it were often used as terms of respect without reference to age. . . . There was thus an antecedent probability, apart from Jewish influence, not only that the Christian communities, when organized, would be governed by a council, but also that in the appointment of the members of such a council seniority would be a prime qualification. And this we find to have been in fact the case. Out of the several names which the members of the Christian councils bore one ultimately survived the rest: they continue to be known to modern times as "presbyters.". . .

If we look at contemporary organizations, we find that the tendency towards the institution of a president was almost, if not altogether, universal. . . . Whether we look at the municipal councils, at the private associations, religious and secular, with which the East was honeycombed, at the provincial assemblies, at the boards of magistrates, at the administrative councils of the Jews both in Palestine and in the countries of the dispersion, or at the committees of the municipal councils whose members sometimes bore in common with the Christian and the Jewish councils the name of "elders" (πρεσβύτερος) , we find in every case evidence of the existence of a presiding officer.

Now although the existence of such a general drift in contemporary organizations by no means proves that the Christian communities were borne along with it, still it establishes a basis of probability for the inference that communities which were so largely in harmony with those organizations in other respects, were in harmony with them also in this.

The main propositions in which the results of that examination may be summed up are two—

(1) That the development of the organization of the Christian Churches was gradual:

(2) That the elements of which that organization were composed were already existing in human society. . . .

But in dealing with them I have arrived at and set forth the view, in regard to the first of them, that the development was slower than has sometimes been supposed, and, in regard to the second, that not only some but *all* the elements of the organization can be traced to external sources.

In 1883 the Greek text of an early Christian writing, found in a hitherto unknown medieval manuscript, was published for the first time—"The

Teaching of the Lord through his Twelve Apostles" (the *Didache*, presumably from the beginning of the second century),[275] a document which among other things contains directions for the conduct of various ecclesiastical officeholders. On the basis of this new source and other early Christian writings, **A. Harnack** soon declared that it can now be seen that "in the oldest Christian congregations the proclaimers of the Word of God held the highest rank and that these consisted of Apostles, Prophets, and Teachers," but that according to the same sources "these Apostles, Prophets, and Teachers were not regarded as officials of the individual congregation, but were honored as preachers appointed by God and designated to the whole Church." And he added: "So far as the origin of the institution of the Apostles, Prophets, and Teachers is concerned, we have to regard it for the present as a free creation of the Christian churches—the oldest, in fact." [276] On the basis of the witness of this new source, then, it became doubtful that the *whole* development of early Christian order was dependent on institutions in its environment, and it was also recognized that in early Christianity there was an idea of the *whole Church* and an articulation of that idea that rested on purely religious presuppositions. Harnack, however, continued to hold fast to the concept of the Christian congregations and their offices as religious societies with their officers, and consequently to insist on a connection of the early Christian communities with the religious societies of their cultural setting.

But precisely these sociological and religio-scientific presuppositions were utterly denied by the jurist **Rudolf Sohm** in his *Kirchenrecht* [Church law], a book that appeared in 1892. Sohm's thesis became a celebrated one: "Church law stands in contradiction to the essence of the Church." To support it Sohm denies that the individual congregation had the character of an association—for that matter, that it had any organization at all—because "church" designates Christianity as a whole, whose organization is "not juridical but charismatic organization." [277] Since therefore the original Church and its "organization" are charismatic in kind, we have to assume a genuine Christian development and cannot think in terms of an adoption by Christianity of religious forms of its milieu. Now Sohm's thesis of the completely antithetical nature of Church and law in primitive Christianity has had the most persistent influence in this area of historico-theological study, despite objection raised to it.[278] For the development of New Testament research, however, it was not this thesis that was of fundamental significance, but the fact that "Harnack practiced throughout a profane and Sohm a strictly religious, method of viewing [church history]." In this way Sohm, from a point of view that in fact was not strictly historical, pushed aside every history-of-religions interpretation of primitive Christian history, but suggested instead that for primitive Christianity "the Church is not from below but from above, not man's work but God's work." [279] But it was not without consequences that it was a non-theologian who turned away from the emerging history-of-religions study of the New Testament and turned back to a point of view that in the narrower sense of the word is theological. The arbitrary use of sources on the part of Sohm the jurist and the extreme form of his fundamental theses meant that his conclusions were almost entirely rejected by theologians, and the result of this was that his important theological findings had at first no effects.[280]

According to the prevailing point of view today, the axiom that office in the Christian Church was originally *not a teaching office,* and therefore *not a spiritual office* in terms of modern church law, is regarded as the most conspicuous and at the same time the most assured result of research. The original task of congregational office, it is held, was that of administration. . . . By means of disciplinary and administrative or cultic activity the office represents the external order of the congregation and therefore exhibits originally "a character that in the widest sense can be called political" (A. Ritschl). It represents, according to the dominant hypothesis, in the main what we might call a secular office, such as we see in corporations, and is inevitably an office which serves the *organization,* the government of the congregation as such, but not the proclamation of the divine Word. . . . According to the prevailing view, then, there were two organizations in the Christian congregation of the earliest period (*ca.* A.D. 60) that are clearly to be distinguished from each other: on the one hand an organization for *teaching,* which rests simply on *charisma* and has nothing to do with external order and administration in the congregation, and on the other an organization for leadership and *administration,* which represents the striving of the congregation for a *system of government* based on law and that gives birth to its organs of management. . . . This basic conception supports the other, viz., that the constitution of the congregation represented originally a kind of *association constitution.*

Until recently the view commonly held was that the oldest constitution of a congregation was modeled on that of the Jewish synagogue. More recently this idea has given way to the other, namely, that at least for the Gentile Christian congregations the closest model for their organization must be sought in the pagan associations of the Roman Empire, associations whose constitution, though with many variations, reflected the constitution of the city and state of the day. According to the former view, the constitution of the Christian congregation would be of Jewish, according to the latter, of pagan, origin. . . . The most recent literature has given up the effort to explain the constitution of the Christian congregation as a copy of that of the synagogue or the pagan association. . . . The finding has prevailed that the constitution of the Christian congregation represents an *original* product of the Christian spirit.

The Church is Christianity as a whole, the Body of Christ, the Bride of the Lord—a spiritual entity, unrelated to earthly norms, including law.

Not that the Church signifies a purely abstract power, remaining invisibly, inactively, and silently in the dark background. On the contrary, the Church is visibly and actively in all the assemblies within Christianity. Indeed, it is likewise visible and active in the gifts of grace that are bestowed upon individual Christians in order to summon them to the service of Christianity. It has its organs, but it is impossible for its organization to be of a legal nature.

If then the great venture must be made and the way into the area of the sources of primitive Christianity be taken with the courage of an explorer—many tracks lead in, but few lead out—a further barrier soon appears in the way of the advancing jurist. A new world soon engulfs him, the world of the Christian life of faith that exercises its power over the whole being of Christianity and in which he is unable to see anything with a jurist's eyes or grasp anything with a jurist's hands. Loose thy shoes from off thy foot; for the place whereon thou standest is holy! Christianity came into the world in an unearthly way, supernaturally. You will never understand it unless you yourself have drunk from the wondrous goblet whose contents assuage the thirst of the soul. Drink, and you will never thirst again. Drink, and you will discover a new world that you have never seen before, the world of the spiritual, overarching, eclipsing the world of the earthly. It is this very world of the spiritual that we must behold if the generation of church law and all its subsequent history are to be understood.

But this world of the spiritual cannot be comprehended with judicial concepts. More than this, its essence stands in opposition to the essence of law. The spiritual essence of the Church excludes every ecclesiastical legal order. The formulation of church law arose in contradiction to the essence of the Church. This fact dominates the history of church law from the earliest era to our own time. And this is the very fact that must be made clear.

Sohm's act of turning away from the religio-historical view of early Christianity had no effect to begin with because the interpretation of the New Testament in light of its environment proved itself in the most varied areas far too influential and far too fruitful. In fact, in the year 1888 no less than three works appeared that showed the importance of the religio-historical research for the historical understanding of the New Testament. From F. C. Baur's time, Jesus' expectation of his speedy return had repeatedly been declared to be impossible, and Jesus accordingly had been detached from the Judaism of his time.[281] The Alsatian pastor **Wilhelm Baldensperger** broke with this pattern. In his study of *Das Selbstbewusstsein Jesu* [Jesus' self-consciousness] he took his departure explicitly from the statement that such an investigation "becomes possible . . . [only] when one takes the messianic world of faith of Judaism into account: indeed, it is in this frame, according to all our sources, that Jesus' picture [of himself] is set, and we have no *a priori* reason to tear it out of that frame." Baldensperger accordingly points out that the Jewish apocalyptic signifies the "renunciation of secular political ideals and the intensification of messianic expectations into the realm of the supernatural," and that therefore the "soil in which Christianity took root" has become known to us. For Jesus' proclamation of the kingdom of God "has . . . undeniably a *messianically*

216

eschatological coloring, that is, it bears the stamp of its origin." Balden-sperger also shrinks by no means from drawing the conclusion that "the founder of Christianity appears less separable from the soil of Judaism than many believe," but then, to be sure, seeks to show on his own part that the work of the *Messiah* in Jesus' instance, in contrast to Judaism, is sustained by religious motives. "It breaks out of *eschatology* and flows into *soteriology*." [282] So in the end, then, the religio-historical view is robbed of its ultimate efficacy by a dogmatic judgment.

In the same way the Rhenish pastor **Otto Everling**, in a study of the Pauline concepts of angels and demons, showed perhaps even more clearly that "the Pauline expressions [are] to be understood in light of the ideas of the apostolic age," and that therefore we have to "become acquainted with contemporary ideas in this area" if we wish to understand Paul correctly. The examination of the whole body of apocryphal and pseud-epigraphical literature of Judaism demonstrates that numerous Pauline statements are traditional, but at the same time it also shows "that exeget-ical science . . . still continues to have the urgent task of effacing, spir-itualizing, and rationalistically modernizing none of the distinctive color of the biblical concepts." On the contrary, the insight into the kinship of the Pauline concepts with those of late Jewish literature demands that we "now understand such expressions of the apostle also within the ideo-logical framework of the time which produced and read such books." It is thereby clear that the task of a historical understanding of New Testament concepts was undertaken with full earnestness, but it is also clear that such an attempt associates the Pauline ideas with conceptual forms "that are highly uncongenial to our way of thinking." [283] And in the same year **Hermann Gunkel** (later an Old Testament scholar), whose first scholarly work examined *Die Wirkungen des heiligen Geistes nach der populären Anschauung der apostolischen Zeit und nach der Lehre des Apostels Paulus* [*The activities of the Holy Spirit according to the popular view of apostolic times and according to the teaching of the apostle Paul*], declared: "Wherever the attempt is made to derive the Pauline circle of ideas, or even the Pauline linguistic usage, directly from the Old Testament, wherever, therefore, the apostle's origin in Judaism is ignored, there we encounter a serious methodological error that must result in a great many misunderstandings. Rather, we can be concerned only with the question of whether Paul is dependent on Pales-tinian or on Hellenistic Judaism." And he expressly advanced the opinion that "in his anthropological expressions and views, if anywhere, Paul will make use of contemporary concepts." Against this methodological background, then, Gunkel concluded that Paul shares "the popular view of the New Testament age," according to which men thought of themselves "in the 'Spirit' . . . the supernatural power of God which works in man and through man." And Gunkel also declared that "so far as naïve realism is concerned, earliest Christianity [is] not [to be distinguished] in any respect from Judaism," and that "the interpreter is not to be troubled by this realism." Here also, then, by relating New Testament thinking to that of its times there is a new recognition that for Paul "the possession of this ζωὴ 'Ιησοῦ [life of Jesus] . . . [is] a reality to him." At the same time, however, by the proof that, according to the early Christian view, "the effect of the Spirit [is] . . . not an intensification of the natural [spirit] that is in all men, but [is] *the absolutely supernatural and consequently divine,*" the early Christian world of thought is made strange and puzzling to the consciousness of modern man, without as yet bringing the theological consequences of this insight into the open.[284]

This placement of early Christianity in its environment had necessarily to raise the urgent question of the relationship of the language of the New Testament to the language of its time. John Lightfoot in the seventeenth century had been the first to make use of numerous parallels from the rabbinical literature for the explication of the New Testament. Now, late in the nineteenth century, **Gustaf Dalman,** tutor in the Old Testament at Leipzig, observed—his personal involvement in this field of study was due to his interest in the Christian mission to the Jews— that "Jesus' words [were] . . . undoubtedly originally in Aramaic." And from this observation he derived "the right and duty" of the scientific study of Scripture to investigate "in what form the words of Jesus must have been uttered in their original language, and what meaning they had in this form for the Jewish hearers." And having first made a grammatical and lexical study of Palestinian Aramaic, he published in 1898 his *Die Worte Jesu* [The words of Jesus], a book which, by drawing on a rich body of late Jewish material for purposes of comparison, examined the important concepts of Jesus' proclamation in order by a "back translation" of the testimony to Jesus' teaching "to get even one step nearer to the original by a fresh apprehension of his message in the light of the primary language and the contemporary modes of thought." [285]

While Dalman drew in this fashion on the late Jewish rabbinical material for an explanation of the conceptual language of Jesus and of early Palestinian Christianity, it remained for **Adolf Deissman,** at that time pastor and lecturer in Herborn, to assume the task of obtaining help for the understanding of the New Testament language and world of thought from the "nonliterary remnants of the environment of the Septuagint and the New Testament." Having stumbled on the importance of these sources as the result of an accidental glance at a publication of papyri,[286] he succeeded, first of all in his *Bibelstudien* [Bible studies] (1895), in determining, with the help of inscriptions and papyri, the meaning of countless New Testament words in the Greek of that time and in proving that the "New Testament . . . as a whole, [is] a monument of late colloquial Greek, and in the great majority of its component parts the monument of a more or less *popular* colloquial language." In addition, by means of comparison with papyri letters that have been preserved, Deissmann was able to show that a difference exists between genuine letters and "epistles" intended for literary publication, and that numerous New Testament letters are genuine letters and must be interpreted as such. And finally, by comparing the books of the New Testament with the nonliterary texts of its environment, he gained the insight that "by its social structure primitive Christianity points unequivocally to the lower and middle classes. . . . Until recently these masses were almost entirely lost to the historian. Now, however, thanks to the discovery of their own authentic records, they have suddenly risen again from the rubbish mounds of the ancient cities, little market towns, and villages." Deissmann then made these findings available to wider circles in his *Licht vom Osten* [Light from the Ancient East], a book frequently republished, in which he presented a very large number of these inscriptions and papyri in admirable fashion and so made possible "new life and depth to all our conceptions of primitive Christianity." [287]

In the investigation of the Greek Bible it is important to free oneself first of all from such a methodological notion as the sacred uniqueness of its texts. And in breaking through the principle, now become a dogma, of its being linguistically sealed off and isolated, we must aspire towards a knowledge of its individual and heterogeneous elements, and investigate these upon their own historical bases. . . .

The early Christian writings, in fact, must be taken out of the narrow and not easily illuminated compartments of the Canon, and placed in the sunshine and under the blue sky of their native land and of their own time. There they will find companions in speech, perhaps also companions in thought. There they take their place in the vast phenomenon of the κοινή [Koine, Greek: "world language"]. . . . Certain elements in them of the popular dialect reveal the fact of their derivation from those healthy circles of society to which the Gospel appealed. . . .

It is thus likewise insufficient to appeal to the vocabulary and the grammar of the contemporary "profane" literature. This literature will doubtless afford the most instructive discoveries, but, when we compare it with the direct sources which are open to us, it is, so far as regards the language of the early Christian authors, only of secondary importance. These direct sources are the inscriptions of the imperial period. Just as we must set our printed Septuagint side by side with the Ptolemaic papyri, so must we read the New Testament in the light of the opened folios of the Inscriptions. . . .

If the Greek texts of the Old and New Testaments are subjected to a linguistic examination, the first impression can only be that linguistically disparate elements are found here side by side. However, the linguistic point of view can be concerned only with the definition and carrying out of our task. A good bit of the unclarity that we have to acknowledge in this connection is due to the fact that we have confused the linguistic point of view and that of the scientific study of religion. From the point of view of the history of religion the sacred texts, despite their lack of linguistic homogeneity, belong together as the records and monuments of two phases that cannot be separated from one another. That is certain. And it is just as certain that the ideas, the concepts, the spirit of the Greek Old and New Testaments are related and that in their characteristic features they differ from the average faith of Graeco-Roman paganism. But these are elements that concern the history of religions and that cannot be regarded as constituting the marks of a specifically biblical or Christian Greek idiom.

Only a single consideration of historically oriented linguistic studies permits us to maintain that biblical writings exhibit a certain linguistic peculiarity, and only, it must be emphasized, in a formal sense: Almost all are to be regarded as monuments of late, nonliterary Greek. In passing this judgment, however, it must be kept in mind that "late Greek" does not designate a sharply circumscribed and wholly controllable factor, but something fluid, something often problematical, something we do not fully know, a piece of living language history and, because of that, something mysterious.

If I am not mistaken, this "nominative" [πλήρης = full (John 1:14)] has been regarded by a pious Silesian commentator of our day as a peculiarly fine dogmatic distinction in the inspired sacred text. In matters linguistic, however, the commentator's piety is not enough. I agree, *mutatis mutandis*, with Hans Thoa [a painter, b. 1839, d. 1924], who once told the Protestant clergy of Baden that it would be more desirable to have a sinner painting good pictures than to have a saint painting bad ones. The present case, therefore, must be decided by cold philological considerations, and philology tells us, on the evidence of papyri, ostraca, and wooden tablets, that πλήρης as used by the people had often shrunk and become indeclinable.

The letter, in its essential idea, does not differ in any way from a private conversation; like the latter, it is a personal and intimate communication, and the more faithfully it catches the tone of the private conversation, the more of a letter, that is, the better a letter, it is.

Literature is that species of writing which is designed for the public: the producer of literature wants others to heed his work. He desires to be read. He does not appeal to his friend, nor does he write to his mother; he entrusts his sheets to the winds, and knows not whither they will be borne; he only knows that they will be picked up and examined by some one or other unknown and insolent. . . .

When for the first time a *book* was subsequently compiled from letters,—it would be piety rather than scholarship that made the beginning here—the age of literature had long since dawned, and had long since constructed the various literary forms with which it worked. That book, the first to be compiled from real letters, added another form to those already existent. One would, of course, hardly venture to say that it forthwith added the literary letter, the *epistle*, to the forms of published literature; against its will, so to speak, that book is merely the impetus to the development of this new literary *eidos* ["form"]. The present writer cannot imagine that the composition and publication of literary treatises in the form of letters was anterior to the compilation of a book from actual letters. So soon, however, as such a book existed, the charming novelty of it invited imitation. . . .

If we rightly infer, from an investigation of ancient literature, that the familiar term *"letter"* must be broken up—above all, into the two chief categories *real letter* and *epistle,* then the biblical "letters" likewise must be examined from this point of view. Just as the language of the Bible ought to be studied in its actual historical context of contemporary language; just as its religious and ethical contents must be studied in their actual historical context of contemporary religion and civilization—so the biblical writings, too, in the literary investigation of them, ought not to be placed in an isolated position. . . . When we make the demand that the biblical "letters" are to be set in their proper relation to ancient letter-writing as a whole, we do not thereby imply that they are products of ancient epistolography, but rather that they shall be investigated simply with regard to the question, how far the categories implied in the problematical term *letter* are to be employed in the criticism of them. We may designate our question regarding the biblical letters and epistles as a question regarding the literary character of the writings transmitted by the Bible under the name *letters,* but the question regarding their literary character must be so framed that the answer will affirm the *preliterary* character, probably of some, possibly of all. . . .

It appears . . . quite certain that the authentic writings of the Apostle are true letters, and that to think of them as epistles is to take away what is best in them. . . . They differ from the messages of the homely papyrus leaves from Egypt not as letters, but only as the letters of *Paul.* . . .

The letters of Paul are not so much sources for the theology, or even for the religion, of the period, as simply for the personal religion of Paul as an individual; it is only by a literary misconception that they are looked upon as the documents of "Paulinism". The result of their criticism from the standpoint of the history of religions can be nothing more than a sketch of the character of Paul the letter-writer, and not the system of Paul the epistolographer; what speaks to us in the letters is his faith, not his dogmatics; his morality, not his ethics; his hopes, not his eschatology—here and there, no doubt, in the faltering speech of theology.

The consistently historical view of the New Testament, which without qualification set its language and thought world into its time, on the one hand assimilated the New Testament to the history of the religions and the spirit of its time—thereby to some extent depriving it of its uniqueness—and on the other had the effect of making the New Testament primarily the witness to a distinct piety of antiquity. Although neither the supporters nor the opponents of the religio-historical way of viewing the New Testament yet clearly saw its consequences, an objection was raised at once from two sides to the history-of-religions method employed in such research. On the one hand, for instance, a conservative critic protests against the thesis "of a group of theologians, most of them younger theologians, . . . that much is to be learned from the reading of the New Testament apocrypha and pseudepigrapha for an understanding of the New Testament especially of the obscure passages," points to "the great gap between the manner of thinking of the apocryphal writings and the sense and spirit of the New Testament books, a gap that yawns at every step before the earnest investigator," and actually declares that even "the comparison of forms of speech and terminologies . . . [may] only be carried on with great caution." [288] And over against "the complete identification of Pauline ideas with those of later Judaism to the point of the silliest of fantasies," a representative of systematic theology had this to say: [289]

If one has given . . . the Jewish passages in question a careful reading and has thus run across many similarities that at first glance are striking but often turn out to be very superficial, he will be astonished at how far in every direction, not only ethico-religiously but also aesthetically, the biblical passages stand above the Jewish. . . . But the method of a theology which believes it possible to treat the sacred words of Holy Writ in just the same way as it does the profane words of a human, secondary literature—a literature in part quite unworthy of attention—with such fantasies calls down upon itself its own punishment. Similarities are there, to be sure, and it is interesting to observe them; but the similarity is that between a stagnant pond that has become a swamp, exhaling all sorts of miasmas, and the fresh, clear, pure stream that is its source. A theology that does not point out this far-reaching difference and which thus actually contributes increasingly to the depreciation of the holy, reverent awe before the Bible, especially before the apostolic word, is not really a genuinely evangelical theology. . . . The decisive factor is the *attitude of faith* with respect to the biblical Word of God, an attitude, it must be insisted, that does not exclude strictly scientific and thorough-going research.

Although such criticism still remained sporadic, especially since the consequences of the new direction of research had not yet clearly emerged, at the same time a systematic theologian at Halle, **Martin Kähler,** made a basic attack on the historical study of the life and teachings of Jesus. In his first lectures, while still a tutor of the New Testament, Kähler had formulated his goal as follows: "The biblical text is to speak to its hearers as though the author, able to employ our idiom, were speaking to us today." [290] Even then (1860), therefore, Kähler had pushed wholly into the background the task of a discovery of the *historical* meaning of the New Testament writings. Now he declared without hesitation that "this whole 'Life-of-Jesus movement' is a blind alley." To be sure, the reason for Kähler's rejection "of the critical method of historical theology that examines sources and undertakes historical and analogical constructions" is also the correct observation that "we do not possess any sources for a life of Jesus which a historian can accept as reliable and adequate," but especially the insight that "the real Christ [is] . . . the Christ who is preached." And Kähler therefore maintains that either we must give up "the God who is manifest," or that "there [must] be another reality of Christ than that of the individual product of biographical scholarship." He therefore declares it to be "the task of the dogmatic theologian, in representing simple Christian faith, to enter the lists against the papacy of historical scholars." [291]

The historical Jesus portrayed by modern authors conceals from us the living Christ. The Jesus of the "Life of Jesus" school is only a modern variety of the fruits of the inventive genius of men, no better than the ill-famed dogmatic Christ of Byzantine Christology; both stand equally distant from the real Christ. . . .

The New Testament accounts are not concerned to afford a view of how Jesus developed; they let him proclaim and manifest himself, but not give information, let alone involuntary information, about himself. . . . Consequently they provide absolutely no grounds for any deduction concerning the nature and form of his earlier development. To be sure, it is evident that the writings of the Old Testament and the way of thinking of his people determined the subject matter of Jesus' views. However, such self-evident observations add little to our knowledge. In addition, when our sources are silent and leave us in the lurch, even though it is in conflict with the whole character of their description, analogy with some other human event must be employed as a research tool. In this connection the attempt to analyze or supplement what we know with the help of psychology is especially popular. Can such an attempt in this area be justified? . . . Will he who has the impression here of standing over against the only Sinless One, the only son of Adam with an overwhelming consciousness of God—will such a one after mature reflection still dare to make that attempt?! Do not suppose you can gain the information [bit by bit like Aesop's] stork [dropping stones in the pitcher]; do not think that all you have to do is simply to increase the amount. The difference lies not in degree but in kind. Furthermore, sinlessness is not just something negative. It is not enough merely to erase the blemishes on our nature. If that is all you do, you end up with a clean slate. So very different in nature, so different that to become like him is possible only by a rebirth, a new creation—how can we hope to conceive and explain his development, its stages and turning points, in terms of the ordinary human pattern? Indeed, if you dig deeper you run into the difficulty: How could he have been sinless in a world, a family, and a people that were full of causes of offence? How could the child have developed purely and surely when in his minority, dependence, and immaturity he was surrounded by temptation and when all possibly well-meant training could at best be only forgiveness? That is a miracle, and it cannot be explained merely as the consequence of an unspoiled disposition. It is conceivable only because this infant entered this earthly existence with a different substance than the rest of us—a substance given him beforehand; because in all forms and stages of the life of his soul an absolutely independent will was at work; because in him God's grace and truth became flesh. With this fact in view, one would be wise to renounce all attempts at giving an account of his spiritual development by means of analogy.

So then, no historical analogy is necessary. Interpreters go back to the conditions and ways of thinking of his environment, to the history of his times and to the Jewish writings of the period that have come down to us. Perhaps in retrospect we can view this attempt in the proper light. . . . Now, if the Jesus of our Gospels is compared with Saul of Tarsus we become immediately aware in fact of a wide gulf that separates the student of the Pharisees and the Master; on the one hand the typical Jew, on whom the formative powers of his people and his time have made such an unmistakably deep and persistent impression; on the other hand the Son of man, whose person and action make us think we are moving in the nonhistorical era of the patriarchs. Accordingly there is a little promise of rewarding results from any return to the history of New Testament times. . . . The biographer who attempts to give an account of Jesus is always in some way a dogmatist, in the pejorative sense of the word. At best he shares the dogmatic position of the Bible. In most instances, however, modern biographers share the biblical point of view only to a very limited extent. In fact, not a few deliberately set themselves against "the antiquated world view of the New Testament.". . .

We have fellowship, then, with the Jesus of our Gospels because it is there that we come to know the Jesus whom our eyes of faith and our prayers encounter at the right hand of God; because we know with Luther that God reveals himself only in his beloved Son, for he is for us the revelation. . . . *What, however, is the effect, the decisive effect, that this Jesus has left behind? According to the Bible and Church history, none other than the faith of his disciples,* the conviction that we have in him the victory over guilt, sin, the tempter, and death. All other effects flow from this one; we measure them by it; with it they rise and fall, stand and fall. And this conviction is summed up in the single confession: "Christ, the Lord."

With this confession, the history of New Testament times had nothing to do, and the theology of Judaism still less. . . .

The risen Lord is not the historical Jesus *behind* the Gospels, but the Christ of the Apostolic proclamation, of the entire New Testament.

The real Christ, that is to say, the living Christ, the Christ who strides through the history of peoples, with whom millions have fellowship in child-like faith, with whom the great heroes of faith have had fellowship in struggle, in response, in victory, and in evangelism—*the real Christ is the Christ who is preached.*

From these fragmentary traditions, from these uncomprehended recollections, from these accounts colored according to the peculiarity of the author, from these confessions of the heart and these sermons on his saving merit, there emerges for us, nevertheless, a living, concordant picture of a Man, a picture we recognize again and again. The conclusion is virtually forced upon us: Here the Man in his incomparable and powerful personality, with his unparalleled deeds and experiences, including his self-manifestations as the Risen One, has engraved his picture on the mind and memory of his own with such sharp and deeply-etched lines that it could not be obliterated, and also not misdrawn. . . .

The fact, then, remains: Whoever agrees with the judgment on the picture of Christ that confronts us will also recognize the miracle that it has been able, in the simple course of events of the faulty tradition left of himself, to make his person distinct and living for the impact on the further development of mankind. What matter, then, if the origin of this picture remains obscure? . . .

If the biblical picture of Jesus Christ means that to us and does that for us, why do we look for more? Why do we seek another?

Even though Kähler little wished to contest the validity of the historical study of the Bible,[292] he nevertheless fails to appreciate the inescapability of historical research in the Gospels and completely denies the usefulness of setting them within the framework of contemporary history. Therefore, though his emphasis on the proclamation character of the Gospels was especially important, his radical rejection of the consistently historical investigation of the New Testament could have little effect at a time when the necessity of unreserved study of the New Testament in light of its own times became more and more unavoidable.

2.
Consistent Eschatology

It was to be expected that research at first should proceed further in the direction taken by Baldensperger, Everling, and Gunkel and turn energetically to the historical connection of Jesus and early Christianity with late Judaism. To be sure, in his small book, *Die Predigt Jesu vom Reiche Gottes* [Jesus' proclamation of the kingdom of God] (1892), **Johannes Weiss**, at that time professor of New Testament at Göttingen, does not at first glance betray that the awareness of late Jewish apocalyptic had affected his interpretation of Jesus' proclamation of the kingdom of God.[293] But the occasional introduction of citations from late Jewish apocalypses[294] to illuminate Jesus' thought and the explicit appeal to Baldensperger make this influence apparent. It first becomes clear from the foreword to the second edition of his book (1900) that J. Weiss, who had convinced himself as Ritschl's pupil and son-in-law "of the uncommon significance of the systematic idea of the kingdom of God which forms the organic center of [Ritschl's] theology," was driven to write his book by the "clear impression . . . that Ritschl's idea of the kingdom of God and the idea by the same name in the proclamation of Jesus were two very different things." Consequently, even in the first draft of his book Weiss pursues the goal "of determining once again the original historical meaning that Jesus associated with the words 'kingdom of God,' " without introducing ideas "that are modern, or at any rate foreign to Jesus' way of thinking." And on an unprejudiced reading of the Gospels with a knowledge of the late Jewish expectations of the future in mind, J. Weiss sees himself driven to the conclusion that in the proclamation of Jesus the kingdom of God is near, but not yet come, and that when Jesus speaks of the kingdom of God as present, his utterances are those of moments of prophetic inspiration. Furthermore, the ethical demands of Jesus are determined by this belief in the imminence of God's kingdom, and Jesus' claim to be the Son of man is likewise oriented only to the future. And J. Weiss does not impose any qualifications on this strictly futuristic, eschatological interpretation of Jesus' proclamation of the kingdom of God, but, to be sure, sees himself compelled to accept the corollary, viz., that modern theology, which does not share Jesus' eschatological orientation, must employ the concept of the "kingdom of God" in another sense than Jesus.[295]

The meaning of this well-authenticated proclamation of Jesus and his disciples seems indeed to be clear: The kingdom (or the rule) of God has come so close that it stands at the door. . . . Consequently it is not because there is a congregation of disciples in which the will of God is done, i.e., the "rule of God" is realized on the part of men, but because the work of Jesus has broken the power of Satan, who above all is the bringer of evil, that Jesus already speaks of a present kingdom. But these are moments of sublime, prophetic inspiration, when he is overcome with a consciousness of victory. . . . Alongside such utterances, however, stands the large number of sayings in which the establishment of the kingdom remains reserved for the nearer or more distant future. In light of that parallelism of religious outlook touched on above, this juxtaposition accordingly declares: Already Satan's kingdom is broken, already the rule of God gains ground, but it has not yet become a historical reality: As Jesus expected it, the kingdom of God has not yet been established upon earth. . . .

Indeed one may possibly say that *in the mind of Jesus* his whole activity is not a messianic but a preparatory mission. For it is apparent from a whole series of passages that Jesus thinks of the establishment of the βασιλεία τοῦ θεοῦ ["the kingdom of God"] as brought about solely by a supernatural intervention of God. Consequently there is no place at all for human activity, and if, to be sure, a main role in this is ascribed to the "Son of man," yet in Jesus' self-consciousness the predicate "Son of man" finds a place, as we shall see later, only by virtue of the intermediate idea of an exaltation (John 3:14). As Jesus now is, a rabbi, a prophet, he has nothing in common with the Son of man but the claim that he is to become that Son of man. So he, too, cannot in any way intervene in the development of the kingdom of God: He has to await, just as the people, God's definitive resumption of his rule. . . .

When will that be? When does the kingdom of God come? So the Pharisees ask, half curiously, half mockingly (Luke 17:20-21). Jesus' answer is difficult to interpret. . . . People felt able, by the combination on the one hand of prophecy and on the other of signs, to decipher, to determine by παρατήρησις ["observation"], how long it would still be until the kingdom of God should come. As the subsequent saying shows, Jesus rejected that procedure. One cannot observe the coming beforehand, one cannot say that "See, here it is," and "See, there it is" are the decisive signs! To prove how wrong this whole method is, he introduces the fact that, with all their calculation and combining, the Pharisees failed to see that already the decisive beginnings of the rule of God were in their midst. And now Jesus shows how suddenly, how unexpectedly and contrary to all combinations the coming of the Son of man will be. Therefore that obscure saying is parallel in content to Mark 13:32: "But of that day or that hour no one knows, not even the angels in heaven, nor the Son, but only the Father." A religious principle is involved here. As long as the time of the end can be calculated, the establishment of the kingdom is still the work of men, but for Jesus it is solely the work of God and therefore in every respect to be left to God.

But there is till another fact to be noted. However uncertain the approaching time of the Second Coming may be, it is conceivable only during the lifetime of the generation among which Jesus worked. This does not contradict what goes before. The end is to come during the lifetime of the generation among which Jesus worked. This does not contradict what goes before. The end is to come during the period of the next ten, twenty, thirty years, but nothing more definite is to be said. But this fixing of a _terminus post quem non_ ["latest possible date"] does not depend at all on any combination, any calculation, but is a direct, intuitive, religious certainty. . . .

Now we ask: How does Jesus think of the events in connection with the establishment of the kingdom by God? The parousia address in Luke 17 emphasizes a number of points. In the first place, the establishment of the kingdom will not be accomplished in some corner, but, "as the lightning flashes and lights up the sky from one side to another, so will the Son of man be in his day." His appearance will be visible to all, seen by all the world. It is then compared with the deluge in the days of Noah. Certainly the suddenness is the _tert. comp._ ["point of comparison"], but next to that emphasis is laid also on the universality and distinctive character of this appearance. But also according to the other parousia address that one can reconstruct from Mark 13, the appearance will be an event that will concern the whole world.

After what has been developed to this point it is probably no longer necessary to say that the "righteousness of the kingdom of God" does not mean the moral perfection which the members _of the kingdom of God_ possess or do, but the δικαιοσύνη ["righteousness"] which is the _condition_ of entrance into the kingdom of God (Matt. 5:20). It is the consequence of μετάνοια ("repentance, turning about"]. And, corresponding to the basic religious mood, it is an ideal of really positive morality just as much as, or perhaps even more than, negatively ascetic. The new righteousness that Jesus demands of his followers, of those who with him wait for the kingdom of God and hope to enter it, the new righteousness in both its negative and positive aspects cannot be understood if it is cut loose from the religious—that is to say, in this instance the eschatological—basis on which it rests: "Repent, for the kindgom of God is at hand." The nearness of the kingdom is the _motivation_ of the new morality.

From the discussion above, then, we see that the kingdom of God as Jesus thought of it is a wholly supernatural entity that stands completely over against this world. It follows from this that in Jesus' thought there cannot have been any place for a development of the kingdom of God _within the framework of this world_. On the basis of this result it seems to be the case that the dogmatic religio-ethical use of this idea in recent theology, which has divested it completely of its originally eschatological-apocalyptic meaning, is unjustified. When one uses the expression in a sense other than Jesus used it, one is in only apparent agreement with biblical usage.

The main point is that Jesus by virtue of his baptismal experience lived on the religious conviction that he had been chosen as Judge and Ruler in the kingdom of God. . . . It ought only to be shown that Jesus' messianic consciousness, as it is expressed in the name "Son of man," shares also in the wholly transcendental, apocalyptic character of Jesus' idea of the kingdom of God and cannot be separated from it.

228

While Jesus at the beginning hopes to live to see the establishment of the kingdom, he gradually becomes convinced that he first must tread the way of death and also by his death contribute to the establishment of the kingdom in Israel. Then he will return on the clouds of heaven to establish the kingdom, and will do so during the lifetime of the generation that rejected him.

Jesus gives no more exact indications of time, since the coming of the kingdom cannot be determined beforehand by observation of signs and calculation.

But when it comes, God will destroy this old world, ruled and corrupted by the devil, and create a new world. Men are also to share in this transformation and become like the angels.

The actual difference between our modern evangelical world outlook and that of the early Christian therefore is this, that we do not share the eschatological mood, namely, that the form of this world is passing away. We no longer pray: May grace come and this world pass away, but we live in the glad confidence that *this very world* will more and more become the stage of a "humanity of God." Another mood has quietly taken the place for us of the actually eschatological, however—and where it is not found, preaching and instruction should do everything to awaken it. The world will continue to exist, but we, the individuals, will soon leave it. Therefore we shall be able in another sense at least to approximate Jesus' mood, if we make the principle of our life the command that a wise man of our day has spoken: Live as though you were dying. We do not wait for a kingdom of God that is to come down to earth from heaven to destroy this world, but we hope to be joined with the Church of Jesus Christ in the heavenly βασιλεία ["kingdom of God"]. In this sense we can enter into the experience of the ancient Christians and pray as they did: Thy kingdom come!

The clear and persuasive arguments advanced by J. Weiss, based solely on exegetical observations, had the result that this small book "attracted much attention" but also "was the object . . . of numerous attacks." [296] In all this it was not really strange that conservative scholars, in spite of their agreement with J. Weiss's emphasis on Jesus' expectations of the future, continued to maintain that Jesus thought in terms of the essentially present character of the kingdom of God.[297] And it is also understandable that liberal scholars characterized the purely future interpretation of the kingdom of God by J. Weiss either as one-sided and exaggerated and wished to hold that Jesus assumed a development of the kingdom of God within the world in addition to the traditional expectations of the future,[298] or actually more or less denied the connection of Jesus' proclamation of the kingdom of God with apocalyptic.[299] For the Jesus who proclaims the imminent end of the world as J. Weiss portrayed him could not be harmonized with the spiritual kingdom of God of the inner life as pictured by liberal "life-of-Jesus" research; and if one could not avoid acknowledging that Jesus expected his imminent second coming, there remained only the expedient of maintaining "that here the inadequacies of the messianic idea had won the final, the only, victory over

Jesus. The promise of the Second Coming is the tribute Jesus paid to the faith of his time. Here, in fact, the fantasy of late Judaism, the enchanted world of ancient popular faith, looms up in Jesus' simple and magnificent consciousness of mission." [300] And there is no need for surprise that even a scholar who agrees with J. Weiss that "Jesus' conception of the kingdom of God is a thoroughly harmonious one, exclusively eschatological in content," goes on, however, to maintain: "Because the world beyond had shifted back in [Jesus'] religious thought from the future into the present, he could free himself from that concentration of mind on the ages to come which robbed the present of all value in the eyes of the pious whose thoughts were eschatologically oriented"; for only so can the kingdom of God demand "of man above all else that he raise his thinking and his striving to the heights of the God who has been presented to him." [301] The consistent relation of Jesus' proclamation to the conceptual world of late Judaism made it indeed all too clear that this proclamation became strange and unintelligible to modern man and therefore could not be accepted as obligatory so long as this consistent history-of-religions view was not yet acknowledged as inescapable. But this is just why it is all the more astonishing that those scholars who later were to become the leading representatives of the history-of-religions view of the New Testament likewise opposed the consistent relation of Jesus to Jewish apocalyptic. **Herman Gunkel,** who shortly before had related the Pauline concept of the Spirit to that of late Judaism, declared that also in his opinion "Weiss's overly rash theses seem to have missed the nuance in which the truth lies" because "the impression [is] given that Jesus' preaching was saturated with eschatology." [302] But it was of especial importance that immediately after the appearance of J. Weiss's book **Wilhelm Bousset,** later to become the most influential representative of the history-of-religions approach to the New Testament, published his book, *Jesu Predigt in ihrem Gegensatz sum Judentum* [Jesus' preaching in contrast to Judaism] (1892), in which he completely affirmed "the demand for a consistent—not merely occasional—use of the world of religious ideas and moods of late Judaism for the understanding of the historical phenomenon of Jesus," but then raised as an objection to the attempt to understand "Jesus from the outset . . . within the framework of Judaism," that "by this procedure . . . an unbiased comparison and a really historical appreciation of the person of Jesus [can] . . . not be obtained." Jesus' piety was "related [only] in outer form to the piety—to the expectation of the imminent end of the world—of late Judaism. . . . The person of Jesus in its entirety, accordingly, is not under the spell of Judaism." [303]

In late Judaism there is no really living power, no creative spirit. The characteristic feature of Judaism merely elevated itself to a mood of purely transcendental, world-denying resignation, a mood for which life has lost its meaning, intimately bound up with a legalistic striving after holiness. . . . What living faith and moral power Judaism still possessed was not enough to fill those new, forceful ideas with inner power and vitality so as to support them in all their purity. Therefore that intermixture of supernatural and this-worldly, of transcendent and politico-nationalistic traits, of world-denying and materialistic, world-affirming moods, was a historical necessity. Late Judaism resembles a building whose foundations have been laid insufficiently strong and too small to be able to carry the mighty pillars and vault that are erected on them, and to which props and other external supports have been added which make the whole ugly and unattractive.

And with this we have obtained the principle that is to guide us from now on in our attempt to understand the main and really characteristic features of Jesus' message. From now on we can maintain with full justice that if here something new was now created, a new, powerful piety that was able to outlast the destruction of Jerusalem, and that if this new thing was not attached to the name of Jesus by accident, then Jesus' message above all and first of all must be understood in light of its contrast to Judaism. . . .

It is further clear from this that for Jesus, who was aware of the nearness of God as the basis of his whole life, that breathless longing, that pathological homesickness for the beyond that we meet especially in the later Jewish apocalypses was something utterly foreign. . . .

The thought of the imminent end does not rob him of directness and spontaneity, and we find not a trace of the reflection that everything is merely transient, preparatory, only a means to an end. This world has not become so old and corrupt that it cannot be a place of joyful activity and creativity. We cannot avoid the impression that, however much the thought of the beyond projects into this life, here nonetheless the present is regarded as meaningful with an incomparable spontaneity and directness, that here there is a figure that has firm ground under his feet.

We may no longer hope, in my judgment, somehow to understand the person of Jesus in its characteristic features against the background of Judaism. With the confident grasp of a faith in God the Father that governed his whole life, Jesus broke through the transcendental, world-denying mood of Judaism at the decisive point. The present, the here and now, is no longer for him a mere shadow and phantom, but truth and reality, and life in it is no illusion, but a life with a very real and worthful meaning. He was not primarily the prophet of repentance but of a new righteousness in the old prophetic fashion, yet in a new and powerful way. More and more life for him came to mean a definite task, that of equipping his group of disciples with his own personal power and purpose. He sees a new epoch, a new and decisive era, beginning with his time, and himself as the personal vehicle of this new epoch. How is it possible in any respect whatever to understand this figure within the framework of late Judaism? Rather, is there not everywhere a palpable contrast? We must go back into prophetic times if we are—perhaps—to discover the seed of the new that comes to flower in the person of Jesus.

God's rule is already a fact. It does not need first to be brought into being. And when Jesus speaks of the mighty growth of God's kingdom, the mustard seed becoming a mighty tree, and of its intensive and powerful activity—it is once again as if the bank of mist were to lift and to open before us the view into the distance—he does not think of the kingdom of God as first coming into being in this process of growth, *perfecting itself in terms of its own being*, but only as a rule of God already in being and now mightily expanding its activity. . . .

Because of the certainty of his faith in God the Father, the whole course of the world that lies ahead is something essentially indifferent to him. Even if the ideas of a development that would stretch over centuries, of a mighty triumph of his message, of a propagation of that message over the whole world, of a conquest of the powerful Roman world empire by that message—even if such ideas had crossed his mind, they could have added nothing to the inner joy, clarity, and assurance of this faith.

Knowledge of contemporary Judaism is necessary to the highest degree if we are to understand the figure of Jesus in its deepest sense and in its historical significance. But from Judaism and its world outlook we never apprehend the figure of Jesus. Judaism and Jesus are at completely opposite poles to each other. It remains true that "the Gospel develops hidden elements in the Old Testament, but it protests against the ruling direction of Judaism."

It is evident that, in spite of his assertion that he had undertaken a fundamentally religio-historical comparison, Bousset rejected the "consistent view of J. Weiss" because it would put Jesus' faith in God the Father and his proclamation of the kingdom of God in a conceptual framework so remote from, and inaccessible to, the faith of the modern theologian that he shrank from doing it. But the insight into the thoroughgoing eschatological nature of the oldest Christian message, once the religio-historical comparison was really taken in earnest, could no longer be overlooked. A year after J. Weiss's study that proved so basic for future "life-of-Jesus" research, a book by **Richard Kabisch** appeared, *Die Eschatologie des Paulus* [The eschatology of Paul], that was to prove equally basic for Pauline research. And, despite the formally very different procedure—J. Weiss uses broad strokes to depict the decisive features of his subject in a striking manner, while Kabisch treats the several letters one after another in detail and then deals with the content of different eschatological concepts—both books supplement each other remarkably. Kabisch also simply observes the text and discovers in the process the eschatological orientation of Pauline theology, just as he sees that Paul's eschatological orientation is consciously dependent on the Jewish concepts of his time. But at one point Kabisch goes beyond J. Weiss, and in this respect he follows O. Everling, whom he often cites, and H. Gunkel, whom he fails to mention: He emphasizes most strongly the antique realism and the singularity of the Pauline doctrine of redemption without inquiring what consequences this insight could have for the significance of Paul in the present. But this very fact makes

Kabisch also a representative of a "consistent" history-of-religions view of Paul.[304]

What was intended by the apostolic preaching was the foundation of a little company that would survive the collapse of the present aeon and would certainly be saved into the blessed future aeon; by the divine Spirit of its Lord, which Spirit was now to be looked to among his subjects as a second person, what actually came of it was a new religion. The eschatology: The Christ comes, he rules the world, he decides forever the fate of individuals and of peoples, therefore he gathers you as his subjects—was the first; the ethics: Therefore he sanctifies you as his subjects according to his will, in his spirit, the spirit of eternal love—and the religion: Regard yourselves in his fellowship as God's children—the second.

This general observation perfectly represents the actual content of the apostolic preaching.

We therefore regard it for general historical reasons as the first task that the research student in the field of Pauline studies must undertake, to familiarize himself in greatest detail and most exactly with all the matters that go to make up the world view, with the anthropological, cosmological, soteriological, angelological, christological, eschatological concepts of his time; that is today, not only with Philo's, but especially with those of the Pharisaic theologians, those who, like the pre-Christian Paul, hoped for and pondered over the messianic kingdom, in what form it would appear and by what means it would be brought about. . . . We may assume that Paul before his conversion, like all his teachers, brethren, and peers, "was zealous for the Law, in order to partake of the reward in the days to come"; and since he regarded this hoped-for blessedness as the goal of all God's religious preparations, so we have first to expect that after his conversion he pursued this goal further, only by different means. Only a thorough exegetical examination of his literary remains that led to contrary results could shatter this presupposition. . . .

This exegesis, however, does not lead to contrary results, but to such as exactly confirm all that we would expect of it from our knowledge of contemporary religion and theology. It shows that also as a Christian he still made the messianic glory the principal object of his life of faith, with the same passionate fervor with which he had striven throughout his lifetime. He who certainly as a Jew, as a Pharisee, hoped for the coming of the Messiah more ardently than all others—for why else, with greater rage than all others, would he have stoned and forged chains for the followers of one whom he regarded as a false messiah?—when he comprehended that the Messiah was already come and consequently had set the end of things in motion, felt himself removed with soul aflame into the midst of the last days. In this lively consciousness of being one of those who have experienced the end of the world, he did not preach an abstract ethic or a religion that comprised merely the present blessedness of a relation of man to God, but he preached the Messiah, the Christ and his kingdom, that is, eschatology. And he carries out his whole tremendous work in the conviction and with the intention of working not only for the present, but also (and rather) for the future. The morality he preaches and the religion he proclaims are above all the way by which one enters that future glory. . . .

The inner direction of his purposes is coherent through and through, coherent, not mechanical, but experienced with all his soul and therefore, created by himself, the content of what he longs for as blessed or abhors as accursed. Therefore coherent through and through is the picture of the blessed future he paints for himself as the future realization of these wishes. It would never happen that he might vacillate uncertainly between different world forms, between contradictory wishes. Into his concept of the kingdom of God images of things that fill the belly and gladden the senses would never flow: never would he report anything contradictory about the question of whether this earth could support the visible establishment of the messianic kingdom with its blessednesses, of whether the action of the realized kingdom of promise could take place in the forms this earth provides and on this earthly stage. Although he drew on the traditions that his time offered concerning these matters, he nevertheless did not take them over indiscriminately, but only fitted such constituents into his picture of the future as had grown from the same ground on which his own messianic temple was built. For this corresponded to a spirit that was filled with one passion; and what did not accord with this passion could find no room in any part of his hope. This passion means: life; and what he fled as the *summa* of all horrors: death. This passion and this abhorrence were the positive and negative pole from which flowed the stream of his messianic hope. . . .

Paul does not know the concept of a metaphorical "life" as an ethical quality. On the contrary, although according to his peculiar metaphysics and anthropology the renewal of the physical life given by Christ, among other things, has also moral consequences; yet always and precisely he connects with the words ζωή, ζῆν ["life," "to live"] and their derivatives the meaning they possess in common Greek usage. Life as being alive, as the abstract designation of the fact of physical existence, no matter with what substance the fact is connected, is the sense which, true to speech usage and the understanding of his Greek-reading readers, lies at the basis of those words. This life as something indestructible, eternal life in the literal sense, . . . is for him the highest good. Obviously provided besides with all things that seem desirable to him and freed from evil. But the fact of its indestructibility, the property of imperishableness, is for him the highest. On the other hand, perishableness, death as physical termination, is the greatest evil. For him there is no other punishment for sin than death, physical destruction. For he can conceive of no form of existence, even if full of torments, that would be more horrible than nonbeing. Dread of this, of ceasing to be, permeates all his thinking.

The characteristic element in Paul's view of the world is just this, . . . that in the glow of his ardent vitality he rejects this whole world, which he regards as subjected to the slavery of corruption, and rejects it not in part and hesitantly, but wholly and deliberately; that without exception, in physical, moral, and intellectual respects, he does not believe it worth stretching out a finger for; a kingdom of Satan and of demonic power that, if the host of its creatures is ever to achieve happiness and life, must be free from this slavery and transformed in the depths of its nature. . . .

It is a most noteworthy feature of the formation of Christianity, a feature associated inevitably with the earliest form of the faith, that the Christianity that manifested itself *is already a part of the last things.* The Messiah was the one who inaugurated the end of the world, the author of the new world order.

And since he had already appeared, that appearance was the beginning of the end. From the concealment of heaven the emergence of the kingly rule with its inhabitants, with its King, had begun; all who, while still in this body, were won by it as its citizens, lived in the last days. Therefore Peter's sermon concerning the outpouring of the Spirit begins with the quotation from Joel: "And it shall come to pass in the last days, saith the Lord"; and consequently this consciousness that *all Christianity is a piece of eschatology* exercises the very greatest influence on the whole practical direction of Paul's life, for the apostle expects from eschatology, from the appearing of the Lord, not merely the end of the world order, but the end of the world itself. Paul's whole ethics, so far as it has the future form of society in mind, is the method of a man who locks up his house to leave it. For now, since the Messiah died and rose again, what actually exists is no longer the earthly world in its earthly order, but only, scarcely hidden beneath the earth cover, the beginning of his heavenly kingdom. And the Christians are already no longer citizens of this earth, but citizens of the material world of the Spirit. Accordingly, a complete account would have to subsume virtually the whole of his doctrine of faith and morals, so far as it is specifically Christian, under eschatology.

A Paul so closely bound up with the Judaism of his time was, however, still too alien for contemporary theology to understand, and so Kabisch's work was largely rejected.[305] The Strassburg tutor, **Albert Schweitzer,** received a similar reception a few years later when, in his *Skizze des Lebens Jesu* [A sketch of the life of Jesus] (1901) he put the alternatives as follows: "Jesus . . . must have thought either eschatologically or un-eschatologically, but not both together." In this second volume of a study of the problem of the Last Supper, Schweitzer sketched a picture of a Jesus who proclaimed the imminent coming of the supernatural kingdom of God and who regarded himself as the coming messiah, who by personal suffering wished to take upon himself the inescapable "woes of the end," and who, for the brief interval until the imminent coming of the kingdom of God, taught an "interim-ethic." For Schweitzer had become convinced that the heretofore insoluble problem of Jesus' Last Supper could only be solved on the basis "of a new conception of the life of Jesus . . . that takes the messianic- and passion-secret into consideration in such a way that its solemn enactment at the Last Supper becomes conceivable and intelligible." This work is "dedicated with sincere respect and devotion to Dr. H. J. Holtzmann by his grateful pupil," although the acceptance of several of Jesus' discourses in the Gospel of Matthew as historically reliable reports, the rejection of the theory of the developing messianic consciousness of Jesus derived by liberal scholarship from Mark's Gospel, and the "consistently eschatological" interpretation of Jesus' message radically contradicted the picture of Jesus the Master of the liberal life-of-Jesus school. Characteristic of Schweitzer's rigidly consistent manner of introducing proof is that in this book on Jesus, the Pauline theology is also derived from Paul's eschatological viewpoint, and Jesus' whole proclamation is regarded in the strict sense as logically homogeneous.[306]

Only that conception is historical which makes it intelligible how Jesus could take himself to be the Messiah without finding himself obliged to make this consciousness of his count as a factor in his public activity in behalf of the Kingdom of God,—rather, how he was actually compelled to make the messianic dignity of his person a secret! Why was his messiahship a secret of Jesus? To explain this means to understand his life. . . .

For the Synoptic question especially, the new conception of the life of Jesus is of great importance. From this point of view the composition of the Synoptists appears much simpler and clearer. The artificial redaction with which scholars have felt themselves compelled to operate is very much reduced. The Sermon on the Mount, the commission to the Twelve, and the eulogy of the Baptist are not "composite speeches," but were for the most part delivered as they have been handed down to us. Also the form of the prophecy of the Passion and the Resurrection is not to be ascribed to the early Church, but Jesus did actually speak to his Disciples in these words about his future. This very simplification of the literary problem and the fact that the credibility of the Gospel tradition is thereby enhanced is of great weight for the new interpretation of the life of Jesus.

If the idea of the eschatological realisation of the Kingdom is the fundamental concept in Jesus' preaching, his whole theory of ethics must come under the conception of *repentance* as a preparation for the coming of the Kingdom. . . .
As repentance in view of the Kingdom of God, even the ethics of the Sermon on the Mount is interim-ethics.

How did Jesus arrive at the conviction that the Baptist was Elijah? It was through a necessary inference from his own messiahship. Because he knew himself to be the Messiah, the other must be Elijah. Between the two ideas there was a necessary correspondence. No one could know that the Baptist was Elijah except he derived this cognizance from the messiahship of Jesus. No one could arrive at the thought that John was Elijah without at the same time being obliged to see in Jesus the Messiah. For after the Forerunner there remained no place for a second manifestation of the kind. No one knew that Jesus took himself to be the Messiah. Therefore in the Baptist men perceived a prophet and raised the question whether Jesus were not Elijah. No one understood in their full bearing the mysterious concluding sentences of the eulogy over the Baptist. *Only for Jesus was John the promised Elijah.* . . .
It is almost impossible to express in modern terms the consciousness of messiahship which Jesus imparted as a secret to his Disciples. Whether we describe it as an identity between him and the Son of Man who is to appear, whether we express it as a continuity which unites both personalities, or think of it as virtually a pre-existent messiahship,—none of these modern conceptions can render the consciousness of Jesus as the Disciples understood it. . . .
In this sense, then, Jesus' messianic consciousness is futuristic. There was nothing strange in this either for him or for his Disciples. On the contrary, it corresponded exactly to the Jewish conception of the hidden life and labor of the Messiah. The course of Jesus' earthly life preceded his messiahship in glory. The Messiah in his earthly estate must live and labor unrecognized, he must

teach, and through deed and suffering he must be made perfect in righteousness. Not till then will the messianic age dawn with the Last Judgment and the establishment of the Kingdom. The Messiah must come from the north. Jesus' march from Caesarea Philippi to Jerusalem was the progress of the unrecognized Messiah to his triumph in glory.

Thus in the midst of the messianic expectation of his people stood Jesus as the Messiah that is to be. He dare not reveal himself to them, for the season of his hidden labor was not yet over. Hence he preached the near approach of the Kingdom of God.

How is it conceivable that the Disciples proclaimed that Jesus had entered upon his messianic existence through the Resurrection, if upon earth he had spoken of his messiahship as a dignity already actually possessed? As a matter of fact the early Synoptic tradition and the view of the primitive Church agree together completely. Both affirm with one voice that Jesus' messianic consciousness was futuristic.

If we had not this witness, the knowledge of Jesus' historical character and personality would be forever closed to us. For after his death all sorts of presumptions arose to obscure the consciousness of the futuristic character of his messiahship. His resurrection as Messsiah coincided with the general Resurrection which should usher in the messianic age—such was the perspective of the Disciples before his death. After his death his resurrection as Messiah constituted a fact for itself. Jesus was the Messiah *before* the messianic age! That is the fateful shifting of the perspective. Therein lies the tragic element—but the magnificent as well—in the whole phenomenon of Christianity.

The primitive Christian consciousness made the most strenuous efforts to fill the breach, trying in spite of it to conceive of Jesus' resurrection as the dawn of the messianic era in the general rising of the dead. There was an effort to make it intelligible as analogous to a somewhat protracted interval between two scenes of the first act of a drama. Properly, however, they already stood within the messianic Resurrection. Thus for Paul, Jesus Christ, who is proved to be the Messiah through the Resurrection of the dead, "is the first fruits of them that sleep" (I Cor. 15:20). The whole structure of Pauline theology and ethics rests upon this thought. Because they find themselves within this period, believers are in reality buried with Christ and raised with him again through baptism. They are "new" creatures, they are the "righteous," whose citizenship is in heaven. Until we grasp this fundamental notion we cannot perceive the unity in the manifold complications of St. Paul's world of thought.

In genuine historical knowledge there is liberating and helping power. Our faith is built upon the personality of Jesus. But between our world-view and that in which he lived and labored there lies a deep and seemingly unbridgeable gulf. Men therefore saw themselves obliged to detach as it were his personality from his world-view and touch it up with modern colors.

This produced a picture of Jesus which was strangely lifeless and vague. One got a hybrid figure, half modern, half antique. With much else that is modern, men transferred to him our modern psychology, without always recognising clearly that it is not applicable to him and necessarily belittles him. For it is derived from mediocre minds which are a patchwork of opinions and apprehend and observe themselves only in a constant flux of development. Jesus, however, is a superhuman personality moulded in one piece.

This Jesus is far greater than the one conceived in modern terms: he is really a superhuman personality. With his death he destroyed the form of his *Weltanschauung,* rendering his own eschatology impossible. Thereby he gives to all peoples and to all times the right to apprehend him in terms of their thoughts and conceptions, in order that his spirit may pervade their "Weltanschauung" as it quickened and transfigured the Jewish eschatology.

It is interesting to note that the reader of this impressively consistent account of Jesus is not aware that J. Weiss and Kabisch already recognize the central importance [in early Christianity] of the expectation of the nearness of the end and had made use of it in setting Jesus and Paul within the framework of late Judaism. Furthermore, since the argument offers scarcely any interpretation of individual passages, the reader cannot learn what Schweitzer himself only decades later reported, namely, that the author of this book, as a result of a sudden observation in connection with the text of the Gospel of Matthew, had been "sorely puzzled" about the conclusion that the activities of Jesus can be understood from Mark's Gospel only and thereby had been "landed in perplexity about the explanation of the words and actions of Jesus, then accepted as historically correct." [307] Since therefore the reader found himself, without sufficient personal and material reparation for it, faced with such a strange Jesus, it was understandable that also Schweitzer's picture of Jesus was at first completely rejected or wholly disregarded. [308] Only when Schweitzer, at the end of an account of the *Geschichte der Leben-Jesu-Forchung* [= The Quest of the Historical Jesus (so runs the subtitle)], presented "consistent eschatology" as the right solution of the question concerning the historical Jesus did there emerge a really dangerous opponent of the picture of Jesus that had hitherto been accepted. To his work, a book that digested an immense body of material, Schweitzer gave the title *Von Reimarus zu Wrede* [From Reimarus to Wrede] because, according to his view, the rationalistic skeptic Reimarus had "first comprehended Jesus' conceptual world historically, that is, as an eschatological world-view," and Wrede's "consistent skepticism" (of which we will speak later) "and consistent eschatology, in their combined impact," have jointly destroyed the noneschatological picture painted by liberal theology. And, apart from David Friedrich Strauss's battle for the strictly historical study of Jesus and the exclusion of the Gospel of John as a source for the historical Jesus by F. C. Baur and H. J. Holtzmann, Schweitzer recognizes only Johannes Weiss's account of *Die Predigt Jesu vom Reiche Gottes* [Jesus' proclamation of the kingdom of God] as a genuine contribution to our knowledge of Jesus, because Weiss had shown "that Jesus' message was solely eschatological." And if as the "result of the insight into the whole course of research in the life of Jesus" comes the realization of "the mistaken interpretation of the historical

Jesus as set forth by modern theology," then at the end appears the picture of the Jesus who proclaimed the imminent kingdom of God and whose eschatology "can . . . only be identified on the basis of the Jewish apocalyptic literature of the period from Daniel to the Bar-Cocheba revolt," as the representation of the historical Jesus that "overthrows the modern portraits." However, it is "not the historical Jesus, but the spirit which goes forth from Him and in the spirits of men strives for new influence and rule . . . that . . . overcomes the world." [309]

When, at some future day, our period of civilization shall lie, closed and completed, before the eyes of later generations, German theology will stand out as a great, a unique phenomenon in the intellectual life of our time. For nowhere save in the German temperament can there be found such a living complex of philosophical thought, critical acumen, historical insight, and religious feeling, without which no deep theology is possible.
And the greatest achievement of German theology is the critical investigation of the life of Jesus. What it has accomplished here is basic and binding for the religious thinking of the future.

It is time that Reimarus was justly treated and that the great historical achievement in his Deistic polemical writings should be acknowledged. His work is perhaps the most splendid achievement in the whole course of the historical investigation of the life of Jesus, for he was the first to grasp the fact that the world of thought in which Jesus moved was essentially eschatological. . . .
In the light of the clear perception of the elements of the problem which Reimarus had attained, the whole movement of theology, down to Johannes Weiss, appears retrograde. In all its work the thesis is ignored or obscured that Jesus, as a historical personality, is to be regarded, not as the founder of a new religion, but as the final product of the eschatological and apocalyptic thought of Late Judaism. Every sentence of Johannes Weiss's *Die Predigt Jesu vom Reiche Gottes* (1892) is a vindication, a rehabilitation, of Reimarus as a historical thinker.

What was the net result of these liberal lives of Jesus? In the first place the clearing up of the relation between John and the Synoptics. . . .
The fact is, the separation between the Synoptics and the Fourth Gospel is only the first step to a larger result which necessarily follows from it—the complete recognition of the purely and fundamentally eschatological character of the teaching and activity of the Marcan and Matthaean Jesus. . . .
But the striking thing about these liberal critical lives of Jesus was that they unconsciously prepared the way for a deeper historical view which could not have been reached apart from them. A deeper understanding of a subject is only brought to pass when a theory is carried to its utmost limit and finally proves its own inadequacy.
There is this in common between rationalism and the liberal critical method, that each had followed out a theory to its ultimate consequences. Rationalism had carried out to the limit its naturalistic explorations of the miracle stories and in so doing had prepared the way for progress under Strauss. The liberal critical school had carried to its limit the naturalistic-psychological explanation

of the causal links between the various actions of Jesus and between the various events of His life. And the conclusions to which they had been driven had prepared the way for the recognition that natural psychology is not here historical psychology, but that the latter must be deduced from certain historical data. Thus through the meritorious and magnificently conscientious work of the liberal critical school the a priori "natural" psychology gave way to the eschatological psychology. That is the net result, from the historical point of view, of the study of the life of Jesus in the post-Straussian period. In [Johannes] Weiss there are none of these devious paths: "behold the land lies before thee."

His *Preaching of Jesus Concerning the Kingdom of God*, published in 1892, has, on its own lines, an importance equal to that of Strauss's first *Life of Jesus*. He lays down the third great alternative which the study of the life of Jesus had to meet. The first was laid down by Strauss: *either* purely historical *or* purely supernatural. The second had been worked out by the Tübingen school and Holtzmann: *either* Synoptic *or* Johannine. Now came the third: *either* eschatological *or* non-eschatological!

There is nothing more negative than the outcome of the critical study of the life of Jesus.

The Jesus of Nazareth who came forward publicly as the Messiah, who preached the ethic of the Kingdom of God, who founded the Kingdom of Heaven upon earth, and died to give His work its final consecration, never had any existence. He is a figure designed by rationalism, endowed with life by liberalism, and clothed by modern theology in an historical garb.

This image has not been destroyed from without, it has fallen to pieces, cleft and disintegrated by the concrete historical problems which came to the surface one after another, and in spite of all the artifice, art, artificiality, and violence which was applied to them, refused to be planed down to fit the design on which the Jesus of the theology of the last hundred and thirty years had been constructed, and were no sooner covered over than they appeared again in a new form. . . .

The study of the life of Jesus has had a curious history. It set out in quest of the historical Jesus, believing that when it had found Him it could bring Him straight into our time as a Teacher and Savior. It loosed the bands by which He had been riveted for centuries to the stony rocks of ecclesiastical doctrine, and rejoiced to see life and movement coming into the figure once more, and the historical Jesus advancing, as it seemed, to meet it. But He does not stay; He passes by our time and returns to His own. What surprised and dismayed the theology of the last forty years was that, despite all forced and arbitrary interpretations, it could not keep Him in our time, but had to let Him go. He returned to His own time, not owing to the application of any historical ingenuity, but by the same inevitable necessity by which the liberated pendulum returns to its original position. . . .

It is not given to history to disengage that which is abiding and eternal in the being of Jesus from the historical forms in which it worked itself out, and to introduce it into our world as a living influence. It has toiled in vain at this undertaking. As a water-plant is beautiful so long as it is growing in the water, but once it is torn from its roots, withers and becomes unrecognizable, so it is with the historical Jesus when He is wrenched loose from the soil of eschatology, and the attempt is made to conceive Him "historically" as a Being not subject to temporal conditions. The abiding and eternal in Jesus is

absolutely independent of historical knowledge and can only be understood by
contact with His spirit which is still at work in the world. In proportion as
we have the Spirit of Jesus we have the true knowledge of Jesus.

The proclamation of Jesus as wholly dominated by the expectation
of the imminent supernatural kingdom of God, Schweitzer had presented as the answer to all debatable questions of previous life-of-Jesus
research, and had accordingly characterized as entirely demolished the
liberal picture of Jesus, based as it was on psychological presuppositions.
On his own part, however, his description of the public activity of Jesus,
with its assumption that as a result of the delay of the parousia Jesus decided to bring about the coming of the kingdom of God by the compulsion of his death, also represented a historical *construction*. It is
understandable that conservative scholars confirmed with satisfaction
Schweitzer's observation concerning "the mistaken interpretation of the
historical Jesus as set forth by modern theology," [310] but went on to
add that "any critical comment on this result of consistent eschatology"
would be "superfluous." [311] And the motives that led a few English
scholars to extend a hearty greeting to Schweitzer's picture of Jesus were
not basically different.[312] On the other hand, it is astonishing that in
Germany not only the liberal but also those scholars who were outspoken
in their defense of the history-of-religions methodology rejected Schweitzer's consistently eschatological Jesus with almost passionate severity.[313]
At the moment when Schweitzer's eschatological picture of Jesus compelled attention, the strangeness of the Jesus set wholly within Jewish
apocalyptic contradicted the traditional concepts so violently that even
critically oriented scholars saw in it an unhistorical distortion of reality.
Schweitzer himself, however, sought still better to demonstrate the accuracy of his historical picture of Jesus as set consistently within the
framework of apocalyptic Judaism by referring to "the road [that leads]
into the history of dogma" as the means of "making intelligible . . . the
transformation of Jesus' teaching into ancient Greek dogma." His
Geschichte der Paulinischen Forschung [= Paul and His Interpreters],
published a few years later (1911), undertook by a critical analysis of
previous research to prove that the theology of Paul is likewise to be
understood wholly on the ground of apocalyptic Judaism, and therefore
in light of an expectation of the imminence of the end that had been
thought through in strictly systematic fashion, while the Hellenization of
Christianity only began after Paul and is recognizable especially in the
Gospel of John.[314]

Theological scholarship has in fact been dominated by the desire to minimize
as much as possible the element of Jewish Apocalyptic in Jesus and Paul, and
so far as possible to represent the Hellenization of the Gospel as having been

prepared for by them. It thinks it has gained something when in formulating the problem it has done its best to soften down the antitheses to the utmost with a view to facilitate conceiving the transition of the Gospel from one world of thought to the other. . . .

The thoroughgoing application of Jewish eschatology to the interpretation of the teaching and work of Jesus has created a new fact upon which to base the history of dogma. If the view developed at the close of my *Quest of the Historical Jesus* is sound, the teaching of Jesus does not in any of its aspects go outside the Jewish world of thought and project itself into a non-Jewish world, but represents a deeply ethical and perfected version of the contemporary Apocalyptic.

Therefore the Gospel is at its starting-point exclusively Jewish-eschatological. The sharply antithetic formulation of the problem of the Hellenization of Christianity, which it always hoped to avoid, is proved by the facts recorded in the Synoptists to be the only admissible one. Accordingly, the history of dogma has to show how what was originally purely Jewish-eschatological has developed into something that is Greek. The expedients and evasions hitherto current have been withdrawn from circulation.

The primary task is to define the position of Paul. Is he the first stage of the Hellenizing process, or is his system of thought, like that of primitive Christianity, to be conceived as purely Jewish-eschatological? Usually the former is taken for granted, because he detached Christianity from Judaism, and because otherwise his thoughts do not seem to be easily explicable. Besides, it was feared that if the teaching of the Apostle to the Gentiles, as well as primitive Christianity, were regarded as purely Jewish-eschatological, the problem of the Hellenization of the Gospel would become so acute as to make the possibility of solving it more remote than ever. . . .

Those who have faced the recognition that the teaching of Jesus is eschatologically conditioned cannot be brought by considerations of this kind, scholarly or unscholarly, to entertain any doubt as to the task which awaits them. That is, to apply this new view to the explanation of the transition to the history of dogma, and as the first step in that direction, to undertake a new formulation of the problem of Paulinism. They will ultimately endeavour to find out how far the exclusively eschatological conception of the Gospel manifests its influence in the thoughts of the Apostle of the Gentiles, and will take into account the possibility that his system, strange as this may at first sight appear, may have developed wholly and solely out of that conception.

To apply the comparative method to Paul would, therefore, generally speaking, mean nothing more or less than to explain him on the basis of Late Judaism. Those who give due weight to the eschatological character of his doctrine and to the problems and ideas which connect it with works like the Apocalypse of Ezra are the true exponents of "History of Religions," even though they may make no claim to this title. Any one who goes beyond this and tries to bring Paul into direct connection with the Orient as such commits himself to the perilous path of scholarly adventure.

The half-and-half theories which represent Paulinism as consisting partly of Greek, partly of Jewish ideas, are worse off than those which more or less neglect the former element. Encumbered with all the difficulties of the Hellenizing theory they become involved in the jungle of antinomies which they discover or imagine, and there perish miserably.

242

The solution must, therefore, consist in leaving out of the question Greek influence in every form and in every combination, and risk the "one-sidedness" of endeavoring to understand the doctrine of the Apostle of the Gentiles entirely on the basis of Jewish primitive Christianity. That implies, in the first place, that the Pauline eschatology must be maintained in it full compass, as required by the evidence of the letters. But merely to emphasize it is not everything. The next point is to explain it. . . .

Not until Pauline eschatology gives an answer to all the "idle" questions . . . will it be really understood and explained. And it must be somehow possible, by the discovery of its inner logic, to reconstruct it from the scattered statements in the documents. We have no right to assume that for Paul there existed in his expectation manifest obscurities, much less that he had overlooked contradictions in it.

Is there, then, any possibility of explaining the mystical doctrine of redemption and the sacramental teaching on the basis of the Jewish eschatological element?

The attempt is by no means so hopeless as it might seem in view of the general consideration that Judaism knew neither mysticism nor sacraments. It is not really a question of Judaism as such, but of apocalyptic thought, which is a separate and independent phenomenon arising within Judaism, and has special presuppositions which are entirely peculiar to it.

We saw in analyzing the "physical" element in the doctrine of redemption and the sacraments that the related conceptions are conditioned by the underlying eschatology which everywhere shows through. It needs no special learning to make this discovery. Any one who ventures to read the documents with an open mind and pays attention to the primary links of connection will soon arrive at this conclusion. That Paul's mystical doctrine of redemption and his doctrine of the sacraments belong to eschatology is plain to be seen. The only question is in what way, exactly, they have arisen out of it. The future hope, raised to the highest degree of intensity, must somehow or other have possessed the power of producing them. If the impulse, the pressing need to which they were the response, is once recognized, then Paulinism is understood, since in its essence it can be nothing else than an eschatological mysticism, expressing itself by the aid of Greek religious terminology.

This *Geschichte der Paulinischen Forschung* [Paul and his interpreters] was intended to be only the introduction to Schweitzer's own *Mystik des Apostels Paulus* [The mysticism of Paul the apostle], but for personal reasons this latter account appeared twenty years later and at that time, in a completely different climate of research, was given a much more favorable reception[315] than had been accorded *Paul and His Interpreters.* For in the first decade of the twentieth century, parallel to the consistent setting of Jesus and Paul in the framework of contemporary Judaism by the representatives of "consistent eschatology," a study of the New Testament had developed, taking its departure from the Hellenistic environment [of early Christianity], whose results and views in the year 1911 stood so impressively before all eyes that, while Schweitzer's demonstration of the basic importance for Paul of the expectation of the end was regarded as proven, his further Jewish-apocalyptic interpretation of Paul, which denied all Hellenistic influences on the apostle, was rejected.[316] In order to comprehend the situation of research at the beginning of our century, we must therefore now direct our attention to the "history-of-religions" research that developed parallel to "consistent eschatology."

3.
The History-of-Religions School

About the same time as O. Pfleiderer, C. F. G. Heinrici, O. Everling, H. Gunkel, and W. Baldensperger pointed for the first time to early Christianity's links with religious concepts of its Hellenistic environment and Jewish-apocalyptic popular piety, a development took place in the study of the religion and the spirit of Hellenism that was to be of decisive importance for the historical investigation of early Christianity. After the scholarly study of antiquities had long concerned itself almost exclusively with the witnesses of classical religion and literature, interest turned towards the end of the nineteenth century, under the influence of research in Germanic religion, folklore, and ethnology, increasingly also to Hellenistic popular belief and syncretism.[317] When in 1890 **Erwin Rohde** published the first half of his masterful study of "the Greek cult of souls and belief in immortality" under the title of *Psyche*, he discovered behind Homeric ideas and customs "rudiments of an outgrown level of culture, . . . an important rudiment of the most ancient belief, reflected in a custom that did not wholly die out when times had changed." And for the understanding of the customs no longer understood even by the author, Rohde referred to the "beliefs of so-called peoples of nature, . . . our indigenous popular legend," or to "a very old idea, widespread among many peoples," and emphasized explicitly that such concepts that we meet among many peoples "arose spontaneously and independently in answer to a common need." [318] While reference was here made for the first time in comprehensive fashion to the prehistory of classical Greek religion and to the help provided by ethnology and folklore for the understanding of these persistent substrata of Greek religiosity, yet just prior to this, in 1899, **Hermann Usener, the real father of the "ethnological school" of the scholarly study of antiquities,** had applied these methods also to Hellenism and emerging Christianity in a history-of-religions study of *Das Weihnachtsfest* [The Christmas festival]. Here the magic-books of the papyri finds are used to familiarize us with the soil on which the pre-Christian gnosis grew. Here the New

Testament reports "that our Savior was the Son of God, born of a chaste virgin" are characterized as "the involuntary, indeed, by the nature of things inevitable, reflection of the divinity of Christ in the souls of converted Greeks," and the whole cycle of birth and infancy narratives of Matthew's Gospel is said to be legend that appears "to have arisen on Greek soil." Here, behind the reports of the baptism of Jesus in the Gospels, the prehistory of these religious ideas is sought, because "inner contradictions in simple mythical pictures" may "probably always be considered as signs of a later compromise." And here this historical question concerning the transformation of original ideas, as this can be deduced from the reports of the New Testament, is characterized as "a genuine act of worship, well-pleasing to God," in the confidence "that the divine kernel of our religion, freed from the human husk of poetry and dogma, will prove itself only all the more effective to coming, more advanced generations as a source of salvation and as a means of lifting the soul to God." [319] One of Usener's pupils, **Albrecht Dieterich**, then turned in 1891 wholly to the "wild, often bottomless ocean of 'syncretism.'" On the basis of a study of the magic-papyri, he pointed out that "the form of religious thinking, not to say of religion; that the men of the Stoa had taught . . . had for long been disseminated among the people" in the Greek world, and drew attention to the fact that the Pauline idea of "the weak and beggarly elemental spirits" (Gal. 4:9) is only to be understood in light of a "magical background" in which "the elements or the stars [are characterized] as demons." He pointed out, further, that the Revelation to John "painted the ancient, powerful picture of the battle between Apollo and the dragon in the old colors as the eschatological battle of Michael and his angels against the dragon and his angels," and that also much in the background of this passage (Rev. 12) is dependent on Greek myth forms. And Dieterich maintained that we have hardly begun "correctly to understand this process of the Hellenizing of Christianity," and that "the problem of the genesis of the Christian religion and its forms, a problem also in this direction so infinitely wide and immense," seems to be the one "that chiefly confronts us today." [320] Consequently Dieterich a decade later, in connection with the publication of a magic-text that he interpreted as a liturgy, made a study throughout all antiquity, ethnology, and folklore of such religious conceptual forms as those of the unity with the Godhead, the eating of the god, the magic inherent in a name, the sonship with God, rebirth, and so forth, and also in this connection brought similar New Testament concepts under consideration and gave them a correspondingly realistic interpretation ("Christ was eaten and drunk by the believers and therefore is in them" [I Cor. 10:16 ff.]; "the strongest evidence for the magical understanding of the earliest rite of baptism" is the reference to baptism on behalf of the dead [I Cor. 15:29-30]; etc.) .[321]

Other scholars soon joined these pioneers of a comparative, historical method in studying Hellenistic religiosity and in relating the New Testament to this history of religion. In 1895 **Paul Wendland** pointed out that the Jewish philosopher Philo was dependent at many points on the Stoic philosophy ("diatribe") that had permeated the popular thought of the day. In this connection he stressed that "If New Testament writings have many concepts and ideas, stylistic forms and conventions, in common with philosophical literature, it is consequently not impossible that the diatribe has already exercised a certain influence on parts of early Christian literature." [322] This shows that he was already aware that a study of the culture and religion of Hellenism was indispensable for the historical understanding of the New Testament,[323] and in an account of *Die hellenistisch-römische Kultur* [The culture of the Hellenistic-Roman world] (1907) that summed up the research of the time but avoided extremes, Wendland pointed out that "Christianity . . . was influenced in many respects by streams of popular thought and by the popular and ephemeral literature produced in that time, but that we today find only too baffling," that "Christianity [shares] with its time the boundless faith in the miraculous," that "already in early Christian literature . . . borrowings of pagan ideas and motifs, reminiscences of, and relationships to, the Hellenistic conceptual world, [increase] with the progressive stages in its development," indeed, "that oriental gnosis had its influence on the special religiosity of Paul and that this factor helps to explain the undeniable difference between Paul's Christianity and Jesus' Gospel." Wendland also, to be sure, will not admit that Jesus' message of the kingdom of God is to be understood eschatologically ("the idea of the kingdom of God is transformed into a spiritual and already present fellowship") . And since in his judgment Christianity as a religion of redemption is to be understood only against the background of "purely pagan mysticism," it follows that Jesus' "picture" stands quite apart "from this [pagan mystical] atmosphere." [324]

In this connection two other scholars remain to be mentioned, men whose contributions to the study of the history of the religion of Hellenism strongly influenced the development of New Testament research. In his monumental book on the religion of Mithra, published in 1899, **Franz Cumont**, the Belgian historian of religion, gave the first inclusive account in the history of comparative religion of a Hellenistic mystery cult and in so doing pointed out numerous parallels between ancient Christianity and the religion of Mithra, though he reserved judgment on the question of a mutual influence on each other of both religions because we "have too inadequate a knowledge of the dogmas and the liturgy of Roman Mazdaism as well as of the history of early Christianity to be able to determine under which mutual influences their simultaneous development took place." [325] In a brilliant account of the invasion of Roman paganism by the oriental religions published a few years later (1907), though he likewise avoided the question of the influence on early Christianity of the oriental religions,[326] he did however demonstrate by examples that "the researches into the doctrines [and] practices common to Christianity and the Oriental mysteries lead almost always beyond the limits of the Roman empire into the Hellenistic Orient" and demanded an explanation above all of "the composite worship in . . . Jewish-pagan communities." [327]

The task of clarifying these oriental antecedents of Hellenism and consequently of early Christianity was taken up by **Richard Reitzentstein.** Already in connection with the publication of two papyri in 1910 he pointed out that "the religious idea, so foreign to us, that the 'word' in itself is at the same time a divine personality [is] to be explained by the union of Stoic and Egyptian theories," and that this idea, already known to Philo, had become current in the Orient and explains the significance of the *logos* concept in the prologue to John's Gospel.[328] In a study that appeared shortly thereafter of Hermetic texts as important documents "of that mighty religious movement . . . which overflowed the West from the East like a flood and first prepared the way for Christianity and then swept it along with it," he tried to prove that "the coalescence of Greek and oriental life of the spirit" was due to Egyptain influences on Hellenistic mysticism. This postulated not only the existence of a "Hellenistic myth of a 'man' from God," but also led to the observation that the peculiar speech formulae of Hellenistic mysticism pervade the whole Gospel of John and therefore that "the remnants of Hellenistic mysticism . . . no less than the Christian writings [must] be regarded as . . . a usable lexicon of the New Testament." [329] With this was properly stressed anew the necessity of drawing on the Graeco-oriental environment of the New Testament for the historical understanding of the New Testament.

In the meantime religio-historical research into the New Testament had already begun, closely connected in both time and content with the first publications by members of the school of classical philology that had undertaken to investigate folklore and ethnology.[330] **Hermann Gunkel,** who a few years earlier had related the Pauline idea of the Spirit to the concept in late Judaism (see above, p. 230), published in 1895 a study of the first and last books of the Bible entitled *Schöpfung und Chaos in Urzeit and Endzeit* [Creation and chaos at the beginning and the end of time], in preparation of which he was able to use, in addition to the help of the Assyriologist H. Zimmern, also the criticism of Albert Eichhorn, whose contributions proved especially stimulating to the earliest investigations carried out by representatives of the history-of-religions school.[331] By means of a vigorous critique of the then current interpretations, Gunkel pointed out that the creation story (Gen. 1) and the vision of the heavenly mother (Rev. 12) cannot be understood on the assumption of Jewish or Christian origin. On the contrary, he argued that behind both passages there stands the Babylonian creation myth which, in the time of late Judaism, had reached Israel also in an eschatological version. In this connection strong emphasis was placed on the need of a historical study of the *tradition*, in particular of apocalyptic texts, and on the consequent insight that when foreign myths are assimilated numerous elements are also taken over without being understood. Reference is also made in passing to the necessity of investigating the *tradition* of Jesus.[332]

In principle, then, a new method for the exegesis of apocalyptic writings emerges, a method that must be distinguished as sharply from the two that have hitherto been used as the view of the nature of the subject matter that lies back of both is different. The first two explanations agree in that they think of the authors of the apocalyptic writings as originators of their material; in accordance with this, such an apocalyptic writing would be the work of a single person, would have arisen out of the situation of a given time, would be a purely literary entity. Of quite another sort, however, are writings that represent in essence codifications of a tradition: the actual originator of the matter embodied in them is not the writer but a whole series of generations; and the matter in the form in which it exists today presupposes a history, possibly of centuries, in which oral tradition also may play a role. Therefore the interpretation must be different: According to the first two methods the object of investigation would be the coherent work of *one* writer, who is to be understood in light of his time; in the case of a codified tradition the exegesis consists in exploring the prehistory of the subject matter, a prehistory that may be very complicated and stretch over a long period, and in explaining the present state of the tradition in light of that prehistory. . . .

It cannot be taken for granted that the apocalyptist freely invented his material, not even that he did what he liked with what he took over; rather, in connection with every new body of subject matter the question is to be raised anew, whether it is to be explained better out of a history of the tradition than out of the mind of man. In this respect especial attention is to be paid to the uncertainties of the text before us; we must investigate whether an oral tradition is to be assumed and, by virtue of its nature, in what form the apocalyptic subject matter existed. . . .

We are perhaps inclined to wonder why this method of paying attention to the history of the tradition has thus far remained so very much in the background—until we recognize the legitimacy of this phenomenon. This, too, is grounded in the literary critical character of modern biblical exegesis: interest lies predominantly in literary questions. . . . Furthermore, more attention has been paid to the writings that document such a tradition than to the history of the tradition at the oral level. We have highly complicated investigations of the synoptic problem, as of the source documents of genesis, but only the beginnings of a history of the early Christian tradition about Jesus, and still no history of the origin and transmission of the patristic tradition. So also in connection with the Apocalypse we have a plethora of source hypotheses, but no history of the apocalyptic tradition.

In the preceding study [of Rev. 12] we observed the juxtaposition of highly concrete and quite attentuated traits and recognized in the former the well-preserved remnants of the old tradition. Since we can take it for granted that the original recension—as everything original—possessed a uniform style, it follows that we have to think of it after the fashion of the concrete traits.

Well then, of what sort are these concrete traits? Characteristic of them all is a certain burning hue, the symptom of a passionately aroused fantasy.

If we yield to this aesthetic impression and go on to ask where we must look for analogies to these traits, the answer must be uttered: in mythology. . . .

If we now are justified in thinking of the original form of the now-no-longer-distinct traits after the fashion of those that have been retained, we then must maintain that the narrative originally was much more colorful, mythological, than it is now. The presently obscured connections and faded individual traits were originally of a mythological nature; and in this very nature we now also recognize the reason why they have been retained in such an enfeebled state.

So a great part of the New Testament speculations—Christology, the doctrine of predestination, the doctrine of the original state, and so forth—bears this form of equating the first and the last.

If the primeval myth of chaos is understood eschatologically, this too fits in this connection. At the end is repeated what was at the beginning: a new chaos will precede the new creation; the monsters of the beginning of time appear on earth a second time. In all this an image of the ancient myth has been taken up: Already the ancient myth that saw in the storm floods of the present a repetition, however pale, of the primeval chaos, had here and there spoken of the monster of primeval times that only "waits," chained in the abyss, "locked in by bolts and bars," and at times attempts to escape the divine power. This picture is developed: The beast of chaos, chained at the beginning by God in the deep abyss, will escape at the time of the end and "ascend" to the upper world. But then, as once upon a time before the creation, he will be overcome again by God. Then chaos will be set aside once and for all; in the new world the battle will not be refought. . . .

In all probability the myth had already been given this eschatological twist when it found its way into Judaism.

Here a small matter brings a greater to light; vis-à-vis this heterogeneous tradition, Judaism and Christianity are closely related phenomena; to the Jewish interpretation of the material the related Christian interpretation attached itself. . . . The Christian interpretation is just as eclectic and inorganic as the Jewish. From the Christian standpoint, also, the fact that the tradition, though so little was understood, was nevertheless handed on, is to be understood only as a result of holy awe before the deep mystery of this revelation. . . .

Chap. 12 of the Apocalypse of John which, whether it grew up on Jewish or Christian soil would contain nothing but confused, muddled, and—now it may even be said—half-crazy phantasmagoria, is, if only rightly understood, a wonderful myth that out of most ancient times speaks to us of the eternal woes and the eternal faith of mankind.

A few months later in his study of the idea of the anti-Christ **Wilhelm Bousset** built on the methodological foundation laid by Gunkel. "With a view to the explanation and interpretation of some obscure passages in the Revelation of St. John," Bousset undertakes a thorough study, covering the period from late Judaism to medieval times, of the tradition of a figure who at the end of days would be opposed to God. He demonstrates that the later sources offer "much supplementary matter needed to fill up the gaps and omissions in the earlier and more fragmentary documents" because "in many cases the eschatological revelations have been passed on, not in written records, but in oral tradition, as an esoteric doctrine. . . . Hence it is not till later times that the tradition comes to light in all its abundance." According to Bousset, however, behind the legend of the anti-Christ stands the primeval dragon myth that has been reworked into the expectation of a simple pseudomessiah. In this way Bousset also emphasizes the necessity of an interpretation of apocalyptic matter in light of the history of the tradition. But he goes still further. He explicitly asserts that for the understanding of the gospel such presuppositions are unnecessary, consequently he invariably removes the message of Jesus from consideration as a history-of-religions matter. The methodological demands set forth in this book for a suitable interpretation of an apocalyptic writing were then put into practice by Bousset in his epochmaking commentary on the Revelation to John (1896), a study in which he made use of the whole body of comparative history-of-religions material to explain the individual apocalyptic images and paid attention to the confluence of different traditions, while at the same time making inquiries into the religious conceptual world of the apocalyptist. Research in light of the history of religion clearly serves here, then, the understanding of the *particularity* of the New Testament text, but does so in the sense of interpreting it in a radically historical way.[333]

In such discrimination lies the whole art of sound exegesis for all apocalyptic writings. Everything depends on clearly distinguishing between what is traditional and what is peculiar to each document. . . .

The method of literary criticism so much in vogue at present will certainly have to modify its pretensions greatly; an end must be put once for all to the reckless use of the knife, and critics must henceforth refrain from laying rude hands on original documents. . . . Before critical analysis can be undertaken a far more accurate knowledge of the substantive connections must be achieved. . . .

Work of a comprehensive character must be undertaken, even though the results produce only extrinsic works. These investigations do not penetrate into the essence of things, into all that lives and has real force in every religion. For the pitch and marrow of all creeds lies in what is special to each, not in what one nation or one religion may have borrowed from another; it lies in the original creations of distinct personalities, not in what one generation may have handed down to another. To understand the Revelation we need a fulness of eschatological and mythological knowledge; to understand the Gospel all this may for the most part be dispensed with.

Behind this anti-Christ saga there lies an earlier myth. As convincingly shown by Gunkel himself, we find in the Old and here and there in the New Testament literature very numerous traces of a primeval creation myth, which was later transformed to an expectation of the last things. As may be seen in Revelation, there existed in the popular Jewish belief the foreboding of another revolt of the old marine monster with whom God had warred at the creation, but who in the last days was again to rise and contend in heaven-storming battle with God. The expectation is not of any hostile ruler and of the oppression of Israel by him and his army, but of a struggle of Satan directly with God, of a conflict of the Dragon with the Almighty throned in heaven. To me the anti-Christ legend seems a simple incarnation of that old dragon myth, which has in the first instance nothing to do with particular political power and occurrences. For the dragon is substituted the man armed with miraculous power who makes himself God's equal—a man who in the eyes of the Jews could be no other than the false messiah.

But the anti-Christ legend is after all unable quite to conceal its origin in a far wilder and more fantastic world of thought and sentiments, from which it has received an indelible impression. During its further development there continually arises behind the anti-Christ the still wilder figure of the God-hating demon, of Satan, ever seeking to thrust him aside. The history of the saga bears on its face the impress of our assumption regarding its origin.

In recent times a new method of interpreting the Apocalypse has been introduced by Gunkel, one we can call the "history-of-the-tradition" method. Here and there this method has already been applied without its practitioners being aware of what they were doing. . . . Whatever you may think of Gunkel's investigations in detail, it remains true that an uncommonly strong traditional element is to be found in all apocalyptic. And it follows from this that if possible the apocalyptic material of such recurring ideas and traditions must be surveyed as inclusively as possible before research into the peculiarity and historical determination of any given apocalypse can get underway. In the interpretation of all apocalyptic Gunkel combines in fine style the history-of-religions viewpoint with that of the history-of-tradition method.

The main task of a commentary on the Apocalypse—provided our view of the whole of the document is the correct one—is fulfilled by obtaining as living a conception as possible of the character of the apocalyptist himself, his piety, and the situation in which he writes. At the same time, however, it must be kept in mind that the writer of the Apocalypse in a large part of his writing, as we already have had occasion to observe, does not create with a free hand and with his own resources; it seems almost as if he had the intention not merely of giving a definite prophecy, but of writing a *corpus apocalypticum,* of organizing a collection of apocalyptic material then in circulation in accordance with a unified point of view. Therefore the second task consists in the careful study of the apocalyptic sources. To be sure, it will always remain more important—this is a point of view far too often overlooked—to determine what the apocalyptist himself did with this than to take a few uncertain steps in the darkness of the apocalyptic tradition that lies back of him. But this latter work also must be done for the very reason that a more exact study of the sources and the tradition that lies at the disposal of the apocalypse provides indirectly a clearer insight into what is precisely peculiar to, and characteristic of, it. Every apocalypse is only properly understood at the moment one succeeds with some assurance in separating the matter it has taken over, from what is peculiar to it. . . .

The apocalyptist is not only a writer who hands on ancient, sacred ideas, often not understood, just as they are, but one who creates *de novo* and who, even where he only takes over matter, views what he has taken over with his own eyes, as this is often surprisingly apparent in quite insignificant alterations. And it is much more important for us to pay attention to this than to trace the apocalyptic material of the Apocalypse to its ultimate stages.

If the history-of-religions view of the New Testament began with what is conceptually the strangest book of the New Testament, the Revelation to John, it soon turned just as naturally to that phenomenon of early Christian history that seemed least to correspond with the Jewish origin of Christianity, viz., the sacraments. In his lecture on *Das Abendmahl im Neuen Testament* [The Lord's Supper in the New Testament] (1898), Albert Eichhorn emphasized expressly that he wished "to proceed in accordance with another method than that usually employed," namely, in accordance with the "history-of-religions" method that directs "its interest to the formation of Christianity as religion." Consequently he tried to demonstrate that the New Testament reports concerning Jesus' last supper were influenced "by the dogma and the cultures of the Church" and that therefore "the original, historical event . . . cannot clearly [be] ascertained." And if Paul thinks of "participating in the body and blood of Christ," we cannot, according to Eichhorn, question this view, although we do not know how it arose. Although he hints at a "gnostic view of religion" as a possible source, Eichhorn is of the opinion that this historical problem is still "not clearly recognized by any scholar"; the step from Jesus to the sacramental cult meal of the Church must therefore still be explained in terms of history-of-religions method.[334]

It is very important for us to recognize the oldest level of the tradition of Jesus, which is preserved for us only fragmentarily. In large part it is overlaid by more recent levels, and only by a critical procedure can the older levels be uncovered. In this endeavor the scholar will be aware that his aim is the same as that of the practitioner of the historico-critical method. On the other hand, it is just as important—yes, we may say, in a certain respect even more important —to recognize the transformation of the older traditions and to appreciate the result of the whole process. In passing I should like here to refer to a folly of historical criticism that we encounter more often than one might think. There are actually people who believe they have to identify the oldest recoverable tradition with the historical event itself. The latest reports, it is held, must be rejected by every theologian trained in historical criticism, while the oldest reports, on the other hand, must be accepted if the accusation of arbitrariness is not to be invited. I confess that I hold this view to be very restricting. In fact, I must simply repudiate it as wholly unscientific. Such critics have the second-rate mind of an actuary; however tolerant I am, I cannot express myself more gently. In reality it is natural that the same factors that were at work, in a way we can recognize, to transform the old within the tradition when it was fixed in literary form, had already played a decisive role at earlier stages. I believe it probable that the most important transformations of the traditions took place in the first decades of the Christian Church. The question arises: why, then, was the older tradition transformed—the tradition that in fact was at the same time the historically more accurate? The answer is: because it did not satisfy the need of the Church.

But why did the idea of eating and drinking the body and blood arise? I emphasize the fact that this question must be raised by all theologians, irrespective of whether they doubt the historical character of our accounts or not. For he who regards our reports as historical must somehow interpret Jesus' words symbolically. Then this theologian has to face the question of how the transformation of symbolism into reality could have taken place. The question exists, then, for all theologians without distinction, except for the few who, in the Lutheran sense, maintain the real presence of Christ's body and blood even in the Last Supper. The answer to our question can only be: We are unable to say. . . .

We do not find the requisite presuppositions of the Eucharist in the area of the Old Testament, where there is no actual sacrament of eating and drinking. Here we have to have recourse to that form of oriental religious view that I characterize for brevity's sake as gnostic. Naturally I call it gnostic in somewhat different sense than the Church historians are accustomed to do. Jewish and gnostic-oriental elements are combined with each other in the Lord's Supper as in the rite of baptism. Baptism for the forgiveness of sins is to be explained on Old Testament presuppositions, while baptism as a bath of rebirth to eternal life, on the other hand, is gnostic-oriental. The forgiveness of sins in the Lord's Supper is Jewish, while the Lord's Supper as a meal that leads to eternal life is oriental. In the Gospel of John we find that baptism effects rebirth and that the Eucharist gives eternal life. This is due to the fact that the Gospel of John generally uses in a Christian connection ideas that already long existed in the religious vocabulary of gnostic religion.

We cannot now document such a sacramental meal that could have afforded the model for the Eucharist; and this is a gap in our historical knowledge. It is the task of the historian to recognize these gaps in our knowledge and to de-limit their extent and significance: more science cannot do, for it cannot bridge this gap. The more exact the historical sense and the historical method, the better we are able to recognize where a steady historical development lies before us and where this is not the case. The difficulty for me lies in the history-of-religions development. Whatever Jesus may have said and done that evening does not enable me to understand the cult meal of the Church, with its sacramental eating and drinking of the body and blood of Christ, as it took its rise in the earliest church, apparently from the beginning.

The task articulated by Eichhorn was soon after taken up by **Wilhelm Heitmüller**, a tutor at Göttingen. In a study of the ideas connected with the use of the name of Jesus in early Christianity (1903) —a study rich in its employment of source material—he not only gave a linguistic explanation for the meaning of the expressions "baptism in the name of Jesus" or "baptism into the name of Jesus" (the expressions denote dedication to Jesus, accompanied by the utterance of his name), but also drew attention to the ancient, and at the same time Jewish, faith in the power and magic virtue of the "name" as the root of the use of the name of Jesus in early Christianity: "Here as there, we have before us the same religio-historical phenomenon. . . . Here, as scarcely anywhere else, we clearly see the close relation of nascent Christianity—a relation that existed from the earliest beginnings of the Church—with the general stream of the history of religion." From this it followed that, according to the belief of early Christianity, the naming of Jesus in connection with baptism had a real exorcistic significance. And in a lecture on *Taufe und Abendmahl bei Paulus* [Baptism and the Eucharist in Paul] which appeared a little later, Heitmüller emphasizes that baptism for Paul was a sacrament with "effects of a mystical and enthusiastic nature" in which faith played no essential role. And in similar fashion, "Christ in the Eucharist . . . [is] the food and the drink that are served" and "the effects of baptism and the Eucharist lie above all in the enthusiastic, mystic side of Pauline Christianity." Then, in particular, Heitmüller tried to prove that in the Pauline idea of the Lord's Supper the primitive concept of devouring the godhead again breaks through, a concept for which also parallels from widely remote religions can be cited: "The Pauline view of the Eucharist . . . is a new shoot on an old branch of the history-of-religions tree of mankind." And while Heitmüller emphasizes expressly that the Pauline views are not to be "characterized as worthless" because "in the end [they] have their root not in the gospel, but in the soil of the general history of religion," he nevertheless raises the question "whether the Pauline views of baptism and the Eucharist can still be valid for us." And Heitmüller also points to the remoteness of this Pauline sacramental mysticism from the preaching of Jesus.[335]

The name-milieu of Judaism and that of syncretistic paganism bear by and large the same features. And this is true not only of these two areas. In spite of many small differences and nuances . . . the Jew and the Babylonian, the Ancient Egyptian and the Hellenistic pagan, have a closely related, almost identical view of the worth of the name, especially of the worth of holy names, and of the use of the name. . . .

255

The value and use of the Jesus-name in earliest Christianity obtain their peculiar, historical light against this background. This foil must be kept in mind as we explore the question of what ideas may have been bound up with the Jesus-name and its use. . . .

We have . . . to assume that not only in postapostolic times, but already in the apostolic age the name of Jesus was believed to be furnished with miraculous powers and was utilized, that is to say, was named, in prophesying, in the doing of mighty acts in general, and in particular in the driving out of demons. . . .

Furthermore, however, in view of our sources it is highly probable that the first seeds of the Christian faith in the name had already sprouted during Jesus' lifetime among the earliest circle of disciples.

Christian faith in the name is not really to be distinguished in principle from Jewish and pagan beliefs. . . .

And if from our point of view we use the categories of magic and superstition for the Jewish and pagan faith in the name, the same categories must necessarily be employed with respect to the faith of ancient Christianity in the Jesus-name.

The solemn naming of the name of Jesus in the rite of baptism is not merely a symbolic form for the confession of Jesus' messiahship, to take one example, but is thought of as bound up with real, mystical, mysterious effects; the effects, however, must be similar *mutatis mutandis* to those that in other connections are ascribed to the use of this name: real seizure by the power that is designated by the Jesus-name, sealing, inward union with the bearer of the name, expulsion of all hostile powers, consecration, and infusion with the Spirit.

Baptism and the Eucharist are means of grace in the sense that they mediate divine grace, divine gifts of grace. But in the first place they are not means of grace in the sense that the term is used in the Reformed tradition, that is, as means by which divine grace awakens faith, and thus identical in function with the Gospel.

After their fashion they are effective, sacramental actions. . . . Obviously faith is presupposed, but it is not apparent that this faith converts or could convert the sacramental effect into an effect that is transmitted psychologically.

The effects of baptism and the Eucharist belong chiefly to the enthusiastic-mystic side of Pauline Christianity, hardly at all to the ethical-personal side. They relate to the possession of the Spirit and to Christ-mysticism.

At the basis of the worth of both acts lies a mystical-natural conception of the religious relationship, from the psychological point of view a primitive, animistic, spiritistic way of thinking.

These views of baptism and the Eucharist stand, therefore, in unharmonized and unharmonizable incongruence with the central meaning of faith in Pauline Christianity, that is to say, with the purely spiritual, personal conception of the religious relationship as this stands in the foreground of Pauline piety and ideology.

On the other hand, we see also that very central elements of the apostle's religious world of thought stand so completely in harmony with the idea of the sacraments that we can say: if Paul had not found baptism and the Eucharist as existing sacraments, he could have produced them entirely on his own.

And not only that, from the point of view of the philosophy of history we must say: he would have *had* to do that, if he wanted by some means to conquer the world with his gospel. For the world that he had to win could not yet endure the purely spiritual view of the Gospel that corresponded most closely to his religious genius; it needed the excitement and the magic of the mysteries and sacraments. . . .

Finally, in the interest of a proper judgment of these Pauline views it must not be forgotten that, however certain it is that sacramental mysticism stands in closest connection with the central points of his piety and ideas, it is just as certain that the apostle's primary interest and the peculiar power of his message did not inhere in it.

It requires no proof that the ideas described to this point did not have their background and their root in what we know as the message of Jesus—if the sparse fragments [we possess] enable us rightly to recognize the essence of this message. In the sober, plain, simple preaching of the coming kingdom, the judgment, the holy Father-God who forgives sins, "the infinite worth of the human soul," the proclamation of the righteousness of the kingdom of God— hard as steel—there is not a syllable of the Spirit-mysticism and Christ-mysticism of the baptism and the Lord's Supper.

Rescued from its isolation the Pauline idea of the Eucharist does not appear in its basic features as something absolutely new and as an original creation of Christianity, but as interwoven with the pre- and extra-Christian religious world of ideas. It is a new sprout on an old branch of the history-of-religions tree of mankind.

In one form or another a primordial longing to enter into direct, real union with deity possesses almost all peoples of the old and new world. There is a primordial conviction of being able to obtain that union by natural media which stand directly or indirectly in contact with the life of the deity and mediate that life in a natural-mystical way. In a form suited to the new conditions, that primordial longing and that primordial conviction express themselves in the primitive Christian Eucharist. (I am not speaking of Jesus' view.) . . .

In light of our scanty sources, however, it is too precarious to wish to affirm a direct dependence on such specific phenomena. We are on safer ground if we point to the general character of the time, a time filled to the full with such ideas. Nascent Christianity lived in an atmosphere which, if you will permit the expression, was impregnated with the bacilli of the mysteries. It grew on a soil that was manured and plowed up, and through the decay and the syncretistic tendencies of a great variety of religions old seeds could sprout and old shoots could take on new life.

To his studies of separate subjects **Hermann Gunkel** now also added a fundamental piece of research. In his book *Zum religionsgeschichtlichen Verständnis des Neuen Testaments* [A contribution to the history-of-religions understanding of the New Testament] (1903) he defended the thesis that "in its origin and development the New Testament religion stood at a few even essential points under the decisive influence of foreign religions and that this influence on the men of the New Testament came by way of Judaism." Taking his departure from the presupposition that "historical knowledge [means] . . . knowledge derived from the historical connection," he therefore pointed out by examples that "the Judaism that developed along certain lines must actually be called a syncretistic religion" and then went on to show by reference to individual features of the Revelation to John, the pre- and post-histories of the Gospels, and the Christology of Paul that in these instances oriental ideas taken over from Judaism were simply transferred to Jesus. From this he reached the startling thesis that Christianity is a syncretistic religion, though, to be sure, the Gospel of Jesus was, as previously, excepted from this judgment.[336]

Our thesis is . . . that *Christianity, born of syncretistic Judaism, exhibits strongly syncretistic features.* Early Christianity is like a river that is the confluence of two great source streams: the one is specifically Israelite, it originates in the Old Testament; the other, however, flows through Judaism from the foreign, oriental religions. Then to this, in the West, is added the Greek factor. It is to be emphasized explicitly that in this connection "Gospel" and "Christianity" are to be sharply distinguished and that in what follows, the discussion first of all is of "Christianity," that is, the religion of the earliest Christian Church, not the "Gospel," that is, the proclamation of Jesus that in the main we reconstruct from the synoptic accounts. . . .

The student of the Old Testament who in the New Testament turns first of all to the Synoptics finds himself in a world in which he soon feels at home; it is pervaded by a spirit with which he is familiar, for he knows it from the noblest prophets; and here he joyfully greets the most magnificent transfiguration of what prophets and psalmists in their finest moments wanted to declare. What is strange in the sayings of Jesus amounts to only relatively little, and even that is no more than what must have been generally recognized in Judaism at the time: The center of what is strange in the gospel is eschatology, especially the doctrine of the resurrection of men at the last day.

That the preaching of Jesus is so relatively free of the mythical element is explained by the person of Jesus himself, whose simple greatness scorns the clever, the fantastic, as well as by the simple circles of the Galilean peasantry from which he issued; these circles, we may suppose, lived in the thoughts of the psalms as in olden times; they had little place for secret, mythical teaching. . . .

But the greatest part of the New Testament, especially the writings of *Paul* and *John,* present quite a different picture. Here the student of the Old Testament finds things wherever he turns for which he has absolutely no analogy and which he cannot understand historically. Think only of ideas such as reconciliation by Christ's death, the mystical union of Christ and the Church, the creation of the world by Christ, among others. . . .

But whoever compares all these doctrines that are foreign to the Gospel will be astonished at the mighty productive power of early Christianity and will have to assume that here an extraordinarily strong foreign factor has played a part. It is not the Gospel of Jesus, as we know it predominantly from the Synoptics, but *the early Christianity of Paul and of John* that *is a syncretistic religion.*

Where are we to look for this foreign factor? At present scholars point almost exclusively to the influence of Hellenism, especially of Alexandrian Hellenism. Let me emphasize once more that this Hellenistic influence, which is not to be treated here, must not be left out of account or minimized. But it is a question whether the assumption [of Hellenistic influence] *wholly* solves the problem. The numerous details that have been presented in preceding sections of this study raise the question of whether the foreign factor is not to be sought *in the Orient itself.* If we look to the Orient we have every right to think first of an influence emanating from *oriental gnosis.* The contact of Paul and John with later occidental gnosis has long been recognized. Let us now recall the picture of oriental gnosis that has been sketched in preceding sections of this study. As a matter of fact, at many points at which it differs from the Gospel, early Christianity agrees with this oriental religious movement. Let us name a few of these points of agreement (there are many others) : the high respect for knowledge; the partition of the world, which often reminds us of dualism; the longing of man for redemption and "rebirth"; faith in the descent of a redeemer-god; the doctrine of the sacraments; the treatment of knowledge as something secret, a concept that plays a large role in the New Testament. John's Gospel is carefully attuned to this tone of infinitely deeper, more secret teachings that ordinary men with hearing ears cannot hear. Indeed, there are also contacts in vocabulary: "the life," "the light," "the word of life," "the vine" as names of aeons. All this should dispose the New Testament scholar to look for contacts not only in the Greek world but also in the Orient. . . .

Christianity is a syncretistic religion. Powerful religious motives that came from abroad were contained in it and throve mightily, both oriental and Hellenistic. For the characteristic feature—we might say, the providential feature— of Christianity is *that it experienced its classical era in the hour of world history when it stepped out of the Orient into Hellenism.* Therefore it has a share in both worlds. However strong the Hellenistic element in it became, the oriental, which was characteristic of it from the beginning, never wholly disappeared. These foreign religious motives must have flooded into the Church of Jesus immediately after Jesus' death. For this reason it would be incorrect (although it is often done) to use the Gospel of Jesus, recovered in large part from the Synoptics, as the only valid standard by which to measure Christianity. Rather, vis-à-vis the Gospel, from which on the one hand it derives, Christianity is a new, independent phenomenon, on the other hand, having its roots also in a soil from which the Gospel did not grow. Therefore this phenomenon cannot be measured only by the Gospel, but bears its standard of measurement within itself.

Gunkel's thesis that foreign religions exercised a decisive influence on early Christianity by way of Judaism was supported at the same time by **Wilhelm Bousset.** In his *Religion des Judentums im neutestamentlichen Zeitalter* [*The Religion of Judaism in the New Testament Age*] 1903) , an account based on the whole tradition of late, nonrabbinical Judaism, he demonstrated that at many points Judaism also could not escape influence by the religious mixing of the Hellenistic age and that these influences "finally [penetrated] to the very center of religion" even in Palestinian Judaism. "In the end it was not just *one* religion that contributed to the development of Christianity, but contact of the religions of the western world of culture, of the Hellenistic period of culture. . . . Judaism was the retort in which the various elements were assembled. Then the new formation of the Gospel was brought into being by a creative miracle." [337] And in a lecture that set these researches in a wider context, Bousset emphasized that Jewish apocalyptic, influenced by Iranian religion, had prepared the way both for the message of the Gospel and for the Christology of the early Church; he sees himself even driven also to admit that "in all probability . . . Jesus himself in individual sayings towards the end of his life [had] reached for this title [i.e., Son of man]" in order thereby "to express his confidence in the lasting triumph of his person and his cause." It was also assumed that Jesus had contact with apocalyptic, which was influenced by Iranian religion. Yet at the same time it is now apparent why these theologians who consciously employed history-of-religions methodology also excepted the message of Jesus from the history-of-religions influence on early Christianity that they had demonstrated: the proof of foreign influence on early Christianity is also to serve to exclude foreign matter from the Gospel, which by these very means is to be preserved as "a creative miracle." Once again and on a new plane the danger appears that earlier became apparent (cf. above pp. 69 ff., 127) in the writings of J. D. Michaelis and F. C. Baur in connection with problems of New Testament introduction, namely, that a decisive *theological* question is to be answered by *historical* means.[338]

The closer we examine the character of the contemporary Jewish hope, the clearer we see how Jesus goes his own way in his proclamation of the kingdom of God. If we look first of all at its outer form, we see little trace of [a belief in] the transformation of things. When Jesus speaks of the anticipated future, he always employs the concept of the kingdom of God to sum up the whole hope. That is to say, Jesus holds fast to the central concept of the ancient popular messianic expectation. If he used the new terms—this world, that world—at all, he did so only very infrequently. So, with the sure hand of a master he spiritualized the popular faith in the kingdom of God by almost wholly denationalizing it. . . .

Nevertheless we may be permitted to say: the Jewish apocalyptic prepared the way for the proclamation of the Gospel and cultivated the soil for it. The idea that the hoped-for new world, the new life of the pious in the future, is by its nature something different and higher, lies seedlike and latent in Judaism. The Gospel caused it to sprout and blossom.

Other-worldly gospel faith develops very quickly. Even Paul articulates it in the purest form. For him the new era is actually other-worldly. In his writings the term "Kingdom of God" retreats wholly into the background. The contrast between this world and the world to come is set forth in all its sharpness. The temporal for him is visible, the eternal invisible. . . . The idea of the beyond begins here to lift its wings. That this could happen so easily is best explained on the assumption that Paul, even before he became a Christian, held an eschatological view such as appears in Fourth Ezra and the Apocalypse of Baruch, for instance. Among Christians, it was Paul to be sure who first of all was the recipient of eschatology's full force and of its ability to arouse the will. He was the first to loose the religion of Christianity from the Law and from the nation, and thereby he stripped the Christian hope of its last traces of this-worldly residue. On the other hand, however, it must be admitted that his basic views of the world of the flesh and of the world of the spirit are anticipated in Judaism.

At many individual points, moreover, the influence of apocalyptic on the Gospel is undeniable. As is well known, from apocalyptic comes the tense and greatly heightened expectation of the nearness of the end that runs through the religion and ethics of the whole New Testament. . . .

In the Gospel it is above all the new conception of the Messiah that is comprehensible in light of Jewish apocalyptic. For we see how this concept in the Gospel becomes something absolutely new, the figure of a heavenly, pre-existent Messiah who will come to judge the world and whose designation is usually the name, Son of man, "human being." As is recognized, in our Synoptic Gospels—but also even in the Gospel of John—this title Son of man has become the actual messianic designation of Jesus. In all probability even Jesus in some sayings towards the end of his life seized upon this title in order to express his confidence in the lasting triumph of his person and cause, in view of the thoughts of defeat and death that pressed in upon him. In any case, the early Church developed the first rudiments of a christological dogmatics in connection with the Son of man title. For the early Church, Christ was already the heavenly "Man" who at some future time was to come as World Judge for world judgment and whom believers in all probability already thought of as preexistent, since the idea of preexistence is interwoven with the idea of the Son of man from the very beginning.

What here takes place is of uncommon symbolic and instructive significance. We see how the forms of ideas that nascent Christianity employed are in many respects already anticipated in its immediate prehistory. A preexistent Christology, as it were, lies hidden in the Son of man idea of Jewish apocalyptic. The structure is ready. Faith in Jesus needed only to move in. And so powerful is the faith of the first disciples of Jesus in their Master that no crown seemed too costly and no concept too lofty. Quite unaffectedly that picture of the transcendent Messiah was applied to him who shortly before had walked upon earth with his disciples.

We have now confirmed two things. On the one hand we have seen that it is probable that the Jewish apocalyptic is not a genuine product of Israelite religion, but that, rather, Iranian apocalyptic played some part in its genesis. On the other hand, we have become aware of a far-reaching influence of Jewish apocalyptic on the New Testament.

It remains for us to visualize the consequence of this study. In the first place, in this consideration we obtain a *critical yardstick*. When we remove, or at least attempt to remove, the many foreign elements that in devious ways have infiltrated the Gospel, we are only responding to a demand inherent in the Gospel itself. That certainly applies in the New Testament to the remnants, for instance, of dualism, of belief in the devil and in demons. As a matter of fact, this process is already well advanced. A purified evangelical piety has actually in practice excluded that belief. . . . So then the history of religion has the last and decisive word. By demonstrating the alien origin of that dualistic series of ideas in the New Testament it stamps the seal of confirmation on the practical development of things that is actually underway. . . .

But also another aspect of the study demands our attention. The rule that all that has come in from alien sources is to be removed is not a universally valid one. It holds true only where what is alien has remained alien, unassimilated. But it does not hold where what was perhaps once alien has amalgamated completely with the spirit of the Gospel to form an essential and fundamental part of it. In this category belongs above all the gospel faith in the beyond. That is part of its indispensable store [of truth]. . . .

And even the garment it wears—the expectation of the immediate nearness of the end of the world—in which those ideas wrapped themselves on their first appearance, seems familiar and dear to us. We understand it as a temporal, gleaming clothing of eternal ideas. . . .

However, it is wrong to assume from all this that we have in the Gospel a conglomerate of different stocks of ideas, a product whose constituents we can separate, whose origin we can reckon mathematically. Rather, after all has been said, the Gospel remains a creative marvel, even if we can form a better idea of the conditions under which it came into being.

What existed before the Gospel was nothing more than the raw material, rudiments, makings, that never developed properly, that never came to anything, ideas that were devoid of faith, fantasies without vital, personal content, speculations without the spark of life. A longing for something higher, for an invisible world, a longing that was chained to this earth by a thousand bonds: a striving for distant horizons, a striving repeatedly frustrated by national narrow-mindedness.

Into this seething, chaotic world the divine creative Becoming had first to appear. The mists had to be dissipated. The personal force by which those chains could be broken had to make its appearance. Only then did the faith in the other-worldly unfold in its divine inwardness, its ethical substance and power, its ability to free personality. Jesus' person and Jesus' Gospel remain a creative miracle.

These basic studies of Bousset already indicate the inadequacy of the hypothesis that early Christianity was influenced by other religions only by way of Judaism. In an elaborate investigation of the *Hauptprobleme der Gnosis* [Main problems of gnostic research] (1907) in which Bousset tried to prove that the gnostic systems of early church history are "branches of the same tree . . . whose roots reach deeply into the syncretistic soil of ancient religion in process of decay," he points out in passing that Paul occasionally echoes the "ancient myth . . . of the redeemer who conquers and chains the *archons* ["the demonic powers"] of this world" ("[God] disarmed the principalities and powers and made a public example of them, triumphing over them in [Christ]" [Col. 2:15]) and goes on to ask whether Paul, when he says that "the *archons* [rulers] of this world . . . have crucified the Lord of glory . . . *without recognizing him*" (I Cor. 2:8), does not know the gnostic myth of "the descent of the redeemer incognito into the world of darkness." [339] The question of syncretistic Jewish and Hellenistic influence on the writings and world of thought of early Christianity having been raised in this fashion was now attacked from various angles. **Martin Dibelius,** personally influenced by H. Gunkel, turned afresh to *Die Geisterwelt im Glauben des Paulus* [*The world of spirits in the faith of Paul*] (1909) but, in contrast to O. Everling (see above, p. 217), properly made use also of rabbinical literature to illuminate the Jewish presuppositions of Pauline ideas. He went on to show the connection of certain features of Pauline Christology with gnostic concepts, and endeavored to demonstrate in particular the *connection* between these concepts of the activity of the spirit world and Pauline theology. In this way, however, not only was the breadth of the history-of-religions question enlarged, but the facts as obtained by the history-of-religions methods were interrogated with respect to their material significance, and as a consequence the *theological* goal of religio-historical research was again made clear. And along with the history-of-religions question, the literary at once emerges. In his study of *Die urchristliche Überlieferung von Johannes dem Täufer* [*The early Christian tradition of John the Baptist*] (1911) Dibelius explicitly designates the investigation of "the literary process of growth" as a presupposition of knowledge of the "history of the *matter*" and, because the originality of a tradition is indicated not by its presence in a literary source but by its existence in the ancient tradition, he undertakes to trace the ancient strands in the synoptic tradition. In this we encounter for the first time the reference to the distinction between the matter transmitted by the tradition and that added by the evangelist and to two different genres in the narrative tradition of the Gospels. In this way are suggested two of the most important findings of later "form-critical" study of the Gospels. And, on the basis of his insight into the character of the gospel tradition about John the Baptist as influenced by Christian motifs, Dibelius emphasizes that the original meaning of the Baptist's baptism can be recognized only by the methods of the history of religions. [340]

Information about many viewpoints of Paul, the Greek-speaking Jew, is certainly to be found in the literature of the apocalypses and moral writings of late Judaism. But the key to all of them will not be found in this way. We dare not forget what distinguishes the man of Tarsus from the Galilean fishermen: rabbinical education. While Paul believed, dreamed, and hoped with his people, he absorbed the wisdom of the Jewish scribes, penetrated into the labyrinth of Jewish exegesis, and accustomed himself to understand the Old Testament in the sense of the developing *halachah* and *haggadah* [i.e., legalistic and edifying interpretation]. In so doing the man and his manner of writing are of the common people, but his thinking is saturated with Jewish elements. And these elements also play no little role in the writings of Paul the Christian. None of the four major letters is free of them. But the lode from which we today can mine similar ideas in abundance is the _talmudic and midrashic literature_.

The main objection that is usually raised to the use of these writings in interpreting the New Testament is the reference to their relatively late date. It must be granted that in general their origin is not early enough to warrant regarding them as contemporaneous with New Testament literature. Consequently, especially since we have to do not with literary dependence but with a community of ideas, a certain caution is obviously to be exercised in using them for purposes of comparison. A categorical judgment, however, that simply rules out the use of rabbinical literature for the exegesis of the New Testament seems to me to be by no means sound. The rule that a religious concept does not date merely from the time of its final articulation, a rule that is beginning gradually to become axiomatic in the field of Old Testament studies, must be recognized as valid also for the study of early Christian history. And it must be true to an even higher degree of a people who managed as did the Jews, to preserve their national character over the centuries only by way of the most meticulous conservation of their tradition. Therefore it is often possible to draw a conclusion as to their original significance from concepts that have come down to us in elaborated form.

The ultimate goal of this study is to demonstrate the _importance_ of the ideas of spirits _in the faith_ of Paul. It was necessary to establish the connection between Paul's belief in spirits and his other religious and theological ideas. . . . But the place of belief in spirits is of special importance in Paul's religion for his eschatology and Christology. We must not exclude these things as peripheral, for individual ideas are found at the very heart of piety: We lose a segment of Pauline faith if we scorn them.

The gospel of Paul also contains, as we shall see, a number of motives from which gnostic speculations have developed. And in particular the ideas we are now to examine [the descent of the Redeemer, Phil. 2:5 ff.] play a large role in the gnostic world of thought. But that must not prevent us from noting that elements of this thought world already are found in Paul's writings. The line that leads from Paul to gnosis is there; the only question is the point at which we use the term gnosticism.

The decline of eschatology, perhaps also the opposition to the cult of angels, led to the ascription of a heightened significance to the work of Jesus that lay in the past; and that had to lead to the formulation of new theological categories. Paul, however, experienced the basic religious ideas of these categories—and his personal experience gave his ideas of spirits a new, Christian character that also became of greatest importance in the time to come. Paul learned from experience that spirits have no further power over the man who has found God in Christ. This experience, which resounds in tones ever new from sayings the apostle variously formulates, can to some extent be described. Paul knows this feeling of freedom from the pressure of the spiritual powers only after he becomes a Christian; it is Christ who has already brought about this situation. So we are compelled to face the question of how far Christ's work extends over the world of spirits.

Paul obtained the answer to this question from the Hellenistic store of ideas. Judged by Hellenistic dualism, this world is the realm of the spirits. When Christ the heavenly being comes to earth, this already means a foray into the camp of the enemy, so to speak. The head of the spiritual powers is Death, and it is therefore a direct consequence of his becoming man that Christ comes under Death's sway. By means of Christ having cast off the chains of Death, ascended to heaven, and been seated at the right hand of God, however, the spirits are overcome. This whole drama can only be played out if the spirits do not recognize Christ at his advent, and if he has previously emptied himself of his heavenly nature. . . .

This outline of the life of the Jesus who came from above, from heaven, constitutes a genuine Christ-myth. . . .

To be sure, the question must be left open whether Paul himself painted in the mythological background of his Christology. . . . In his letters he did not emphasize the mythical elements of his thinking, but in any case this background is there; and passages such as Phil. 2:5 ff. and II Cor. 8:9 assume it to such an extent that we must suppose that Paul on occasion said more about it than can be read in his letters at any rate. . . .

When we survey the situation we must conclude that in the phrases "he emptied himself" and "he became poor," Paul also made use of features of the myth of the descent into hell. For it is only if the *kenosis* ["self-emptying"] is related to the world of spirits that we can understand that Christ's transformation back into heavenly glory signifies a *victory over the world of spirits*. To be sure, Paul was only concerned with this *result*, not with the *mythical narrative* of how this result came about. And also this demonological consequence of the redemption effected by Christ retires in Paul's total view before the other, the soteriological. What was important to him above all was what men obtain as a result of this victory won by Christ, and not what the spirits suffer because of it. For Paul's religion is no mythology, but a living, personally experienced faith.

If the religious conditioning of the writing of the Gospels excludes "objective" representation which is in the modern sense historical, on the other hand the unliterary character of the Gospels also guarantees the possibility that ancient and original matter is well preserved in the reports. For the writers did not aim at being authors, but at preserving and handing on tradition. That they polish the stones they have assembled, fit them one to another, give them shape, does not always prevent us from recognizing the natural state of these stones. . . .

Literary work on the Gospels is not exhausted by the research methods of literary criticism. The miscellaneous material that the Gospels present confronts us in different form. Often the additions of the collector are easily distinguished from what he has collected: *references to the change of place and time,* remarks of *a pragmatic sort, isolated sayings of the Lord,* reproduced in accordance with the oral tradition, that are often attached to one another only by a catchword, finally, the so-called *summary reports,* with general references to the healing of sick persons. But even the tradition that already lay before the evangelists in a fixed oral or literary structure reveals different forms that we can still clearly distinguish in part. Individual sayings or groups of sayings were readily combined with other sayings of the Lord that deal with the same theme to constitute a *composite address,* or were provided with *reference to the (real or supposed) situation.* This genus is closely related to the Gospel narratives. In the case of the latter, also, at least two stylistic species can be distinguished, and by these forms we can recognize the points of view

265

that were responsible for their formulation: The one kind makes a saying of the Lord central to or the conclusion of a brief description of the situation—these narratives are formed in the interest of the missionary proclamation and are intended to corroborate views or instructions of the preacher with an example taken from the Lord—and could therefore be called *paradigms;* the other kind shows the use of a broader brush. The narrator is interested in detailed descriptions that at times take even minutiae into consideration. It is usually not a normative saying of Jesus that forms the point, but a significant and usually miraculous act. The whole is not narrated to regulate the life of the Church by a command of the Lord, but to hand on to posterity an account of a miraculous happening *ad maiorem gloriam Christi* ["to the greater glory of Christ"]. In accordance with their technique we could call this kind *short stories* [novellen].

Besides these laws of form, laws that have to do with content, that is, above all religious points of view, exercised an influence on the development of gospel tradition. For the authors of the Gospels examined the traditions neither with the critical eye of a historian nor with the uncritical but also detached outlook of the reporter—they selected and reproduced them under the influence of an evangelistic and apologetic point of view: they were to be the message of salvation that would strengthen the faith of friends and repulse the attacks of opponents.

The parallels from the history of religions . . . can instruct us concerning the ideas that for men of antiquity were bound up with such actions [i.e., baptisms]; they can explain for us the relation between superterrestrial values and the material means that serve to constitute them; in short, they can assist us to a better understanding of the ancient ideas about sacraments. So, if the history of religions environment of John's baptism is examined, this baptism itself will become clearer to us and, along with that, the origin of the Christian baptism.

The problem of the influence of his Hellenistic environment on Paul was pursued by **Rudolf Bultmann,** a pupil of J. Weiss, by means of a demonstration (1910) that in his letters Paul exhibits a clear relationship to the style of the popular philosophical sermon, the diatribe,[341] and that at this point the dependence doubtless lies on the part of Paul. At the same time, however, Bultmann emphasizes that, despite such dependence, the difference between the Pauline proclamation and the popular philosophical sermon is greater than the similarity and that an examination that concerns itself with content must be combined with one concerned with form. Therefore Bultmann followed his stylistic study with a comparison between the religious factor in the ethical instruction of the Stoic Epictetus and the New Testament (1912). In this piece of research were stressed the great difference in the faith in God and, in particular, the absence of a redemptive history among the Stoics. Furthermore, the insight emerges that the comparison of the living faith in God of the New Testament with the intellectualistic religion-tinged ethic of Epictetus, makes comprehensible the superiority of New Testament religion to the Hellenistic religion of the educated [of the day].[342]

The view acquires worth only if we evaluate the individual writer in relation to the literary genre or genres to which his writing aspires to belong or actually does belong. Only then can we balance out: What is foreign to him, what is his own? What is dead form, what is living spirit? Where does the material follow old tracks, where does the author make the ancient form his own? Only then has his literary distinctiveness been recognized.

This truly literary-historical view of the New Testament is new . . . .

The work that lies before you sees it as its task, then, to demonstrate that the Pauline letters exhibit a relationship to a certain literary genre. This genre, as has long been recognized, is the _genre of the diatribe_. . . .

The letters of Paul are genuine letters; each is wholly the result of a peculiar situation and temper. Paul did not reflect on their style, but wrote (or, rather, dictated!) as he always expressed himself, whether in writing or orally. . . .

And if we now discover that the style of his letters is related to the style of the diatribe, we may be permitted to conclude that also Paul's oral preaching demonstrated this relationship. Indeed, the relationship in this latter instance will have been still greater; for the style of the diatribe is not really sermon style; it is the style of the Cynic-Stoic popular preaching. . . . However, the _result_ of our study can help us obtain a picture of the style of the Pauline sermon.

Paul's preaching is cast in part in forms of expression similar to those of the preaching of the Cynic-Stoic popular philosophers, forms such as the diatribe. In conclusion, we have no desire to hide the fact from ourselves that the impression of difference is greater than that of similarity. However, we must not for that reason underestimate the similarity. . . .

The similarity as to mode of expression rests on _Paul's dependence on the diatribe._ . . .

It is appropriate to inquire further whether also certain thought content, certain ideas, are taken over by Paul together with those forms. In this connection we can think in the first instance of concepts such as freedom and slavery. . . . In such questions we achieve nothing by the demonstration of stylistic similarity _alone_, but this has to go hand in hand with the investigation of the content. Nevertheless, the demonstration of stylistic similarity can be a clue as well as a control for the investigation of content.

How very remote is this resignation that hides beneath the name of faith in providence, from New Testament faith in providence!

The decisive difference is this: Epictetus does not know the _living_ God, that is, the God who directs nature and history according to his purposes, whose leadership of peoples as of individuals is a work of education. He cannot know him because he lacks the concept of revelation. So the assertion that everything happens according to God's will remains an empty one. For Epictetus only knows what happens, not what God's will is. . . .

And as there is no redemptive history on a small scale, so there is also naturally none on a large one. Error and truth were possible at all times, and the rational man could always recognize and choose the truth. So it has always been. Nothing new has ever appeared. Just as there is no history of the individual, so there is also no history of mankind. And in this there is lacking the frame of mind of enthusiasm, which is characteristic of New Testament religion: the consciousness of standing at the end of the old, of detecting in oneself the powers of the new age, of possessing a God-given wealth that is not accessible to any reflection or comprehension, that must unfold ever more sublimely from glory to glory: all expressions of the consciousness of a personality awakened to its own [true] life.

Looking back from this point of vantage, the irreligious character of [Epictetus'] faith in providence and in God becomes clear to us once more: the faith in providence cannot imply a divine direction of history; as faith in the *logos* in things that happen, it signifies only the eternal sameness of what happens.

But what, then, do we learn for the New Testament from the comparison? We wish to be cautious: A little light has been thrown on only a very limited area of the large, complicated Hellenistic culture, and we believe we have seen a relationship and a sharp contrast between it and the New Testament. These factors: Stoicism tinged with religion on the one hand, and New Testament religiosity on the other, have come into contact because of the historical situation. We may be permitted perhaps to attach two conclusions in the form of questions:

1. Was it not inevitable that the relationship which unquestionably exists between the moral ideas of Stoic instruction and the New Testament should provide the New Testament with positive points of contact for its proclamation?

2. The religion of the New Testament could give just what this Stoic instruction lacked: the power and enthusiasm of a living religion, the new estimate of the worth of the individual, and the power to awaken the human soul to its own [true] life. Does this not throw a ray of light on the historical situation? Does this not contribute in small part to an understanding of the struggle with the spiritual powers and help to explain the triumph of the religion of the New Testament?

Although Dibelius and Bultmann, even while making full use of the history-of-religions method, clearly emphasize the individuality of the New Testament message, **Richard Reitzenstein,** in a lecture (enlarged by numerous excurses) on *Die hellenistischen Mysterienreligionen* [The Hellenistic mystery religions] (1910), goes considerably further in relating the New Testament, especially Paul, to Hellenism. Against the background of a lively description of Hellenistic syncretism he portrays Paul as a Hellenistic mystic and gnostic who had read Hellenistic literature, who shares with the Hellenistic mystics the ecstatic experience of the duality of his own personality, and who demonstrates by his vocabulary that the gnosis is pre-Pauline. Here, then, the process of relating Paul to pagan Hellenism, begun by Bousset, is pursued consistently, without expressly raising the question of Paul's theological peculiarity.[343]

If it is the task of the philologian to give vital expression to the growth of the spirit throughout the whole of antiquity, and therefore not least to that development during the closing era of the ancient world, he will not be able to avoid also inquiring into the earliest development of Christianity. And even if he wanted to limit himself arbitrarily to paganism, there is much in the latter he would be quite unable to understand without reference to early Christian literature, its language and conceptual development, and to the perception of life and cultus of the communities.

Only when the existence and significance of a *religious literature* is firmly set in Hellenism and when the nature of Paul's linguistic borrowings points to a literary intermediary, does the possibility of an explanation present itself. The thinking of Jews who remained loyal to the Law was already influenced, not by Greek philosophy, but no doubt by that literature of edification and revelation already colored by it, a literature that exists at all sorts of levels between theosophical speculation and magical prescription. Such a state of affairs is readily conceivable, especially in the Diaspora, and in this respect, the picture of Philo, similar in spite of all its difference, can again help us to an understanding. There can be no doubt that this influence helped prepare the way for that powerful inner experience that then broke the apostle loose from his ancestral religion and that the same influence must later have grown stronger during the two years of lonely inner struggle for a thorough grounding in the new religion. A renewed study was necessary from the moment at which the apostle prepared himself with full devotion for the task of presenting the Gospel among the Greeks. He had to get acquainted with the language and conceptual world of the circles he wished to win and to find norms—for worship, to take but one instance—for the congregations he wished to found but which he could not fashion according to the model of the primitive church. So is it really inconceivable that he, or perhaps his predecessors, reshaped existing forms?

Indeed, we have an absolutely certain proof of, and at the same time a graduated scale for, the strength of even the indirect influence of Hellenism on the apostle. I mean, of course, the apostle's language. We must examine the words that are used technically in a context whose origin is doubtful. . . .

[The apostle] must have read Hellenistic literature; he speaks its language and has made its ideas his own. And these ideas associate him necessarily with that very circle of thought that grew out of the new life experience that extends beyond the limits of Judaism. . . . Though much, very much, in his thinking and experience may have remained Jewish, he is indebted to Hellenism for his belief in his apostolate and his freedom. Herein lies the greatest, and for the history of the world, the most significant of the ancient mystery religions.

I regard as most decisive . . . a strange, and for us at first scarcely comprehensible, sense of the duality of his own personality that seems to me not infrequently to break through Paul's writings. . . .

The same sense of being two persons (that of the weak man and that of the divinized being) by which alone these sayings [Gal. 2:20; II Cor. 12:2-5] can easily and naturally be explained, is in my judgment to be accounted for only by the miraculous combination in Paul of tremendous inflexibility, of almost superhuman self-assurance of the pneumatic ["Spirit-filled man"] and of the groaning and longing of the poor human heart. Granted that such an experience is not acquired secondhand or simply transferred from a foreign religion to one's own; nevertheless it becomes more conceivable in detail if we can demonstrate something similar in the mood of the time. We find this feeling of a double personality in the fullest sense of the term in the literature and religion of the Mysteries, and we find it, furthermore, in gnosticism which

269

grew out of the Mysteries. Here also the pneumatic is basically a divinized being and one who, in spite of his earthly life, is transported into another world that alone has worth and truth. . . . That basic Hellenistic feeling we meet already in [Paul], and those who adopt the approach of the history of religions are permitted to place him, not as the first, but probably as the greatest, gnostic in the whole sequence of development.

Reitzenstein's observations, however impressive, were presented unsystematically. In his *Kyrios Christos* **Wilhelm Bousset** came to the philologian's support with a comprehensive history-of-religions account of the "history of faith in Christ from the beginning of Christianity to Irenaeus." For the account of the origin and development of Christian piety given in this book he expressly "removes from operation . . . of the double barrier," that is, (1) "the barrier of separation between . . . the theology of the New Testament and the history of the dogma of the ancient church" and (2) "the barrier of separation between the history of the religion of early Christianity and the general development of the religious life that surrounds Christianity in the first bloom of its youth." Bousset therefore consistently avoids any discussion of the New Testament canon and of the presupposition of the uniqueness of the New Testament message. From this vantage point he asserts first of all that "in the confession of Jesus as Son of man [we] have before us the conviction of the primitive Christian community, . . . a coherent and self-contained church dogmatics," but then leaves open the question of "whether with respect to matters of detail this church dogmatics can make use of genuine sayings of Jesus concerning himself." The impression awakened in the souls of men by Jesus found its expression in that title, which was taken over from Jewish Son-of-man dogmatics, and on the basis of this belief the tradition of Jesus was reshaped. In similar fashion to Dibelius, Bousset tried to recover the oldest tradition by separating individual tradition from the finished Gospels. However, the primitive Hellenistic Gentile church now takes its place by the side of the primitive Palestinian church—and in this lies a new and very significant observation. And it was first in the former, according to Bousset, that the worship of Jesus as "Lord" (*Kyrios*) originated.[344] But this worship of the *Kyrios* grew out of the cultus in connection with the pagan worship of cult deities, to whom this title was given. So the worship of the heavenly Lord in the *present* took the place of the original expectation of the coming Son of man, and a dangerous opponent of primitive Christian eschatology sprang up. Against the background of this Hellenistic church, Bousset then describes Paul's piety of redemption, a piety which "grew on the soil of Hellenistic piety" and which transformed Christianity into a supernatural religion of redemption, and then, further, "the high-strung mysticism" of the Gospel of John, a mysticism that wishes to attain "divinization by means of the vision of God" and that is rooted "in the soil of Hellenistic mysticism." Although in all this it is occasionally stressed that Paul puts "the freeing [of men] from sin and guilt" in the place of the Hellenistic freeing [of men] from transitoriness and that thereby "the ethos of the Gospel calls attention to itself," nevertheless in all stages of its development early Christianity is regarded purely as a part of a history-of-religions development, while now as before, "the Gospel of the forgiveness of sins as Jesus proclaimed it" remains excepted from this classifying of the New Testament within the history of religions.[345]

One cannot avoid the impression that in the bulk of the Son-of-man sayings we have the deposit of the theology of the primitive church. That is the certain and given point of departure. All that is uncertain is whether and to what extent a few of the Son-of-man sayings are to be traced back to Jesus. . . .

All these observations point to the conclusion that at least in certain apocalyptic circles the title "the" Son of man for the Messiah could very probably occur. And furthermore, our gospel literature itself, within which the title Son of man . . . can be traced back to the oldest (and therefore Palestinian) sources, proves beyond question that that transition to the title Son of man actually took place. . . .

But with the title—and with this we are brought face to face with a fact of the most decisive importance—the primitive church took over also what the title stood for, that is to say, the total content of the ideas associated with the term. To be specific, that remarkable transcendental concept of the messianic figure is combined with the Son of man. . . . As soon as the symbol in Daniel is interpreted messianically, the Messiah had to become a superterrestrial figure. . . .

And now we can demonstrate how along with the title Son of Man the entire Son-of-man dogmatics already formulated in Judaism, enters the theology of the primitive church. As in Daniel's vision of the judgment of the world the "Son of man" appears by the side of the Ancient of Days, as Enoch in primeval times views one formed like a man by the side of God, so Jesus in the faith of the primitive church is above all else the Son of man, enthroned at the right hand of God or of God's power. From the point of view of the new faith only one thing is added to this picture of the Son of man enthroned in glory, and that is the thought of the *exaltation* of the earthly Jesus of Nazareth to the dignity of the Son of man, something Jewish Son-of-man dogmatics naturally could not conceive. . . .

In similar fashion the coming of the heavenly Messiah was transferred to Jesus and his parousia. He is to appear on the clouds of heaven (Mark 14:62), in the glory of the Father, surrounded by the angels (Mark 8:38).

But in all this what remains most important and most central is the fact that the unshakable conviction arose in the souls of the disciples that Jesus, despite his death and apparent defeat, indeed, because of all that, has become the supernatural Messiah in glory. . . .

Furthermore, however, it was . . . of tremendous importance that in contemporary apocalyptic a picture of the Messiah stood ready that now seemed to provide the key to the whole weird puzzle that confronts the disciples. Jesus' disciples salvaged their hopes, which no doubt had already been raised during Jesus' lifetime, by reshaping them in higher and more majestic terms. They threw around their Master the kingly mantle that was at hand, put the highest crown they could reach on his head, and attached themselves to Jesus the Son of man, who through suffering and death had entered into glory. . . .

"Mark" and the "logia" are not the creators of the gospel tradition. Behind them lies perhaps a generation of oral tradition. And it was this tradition, not a literary personality, that stamped its character on the synoptic framework. Above all, it is still abundantly clear that the *individual*, closed pericope and the *individual* logion (or the individual parable), as the oral tradition is accustomed to transmit them, constitute its germ cells. . . .

The passion story . . . possessed from the beginning—this is a fact that is still insufficiently grasped—a different character than the other sections of Mark's Gospel. In it the narrators were not content with a few disconnected recollections and separate accounts. As far as we can look back over the process of transmission, the passion story seems to have provided a connected report— one perhaps already given literary form at a very early date. . . .

It is now to be demonstrated not only that the primitive church was responsible, at least in large part, for introducing the explicit messianic self-testimonies of Jesus into the tradition, but also that to a great extent it reshaped the gospel tradition in general in the interests of placing greater emphasis on, and giving greater prominence to, the person of Jesus and its significance. . . .

Only because the Church put the figure of the heavenly Son of man, the Ruler and Judge of the worlds, behind the Gospel of Jesus and let his glory, half-concealed, half-veiled, shine in transparent fashion through his story; only because it painted the picture of the peripatetic Preacher against the golden foil of the miraculous, enveloped his life with the luster of fulfilled prediction; only because it placed him in this way into a great, divine redemptive history and let him appear as its crown and culmination; only so did it enable the picture of Jesus of Nazareth to produce the desired effect. For the purely historical is never effective, but only the living, present symbol by which a person's own religious conviction is given transfigured expression. . . .

Between Paul and the primitive Palestinian church stand the Hellenistic congregations in Antioch, Damascus, Tarsus. . . . In any case the apostle underwent his development as a Christian on the soil of the Hellenistic church. He did not create this Hellenistic church, nor did he determine its singularity from the beginning. It is one of the most important of the established facts that the universal religious congregation at Antioch, composed of Jews and Greeks, came into being without Paul. . . . Where the apostle appeals to the tradition, however, it is, according to all the evidence, not to the tradition of Jerusalem, but in the first instance to that of the Gentile Christian congregation at Antioch. . . .

What the κύριος ["Lord"] meant for the first Hellenistic Christian churches stands before us in clear and living colors. It is the Lord who rules over the life of the Christian fellowship as it expresses itself especially in congregational worship, and therefore in the cultus. The congregation assembles about the Lord in believing reverence, confesses his name, baptizes by calling upon his name, gathers round the table of the Lord Jesus, utters the fervent petition, "Maranatha, Come, Lord Jesus,". . . Consequently the congregation gathers as a body about the Lord as its head, to whom in the cultus it pays its homage of reverence. . . .

The survey shows that the title "Lord" encompasses an area in the history of religions that can still be delimited with some confidence. The title penetrated the Hellenistic-Roman religion from the East. Syria and Egypt were actually its native habitats. That it plays the major role in the Egyptian-Roman worship of rulers is only one aspect of the general phenomenon. . . .

It seems as if the title "Lord" was given especially to the divinities that stood at the center of the cult of the fellowship with which we are concerned. . . .

Antiochian Christianity and that of the other primitive Hellenistic congregations came into being and developed in this atmosphere. In this milieu the young Christian religion took form as a Christ cult, and from this environment the summary formula "Lord" was also taken over to designate the dominating place of Jesus in divine worship. . . . Such processes took place in the unconscious, in the uncontrollable corporate psyche of a congregation. That was inevitable. It lay, so to speak, in the air that the first Hellenistic congregations of Christians should give their cult hero the title "Lord." . . . Kyrios-faith and Kyrios-cult represent the form that Christianity assumed on the soil of Hellenistic piety. . . .

It now becomes clear that it was no accident that we did not meet the title "Lord" in the gospel tradition on Palestinian soil. Such a development would not have been possible there. This insertion of Jesus into the center of the cult of the believing community, this remarkable doubling of the object of reverence in worship, is only conceivable in an environment in which Old Testament monotheism no longer prevailed unconditionally and with absolute certainty. . . .

In its environment nascent Christianity *had to* take on this form of *Kyrios*-faith and *Kyrios*-worship. There was no alternative. . . .

And at the same time the *Kyrios* of the Hellenistic church became a present, palpably living entity. The *Son of man* of the primitive church derives from the Jewish eschatology and remains an eschatological entity. . . . The *Kyrios* of the primitive Hellenistic congregation, however, is a *present entity* in the cult and in worship.

In this presence of the *Kyrios* in worship, in the experiences of his palpable reality, there grows from the beginning a powerful opponent of the primitive Christian eschatology. . . . Quite unnoticed, very gradually, the center of gravity begins to shift from the future into the present. *Kyrios* cult, worship, and sacrament become the most dangerous and the most significant opponents of the basic eschatological mood of primitive Christianity. When the former will once have fully taken shape, the latter will have lost its *élan* and the impetus that carried everything with it. The development will be as follows: The Son of man will be to a large extent forgotten and will remain in the Gospels as an unintelligible hieroglyph. The future belongs to the *Kyrios* who is present in the cult.

According to the popular notion the Spirit is related above all to worship and cult, while according to Paul he is the basic fact of the whole life of the Christian.

This almost violent remolding of the conceptions of the Spirit within Christianity must have been the work of the apostle. Who else in the whole Christian Church could have accomplished this change but the Spirit endowed apostle? Out of naïve community enthusiasm he created a *religious psychology* with a character all its own.

If we wish to recognize this peculiarity we must lay emphasis above all on the fact that also in Paul's thinking the Spirit appears as a wholly supernatural entity. This rough supernaturalism with its origin in the popular view of the Spirit as the divine wonder-working power has already contributed to the apostle's point of view. Indeed, because Paul now places not only the high points and extraordinary events but the whole Christian life under the power of the Spirit, that naïve belief in miracle becomes a crudely supernatural, overall view according to which really the whole Christian life is a miracle and is subject to a power outside itself. . . .

For the apostle, the pneumatic who is filled with the Spirit of God and the old man are two different beings, completely separate from one another. They have almost nothing in common save the name. Only the way of divine miracle leads from the one to the other. . . . Just as the ecstatic has ceased to be him-self and feels himself in the grip of a foreign power, so it is with Paul's pneumatic Christian: in him the natural being has wholly ceased to be. . . . But the most remarkable is this: Paul extended this way of thinking to include the whole Christian life. His life as a Christian is subject to a higher power that puts to death the ego: I live indeed no longer, but Christ (or, as the case may be, the Spirit) lives in me. . . .

Where in Paul's environment do we discover a similar one-sided view? When we put this question in this direct and sharp way, two instances stand out from the very beginning: first, Old Testament religion, and then the Gospel of Jesus. . . .

On closer inspection parallels appear in the history-of-religions milieu of Paulinism. We shall have to direct our attention to those hybrids in which philosophy and faith determined by oriental ideas, intellectual reflection and ancient Mysteries, speculation and religio-ecstatic mysticism, became intertwined into wonderful forms. . . .

So the Pauline doctrine of the *pneuma* ["spirit"], with all its consequences, stands in a great network of relationships. In his turbid anthropological pes-simism, in the dualistic and supernatural formulation of his doctrine of redemp-tion, Paul followed a mood of the time that even then had already deeply stinted many spirits.

It is not the "historical Jesus" nor, so far as we can see, or in particular the Christ who appeared to Paul at his conversion and whom he identifies with the pneuma ["spirit"], but the Kyrios reverenced in the worship of the com-munity. Now, I believe, we may venture to draw the comparison: Just as the Spirit in Paul's thought is transformed from the element which determines and characterizes the Christians' cultus into the supernatural factor that governs the whole Christian life, so for Paul, the Lord that is present in the Christians' cultus becomes a power that fills the whole life of the Christian with its presence. . . .

We are now in a position to take a look also at the development and growth of the Pauline Christ-mysticism and the formula "to be in Christ, in the Lord" that sums it up. All that grew out of the cult. The *Kyrios* who was present in the cult became the Lord who rules over the whole personal life of the Christian. Paul's idea of the Spirit, likewise reinterpreted and expanded from the cultic into the ethico-religious, is the vehicle for the introduction of Christ mysticism.

One can scarcely avoid the impression that Paul's whole theory of redemption and the piety associated with redemption developed on the soil of Hellenistic piety. The myth of the suffering, dying, and rising god is extraordinarily widespread in Hellenistic religions influenced by oriental ideas. Above all it belongs to the characteristic traits of almost all so-called mystery religions.

In mystical fellowship the devout man experiences what the divine hero as a prototype experienced previously and in principle. The experience of the believer is but the victorious outcome of a beginning once established. Make the connection and the electric current flows.

This parallel becomes even closer when we observe that, as those Hellenistic speculations developed out of the cult of the dying and reviving god, so also the sacrament stands quite clearly and distinctly back of Paul's statements about dying and rising with Christ (cf. Rom. 6; Gal. 3:26-27). . . . Out of the baptismal mystery of the community's religion Paul also made a spiritual experience that in its fundamental significance controls the whole life of the Christian and gives him a conquering power and an incomparable impetus.

The great idea that he [the author of the Fourth Gospel] grasped, not consciously, of course, but instinctively, was that of reading myth and dogma back into history. To some extent that had already happened when the primitive church read its Son-of-man dogma and its proof through miracles and prophecies back into the life of Jesus, but now it was necessary to dissolve history wholly in myth and make it become transparent for this [myth].

The author of the Fourth Gospel succeeded in doing this. What he sketched in his new life of Jesus was the Son of God (or God himself) walking upon earth. . . .

"And the word became flesh." The Fourth Evangelist carried out his program. What he sketched is the *Logos*-God traveling over the earth. And yet from the same Gospel again and again there sounds the note: *Ecce homo*. He rescued from abstraction the Pauline message of the "Spirit-Christ" and his own message of the supernatural Son of God (the *Logos*) and made them alive and visible. He saved and gave expression to what little of humanity in the picture of Jesus was still to be retained on the soil of this inclusive view. He reconciled myth with history to the extent that such reconciliation was still possible. . . .

So, with their notion that one receives life by "seeing," with their ideas of the wonder-working Word, of faith, knowledge, truth, light and darkness, light and life, the Johannine writings are rooted in the soil of Hellenistic mysticism. This does not detract from the Evangelist's originality. Indeed, it is only from this point of vantage that we understand the magnificent conception he proclaims: "Everyone who sees the Son . . . [has] eternal life" [John 6:40]. For this is the new thing that the author has to say to the world about him: Not by looking to the starry heaven, to its *pleroma*, the fullness of the glorious, godlike beings that walk there, not by the vision of deity that the *myste* ["the initiate"] experiences as the high point of sacred consecration, not by such means does one obtain eternal life or exaltation into the world of the divinity. *Here* is the fullness of grace, here is light and life, here is gnosis brought to its completion: "Every one who sees the Son and believes in him . . . [has] eternal life." . . .

Despite the fact that he wrote a further Gospel, John is basically even a bit more remote than Paul from the preaching of Jesus. The Gospel of the forgiveness of sins, as Jesus preached it, has disappeared even more completely, and in its stead comes the message of redemption and of the Redeemer. Instead of the Savior of sinners, stands the Friend of his own, he to whom the friends give themselves as a possession in a quiet and transfigured mood, as to one who has for them the words of eternal life.

The thorough integration of primitive Christianity into the Hellenistic religious history was carried out by Bousset by paying no attention, or scarcely any, to the results of research on the part of the school of consistent eschatology. That this did not have to be the only and unavoidable way of practicing the history-of-religions method was demonstrated by **Johannes Weiss** in his pioneering treatment of *Das Problem der Entstehung des Christentums* [The problem of the origin of Christianity]. Weiss also begins with the methodological presupposition that it is the task of historical scholarship "to show that a historically somewhat later phenomenon is the necessary outcome of its prehistory and the fruit of its environment" and that, therefore, in actual life "there is no such thing as an 'origin' in the sense of an entirely new creation," but rather, "the 'new' . . . is always in large measure a 'regrouping' of older elements." Although Weiss therefore properly demands that Christianity be regarded as "a historical phenomenon, however, with all that involves," he explicitly maintains that Christianity is not understood "if one does not appreciate its special form and its differences of mood and feeling vis-à-vis the mystery cults" and does not find . . . an explanation . . . for the inner life of the new religion, for those inner mainsprings of its faith and action." But Weiss discovers this special form of Christianity in the "basic conviction that holds the whole together" of "living in the final era of the world," and he designates "this 'dramatic' element in primitive Christianity," this "already almost completed entry of the future into the present," as the "real subject that demands from the history of religions an explanation." It turns out then, however, that this primitive Christian consciousness of history goes back to the event of the "person of Jesus" and that therefore the faith in Jesus' messiahship awakened by the Easter experiences must go back to the faith of the disciples of Jesus during Jesus' lifetime. In this way it appears that the marks of the primitive Christian faith in Christ regarded as basic by the history of religions actually have their roots in Jesus himself, and that even in the earliest church the expectation of the imminent return of Christ was already combined with worship of the exalted Lord, in other words, with the Christ cult. In his comprehensive, masterful account, *Das Urchristentum* [Earliest Christianity], Johannes Weiss could therefore combine the knowledge of the basic eschatological orientation of the primitive church, which had its starting point in Jesus (Weiss died before his book was completed and in its unfinished state it lacks an account of Jesus), with the insight into the significance for the origin of Pauline theology of the Hellenistic Christian Church as well as of Hellenistic paganism, without overlooking Paul's basically eschatological outlook. And Weiss also properly emphasizes that the eschatological myth of early Christian faith is already held by Jesus. But, in spite of such cautious and convincing use of the history-of-religions method, Weiss did not hesitate to acknowledge also a "supernatural ground" for the origin of the primitive community's Easter faith and so to return decisively to the posing of theological questions.[346]

The positive question now becomes all the more urgent, namely, What then actually was the element that bound the earliest circle of disciples together? What was the organizing idea of earliest Christianity? . . .

Wherever in the final analysis eschatology may have come from, at any rate its thought is genuinely Jewish to the extent that it still demands a powerful *external justification* for faith in God and a brilliant, positive, *external recognition* of insufficiently compensatory justice here below. But . . . already long before the rise of Christianity this eschatological mood was in conflict with a piety focused on the present that, strictly speaking, stands in contradiction to eschatology. For every one who in this life experiences the help and grace of God and has learned to put his trust in them has thereby basically overcome the metaphysical dualism and the tension with respect to the future. We now observe this also in Jesus' message. Here the quite thoroughly non-eschatological faith in God stands cheek by jowl with the eschatological mood as an element that can scarcely combine with it. . . .

So we have to conclude that what actually bound the circle of disciples together was not the message of the kingdom in general, and also not merely the special ardor and intensity of the expectation of Jesus. What bound them to him was in a real sense *his person.* In him they set their hope; *from him* they expected the decisive change. The disciples' mood even during Jesus' lifetime must already have been more than hope in the kingdom of God; in some sense it must also already have been a *faith in Jesus.*

So then, what actually created history would not have been the eschatological current of the times as a mass mood, but, in the last analysis, the personality of Jesus. . . .

Now the appearances could be a proof of [Jesus'] messiahship for the very reason that this *already had been called into question.* Only because [Jesus'] death seemed to be evidence *against* his messiahship could the exaltation be regarded as evidence *for it.* Furthermore, it follows that the temporary disillusionment of the disciples was grounded on the fact that they had not only learned from him to hope for the kingdom of God but that they had also expected that he would be the king of this realm, as emerges from the comment made by the Emmaus disciples: "But we had hoped that he was the one to redeem Israel" (Luke 24:21). All this shows that the messianic question was raised already during Jesus' lifetime. . . .

We are therefore thrown back on the so-called "messianic consciousness" of Jesus as the ultimate basis for the messianic faith of the first disciples. Here we have the *ultimate puzzle for him* who reflects on the origin of Christianity. . . .

Even for the living Jewish hope the messiah was nothing but an abstract concept. . . . For the disciples, however, the heavenly Messiah bore the concrete *personal* features of Jesus. By this means [the first believers] left the realm of fantasy for that of reality. From the eschatological standpoint, also, it is a tremendous forward step that these men no longer wait for some messiah or other, but that they already know who he will be. . . . Thereby the warmth and inwardness, the personal element, enters this new religion, a fact that became so important for its history. Even in the primitive church the word "Lord," or "our Lord" (*Marân*), already took on another tone in contrast to its earlier one. . . . The question arises, whether it is historically and psychologically conceivable that even in the primitive church, among the personal disciples of Jesus, the step from moral dependence to religious worship, from discipleship to Christ cult, was followed through.

The outcome . . . that this religious worship of Jesus developed very quickly beyond the circle of disciples and that it must be ascribed, even though within certain limits, to the earliest circles [of believers] will not surprise him who is familiar with the religio-historical environment of early Christianity. We are aware of how difficult it is in principle to draw the line between divinity and humanity and of how often it has been transgressed in concepts of apotheosis and incarnation in viewing "divine men.". . .

We are therefore justified in saying that this pre-Pauline Christianity, with its messianic faith and its beginnings of the Christ cult, already possessed the essential features of the later religion. And when in light of this we raise the question of its origin, we believe we have shown that it can finally be answered only by reference to the effects of the personality of Jesus. . . .

The faith of the earliest Gentile Christian congregations is not fully described when we emphasize only the Christ cult and the Mystery faith in the death and resurrection of Christ. We must also mention here the conviction of the imminent end of the world and the *expectation of the parousia.* If the Christ religion had been only the cult of a *Kyrios,* such as Sarapis or Asclepius, this eschatological-apocalyptic apparatus would have been missing. . . . The Lord Jesus is he who saves from the coming wrath, and the "deliverance" for which his believers hope is that wholly determined by the future world judgment. This concentration on the parousia, which *will bring with it* the actual and overwhelming confirmation of the Lord, is an inheritance from Jewish apocalyptic messianism. Furthermore, there is still much of the Jewish messiah in the *Kyrios* of the Gentile Christian communities.

Generally speaking, it was [in Antioch] . . . that the character of the new religion as being especially the veneration of the Lord in heaven received its full and firm imprint. . . .

In this way, as the eschatological and messianic features in the conception of Jesus are falling more and more into the background, a new factor enters into the new religion. . . . With the subsidence of the national factor, the eschatological factor also subsided to a position if not actually secondary, still a little behind the foremost. The relationship with the Risen Lord of course maintained its eschatological perspective; the parousia of Christ remained as an event of the most extreme importance, especially for those members of the church who had come from Judaism. But the majority of the Gentile Christians had now been granted a new *religion of the present.* . . .

278

Even when they were still predominantly Jewish Christian in character, the churches which arose on Hellenistic soil came in close contact with the ideas of Hellenistic religion, especially with the mystery cults and the mysticism whose importance for primitive Christianity we are coming to recognize more and more clearly. Especially prominent was the conception of a rebirth or of a participation in dying and rising again with the dead and risen Christ. This conception seems to have been still lacking in the primitive church but it emerged suddenly in Hellenistic circles.

What distinguishes Paul's religion from ours was the all-inclusive scheme of its world-view: the consciousness of living in the last days of the world. . . . This was . . . the essential thing in the religion of primitive Christianity and of Paul. It spoke of a wholly definite historical action of God. In the language of religious scholarship, it would be said that this religion in contrast to a more abstract, quiescent, rational representation of God had a "myth" as its basis, a tale of how God had done these world-transforming things at a wholly definite time and that he had thereby provided the conditions for a new kind of life. That is also the common element between the faith of Paul and the religion of Jesus, except that Jesus expected this decisive world changing act in the future, while Paul had made the discovery that it had already happened.

Nevertheless the preaching of Jesus and the faith of the ancient churches in general consider the kingdom of God as still future; in any case, the kingdom has not as yet succeeded in establishing direct contact with this world. But Jesus has the conviction that God has already taken the decisive step for the founding of his dominion: through his Spirit and Jesus himself, he is pushing back the kingdom of evil and his kingdom is thus already asserting itself powerfully in the world—visible only, of course, to the eye of faith. Moreover, the primitive community, though it must still wait for the return of the Messiah to this world, yet believes that his rule has already begun in heaven, as also has his subjugation of the spirit-world; the decisive beginnings have already taken place. . . .

It is from this point of view chiefly that the peculiar double aspect of redemption in Paul is to be understood. . . .

The idea just expressed is essentially of an eschatological nature: it is an anticipatory hope for the future; it is, therefore, mythological, gnostic. It is not to be understood apart from those mysterious supernatural events which took place at the crucifixion and resurrection of Christ, nor apart from the dualistic antithesis between God and the cosmic powers from whose authority the Christian has now been torn away. . . .

If mystical experience is the anticipation of future blessedness here and now, then mysticism is in a sense the abrogation or overcoming of eschatology. Then in so far as the eschatological hope still prevails in the religion of Paul, to that extent it is not mystical. But this hope is very pronounced with him; therefore there is very little room for mysticism in his religion. . . .

A tempestuous enthusiasm, an overwhelming intensity of feeling, an immediate awareness of the presence of God, an incomparable sense of power and an irresistible control over the will and inner spirit and even the physical condition of other men—these are ineradicable features of the historical picture of early Christianity.

We are far from being inclined to deny the supernatural origin of these phenomena. Anyone who is accustomed to find fresh strength and uplift in prayer will recognize at once what early Christian belief in the Spirit implied, and no amount of scholarship is adequate to explain it away. Religious experience is an era which in the end resists analysis and rational explanation. Yet since scientific self-restraint in view of the inexplicable requires us to recognize a factor not to be measured by scientific means, it is precisely for this reason that we are obliged to ask whether or not in addition to the supernatural factors which alone impressed the early Christians, there were other factors involved in this enthusiasm, factors which may be much more readily understood by us. We must ask about the human and historical antecedents of this inspiration, and its psychological conditionings. . . .

The study of Paul presented in the foregoing chapters, has resulted in a picture of extraordinary variety. We have seen for ourselves that all the spiritual currents of the time have met in him: Old Testament prophetic piety and rabbinical Judaism; Hellenistic-Jewish enlightenment and Stoic ethics; syncretistic Hellenistic mysticism and dualistic, ascetical Gnosticism. In addition the strong imperatives of the ethical preaching of Jesus are present, the vivid, eschatological emphasis on the end of the age which is found in the Baptist, in Jesus, and in the primitive church, and above all the victorious conviction that the salvation of the final age has already come. All this is held in unity by the personal, thankful, humble consciousness of having himself experienced the grace of God and of having been won forever by the love of Christ. It is in this that the man's variegated world-view and mode of thought, full of contradictions as they are, have their unifying principle. In this personal religious experience which he concisely calls his *faith*, he possessed the power to accomplish his task and to place his thought in the service of his actions.

4.
The Radical Historical Criticism

The attempt to view the New Testament without reservation in light of the history of its own times, to which research felt itself called, at the end of the nineteenth century by its consistent relating of early Christianity to the religions of its time, had led, as we have seen, to the consistently eschatological view of the New Testament on the one hand, and to the history-of-religions view on the other. While in general these two research approaches were at odds with each other, J. Weiss had tried to combine them both. Side by side with these two approaches, however, there ran, from the beginning and with the same object in view, radical historical critical analysis of the New Testament sources and of early Christian history, whose representatives in part were also engaged in the narrower sense in history-of-religions research. This critical method addressed itself in the same way to the Synoptic Jesus, to Paul, to the Gospel of John, as well as to conventional evaluation and methodological treatment of the New Testament Canon as a whole.

About the same time that J. Weiss, H. Gunkel, and W. Bousset by their fundamental works founded the consistently eschatological and the history-of-religions studies of the New Testament, **Julius Wellhausen** published the first edition of his *Israelitische und jüdische Geschichte* [Israelite and Jewish history] (1894). Fifteen years earlier the gifted Old Testament scholar and Arabist had published his *Geschichte Israels* [History of Israel] which, by its reversal of the sequence of the sources of the Pentateuch, had offered a completely new picture of the history of Israel. While it was welcomed by many, it also roused such violent opposition that Wellhausen transferred to the philosophical faculty as instructor in Semitic languages.[347] As a consequence Wellhausen's interest had turned increasingly to the New Testament, and therefore his *Israelitische und jüdische Geschichte* included a penultimate (and in later editions a final) chapter on "Das Evangelium" [The Gospel]. Here Jesus appears as preacher of a rule of God that begins in the present as a fellowship of love and as one who is related to God as a child is to his father,

281

"not because he is unique by nature, but because he is man; he always uses this general generic name with emphasis to designate his own ego." "Son of man" in the sense of a messianic title is therefore a false Christian translation of the word "man" that Jesus used; "by his death and resurrection Jesus first *became* the Son of God, i.e., the Messiah, a dignity to which he had laid no claim during his lifetime." And the first Christians distorted the true content of the earthly history of Jesus "by bringing his *person* into contact with eschatology." [348] Here the liberal picture of Jesus appears not only uneschatologically, but also unmessianically, and the rise of the faith in Jesus as the messiah is located in the primitive church.

Then, in brief commentaries on the three Synoptic Gospels which became important because of numerous individual observations and an acute analysis of the context of the material, Wellhausen sought to furnish proof that the Gospels cannot be used as sources for a history of Jesus, but offer only testimony to the messianic faith of early Christianity.[349] As a delayed "preface to my interpretation of the first three Gospels," he followed these commentaries with an *Einleitung in die drei ersten Evangelien* [Introduction to the first three Gospels] (1905), in which he summed up the literary and historical results of these commentaries, which, he tells us, had been written as "a piece of pioneer work in exegesis." In this *Introduction* Wellhausen emphasizes that the tradition underlying the Gospels had already selected its material with dogmatic intention and that the Evangelists were wholly responsible for its context in the Gospels. Jesus regarded himself only as a teacher and never speculated on his return as Messiah; when he accepted the messianic title conferred on him by his disciples, he did so only as an accomodation to popular Jewish belief. Wellhausen categorically rejects the views of "consistent eschatology," but, it must be admitted, himself offers a contradictory picture by designating Jesus on the one hand as a Jew, not as the Christ, and on the other by representing the non-Jewish element in him as really characteristic. So, by acute criticism of the gospel material Wellhausen, despite his rejection of the history-of-religions method, discovers a Jewish Jesus that closely resembles the one portrayed by the history-of-religions school.[350]

The ultimate source of the Gospels is oral tradition, but this contains only scattered material. The units, more or less extensive, circulate in it separately. Their combination into a whole is always the work of an author and, as a rule, the work of a writer with literary ambitions. . . .

The passion story need not be excluded from the judgment that the Gospel of Mark as a whole lacks the distinctive marks of a history. Our curiosity remains unsatisfied. Nothing has motivations indicated or is explained by preliminary observations. The pragmatic nexus is missing as is the background.

Of chronology there is not a trace. Nowhere is there a fixed datum. To be sure, there is a geographical orientation, and as a rule the situation is specified, although often in indefinite terms: a house, a mountain, some solitary place. But the topographical connection of the event, the itinerary, leaves almost as much to be desired as the chronological; seldom if at all is there any indication of a transition in a change of scene. The separate units are often presented in lively fashion, without irrelevant or merely rhetorical means, but they usually stand side by side like anecdotes, *rari nantes in gurgite vasto* ["solitary swimmers in a vast whirlpool"]. They are inadequate as material for a life of Jesus. . . . Mark does not write *de vita et moribus Jesu* ["about the life and conduct of Jesus"]. He has no intention of making Jesus' person manifest, or even intelligible. For him it has been absorbed in Jesus' divine vocation. He wishes to demonstrate that Jesus is the Christ.

[Jesus] speaks of himself most explicitly in the parable of the sower [Mark 4:3 ff.]. . . . He reflects, just as any other teacher could, on the uncertain success of the words he had directed quite generally to everyone. And this shows that he regards teaching, about the way of God, of course, as his actual vocation. . . .

Finally, attention must still be drawn to Jesus' remark at the end of his sayings at the Last Supper (Mark 14:25): "I shall not drink again of the fruit of the vine until that day when I drink it new in the kingdom of God." He regards himself there as one of the guests at the table at which the chosen will sit when the kingdom of God has come without aid from him; everyone else would have been able to express in similar fashion the hope that he would sometime share in the joys of the kingdom. He has no thought of his own parousia as messiah. . . .

If it is true that Jesus did not in advance teach his disciples of his death and resurrection, it is even more certain that he did not teach about his parousia. There are some very advanced theologians who indeed maintain that this assertion rests solely on the fact that Jesus' parousia, which is anticipated in the immediate future, in the sayings ascribed to him, actually did not take place. They hold that Jesus in this fashion is to be relieved of fanaticism and false prediction. One must let such vigorous spirits rave on and regard it as apologetic infirmity when on this point contradictions in the tradition are pointed out. . . .

The eschatological hope first became intense among the earliest Christians, who attached it to the person of Jesus. They lived on upon earth in his fellowship and in it possessed heavenly citizenship. He was their head and also the head of the future kingdom. In fact, it was he who had brought it down for them and had let them into it. Through him they were confident about and at home in their future abode; they longed for it, just as they longed for him himself, their old, familiar friend. After the bridegroom was taken from them they mourned upon earth. This personal coloring of the primitive Christian hope is foreign to Jesus, though it gave that hope an extraordinary vitality, an enthusiastic ardor. For Jesus the bridegroom has not been taken away, and he could not long for his return. Furthermore, his way of life was not so eschatologically oriented as that of his disciples, who renounced the world in order to prepare themselves for his advent. Some ignorant people have had the audacity to maintain that he himself regarded his ethics as a provisional asceticism that was to be observed only in the expectation of the nearness of the end and that had to be observed only until that end arrived. Certainly

Jesus himself did not so regard it. On the contrary, it was an ethic that set forth the eternal will of God, on earth as it is in heaven; he rejected the practices that had no inner meaning or worth. . . .

The Gospel means Christianity, no more, no less. Jesus was not a Christian, but a Jew. He proclaimed no new faith, but taught the doing of the will of God. The will of God, for him as for the Jews, lay in the Law and in the rest of the Holy Scriptures that were ranked with it. But he pointed to a way of fulfilling it other than the one the pious Jews, guided by their professional leaders, regarded as correct and followed punctiliously. . . . It can occasion no surprise that it appeared to the Jews as if he wished to destroy the principles of their religion. That certainly was not his intention, for he was sent only to the Jews and wished to remain within Judaism—and perhaps he was viewed with suspicion also because he regarded the end of the world as imminent. The break [with Judaism] first came about as a consequence of the Crucifixion, and for practical purposes first with Paul. But it was actually dormant in Jesus' own teaching and in his own attitude. The non-Jewish element in him, the human element, may be regarded as more characteristic than the Jewish. . . . It is not just since yesterday that the historical Jesus has been elevated to a religious principle and has been played off against Christianity. There does exist a more rewarding occasion for distinguishing between his intention and his effect. But in spite of this he cannot be understood apart from his historical effect, and if he is cut off from that it is difficult to do justice to his significance. . . . Without the Gospel and without Paul, however, Jesus remains a part of Judaism. He held fast to it, although he had outgrown it. We cannot go back to him, even if we wanted to. . . . He would not have become a historical figure had it not been for his death. The impression left by his career consists in the fact that it was not ended but abruptly interrupted after it had scarcely begun.

Wellhausen's critical analysis of the Gospels to a considerable extent coincided with that of the history-of-religions school, although he rejected the methodological presuppositions of consistent eschatology as emphatically as he did those employed by the history-of-religions school.[351] But the most consistent representative of the radical criticism of the Gospels, the New Testament scholar from Breslau, **William Wrede,** identified himself expressly as a pupil of A. Eichhorn.[352] In 1901 Wrede published his sensational book, *Das Messiasgeheimnis in den Evangelien* [The Messianic secret in the Gospels] in which, in "contrast to the conventional critical treatment of the Gospels" and without fear of being reproached for a "radical criticism," he produced the proof that liberal criticism's assumption of a development of Jesus' messianic consciousness, in Mark's Gospel cannot be demonstrated, but that on the contrary it is the Church's theological concept of the "messianic secret" that is basic to the Gospel of Mark and that from it the messianic consciousness was read back into the life of Jesus. Wrede achieved this understanding by means of a proof that recalls the methodology used by D. F. Strauss, the proof, namely, that both the critical and the conservative attempts at a psychologizing depiction of the life of Jesus cannot be supported from the text of Mark's Gospel: "The study of the life of Jesus suffers from psychological conjecture, and this is a kind of historical guesswork." Whereas the tradition that lay before Mark represented Jesus as a teacher and doer of mighty works, Mark, in light of his dogmatic concept, created a connection between the separate facts, "but it is the connection of imagination, not of historical development." This idea of Jesus' secret messiahship could only have arisen at a moment when "the Resurrection was thought of as the beginning of the messiahship." It is to the faith of the Church, then, that we owe the picture of Jesus as it is drawn for us by the earliest Evangelist, and the figure of the historical Jesus that stands back of it is recognizable only in very uncertain outlines.[353]

Exegesis has been unable to explain Jesus' repeated command to remain silent about his messianic office—repeated to his very last days. For it has not discovered an illuminating *motive* that could conceivably be ascribed to the historical Jesus and be applicable to all individual instances. In all this it has employed for the interpretation of the Marcan reports, views the possession of which by the evangelist cannot be proven, to say the least. Basically, however, it has had little concern for Mark himself, and has tended rather simply to bypass him in order to go back directly to the life of Jesus. And yet we have these accounts only from Mark. . . .

In Jesus' story we have so far discovered no motive that would explain for us, illuminatingly and satisfactorily, his conscious self-veiling as it is describe by Mark. It is no more likely that *Mark* explained this attitude of Jesus, which is uniformly expressed in many separate accounts, on the basis of the peculiar conditions, relationships, and events of the historical life of Jesus. I go further and maintain: *there can be no question at all of a historical motive;* to put the matter positively, *the idea of the messianic secret is a theological concept.*

A passage to which comparatively little attention has been paid provides the key to the view. To me, at least, it has actually been the point of departure for the understanding of this whole sequence of ideas, and to that extent I regard it as one of the most important passages Mark wrote. It is the command that Jesus issues after the transfiguration (9:9) : And as they were coming down the mountain, he charged them to tell no one what they had seen, *until the Son of man should have risen from the dead.* . . .

Let us courageously lay hold on the idea to which our investigation has led us. We have seen that during his earthly life Jesus' messiahship is completely a secret and should be so; no one apart from Jesus' confidants is to learn of it; but with the Resurrection comes the unveiling.

This in fact is the determining idea, the pith of Mark's whole conception. . . .

I called Mark's idea a theological idea in order to express thereby the idea that it does not possess the character of a historical concept, whether historically correct or only deduced from history. But the theological nature of the idea first becomes quite clear when we ask how Mark thought of the actual *object* of keeping the matter secret. The briefest and for us the most important answer runs: it is thought of as wholly supernatural. . . .

It follows that Jesus' being and what is related to it is by its very nature, in and for itself, a secret, not merely a secret of his consciousness, but so to speak an objective secret. To be sure, it by no means follows from this that the secret must always remain a secret during Jesus' earthly life that he himself is incessantly concerned with *keeping* it a secret. Rather, this idea is so far not wholly intelligible. For the time being we only establish the fact that the concealment of the messiahship in Mark is accompanied by a theological, non-historical concept of the messiahship, stands in relation to it, and gets a definite meaning because of it. . . .

We discover two ideas in Mark:

1. As long as he is on earth, Jesus keeps his messiahship secret.

2. Of course, Jesus reveals himself to his disciples, though not to the people, but in his revelations he remains for the present incomprehensible even for the disciples.

At the root of both ideas, which often overlap, lies the common notion that the real comprehension of what he is begins only with his resurrection.

This idea of the secret messiahship is significantly expanded in Mark. It dominates many of Jesus' sayings, numerous miracle stories, and, in general, the whole course of the historical narrative. . . .

If the idea of the secret messiahship has been properly defined, it follows immediately that *Mark possessed no knowledge of when Jesus became known as Messiah,* in fact, that in the historical sense he had no interest at all in this question. . . .

Modern research into the Gospels ordinarily proceeds on the assumption that Mark in his narration of the story had clearly in mind the approximate, though not the exact, sequence of the life of Jesus. It assumes that *he is familiar with the life* of Jesus, that he presents the individual features in accordance with the actual circumstances of this life, according to Jesus' thoughts and feelings, and links the events he describes together in light of historical and psychological considerations. . . .

This view and this procedure must be regarded as false in principle. It must be said openly: *Mark no longer has any real conception of the historical life of Jesus.* . . .

It is obvious that Mark possesses a whole series of historical and historically oriented ideas.

Jesus appeared as a teacher, and mainly in Galilee. He is surrounded by a circle of disciples, travels about with them, and gives them instruction. Among them are a few of his special intimates. A larger group often attaches itself to the disciples. He likes to speak in parables. In addition to his teaching, he engages in doing mighty works. This latter activity causes a sensation and he is swamped. He deals especially with those suffering from demon possession. So far as he meets the people at large, he does not disdain the company of tax collectors and sinners. With respect to the Law, he takes a more liberal position. He encounters the opposition of the Pharisees and the Jewish hierarchy. They plot against him and seek to entrap him. They finally succeed after he has set foot not only in Judea, but in Jerusalem itself. He suffers and is condemned to death. The Roman authorities cooperate in his condemnation. . . .

But the fabric of this portrayal as we have it first comes into being by adding a strong woof of dogmatically oriented ideas to the warp of these general historical reminiscences. . . .

These elements, and not those that are specifically historical, represent what is moving and determinative in Mark's account. They give the color. It is in them, naturally, that the writer's interest lies and it is to them that he directs his thinking. Consequently it remains true: taking the account as a whole, the Gospel no longer offers a historical *view* of the real life of Jesus. Only pale remnants of such a life have been transmuted into a supernatural creation of faith. In this sense the Gospel of Mark belongs to the history of dogma. . . .

The view that Jesus becomes Messiah only after his death is certainly not merely early, but the earliest of which we have knowledge. If the earthly life of Jesus had been regarded from the beginning as the actual life of the Messiah, it would hardly have occurred to anyone at a later time to regard the Resurrection as the formal beginning of his messiahship and the appearance in glory as the *one* advent of the Messiah. . . .

This earliest idea of Jesus' messiahship was now more and more shunted aside. What is decisive in this is not that the earthly Jesus *was called* the Messiah, or that people said, God *has* sent the Messiah; it would still be possible to understand that to mean: he is here whom we now may expect as the Messiah. Rather, what is of consequence is that the events of the past life of Jesus received a new weight and took on a new appearance. . . .

To some extent parallel to this growing importance of the life of Jesus went a weakening of the first hope, a decline of the faith, not in the parousia, but in the immediately impending parousia.

So the judgment that Jesus *was* the Messiah gained increasingly its own independent content and significance. A new, *specifically Christian* concept of the Messiah arose that cannot be distinguished sharply enough from the earlier, a concept of a very complex kind. To a large extent it came into being because an abundance of new predicates were added to the inherited messianic concept by which the old predicates took on a new appearance, or because everything of any consequence that was known, or thought to be known, of the life of Jesus was accommodated to the concept of the Messiah itself.

The dating of the messiahship from the Resurrection is not in any case a Jesus' idea, but that of the Church. It presupposes the experience of the appearances of the Risen One. . . .

There remains scarcely any other possibility than that the concept of the secret arose at a time when nothing was yet known of a messianic claim by Jesus while upon earth, at a time when the Resurrection was thought to be the beginning of the messiahship. . . .

In my judgment this is the origin of the idea that we have shown to be in Mark. It is, so to speak, a transitional concept, and *it can be designated as the aftereffect of the view that the Resurrection is the beginning of the messiahship, as a concept that arose at a time when the life of Jesus is being filled positively with messianic content.* . . .

If my deduction is correct, it is of importance for critical examination of the historical life of Jesus itself. If our view could only arise at a time when nothing was known of a public messianic claim on Jesus' part, we seem to have in it *a positive, historical testimony that Jesus did not actually represent himself as the Messiah.* However, this question is not finally answered here.

Wrede's *Das Messiasgeheimnis* [The messianic secret] appeared at almost the same time as A. Schweitzer's *Messianitäts- und Leidensgeheimnis*

[The mystery of the kingdom of God]. And a little later Schweitzer greeted Wrede's "consistent skepticism" as an ally in combating "modern historical theology," overlooking the fact, to be sure, that what his view had in common with Wrede's did not extend beyond their joint rejection of the psychological edifice erected on the Marcan report by liberal research,[354] since Wrede, in direct opposition to Schweitzer, actually questions the historical reliability of the Marcan report and suspects a Jesus for whose message the expected impending coming of God's rule is by no means fundamental. Nevertheless the effect of Wrede's critical analysis of the Gospels, from the standpoint of method so apparently logical, was extraordinarily great whether in violent rejection or in partial acceptance.[355] At first no one wholly agreed with Wrede. The reaction of **Wilhelm Bousset** may be cited as probably the most characteristic. Under the influence of Wrede's argument, Bousset at first offered an account that considers as a stronger possibility the historicity of Jesus' messianic claim, but only "with the utmost reserve and on the assumption that Wrede's objections . . . can be met." Soon after in his booklet on Jesus, however, he dismissed Wrede's theory as untenable, although he ascribed the messianic idea to Jesus "only with many misgivings" and expressly asserted that Jesus did not overstep "the bounds of the purely human." [356] Consequently the liberal picture of Jesus was demolished not only by the criticism of the history-of-religions school, but also by literary criticism.

The radical criticism of both the traditional and the liberal picture of Jesus naturally involved also a fundamental change in the traditional view of the historical relation between the primitive church, especially Paul, and Jesus. **Paul Wernle,** a tutor at Basel who in his student days at Göttingen had been strongly influenced by J. Weiss, W. Bousset, and W. Wrede, in his dissertation on *Der Christ und die Sünde bei Paulus* [Paul's idea of the Christian and sin] (1897) had already presented the radical thesis that Paul regarded Christians as free of sin. This understanding of Paul, which he had achieved by purely exegetical methods, he based on "[the apostle's] enthusiastic expectation of the parousia." [357] In his presentation of *Die Anfänge unserer Religion* [The beginnings of Christianity] (1901), a book written with traces of inspiration, he had, to be sure, held to the "superhuman self-consciousness of Jesus" expressed in messianic form and to the eschatological character of Jesus' message, but he had characterized both conceptions of Jesus as inadequate and had emphasized that "Jesus' greatness begins in every case where he sets himself free from these Jewish presuppositions." Even in his description of the early church he had characterized "the opinion . . . that the doing of God's will presupposes faith in Jesus, and is . . . only possible in the company of the faithful" as "the first fatal step away from Jesus toward orthodoxy." And in his extensive discussion of Paul, Wernle actually declares that "the introduction of Christianity into the history of the world is entirely the work of Paul," that Paul "came to be the greatest minister of the Gospel," and that one must stand "in silent amazement at his greatness as a thinker." Furthermore, a remark that Wrede made to Wernle as a student to the effect that Paul was "the corrupter of the Gospel of Jesus" [358] obviously made a lasting impression on Wernle the scholar. For in the course of Wernle's book Paul now appears as a theologian who as a churchman had a disastrous influence, who made himself utterly remote from Jesus by his emphasis on sacrament and Church, and thereby assisted in the bringing into being of Catholicism. As an "inevitable consequence of an exclusive emphasis on feeling" in Paul's piety, there began "the deterioration of morality." Accordingly, in light of "the predominance of St. Paul's theology," the task of present-day theology is said to be "again to bring into the foreground Jesus' own personal religion, and to hold this up as a word of warning to our age." Consequently, the slogan was coined, "Back from Paul to Jesus." [359]

The foundation of the sect, however, brings about the first great change in the new religion. It can be traced in a certain increasing rigidity both without, where it becomes exclusiveness, and within, where it becomes legalism. Between the brethren and those that are without, a fixed barrier has been set up by the institution of baptism and a formulated profession of faith in the Messiah.

The words "believer" and "unbeliever" come to be used as shibboleths, and take the place of "fruits" as the marks of distinction given by Jesus himself. True, it cannot be forgotten that doing God's will alone leads into God's kingdom. But the opinion very soon gains ground that doing of God's will presupposes faith in Jesus, and is, therefore, only possible in the circle of the faithful. That is the first fatal step away from Jesus toward orthodoxy. Jesus had by preference taken as his types unchurchly people like the publican, the Samaritan, the prodigal son. In people such as these he could trace much more clearly the really important things, humility, love, repentance. But it becomes a principle that outside of the sect of Jesus there is no salvation safety, and that all good works—even the best—done by those without are worthless, or at most form a step towards the righteousness which can be reached by the faithful alone. . . .

Speaking generally, all this theological activity betrays a certain dilettantism, and a want of creative power betrays itself thoroughly in this theological concern. These early Christians have experienced something altogether vast in Jesus, but in order to express it their own speech fails them. So they turn to the Jewish categories nearest at hand and attempt to confine the inexpressible into them. After all, how very petty are these first Christian ideas about Jesus compared with the deeds of Jesus himself and his own inner life. The real superiority of the new religion over the old is more concealed than expressed by the earliest Christology.

No one will blame these early Christians because of their transference of Jewish ideas to Jesus. The same hero-worship, the same faith which moved them to speak with tongues and enabled them to face the martyr's death likewise impelled them thus to formulate their creed. The great picture presented by this first Jewish Christology, quaint and extravagant as it is, is inspired by pure love and enthusiasm. But in it lies the danger of all dogmatic thinking, viz., that dogma takes the place of realities and represses them. What is new and emancipating in Jesus is embalmed by these Jewish ideas.

In regard to both sacraments Paul is a man of tradition, not a creator. . . .

The community must have its outward symbols and its means of edification, and these things must be so regulated that they are really of use to the community. And though we have here much that is new and that goes beyond what Jesus taught, yet the purely moral character of his Gospel is left inviolate. But through Paul a new value comes to be attached to acts of worship which cannot be harmonized with the teaching of Christ. At Corinth Christians had themselves baptized a second time for deceased relatives, and Paul appeals to this in his defense of the Resurrection. That is a heathen conception of baptism which turns into an *opus operatum* ["act efficacious in itself"], and as such a guarantee of blessedness. While in this case Paul simply accepts the superstitious view without saying anything, he is himself actually the cause of it in the case of the Lord's Supper. To please his Greek converts he compares it to the Greek and Jewish sacrificial feasts. He is the first to contrast holy food with all other that is profane, and bids us see in the sickness and death of many Christians the judgment upon their profane participation in the holy meal. Now that was an accommodation to Greek superstition which as a direct consequence led to the establishment of a religion of a lower, less spiritual nature. But the mere fact that an extraordinary value is attached to ceremonial acts is in itself fatal. . . .

All those superstitious statements to which allusion has been made are in Paul's hands means to an end: in the one case, that of baptism, to prove the Christian hope; in the other, that of the Lord's Supper, to secure decency and good order in the congregation. It is unhealthy, not for Paul himself, but for the future history of his community. Henceforth participation in divine worship takes its place side by side with trust in God, and two kinds of religion or of communion with God, begin to compete with each other.

The Cross, the Resurrection, the Son of God who descended from heaven— these are the three great innovations of Pauline Christology. In the Gospel of Jesus they are almost entirely wanting, yet Paul's object is to express the gospel ideas by means of them. The comparison between the Master and the disciples is especially instructive:

1. *Jesus.* God is our Father from the beginning of time and everywhere. He showers down his love upon us by the gifts of food and raiment, by abundant pardon, by deliverance from the evil, by the promise of the kingdom that is to come. All that Jesus does and says is meant to confirm man's faith in the love of God the Father.

Paul. In the Cross of Jesus God shows the whole world his forgiving love. Without that there is no certainty of reconciliation. Only he that believes in the Cross has the true God.

So speaks the ecclesiastical apologist according to the principle that outside of the Church—that is, the community of those that believe in the Cross— there is no salvation.

2. *Jesus.* The kingdom of God is at hand. It is to be the goal of longing and the power of the new moral life. Jesus leads his disciples onward to walk in the light of eternity.

Paul. The resurrection of Jesus is the proof that the world to come is already breaking into the present. Even now the Christian is risen with Jesus and has entered into life eternal.

So speaks the apologist, who is bound to give palpable proofs for the promised realities, and thereby confuses facts and postulates.

3. *Jesus.* Through his teaching and his example he redeems men, so that they become the children of God, and lifts them up to a life of love and humility.

Paul. The Son of man came down from heaven upon earth so that we might have a pattern in his self-humiliation, and through him become the children of God.

So speaks the apologist, who himself knew not Jesus, for whom therefore the mythical picture had to achieve what the impression made by Jesus gave to the earlier disciples.

The consequences of the great innovation were boundless. Jesus was presented to the Greeks in the shape of a dramatic myth. Once again they had a story of the gods, one that derived from the most recent past. And this conconquered the world. The simple teaching of Jesus of Nazareth would never have been able thus to win its way to victory simply because at that time the world was not yet ripe to receive the impression of so pure a personality. What was great and redemptive in Jesus had to allow itself to be wrapped up in heavy dogmatic dress; in which even for Paul it lives and works mightily. In spite of all it must be deemed fortunate that Jesus was preached to the world through Paul. Along with the ideas about him came Jesus himself.

Paul would have baptism regarded as a miracle and a mystery. The baptized convert should believe that he steps forth from the water a different person from what he was when he entered it. In like manner he taught that the Lord's Supper was a meal at which one eats no ordinary bread and drinks no ordinary wine, but partakes of the body and blood of Christ. It was a spiritual food and a spiritual drink—i.e. a channel for the mediation of the powers of salvation. It is hard to understand how Paul, who elsewhere always connects redemption with the Spirit of Christ, here all at once attaches a value to the body and blood, i.e. to that which was after all perishable in Jesus. The reason probably is that he found here an institution already existing which could only with extreme difficulty obtain a place in his spiritual doctrine of salvation. But he did find a place for it, and thereby made it a sacrament. It seemed to a teacher of heathens valuable to make redemption clear to believers through individual cultic acts. As a matter of fact this only confused them, dragging them down from the spiritual sphere into that of natural magic. It appears to us at the present day exceedingly strange that the hero of the Word should at the same time have become the creator of the sacrament. As every one who knows anything about Paul knows, he himself needed no ceremonial magic, since the Spirit within him testified to him of God's love, and Jesus had set him free from ceremonial performances. But through taking up the sacraments into his doctrine of redemption, he shares in the vise of the Catholicism which pronounced him a saint and made him dead. . . .

Whoever examines Paul's doctrine of justification, laying aside all Protestant prejudices, is bound to pronounce it one of his most unfortunate creations. The word "justify," with the new meaning attached to it, is ambiguous; the position of God who as judge declares the sinner to be righteous, is confusing; the value attached to the creed of the Church as the decisive factor in the judgment is fraught with evil consequences, and the proof from the Old Testament is arbitrary and artificial. Paul fought for the universalism of Christianity and the substitution of the religion of love for that of legalism: What he really attained was to institute in the Christian Church a new law of faith and confession, with the return of all the Jewish sins of narrowness, fanaticism, and the restricted conception of God. But in spite of all, a great and profound thought lies hidden beneath the defective outer form. God is our Father, who freely gives to us whether we deserve it or not, and we men, just as we are, his children are to live by his love. This thought is at once strengthened and demonstrated by the fact of the manifestation of Christ. To the kernel though not to the husk we Protestants certainly owe the deepest reverence.

Stimulated by Wrede, Wernle had drawn repeated attention to the great step from Jesus to Paul. Shortly thereafter, a pastor, **Martin Brückner,** likewise personally influenced by Wrede, in an exceptionally clear study of *Die Entstehung der paulinischen Theologie* [The origin of Paul's theology] (1903) attempted to demonstrate "that Paul's picture of Christ arose quite independently of the historical personality of Jesus." He pointed out that "the combination of the two disparate pictures of Christ," in Pauline Christology—that of the preexistent, heavenly man and that of the earthly man, Jesus—is explained by the fact that Paul introduced the episode of Jesus' incarnation into the inherited Jewish picture of the heavenly Messiah, with the result that it was not the earthly life of Jesus but the Jewish messianic doctrine which gave form to Paul's faith in Christ.[360]

Paul was convinced by his conversion that Jesus was the Messiah. This conviction rests on the arbitrary combination of two disparate pictures of Christ that Paul had carried about with him before his conversion: a picture he had as a Jewish theologian, and the picture of the crucified Jesus (*conveyed to him by*) the faith of the primitive church. . . .

The passage in Philippians [2:5 ff.] shows that, according to the Pauline view, the divine form of being of the Preexistent One, the form into which also he returns after death on earth, is the only one that corresponds to the essence and the nature of the Christ, while the Incarnation, together with the Death, is a transitory episode that is in absolute contradiction to the essence and the nature of the Christ. This state of affairs, then, confirms the suspicion aroused by the study of Paul's conversion that the heavenly nature of the Christ corresponds to Paul's picture of the Messiah, while his earthly appearance contains the new features that through his conversion are brought over from the primitive church into his picture of Christ. In the passage under consideration Paul has now so combined the two disparate parts of his picture of Christ that he has sublimated the earthly appearance of Jesus up to the time of his death on the cross into a self-denying act of the preexistent Christ. By so doing he made Christ for the first time into a functioning heavenly being. . . .

When the Incarnation is removed from the Pauline picture of Christ . . . the concepts of preexistence and parousia remain basically undisturbed. On the other hand, the removal of this one episode tremendously simplifies Paul's whole picture of Christ. To put the matter more precisely, the pictures of the preexistent and postexistent one now coalesce of themselves into the *one* picture of the heavenly Christ and Son of God, one who before every creature came into being as the exact likeness of God and the archetypal image of man, and who now lives hidden with God as a heavenly spiritual being in divine form, until at the end of the days he appears from heaven in divine power as an emissary of God, destroys the powers opposed to God, presides over the judgment, and establishes the kingdom of God, in order in the end to hand over the rule to God himself. . . .

That the Messiah as the preexistent Son of God in heaven with his retinue suddenly steps forth from concealment, that he protects his own and destroys the enemies, that he presides over the judgment on Satan and his hosts, that at his coming the righteous are raised by him, yes, even the thought that his rule is of limited duration and that he in the end retires for eternity before the sole lordship of God: All these are features that frequently recur in the Jewish apocalyptic, not only individually but in combination, and thereby betray that indeed the whole of Paul's picture of the Messiah belongs in this connection and is taken over into his Christian view almost unaltered from his Jewish past. . . .

Paul's messianic hope had to be limited to the Jewish nation because as a Jew Paul had not been able to give any basis for its universal formulation. As soon as he could perceive such a basis in the death of Jesus, the offence was lifted for him and the obstacle to his conversion was transformed into the power that brought this about. The presupposition of such a ground was actually provided for him in his Jewish idea of the Messiah as the preexistent heavenly man. For through it Paul was able to conceive of Jesus' humanity and death on the cross as the world-redeeming act of the preexistent Son of God. The fact that Paul laid hold of this idea made him a Christian and the Apostle to the Gentiles. . . .

So then the historical origin of Pauline Christology explains the various features of this remarkable picture of Christ. But it also helps us at the same time to understand wherein consists the new and valuable in the Pauline Christology: not in the metaphysical features of the preexistent Son of God and heavenly man that come from Hellenistic Judaism, but in the personal act of his becoming man. Since Paul regarded Christ's incarnation as the proclamation of God's Father-love and as Christ's personal act of love and obedience, he included in his Jewish picture of Christ the gist of what Jesus brought to the world.

While Brückner combines the point of view of the school of the history-of-religions with historical criticism to demonstrate the historical hiatus between Jesus and Paul, the French Protestant **Maurice Goguel,** who was to become the main representative in France of critical research into Christian origins, begins his dissertation for the licentiate on *L'apôtre Paul et Jésus-Christ* [The apostle Paul and Jesus Christ] with the explicit claim that a "strictly historical methodology" is the only legitimate one for such an investigation. A comparison of Jesus' message with the theology of Paul in all its detail shows, according to Goguel, that the most striking differences between Jesus and Paul consist in their respective Christologies and doctrines of salvation, and that Paul made of the Gospel something wholly new. However, in spite of the considerable differences to which he draws attention, Goguel does not wish to admit that a real contrast exists between Jesus and Paul, but seeks rather to show—and at this point he clearly abandons the "strictly historical methodology" and recognizes a theological approach to the subject—that Paul carried out in the best possible way the theological task unavoidably involved in the situation at the beginning of Christianity.[361]

For Paul, Christ by his very nature is a unique being who differs from other men in that he preexisted before his incarnation and during his life as a man was perfectly holy. His holiness is of the same nature as God's, that is to say, he partakes of God's essence.

The Master's thought differs noticeably from that of the Apostle. No doubt Jesus has a clear consciousness of his perfect holiness, but this holiness is for him the result of constant effort, of a persevering struggle against temptation. Jesus felt himself to be different from other men, but mainly because of his inner communion with the Father. None of his preserved sayings contains an explanation concerning his essence. The same can be said with respect to the notion of preexistence, which is found very clearly in Paul and of which not a trace could be found in Jesus. . . .

But the point at which the difference is most apparent is certainly the question of Christ's death. For Paul [Christ's death] signifies the condemnation of sin, the condition of the sinner's justification and of his reconciliation to God. According to Jesus, God did not have to become reconciled to the world. He wishes for love's sake to forgive the sinner, and the latter is justified provided he renounces his sins and breaks with what separated him from God. We have seen that Jesus believes in the efficacy of his death, but this death takes place in order to introduce the kingdom of God and not in order to obtain the forgiveness of sins, for to those who approach him he says: "Thy sins are forgiven thee," never, "Thy sins will be forgiven thee." For Paul the death is the essential element in Christ's work. No doubt for Jesus it is something other than a simple accident, but it is not the actual reason for his coming to the earth. . . .

So then between Paul's Christology and Jesus' teaching concerning himself there are differences that without exaggeration can be called fundamental. . . .

The idea of a supernatural salvation, communicated through mysterious rites by the mediation of a divine institution, the Church, is completely foreign to the thought of Jesus. Furthermore, the idea that the Gospel is a supernatural wisdom cannot be found among his thoughts. . . .

The importance of the innovation of which Paul was the author has been very considerable. Out of the community of the faithful he made the Church, that is to say, a supernatural reality with its hierarchy and sacraments; or at least he laid down the principles that in their development had to lead to the idea of the divine institution of the Church and to the doctrine of the sacraments.

On the other hand, Paul planted the germ that had to bring about the transformation of the Gospel, the proclamation of salvation in the form of a religious philosophy. He is thereby in a certain sense the forerunner of the Gnostics and, in a very general way, of all Christian thinkers.

All the differences between Jesus and Paul that we have noted can, as we have indicated, be reduced to two. The first is that Paul founded a Christology; the second, that in his theology a doctrine of salvation has replaced the proclamation of the kingdom. . . .

Two causes above all seem to us to have determined the evolution of Christianity from Jesus to Paul: on the one hand, the difference in time and the particular perspective that the Gospel had to take for people who envisaged it wholly from the point of view of the death and resurrection of Christ; and on the other, the powerful systematic spirit of the apostle Paul who was the first to understand the Gospel not only as a believer, but also as a theologian. . . .

If we had to sum up in a word the opinion we have set forth in the preceding pages, we should willingly say that what characterizes Paulinism and distinguishes it from the teaching of Jesus Christ is the fact that it represents a theology. . . . Jesus was not, and could not have been, a theologian because the work he had come to accomplish was more important than theology. Paul on the contrary was a theologian, in fact, the first Christian theologian.

In conclusion we can say that Paul's role in the history of Christianity has been not only useful and fruitful but also, we do not hesitate to say, providential. At a moment when the appearance of a theology was a matter of life or death for Christianity, he created a system which, by its fidelity to the teaching of the Lord, has been proven to be the best possible.

But in the field of Pauline studies the real radical was **William Wrede.** In an influential little book on Paul of which A. Schweitzer was to say, "It belongs, not to theology, but to the literature of the world," [362] Wrede was the first to draw the consequences of a radically historical representation of the apostle. For here Paul appears as the theologian who transferred to Jesus the figure of the Christ familiar to him as a Jew, without having been influenced in any essential respect by Jesus' person and teaching. Indeed, Paul is not characterized in any sense as the successor to Jesus but as the founder of Christianity as a religion of redemption, and consequently appears in a light that leads to the alternative, "Jesus or Paul." At the same time, however, Wrede's acute historical perception also enabled him, in a way hitherto unknown, to recognize so clearly the reality of the redemption and the basic eschatologico-historical element in Pauline theology that at a later time new reflection on the kerygmatic character of Pauline theology could take its departure from this radically historical picture of Paul.[363]

The total theory of things which is put forward in the apostle's writings includes a wealth of theological hypotheses, propositions, and inferences: Christianity as a whole appears, to a certain degree, as a structure of thought.

What then is the relation between this and Paul's religion? The answer is, the two cannot be separated. *The religion of the apostle is theological through and through: his theology is his religion.* . . .

The most characteristic utterance of Paul about God is . . . this, that he sent Christ for the salvation of men. That is to say, the whole Pauline doctrine is a doctrine of Christ and his work; that is its essence.

These two, the person and the work of Christ, are inseparable. The apostle had not reached a conception of Christ as a detached object of doctrine, which may be considered without reference to his significance for the world. Paul's essential thought of him is simply this, that he is the redeemer. . . .

What *we* prize in the man Jesus plays no part whatever in the thought of the apostle. Nothing is further from him than religious veneration for a hero. The moral majesty of Jesus, his purity and piety, his ministry among his people, his manner as a prophet, the whole concrete ethical-religious content of his earthly life, signifies for Paul's Christology—nothing whatever. The "manhood" appears to be a purely formal thing. . . .

In our view, no doubt, manhood includes more than this. And if a man is a being who possesses human thought, feeling, and will—not merely in a universal sense, but in his own definite, individual way—then this Christ is not a real man. The truth is, Paul lacks the idea of personality, of human individuality; and therefore the humanity of Christ, as he conceives it, remains for us an intangible phantom. . . .

One thing is clear throughout: Christ had within himself no reason whatever to live through a period in the form of a man, which for him betokens nothing but loss. The reason lies in the man alone. For his salvation, if we may anticipate, depends entirely on the death and the resurrection of Christ. For this reason, and for no other, there was need for the Incarnation. In effect, the Son of God becomes a man in order to die and to rise again. Hence it becomes clear how this doctrine of Christ flows into the doctrine of redemption and cannot be understood without it. . . .

The whole Pauline conception of salvation is characterized by tension; a tension which presses forward towards the final solution, the actual death. The earthly life is not the setting in which salvation comes to its conclusion.

In this connection we should keep before our minds with especial clearness a fact which ought never to be forgotten when we are dealing with Paul. He believed with all his might in the speedy coming of Christ and the approaching end of the world. Accordingly in his view the redemptive act of Christ, which lay in the past, and the dawn of the future glory lay close together. . . .

It has been maintained that Paul altered the view of salvation held by the earliest community by shifting the stress from the future to the past, stressing the blessedness of the Christian as already attained and emphasizing faith instead of hope. It is easy to see that this is assuredly but a half truth. All references to the redemption as a completed transaction change at once into utterances about the future. . . .

There are deep-reaching differences between the Pauline doctrine of the redemption and the ideas of modern belief.

In the first place, the modern view is apt to relocate salvation within man himself, or in his conscience. . . . But Paul does not in the least perceive salvation in all these subjective states of consciousness; rather it is in its own nature something objective, a change in the very nature and conditions of existence. Another matter is of equal importance.

We have several times deprecated a one-sided ethical interpretation of Pauline doctrine. Its prevalence derives from the fact that people do not recognize the remoteness of modern thought from that of Paul. In our view sin is altogether a matter of the individual will, if not necessarily of the conscious will. We are accustomed to draw a strict distinction between the merely natural and the moral. *Paul knows no such distinction.* For him, flesh and sin cohere indissolubly together, even in the case of believers. And therefore redemption does not bring with it merely an ethical revolution. It signifies rather *a change in the nature of humanity,* and the ethical change is derivative from this. . . .

Here again a very considerable difference from the modern conception comes into view. An objective redemption is indeed not unknown to dogmatic and popular exposition of to-day; but the present-day doctrine of salvation is always thinking of what happens in the individual man. It asks how the process which imparts the benefit of Christianity goes on, and must necessarily go on, in the individual soul. . . . This whole chapter is absent from Pauline teaching. The reason is that in his doctrine he is not thinking of the individual at all, or of the psychological processes of the individual, but always of the race, of humanity as a whole. Death with Christ is a general fact, not an event transacted in the individual soul or connected with that soul's special experiences and feelings.

And because it is with the race that Paul is concerned, his mode of thinking is purely historical. All his thoughts about salvation are thoughts about a series of events, in which God and man take part, whose scene is on earth and also in heaven—it proceeds, properly speaking, in both places at the same time. Paul has always before his eyes great periods of human development, and thinks in terms of the temporal distinctions, past, present, and future. All the leading ideas of his theology bear this historical stamp. . . .

What was the origin of the Pauline conception of Christ? For those, indeed, who see in Jesus what Paul saw, a supramundane, divine being, no problem arises. But those who take Jesus for what he was—an historical human personality—perceive an enormous gulf between this man and the Pauline Son of God. Not a generation had passed away since the death of Jesus, and already his form had not only grown into the infinite, but had been utterly changed. How did that come to pass?

The picture of Christ did not originate in an impression of the personality of Jesus. This view has often been maintained, but never proved. . . .

There remains only one explanation: *Paul believed in such a celestial being, in a divine Christ, before he believed in Jesus.* . . . The man Jesus was really, therefore, only the bearer of all those mighty predicates which had already been established; but the blessedness of the apostle lay in this, that what had hitherto been a mere hope he could now regard as a tangible reality which had come into the world. . . .

The question concerning what influence Jesus' preaching had on Paul hardly brings many essential facts to light. But it is not after all the decisive question. The main question is what was *the real distance between Pauline doctrine and the preaching of Jesus?* . . .

297

In Jesus everything aims at the personal character of the individual. Man should yield his soul whole and undivided to God and God's will. . . .

In Paul the central point is an act of God in history but transcending history, or a complex of such acts, which impart to all mankind a finished salvation. Whoever believes in these divine acts—the incarnation, death, and resurrection of a celestial being—receives salvation.

And this, which to Paul is the sum of religion—the framework for the construction of his piety, without which it would collapse—can this be a carrying forward or a remoulding of the gospel of Jesus? In all this where is the gospel to be found which Paul is said to have understood?

Of that which is to Paul all and everything, how much does Jesus know? Nothing whatever. . . .

To reproach Paul is idle. He did not put a religion together by mere caprice, but was guided by internal and external necessity. But the facts themselves must not be whittled down. And, if we do not wish to deprive both figures of all historical distinctness, the name "disciple of Jesus" has little applicability to Paul, if it is used to denote a historical relation. In comparison with Jesus Paul is essentially a new phenomenon, as new as he could possibly be, considering the large basis of common ground. He stands much further away from Jesus than Jesus himself stands from the noblest figures of Jewish piety. . . .

We see then that in the very first decades of nascent Christianity a great leap forward was made in the development of the religion itself. At first sight extremely perplexing, this becomes on a nearer view intelligible. Paul had had no contact with Jesus himself, and was therefore much further removed from him than his nearness in point of time would indicate. His faith had been achieved through a "revelation," and in consequence he was able to apprehend and interpret the vision of Jesus by means of ideas about Christ whose origin was quite independent of Jesus the man.

Another thing must be remembered. Between Jesus and Paul stands the original community. It is the precondition of Paul's existence, and forms beyond doubt a kind of bridge from the one to the other. . . . And yet the divergence between the mother church and Paul is very great, and in truth greater than the parties themselves knew.

Even more important is the question what it was that Paul the theologian effected; *how* he remoulded the new religion. The least part of it is his introduction of a considerable rabbinical element into Christianity. On the other hand everything is summed up when we say he made Christianity the religion of redemption.

No one who sets out to describe the religion which lives in the sayings and similitudes of Jesus could by any chance hit on the phrase "religion of redemption." It is true that the idea of redemption plays a part in the future hope, the kingdom of God, but it does not belong to the essence of the matter. The emphasis falls on individual piety, and its connection with future salvation. But for Paul religion *is* an appropriated and experienced redemption.

That which redeems, however, is by no means to be found within man himself, but outside of him in a divine work of redemption, which has prepared salvation for mankind once for all. In other words it lies in the history which has been transacted between God and man, the "salvation history" or the "saving acts." Paul's whole innovation is comprised in this, that *he laid the foundation of religion in these acts of salvation, in the incarnation, death, and resurrection of Christ.* . . .

It follows then conclusively from all this that Paul is to be regarded as *the second founder of Christianity.* As a rule even liberal theology shrinks from this conclusion. But it is not to be evaded. For demonstrably it was Paul who first—even if a certain preparatory work had already been done—introduced into Christianity the ideas whose influence has been deepest and most wide-reaching in its history up to the present time. . . . Compared with the first, this second founder of Christianity has even exercised beyond all doubt the stronger, though not the better influence. True, he has not dominated everywhere, especially not in the life of simple, practical piety, but throughout long stretches of church history—one need but think of the Councils and dogmatic controversies—he has thrust utterly into the background that greater Person, whom he meant only to serve.

Naturally the rest of the New Testament, and in particular the Gospel of John, was also subjected to this radical historical criticism. In a book that became celebrated, *L'Évangile et l'Église* [*The Gospel and the Church*] (1902), **Alfred Loisy,** the Catholic theologian who had been removed from his ecclesiastical teaching office a decade earlier because of his critical attitude toward the Bible, had characterized "the Gospels . . . as a product and witness of the ancient faith" of the primitive church and the Fourth Gospel as "a symbolic description of the truth" of Christ and as the visible revelation of the eternal word.[364] In so doing he challenged the historical character of the Johannine report. In his great commentary on John's Gospel that appeared soon after he denies that the Fourth Gospel has any real historical worth in comparison to the Synoptics and sees in it an allegorical account of Christianity from the end of the first century that came into being essentially uninfluenced by foreign religions but that in spite of this purely theological character represents "one of the foundation stones of the Christian edifice." [365]

Thanks to the predominance of the dogmatic point of view, the Gospel of John is a perfectly coherent work, all of whose parts correspond to and complete one another, without betraying in any way the fact that its separate parts have been compiled, or even combined. . . . On this point, as on many others, the difference from the Synoptics is altogether remarkable. The evident conclusion is that the Synoptics are almost impersonal works, collections of traditional reminiscences, while of them all the Fourth Gospel is a personal work, which from beginning to end bears the mark of the great genius who created it. . . . All the materials the author has utilized have been passed through the crucible of his great intelligence and his mystical soul. Thence they have issued transformed, intimately interpenetrated and combined with one another by the idea of the eternal Christ, the divine source of light and life.

The Fourth Gospel is therefore not to be interpreted as the simple expression of traditional recollections, as the authentic and exact witness to a teaching that Christ gave in the course of his ministry. All the work of Christian thought since the resurrection of the Savior finds its echo there, and he who has summed it up in an original and brilliant synthesis has not left out of consideration the situation of the Church at the time at which he wrote and the particular needs of the milieu in which he lived. He was more a theologian than a historian; but he was still more an apologist than a theologian. His theology serves to prove the legitimacy of Christianity in light of contemporary Judaism. . . .

In view of this character of the Fourth Gospel, the ancient method of exegesis, which consisted of juxtaposing the assertions of the Gospel of John with those of the Synoptics, seems to be definitely doomed, although it is still practiced today by learned exegetes. The elements that one would like to combine are not of the same nature. In general it can be said that the Synoptics cannot be complemented by John, nor John by the Synoptics. The Synoptics are the true historical sources touching on the life and teaching of the Savior; John is already an ecclesiastical witness and represents the faith of the Church, the Christian religious movement at the end of the first century, as much as, and more than the historical reality of the Gospel.

The evangelist seems to have a supreme indifference with regard to history. Not only does he select out of the tradition what suits his purpose, but without the slightest scruple he corrects and supplements the tradition to maintain the equilibrium of his allegorical pictures. As a result the measure of the historical truth that inheres in his book has not been maintained there by considered reflection, but quite simply because it could serve his purposes. He was ready to conserve more of it, as well as to sacrifice still more of it, if the success of his teaching had demanded that of him. For him truth and imagination mingle in the unity of the symbol. . . .

It seems, therefore, that in the Gospel of John allegory has been extended as far as possible in order to leave nothing outside it that could be called alien to its law. . . .

Allegory is the characteristic trait in the Johannine teaching. It extends into the narratives, which are profound symbols whose secret the author half uncovers only for moments. It extends also into the discourses, where Christ continuously speaks in figurative, ambiguous language which the evangelist himself assumes to have been unintelligible to those who heard it. So the Fourth Gospel in its entirety is nothing else than a great theological and mystical allegory, a work of learned speculation that, so far as form is concerned, has nothing in common with the preaching of the historical Christ. . . .

This Christ is doubtless no metaphysical abstraction; he is alive in the soul of the evangelist, in the faith of the Church, in Christian feeling. But such a Christ, wholly spiritual and mystical, however true he may be in his manner, is not he who lived upon earth, for he is not subject to the conditions of time and of terrestrial existence.

The historian is obliged to choose between the synoptic mode of presenting the ministry of Christ in Jerusalem and the Johannine mode of introducing the Passion, for the two are incompatible, to say nothing of the impossibility of giving any reasonable explanation of the silence of the synoptic tradition about the resurrection of Lazarus. And the critic cannot hesitate an instant, for the Johannine account is obviously a theological and transcendental interpretation, by no means a philosophical one in the modern sense of the word, of the facts whose original appearance the synoptic report has preserved more or less perfectly. . . .

One can say that the human has disappeared and has been effaced before the divine; that the doctrine of the Incarnate Word has transformed the Gospel into a theological dogma that has preserved scarcely even the appearance of history; that the manifestation of the glory of which the evangelist speaks is detached from the reality; that Christ himself is no longer a truly human being.

From the point of view of an "impartial science" Loisy had radically divested the Gospel of John of all historical worth and had understood it only as a witness to the Church's faith. To this judgment **William Wrede** now added the religio-historical conjecture that the religious categories of the evangelist come from tradition of a gnostic sort and that the whole Gospel is written because as an aid in the battle of the early church with late Judaism "the earlier Gospels . . . did not at all suffice." Consequently the Gospel of John for Wrede is not "a historical but a theological document" and can be understood exclusively as a witness to the Church's faith in Christ.[366]

The actual center of gravity of our book lies in the discourses, so far as they interpret history or reduce it to formulae, and so far, on the other hand, as they quickly leave the concrete historical events and hasten away to the height of the loftiest questions.

In terms of their form the discourses reveal themselves at once as literary compositions, even to the relatively unschooled observer. They are not compilations of fragments of the tradition of the preaching of Jesus; they are long, connected accounts of the same sort, from *one* lump and of *one* mold.

In terms of content, however, they reveal themselves just as readily as dogmatic disquisitions. Everything in them aims at formulation of doctrine. And this doctrine concerns *the person of Jesus and his higher nature.* To put the matter in other words: The discourses presuppose a *Christological dogma,* and this they preach and seek to support.

A study of the content of the discourses shows that we do not have to do here with historically authentic speeches. It is not, however, just a matter of reworking authentic material—these discourses are much too homogeneous in form and content for that—and also not just that of a further development of sayings and thoughts that ultimately derive from Jesus, for no one yet has been able to pinpoint the sayings or thoughts of Jesus that are here said to have been further developed. Rather, we have before us simply free compositions of one and the same author, compositions that rarely contain even a reminiscence of anything that originally comes from Jesus. . . .

Scarcely anything is so noteworthy and so striking in the actual narrative as the quite peculiar lack of vividness that appears in the presentation of the historical course of events. . . .

This lack of vividness reveals in many ways at what a distance the evangelist stands from the historical life of Jesus. For an author who has in mind really distinct pictures does not compose such a narrative as our evangelist's. This is true even if he is intent on emphasizing certain ideas, and even if time has

301

caused the experience or firsthand report to fade, or has completely obliterated its detail.

> The doctrine of the Gospel of John is doctrine about Christ. . . .
>
> It is apparent that the leading idea of this doctrine of Christ is that Christ brings the truth from above and communicates it to men. . . .
>
> In other words, Christ in reality is not only the bringer of the message, but also its actual content. . . . Jesus was a historical personality, an individuality. Instead of portraying him as such, the evangelist shows us a divine being who roams majestically over this earth as a stranger and whose "humanity" is purely transparent, in order to let the divine light shine through upon earth.

> Of all the doctrines the evangelist consciously and intentionally represents, . . . I should like to distinguish the religious ideas, which furnish as it were the linguistic material for the expression of those doctrines and that form the underpinning of his religious and theological thinking, although he himself is unaware of it. . . .
>
> All such ideas, concepts, pictures are not really intelligible either from the Synoptic Gospels or from the Pauline letters. Furthermore, they cannot be regarded as the creation and peculiar property of the author. . . . I am inclined to believe that some sort of gnostic views lie back of the Gospel.

This radical approach to the New Testament, which not only severely limited the historical worth of the New Testament writings, but also basically inquired *only* into the place of the New Testament writings and their content in relation to the historical development,[367] on historical considerations necessarily put into question the uniqueness of the New Testament as a whole. The Göttingen orientalist **Paul de Lagarde,** with his thesis that theology was "exclusively a historical discipline"[368] was to become a precursor of the history-of-religions school.[369] As early as his essay "Uber das Verhältnis des deutschen Staates zu Theologie, Kirche und Religion" ["Concerning the relation of the German state to theology, church, and religion"]—first published in 1873 to defend that thesis—he expressly maintained that "the New Testament Canon [is] nothing but the collection of the books which the early Catholic Church found suitable for service as weapons in its conflict with the heretics and sects of the second century," and therefore concluded that, so far as the historical understanding of the primitive Christian era is concerned, the Canon must be left out of consideration and all documents from that time are to be employed.[370]

> It should be evident that in pursuing a historical investigation one should forget all about the New Testament as a collection and seek quite simply to answer the question of the sources of knowledge of the [Christian] religion, non-Catholic, to be sure, but with the same origin as Catholicism: All documents of primitive Christian times—books, monuments, statutes, cultic usages—when employed in the manner customary in historical studies and validated by long

practice and significant results, together throw light on the beginnings of our religion. The question is simply a historical one: since Jesus, or, if you prefer, the Gospel, appeared at a certain moment in history, therefore our knowledge of Jesus and the Gospel can be obtained in no other way than that by which historical knowledge in general is acquired.

When he was first appointed to the faculty at Halle (1886), Albert Eichhorn, whom we have already met as one of the spiritual fathers of the history-of-religions school (see above, pp. 249, 253-55), had defended, among others, the thesis that "New Testament introduction must be the history of early Christian literature." By this he meant that the historian should not study the books of the New Testament any differently from the rest of early Christian literature.[371] Then, a decade later, **Gustav Krüger,** church historian at Giessen, presented the thesis at a university convocation that "the existence of a 'New Testament' science, or a 'science of the New Testament,' as a special historico-theological discipline [is] one of the chief impediments to a study of primitive Christianity and therefore also of the New Testament itself—a study that would prove fruitful and lead to assured and generally accepted results." Consequently he demanded that, "for the 'history of New Testament Times' and the 'history of the apostolic age' . . . there should be substituted a general history of early Christianity; for 'introduction,' a history of early Christian literature; for 'New Testament theology,' a history of early Christian theology." And he declared explicitly that the "dogma of the New Testament . . . taken from the toolbox of the Catholic Church," can only lead to the false conception of a "specifically 'New Testament' structure of thought" and that therefore this dogma should be wholly abandoned.[372]

The "dogma of the New Testament" is actually one of the leading dogmas of the Catholic Church which, like so much else, the evangelical churches have taken over uncritically. When it has once been abandoned there is to be no talk of treating the New Testament books and the theology embedded in them as independent of time and space: in fact they are to be, and can only be, understood in light of their time and environment. But if there is a basic acknowledgment of the rightness of this approach and with it the justification for writing a history of early Christian literature in which the whole inventory of this literature is subjected to a critical illumination and in which one builds on the basis of the literary interconnections—similar tasks would be involved in writing the history of early Christian theology—yet scholars continue to believe that they should demonstrate respect for the New Testament and that by it alone can they do justice to its classical significance for our religion by subjecting it to an examination in isolation from other literature. And in the course of so doing they make it appear again as something unique. Or they abandon this position so far as they themselves are concerned, but hold that the time is not ripe, that theological scholarship in our day is not sufficiently advanced to tolerate another approach. Now, I believe that one can be fully convinced of that classical significance of the New Testament, as a Christian, as a theologian, as a historian, that one can also agree that a respect appropriate to their importance should constantly be paid to the New Testament documents in exegetical and historical lectures, without, however, being in favor of treating them in isolation. And, whatever you may think of our scholarship, you do not need to be so pessimistic as to regard it as incapable of functioning in accordance with a proper perception.

Shortly thereafter **William Wrede** published a lecture "Über Aufgabe und Methode der sogenannten Neutestamentlichen Theologie" [On the task and method of the so-called New Testament theology] (1897) in which, making specific reference to Eichhorn, Lagarde, and Krüger, he likewise demanded that a "history of Early Christian religion" be substituted for the "biblical theology of the New Testament," a history that would take all early Christian writings into consideration, that would deliberately ignore the Canon, and consequently would really grapple for the first time with the historical task and that would leave out of account all questions of revelation.[373]

Scholarship has recognized that the old doctrine of inspiration . . . is untenable. For logical thinking there can be no such thing as a cross between inspired writings and historical documents. . . . From given documents biblical theology seeks to recover the actual state of affairs, if not the external conditions, then the spiritual conditions: It seeks to understand them as objectively, as correctly, as saliently as possible—that is all. What the systematic theologian makes of its results, how he accommodates himself to them, is his affair. Like every other genuine science, its purpose is involved in its very being, and it behaves coyly towards every dogma and every systematic theology. . . .

In view of this, everyone who wishes to concern himself with New Testament theology in a scholarly way must demonstrate first of all that he is capable of concern for historical research. A pure, disinterested concern for knowledge, a concern that accepts *every* result that emerges, must be his guide. He must be able to distinguish his own thinking from that alien to it, modern ideas from those of the past; he must be able to prevent his own view, however dear, from exerting any influence on the object of research, to hold it so to speak in suspension. For he only wishes to discover how things really were.

It may perhaps be objected that New Testament theology, so understood, entirely forfeits its peculiar theological character. In its procedure it is not to be distinguished in any way from any branch of the history of thought, in particular from the history of religion. That, too, is wholly correct. . . .

If the New Testament writings had their origin in the course of a history and are the witnesses to and documents of this history, then we are faced at once with the question of why our discipline is concerned just with these writings, and only with these writings. The answer runs: because they alone belong to the Canon. But this answer is unsatisfactory. When once the doctrine of inspiration is given up, the dogmatic idea of the Canon cannot be retained. . . .

It is very difficult to define the boundaries at all points between the canonical and adjacent noncanonical literature.

Therefore, if the New Testament writings are not to be understood from the point of view of a "subsequent experience" with which they originally had nothing whatever to do, then they are not to be considered as canonical documents, but simply as early Christian writings. Then the historical concern clearly demands that from early Christian writings as a whole *everything that is related historically should be examined together.* The boundary of the material of the discipline is to be placed where a real break in the literature becomes apparent. . . .

Holtzmann holds that the task of New Testament theology is to give a historical account of the religious and ethical content of the canonical writings, or to make a historical reconstruction of the religio-ethical world of thought they reveal. In opposition to his view I would say: The discipline has to give an account of the history of early Christian religion and theology. . . .

What are we really looking for? Ultimately we wish in any case to know *what was believed, thought, taught, hoped, demanded, and striven for* in the earliest period of Christianity, not, however, *what certain writings* on faith, doctrine, hope, and so forth contain. . . .

There can be no doubt that this approach of ours shows in the first place how absolutely necessary it is to go beyond the limits of the New Testament. If I ask what was the content and the development of Christian faith and thought at a given period, it is immediately apparent that the answer to this question must take into consideration all the material that comes from this period. In this connection it no longer makes any sense therefore to propose any external distinction between writings that are related essentially. . . .

On the contrary, it is clear that *no fixed literary limits can be drawn at all.* Not only what falls within the period under consideration is pertinent, but even what lies outside that period and yet indirectly provides information about it. . . .

Furthermore, an exact *temporal* demarcation cannot be specified. . . .

It can only be said that the line of demarcation can be drawn where new movements in the Church have their point of beginning, where new ideas become potent in it and the old has outlived its usefulness. This point in literature coincides *more or less* with the transition from the Apostolic Fathers to the Apologists. . . .

The name that suits the situation is the "history of early Christian religion." or, as the case may be, the "history of early Christian religion and theology." If it is objected that this is not New Testament theology, this is strange. The name is obviously determined by the subject matter, not vice versa. . . .

Now, it cannot be denied that biblical theology as it is practiced today is much less than the history of the apostolic and postapostolic age, though the two go side-by-side as do the history of dogma and church history. In the true, strict sense, biblical theology is not a historical discipline at all. Would that it were to become one!

It was the practitioners of the history-of-religions method of New Testament research who fulfilled this wish of Wrede's. **Paul Wendland** followed up his account of the culture of the Graeco-Roman world (see above, p. 247) with a *Geschichte der unchristliche Literaturformen*

[History of early Christian literary forms] in which he was compelled by "strict adherence to the point of view of form . . . to go beyond the arbitrary limits of the Canon" and at times also to take into consideration the apocryphal literature up to and beyond the middle of the second century. Although the results of this method generally do not differ markedly from the views of scholars representative of the history-of-religions and the radically historico-critical schools, nevertheless Wendland by his assertion that the "insight into the earlier stage and the peculiar character of the oral tradition [is] an essential condition" for the understanding of the Gospels, points in the direction of future developments. For the study of these preliterary stages of the gospel tradition leads not only to the important observation that "the formation and also the selection of material [were determined] not by a historical but by an edificatory interest," but above all the analysis of Mark's procedure points up the perception that the individual traditions at Mark's disposal "had the natural tendency to circulate without any reference to place and time," that "only the passion story [had] preserved a comparatively certain sequence of accounts," and that "Mark [was] more an assembler and redactor than an author." At the same time these purely literary observations gave a fruitful indicator for the response to the question concerning the theological motivating forces for the formation of the earliest gospel tradition.[374] Almost at the same time **Heinrich Weinel,** a New Testament scholar at Jena, published his *Biblische Theologie des Neuen Testament* [Biblical theology of the New Testament]. Despite its title, the book explicitly declares that "the undertaking of biblical theology" has "proceeded on false assumptions and therefore [has] suffered shipwreck," and that its place should be taken by "a history of the religion of earliest Christianity." This task, however, demands the use also of the apocryphal books as sources, and, as a consequence, following the sections on Jesus, the early church, and Paul, there is an account of "The Christianity of the Evolving Church" for which the Apostolic Fathers are prime sources. Although Weinel's account fulfills Wrede's requirement that noncanonical as well as canonical sources should be used for a study of early Christianity and also embodies the historical perspective of the history-of-religions school, it fails abysmally to measure up to Wrede's ideal of "a history of the apostolic and post-apostolic age" that would be "in the true, strict sense . . . a historical discipline" (see above, p. 305). For, while Jesus' religion is characterized as "an ethical religion of redemption" and this is regarded as "the real content of the new religion that Jesus brought to the world," the origin of the Christ cult in the primitive church appears as "a serious change in Christianity . . . even before Paul" by which "the aesthetic religion of redemption overpowers the Gospel." And, with reference to the Apocalypse of John, with its Jewish pictures of the future, it is emphasized that "the aesthetic religion of redemption . . . in an eschatological form increasingly prevailed in Christianity." Therefore, since the development that led to the piety of the Church is not recognized as "a direct continuation of the ethical religion of redemption," the religion of Jesus is used as a standard for judging the worth of the history of early Christianity. So then, while the "dogma of the New Testament" is not used to evaluate this history, a *theological* yardstick is still applied. So, in spite of the author's purpose "to give an account of the religion of Jesus and its first development in his Church from psychological and broadly historical points of view," the theological task is undertaken.[375]

Hermann Gunkel had once expressly declared (1904) that history-of-religions research must take the fact seriously . . . that *religion,* including *biblical* religion, has its history as does everything human," and that therefore "the history-of-religions point of view [consists] . . . in paying constant attention to the historical context of every religious phenomenon." [376] However, in an assessment of the history-of-religions movement published in 1914, while emphasizing once again the radically historical viewpoint of the history-of-religions school, he maintained just as vigorously that its interest had always been directed in the first instance at the history of biblical religion and that the special significance of Holy Scripture had remained fundamental also to history-of-religions research.[377]

How are we to explain the opposition encountered from so many when, as a matter of fact, we desire nothing but what has long been taken for granted in all other historical disciplines, and what is anything but new even in theology? The reason for it is not certain youthful aberrations which, however deplorable they may be, are difficult for a young, effervescent spirit to avoid in all serious effort at scholarly discipline and which, because of human frailty, no new movement can escape. On the contrary, the ultimate reason was that we determined to employ the principles of historical research with whole-hearted, inexorable seriousness, and that because of this we came into more or less violent conflict with almost all earlier theological tendencies. . . .

When we spoke of history-of-religions, we always had first in mind the history of *biblical* religion. Involuntarily we combined the two great words that seemed to us the leading lights of our life, the words "religion" and "history." It is *inspiration* that coined the expression in this sense. A marvelous picture stood before our mind's eye, impressing and charming us: biblical religion in all its glory and majesty. We came to see that such a phenomenon can be understood only when it is comprehended in terms of its history, its evolution. To know this religion in its depth and breadth, to trace its tortuous paths, to get some inkling of its deepest thoughts at the hour of its genesis—this seemed to us a noble task. . . .

Our historical labors relate to a book that from time immemorial has held a unique place and that was regarded by our forefathers as a gift of God himself. This special significance of Holy Scripture is the historically given foundation of all biblical research. While the doctrine of inspiration has long since been abandoned or seriously modified, it still exercises an influence on men's minds, wherever they are, and for this reason all studies of the Bible have an interest to which they would not otherwise be entitled. The scholarly study of the Bible lives and feeds on this special significance of everything biblical.

5.

The Opposition to the View of the New Testament Advanced by the School of the History-of-Religions and Radical Historical Criticism

While the history-of-religions and the radical historico-critical school of New Testament investigation enjoyed great success and exercised wide influence during the years before World War I, the methods it employed aroused sharp and vigorous opposition in wide circles of theological research. This opposition was by no means only the result of unreadiness to accept new knowledge; rather, it contained also important stimuli to the new beginning of New Testament research after the First World War. It is noteworthy, furthermore, that this opposition came from the ranks of representatives of a consistently historical, as well as from those of a conservative view of the New Testament. The two men whom the leaders of the history-of-religions school characterized as their spiritual fathers[378] protested quickly and most vigorously. In 1899 **Julius Wellhausen** declared, vis-à-vis Gunkel's hypothesis of a Babylonian origin of certain material in the Revelation to John, that it is "of methodological importance . . . to know that there is, in fact, material in apocalypses that is . . . not always thoroughly permeated with the author's conception; . . . however, where this material originally comes from is methodologically a matter of no consequence." The exegete "can be satisfied if he is successful in determining in what sense the apocalyptist himself understands his material; he has no need to inquire further." [379] And with reference to A. Schweitzer's consistently eschatological derivation of Jesus' ethic from the expectation of the nearness of the end, Wellhausen declared that "ignorant men have had the audacity to assert" that "Jesus regarded [his] ethics as a provisional asceticism that was only to be observed in expectation of the imminent end and had to be observed only until that end." [380] At the appearance of Gunkel's book on *Die Wirkungen des heiligen Geistes* [The activities of the Holy Spirit] (see above, pp. 217-18) , **Adolf Harnack** had said that Gunkel had combined "his knowledge of basic religious phenomena with a questionable atavistic theory of the history of religions" and that therefore "the history of the Christian religion, if its special character is not to be effaced, [can] only with great reservations [tolerate] the application of this way of think-ing." [381] In an academic address on "Die Aufgabe der Theologischen Facultäten und die allgemeine Religionsgeschichte" [The task of the theological faculties and the general field of the history of religion] (1901), he now turned against the proposal "to expand [the theological faculties] into a faculty of the general history of religion." He did not reject the proposal because there is "a special method by which the Christian religion, in contrast to others, is to be studied." Rather, "the theological faculties [should] remain faculties for the study of the *Chris-tian* religion because Christianity in its pure form is not *a* religion along with others, but *the* religion"; "he who does not know this religion, knows none, and he who knows it, together with its history, knows all." [382] Harnack therefore repudiates the history-of-religions view of Christianity on clearly theological grounds because the Christian religion, by virtue of its superiority to all other religions, does not tolerate in-corporation into a general history of religion. And in a discussion of the history-of-religions methodology in the fourth edition of his *Dog-mengeschichte* [History of dogma] (1909), Harnack accordingly char-acterized this direction of research as faulty because by its exaggeration of the mythical and primitive elements in the Christian religion it shows an inadequate understanding of the nature of higher religion. [383]

A word should be added with reference to the history-of-religions method, which plays a role in a series of new studies of the early history of dogma. It was an observation of the Enlightenment that this dogma stands in the closest connection with Hellenism, an observation to which this textbook has lent the strongest confirmation. In this way, so we are led to believe, the history-of-religions method received recognition; for it was related and applied to the very heart of the Christian religion, to the definition of faith itself. But things turned out differently. When Usener extended his mythological re-searches to include also hagiology and primitive Christian developments and found here familiar mythic tales—though he was by no means the first to do so—when research into the Old Testament and its Babylonian background recognized that oriental matter intrudes upon the New Testament by way of the Old (something that, with reference to the devil and cognate matters, for example, had long been known) ; and when, finally, a few New Testament obscurities appeared illuminated by analogy; the cry then was suddenly raised that a new methodological principle for the study of the history of the early church and of early dogma had been discovered, viz., the history-of-religions. It is not to be wondered at that philologians heeded the cry, for they are accustomed to avoid theological studies as an arcane science. But it is re-markable that even theologians declared that they were convinced of the novelty of the matter and hastened to found a history-of-religions school. To say that even they had read too little, and that a new generation has the right to flaunt a new flag, are insufficient explanations. The causes lie deeper. They are to be sought in an overestimation of the mythological and folkloristic elements that even the Christian religion naturally carried with it from the beginning.

This overestimation, again, had its origin in the underestimation of the culture and religion of reflection vis-à-vis the "original," and consequently in the deficient understanding of higher religion, that is to say, of religion in general. This brings us fortunately to the point that the romantic school reached a hundred years ago. But it is questionable whether the new romanticism has as much to say to us as the old, and whether it will last any longer than the latter. The "logos" [= reason] stands again at the door! So far as the historical studies of this "school" are concerned, we have certainly learned much from them with respect to secondary problems and minor points; but what was new with reference to major problems proved for the most part not to be true, and what was true proved not to be new; for we cannot possibly call it new, when it is demonstrated in matters of detail that Jewish Christians exhibit elements of late, syncretistic Judaism and that Hellenistic Christians bear the impress of Hellenism, not only in head and heart, but also in the very clothes they wear. However, with reference to all the derivatives and borrowings from ancient religions by Judaism and Christianity (in practices, customs, sacred narratives, and formulae), there has been no carefully controlled investigation of whether and in what order the meaning and value of what has been appropriated has been transformed to the point of total sublimation and poetic arabesquerie. The fact that the duty of inquiring into this is not recognized as urgent is characteristic of the romanticism that would still like to enjoy as though it were an original crude product what has ever been in the process of change.

Adolf Jülicher expressed himself in similar fashion. In an academic address on the task of church history (1901), in which he included "the representatives of the New Testament disciplines [among] the church historians," he declares that of course he "expects [for church history] as little significant gain as danger," but then goes on to say that "from the urge of our modern historians of religion to get results and build hypotheses [he] is more afraid of confusion and distraction . . . for biblical research . . . than he is hopeful of a thorough disposal of useless chaff." [384] Jülicher followed up these warnings with a vigorous rejection of A. Schweitzer's "dogmatic, nonhistorical, criticism" of the tradition of Jesus.[385] And then, while fully acknowledging the scholarly accomplishments of Bousset and Wrede in their accounts of Jesus and Paul (see above, pp. 270, 284 ff.), he showed, in his methodologically exemplary book on *Paulus und Jesus* [Paul and Jesus] (1907), that the gulf between Jesus and Paul was really less deep than they (especially Wrede) viewed it, and that at all essential points Paul is in agreement with the primitive church, which stood on the other side of Jesus' death on the cross. So, to a more thoroughgoing historical criticism, Paul's theology appears as an appropriate development at a new historical level of the Gospel Jesus preached.[386]

Even if we ignore a few of Wrede's gross exaggerations, Paul's "Christ mythology" seems like a violent distortion of the picture of Jesus, great in its simplicity, that we have gained .from the Gospels. Jesus himself never spoke of his preexistence, of a form of a servant that he had to take upon himself, of a substitutionary act that he wished to perform by his sacrificial death. He promises the forgiveness of sins from case to case, and nothing is further from his thoughts than that before his appearance there had been no one who was righteous, no one who was sure of salvation. We conclude, then, that not a single link of this remarkable chain of Pauline theology comes from Jesus. There can be no shadow of doubt that it had its origin in Paul's own thought. Did it, however, seem so frightfully strange to the Christians of the primitive church, especially to those of their number who had seen the Lord with their own eyes? We hear nothing of a protest of other Christians against the Pauline *picture of Jesus*. . . .

In the attitude toward the Jewish law and in the magnificent demolition of all nationalistic-Jewish barriers, Paul and the Jerusalem Christians did not understand one another. Paul has the *spirit of Jesus* on his side. . . . Where, however, Paul breaks completely new paths, paths that are separated by a wide ditch from the Gospel of Jesus, as in the doctrines of atonement, redemption, and the person of Christ, he has the *primitive church* on his side: In these directions he represents only the great, new interest of the Church which believes in Christ against those who disputed both Jesus' *saving death* and his resurrection. Jesus' death, in fact, had imposed new tasks that needed new means for their accomplishment. What others with great effort defended against Jewish scorn, Paul chose as the main weapon against the religion of the enemy and thereby demonstrated that he was equal to the situation. . . .

Paul had submitted to the influence of the person of Jesus, at first involuntarily, but then of his own free will: At that time no one entered "the Church" as a believer, still less as an apostle, without subjecting himself to this influence. Also he was not lacking in the ability to understand Jesus. It is a gross underestimation of the influence of Jesus on his early disciples to credit Peter with accepting Paul as a brother simply because he acknowledged the death of Jesus on the cross as that of the Messiah and accordingly to assume that he did not employ other criteria for determining whether one could belong to the Church. No, *Paul's Christianity also grew in the soil of the primitive Jerusalem Church,* and although Paul on occasion criticized the person of Peter, he never criticized the Gospel Peter preached. . . .

Once Jesus himself was no longer on earth, the religion of Jesus could not remain in its original simplicity. . . . The Gospel necessarily assumed the character of a philosophy of history because it now set itself the task of solving by scientific means the riddle of its history.

This brings us now to the final, decisive point: the difference in the situation that Paul faced, as against that in which Jesus had undertaken his work.

Jesus' death on the cross lies between them. It had not belonged to the Gospel of Jesus. For Paul it was the point of departure and permanent focal point of all his preaching. . . .

How now are we to answer the question respecting the founder of Christianity? Is Paul really the "second founder of the Christian religion"? Actually, a religion cannot be founded; the expression can only be applied to a religious community, in this instance the Christian *Church*. But Paul did not in any case found the latter, for it had already been in existence for some time before he joined it. To be sure, even Jesus did not intend to found the Church: certainly *we* will no longer credulously seek to equate the kingdom of heaven with our church. The Church in the Pauline sense—as the community of the saints, of those who have entered by faith into the enjoyment of the saving merits of Christ's death and ressurection—exists from the time of the first believers of this sort, that is, from the time of the first Easter. Accordingly, one may say in the Pauline sense: Jesus Christ founded the Church by his death. To put it more precisely: the Church came into being when believers in Jesus came to think of the death of Jesus Christ for the first time as a *saving fact*.

All Paul's theological creations (albeit very far-reaching in implication) are only *deductions* of a scribal nature from *this* central act of faith. If the religion of Jesus underwent any decisive transformation whatsoever, that transformation took place before Paul's conversion. . . .

From the power of the faith of the disciples, who after the horrendous collapse of all their hope rallied to a conviction that was never again to be shaken— "and he was indeed the Son of God"—we must infer . . . an infinitely stronger power in the man from whom this faith proceeded. And since a great deal of theology was added to the gospel of Jesus, though *not a single* fundamental element in the religio-ethical ideal that was propagated in the primitive Christian Church, it is correct to assert that Christianity (if one intends this ambiguous word to convey anything at all that is definite) has no other beginning than the gospel of Jesus. . . .

To be sure, Paul made a new beginning. . . . But did he remove Jesus in order to put his Christ in Jesus' place? That he did not do, although through his work the picture of Jesus was in danger of being snatched from the sight of many. . . .

Paul did not put his theology in the place of the religion of Jesus, but all around it. . . . And also he did not displace Jesus, as it were unconsciously, by his overpowering influence. His influence has been stronger only in the instance of theologians who, like himself, were preeminently concerned to improve the weapons for the defense of their Christianity. The Church did not understand the synthetic intricacy of Paul's concepts. It honors him as the apostle of the *assurance of salvation* based on the blood of Christ. What else it took over from them with especial gratitude was not what was peculiarly Pauline, but the religious ideas or world outlook of Jesus, which Paul with the help of the early church had received from Jesus.

Jülicher's criticism of the picture of history sketched by the history-of-religions school employs the same methodological presuppositions as the latter, but leads to a more penetrating historical outlook. In a survey of the *Probleme des Apostolischen Zeitalters* [Problems of the apostolic age], **Ernst von Dobschütz**, a New Testament scholar at Jena and a pupil of A. Harnack, raises the following express objection to history-of-religions research: "The finger is placed on what attracts our attention, instead of on what Christianity had to attract the attention of people in those days. There has not been an overdose of historical methodology: On the contrary, the historical methodology has not been historical enough." And he properly points out that the historical task is only fulfilled when the triumph of Christianity over the religiosity of antiquity is explained.[387]

Carried away by the new discovery that things were different then than now, filled with much new knowledge that this insight undoubtedly has afforded us, there are those who see everywhere only what diverges from Christianity as we know it, what is strange to us. Now, in contrast to the Christianity of our day, it is certainly characteristic of early Christianity that vision, speaking in tongues, formulae of blessing and cursing, and abstinence from marriage, wine, and meat played a large role in it. But was it also characteristic of early Christianity in its own time? Is it right to describe Christianity on Gentile soil essentially as an enthusiastic movement in which ecstatic experiences of all sorts played the main role, in which the "Spirit" manifested itself in all kinds of remarkable phenomena? Such a description characterizes it as only one of the many religious movements of its time, without doing justice to its singularity. In my judgment, the fundamental defect of this way of thinking lies just here. . . . In our attempt to put ourselves back entirely into that ancient time, we must gradually come to the point where we are struck no longer by what Christianity of those days had in common with the religiosity of the time, but by what distinguished it, by what in Christianity attracted the people of that time. Only then shall we be justified in speaking of a truly historical history-of-religions view of things. . . .

Undoubtedly there was already a Christian Gnosticism in Paul's day, in Phrygia, for example—Paul writes the Letter to the Colossians to combat it. Undoubtedly magical concepts dominated the thinking of many young Gentile Christians, for example, in Corinth when they had themselves baptized on behalf of deceased relatives (I Cor. 15:29), to say nothing of the high estimate placed on glossolalia ["speaking in tongues"] and similar phenomena. Undoubtedly asceticism very soon began a violent struggle with the Gospel, to which in my opinion it was basically wholly foreign, and in that struggle was often victorious. But one must be on one's guard against generalization and exaggeration. If Christianity from the beginning had been nothing more than such a syncretistic religious structure of an ecstatic, magical, ascetic sort, it would not have been worth outliving those sects of the Ophites, etc. And in accordance with the brazen laws of history, it would have had to perish instead of finally emerging as victor (although often a battered victor) in the gigantic struggle with all the powers of the ancient world. There must have been something in Christianity which was different from that religiosity, a power that raised it above all those formations. This distinctive element is the Gospel and the impression it conveyed of the person of Jesus Christ. The major defect of this history-of-religions point of view, in my judgment, is that it underestimates the importance of this factor for the whole development. . . .

Though man's sinful nature may indeed have stood in the way of a full working out of the revelation given us in Jesus, though religion as he lived and taught it may have undergone all kinds of adulterations, restrictions, and foreign admixtures in its immediate environment and in its directly subsequent history—that this happened seems certainly to have been demonstrated; I regard this as a historical contribution of most recent research but it still is necessary above all to clarify the effect of the Gospel, the positive element that proceeded from the person of Jesus, on which all the centuries of Christianity's history feed.

Then even representatives of the consistently eschatological and history-of-religious research themselves agreed with these warnings and crit-

314

icisms which sought, not to question the right of a radically historical view of the New Testament, but rather to reinforce it. We have already seen that **Albert Schweitzer**, in his *Geschichte der paulinischen Forschung* [Paul and his interpreters], radically refused to recognize any dependence of Paul on oriental or Greek ideas and demanded that we endeavor "to understand the doctrine of the Apostle to the Gentiles entirely on the basis of Jewish primitive Christianity" (see above, pp. 241-44). Accordingly Schweitzer regarded the assumption of any connection of Paul's sacramental ideas with the Hellenistic mysteries as wholly impossible and even maintained that Reitzenstein's proof of the relationship of Pauline concepts to the language of the mystery cults proves on the contrary that "Jewish Hellenism and Greek philosophy had practically no part" in Paulinism.[388]

What are the results to which the students of comparative religion have to point in regard to the Lord's Supper? They are obliged at the outset to give up the attempt to explain it on the basis of the Mystery-religions, or even to point out in the latter any very close analogies. In place of this they attempt to make intelligible both the meal which formed part of the mystery-cults, and that of Pauline Christianity, as growths which develop from scattered seeds of ancient conceptions of the cultus-eating of the divinity and spring up from the soil of syncretism in two different places at the same time. Neither in the one case nor the other, however, can they render this even approximately probable. Up to the present, therefore, neither a direct nor an indirect connexion between the cultus-meal of Paul and those of the Mystery-religions has been shown. . . .

The sacramental views of the Apostle have thus nothing primitive about them, but are rather of a "theological" character. Paul connects his mystical doctrine of redemption with ceremonies which are not specially designed with reference to it. It is from that fact, and not from a specially deep love for Mysteries, that the exaggeratedly sacramental character of his view of baptism and the Lord's Supper results. It is in the last resort a question of externalisation, not of intensification.

It is therefore useless to ransack the history of religions for analogies to his conceptions. It has none to offer, for the case is unique. The problem lies wholly within the sphere of early Christian history, and represents only a particular aspect of the question of Paul's relation to primitive Christianity. . . .

Paulinism is thus a theological system with sacraments, but not a Mystery-religion. . . .

Of eschatology in the late Jewish or early Christian sense there is not a single trace to be found in any Graeco-Oriental doctrine.

Therefore, the Mystery-religions and Paulinism cannot in the last resort be compared at all, as is indeed confirmed by the fact that the real analogies with both the mysticism and the sacramental doctrine are so surprisingly few. Reitzenstein's attempt has not succeeded in altering this result, but only in confirming it. What remains of his material when the circle of ideas connected with the thought of "re-birth" is eliminated, and the all-pervading eschatological character of the fundamental ideas and underlying logic of Paulinism are duly considered in making the comparison?

And **Paul Wernle,** who himself had contributed to the history-of-religions interpretation of early Christianity (see above, pp. 288-92), joined the representatives of the school of consistent eschatology as a critic of the religio-historical method of research. To Bousset's *Kyrios Christos* he opposed "unvanquished scepticism" vis-à-vis the history-of-religions derivation of Pauline Christology and demanded that progress in the Christology of the early church be explained by inner Christian developments.[389]

I now confess my present unvanquished skepticism with respect to the new way the history-of-religions school has *of speaking* offhandedly *of a myth of the dying and rising divine savior* as a comprehensive idea found everywhere in the Orient. . . . I do not doubt the fact itself, namely, that individual instances of such cult myths were connected with a cult mysticism, as Bousset describes. But I do confess that the way from these myths and mysteries to Paul seems much longer to me than to Bousset, and that according to our sources we have in fact a much shorter way before us, especially since Paul's reference to "folly to the Gentiles" (I Cor. 1:23) clearly shows how strange his teaching of the death of Christ sounded to his Hellenistic auditors. If it is true that the death, *the death of Jesus on the cross and his resurrection, became a center of the faith of the entire Christian community,* not because of the influence of any myth, but because it was necessary to contend zealously with the Jews concerning Jesus' death and his messiahship, despite this death, why then does Paul need, does our contemporary explanation need, the *detour* by way of those Hellenistic myths and mysteries? That this death on the cross could and must lead a ponderer such as Paul to the most varied explanations is so understandable, so compelling that I too have no need of any alien myth as a cause of it. But [what about] the *sacramental* character of the Christ mysticism, which revolves about the death and resurrection of the Christ, comparable to the cultic mystical ideas which attach themselves to those myths? The parallel, however, is more apparent [than real]. *Early Christianity has no knowledge whatever of a genuine mystery of being crucified and rising again;* furthermore, baptism as practiced by the early church will have been so simple a custom that, taken strictly, it cannot possibly be compared to these Mysteries. . . .

It was by personal experience, not by baptism, that Paul attained to a new life, as emerges especially clearly from Gal. 2: *this new life in most intimate fellowship with his Christ is the true origin of Paul's mysticism,* although *the language with which it is described* may reflect Hellenistic influences. And because it arose as a result of Paul's personal experiences, it also disappeared with them. . . .

It is almost an axiom for Bousset that the entire progress of the Christology of the early church down to the time of Paul is to be explained by history-of-religions factors, that is, by change in the milieu of the Gospel. Neither the rabbinical roots of Pauline thought, nor Paul's familiarity with a definite Christology of the primitive church, nor, finally, his conversion experience, are pursued seriously for understanding his Christology. . . . The Hellenistic milieu, the mystery religions of Syria and Asia Minor, the pessimistic current of the time—all these external contemporary factors are to explain everything that may appear as new in Paul when his thought is compared with that of the primitive church. In my judgment this application of the history-of-religions method is a relapse into old rationalistic traditions of the beginning of the last century, from which the research in depth of German idealism was said to have rescued us. I can regard Pauline thought least of all as a mere product of the milieu, an intrusion of Hellenism into the thought world of the Gospel. It seems to me that Paulinism obviously reveals that it has its deepest and decisive root in powerful, wholly personal, inner experiences, and that everything that incidentally may go back to environmental influences (and which I, too, would not wish to deny) could still be only ways of expressing his inner experiences and his own processes of thought. For my part, just one truth emerged from the entire investigation, viz., that in the first instance we have to understand Paul in light of himself and that every insight from history-of-religions analogies must remain peripheral.

Although such critically minded scholars—even some who themselves worked with the history-of-religions method—recalled their contemporaries to an inward, Christian view of the New Testament and to the theological task, it is self-evident that conservative scholarship raised even more vigorous objection to the new direction of research. In a survey of earlier work on *Biblische Theologie* [Biblical theology] (1897), **Martin Kähler**, whose basic objection to the historical study of Jesus we have already noted (see above, pp. 222-25), declares right at the beginning of his survey of history-of-religions research "that for the conclusions of biblical research, as of all theology, 'historical' may well be an adjective, but not a noun." He asserts that "to regard and to treat the writings of both Testaments simply as documents for the history of a religious people and of the early church" is "an unhistorical procedure. . . . In the same measure that 'historical' can only be an adjective, so in this instance 'biblical' must be the determining word." [390] While Kähler in this fashion challenges completely the justice of a consistently historical treatment of the New Testament writings, the systematic theologian **Max Reischle**, an independent pupil of A. Ritschl, in an admirably objective investigation of *Theologie und Religionsgeschichte* [Theology and the history of religion] (1904) staked out the boundaries of this radical historical study of the New Testament with much greater care. While expressly declaring that theological and general history-of-religions procedure must use "the same methods and principles of historical research," he nevertheless warns the history-of-religions scholars against "the tendency to evolutionary constructions," against the inclination "to portray" the original religious experience "as drastically and bluntly as possible," and against "the overestimation of the form vis-à-vis the content." Further, he demands that "the individual phenomena of history [be] first understood in light of its own process of development" and that "only then" should resort be made "to the hypothesis of foreign influence" and wishes to assume a "borrowing from foreign religions,"

317

least of all "where the genuinely personal religious life begins." In all these remarks Reischle is in far-reaching agreement with the objections of the "critical" scholars we have already cited, but at *one* characteristic point he goes beyond them: He requires of the theologian, because of his responsibility to the Christian community, recognition of the *special* significance of the New Testament, and consequently special caution in the assumption of the dependence of the New Testament on alien religions. And it is his hope that the theologian in his research should bear witness to his conviction of the activity of God in history; in other words, that even as a historian he should reach expressly theological judgments.[391]

One must be doubly careful in asserting *borrowings*. It is a *regulating principle* of all historical scholarship that *it attempts in the first instance to understand* the individual phenomena of history *in light of their own process of development* and *only then resorts to the hypothesis of an alien influence.* Above all and as a further consideration, the theologian has a duty which is not merely an opportunistic calculation, but his vocation to serve the Christian community: namely, that of exercising special caution. . . .

The Christian fellowship . . . requires theological scholarship as well as historical theology, and in the interests of its life always produces them. Just as the scholarly knowledge of law and its history is necessary for the administration of justice, so is the historical understanding of Christianity necessary for the Christian community and its practice of the Christian religion.

The theological interest relates the whole body of historical material at the same time to *the needs of the present,* however. . . .

All this throws light on those theological viewpoints that prevail in the biblical and historical disciplines, viewpoints that are ruled out by representatives of the history of religions school as "unhistorical," as, for instance, the *"dogma of the New Testament."* Even on scholarly grounds one can doubt whether it is right to replace "New Testament introduction and theology" by a "history of early Christian literature and religion." In any case the New Testament presents itself to *our* research as a whole. Is it then not also scientifically correct to subject this whole, like any other collected work of history, in the first instance to *analytical* investigation? . . . But, quite apart from this historical viewpoint, the New Testament has its *special significance* for the entire history of the Christian Church, whose doctrine is built on this foundation and has repeatedly been renewed from this source. And, likewise, in *the Church of our day* it determines the preaching, the liturgy, the instruction, the exhortation. Therefore the prospective servant of the Church positively requires a more exact knowledge of the New Testament writings. . . .

When we assert a self-revelation and activity of God in history and in its prophetic personalities, we are making *rather a declaration of faith*, a declaration that is not grounded on the inexplicability, but on the worthful content, of the life that presents itself to us in history. By it an impression is made on our conscience and our trusting heart, and thereby the faith judgment is awakened, viz., that in that life God himself reveals himself to us. For us

Christians it is above all on the personal life and the spiritual influence to which the early community bears witness that that judgment depends. . . .

When this conviction is a living one for the theologian, when it is not merely an aesthetic notion nor a fortuitous, subjective opinion or matter of custom, but a personal apprehension of the highest reality that gives meaning to his life and to the whole world, then it must also be expressed by him in terms of biblical, historical theology. Not that he should now produce edifying phrases! That conviction in any case will be manifest in the *tranquil attitude of reverence* toward history, in which God's work reveals itself to him. What prejudices many from the outset against this direction of scholarship science is that not infrequently this reverence is lacking in modern history-of-religions work, that profane expressions are applied even to what for others is holy. But I regard it furthermore as unobjectionable, even as quite natural, when the theologian who works with the history of the Old and New Testament or of the Church and of dogma at the high points *expressly emphasizes* the extent to which this history, comprehended at its central point in the person of Jesus Christ and in the inner theological relationships of that person, grounds the faith for us on an activity of God within history. When he undertakes to do that, however, he is clearly to stress the fact that in so doing he passes over from the task of historical exegesis into the teleological overall view of history, from the account of history into the Christian philosophy of history, from the scientific process of proof into the witness to faith, a faith, it should be noted, that is not merely his "subjective postulate," but the Church's faith which exercises an inward compulsion on us by virtue of its very content, not by means of logical coercion to be sure, but by an obligation of our conscience.

The judgment of the conservative scholar **Paul Feine** (1904) is considerably more strict: The history-of-religions picture of early Christianity is a caricature; the picture of Christ held by the early Church and Paul goes back to the earthly appearance of Jesus and to living experience, not to conjectured conceptual forms. Over against the investigations carried out by the history-of-religions school must be set the *firm* fact that a divine life became a reality in Jesus. In view of this, then, Feine demands a prior decision of faith and the indispensable condition of an appropriate historical consideration of early Christianity.[392]

When we read such assertions, especially those of Gunkel, there is reason to wonder whether a Christian theologian is actually writing, whether such amazing ignorance of the vitality of the Apostolic Church can be credited to serious scholars. But very soon we become aware of the reason for so great a distortion of viewpoint: Correct observations of a formal relationship are brought into play so onesidedly and so lacking in each instance proper evaluation of the underlying content and the motivating ideas that a caricature of the Christian religion is drawn.

We must raise the most emphatic objection to the claim that Christianity is the inevitable product of the development of the religious spirit of our species, towards whose formation the whole history of the ancient world strove, in whose formulation all spiritual products of the Orient and Occident have been utilized and at the same time ennobled and harmonized. We believe that the history of the ancient world prepared the way for Christianity; it can be demonstrated that the learning of the Orient and the Occident is fused in the theology of the ancient church; yet the Christian religion is assuredly not the product of a development immanent in mankind, but rests on a decisive act of the living and gracious God. It rests solely and alone on the person of our Lord who, in his historical appearance and efficacy, is an unfathomable miracle of God. . . .

There would be no Christianity today if the disciples had not been rescued from their deep despondency after Jesus' death and thus for the first time made his disciples in the full sense of the word by the apprehension of the Risen Christ and by the power of the Holy Spirit that he bestowed upon them. . . . It was not the impact of Jesus' character that made them Christians —though we must not underestimate its great influence—but the divine power that Jesus made effective in them. The picture that the earliest church drew of Jesus is no ideal picture, but the picture of his earthly appearance in the light of his heavenly exaltation. In like manner Paul is basically misunderstood when his proclamation of the heavenly Christ is traced back to this heavenly figure that was already in his consciousness before it presented itself to the sight of his eyes on the road to Damascus. . . . One has to throw to the winds all the emphatic assertions of the apostle himself regarding the experience of his conversion and the transformation it effected if one is to subscribe to the opinion that Paul already during his pre-Christian life bore in his mind the basis of his Christian messianic proclamation. He knows no better way of representing what life brought him in his conversion than by the metaphor of God's call at Creation: "Out of darkness let there be light." After that experience, his life received a totally different content. Since then he proclaimed the heavenly Christ because he had seen and experienced him. . . .

The most crucial declaration of the whole apostolic church—a common declaration, however clearly it may differ in detail—is this: By the Christ who has been raised to the divine office of Lord the faithful know themselves to be filled with a new vitality that lifts them above their former sinful condition and above the life of this world. Heavenly powers have taken possession of them and assure them of divine sonship and of citizenship in the heavenly world.

Modern religious scholarship is at fault when it fails to take as its starting point this experience peculiar to Christianity and first from this stance to examine the parallels in other religions, or when it fails to make at least the attempt not to efface what is distinctive. History-of-religions research in recent years often gives the impression that even biblical Christianity is more or less dependent on heathen myths and mysteries in all decisive assertions of faith; that the boundary lines even between early Christianity and the nature religions of that time were fluid and that by becoming strongly mythologized the Christian religion immediately after its origin was diverted from the way that Jesus had set before it. On the other hand, if we take our departure from the historical Christ and from the experience peculiar to Christianity, we can readily acknowledge the relationship between Christian and extra-Christian concepts and cooperate disinterestedly in the enlargement of our religio-historical knowledge, without running the danger of being led astray into an underestimation of what is Christian. For such studies cannot alter in the slightest the great, established fact that through our Lord Jesus, Christ became a reality among men, and that in every individual what men have hitherto only sought after in anticipation and in the area of natural occurrence—a life from God and in fellowship with God—can become truth and reality.

When then R. Reitzenstein's book on *Die hellenistichen Mysterien-religionen* [The Hellenistic mystery religions] appeared (see above, pp. 268-70), **Georg Heinrici,** who himself had decisively demonstrated the historical connections of the early Christian Church offices with those of the religious associations of that time (see above, pp. 210-12), raised the question: "Is early Christianity a mystery religion?" (1911) and emphasized that, in spite of "many surprising connections with the mystery cults," especially apparent in Paul and the Gospel of John, early Christianity was characterized by and triumphed because of the union of religion and morality, rather than by and because of the high regard for ecstasy and the physical effect of the sacraments that was peculiar to the mystery religions.[393]

When Christianity was proclaimed it proved itself victorious over and superior to all mystery cults; even the powerful gnostic movement and the enthusiasm of the Montanists were not able to stay its course. Would that have been the case had it operated with the methods of mysticism? A victorious world view conquers by means of new powers. Christianity finds its power, not in ecstasies and visions, not in superstitious practices, not in impressive cult acts, not in ascetic assaults, on the joy of living, but in offering nourishment for the soul, which gives joyousness of life and comfort in death. It therefore possessed something that the mystery cults lacked. . . . The superiority of Christianity is demonstrated above all in the unity—a unity it takes for granted—of religious certainties and the obligation to moral action. "In Christ Jesus [nothing is of any avail], but faith working through love" (Gal. 5:6). The Christian Church, a fellowship of like-minded people that rises above all national and social limitations, grew up by virtue of this unity of religion and morality, a unity in which faith assures the purity of motive for moral action. There is nothing with which it can be compared. When Patristic thought likes to conceive Christianity as philosophy, it thereby bears witness to a tendency to the construction of an ethico-religious conviction. When, after the Church had become a force in the ancient world, the simple rooms where Christians assembled were displaced by the basilicas, the halls of free intercourse and exchange, rather than by a cult temple, this basic tendency was confirmed. When in early Christian art Jesus is represented predominantly by the simple picture of the good shepherd or the youthful teacher—how remote all this is from the cult picture of the steer-slaying Mithra or the awesome idols of obscure mystical cults! It is clear that the idea of a cult god after the model of the Hellenistic mysteries is absolutely foreign to the Christian perception. If therefore we were to characterize Christianity as a whole, we could better call it an anti-mystery than a mystery religion. Actually, it is neither of these. Its peculiarity is appropriately paraphrased as "worship of God that corresponds to reasoned understanding" (λογικὴ λατρεῖα, Rom. 12:11). This striking and carefully chosen expression, which Paul uses only once, is more correctly understood in light of the linguistic usage of popular philosophy than in that of analogies from Poimandres: for this "reasonable worship" manifests itself in the hallowing of the body and the renewal of the mind: its fruit is a sure judgment of what is the will of God. Christianity does not proclaim a redemption from the body by asceticism and withdrawal, but a transfiguration of the body by a way of life in the Spirit.

Kurt Deissner, a New Testament scholar at Greifswald, then followed this summary demarcation of early Christianity over against Hellenistic mysticism with a very careful study of *Paulus und die Mystik seiner Zeit* [Paul and the mysticism of his time] (1918). He pointed out, on the one hand, "that that picture of the pneumatic and gnostic, so related to Hellenistic mystical concepts, which Reitzenstein reads into Pauline thought, into Paul himself, is in keeping rather with Paul's opponents, belongs accordingly in the thought world of those with whom Paul contends in the Letter to the Corinthians," and that therefore "the whole body of Paul's doctrine must stand in opposition to Hellenistic mysticism, just as Paul himself does to his Corinthians adversaries." And, on the other hand, he complemented this negative conclusion with the positive demonstration that "the new life into which Paul enters by fellowship with the death and life of Christ" can be understood, "not in that partly physical, partly hyperphysical sense, but only spiritually and personally," and that the "terminological borrowings from the piety of the Mysteries" must not be allowed to obscure the fact "that we have to look for the sources of the idea of 'dying with and rising with Christ,' not in an extra-Christian religiosity, but in the apostle's own personal experience of Christ." And in the second edition of the book Deissner adds the comment that Paul "does not belong under the category of mystical piety, but represents the type of prophetic piety," and therefore stands in sharp opposition to mysticism. The question of the meaning Paul gives to the terminology he has in common with his Hellenistic environment leads, then, to a demarcation of Paul over against this environment and along with that, on the one hand, to a relativization of the observations of the history-of-religions school and, on the other, to a more acute formulation of questions concerning the distinctiveness and the peculiar intention of the Pauline message.[394]

Consequently the gnosis of mysticism is fundamentally *ahistorical:* It has no inner relation to the events and occurrences of history. The Pauline gnosis, on the contrary, originates . . . in the historical fact which, for the apostle, is the focal and turning-point of all history: in the crucified Christ. As a result of this close connection with history the apostle's gnosis is from the first divested of all mystical magic. . . .

Similarly, with reference to the ecstatic experience that Paul reports in II Cor. 12:1 ff., we must also insist that *the apostle evaluates the* ὀπτασίαι καὶ ἀποκαλύψεις ["visions and revelations"] *in a sense different from that of mysticism and does not accord them the place within the framework of his piety that the ecstatic experiences have within the mystical religiosity. . . .*

If Paul had actually placed a stress on these matters, he would have had to betray the intention of influencing and educating his congregations in this sense. Consequently we must take it for granted that Paul was not an "ecstatic" and that his piety is not to be judged as ecstatic. . . .

If this hope is a basic element of the apostle's religiosity, it follows that his piety is characterized by a certain tension: There are for him no high points of assurance in faith from which he does not at the same time allow his gaze to rove into eternity even while he is aware that the religious consummation—the vision of God, and direct fellowship with Christ—are attainable by the Christian only in the other world. It would be utterly wrong to wish to speak in this connection of a change in the apostle's religious attitude, however, as though at certain high-pitched moments of his life he attained a marvelous height of fellowship with God or Christ, from which he sank down soon thereafter or in other situations. If this were the case, the apostle's piety then would certainly closely approximate the mystical, which is characterized by this very reversal of religious feeling in which the condition of most direct nearness of God is dissolved by the feeling of God's remoteness. Rather, the apostle possesses both these: the greatest assurance of faith and the consciousness of an inability as yet to reach the religious consummation. The two are *interspersed*, not side-by-side and by turns. "Faith" and "hope" do not supplant each other but belong intrinsically together. . . .

The merely relative value he placed on the enthusiastic effects of the Spirit, such as speaking with tongues (I Cor. 14:18) and visions (II Cor. 12:1 ff.), may nevertheless be regarded as a tribute paid by the apostle to the mystical piety of his age: *But these things did not determine . . . the essence of his piety. . . .*

The consciousness that Jesus is the *Lord,* to whom he is without question subordinated, is as peculiar to his piety as the conviction that all gifts are to be attributed to the *love* of Christ and that this love means something much higher than all other workings of the Spirit, such as prophecy and knowledge. Yes, his thoughts about atonement, his ideas of the saving worth of Christ's death (Rom. 3:25), appear in quite a new light and are also more intelligible to modern man if we pay attention to the fact that those two divine principles: holiness and love, are of fundamental importance to his idea of atonement. In Christ's death on the cross God presents himself to the apostle as the one who is righteous and at the same time the one who *justifies*. We can restate this experience in our own words after this fashion: In the death of Jesus, God, who is not mocked, makes his *holy* will known to mankind in all clarity and yet, at the same time, declares that he does not purpose the death of the sinner, but in his saving love forgives man by absolving him from his sins. Consequently the one simple experience of the holiness and love of Christ is basic even to the apparently complicated trains of thought of the Pauline Christology. And we make no mistake when we assert that this spiritual and personal element that we have at last discovered at the very heart of Pauline piety in his Christology lifts the apostle far above the mystical religiosity. Whoever ignores the *historical situations* that frequently impelled the apostle to engage in polemics against mystical piety or piety related to mysticism, will be readily inclined—on the basis of the ideas that Paul no doubt shares with mysticism, but to which in

323

our judgment he gives new meaning—to draw far-reaching conclusions concerning the inner contact of the apostle with this piety. Nevertheless the historically well-founded observation that Paul had to *battle* against mysticism leads to the result that at the main points Paul sharply distinguished his piety from mysticism and in so doing set ideas and motives in motion that are also still able to provide valuable guidelines in Christianity's attempt to come to terms with *modern* mystical currents of thought.

Deissner's book, published towards the end of the First World War shows, therefore, that the work of the history-of-religions school is widely recognized as indispensable, but that the method of its proper use must still be discovered. And this set the stage for one of the tasks that faced New Testament research after World War I.

Part VI
The Historical-Theological View of the New Testament

1.
The Literary Problems

The First World War denotes a decisive turning point for New Testament research. While it is true that during the first years after the war
there appeared many studies of literary and historical problems that
had their spiritual roots in the researches of the history-of-religions
epoch, nevertheless these studies were characterized in part by new and
more far-reaching ideas; but at the same time a revolutionary change took
place, especially in German-speaking postwar theology, which took its
departure from New Testament exegesis and compelled all New Testament research to undertake a radical reconsideration of its task. Naturally
the catastrophe of 1918, with its collapse of culture optimism and of
confidence in the power of rational thinking, played a decisive role in
this return of New Testament research to a properly theological way of
posing the issues.[395] But the political and social catastrophe only brought
to light in the area of theology a crisis of the cultural consciousness and
of all scholarly activity whose beginnings go back into the decade before 1918. The effort of the humanities to free themselves from the
dominance of the natural sciences, the insight into the deadening character of a *merely* historical view of the present, the return to the organic
and the irrational, all are already characteristic of the spiritual development during the period before the collapse of 1918, a development to
which the theological disciplines also made a contribution.[396] And
though the spokesmen of a *faith* theology were dominated by the conviction that, in response to "a time that is gone, the work of a century that
lies behind us and is over and done with," all that is still possible is "an
obituary, full of piety, full of tribute and gratitude, but an epilogue for
those who can still look only forward, no longer backward," [397] nevertheless we cannot overlook the strong threads that bind the new depar-
tures at the end of the First World War with the research of the preceding
epoch. Nevertheless the research of the present is still so firmly rooted
in the new stances that became manifest after 1918 that today the

permanently important features of this development can only be sketched in very broad outline.

Though the years after World War I led to a new orientation of New Testament scholarship, this new orientation does not exclude the fact that in many areas of research scholars also continued consciously along paths that had already been trodden at the beginning of our century. That is true beyond all doubt of textual criticism. By their grouping of manuscripts into text families and their methodical demonstration of the value of these "families," B. F. Westcott and F. J. A. Hort had shown that only in this way can the really ancient forms of text be discovered and a text reconstructed that will approach as closely as possible to the original (see above, pp. 185-86).[398] **Burnett Hillman Streeter,** a New Testament scholar at Oxford, carried this insight a step further (1924). Building on earlier research, he succeeded in discovering in a few late manuscripts the text of the church in Caesarea in Palestine that was already used in the third century by the church father Origen. In Streeter's opinion this text can be properly placed alongside the three great text recensions already known. "The result," Streeter adds, "is materially to broaden the basis of early evidence for the recovery of an authentic text."[399] While it is still an open question how far *in matters of detail* this genuine discovery has broadened the basis for the recovery of the original text of the New Testament, the manuscript basis for the recovery of the original New Testament text has been materially broadened by the publication of a large number of papyri manuscripts since the Caesarean text was discovered, and independently of it. Until about 1935 only individual papyrus leaves with the New Testament text from the time prior to the origin of the earliest extant complete vellum manuscripts of the New Testament (fourth century) were known. But since that time, in addition to the papyrus fragments of the New Testament from the second century, which were quite small, but epoch-making because of their age, extensive papyrus manuscripts of large parts of the New Testament from the third century have come to light, manuscripts that have pushed back our knowledge of the transmission of the New Testament by from one to two centuries.[400] A few of these extensive papyrus texts have confirmed Streeter's discovery of a new text family, with the result that new methods and possibilities for the study and determination of the original text of the New Testament have been opened up from two directions.

Following the First World War studies in the area of literary criticism of the New Testament and related source research were also carried on in basically the same direction as in the preceding period. But now a new hypothesis of the literary relationship of the Synoptic Gospels to one another was advanced and was able to attract considerable support.

In his *The Four Gospels* (1924), the significant work to which reference has been made above, B. H. Streeter applied the thesis of the varying geographical origin of the branches of the text tradition also to the sources of the Synoptics and, on the basis of a careful study of the peculiarities of the material transmitted solely by Matthew or Luke, replaced the almost universally accepted two-source theory (see above, pp. 148 ff.) with a four-document hypothesis which has been widely accepted in the English-speaking world. Streeter assumes that the Gospel of Luke arose from the fusion of the Gospel of Mark with a document he calls "Proto-Luke," into which the "Sayings-Source" had already been worked, while Matthew enlarged Mark's Gospel with material from the Sayings-Source and a further special tradition. What distinguishes this hypothesis is not the assumption of further sources of the Synoptic Gospels in addition to Mark and the Sayings-Source (such hypotheses have been advanced in the most varied forms both before and after Streeter's time),[401] but the ascription of the essential constituent parts of Luke's Gospel to a narrative source independent of Mark and the consequent conclusion that "as historical authorities" Mark and Proto-Luke "should probably be regarded as on the whole of approximately equal value," which means that "far more weight will have to be given by the historian in the future to the Third Gospel, and in particular to those portions of it which are peculiar to itself." Although Streeter expressly avoids any attempt at an exact determination of which words or narratives belong to the individual sources, it is nevertheless his opinion that "the final result of the critical analysis which has led to our formulating the Four Document Hypothesis is very materially to broaden the basis of evidence for the authentic teaching of Christ." [402] The development of the method of literary criticism through the separation of sources as a means of discovering a more certain knowledge of the history of the tradition shows that Streeter's study, like many similar ones, is based on the conviction that through source analysis one can retrace the steps backward from the primitive church's historical picture and faith in Christ to the beginnings of Christianity, and in particular back to the historical Jesus.

But this assumption was now questioned by a new view which was adopted first toward the Synoptic Gospels, and then toward numerous other New Testament writings. This view which emerged immediately after the end of World War I came to be known as the form-critical method. To be sure, the study of *Der Rahmen der Geschichte Jesu* [The framework of the story of Jesus] by **Karl Ludwig Schmidt**, a New Testament instructor at Berlin, which appeared in 1919, carries the subtitle *Literarkritische Untersuchungen zur ältesten Jesusüberlieferung* [Literary-criticial studies of the earliest Jesus tradition], but this designation is misleading, for, by a careful analysis of the references to place and time, first in Mark's Gospel and then in the two other Synoptics, Schmidt demonstrates that the classical two-source theory must be enlarged to include the insight that behind both sources, and behind our Gospels in general, stand individual reports orally transmitted, which the evangelists have linked together at secondhand without any knowledge of the historical connection in accordance with principles based on their content, or even on pragmatic grounds. Only the passion story was narrated from the beginning as a connected whole. Even more important than this distinction between framework and individual tradition was the recognition that the individual tradition has its "life situation" [*Sitz im Leben*] in worship, so that the tradition about Jesus owes its preservation and formulation, not to historical concerns, but to interest that are related to faith. All this, to be sure, questioned the possibility of writing a "life of Jesus in the sense of a developing history of his life," but directed attention instead to the religious motives to which the gospel tradition owes its formulation and transmission. A little later, in an essay on "Die Stellung der Evangelien in der allgemeinen Literaturgeschichte" [The place of the Gospels in the general history of literature] (1923), K. L. Schmidt pointed to the fact that the Gospels are "originally nonliterary rather than literary documents," "cultic books for ordinary folk, or even popular cultic books," and consequently "an expression of a religious fact, a religious movement." [403]

The earliest transmission of the tradition about Jesus was in the form of "pericopes," that is, individual narratives and independent sayings that were transmitted within the Christian community in large part without specific chronological or topographical indication. Much that looks as though it were chronological and topographical is only the framework that was imposed on the individual units. Set, then, in a connection within the literary transmission, unattached at the beginning and ending with the opening and closing phrases of related pericopes, they were often given the appearance of chronological and topographical notices. In most cases, however, it is apparent that these accessories are "framework." Such a fundamental methodological idea, impressed upon me by the analysis of the Synoptic Gospels and not applying by and large to the passion story, must not, of course, be exaggerated to maintain that the earliest tradition of Jesus was devoid of any topography and chronology. There are many statements which, by pointing to a fixed connection within individual narrative complexes, undoubtedly have a genuine chronological and, above all, topographical character. Viewed as a whole, however, only broken bits of an itinerary can be recovered. The fact that the narrative introductions reveal a remarkable diversity, that they occur at random, without regard for the proper connection of the succession of events with the individual narratives, demonstrates again and again the "framework" character of this tradition. The earliest narrators or transmitters of stories about Jesus paid little or no attention to their connection one with another, but were wholly concerned with the pictorial presentation of the individual pericopes as they met the needs of public worship. If the origin of Christianity is the emergence of a cult—in recent years this conclusion has increasingly been accepted—it is therefore clear that the origin of early Christian writings must be understood in light of their setting within the cult. In my judgment the significance of the early Christian cult, of the practices of public worship, can scarcely be over-estimated. The earliest tradition of Jesus is cultically determined, and therefore pictorial and suprahistorical. . . .

What there is of chronology and topography in the Gospels serves as a framework. An individual item of the framework can easily be changed or may even fall out. It is a peculiarity of popular narratives of such a sort that sometimes they contain chronological and topographical material, and sometimes not. In other words, sometimes they are framed pictures, sometimes unframed. And in this respect the collectors of these narratives have not on the whole made sweeping changes.

What we have discovered so far in our examination of the sketch of the life and work of Jesus has little or no bearing on its closing section, which deals with Jesus' suffering and death. We have seen that the structure of the account of Jesus' public ministry has little to tell us of chronology and topography. Individual stories or, as the case may be, complexes of stories, exist in abundance and do not stand in any certain sequence of events, but are offered within a sketch that has only the value of a framework. By and large every individual narrative has the character of a self-contained pericope, sometimes framed, sometimes more or less unframed. . . .

The passion story requires a different literary appraisal. It is the only portion of the Gospels that gives topographical and chronological detail, even to the day and the hour. It is readily apparent that in this instance a consecutive narrative was in mind from the outset. Whoever reads the first words of the whole, knows that the account must end in catastrophe: One thing leads to another with compelling necessity and logic. There is an explanation of the fact that from the standpoint of form the passion story occupies in every respect a special place within the gospel tradition. In giving it we must take our departure from the usage of pericopes, about which we have already had frequent occasion to speak.

In the assemblies of the Christian community for public worship, and in the assemblies which the missionary arranged for the purpose of winning new Christians, the self-contained reports of individual acts or words of Jesus played a role. In this connection the two kinds of assemblies did not need to be strictly distinguished from one another; the congregational assemblies were not rigorously exclusive, and if interested outsiders took part in them, such assemblies were thereby enabled also to serve the purposes of the Church's mission. . . .

How is the passion narrative to be fitted into this scheme of things? The individual narratives of this account satisfied neither the need of the narrator, nor that of the liturgy, nor that of the apologist. From the standpoint of the narrator certain aspects of this account such as Judas' betrayal, the preparation for the passover meal, the trial before Pilate, carried no proper weight. It is quite different with the account of the institution of the Lord's Supper and Jesus' crucifixion. Such an appraisal of the individual story is still clearer [when the latter is viewed] in connection with the conduct of public worship and the missionary program. Many of the narratives of the passion story have neither cultic nor even apologetic power. Their force is apparent only in combination where certain passages are necessary as a preparation for other passages. The passion narrative will have been read out in public worship as a *lectio continua* ["continuous lection"]. Only as a whole could it give the answer to a question that repeatedly emerged during the missionary period of the Church: How could Jesus have been brought to the Cross by the people which had been blessed with his signs and wonders?

It was in this different way that the passion story played its special role.

J. G. Herder's ideas about individual forms and the witnessing character of the earliest tradition of the Gospels; Weizsäcker's evidence for the motivating forces of the synoptic tradition; F. Overbeck's insight into "primitive Christian literature" as different from all later Christian literature and as recognizable by its literary forms; A. Deissmann's recognition of the popular character of primitive Christian writings; J. Wellhausen's proof of the dogmatic purpose involved in the choice of the tradition incorporated in the Gospels and of the creation by the evangelists of the connecting links within the Gospels; the observation made by P. Wendland and W. Bousset that from the outset the character of the individual units of the gospel tradition differed from that of the connected passion story (see above, pp. 79 ff., 167 ff., 199 ff., 218-21, 281-84, 305-06) —all these ideas had prepared the way for the insights of the form-critical view of the gospel tradition.[404] But K. L. Schmidt and his like-minded colleagues, M. Dibelius and R. Bultmann, owe the most potent stimuli to the writings of the man who, after having cooperated in founding the history-of-religions school, transferred his interests to Old Testament research—Hermann Gunkel. Gunkel's method of recovering the original traditions and of discovering the spiritual presuppositions of the formation of these traditions (*Sitz im Leben* or "life situation") — a method applied especially to the Old Testament legends of the patriarchs and to Old Testament songs—prepared the way in decisive fashion for the investigation of the gospel traditions by K. L. Schmidt and the other form-critics.[405]

The new direction in research received its name from *Die Formgeschichte des Evangeliums* [*The form history of the Gospel* (a title paraphrased by the English translator as *From tradition to Gospel*)] by **Martin Dibelius,** a programmatic book which appeared almost contemporaneously with Schmidt's analysis.[406] The intimations that Dibelius had already given of the character of the gospel narrative matter as tradition and of its different genera (see above, pp. 263-66) are here elaborated into a well-rounded picture of the origin of the gospel tradition and its place in the history of early Christianity. The two basically different narrative forms, "paradigms" [= pronouncement stories (Vincent Taylor)] and "novelettes" [= tales (B. L. Woolf)], are related with their different functions to the life of the early church; we are shown how the growing orientation to the world of Christianity originally alienated from the world expresses itself in the development from one genus [of tradition] to another, with the result that in this book form-critical distinction [of types or genera] becomes a tool of historical criticism; and, finally, we are enabled to discern what motives of faith played a role in the first combination of the tradition into an integrated report by Mark. The application of criteria based on the historical differentiation of types [of tradition] and the inquiry into the religious motivation involved in the formation of the tradition lead to a new insight into the historical value of the tradition of the Gospels and the concepts of early Christian faith.[407]

The literary understanding of the synoptics begins with the recognition that they are collections of material. The composers are only to the smallest extent authors. They are principally collectors, vehicles of tradition, editors. . . .

The position taken by the evangelists in forming the literary character of synoptic tradition is limited. It is concerned with the choice, the limitation, and the final shaping of material, but not with the original moulding. The form in which we hear of the words and deeds of Jesus is only in a certain degree due to the personal work of the evangelist. . . . What took place previously was the formation and growth of small separate pieces out of which the Gospels were put together. Even these little pieces obey the laws of Form-construction. They do it all the more as in the development of *their* form the individuality of an original writer played no real part. To trace out those laws, to make comprehensible the rise of these little categories, is to write the history of the Form of the Gospel. . . .

To understand the categories of popular writings as they developed in the sphere of unliterary people we must enquire into their life and, in our special case which deals with religious texts, into the customs of their worship. We must ask what categories are possible or probable in this sociological connection.

On the other hand, if it becomes clear that certain categories are contained in the majority of the texts, we must measure them up by those researches and determine whether they reveal relationships to particular modes of life and of worship. That research and this determination together constitute our problem. . . .

Because the eyewitnesses were at the same time preachers, what they had experienced must have come out amongst the people—here we see the reason for the propagation of the gospel. And this propagation remained subject neither to personal taste, nor to the circumstances of the hour, but took place in a regular manner in the service of certain interests and for the purpose of reaching certain goals. This is where we begin to catch sight of the law, according to which the formulation of the tradition was perfected. . . . *Missionary purpose was the cause and preaching was the means of spreading abroad that which the disciples of Jesus possessed as recollections.* . . .

If what was preached was a witness of salvation, then, among all the materials which were related, only this one, the Passion, was of real significance in the message. For what it dealt with was the first act of the end of the world as then believed in and hoped for. Here salvation was visible not only in the person and the word of the Lord, but also in the succession of a number of events. To set these matters in their proper connection corresponded to a need, and all the more as only a description of the consequences of the Passion and of Easter resolved the paradox of the Cross, only the organic connection of the events satisfied the need of explanation, and only the binding together of the individual happenings could settle the question of responsibility. Here we meet with the interests of edification, of the most primitive theology, and of the simplest apologetics, which certainly, for the time, tended to the relating of the Passion story in its historical circumstances. . . .

The description of the deeds of Jesus was not governed by the same interests in the course of preaching. These events had only an incidental and not an essential significance for the understanding of salvation. . . .

The narratives of the deeds of Jesus could only be introduced as *examples* in support of the message. . . . If the custom of the preacher, as we may in all probability conclude, was to illustrate his message by relating examples, and if this constituted the oldest Christian narrative style, we can perhaps give the name of paradigm to this category of narrative. . . .

[Only the edificatory stylization characteristic of the sermon, something which excludes complete objectivity, is the guaranty that we are dealing with old and relatively good tradition. Only narration in which they were personally involved was possible to those first Christians; neutral reports, if we had them, would be *ipso facto* suspicious. . . . Their report is certainly not comparable to a stenographic account but, because it is noticeably adjusted to the sermon, it may be accepted as ancient and as reliable as is possible under these circumstances. . . .]

The Paradigm reveals itself in fact as the narrative form whose use we could assume in the preachers of the Gospel. It is the only form in which the tradition of Jesus could be preserved at a time when a yearning for the end and a consciousness of estrangement from the world would still entirely prevent concern for a historical tradition or the development of a literature in the technical sense of the word. What "literature" and what "history" was present in the churches lived only within the sermon and by means of preaching. . . .

In the sermon the elements of the future Christian literature lay side by side as in a mother cell. The more Christianity reached out into the world, and the more the separate needs were distinguished, then the more the various means were separated from each other with which these needs were met in the Churches. For the further development of evangelical tradition the *story-teller* and the *teacher* appear to have been of special significance. . . . The sources have nothing to say of the tellers of tales. Nevertheless there were such, who could relate stories out of the life of Jesus broadly, with color, and not without art, as with every certainty we may conclude from the existence of such stories. We are concerned now with a number of narratives which I excluded from observation in the preceding Chapter. Their formulation shows clearly that they were not created for the aims of preaching, and that they were not repeated as examples as opportunity arose in the course of preaching. There is found here exactly that descriptiveness which we missed in the Paradigms; that breadth, which a paradigmatic application makes impossible; that technique, which reveals a certain pleasure in the narrative itself; and that topical character, which brings these narratives nearer to the corresponding categories as they were to be found in the world outside Christianity. . . . In order to describe this second category, we may best use the term "Tale" (Novelle). . . .

It is not Jesus as the herald of the Kingdom of God with His signs, demands, threats and promises, who stands in the centre of these stories, but Jesus the miracle-worker. *The Tales deal with Jesus the thaumaturge.* . . .

One has to do then with *Epiphanies* in which the divine power of the divine wonder-worker becomes manifest. . . .

[The hope of the end of the world that determined all their thinking meant that Christians to begin with were able to produce a kind of literature only indirectly by way of the sermon. This limitation no longer existed to the same extent at the time the old stories were expanded and the Tales were created. Christianity begins to accommodate itself to the world. A new element enters into narration, certainly not accidentally, certainly as the consequence of pious faith and intention, so that it becomes different from at first: there is now a delight in description, and artistic media, however simple, are employed. All this means that Christians are now at home in the world.] . . .

Tales, in accordance with their own nature are, at best, further removed from the historical text than the Paradigms.

The only long connected passage of a narrative kind given in the old tradition was the Passion story. . . . The tradition of Jesus' words consisted of individual stories and sayings. If one wished to give the Church a connected presentation one must undertake to bring them together and provide connecting links.

As far as we can see the first who undertook this work was the composer of the Gospel of St. Mark. . . . In the main body of his book, which deals with the work of Jesus, Mark brought together in his own way passages from the tradition preserved in the Churches, i.e. what were essentially Paradigms, Tales, Sayings . . . of Jesus. . . .

The most significant of all the means used by the evangelist for creating a lively connection among the fragments of tradition has not yet been mentioned. This has to do with the *interpretation of tradition.* The evangelist, in making his collection, strives to do this by setting a number of traditional events in a particular setting. He shows how and why they must have taken place in accordance with the Divine Plan of Salvation. . . .

[His purpose is] to represent Jesus as the Messiah.

The fortune of primitive Christianity is reflected in the history of the Gospel Form. The first beginnings of its shaping hardly deserve to be called literary. What Form was present was determined by ecclesiastical requirements arising in the course of missionary labour and of preaching. . . . But pleasure in the narrative for its own sake arose and seized upon literary devices. The technique of the Tale developed, and lent meanwhile a fully secular character to the miracle stories. . . . Already between the lines of the Gospel Form one can see that the faith of Christendom moved from its fundamental alienation from the world and its self-limitation to the religious interests of the Church, to an accommodation to the world and to harmony with its relationships. . . .

The Gospel Forms bear clear witness not only to these developments, but also to the *subject matter.* The earliest formal constructions, the Paradigms, give us insight into a class of man to whom all literary effort, every artistic aim, each emphasis upon personal impression in the course of the narrative, is completely strange. . . .

The significance of the history of the Form of the Gospels for the historical criticism of the evangelical tradition is by no means exhausted with such an illumination of the circumstances. Indeed, the formal criteria seem to me perfectly fitted to exclude the subjective judgment which easily makes itself felt as a matter of experience in the examination of the historicity of the evangelical narratives. The undoubted impression that more trustworthiness belongs to certain stories than to others can be more exactly settled with the differentiation between Paradigms and Tales. It can be rooted in the nature of the tradition and finally become a certainty. In their connection with preaching the Paradigms possess a means of protection against unhistorical extensions and other corruptions. Just because the simplest preaching of Jesus itself made use of it, it may be traced back as a category to the generation of eyewitnesses. Indeed, unprejudiced reading of these stories shows that their trustworthiness is not subject to such great questions as that of the Tales. The impression given to many unprejudiced readers of the life of Jesus in the Gospels, that it was narrated in a true, human, simple, and artless manner—this impression ascribed by many theologians to the Gospel of Mark—rests fundamentally neither upon this one, but to a large extent upon the paradigmatic narratives alone.

Soon afterwards the *Geschichte der synoptischen Tradition* [History of the synoptic tradition] by **Rudolf Bultmann** (1921), which had been completed in all its essential content before the works of Schmidt and Dibelius appeared, took a place alongside Dibelius' broadly constructive and programmatic volume which had preceded it. Employing an analytic method which took its departure strictly from the tradition as it exists, Bultmann undertakes "to give a picture of the history of the individual units of the tradition." He, too, proceeds from the view that the tradition was originally comprised only of separate units. In fact, he makes this assumption even in the case of the passion story. But he extends his examination to all the content of the Synoptic Gospels, inquires into the historical origin of every individual unit, and in so doing makes much more use than Dibelius of the history-of-religions approach and, together with that, of the difference between the early Palestinian and the early Hellenistic church, which the representatives of the history-of-religions school had recognized. In all this a very large role was attributed to the creative influence of the Church on the formation and embellishment of the tradition of Jesus, and strong emphasis was laid on the fact that the literary type of the "Gospel" as created by Mark has its roots in the preaching and the worship of the Hellenistic congregations. In Bultmann's study, then, there is also a strong emphasis on the character of the gospel tradition as conditioned by faith.[408]

For the most part the history of the tradition is obscure, though there is one small part which we can observe in our sources: how Marcan material is modified as worked over by Matthew and Luke. . . . If we are able to detect any such laws, we may assume that they were operative on the traditional material even before it was given its form in Mark and Q [the Sayings-Source], and in this way we can reason by inference back to an earlier stage of the tradition than appears in our sources. Moreover it is at this point a matter of indifference whether the tradition was oral or written, since as a result of the unliterary character of the material one of the chief differences between oral and written traditions is lacking. . . .

The aim of form-criticism is to determine the original form of a piece of narrative, a dominical saying or a parable. In the process we learn to distinguish secondary additions and forms. . . .

[I differ from Dibelius not only in terms of differing judgments in many matters of detail . . . but also with respect to the larger task I have set before myself. In the first place. I examine the Synoptic materials, especially the discourse matter, more fully, and, in the second place, I pursue the history of the several units more thoroughly and endeavor to recognize the laws by which they were transmitted, while he is basically concerned to comprehend their essential character. Furthermore, I believe that in my investigation concern for the one chief problem of the history of primitive Christianity, namely, the relationship of the primitive Palestinian and Hellenistic Christianity, has been made more consistently fruitful for the history of the tradition than is the case with Dibelius. . . .

I believe it a gross exaggeration to maintain (as Dibelius does) that the sermon stands at the beginning of all the spiritual production of primitive Christianity. . . . Apologetics and polemics as well as concerns for the strengthening of the church and for discipline, to say nothing of scribal activity, are also to be taken into account. . . .]

It cannot be maintained that the Passion story as we have it in the Synoptic Gospels is an organic unity. Even here what is offered us is made up of separate pieces. For the most part, though it does not indeed apply to them all, they are not dependent upon their context in the Passion narrative. Thus e.g. the story of the anointing, of the prophecy of the betrayal, of the Last Supper, of Gethsemane, of Peter's denial. . . . For such particular stories, once they were joined together into a whole, it was essentially the nature of the facts that determined the particular order. Another set of particular stories admittedly consists of supplementary embellishments of individual moments in a narrative that had already been knit together, as e.g. the stories of the Preparation of the Passover, the Hearing before the Sanhedrin, and of Herod and Pilate.

Even if it can be said in general that the Messianic outlook had little significance in Hellenistic Christianity, but that the figure of Jesus was conceived of in mythical and cultic categories, it would still be wrong not to take account of the high proportion of Hellenistic Christianity which came out of Jewish-Hellenistic circles. Unfortunately the picture of *Jewish-Hellenistic Christianity* is still very obscure and its exploration has hardly begun. It is certain that there was a strong Jewish-Hellenistic Christianity, and a chief proof is the fact that the history of the Synoptic tradition appears in a Greek dress. I do not believe it is possible to state sufficiently sharply the contrast in the N.T. Canon between the Synoptic Gospels on the one hand and the Pauline letters and later literature on the other. It must still be a puzzle to understand why

Christianity, in which Pauline and post-Pauline tendencies played so dominant a role, should also have the motives which drove it to take over and shape the Synoptic tradition out of the Palestinian Church. And this puzzle can only be solved by recognizing that there were strata of Hellenistic Christianity of which so far little is known, and on the further working out of which everything must depend. This will enable an important place to be given to the Jewish-Hellenistic element. . . .

The editorial activity of Mark (and his predecessors) which have described essentially rests upon literary motifs, even though they are mixed with dogmatic motifs in the picture of Jesus as the constantly attacked teacher and healer, and in the idea of the Twelve. But apart from this Mark is influenced by dogmatic motives . . . Dibelius' characterization of Mark as the book of secret epiphanies is just right. On the one hand the life of Jesus is represented as a series of revelations. Baptism and Transfiguration are alike epiphanies in Mark's view: the stories of the stilling of the storm and of the walking on the water report epiphanies just as much as the feeding stories. So do the healings wrought by the Son of God, especially the exorcisms of the demons which by their supernatural powers recognize the Son of God. In addition to this Jesus reveals himself to his own in the esoteric instruction of the disciples. . . . Yet on the other hand a veil of secrecy is drawn over the revelations: the demons must be silent, those who are healed must not talk about the miracle. Jesus sought solitariness and concealment; he told parables in order to conceal the secret of the Kingdom of God. . . . The disciples must not speak about what they have seen and heard until his resurrection, indeed they cannot yet themselves enter properly into the secret of his Messiahship; the incapacity to understand lay like some sorcerer's ban on them all. The dogmatic element in all these features has long been recognized. For the author they are the means of writing a life of Jesus as the Messiah, in so far as he was able to do so on the basis of the tradition available to him and under the influence of the faith of the Church, in which he stood. . . . In any case the author has succeeded by making use of the means available to him, in setting the tradition in a certain light, in impressing it with a meaning such as it needed in the Hellenistic Churches of Paul's persuasion; in linking it with the Christological Kerygma of Christendom, in anchoring the Christian mysteries of Baptism and Lord's Supper in it and so giving for the first time a presentation of the life of Jesus which could rightly be called εὐαγγέλιον Ἰησοῦ Χριστοῦ ["the gospel of Jesus Christ"] (Mk. 1:1). . . .

This is fact marks the purpose of the author: *the union of the Hellenistic kerygma about Christ*, whose essential content consists of the Christ myth as we learn of it in Paul (esp. Phil. 2:6 ff.; Rom. 3:24) with the *tradition of the story of Jesus*. . . .

The outcome of the development we have exhibited is the Gospel, which we meet first of all in the three forms of the Synoptists. What can we say about it from the point of view of the history of literature?

The motives that have led to its formation are plain. *The collection of the material of the tradition began in the primitive Palestinian Church.* Apologetic and polemic led to the collection and production of apophthegmatic sections. The demands of edification and the vitality of the prophetic spirit in the Church resulted in the handing on, the production and the collection of prophetic and apocalyptic sayings of the Lord. Further collections of dominical sayings grew out of the need for paranesis ["exhortation"] and Church discipline. It is only natural that stories of Jesus should be told and handed down in the Church—biographical apophthegms, miracle stories and others. And just as surely as the miracle stories and such like were used in propaganda and apologetic as proofs of messiahship, so it is impossible to regard any one interest as the dominant factor; as it is generally not right to ask questions about purpose and need only; for a spiritual possession objectifies itself also without any special claim.

With all this the Church did not itself create any literary genres but took over traditional forms that had long been used in Judaism, and which—so far as dominical sayings are concerned—Jesus himself had used. That such forms were ready to hand encouraged the relatively rapid precipitation of a somewhat fixed tradition. Yet with all this the type of the Gospel was not yet formed, but only in preparation. For these methods served only for the handing down of isolated sections. And when such sections were finally collected and fixed in written form and in this way underwent naturally enough some process of editing . . . then the result was only some enumerations and summings up. . . . For the idea of a unified presentation of the life of Jesus, knit together by some dominant concept, which first constitutes the Gospel, was obviously far removed from the Palestinian Church. . . .

It is possible to hold that a coherent presentation of the life of Jesus on the basis of a tradition of separate sections and small collections had to come at some time. The more the wealth of the oral tradition dried up, the more the need would grow of a collection as full and definitive as possible. And it seems but natural that the tradition which had an historical person at its centre should have been conceived in the form of a coherent, historical, biographical story. But this consideration by no means suffices to explain the peculiar character of the Synoptic gospels. Indeed their lack of specifically biographical material, their lacunae in the life story of Jesus are due to their presentation being based on the then extant tradition. But their own specific characteristic, a creation of Mark, can be understood only from the *character of the Christian kerygma*, whose expansion and illustration the gospels had to serve. . . . The Christ who is preached is not the historic Jesus, but the Christ of the faith and the cult. Hence in the foreground of the preaching of Christ stand the death and resurrection of Jesus Christ as the saving acts which are known by faith and become effective for the believer in Baptism and Lord's Supper. Thus the kerygma of Christ is cultic legend and the *Gospels are expanded cult legends.* . . . Which all amounts to this: The tradition had to be presented as a unity from the point of view that in it he who spoke and was spoken of was he who had lived on earth as the Son of God, had suffered, died, risen and been exalted to heavenly glory. And inevitably the centre of gravity had to be the end of the story, the Passion and Resurrection. Mark was the creator of this sort of Gospel; the Christ myth gives his book, the book of secret epiphanies, not indeed a biographical unity, but a unity based upon the myth of the kerygma. . . . Matthew and Luke strengthened the mythical side of the gospel at point by many miracle stories and by their infancy narratives and Easter stories. But generally speaking they have not really developed the Mark type any further, but have simply made use of an historical tradition not accessible to Mark but available to them. There was no real development of the type of Gospel created by Mark before John, and there of course the myth has completely violated the historical tradition. . . .

It seems to me that while we need analogies for understanding the individual components of the Synoptic Tradition we do not need them for the Gospel as a whole. . . . It has grown out of the imminent urge to development which lay in the tradition fashioned for various motives and out of the Christ-myth and the Christ-cult of Hellenistic Christianity. It is thus an original creation of Christianity. . . . So it is hardly possible to speak of the Gospels as a literary genus; the Gospel belongs to the history of dogma and worship.

It was not the theological consequence of this method, but no doubt Bultmann's "critical radicalism," his "much-berated skepticism" [409] concerning the historical reliability of the tradition of Jesus, that brought the form-critical method into more or less great disrepute among many, since it seemed overly much to dissolve the historically recognizable basis of the Christian faith in the person of Jesus.[410] On the other hand, however, the new method proved to be not only an indispensable aid to the discovery of the leading motives in the transmission of the tradition of Jesus, but actually also an important tool for the recovery of the earliest layer of this tradition itself and, as well, a means of access to the historical foundation of the earliest Christological interpretation of the person of the historical Jesus.[411] In fact, inquiry concerning the earliest literary units and the "life situation" [*Sitz im Leben*] of the earliest Christian tradition was necessarily extended even beyond the Gospels to other New Testament writings.[412] While M. Dibelius looked for the early traditional matter in the Book of the Acts, and in so doing tried to lay a new foundation for the presentation of the earliest Christian history,[413] it was the Breslau New Testament scholar Ernst Lohmeyer, once a student of A. Deissmann and M. Dibelius, who applied the form-critical method also to the Revelation to John and to the Letters of Paul. In an influential treatment of the "Hymn to Christ" in Paul's Letter to the Philippians (2:5 ff.), he proposed the thesis, based on form-critical but also on history-of-religions and historico-theological observations, that this bit of poetry is a pre-Pauline hymn taken from the eucharistic service of public worship, and that a Christological point of view is revealed in it which shares with Iranian cosmology the metaphysics of two worlds, but which in essential matters is dependent on Jewish ideas and forms a preliminary stage of the idea of Christ in the Gospel of John. Here the form-critical investigation serves not only to disclose older cultic or theological traditional matter, but also this literary analysis lends itself at the same time to a new kind of history-of-religions inquiry and is combined with an interpretation which pays attention to the message of the text but is not wholly free of obscurities, and which in Lohmeyer's instance reflects powerful influences of idealistic philosophy.[414] Along with that, however, this work of Lohmeyer's is at the same time a witness to two further new beginnings in New Testament research after the First World War, of which we shall have to speak at a later point.[415]

The question of the meaning of the early Christian concept of *Kyrios* ["Lord"] touches on the ultimate problems of early Christian religion and its history; it has come alive again and its importance has been recognized since the publication of *Bousset's* familar work. The discussion it has sparked and still continues to fan, feeds, to be sure, almost solely on the question of the historical origin of the name. . . . But the other question is also possible, namely, whether to that early Christian faith this very figure was not in the deeper sense the unknown, and the name *Kyrios* was able to speak of a revelation which first unlocked a suspected secret of this figure. . . .

This question means nothing else but that of the earliest content with primitive Christianity found in the concept of the "Lord." . . . In the Pauline letters, as the earliest documents of the primitive church, there is only one passage in which the concept of the *Kyrios* is actually central to a well worked-out course of thought; this passage is the so-called *locus classicus* ["classical passage"] of Pauline Christology in the Letter to the Philippians. It forms therefore the point at which this study begins and to which it repeatedly returns. . . .

It has often been observed that this period is more strictly constructed and more carefully arranged than other more epistolary passages of the same document. . . .

Christ's course from heaven to earth to death is described in three strophes, and in another three are presented his exaltation over the world. . . .

All these observations . . . compel us to conclude that here we have no ordinary piece of epistolary speech and no rhetorically heightened prose, but a carefully composed and meticulously balanced strophic structure, a *carmen Christi* ["hymn to Christ"] in the strict sense. . . .

Was it . . . composed by Paul at all? To be sure, other hymnic passages from Pauline letters are familiar to us. But even the lofty song to love, which comes first to mind both because of its poetic form and its opening words, does not exhibit the careful strophic structure and the meticulous arrangement in detail that this poem possesses. If even this general observation makes it doubtful that Paul is the poet, then the linguistic features of the poem make it certain that he is not. . . . All these factors make it necessary to conclude that this poem represents a creation foreign to Paul which he simply took over; it is a sort of traditional early Christian anthem. . . .

Even for the Philippians the psalm must have had the character of a *kerygma* of Christ ["proclamation of the essence of the Christian gospel"] which claims to be authoritative; it could not otherwise have been referred to Christ as a sacred utterance. We draw, then, the further conclusion that it is a bit of that tradition which Paul did not create, but only handed on; that it represents the common inheritance of the early Christian churches. . . .

Thus this psalm becomes one of the most perfect creations of primitive Christian poetry, which is otherwise almost wholly lost. The power of language and spirit, with which a still greater content is combined in a form that is completely appropriate, elevates it as the great work of a nameless poet. Among the early Christian literary witnesses, only a few of the poems in the Revelation to John are worthy to stand beside this poem on the ground of the comparable perfection with which form and content are harmoniously blended.

Now it is characteristic that it is only the antitheses of divinity and human-ity that are designated in terms of the forms they assume. It is not sinfulness and holiness, not transitoriness and imperishability, not power and impotence, that are set in contrast, but just human and divine form. Death, like a dark shadow, is associated with the human form; therefore we may conclude that the concept of life is necessarily bound up with that of the divine form. A second contrast is immediately added to this first. The divine form lives in the sphere of being, and this being is referred to on two occasions; the human form exists in the sphere of becoming and this also is spoken of twice. Becoming and death, then, define the human form of existence, while the divine form is defined as life. The inclusive concept which makes these antitheses possible is that of form; that which overcomes them is that of the pure, divine deed. Therefore these two words belong closely together. The essence of this form is determined by its deed, and the deed by the peculiarity of the form. . . .

Consequently the necessity of the antitheses of God and man, of heaven and earth, becomes apparent from the relationship of form and deed and their metaphysical definition. . . . On the basis of this theoretical presupposition, accordingly, there arises the necessity of the myth; and such a myth must only deal with the religio-metaphysical interpretation of the existence of the world and of men. . . .

No doubt this state of affairs in the first instance is nothing else but a necessary definition of the concept of faith, but what is peculiar to it lies in the relation of the axiom of faith to the metaphysical conception of two worlds, two worlds which stand in dialectical opposition. If we inquire into their historical determination, we find only one genuine analogy on Middle Eastern soil, viz., the message of Zarathustra. With grandiose onesidedness Zarathustra made the norm of the moral the final determining factor and the ultimate basis of all natural and historical existence. In it the religio-ethical deed deter-mines also the form and the meaning of divine existence, just as the state of religious existence of the believers is dependent on it. . . .

The word "servant" can only mean that the most extreme human abasement is necessary and demanded by the divine significance of this figure. Both, then, must coexist in him: he is "servant" as a sign both of his human abasement and his divine exaltation. This double sense is connected paradigmatically with the concept of "servant" only in the *Ebed-Jahwe* ["Servant of the Lord"] poems in Second Isaiah, above all, that in chapter 53. So then, the view of the historical life of this divine figure has been influenced by the ideas of the Isaiah of the Exile. . . .

We need to sum up and round off the results of our detailed examination. The psalm that lies before us, so compact both in form and in content, seems however to be everything else but a psalm. For where in this passage would there be a word of the salvation or damnation, of the distress or the blessedness, of a believing soul or congregation? Where at all any reference to a believing "I"? Almost all other psalms we know, Jewish or early Christian, cannot dispense with these elements, and when they speak of the acts of God, experi-enced or hoped-for, the psychic trait, which gives them a direct significance for the heart, is never lacking. This passage speaks of an event that is beyond all human conception, that has nothing to say of the distresses and joys of the heart, but speaks all the more eloquently of the powers of God and the world. And this occurrence between heaven and earth is described in straightforward but carefully weighed language, and at the same time with an unruffled objectivity, as though the psalm dealt with a natural event, or with a narrative out of the distant, unnamed past. Accordingly, it assumes a mental attitude on the part of the writer of this psalm to which the problems of the believing soul are remote and to which the problem of the natural and historical world is all-embracing, or to put the matter perhaps more precisely, for which the questions of the salvation of one's own soul are taken up in the greater question of the meaning and fate of the world and are solved only together with and as a part of it. No doubt there are related psalms scattered among Jewish apocalypses, but this particular psalm lacks the immediacy of the visionary experience. Here the poet sees, not in a state of apocalyptic ecstasy, but in light of a clear perception of what is occurring. Consequently it would be possible to describe the psalm in modern terms as an ideological poem in the form of a myth. . . .

The psalm was handed on to Paul, and by him to his congregations; it possesses enough inherent authority as "a firm prophetic word" to give his life and theirs goal and direction. Consequently it can hardly have been an ordinary part of public worship, in which, to quote Paul, "each one" presents "a hymn, a lesson, a revelation, a tongue, or an interpretation" (I Cor. 14:26); for how the possibility of a tradition of sacred utterances could result from such freedom remains unclear. Furthermore, this psalm seems to demand a place in which the faith of the congregation gathers wholly round its eschatological goal. Both elements, the holiness and necessity of the tradition and the eschatological determination of the expression of faith, seem in early Christianity to be combined only at one place, namely, at the celebration of the Eucharist. . . . Consequently it is probable that this hymn also was a bit of the earliest eucharistic liturgy. And this, too, seems clearly to confirm its Palestinian origin. . . .

However, even if this psalm was a prayer of thanksgiving in the celebration of the Eucharist, it remains nonetheless the creation of a nameless poet and prophet; for in the power of its construction, in the transparent depth of its ideas, only a little that the New Testament has handed down to us of the original and lofty testimonies to its faith is to be compared with it; it presupposes the almost impersonal and spirit-directed vision of a poet, to whom the "vision of his glory," that is, of a divine purpose and its realization in history and the world, is all that matters. And again we perceive a connection with the magnificent words of the prologue to the Gospel of John: "We have beheld his glory." But this psalm is earlier than John, and earlier even than Paul. Therefore it is one of the most precious documents of earliest Christianity and an illuminating example of the rich and varied forces that were alive in it.

2.
The New History-of-Religions Approach

Studies employing the history-of-religions school's view of the New Testament had endeavored increasingly to see the New Testament in relation to Hellenistic-Jewish religiosity, and then also to Hellenistic-pagan religiosity; in the course of this the ideological world of Jesus was represented to a great extent without relation to his environment. The evidence presented by John Lightfoot, Gustaf Dalman, and Adolf Schlatter that important presuppositions for the understanding of early Christianity are to be found in the extensive literature of late rabbinical Judaism was scarcely any longer considered.[416] All this changed overnight when, beginning in 1922, the Brandenburg pastor **Paul Billerbeck** began the publication of his four-volume *Kommentar zum Neuen Testament aus Talmud und Midrasch* [Commentary on the New Testament from the Talmud and the Midrash]. By means of reliable translations and introductory comments, the extensive literature of rabbinical Judaism, hitherto virtually inaccessible to the non-specialist, was made intelligible in this massive work in the form of a commentary on the words and content of all New Testament passages that interpreters need in any way to take into account. The author's express purpose was "to collect, to sift, and to make conveniently available in reliable translation all the material from late Jewish literature that is useful for the interpretation of the New Testament." Decades of self-denying work on the part of a pastor had in this way opened up the possibility of getting "to know the Judaism of that time in terms of its life and thought," [417] and so countless studies in the field of late rabbinical Judaism which have been concerned with the problem of the objective relation of early Christianity to its Jewish environment have profited from Billerbeck's great work, and translations of many rabbinical writings in their entirety owed their inspiration to it.

Although Billerbeck's commentary laid a new foundation for the history-of-religions study of the New Testament, this standard work was nevertheless only an especially effective and permanently useful product of a more far-reaching new orientation of this enterprise. Even before Billerbeck's first volume appeared, a New Testament scholar at Griefswald, Gerhard Kittel, had begun the publication of a translation of one of the earliest rabbinical commentaries,[418] together with brief comments on its bearing on the New Testament; a few years later he brought out a comprehensive study of *Die Probleme des palästinischen Spätjudentums und das Urchristentum* [The problems of late Judaism and primitive Christianity] (1926). In this latter book he not only points out that recourse to the rabbinical literature is indispensable to the understanding of the earliest form of primitive Christianity and emphasizes that the history-of-religions setting of Palestinian Judaism is wholly in conformity with that of early Palestinian Christianity, but also by means of a comparison of the ethic of Jesus with that of the rabbis, he attempts to demonstrate both the far-reaching similarity and the radical differences between the two religions. The religio-historical approach in this instance is therefore quite deliberately put at the service of the theological task of isolating the distinctiveness of the early Christian proclamation.[419]

In recent decades New Testament research within Protestant theology has received a strong impulse from the discipline of comparative religion. Scholars have begun deliberately to give beginning Christianity its due place in the world of non-Christian cultures and religions.

In all this it is one of the remarkable paradoxes that, as the history of science shows again and again, a beginning is frequently made with what is remote, rather than with what is near. . . . Every sensible person will agree with the observation that it is important and meaningful to investigate the Hellenistic-Oriental influences on the consolidation process of Christianity. At the same time, however, it must be established beyond all dispute that the first phase in the history of the development of Christianity—chronologically the earliest, but also the one fundamental to all that was to follow—was provided by that basic Palestinian factor.

Consequently it can and must be asserted that, *along with* and *prior to* all Hellenistic–Near Eastern analogies for the study of early Christianity, the question of its relation to late Palestinian Judaism must be faced. Even at the risk of uttering banalities, we must declare again and again that Jesus himself was beyond all doubt a Jew and a Palestinian and that his disciples and the earliest Christian Church, as well as he himself, belonged to Palestinian Judaism. . . .

The genuine part of late Judaism, the part with firm roots, is Palestinian Judaism. . . . And so far as the relation of late Judaism and early Christianity is concerned, it is clear that the connections between the two entities that are characterized as primary have to do entirely with Palestinian Judaism. So it is methodologically appropriate and unavoidable to concentrate our attention first of all on this part, as on the principal item of the problem.

The history-of-religions situation of early Palestinian Christinaity corresponds to the historical situation of Palestinian Judaism, just as does its linguistic situation. No one questions that at many points the religious views and doctrines passed over directly from the environing Judaism into early Christianity. . . .

The nearer we come to the beginnings of Christianity, the more precarious becomes the basis of the history-of-religions orientation, and consequently the more difficult the sober evaluation of real or alleged parallels. But if we raise the questions in light of Palestinian Judaism, from which early Christianity emerged, the result is at once a great increase of the material for comparison and, as a consequence, a foundation much less exposed to constructive fantasy. Therefore, in terms of content as of method, it remains essential to incorporate the history of religion of early Christianity into the history of religion of late Palestinian Judaism. . . .

The problem of the comparison of the matter of religion remains at all times the most important part, the crowning feature of the task for the one who seeks to discover the external and internal relationships of the two religions.

In posing the issues within this group of problems it is certainly well to reach an understanding immediately about the goal of the research. In the sense of a scientific undertaking, this goal can be but one: to comprehend the special nature of the one and the special nature of the other religion. . . . Judaism is that religion which is basically most congenial to Jesus' ethical demand. . . . But by this approach *the basic question of all comparison of religion* is introduced: . . . *measured by this Judaism, where is the element of the new, the different, in Jesus and his gospel?* . . . There is not a single one of the ethical demands of Jesus of which one might maintain *a priori* that, as an individual demand—observe carefully that I am speaking it as an individual demand—it is something absolutely singular; that it could not occur also on the soil of non-Christian Judaism; that it would not be possible also there— perhaps ever so seldom, but nevertheless basically possible! This means that the singularity of early Christianity as a religious and spiritually historical phenomenon cannot be found in any individual demand, be it ever so lofty. . . .

Both Jesus and the Judaism of his time have their roots in Old Testament piety. . . .

Only when this common native soil is determined can we begin to find a clue to the difference. It lies first in the fact that in the case of Jesus all those multiplicities of levels are overcome. A *concentration* has been achieved, such as we find nowhere in Judaism. . . .

To be sure, both Jesus and the scribes have their roots in the Old Testament; but for Jesus this connection is the cohesive factor for the totality of his life. . . .

But all this draws attention to the second great difference between Jesus' demand and the ethic of Judaism. It can be reduced to the formula: the *absolute intensity* of Jesus' ethics. Jesus' demand is formulated as an absolute. . . .

The absoluteness of the ethic of Jesus is only comprehensible from one single psychological vantage point: from *Jesus' consciousness of himself and* of *his mission*. The heart of the new religion—beyond all questions of reality and illusion conditioned by a given ideology—is nothing but the historic fact of the consciousness both of God and of absoluteness on the part of its founder. . . .

We have now determined the two great components that comprise the Gospel of Jesus and the whole of early Christianity, and of which at no time is one to be found without the other; in the deep accord between the two we discover the singularity of the new religion. The *one* component is this: direct and vital assimilation of what values the development of the history of the Israelitish-Jewish religion had to contribute. But the *second* component is: Jesus' consciousness of absoluteness, of fulfillment, of God's kingdom. . . . The point at which Jesus' consciousness of mission coincides with his claim that *fulfillment* has come about in his person is the point at which he ceases to be a Jew and his Gospel ceases to be a branch of Judaism. . . .

Just *because* his claim is related to what for Judaism is the *given*, Jesus becomes an offense to Judaism. For to the extent that he takes over the ancestral inheritance of Judaism, there arises the new religion, a religion that is no longer Judaism, but the Christ religion. Christianity has its history of religious distinctiveness in the fact of the person of Jesus himself.

The combination of the form-critical view with the renewed question concerning the late Jewish environment of the New Testament proves even more clearly fruitful in the studies (unfortunately published only as fragments) of **Julius Schniewind,** New Testament scholar at Halle, on the origin and history of the New Testament concept of the "good news" (i.e. gospel). Schniewind pointed out that Jesus' message of the Gospel proclaimed at the end of the days has its roots in the Old Testament, in the writings of Second Isaiah (Is. 40 ff.), and that these ideas remained alive, not in Hellenistic, but rather in Palestinian, Judaism and from this source influenced Jesus and early Christianity. Thus the history-of-religions way of posing problems provides a reply to the question of the life situation (*Sitz im Leben*) of a central New Testament concept and helps to make the actual meaning of the concept comprehensible.[420]

That in its ultimate *content* Jesus' message is "good news" is a statement that seems incontrovertible. It naturally remains true even if Jesus never used the *expression* "gospel" [evangel]. . . .

Where does the expression "gospel" come from? Did Jesus use it or not? If he used it, how did he hit upon the expression? Did it already have a history? Rather: did the idea, did the view, already have a history *before* Jesus' time? And to what extent did Jesus reshape the view? . . .

The whole emphasis of our study must naturally fall upon the content of the concept. . . . We have learned from the form-critical approach to regard questions about *content* as decisive. All scholars lay emphasis on the task of discovering the *historical situation* of every individual λόγιον ["saying"] from its structure.

Whether a saying comes from Mark, from Q, from a hypothetical primitive Mark [*Urmarkus*], from the material peculiar to one of the evangelists, from Special Luke or Special Matthew: None of this has any bearing on whether or not a saying is authentic. All depends on whether and how, in terms of content, a saying must be understood as an expression of the situation of Jesus, of Judaism, of the early church, or of the Hellenistic Christian community.

Greater certainty could be obtained only by a detailed examination of the Jewish world of ideas. . . . But even when we seek to understand our concept as originating either in Judaism or the early church, or, indeed, as from Jesus himself, we must take into account all the more carefully the assured results of classical philology.

The idea of the "good news" [gospel, evangel] took its rise with Second Isaiah. To be sure, *neither in the Old Testament nor later in Judaism* did *the substantive for "good news"* become a technical expression *for a message of God: but the verb is a religious term* from Scond Isaiah's time. . . . *In Second Isaiah the "good news" is the vehicle of the effective "word of Yahweh."*

In Second Isaiah, as in the Psalms, the religious note sounds in a complete symphony: The rule of Yahweh as King, salvation, righteousness, the new, miraculous age—they *are coming;* they are already *here.* They are already here in the word, and what is meant by Yahweh's word and Yahweh's act applies to all peoples. It is proclaimed in the cult. The "good news" announces Yahweh's act. . . .

Second Isaiah's eschatology continued to exercise the strongest influence. . . . Eschatology revives in the very period of the New Testament; interest in the "word" is newly awakened; once more the hope of the coming good news comes alive. . . .

The *Septuagint adds no new traits to the picture we have gained.* It exhibits no tendency to define our ideas more precisely. On the contrary, *traces of a serious misunderstanding are clearly to be recognized.* . . .

Our Old Testament researches have shown us that in the Old Testament the idea of the "good news" is closely related to the idea of the "word of Yahweh." *Here* we discover the background of the early Christian view of things. . . . It is the ideological world of Second Isaiah that prevails in rabbinism and in the New Testament, and the terminology must be evaluated in light of this ideological world.

The use of rabbinical matter contributes therefore both to the understanding of the New Testament text and to its differentiation from contemporary Judaism. Consequently it is a matter of no surprise, and even signifies a new and beneficial line of investigation, that modern, historically oriented Jewish theology turned to the question of how we are to judge the distinctiveness of the New Testament and of Jesus in particular and their relation to rabbinic Judaism. In a long line of other scholars[421] it was especially **Claude G. Montefiore**, the leader of English liberal Judaism, who in this connection raised the decisive question. He followed his comprehensive commentary on the Synoptic Gospels[422] with another work that likewise took its departure from an exposition of the sayings of Jesus in the Synoptics, namely, his *Rabbinic Literature and Gospel Teachings* (1930), a book which, fully recognizing the achievement and relevance of Billerbeck's collections, undertakes to show that Billerbeck nevertheless repeatedly tries improperly to demonstrate an originality on Jesus' part at points where Jesus plainly finds himself in agreement with the teaching of the rabbis. Despite all Jesus' criticism of rabbinic legalism, Montefiore not only claims to show that Jesus stands decidedly closer to the rabbis than Christian theologians are ready to admit, but also to demonstrate that Jesus' teaching can make no claim to superiority in comparison with the rabbis. In this fashion this extremely objective investigation shows that the history-of-religions method of comparison inevitably leads to the question of the actual meaning of the text and to one's personal attitude toward its message.[423]

I have to admit that the "parallels" are not allowed to speak for themselves, for I have added a certain amount of commentary. . . . I am, I fancy, rather less concerned than most Jewish writers either to bring Rabbinic teaching on the religious and ethical topics touched on in the Gospels to the exact level of the teaching of Jesus, or to depreciate the teaching of Jesus when it appears (to Christian writers) to rise above the Rabbinic level. On the other hand, whereas a main interest for most Christian writers is to vindicate, so far as they can, the originality of Jesus, and, for that purpose, the question of dates is for them a matter of utmost importance, for *me* the question of dates is of very little importance at all. . . . A given parallel to a Gospel saying may be much later than Jesus: from the point of view of chronology, the originality of Jesus is completely vindicated. . . . To me, and for *my* purpose, if it is a true parallel, in the sense of being characteristic and "on the line," its value and interest are largely independent of its date. . . .

It is difficult for the Christian commentators to have it both ways. If the Rabbis consciously and habitually taught that one must love one's fellow-Israelites, but that one need not love, and that indeed one might hate, the non-Jew; if they taught the identification of the non-Jew with the enemy, then it is very strange that Jesus, who *ex hypothesi* is teaching a new doctrine—universal love, the love of all men without distinction of nationality—does not definitely tell his disciples either that neighbour is to include the non-Jew as well as the Jew, or that by enemy he means the national and public enemy, the idolater and the Roman, as well as the private, Jewish enemy. . . .

I do not mean for a moment to imply that, when the occasion arose, Jesus would not have urged his disciples, or would not have urged his fellow-Jews, to show mercy and love to a needy Roman or to a needy Greek. . . . All that I am concerned about is the meaning and the implication of this section in the Sermon on the Mount [Matt. 5:43-48]. And *about this section* I contend that it does not consciously and designedly teach, in contrast to current particularism, the universality of love, the love of all men without restriction of race and nationality.

The truth is that the Rabbis are not entirely of one mind on the matter of loving or hating the non-Jew. It would be unjust to sum up the matter by saying that the Rabbis generally taught that it is right and permissible to hate the Gentile. On the other hand, it would be hardly less unfair to say that the Rabbis taught that the love which was to be shown to the Jewish "neighbour" was to be extended equally to all men, whatever their race or nationality or creed. One can hardly quote any unequivocal utterance from the Rabbis which goes as far as this. . . .

From the vast compass of the Rabbinical literature it is not difficult for S. B. [Strack-Billerbeck] and others before them to choose out a number of passages which illustrate Rabbinic hatred of the non-Jew, of the heathen world. . . . Indeed, . . . I could quote passages . . . which illustrate the intense particularism of the Rabbis, a particularism which often passes over into contempt and hatred of the "nations." On the whole, I think we must allow that this particularism is their more prevailing mood. . . .

Still one must also observe caution on the other side. If, as regards any particular ordinance of the Pentateuchal Law, the Rabbis pretty well always interpreted the Biblical *Rea'* (neighbour) to mean "Israelite only," it is no less clear that their word *chaber* [companion], and still more their word *beriyyoth* (creatures), by no means always excluded, but, on the contrary, often included, the non-Jew, or, at the least were intended to mean men in general. . . .

Thus the evidence would seem to show that the Rabbis could and did, in the abstract, and as a general religious doctrine, teach that one must love, and do good to all the "creatures," all the children of men, created by the One God. . . .

I am not clear that Jesus was definitely enlarging the range [of the love commandment], but as to the private enemy (the enemy of whom you are not thinking about his race, or nationality, or religious opinions) my verdict would be that Jesus unites himself with the *very* best Rabbinic teaching of his own and of later times. It is, perhaps, only in trenchantness and eager insistency that he goes beyond it. There is a fire, a passion, an intensity, a broad and deep positiveness, about these verses, which is new.

Billerbeck's object is to stress the immense difference between the poor, verbal, legal "righteousness" of the Rabbis and the glorious, evangelical "righteousness" taught by Jesus. . . . The old Jewish (*i.e.* Rabbinic) religion is, he says, a religion of redemption by oneself and one's own power; it has no room for a redeemer and saviour who dies for the sins of the world (iv. p. 6). . . . That sentence is largely true, especially the second part of it. But it is not wholly true to say that the Rabbinic religion is one of "völligster Selbsterlösung" ["redemption by oneself alone"]. . . . It is not wholly true, just because the Rabbis never worked out a complete and consistent theological system. . . .

It cannot be fairly said, without many saving clauses, that the Rabbinic religion is one of complete self-redemption. The enormous mass of Israelites did *not*, in Rabbinic opinion, completely fulfil the Law, and so far as they did fulfil it, they did not fulfil it (in their own opinion) entirely from their own strength and by the power of their own free-wills. Nor would it be true to say of the vast majority of the Rabbis that they believed that they were sinless people who, so far as they were concerned, needed no Day of Atonement and no divine forgiveness. They did not believe this, I think, either about themselves or about one another. . . .

The Law is the true antidote to the *Yetzer* [= evil impulse], but the antidote must be rightly used. Practice is the condition of right study. The finest medicine falsely used can become a poison. Such is Rabbinic soteriology. Can it rightly be so sharply opposed to the soteriology of Jesus? I hardly think so. . . .

The alleged sharp opposition between the soteriology of Jesus and the soteriology of the Rabbis has, I think, been shown to be uncritical. It is forced out of, and into, the texts. Historically, this sharp contrast cannot be maintained. Jesus was not so far from the Rabbis, nor were the Rabbis so far from Jesus. That is not to say that the legalism of the Rabbis would have been accepted by, or acceptable to, Jesus. It would not. But it does mean that, as far as God's grace and human effort and freedom of will and human weakness and human repentance and God's forgiveness are concerned, the Rabbis and Jesus were by no means poles asunder. . . . In truth the religion of the Rabbis cannot justly be described . . . as a religion of works as *contrasted* with a religion of grace. It is a religion of both . . . works *and* grace. For the works are never adequate without the grace, though the grace may be given without the works. . . .

We cannot *prove* the "grace" or the "help." We cannot quantitatively divide up any action into our part and God's part. But we may none the less believe in both. The *Stückwerk* [piece-work] seems right. It is *not* all God's grace. It *is* partly man's own effort. . . . Both the "righteousness" of the Rabbis and the "righteousness" of Jesus are excellent righteousnesses. Each thought that the other was quite inadequate for the entering into the Kingdom of Heaven. Yet surely here were Jesus and the Rabbis equally in error. For both righteousnesses, honestly pursued, are acceptable unto God.

It would certainly have meant abandoning the really historical view of the New Testament if research had been satisfied with the Palestinian-Jewish background of the New Testament and had ignored the insights that the history-of-religions school had achieved. The broadening of the scope of the history-of-religions method of setting the issues had to lead, rather, to an energetic attempt to take into consideration also the relationships of late Judaism to its environment as well as the influence of this non-Jewish milieu on early Christianity. When **Ernest Lohmeyer** wrote his interpretation of the Revelation to John (1926), he saw himself driven, as his predecessors had been, not only to refer again and again to the dependence of the book on Jewish apocalyptic, but also to emphasize its familiarity with the "myth of the original divine man, which Reitzenstein brought to our attention," and to point out that these mythological concepts must have been known to the author of the Revelation to John in a Jewish version; that, therefore, a "Jewish gnosis" can be recognized as a presupposition of the Christian apocalypse.[424]

Full understanding of the uniqueness of the Apocalypse can only be attained when one knows the tradition it used and the manner in which it used it. Paramount among the sources of this tradition is the Old Testament. . . . Other sources of the Apocalypse can be determined only with difficulty. Certainly some Jewish apocalypses and pseudepigraphs belong among them. Nevertheless, however frequent the contact . . . here it is still only the often identical tradition that is to be recognized, not its fixed form in a specific book. . . . This tradition itself is varied and rich; its elements do not arise out of a closely guarded Jewish source. On the contrary, their origins are diverse and often of a contradictory nature. But, whatever of alien or of most alien origin may have gone into it, nowhere does it deny the nature and thoroughness of Jewish reformulation. . . . This sort of "spiritual" [pneumatic] interpretation is not only a sign of the priestly and scribal training of the seer, but also a sign of a great complex within the history of religions, not yet explained in detail, which is confirmed by the distinctiveness of the total religious outlook of the Apocalypse. It is the stream of "Jewish gnosis" which, from the time of the Exile, must increasingly have pervaded the, so-to-speak, non-official Jewish piety. Its sources, often discernible with difficulty, lie in individual sections of Jewish apocalypses and pseudepigraphs, in Jewish-Alexandrian hermeneutics —although this latter is permeated with the legacy of the Hellenistic spirit —in "Johannine" writings and writings of the "Johannine" school, and in Manichaean and Mandaean documents. Under the safe protection of the Old Testament, this gnosis preserves the much-mixed legacy of Near Eastern piety.

The necessity of looking for a Jewish gnosis or its oriental roots then also became evident, especially in interpreting the Johannine writings. In an article published as early as 1923, **Rudolf Bultmann** had shown that "Der religionsgeschichtliche Hintergrund des Prologs zum Johannes-Evangelium" ["The religio-historical background of the prologue to the Gospel of John"] is a Jewish Wisdom myth which, on its part, represents only *one* example of the oriental myth of the heavenly primal man, a myth which can be recognized especially clearly in the Mandaean writings. Bultmann thus not only develops ideas of H. Gunkel and W. Bousset about the significance of the oriental redeemer-myth for the thought-world of the New Testament, but also, and more importantly, adopts R. Reitzenstein's reference in his later works[425] to the significance of the Mandaean writings for knowledge of this oriental redeemer-myth, and in so doing resumes an hypothesis that J. D. Michaelis had advanced as much as 130 years earlier.[426] The possibility of making use of these texts was now opened up by the fact that the Göttingen orientalist **Mark Lidzbarski** had published accurate translations of the writings of this religious group, which still exists in a small community along the Euphrates.[427] As a result Rudolf Bultmann was shortly thereafter (1925) able to follow his work on the prologue to John's Gospel with a comprehensive essay that dealt with "Die Bedeutung der mandäischen und manichäischen Quellen für das Verständnis des Johannesevangeliums" [The importance of the Mandaean and Manichaean sources for the understanding of the Gospel of John]. By assembling numerous citations, above all from Mandaean, but also from Manichaean and early gnostic Christian, writings, he was able to demonstrate that this literature is based on a redeemer-myth that was taken over in an abbreviated form by the author of the Gospel of John, and for that reason, despite the disparity in age of these writings, is undoubtedly pre-Christian. Oriental mythology therefore serves in this connection to illuminate the origin and the historical setting of an early Christian writing, but also at the same time to make the actual content of the message of the evangelist more intelligible to modern man. The history-of-religions approach to the problems of the New Testament is in this way part of a theological task.[428]

The ancient *myth of Wisdom* is now clearly recognizable: The preexistent Wisdom, God's companion at Creation, seeks a dwelling upon earth among men; but she seeks it in vain; her preaching is rejected. She comes to her own, but her own do not receive her. So she returns to the heavenly world and dwells there in concealment. To be sure, men now seek her, but no one any longer is able to find her; God alone knows the way to her. . . . There are . . . exceptions; there are individual blessed ones among the *massa perditiones* ["mass of the lost"] to whom Wisdom reveals herself, who receive her, and who consequently become friends and prophets of God. . . .

The proof that the Logos speculation of the prologue to the Gospel of John is based on the Wisdom speculation that we meet in the sources of Judaism seems to me to have been provided with relative certainty. And now at this point we can at last raise the question why the figure we meet in Judaism as Wisdom is called the Λόγος ["Word"] in John's prologue. . . . Now, no doubt the prototype does not, or at least not directly, come from pagan tradition but from Hellenistic Judaism, on which the Gospel in other respects is also dependent. We must . . . assume that . . . in Hellenistic Judaism Logos replaced the earlier Wisdom.

The one she has sent speaks what Wisdom speaks, and conversely: The words of him who is sent are the words of Wisdom herself. *Wisdom herself appears, reveals herself, in the one who is sent.* . . .

It is basically Wisdom herself who repeatedly. comes down to earth from her concealment and incorporates herself in her emissary, the prophet. . . .

And we find this idea . . . in a series of sources, and we owe it to Reitzenstein that they have been set in this context. The divine figure, who is pre-existent and the embodiment of all knowledge and who appears on earth in his own person or incorporate in his emissary, we know from the speculations of the Manichaeans. . . . In like manner, among the Mandaeans the divine figure of the primal man appears on earth as Manda d'Haije, that is, as knowledge of life, to bring life. . . .

On the basis of the material that has come to light and can be scanned, it seems to me that one thing . . . can be said, viz., that the *name "Wisdom" is not essential*, any more than the female sex, *to the divinity who brings revelation*. . . .

We cannot dismiss the question . . . of whether the designation of the Revealer as "Word" is not even older.

It must have become clear that in [John I] vss. 1-13 a prototype has been employed whose content and course of thought are the same as in Jewish Wisdom speculation. Perhaps it has also become probable that the view set forth in the Johannine prologue belongs in the wider context of Near Eastern speculations about a divine Revealer who is incorporate in an emissary upon earth. . . .

In the context of the speculation reconstructed by Reitzenstein in his last published works and designated by him as Iranian, probably still another reference . . . is necessary to the very great influence on the *Christology of the entire Gospel of John,* of the idea of the Redeemed Redeemer, i.e., of the divine being, the heavenly "Man," who has come down to earth as the Emissary of God, as Revealer, has taken upon himself human form and, after the completion of his vocation as Revealer, returns to the heavenly world, is exalted and transfigured and receives the office of Judge, and all that because he is the "Man." . . .

If my hypothesis is correct, then the Gospel of John is proof in a new

? sense of the extraordinarily early penetration of primitive Christianity by oriental-gnostic speculation.

The place of the Gospel of John in the history of early Christianity is . . . a puzzle which, in my judgment, has not yet been solved, even today. . . .

The Gospel belongs neither to Palestinian Christianity, as it is attested by the Synoptics, nor to the type of Hellenistic Christianity represented by the Pauline congregations or that to be seen in Hellenistic Jewish Christianity, as the latter is testified to, for instance, by I Clement, the Shepherd of Hermas, or the Letter to the Hebrews or of Barnabas. . . .

Yet the Gospel of John seemed understandable as a special type within Hellenistic Christianity. . . . Nevertheless despite all analogies, the Gospel of John cannot be regarded as a representative of the piety of the Hellenistic mystery cults; what distinguishes it from Paul, distinguishes it also in part from the Mysteries. . . . The Christology is not determined by the cosmic catastrophe, or the dying and rising of the cult god, or the idea of revelation. And Jesus does not reveal anthropological and cosmological or theological secrets, but only one thing: that he is the Revealer.

This brings us to the second great puzzle of the Gospel of John. If the Gospel is considered by itself, *what is its central idea, its fundamental conception?* No doubt it is to be found in the repeated assertion that Jesus is the one whom God has sent (e.g., 17:3, 23, 25), who brings the revelation by words and deeds. . . . But therein lies the puzzle: What is it actually that the Jesus of the Gospel of John reveals? While it is expressed in many different ways, it is yet always only the one thing: *that* he was sent as Revealer. . . .

If we wish to make further progress we must maintain the position that the ever-recurring assertion must provide the solution: that Jesus has been sent by God, lives in union with the Father, and as such brings the revelation. More must lie behind this assertion than at first glance it appears to say. In fact, hidden behind it is a mighty myth, and to recognize this is to take the first step towards a correct understanding of the Gospel of John. Aids in assisting us to such an understanding are the Mandaean texts, actually unlocked for the first time for scientific use by the Lidzbarski editions, and the new discoveries of Manichaean sources. . . .

The redemption myth, which is to be recognized in all the sources to which we have referred, can be briefly summarized as follows: The emissary who comes from heaven brings to the soul imprisoned on earth revelation concerning its origin, its homeland, and its return to this homeland. The one who is sent appears in earthly, human garb, but ascends in glory. Parallel to this soteriological myth is a cosmological one: The figure of him who is sent corresponds to the figure of the heavenly world into matter and was overcome and imprisoned by the latter. Now, since the figure of the emissary was assimilated to that of the primal man, the one who is sent appeared also in his earthly manifestation as imprisoned and oppressed, and his ascension is also his own redemption; he is the Redeemed Redeemer. In turn, the fate of the primal man is nothing else than the fate of the individual soul; the redemption of souls is the freeing of the primal man and thereby the end of the earthly world, whose origin and continuance were made possible by the connection of the particles of light of the primal man with chaotic matter. Consequently, then, in the final analysis the fate also of him who is sent and that of the soul are related; in fact, the one who is sent is nothing else than a faithful copy

352

of the primal man, an exact likeness of the soul, which recognizes itself in him. . . .

Our main purpose . . . has been achieved if it has become clear that the Gospel of John presupposes the redemption-myth we have outlined above and is only comprehensible against its background. Though the sources that bear witness to the myth may be later than the Gospel of John, nevertheless there can be no doubt about the greater age of the myth as compared with the Johannine Gospel. No one who studies the texts in question can entertain the notion that that mythology, elaborate and multiform despite its basic uniformity of thought, developed out of John's Gospel. . . . The conclusive proof . . . emerges when one observes that [in John] is lacking a decisive part of the redemption-myth without which it is basically unintelligible: the idea of the parallelism between or even the identity of the Redeemer with the redeemed (the one or the many). It is just this . . . idea . . . that is missing in the Gospel of John. Very closely related to this lack is the fact that the Johannine Gospel is interested neither in cosmology and anthropology, nor in the fate of the soul. That myth rests, in fact, on a definite view of man as a particle of light which derives from the heavenly world and is imprisoned in matter, and this view in turn is related to a cosmology that understands the creation of this world and of man as the result of a conflict between light and darkness. Above all, however, a major interest in the fate of the soul after death resides in the realm of that myth; the myth is concerned with how the soul may complete its journey to the world of light. . . . All that is lacking in the Gospel of John. And it is consequently evident that we must regard the ideas and images of that myth as the material from which the Gospel of John constructed its picture. The myth is what is primitive. . . .

We may add that, as is well known, individual traces of the myth may be detected and inferred in the pre-Christian era. I remind you in brief of the figure of the "Man" in Jewish apocalyptic, of the figure of "Wisdom" in Jewish speculation, and of the "Man"-speculation in the writings of Philo and of Paul.

All this has not yet solved what at the beginning we called the second puzzle of the Gospel of John, but it has brought the solution nearer. Within the framework of the myth, the revelation that the emissary brings is limited to the fact that he is the Revealer, has come from the heavenly world, and returns to the heavenly world. It can so limit itself because the one who is sent, the Redeemer, and the redeemed stand in fact in the actual relationship of parallelism or identity. . . . Therefore the one who is sent needs to reveal nothing but his own person. In so doing he reveals to the believers what they need to know for their salvation. So then, it is understandable to begin with that the Johannine evangelist, who sketches his picture within the framework, and with the materials, of the myth, has no occasion to put special revelations into the mouth of his Jesus. And yet this answer is only half-satisfactory, for that decisive and basic idea of the identity of the Redeemer with the redeemed, as well as the reflection on the fate of the soul, is lacking in the Gospel of John. All this seems to make the puzzle of the Johannine Gospel even greater. At the same time, however, it becomes clearer. The author is interested only in the *fact* of the revelation, not in the *content*. . . . But there remains still another possibility, namely, that the idea of revelation is construed radically, that is to say, that no attempt is made to describe its content, whether by speculative propositions or conceptions based on psychic states, because both would reduce revelation to the sphere of the human. We cannot say of God.

how he is, but only *that* he is. . . . The contrast between the revelation and "sound human understanding" extends throughout the whole Gospel. The numerous misunderstandings in the dialogue are not a technique of the author, but are deeply rooted in his conception of revelation. Revelation can be represented only as the destruction of all that is human, as the rejection of all human questions, as the refusal of all human answers, as the casting of doubt upon man's very being.

The exegetical significance of the Mandaean and related texts now seemed so apparent that numerous studies which made use of these texts for the interpretation of New Testament writings appeared in rapid succession. The Göttingen New Testament scholar **Walter Bauer** published a commentary on the Gospel of John which appeared at almost the same time as Bultmann's essay. In it he argued that there was a Judaizing gnosis in addition to the pre-Christian pagan gnosis, that we find in Mandaeanism a "very original form of syncretistic gnosis which developed independently of Christianity," and that the Gospel of John and Mandaeanism "must both have sprung from the same milieu of thought and share in the same store of ideas, symbols, and images, and more generally of religious outlook and language." [429] When E. Lohmeyer in his commentary on the Revelation of John referred to the oriental myth of the primal man (see above, pp. 349-50), he documented this myth likewise with Mandaean texts. And soon after this **Hans Windisch,** a New Testament scholar at Kiel, made use of the Mandaean writings in his interpretation of the Letter to the Hebrews because "the foundation of the Mandaean religion is an oriental gnosis that fused very early with a Jewish and then with a Christianized gnosis." As a result, the Mandaean writings can "serve as oriental commentaries." [430] The discovery of the oriental-mythical background of parts of the New Testament deepened the insight into the historical conditioning of the New Testament message, but at the same time also created the possibility of a penetrating answer to the question of the meaning of this message.[431]

This continuation of the work of R. Reitzenstein, W. Bousset, and others seemed to have opened up a new and very promising way of helping us to understand the history of early Christianity and its world of thought. However, it also gave rise at once to a vigorous opposition, both generally and in terms of specific issues. **Karl Holl,** the church historian at Berlin who was known in particular as an authority on Luther, delivered a lecture in 1925 on "Urchristentum und Religionsgeschichte" [Early Christianity and the history of religion] in which he asserted that, despite all pagan influences on the ancient church, Christianity was by no means a syncretistic religion, but by virtue of Jesus' message about God, was from the beginning something new. He even disputed the conclusion that Paul at essential points had been influenced by Hellenism.

Consequently the use of Hellenistic parallels seemed quite unnecessary for a pertinent answer to the question of what is singular in early Christianity.[432]

Although certain deletions and abbreviations may be made in matters of detail, what is essential seems nevertheless assured: the ideas of redemption and judgment, of Kyrios ["Lord"] worship and Kyrios mysticism, of sacramentalism and the religious orientation of public worship—all this Christianity has in common with other religions. Accordingly, the judgment seems well-founded. Christianity is a syncretistic religion; it did not become so for the first time in the second or the fourth century, but was so from the beginning. At least as early as Paul's time, but basically already with Jesus. Or, as someone has put it even more bluntly: only the names changed; the matter remained the same.

For all that, at the very moment when Christianity is resolved in this way into its constituents it seems to me that a question arises that cannot be dismissed: *what then enabled Christianity to triumph over the other religions?* I regard it as the most serious defect of contemporary history-of-religions research that it almost completely ignores this simple question. . . .

And yet it is a fact, a fact that is obvious to all, not only that Christianity in the end remained alone in the field, but also that its adherents as compared with the representatives of all other religions, always felt themselves to be something apart. Such a fact must surely have its reasons. . . .

At some point there must be an error in the whole calculation. There is one, at any rate, and it occurs right at the beginning. At least so far as it concerns Christianity, the whole approach is from the wrong point of view. It looks everywhere only for similarities and believes that by so doing it can ascertain the essence of Christianity. But the force of religion never consists in what it has in common with others, but in what is peculiar to itself. Christianity can only have *triumphed* by virtue of something that *distinguished it plainly* and set it apart *as religion;* by something quite special, leaving out of consideration whatever stamp it placed on what it borrowed. . . .

Jesus proclaims . . . a God *who is concerned about sinful man;* in fact, to whom one who is brought low by circumstances stands particularly close. . . .

So then, if one wishes to treat Christianity under the common designation of a religion of redemption, one must immediately add that in this instance we have to do with an idea of redemption of a quite unique kind. In all other doctrines of redemption, faith in deliverance is based on the conviction of man's indestructible nobility or on a belief in a metaphysical homogeneity of the soul with God: the divine in man must finally enter into its own. In contrast to this, Jesus sees a deep gulf between God and man. . . .

A faith in God as Jesus preached it, according to which God gives himself to the *sinner*—this was the death of all serious moral effort; this was nothing other than blasphemy. That is why the Jews crucified Jesus. . . .

Jesus' idea of God, therefore, is certainly *new*. It flew in the face of all that serious moral reflection had come to believe concerning the relation of God to man and that sound human understanding to this very day thinks of alone as right. It is all the more amazing, then, that Jesus once again grounds an ethic—and the strictest imaginable sort of an ethic at that—on this very idea of God that seemingly dissolves all morality. . . .

But if in this way Jesus stands alone and unique as an innovator, is it then not *Paul* who involved Christianity in syncretism?

Scholars today paint for us a picture of Paul in which the Jew Paul has as good as disappeared and has been replaced with the Hellenist. . . .

In all this I cannot suppress the suspicion that present-day scholars only represent that in Paul as vital which seems in some way acceptable or intelligible to themselves. In any case, Paul thought of himself otherwise than they conceive him. He felt himself as much opposed to Hellenism as to Judaism. He it was, in fact, who coined the saying about the Cross: "a stumbling-block to Jews and folly to Gentiles." With reference to Hellenism, then, he sees himself separated from it by a broad gulf. And I believe that Paul, too, like every historical personality, is entitled to demand that he be understood in the first instance as he understood himself. . . .

The entrance to the deepest levels of Paul's thought is blocked when one seeks to understand his views in light of Hellenistic ideas. Reitzenstein went that way, having described it as methodologically the only right one. He believes that he is able to show "that all passages in Paul which deal with πνεῦμα ["spirit"] can be explained by Hellenistic usage." But he failed utterly, in fact he did not even try, to derive from Hellenism the *moral content* that unquestionably for Paul was bound up with his view of πνεῦμα. . . .

Reitzenstein's demand that we begin with Hellenistic linguistic usage would be justified if Paul had been able to borrow the concept of πνεῦμα only from books. But the fact is that Paul knows πνεῦμα—not the "concept" of πνεῦμα, but πνεῦμα itself—*from life;* from the life of the primitive Church, where πνεῦμα was present only as a *reality.* . . . To this that for him was *obviously* the given, Paul makes his own peculiar contribution, and in light of it, then, he is in the first instance to be understood.

The consciousness of possessing the Spirit was wholly native to the early Church itself, having originated quite independently of any foreign pattern. The impulse to it came . . . from the appearances of Christ. . . .

If Paul's teaching as a whole is laid beside the preaching of Jesus, we can but wonder at the sureness with which Paul, who had never heard Jesus speak, nevertheless grasped the decisive elements in his gospel. To be sure, everything is expressed theologically, but no one in the early Church grasped the meaning that lay embedded in Jesus' thought of God so fully as he. But to say this is also to say that, even if everything were to hold true that these days is asserted concerning Hellenistic influence on Paul, Paul would not therefore be the one who delivered Christianity into the arms of Hellenism. On the contrary, it was he who preserved Christianity from submersion in Hellenism.

Adolf von Harnack [433] agreed heartily with K. Holl, promptly declaring his article to be "the best discussion of a major problem of early Christian history that has been published during the last generation." Harnack therewith renewed his earlier rejection of the conclusions of the history-of-religions school by seeking to link exclusively to late Jewish piety not only early Christian belief in the Resurrection, but also Pauline and Johannine theology, and to derive everything essential in early Christian faith and life from the Church's own experience. In all this he completely disregarded the most recent theses of the influence of Jewish gnosis.[434]

It is a widespread opinion today, and one that is regarded as the judgment of scholarly research, that the proclamation of Jesus as the crucified and risen Savior, as the supernaturally begotten Son of God, and as the Prince of life who descended into the realm of the dead and ascended into heaven, had its origin in myths which were widespread at that time as we know. If this judgment is legitimate, so far as it relates to the first article (the Death and Resurrection), it means the end of historical Christianity, though the Gospel of Jesus remains untouched, at least in part; in comparison with it, the other two articles are of subordinate importance.

Investigation of when and in what way the main articles of the Christian confession arose, however, contradicts the hypothesis that it is to be explained by the taking over of the myth of a god who had died and been revived. Rather, it rests originally on itself, that is to say, on facts that were really experienced; for Jesus Christ was a real person and really died—died, in fact, a death on the Cross, something no myth had anticipated; . . . and his disciples saw him, and had no doubts of the reality of the vision. And there is not the slightest evidence that these visions were suggested by a myth that had long been familiar to the disciples. On the contrary, no tradition leads us to assume that in the circles from which Peter and the first disciples came, or in the contemporary pious Judaism of Palestine, such a myth was known at all, or even had any place within religion. . . .

Only when the singular and astonishing character of the experience has been clearly recognized is there any justification for the further question of whether in the course of the development the ancient, widespread, and multiformed myth of the god who had died and been revived . . . gained any influence on Christian faith and worship. This question is to be answered in the affirmative. . . .

But even the articles of faith concerning the supernaturally born Son of God and the Prince of life who descended into the world of the dead and ascended into heaven did not *originate* from borrowed myths. . . .

Paul was a theologian who seized upon his own inner experience and made it the point of departure of his theological thinking.

He was a Jewish thinker—living in the Old Testament, a product of Pharisaism—both when he investigated the facts of the case and when he advanced his arguments. He was influenced only secondarily by the language of the Greek Mysteries—probably not at all by the Mysteries themselves—and by the popular idealistic philosophy of the Greeks. He did not derive from them his assiduous quest for knowledge.

At the center heart of his message, he place reconciliation to God as Jesus preached it and consequently the person of Jesus, through whose work the elect are justified. The statement is untenable that he came up with a finished Christology about Jesus that had originated in late Jewish dogmatics: in the first place because he had no finished Christology at his disposal, and in the second place because the conviction that Jesus now reigns as the Exalted One was obtained by him from the image and activity of the historical Jesus (sovereignty in humility), from his work of obedience, crowned by his death on the Cross, and from his Resurrection. . . .

During the two generations after Paul there was but one theologian . . . *That one* was John. . . . Despite its background of difficult problems, John's theology, presupposing the basic elements of Paulinism, was a mystical fugue on great themes about the "grace and truth" that were brought into being by the incarnation of the Son of God. . . . Furthermore, back of John's theology, just as back of Paul's, lies the apostle's own Christian experience as point of departure and object, but Paul knew how to develop it in a psychologically gripping manner. This John was unable to do. He expressed it in profound abstractions, whose precise meaning he left to like-minded souls to determine. He is misunderstood, however, when an attempt is made to develop a gnostic metaphysical system from these abstractions. They are construed wholly in religious terms and have only certain stock phrases in common with the idealistic philosophy of the age and with the wisdom of the Oriental Mysteries—stock phrases that have a different meaning and purpose in Johannine than in Greek or oriental usage. Johannine theology is Christian mysticism; however, its native soil is not the Greek philosophy of religion, but late Jewish piety and mysticism.

But even where the integration of the early Christian world of thought into its contemporary history-of-religions setting was not so fundamentally repudiated, the use of the Mandaean texts, and with that the assumption of the influence of the oriental redeemer-myth and of Jewish gnosis on the New Testament were frequently vigorously protested, as well by critical theologians as by conservatives. The important Catholic exegete **Marie-Joseph Lagrange** (1928) conceded the great age of the Mandaean religion, to be sure, but wanted to account for every contact between the Gospel of John and the Mandaean texts by postulating the dependence of the Mandaeans on John's Gospel: "The divine emissary of the Gospel of John and that of the Mandaeans have no really impressive similarity, except when the Mandaeans have in mind the Gospel tradition, particularly that of the Fourth Gospel." And from this Lagrange drew the conclusion that the Gospel of John "was not dominated by a gnosis which was the root of both the Johannine Gospel and of Mandaeanism. They move in two different worlds." [435] Similarly the Protestant critic **Maurice Goguel** (see pp. 293 ff.) (1928) protested that "for several years a kind of Mandaean fever seems to have gripped a part of German criticism";[436] and even **Alfred Loisy,** the radical critic of the history-of-religions school (see pp. 299 ff.), declared (1934): "Mandaeanism as such has no bearing on the discussion of Christian beginnings: it is itself to be understood only in light of developed, long-established Christianity" and wanted only to admit that "the predecessors of the Mandaean gnosis to a rather significant extent preceded Christianity and influenced its development." [437] But what made the greatest impression was a brief "Beitrag zur Mandäerfrage" [Contribution to the Mandaean question] by **Hans Lietzmann** (1930), the scholar who succeeded to the chair at Berlin which A. Harnack had held and who was noted for his strictly philological and scientific studies of religion. By presenting evidence that the accounts from the Mandaean texts about John the Baptist were first introduced into the Mandaean writings in the Byzantine-Arabian era and that the Mandaean baptism is dependent on the Syrian Christian baptismal ritual, he sought to prove that the Mandaean religion has no roots in pre-Christian times, and consequently has nothing to contribute to our knowledge of the gnostic presuppositions of early Christianity.[488]

The Mandaeans have no connection whatever with the disciples of John; the extant writings, as well as their ritual practices, have been strongly influenced by the developed Christianity of the Church. They cannot be regarded in any way as witnesses to a movement existing since the days of primitive Christianity. This can be demonstrated. . . .

The name of John the Baptist and the stories about him occur only in the Arabian period, in the latest stratum of Mandaean literature. . . . From this it necessarily follows that the figure of John was taken over into the Mandaean religious fantasy first in Byzantine-Arabian times and under Christian influence. Accordingly, there can be no talk of a historical connection of the sect with the disciples of John.

The entire complex of rites of Mandaean baptism is an imitation of the baptismal ritual of the Syrian Christians. . . .

The celebration of Sunday makes it probable that impulses from Christianity determined the form of their religion as it lies before us. . . . In later times—perhaps as late as the Arabian era—an older oriental-gnostic religion was permeated in several stages by a Nestorian Christianity bereft of content and thus was transformed into a syncretistic Christian gnosis. This admonishes us to exercise the greatest care in our analysis of the texts, and wholly invalidates the uncritical employment of all their strata for the interpretation of the New Testament—a practice that is only too common in our day. The Mandaean texts enable us to study the Christianization of an oriental gnosis, rather than the gnostic foundations of early Christianity.

This judgment of Lietzmann's seemed to many to give the coup de grace to the use of Mandaean texts in particular, and to the assumption of an oriental-Jewish gnosis in general, for the explanation of certain parts of the New Testament world of thought. Even R. Bultmann admitted to having been convinced by Lietzmann's evidence that Mandaeanism *in the form we know it* represents a late religious form, dependent on Syrian Christianity, but added quite properly: "The question of whether the analysis of the Mandaean body of writings can make probable or establish an ancient gnostic tradition is one that has not been silenced by Lietzmann's findings." [489] In fact, the question of an oriental-Jewish gnosis as the native soil of a part of the New Testament ideological world continued to be discussed and became important for other New Testament writings in addition to the Johannine,[440] for the similarities in language and in the world of thought cannot be denied and demand a satisfactory explanation.

The question of the nature and the origin of a Jewish gnosis and its relation to early Christianity now entered an entirely new phase beginning in 1947 with the discovery of the literary remains of a Jewish sect in the caves at Qumran on the Dead Sea.[441] Although the publication, translation, and interpretation of these extensive texts is still in progress, as is the determination of the historical relationships of the life and teachings of this community, it can nevertheless now be said that the basic views of this Jewish group, either a community of Essenes or of a closely related sect, correspond closely to all that we have learned earlier from Mandaean and Jewish texts about a Jewish gnosis,[442] except that in this *Jewish* form of the gnosis we do not again encounter the myth of the divine emissary that can be detected in the Mandaean texts and that also lies behind the Gospel of John. The efforts since the First World War to advance our knowledge of important parts of the New Testament by the discovery of the oriental-Jewish redeemer-myth and of a Jewish gnosis have therefore taken on today a new currency, without, however, having led as yet to sure and generally accepted results.

In the interest of a really *objective* understanding of the New Testament world of thought and in order to determine its *singularity,* the need of setting the New Testament in broad outline in its religio-spiritual historical milieu now also led at the beginning of the thirties to a new scientific undertaking, the preparation of the *Theologisches Wörterbuch zum Neuen Testament* [Theological dictionary of the New Testament]. It was not A. Deissmann's efforts to find the place of the language of the New Testament writers within the Greek of its day and thereby to explain it which provided the stimulus to this new work.[443] As early as 1928 **Walter Bauer** had already brilliantly met Deissmann's demand for a New Testament dictionary which would do justice to our knowledge of Greek lexicography and linguistic science, and he continued to enlarge and improve it in subsequent editions.[444] The new cooperative venture, initiated by **Gerhard Kittel,** is rather in the succession of Cremer's *Biblisch-theologisches Wörterbuch der Neutestamentlichen Gräcität* [Biblical-theological dictionary of New Testament Greek idioms].[445] But while Cremer wished to illuminate "the language of the Holy Spirit," the *Theological Dictionary* undertakes the more modest task of "making apparent . . . the new content of individual concepts" by means of *"intrinsic* lexicography." [446] The methodological presuppositions that were basic to this new undertaking are best set forth by G. Kittel, the editor, in his inaugural address at Tübingen, published (1926) a few years before the appearance of the first volume of the work (1933, the dictionary is not yet complete). Although Kittel himself had devoted his attention especially to research into the relation of early Christianity to Palestinian Judaism (see above, pp. 343 ff.), he expressly emphasizes in this lecture that the historical setting of the New Testament requires consideration of its Hellenistic, as well as of its Palestinian-Jewish, environment and that early Christianity took over many things from the Hellenistic religions. To be sure, he qualifies this statement by adding that Hellenism only lent color to early Christianity, whereas early Christianity was aware of itself as the fulfillment of Judaism. Finally Kittel declares that the demonstration of the essential nature of early Christian religion is the ultimate goal of the indispensable comparison of history-of-religions material.[447]

In a peculiar way Christianity is a religion of *two* cultures. Its homeland is Palestine; its native folk, Jewry. But the area in which it expanded is Asia Minor, Greece, Egypt, Italy: the world of Hellenism. . . . Necessarily, then, all historical description of the cultural setting and religious background of the New Testament has two concerns: the Palestinian environment and the Hellenistic environment. . . .

While it must be insisted that both factors, Judaism and Hellenism, are unconditionally important for early Christianity, it must be emphasized just as strongly that this importance and this influence are in both instances structurally of a wholly different order. . . .

Whenever contacts, adjustments, and mutual influences took place between early Christianity and Hellenism, the phenomenon is wholly of the same order as must always occur and reoccur wherever a religion penetrates a distinct but completely foreign cultural area. Because religion is an affair of living men, the garment it wears must bear the colors characteristic of its milieu. . . .

The interaction between primitive Christianity and Hellenism belongs to this whole category.

The relation to late Judaism, however, is something different, wholly and in every respect. It is the relation to that culture which is the bearer of tradition for the new religion—but the bearer of tradition of something which is more than the mere color of its coat, of something that constitutes its own innermost sanctuary. The interaction here is very varied and preeminently a critical and combative one, both in Jesus' case as in the instances of Paul and John. But this critical attitude is not, as it is in relation to paganism, one that radically disavows the other religion. On the contrary, in all its struggle its only wish is to rediscover the roots that lie below the rank overgrowth and excrescences, that is to say, the divine promise and the divine purpose enunciated by Mosaic and prophetic religion, and from this point of vantage to complete and fulfill them. . . .

If we thus locate the New Testament in the context of its environment, what, then, is the meaning of this undertaking? Naturally a manifold one: We recognize the linguistic, the historical, the cultural, and the literary relationships and limitations that were put at the disposal of emergent Christianity. But naturally the ultimate significance in this instance, as in all historical research closely related to life, is and remains the wish by comparison to discover more clearly and distinctly the actual and singular nature of the historical phenomenon. And that for theology means the kernel and essence of early Christian religion. . . .

Consequently the meaning of all work in the field of comparative religion as it affects early Christianity ultimately is not to deprive early Christianity of its singularity, but to emphasize it.

As a result almost all the articles of the *Theological Dictionary*, articles on all religiously significant words of the Greek New Testament by a great many different scholars, are so constructed that an account of the development of the respective words and concepts in the Old Testament and in late Judaism is followed by a corresponding section on Greek and Hellenistic usage. The contribution of both sections serves to bring out the distinctiveness of the New Testament idea. It is almost inevitable that a large number of the contributors should not only differ in their estimate of the history-of-religions influences on early Christian thought, but should also vary greatly in their judgment of the relationships of the various concepts to Hellenism. But it was rightly said as early as the appearance of the first volume that "the authors of this work at least agree that the language of the New Testament is thoroughly permeated and transformed by the Christian spirit and Christian thought in its historical development." [448] Accordingly, then, the new form of history-of-religions study of the New Testament, just as the new way of posing literary questions, is revealed as a part of the effort to understand what is meant by the *central concern* of the New Testament, and of this transition to a theological consideration of the New Testament after World War I we shall have to speak in the following and concluding section of this history of New Testament research.

3.
The New Emphasis on Theological Interpretation

Already at the beginning of our century, when the history-of-religions and the radical historical-critical schools of New Testament research were at the height of their influence, opposition had arisen both from critical and from conservative scholars, not only to individual results of such critical work, but also to the fundamentally presuppositionless approach to the New Testament that was characteristic of it (see above, pp. 309 ff.). But it was not until the catastrophe of the First World War and the cultural and scientific crisis which it precipitated [449] that the demand for a theological approach to the New Testament found a lively echo.[450] The decisive impetus to New Testament research in this direction came actually from outside the ranks of professional New Testament exegetes. In 1919 the Swiss pastor **Karl Barth,** once a pupil of A. Harnack and an assistant editor of *Die Christliche Welt* [The Christian world],[451] the most influential organ of free Protestantism, published a commentary on the Letter to the Romans that owed its genesis to the preacher's need of interpreting the biblical text, a need that had gone unmet "because at the University [the author] had never been brought beyond that well-known 'Awe in the presence of History' which means in the end no more than that all hope of engaging in the dignity of understanding and interpretation has been surrendered." [452] In the preface Barth characterized historical biblical research as only prolegomena, demanded that we endeavor to see "through and beyond history into the spirit of the Bible," and then offered an interpretation that did not inquire about Paul's message to his original readers, but related the biblical text directly to the situation in which modern man finds himself. From lectures delivered about the same time it is even more apparent that in his exegesis Barth wished to allow the Bible to speak, not as a collection of human documents, but as the Word of God itself.[453]

Paul, as a child of his age, addressed his contemporaries. It is, however, far more important that, as Prophet and Apostle of the Kingdom of God, he veritably speaks to all men of every age. The differences between then and now, there and here, no doubt require careful investigation and consideration. But the purpose of such investigation can only be to demonstrate that these differences are, in fact, purely trivial. The historical-critical method of Biblical research has its rightful place: it is concerned with the preparation of the intelligence—and this can never be superfluous. But, were I driven to choose between it and the venerable doctrine of Inspiration, I should without hesitation adopt the latter, which has a broader, deeper, more important justification. The doctrine of Inspiration is concerned with the labor of apprehending, without which no technical equipment, however complete, is of any use whatever. Fortunately, I am not compelled to choose between the two. Nevertheless, my whole energy of interpreting has been expended in an endeavour to see through and beyond history into the spirit of the Bible, which is the Eternal Spirit. What was once of grave importance, is so still. What is to-day of grave importance—and not merely crotchety and incidental—stands in direct connection with that ancient gravity. If we rightly understand ourselves, our problems are the problems of Paul; and if we be enlightened by the brightness of his answers, those answers must be ours. . . .

The understanding of history is an uninterrupted conversation between the wisdom of yesterday and the wisdom of to-morrow. . . .

It is certain that in the past men who hungered and thirsted after righteousness naturally recognized that they were bound to labor with Paul. They could not remain unmoved spectators in his presence. Perhaps we too are entering upon such a time. Should this be so, this book may even now be of some definite, though limited, service. The reader will detect for himself that it has been written with a joyful sense of discovery. The mighty voice of Paul was new to me: and if to me, no doubt to many others also. And yet, now that my work is finished, I perceive that much remains which I have not heard and into which I have not as yet penetrated. My book is therefore no more than a preliminary undertaking. Further co-operation is necessary. . . .

It is not the right human thoughts about God which form the content of the Bible, but the right divine thoughts about men. The Bible tells us not how we should talk with God but what he says to us; not how we find the way to him, but how he has sought and found the way to us; not the right relation in which we must place ourselves to him, but the covenant which he has made with all who are Abraham's spiritual children and which he has sealed once and for all in Jesus Christ. It is this which is within the Bible. The word of God is within the Bible. . . .

The Bible is the literary monument of an ancient tribal religion and of a Hellenistic cultic religion of the Near East. A human document like any other, it can lay no *a priori* dogmatic claim to special attention and consideration. This judgment, announced in every tongue and believed in every territory, we take for granted today. We need not continue trying to break through an open door. And when now we turn our serious though somewhat dispassionate attention to the objective content of the Bible, we shall not do so in a way to provoke religious enthusiasm and scientific indignation to another battle against "stark orthodoxy" and "dead belief in the letter." For it is too clear that intelligent and fruitful discussion of the Bible begins when the judgment as to its human, its historical and psychological character has been made and *put behind* us. Would that the teachers of our high and lower schools, and with them the progressive element among the clergy of our established churches, would forthwith resolve to have done with a battle that once had its time but now has really *had* it! The special *content* of this human document, the remarkable *something* with which the writers of these stories and those who stood behind them were concerned, the Biblical *object*—this is the question that will engage and engross us today. . . .

It is the peculiarity of Biblical *thought and speech* that they flow from a source which is above religious antinomies. The Bible treats, for instance, of both creation and redemption, grace and judgment, nature and spirit, earth and heaven, promise and fulfillment. To be sure, it enters now upon this and now upon that side of its antitheses, but it never brings them pedantically to an end; it never carries on into consequences; it never hardens, either in the thesis or in the antithesis; it never stiffens into positive or negative finalities. . . . It always finds as much and as little in the Yes as in the No; for the truth lies not in the Yes and not in the No but in the knowledge of the beginning from which the Yes and the No arise. . . . Biblical dogmatics are fundamentally the suspension of all dogmatics. The Bible has only *one* theological interest and that is not speculative: interest in God himself.

The reaction to this new kind of interpretation was sharp. Our interest lies, however, not in the voices that maintain that Barth misrepresents Paul's ideas,[454] but in the reservations with respect to Barth's nonhistorical method of interpretation as a whole. **Hans Windisch** admitted that the book had "a genuinely prophetic ring," but went on to say that "the Eternal Spirit" which Barth wished to apprehend was actually the spirit "which actuates the author." [455] **Adolf Jülicher** raised more basic objections, accusing Barth of an actual rejection of history and of putting himself before Paul.[456]

Karl Barth is a man of two worlds. Two souls are at war with one another in his breast. One of these also knows that the interpretation of a very difficult text from most ancient times, preserved in a foreign language, regardless of what matters the text deals with, is a task that can be carried out only with all the aids of a widely ramified science, with the deepest possible immersion also in the ever instructive process of its development, and in whose performance we have to take into consideration both lacunae in the transmission of the text and obscurities in its presentation, if not actually of discrepancies and contradictions in the author's ideas. And the other, for which the understanding of a book of the Bible is limited to the citizens of the new world, e.g., Karl Barth, and for which it is absurd, for example, to write a book about Christians and sin in which there is still room only for the Christians and grace; for the kingdom of God which was destroyed by the Fall of man is now restored once more by God's faithfulness in full purity in the Risen Christ. Barth formulates his point of view in order that, as one which stands above historical criticism and above the doctrine of inspiration, it will hopefully enable him to see through the historical into the spirit of the Bible, which is the Eternal Spirit. By this he means to say that the others before him only apprehended the historical element [in Scripture]; he proceeds, not contrary to the historical element, but through and beyond it to the spirit. . . . The great gifts of the author enable him to make a powerful impression with his translation of the Pauline world of ideas into the present. Because he is so aware of what he wishes to do and of what the thrust and core of truth mean to him, and because he has learned how to move the spirits [of men], he forces Paul in his entirety into his frame of reference. He believes he is taking his place beside the Apostle, while the rest of us calmly take our stand over against him as observers; that he quite often puts himself in front of Paul is a fact he declines to note. . . . One will indeed gain much, possibly very much, from this book for an understanding of our times, but scarcely anything new at all for an understanding of the "historical" Paul.

But within two years after its publication **Barth** was able to bring out a second, revised edition of his commentary "in which the original has been so carefully rewritten that it may be claimed that no stone remains in its old place." Once more, by its debate with critics, the preface to the second edition shows very clearly what is Barth's concern: The historical interpretation presented in earlier works cannot really be called interpretation in any sense of the word; the task, rather, is to arrive at a perception of the *inner dialectic of the matter* by making the wall between then and now as transparent as possible. The "inner dialectic of the matter" which it is our task to apprehend, Barth now called the " 'infinite qualitative distinction' between time and eternity, and thereby showed that he looked for an understanding of the text with a quite definite theological presupposition in mind. This is also apparent from a lecture delivered about the same time in which he disputed the right of theology, including New Testament interpretation, to be a science like other sciences, and regarded its task as one of articulating the Word of God.[457]

This second . . . edition also is concerned only with prolegomena. . . . There can be no completed work. All human achievements are no more than prolegomena; and this is especially the case in the field of theology. . . .

This book does not claim to be more than fragments of a conversation between theologians: It is quite irrelevant when Jülicher and Eberhard Vischer announce triumphantly that I am—a theologian. I have never pretended to be anything else. The point at issue is the kind of theology which is required. Those who urge us to shake ourselves free from theology and to think—and more particularly to speak and write—only what is immediately intelligible to the general public seem to me to be suffering from a kind of hysteria and to be entirely without discernment. Is it not preferable that those who venture to speak in public, or to write for the public, should first seek a better understanding of the theme they wish to propound? . . .

I earnestly desire to speak simply of those matters with which the Epistle to the Romans is concerned; and, were someone competent to do this to appear, my work would at once be superseded. I am in no way bound to my book and to my theology. As yet, however, those who claim to speak "simply" seem to me to be—simply speaking about something else. By such simplicity I remain unconvinced.

I have been accused of being an "enemy of historical criticism." Such language seems to me nervous and high-strung. Would it not be better to discuss the point at issue quite calmly? I have, it is true, protested against recent commentaries upon the Epistle to the Romans. . . . [But] I have nothing whatever to say against historical criticism. I recognize it, and once more state quite definitely that it is both necessary and justified. My complaint is that recent commentators confine themselves to an interpretation of the text which seems to me to be no commentary at all, but merely the first step towards a commentary. Recent commentaries contain no more than a reconstruction of the text, a rendering of the Greek words and phrases by their precise equivalents, a number of additional notes in which archaeological and philological material is gathered together, and a more or less plausible arrangement of the subject-matter in such a manner that it may be made historically and psychologically intelligible from the standpoint of pure pragmatism. . . . Even such an elementary attempt at interpretation is not an exact science. Exact scientific knowledge, so far as the Epistle to the Romans is concerned, is limited to the deciphering of manuscripts and the making of a concordance. Historians do not wish, and rightly do not wish, to be confined within such narrow limits. Jülicher and Lietzmann, not to mention conservative scholars, intend quite clearly to press beyond this preliminary work to an understanding of Paul. Now, this involves more than a mere repetition in Greek or in German of what Paul says: it involves the reconsideration of what is set out in the Epistle, until the actual meaning of it is disclosed. It is at this point that the difference between us appears. There is no difference of opinion with regard to the need of applying historical criticism as a prolegomenon to the understanding of the Epistle. So long as the critic is occupied in this preliminary work I follow him carefully and gratefully. . . . When, however, I examine their attempts at genuine understanding and interpretation, I am again and again surprised how little they even claim for their work. . . . For example, place the work of Jülicher side by side with that of Calvin: how energetically Calvin, having first established what stands in the text, sets himself to re-think the whole material and to wrestle with it, till the walls which separate the sixteenth century from the first become transparent! Paul speaks, and the man of the sixteenth century hears. The conversation between the original record and the reader moves round the subject-matter, until a distinction between yesterday and to-day becomes impossible. . . . The critical historian needs to be more critical. The interpretation of what is written requires more than a disjointed series of notes on words and phrases. The commentator must be possessed of a wider intelligence than that which moves within the boundaries of his own natural appreciation. True apprehension can be achieved only by a strict determination to face, as far as possible without rigidity of mind, the tension displayed more or less clearly in the ideas written in the text. . . . Intelligent comment means that I am driven on till I stand with nothing before me but the enigma of the matter; till the document seems hardly to exist as a document; till I have almost forgotten that I am not its author; till I know the author so well that I allow him to speak in my name and am even able to speak in his name myself. . . .

What, then, do I mean when I say that a perception of the "inner dialectic of the matter" in the actual words of the text is a necessary and prime requirement for their understanding and interpretation? . . . I know that I have laid myself open to the charge of imposing a meaning upon the text rather than extracting its meaning from it, and and that my method implies this. My reply is that, if I have a system, it is limited to a recognition of what Kierkegaard called the "infinite qualitative distinction" between time and eternity, and to my regarding this as possessing negative as well as positive significance: "God is in heaven, and thou art on earth." The relation between such a God and such a man and the relation between such a man and such a God, is for me the theme of the Bible and the essence of philosophy. . . . Questioned as to the ground of my assumption that this was, in fact, Paul's theme, I answer by asking quite simply whether, if the Epistle is to be treated seriously at all, it is reasonable to approach it with any other assumption than that God is God. . . . Paul knows about God what most of us do not know; and his Epistles enable us to know what he knew. It is this conviction that Paul "knows" that my critics choose to name my "system," my "dogmatic presupposition."

Precisely as a member of the *universitas literarum,* theology is a signal, a distress signal that something is out of order. There is an academic need which in the last analysis, as might be inferred, is the same as the general human need we have already described. Genuine science is confessedly *un*certain of itself— uncertain not simply of this point or that, but of its *fundamental* and ultimate *presupposition* . . . . And a question mark *is* actually the ultimate fact of each of the sciences.

So the university has a bad conscience, or an anxious one, and tolerates theology within its walls; and though it may be somewhat vexed at the want of reserve shown by the theologians when they deliberately ask about a matter that cannot with propriety be mentioned, yet, if I am not mistaken, it is secretly glad that some one is willing to be so unscientific as to talk aloud and distinctly about the undemonstrable central Fact upon which all other facts depend—and so to suggest that the whole academic system may have a meaning. Whatever the individual opinion of this or that non-theological academician may be, there is a general expectation that theology will attend to its duties and give an answer (let him beware of doing it too well!) to what for the others takes the shape of a question mark in the background of their secret thought. He does his duty when he represents as a *possibility* what others have known only as an impossibility or a concept of limitation, and so he is expected not to whisper and mumble about God, but to *speak* of him: not merely to hint of him, but to know him and *witness* to him; not to leave him somewhere in the background, but to disregard the universal method of scholarship and place him in the foreground. . . .

As a science like other sciences theology has *no* right to its place in the university; for it becomes then a wholly unnecessary duplication of disciplines belonging to the other faculties. . . .

To assign a proper place to our task in the totality of human life, nature and culture is possible only if one can at the same time assign a place for this totality within the world and creation of God. But from the human viewpoint this question must forever remain a question. And so our task must be assigned to the place of the unassignable. . . .

And it must be equally well remembered as we look toward our task that only God *himself* can speak of God. The task of theology is the word of God. This spells the certain defeat of all theology and every theologian.

Because it made a dialectical separation between God and the world and depreciated history, this new "attempt" at understanding the "actual meaning" of the Letter to the Romans also roused vigorous criticism of its content.[458] More important, however, was the renewed charge by **Adolf Jülicher** that the book was "an act of violence perpetrated on the sacred documents" which "has its origin in the *hubris* [= pride] of the pneumatic [= one who believes himself guided by the Spirit,]" because "genuine scholarship" can ascertain "what the writer wanted to say" only "by the same methods . . . that it uses to determine the text." [459] This clearly raised the question of which way can lead to an *objective* understanding of the biblical text. But most important of all, the methodological correctness of this manner of interpretation was put into question, which in turn focused serious attention again on the long neglected hermeneutical problem. **Rudolf Bultmann,** who declared himself "quite at one" with Barth "in the conception of the task of the interpretation of the text," saw himself compelled to say that this "commentary does violence to the individual life of the Letter to the Romans and to the riches that are Paul's." He held it to be "an impossible assumption that the 'inner dialectic of the matter' must be adequately expressed everywhere in the Letter to the Romans," maintained "that no man—not even Paul— always speaks with the central point in mind," and consequently asserted that criticism of what Paul had to say of the "central point" is "inseparable from exegesis and actual history in general." [460] While all this made it clear that Barth's exegetical concern for the central matters in the New Testament "has simply bypassed the sphere of history," [461] the question of *suitable* and therefore the appropriate scholarly approach to the New Testament came clearly to the fore when in 1923 **Adolf von Harnack** directed "Fünfzehn Fragen an die Verächter der wissenschaftlichen Theologie unter den Theologen" [Fifteen questions to the despisers of scientific theology among the theologians], and **Karl Barth** undertook to answer them. Harnack had asked whether historical knowledge is not necessary to the understanding of the Bible and whether there is another theology than that which relates itself to every other scholarly discipline.[462]

Is the religion of the Bible, are the revelations in the Bible, something so *clear and unequivocal* that no historical knowledge or critical reflection is needed to understand its meaning correctly? Contrariwise, are they something so *incomprehensible and indescribable* that one must simply wait until they are illuminated in the heart by the inner light, since no human function of soul or mind can apprehend them? Or is it not more probable that both assumptions are false and, if we are to understand the Bible, do we not need historical knowledge and critical reflection in addition to inner openness? . . .

Admitting to laziness, shortsightedness, and countless ills, is there any other theology than the one that stands in firm relationship and kinship *with scholarship in general?* And if there is such a one, what power of conviction and what worth has it?

Barth's answer was to equate the task of theology with that of preaching and to declare again that historical understanding was only a *pointer* to the *witness* of the Bible, which witness disclosed itself only to faith.

The task of theology is one with that of preaching. It consists in appropriating the Word of Christ and passing it on. Why in all this ought it not to be possible for "historical knowledge" and "critical thinking" to perform a preparatory service? . . . The sentence that so repels you and others, the sentence, namely, that the task of theology is one with that of preaching, is *unavoidably* the *platform* on which I stand. I take it for granted, of course, that the preacher by right has to proclaim "the Word," and not, for instance, his own understanding, experience, maxims, and reflections. . . . But if the task of the preacher is to pass on this "Word," it is also that of the theologian (who is practically in personal union with the preacher) . . . .

Theological activity therefore is not really a matter of separating from the historical-critical method of biblical and historical research, developed especially during recent centuries, but one of incorporating the method and the more acute addressing of questions to the text to which it has given rise into theological work in intelligent fashion. . . . As I see it, the theological function of historical criticism in particular is to make it clear . . . to us that . . . in the Bible we have to do with witnesses, and again *only* with witnesses. And I maintain that since the days of D. F. Strauss, this is the function it has actually *fulfilled* among us, excellently after its fashion, although widely not understood and, above all, itself unaware of what it was doing. . . .

"Inner openness"—experience, occurrence, heart, and so forth—on the one hand, and "historical knowledge" and "critical reflection" on the other, are possibilities that can equally be beneficial, of no account, or harmful for the "understanding" of the Bible. The Bible is "understood" neither by the latter nor the former "function of soul and mind," but by reason of *the* Spirit that is *identical* with its content, and that in *faith.*

Over against this Harnack wished to hold fast to the separation of theological scholarship from preaching and to assign the former a place with all other scholarship; in the end he saw only the possibility of emphasizing the gulf that separated him from Barth.

In life, to be sure, theological scholarship and bearing witness are often enough mixed up; but neither the one nor the other can remain healthy when the demand that they be kept separate is disregarded. . . . Thanks to its subject matter a scholarly theological presentation can arouse warm feelings and edify; but the scholarly theologian *who makes it his object* to arouse warm feelings and to edify lays strange fire on his altar; for, just as there is only *one* scientific method, so there is also only *one* scholarly *task*—the pure knowledge of its subject matter. What comes its way in addition to this is an incalculable gift. . . .

The task of theology is one with the task of scholarship in general; the task of preaching, however, is the pure presentation of the Christian's task as a witness to Christ. You transform the chair of theology into a chair of preaching (and wish to distribute what is called "theology" among the secular disciplines); on the basis of the whole course of church history, I predict that this understanding leads, not to edification, but to dissolution. . . .

I deeply regret that your answers to my questions only reveal the size of the gulf that separates us; but it is not a matter of my theology nor of yours, but only of how the Gospel is properly taught. If your method is to become dominant, the Gospel will no longer be taught at all, but handed over exclusively to the revivalists, who create their understanding of the Bible on their own initiative and set up their own authority.

While the majority of critical as of conservative theologians repudiated Barth's "theological exegesis" after this fashion, nevertheless the Swiss theologian's warning that theological scholarship must learn again to seek out the "central matter" was undoubtedly what gave the decisive impetus to a comprehensive rethinking of the task and method of New Testament research. Support came at the same time (1922) from the demand of another systematic theologian, **Karl Girgensohn** of Greifswald, that historical exegesis be supplemented with a higher exegesis ("pneumatic exegesis") directed by the divine Spirit.[463]

In scholarly theology today the most important approach to an understanding of Scripture is that of historical criticism. In fact, we may almost say that in the first instance it is the only approach. The great trouble with that, however, is that the Christian Church by no means understands Scripture only in the light of historical criticism, or even predominantly in its light. The Church is aware that the Bible makes quite other claims on men, so that it cannot be only the object of philological criticism, or be understood only historically. . . .

None of us today, to the extent that he claims to be treating his source material in scholarly fashion, may employ a historical text in such a way as to bring it naïvely into the present. Every text must be interpreted precisely in terms of its historical context. . . . In many respects this represents a significant step forward. On the other hand, however, *this does not bring the historical text nearer to us, but actually removes it farther from us.* Automatically it is no longer a text for the present, but one of its own time, set at a historical distance from us. . . .

There is no need to fall into the arms of historical criticism. We calmly hand over to it everything in history that is human and psychic in nature. . . . Everything that is human and natural in history is subject to the general laws of event within time and space and is therefore in the domain of the general laws that govern human scientific thinking. But, we add, only that. Wherever in biblical history there is a revelation of the eternal Spirit of God, there man's rational, scientific yardsticks are no longer applicable. *The critics should leave the eternal Spirit of God to the simple, childlike faith of the Church.* . . . The really living Spirit of Scripture is only to be comprehended by a quite indefinable and ultimately indescribable personal experience of the Word of Scripture. He who has this experience, knows the Spirit, and he who has it not will never comprehend it. . . . From the historical and psychological manner of viewing religious experience we should lift ourselves to the knowledge of the activity of the divine Spirit in it. Thus we lift ourselves above all categories of the life of the human soul to the objective bases of all subjective faith. Only in this way do we attain to the true Scripture, to the Bible as *pneumatically* understood.

In place of the traditional one-stage view of Holy Scripture, a view in which the historical, dogmatic, and edifying problems all lie so to speak on the same plane, there must appear a two-stage view in which the purely human and historical method of studying Scripture is distinguished from the pneumatic . . . do I think I should be allowed to expect of the theologian the spiritual mobility and versatility which will enable him to consider the same object, namely, Holy Scripture, at one stage purely historically, philologically, and critically, and at another stage under the viewpoint of faith searching for and attaining to his eternal salvation. The pictures we obtain in this way will be very different. Nevertheless, if theological development is in a healthy state, they will not cancel out or contradict each other, but mutually supplement and correct each other.

To be sure, Girgensohn's demand for a "pneumatic exegesis" was largely rejected on the ground that the Spirit of God cannot be made a presupposition of a scholarly method, and even his demand for an exegesis of Scripture at two levels met with only scattered approval.[464] But the concurrent impetus provided by Barth and Girgensohn compelled New Testament exegesis and the study of the content of the New Testament writings as well, to rethink its *theological* task. However, the works of the three main representatives of the new "form" and history-of-religions view of the New Testament which appeared shortly thereafter showed with striking clarity that this new orientation raised a problem that was not easy to solve.

Rudolf Bultmann, who had declared himself in agreement with Barth's exegetical goal (see above, p. 369), continued nevertheless to maintain without qualification that "there can be only *one* method for scientific New Testament research," namely, "the *historical.*" But he now tried to show that the object of this scientific interrogation, the New Testament as provided by the Church, makes the work of exegetes a theological activity and that a scholarly understanding of the New Testament as a historical phenomenon is only possible when the exegete allows the text to put his own self-understanding in question and to summon him to decision. On the basis of these methodological presuppositions Bultmann wrote his book on *Jesus* (1926), in which Jesus' teaching is interpreted as a call to decision in response to the Word spoken by Jesus. The situation of the man encountered by the Word of Jesus is so described that his present is determined by God's future.[465]

The decisive question is just this: Are we to approach history in such a way that we recognize its *claim on us*, that it has *something new* to say to us? If we abandon neutrality in relation to the text, this means that the *question concerning its truth* dominates exegesis. Ultimately, then, the exegete is not interested in the question: How are we to interpret what has been said (thought of only as something articulated) in its historical and temporal setting, in its historical and temporal context? Rather, in the end he asks: What is the passage referring to? to what realities does the articulation lead? . . . By seeking to understand it as a pointer to its real content, exegesis of "central matter" seeks to deal seriously with the original and genuine meaning of the word "word." . . .

In general it may be said that the area of "what is meant" reaches as far as the possibilities of man extend. Whether the interpreter can enter into it depends, then, on how far he is open to the range of what is possible for man. In the end, therefore, the question regarding the possibility of understanding a text depends on what openness the exegete has to the existential possibility as a human possibility, what interpretation the exegete has of himself as a man. . . .

The single guarantee of the *"objectivity" of exegesis* or assurance that the reality of history is expressed in it is just this: that the text makes an impact on the exegete himself as reality. . . . The possibility of an "objective" exegesis is only vouched for by the pertinence of history itself. And this takes form as "Word" only where the exegete is ready to allow the text to speak as an authority. . . .

We try to understand in what respect the text is its author's explanation of his conception of his existence as an existential possibility. In connection with this question we would seek light on our own existential possibility.

The exegesis of the New Testament becomes the task of one who stands in the Church's tradition of the Word. . . . Just as there is, then, no special method of theological exegesis, there is also no possibility of justifying a theological exegesis of the New Testament "in principle." The proper interrogation of the text can only be interrogation made in faith, that is, one grounded in obedience to the authority of Scripture. . . .

Exegesis can proceed only from the interpretation of the word. Since the work of exegesis is conceptual work and since the word of the text is never the central matter itself, but only an expression of the central matter, the latter is open to the exegete only when he understands the word. . . . This legitimates, indeed demands, the whole historical and philological work on the New Testament, a work that acquires its special character from the fact that the New Testament was written in Greek. . . .

In the actual course of exegesis, historical and theological exegesis stands in a relationship that does not lend itself to analysis, because genuine historical exegesis rests on the existential confrontation with history and therefore coincides with theological exegesis, provided that the right of the latter rests on the same confrontation. . . .

That I have a foreknowledge of my possibilities rests on the fact that occasionally a text opens a possibility of understanding my own existence. . . .

Only on this presupposition can we understand what a text says. The text will not acquaint me with remarkable things in it that were hitherto unknown, will not mediate knowledge of unfamiliar events, but possibilities are opened to me which I can only understand to the extent that I am open to my possibilities and am willing to let myself be opened. I cannot accept what is said simply as information. On the contrary, I understand it only as I affirm or deny it. It is not as if I were first to understand and then to assume a position, but the understanding takes place only in the act of affirmation or denial. For what is involved is the opening up of my own possibility, which I understand only as I appropriate it as mine or reject it as a corruption of my own self. Accordingly, understanding is always at the same time the act of choice, decision. . . .

The work of the exegete becomes theological, not because of his presuppositions and his method, but by reason of its object, the New Testament. His character as a theologian consists in the fact that the Church has referred him to the New Testament, which he is to interpret. It is not what he can do by reason of his presuppositions, his methodological approach, his conceivable gifts as a pneumatic, that makes his work theological. The work of research into the New Testament is just as secular as research into any other historical source. It is the New Testament itself, which he only serves, that bears the responsibility for the theological character of his work. What he hears as a scholar is profane; what alone is holy is the word as it stands written.

If this book [*Jesus and the Word*] is to be anything more than information on interesting occurrences in the past, more than a walk through a museum of antiquities, if it is really to lead to our seeing Jesus as a part of the history in which we have our being, or in which by critical conflict we achieve being, then this book must be in the nature of a continuous *dialogue with history*. . . .

Therefore, when I speak of the teaching or thought of Jesus, I base the discussion on no underlying conception of a universally valid system of thought which through this study can be made enlightening to all. Rather the ideas are understood in the light of the concrete situation of a man living in time; as his interpretation of his own existence in the midst of change, uncertainty, decision; as the expression of a possibility of comprehending this life; as the effort to gain clear insight into the contingencies and necessities of his own existence. . . .

Jesus calls to *decision*, not to the *inner life*. . . . Jesus knows only one attitude toward God—*obedience*. Since he sees man standing at the point of decision, the essential part of man is for him the will, the free act. . . .

The future Kingdom of God, then, is not something which is to come in the course of time, so that to advance its coming one can do something in particular, perhaps through penitential prayers and good works, which become superfluous in the moment of its coming. Rather, the Kingdom of God is a power *which, although it is entirely future, wholly determines the present*. It determines the present because it now compels man to decision. . . .

Jesus sees man as standing here and now under the necessity of decision, with the possibility of decision through his own free act. Only what a man now does gives him his value. And this crisis of decision arises for the man because he is face to face with the coming of the Kingdom of God. . . .

It must again be stressed that the eschatological message of Jesus, the preaching of the coming of the Kingdom and the call to repentance, can be understood only when one considers the *conception of man which in the last analysis underlies it,* and when one remembers that it can have meaning only for him who is ready to question the habitual human self-interpretation and to measure it by this opposing interpretation of human existence. Then it becomes obvious that the attention is not to be turned to the contemporary mythology in terms of which the real meaning in Jesus' teaching finds its outward expression. This mythology ends by abandoning the fundamental insight which gave it birth, the conception of man as forced to decision through a future act of God. To this mythology belongs the expectation of the end of the world as occurring in time, the expectation which in the contemporary situation of Jesus is the natural expression of his conviction that even in the present man stands in the crisis of decision, that the present is for him the last hour. . . .

Thus it has . . . become clear in what sense God is for Jesus God of the present and of the future. God is God of the present, because His claim confronts man in the present moment, and He is at the same time God of the future, because He gives man freedom for the present instant of decision, and sets before him as the future which is opened to him by his decision: condemnation or mercy. God is God of the present for the sinner precisely because He casts him into remoteness from Himself, and He is at the same time God of the future because He never relinquishes His claim on the sinner and opens to him by forgiveness a new future for new obedience. . . .

Jesus is therefore the bearer of the word, and in the word he assures man of the forgiveness of God. . . . Man is constrained to decision by the word which brings a new element into his situation, and the word therefore becomes to him event; for it to become an event, the hearer is essential.

Therefore the attestation of the truth of the word lies wholly in what takes place between word and hearer. . . . There is no other possibility of God's forgiveness becoming real for man than the word. In the word, and not otherwise, does Jesus bring forgiveness. Whether his word is truth, whether he is sent from God—that is the decision to which the hearer is constrained, and the word of Jesus remains: "Blessed is he who finds no cause of offense in me."

Bultmann's applying his demand for decision to the existential understanding of the text being studied thus seeks to perform a theological function within the Church of the Word; that is to say, to be a scholarly interpretation arising from faith, in connection with which the mythical conceptual form of Jesus' thought world is understood as a temporarily conditioned form of expression, for describing the present situation of the believer.[466] **Ernst Lohmeyer,** however, immediately protested that Bultmann's presentation of Jesus, ostensibly a historical book, fails altogether to deal with the historical problem of the figure of Jesus because Bultmann articulates only "the personal experience of faith in and within history"; and he charges Bultmann with obliterating the boundaries between faith and knowledge and consequently of offering dogmatics rather than historical science.[467]

It is one of the characteristics of Bultmann's book on Jesus that it waives all claims to deal not only with anything biographical, but also with all questions concerning Jesus' "person," and with deliberate onesidedness makes

Jesus' work the sole object of consideration. In a certain sense it is a book about Jesus without Jesus. . . .

It is evident that what Bultmann tries to isolate as the historical content of Jesus' proclamation is nothing else than the apologia for his own religious position. As such it is eloquent and powerful. With imperturbable self-satisfaction the fact of faith is everywhere represented and demanded. The peculiar strength and at the same time the scholarly weakness of this book lie in the fact that it so unerringly directs attention to this. In so doing the thesis of faith is not critically justified nor is the historical problem of the figure of Jesus raised, to say nothing of being answered. And yet it claims to be a historical book, and in many sections it is such. . . . So limiting the book to the "work of Jesus" means introducing the "humanistic" concept of culture, which Bultmann elsewhere vigorously denounces. In a special way, however, these relationships are complicated in the history of faith. For it is part of his idea that here a "work" is inseparable from him who performs it. The life and being of him who performs a work are the only possible and only necessary representation of what faith means. Consequently it is impossible to limit to his "work" a presentation of Jesus. . . .

But with all this is already raised the great problem of history which Bultmann touches on briefly in the opening words of his book. What he wishes to give, accordingly, is not "as it were a neutral view" of history. On the contrary, he demands a "personal encounter with it." He demands "the continuous dialogue in which the writer of history questions his subjectivity and is ready to listen to history as an authority." . . . But what then do these remarks reveal? Nothing else than the personal experience of faith in and within history. To be sure, he is compelled to relate the totality of history to the possibilities of his personal act. He finds everywhere only the meaning of his own life situation. Whatever form the historical facts may take, he remains always untroubled by them, and knows that he stands at a permanent distance, over which it is possible for him to listen to history to recover his own meaning from its course. Wherever he touches on history, then, everything for him becomes personal encounter. So it becomes understandable that the "work of Jesus" is dominant in this book (it is the *meaning* of one's own faith that is discovered in it), that it is viewed not in light of its historical certainty, but of its religious originality (it is the meaning of *faith* that becomes so vital). But it is also the principal fault of this book that it wishes to make the viewpoints of faith invariables of scholarly research. Accordingly, not only is the problem of this figure and of his historical presentation ignored, but also the purity of the assertion of faith is adulterated, for the boundary between faith and knowledge is now obliterated, faith is transferred from its own field to that of scholarship, and scholarship is subordinated to the dogmatic setting of faith.

When professional exegetes attempted to bring out the message of the New Testament by theological exegesis, therefore, they met the protest of other professional exegetes that the interpretation they offered was not historical interpretation but dogmatic reinterpretation. This illustrates at once the persistent problem of how scholarly research into the historical meaning of the ancient New Testament texts can be so related to personal readiness to listen to the Word of God which speaks through

the text—a readiness demanded by the special character of *these* texts—
that no violence is done to the historical uniqueness and distinctiveness
of the text. And when Bultmann then made use of concepts of existential
analysis taken over from the philosopher Martin Heidegger to pursue
his question of the understanding of human existence exhibited by the
text,[468] the objection was raised from various quarters that his use of
the analysis of being by the atheist Heidegger made it impossible for
him to obtain a correct understanding of the New Testament statements.[469]

Shortly before **Ernst Lohmeyer** published his criticism of Bultmann's
Jesus, he himself had issued a study of the concept of religious community
as "the foundation stone of primitive Christianity." In this research,
which he referred to as critical-historical and as seeking to be neither
"purely theoretical" nor "purely historical," he declares that, "by reference to the concrete facts of the primitive Christian community, the attempt is made to show the objective motives which join its various parts
together and to illuminate by those facts the characteristics of any concept
of a religious community." Historical inquiry in this instance, then, is to
serve "to reveal the permanent objective validity of the problems and the
unity of their relationships by reference to the historical "once and for
all." In the process it becomes apparent that the early Christian Church,
which thinks of itself as living with the imminent end of the age in
view, is actually living in an eternally timeless present, that the kingdom
of God is a reality that exists outside all time, and that faith "construes"
the totality of history as something closed. And in his commentary on
the Revelation to John (see above, pp. 349-50) Lohmeyer adds that in
the primitive church the inherited eschatology had been transformed into
a timeless happening; that past and future had become interchangeable.[470]

The "Church of God" in its local as well as its more or less ecumenical form
is never more than an anticipation of the ultimate universal fellowship which
the "time of the end" will bring. But this goal of an eschatological universality
and every stage along the way to that goal, represented by the individual
congregations or even by the totality of the congregations, are one and the
same. To adapt Hegel's words, the "Church of God" exists only in accordance
with the norm of the "present tense," in view of which a "not-yet" or a "no-
longer" is irrelevant; it "essentially is." . . .

"The kingdom of God" which is at hand is nothing that comes into being
within time—there is no religious concept of "becoming"—but something that
is in being for this and all times, but consequently it is also a reality outside
all time. And faith is nothing less than finding a place within this reality. . . .
The present and the future, therefore, are not to be disentangled; they are the
expression of a timeless factuality of the concept of the kingdom of God. . . .
If the experience of the meaning of faith and the experience of the meaning

of history belong inseparably together, if the totality inheres in faith, which it surveys as it were in an eternal instant, then faith is compelled to construe this totality as something closed and rounded off. . . . By means of the function of chronological order the believer experiences the meaning and reality of his God; its flow in all its irresistible continuity offers him the discreet signs of a divinely fulfilled time. It is no accident that the saying about the time that is fulfilled first occurs in the primitive early church. . . .

Eschatology in the traditional sense has become in the Revelation to John a kind of outworking of authentic faith, belonging to it, to be sure, but nevertheless separable from it. No apocalyptic power, not even any juridical authority of God, can interfere with the relationships of the believers to God and Christ, any more than anything can be added to the eternal and divine dignity of Christ; he is the beginning and the end, the first and the last; he spans all ages of ages. What alone the time of the end can and will bring is a manifestation of what has been from all eternity and is fulfilled in the death of the Lamb, that is, in a historical occurrence. But that means that every eschatological event, without detracting at all from its urgently immediate futurity, has been transformed into a timeless event of which then it can be said that it was, and is, and is to come. . . . If the eschatological events in terms of their timeless meaning are subsumed under faith, and that means are already closed and completed in the eternal and historical being of Christ, then they are nothing else than as it were a repetition of something that has already happened, or a manifestation of what is eternally present. Past and future have become as it were interchangeable, because both have been abrogated in the timelessness of God and Christ.

In reviews of both these books **Rudolf Bultmann** declared himself in agreement with Lohmeyer "that it is not enough . . . to explain the sources historically and philologically, but that a genuine interpretation can only be given when the concepts are understood in light of the matter they are intended to convey," in other words, by exegesis of the "central matter." It is therefore significant that he now objects that Lohmeyer ultimately reinterprets the statements of the New Testament as a Platonic philosophy of history in which the concrete "now" and "then" are lost and the "time that is fulfilled" of early Christian faith becomes the timelessness of Platonic thought. Lohmeyer on his part, then, must admit that, though he wanted to furnish exegesis *in depth,* what he actually offers is a philosophical reinterpretation of the historically given elements of early Christian thought. In this connection Bultmann specifically emphasizes that Lohmeyer's methodological error is to be sought, not in the use of philosophical conceptuality as such, but in dependence on the content of a specific philosophy.[471]

Perhaps the author will say that he has also been aware of everything in primitive Christian views against which I have taken a stand in opposition, that it was just these ways of thinking that he wished to make intelligible, to interpret. There is a meaning hidden in them that must first be brought out.

Now, I do not wish to deny that all phenomena *can* be interpreted as the author does. But it must be made clear that in such a case the statements of the sources are not allowed to say what they are intended to say, but are interpreted in the sense of a philosophy of history based on Hegel. Primitive Christianity is not investigated as to how it thought about man and history on its own part, but it provides the material for constructing a particular philosophical view of history. . . .

The problematical element in the Hegelian philosophy of history, the relationship of the general and particular, of spirit and matter, is ultimately Greek, especially Platonic. And it is in its Platonic form that it has influenced the author. . . . Against this background of Platonism, then, history may still be interpreted in an idealistic sense, especially in terms of Hegelian idealism, and the actual problem of the theological understanding of history, the problem of the "time that is fulfilled," must become the Platonic problem of the "marvelous essence of the moment."

The author is not practicing theology, but perhaps philosophy. In any case he has fallen into a definite way of thinking of the philosophical tradition. Will he answer that I on my part have fallen into another philosophy? This is a charge that I could accept. If philosophy is understood as a system of all truths, of all knowledge of what is, then theology, to be sure, is incompatible with such a philosophy. For it cannot let philosophy assign it its object or proper method of procedure. But if philosophy is understood as a critical science of being, that is to say, as a scholarly discipline whose task it is to control by its concepts of being all positive scholarly disciplines which have to do with what is, then philosophy certainly renders theology an indispensable service.

For, since theology as a scholarly discipline speaks in concepts, it is always dependent on the everyday, traditional ideological structure of its time, and therefore dependent on the tradition of earlier philosophy. It has no more pressing concern than to learn from a given living philosophy of its time, since this philosophy has to perform the critical task of analyzing the everyday traditional conceptual structure. To this extent theology is always dependent on philosophy, or to put the matter more accurately, philosophy performs for theology its ancient service as *ancilla theologiae* ["handmaid of theology"]. As soon, however, as theology imagines that it can have light thrown on its subject matter by philosophy, it makes itself dependent on philosophy in the content of its propositions; the relationship is reversed, and theology becomes *ancilla philosophiae* ["handmaid of philosophy"]. It seems to me that the author has been overtaken by this danger.

A striking peculiarity of Lohmeyer's commentary is his conception of the *eschatology of the Apocalypse.* He proceeds on the assumption that believers basically have everything as a present possession that any future can bring. . . . It is not the individual but only the Church that still needs fulfillment in the future; for the latter lives in tension between its fulfillment in God and Christ and its imperfectibility in history. . . . All these turnings and twistings, so far as I can see, are only vain attempts at resolving the eschatology of the apocalyptist into a form of Platonism. . . . He understands the eternity of which faith speaks as timelessness, and consequently the historical events as a manifestation of "eternal" norms. . . . Just as in his essay "Vom Begriff der religiosen Gemeinschaft" ["On the idea of the religious community"], the author may have fallen victim to Greek thought, with its dualism of norm and phenomena, of general and particular. . . . In my judgment the apocalyptist is concerned to an astonishing degree with time and history, but not, to be sure, in the sense of an observing historian, but in that of the man who belongs within time and has a part in history, who takes time and history seriously because he knows that nowhere except *in* time and history do supermundane and subterranean powers meet man, that faith does not transfer one into timelessness but makes time urgent, that faith is only genuine when it takes its stand within time. . . . The writing of the apocalyptist from the first line to the last is governed by the glimpse of a concrete "now" and a concrete "then."

The works of Bultmann and Lohmeyer, written deliberately as theological exegesis, show then how both scholars demonstrate in their own way that even when scholarly exegesis keeps itself basically free of dogmatic and confessional presuppositions, if it takes the idea seriously that the New Testament text is to speak to the reader, because of philosophical presuppositions it inevitably incurs the danger of depriving the historical reality of its concrete singularity and its past and thereby of falsifying it. And a quite similar state of affairs can be observed about the same time when **Martin Dibelius** made the attempt to demonstrate the meaning for the present of the thought of early Christianity as revealed by scientific research. In a book entitled *Geschichtliche und Übergeschichtliche Religion im Christentum* [*Historical and suprahistorical religion in Christianity*] (1925) he tried, on the strength of an examination of Jesus' message and of the relationship of early Christianity to the "world," to answer the question "whether in view of the way historical and suprahistorical life are related to each other in Christianity, (that is, in its classical period . . .) we have any right at all to move on from a segment of history to God." He establishes the fact that in primitive Christianity a "new life" is at work which breaks forth from a timeless ground and for which the historical forms of expression, including that of the expectation of the End, are unessential. This timeless Gospel has no interest in the "world," but contains an ethos which had to work itself out in the world; this suprahistorical cannot be recognized by the methods at the disposal of the historian, however.[472]

Jesus' sayings and deeds themselves are historically conditioned and require historical investigation. . . . Such an investigation . . . shows that everything Jesus says and does within his time is only a paraphrase of a being superior to time. . . . Here nothing is intended, nothing brought to light, and nothing new advanced—at least, nothing new in our sense of the word. Here a stream of life is putting itself into operation, requiring no specifying of a goal to be sure, and it is not an elucidation but a falsification when this life is rationalized by raising it to the level at consciousness. . . . The main thing is not *what Jesus says and does*, but *what he means with reference to the kingdom of God.* For the former is once and for all conditioned by the occasion, while the latter is independent of person and occasion; the former represents the form of Jesus' work, while the latter portrays its meaning.

Only when we are compelled by the presupposition of belief in the End . . . . to distinguish between form and meaning in Jesus' work do we recognize how belief in the End lifts up the Gospel *into the unconditioned*. If it were not for the fact that Jesus repeatedly spoke of the kingdom of God and therefore renounced any organization at all of this world it would be possible to understand his sayings as doctrine and his deeds as reform. In this case both would be conditioned by time, borne perhaps by a timeless intuition, but nevertheless directed to goals that are to be realized in this world and in this age. Since in truth, however, the Gospel is redeemed and motivated by faith in the kingdom and in the End, it is clear then that Jesus renounces all reconstruction of this world. . . . When, then, in view of the approaching kingdom he demands this or that behavior of an individual, he has no concern to establish such an ethical practice in this world, but he intends by such a command to help the individual to attain the inner attitude necessary at the turning-point in world history. . . . *The commands for human behavior*—no longer capable of being carried out in the old world and unnecessary in the new—only *describe a human attitude;* what looked like an *ethic* conditioned by a purpose is an unconditional ethos—a new being in view of the kingdom, in the atmosphere of eternity which is free to all conditions, in the nearness of the God who is entering the world.

So ultimately Jesus' sayings stem from a timeless ground: the consciousness of the nearness of God, before whom all that the world deems essential becomes unessential. And they have a timeless goal, viz., that of creating men who can live in this nearness. They are spoken out of eternity to eternity, over and beyond any given time—but they pass from man to man within a given time and make use of means that are temporarily conditioned. . . . The faith in the End, itself conditioned by time and history, is nevertheless the historical garment of the suprahistorical. Only because he looked beyond time and viewed the End was Jesus able to speak so unconditionally and to act as he did. . . .

The task was to illuminate the characteristic features of the Gospel in Jesus' work and word. I have attempted to exhibit the faith in the End, the consciousness of the nearness of the kingdom, as the procreating soil in which all expressions of Jesus in speech and deed have their origin. This faith in the End is neither merely a chronologically historical residue nor merely an erroneous view of world history (however certain it is that this world outlook is historically conditioned by time and erroneous), but it is the form in which the new being revealed itself in the world—beyond time, but nevertheless with the highest actuality of the approaching hour that will mark the turn of the ages. . . .

In the Gospel there is no interest which would be directed toward the reconstruction of the world and which therefore would ascribe independent worth to it. The gospel ethos, however, which seeks to transform man rather than the world which has fallen under the power of the End, does contain an abundance of motives which could provide an impetus and had to provide an impetus if the world was to survive. . . . The sayings of Jesus offer then neither an ethical program nor even the principles of an ethical reconstruction of the world; their ethos, however, contains wholly unconditioned motives which are not at all directed at a reconstruction of the world. Let me recall again in this connection that this very neglect of the relationships which belief in the End contributed offers the guarantee of the timelessness of the Gospel. . . .

An attempt has been made in this study to view separately what is historically conditioned and what is suprahistorical, that is to say, unconditioned, each in its strength and each in its right. An attempt . . . was made to demonstrate that under *one* point of view even in early Christianity everything was ensnared in the historical concatenation and nothing is exempted from the relativity of historical event. Under *another* point of view that is not oriented to the historical, the suprahistorical, as it is observable in the classical testimonies of early Christianity, is rather the perceptible background, perhaps in its pure unconditionedness not fully comprehensible to us, but always revealing itself to our presentiment and our willing as the background of all early Christian life. . . .

The perception of the suprahistorical, that is, of the unconditioned that stands back of the relative phenomena, is achieved on a completely different plane than the recognition of the historical. . . . The perception of the suprahistorical is not attainable with the methods of knowing at the disposal of the historian. But it also escapes the theoretical formulation of the dogmatist; for its formulations, thanks to its language and the concepts available to it, are always conditioned by time and consequently burdened with the world; to make adequate statements about the divine lies beyond human capacity. . . .

Only he becomes aware of the new being which came into the world with Jesus, a new being full of the deepest shock with respect to God's judgment and of the highest bliss by virtue of God's grace, who attempts to lead his life and shape his world in light of this background of the Gospel. . . .

It is clear that Dibelius also raised the question of the central matter intended by the proclamation of Jesus and early Christianity in order in this way to recognize the New Testament message's significance for *the present*.[473] But it is just as clear that by his separation of the historical and the suprahistorical he not only identified himself with rationalism, but against his will debased the importance of the unique historical event, and so **Rudolf Bultmann** could object that his concepts were unsuited to express what he wants to say, in fact, that romantic presuppositions lead to a complete misrepresentation of early Christian eschatology.[474]

By his differentiation between the historical and the suprahistorical the author in some sense reaches back over more than a hundred years of development to tie into the tradition of rationalism, which had tried to justify—within theology—its pietistic relationship to the early Christian tradition by just that very differentiation. . . .

In accordance with the author's presuppositions the question of the particular distinctness of the divine in Christianity had probably to be a question of the character of the suprahistorical. . . . It is my opinion that history in its actual significance as a real event is ignored. . . . In this study history has completely lost its significance. . . . If we speak seriously of revelation in history, the letters of the alphabet belong at any rate to it, and the stream of historical life is of no help to us since it is only the great concatentation of happenings all of which are conditioned. So the "new being" becomes simply part of a series of relativities. . . .

I believe that [Dibelius'] concepts are wholly unsuitable to express what seems to be in his mind, that rather with these concepts he falls into the relativism and psychologizing from which it is apparent he wishes to escape. I am also of the opinion that responsibility for the lack of a genuine theological structure of ideas rests not on the author himself but on our confused theological situation. . . . The author is a *romanticist*, except that a little modern value philosophy is mixed in with his romanticism. . . .

For Dibelius, however, the "relationship to the world" must always appear as an apostasy partly because he does not see that the "unconditioned" is only encountered by man in his temporality, that is to say, in the "now" of his concrete historical existence in time and also because he always believes he must keep a sharp look-out for a supratemporal "being." . . . He does not interpret the present by the future, but by the past, which, whatever else it may be, is the very opposite of Christian eschatology.

The example of the historical and theological work of these three scholars clearly illustrates the difficulty before which New Testament scholarship saw itself placed when it felt itself obliged to engage in the task of combining strictly historical research into the New Testament with the insight into the normative and faith-evoking character of these writings. Furthermore, most areas of research to which New Testament scholarship now applied itself under the stimulus of the newly won methodological presuppositions responded appropriately, and as research proceeded the methodological difficulty with which scholars had to continue to wrestle emerged more clearly.

First of all there is the question of the expectation of the End in early Christian thought and its permanent significance. Bultmann, Lohmeyer, and Dibelius had acknowledged without qualification the central importance of the expectation of the End for the thought of Jesus and early Christianity, but in their effort to interpret this early Christian faith for men of today they in various ways incurred the danger of imposing concepts taken from a modern philosophical system on the primitive Christian belief in the End and thereby of reinterpreting its strictly temporal quality. How difficult the task was thus became apparent: Namely, while acknowledging the factual evidence provided by the history-of-religions, one must avoid a mere confirmation of ideas that belong to the past. The problem was accentuated by the fact that research had to contend with two extreme and mutually exclusive views. On the one hand the view advanced by the "consistent eschatology" of Albert Schweitzer (see above, pp. 235 ff.) and his followers continued to have its representatives, according to which the fundamental faith of early Christianity is to be found precisely in the strictly temporal expectation of an imminent end of the world, a view that obviously soon proved to be false and by so doing compelled the early church to put something else in its place.[475] On the other hand, in a lecture delivered at so early a date as 1927, **Charles Harold Dodd**, probably the leading English New Testament scholar of modern times, interpreted Jesus' proclamation of the kingdom of God as declaring that Jesus preached the kingdom as a power at work in the present, a power which develops under historical conditions and continuously discloses itself. In his subsequent book on *The Parables of the Kingdom* (1935) he undertook to demonstrate in detail that Jesus proclaimed the kingdom of God as a reality of the present and that the eschatological predictions were really symbolic in character and expressed the supratemporal significance of the divine events which became manifest in Jesus. All the parables of Jesus accordingly are interpreted as references to the hour of decision which men face in the presence of Jesus and to the growth of God's kingdom that had its beginning with Jesus. The predictions of the end of the age that are contained in the Gospels must then have originated in a misunderstanding on the part of the early church.[476]

In the healing and restoring powers that are freed in his own ministry Jesus finds a genuine coming of the kingdom of God. However, he does not consider the powers in any sense as magical or as exerted on men from without. "Thy faith hath saved thee." Faith is an attitude toward God. Therefore, by bringing a new attitude toward God, Jesus brought also new divine powers, and by this means the kingdom of God had come among men. So we must find the kingdom of God in beneficent powers which are freed here and now by human faith in the deepening of life.

The parables of growth represent the kingdom of God as it develops under historical conditions. . . . They speak of the kingdom of God as a *process* that operates through a community, or as a *principle* that creates a community, through which the kingdom of God attains growing power in the world of men.

The decisive point, however, is that, in place of the abrupt contrast between this age and the next which we meet in apocalyptic—so complete a contrast that only a catastrophic abolition of this order and its replacement with a supernatural order can "reveal the kingdom of God"—we have the thought of a progressive revelation of the kingdom of God in this historical order. . . .

In the earliest tradition Jesus was understood to have proclaimed that the Kingdom of God, the hope of many generations, had at last come. It is not merely imminent; it is here. . . .

This declaration that the Kingdom of God has already come necessarily dislocates the whole eschatological scheme in which its expected coming closes the long vista of the future. The *eschaton* has moved from the future to the present, from the sphere of expectation into that of realized experience. . . .

Here then is the fixed point from which our interpretation of the teaching regarding the Kingdom of God must start. It represents the ministry of Jesus as "realized eschatology." . . .

If therefore [Jesus] did designate Himself as Son of Man, He must have expected that He would be victorious after death. It is therefore credible that

He predicted not only His death but also His resurrection. It is noteworthy that nearly all of these predictions in Mark are of the form, "*The Son of Man* will suffer, die and rise again." . . . The term "The Son of Man" is in its associations eschatological. Its use in these predictions seems to indicate that both the death and the resurrection of Jesus are "eschatological" events. . . .

Jesus declares that this ultimate, the Kingdom of God, has come into history, and He takes upon Himself the "eschatological" role of "Son of Man." The absolute, the "wholly other," has entered into time and space. And as the Kingdom of God has come and the Son of Man has come, so also judgment and blessedness have come into human experience. The ancient images of the heavenly feast, of Doomsday, of the Son of Man at the right hand of power, are not only symbols of supra-sensible, supra-historical realities; they have also their corresponding actuality within history. Thus both the facts of the life of Jesus, and the events which He foretells within the historical order, are "eschatological" events, for they fall within the coming of the Kingdom of God. The historical order however cannot contain the whole meaning of the absolute. The imagery therefore retains its significance as symbolizing the eternal realities, which though they enter into history are never exhausted in it. The Son of Man has come, but also He will come; the sin of men is judged, but also it will be judged.

But these future tenses are only an accommodation of language. There is no coming of the Son of Man "after" His coming in Galilee and Jerusalem, whether soon or late, for there is no before and after in the eternal order. The Kingdom of God in its full reality is not something which will happen after other things have happened. . . .

The predictions of Jesus have no long historical perspective. They seem to be concerned with the immediate developments of the crisis which was already in being when He spoke, and which He interpreted as the coming of the Kingdom of God. . . .

It seems possible, therefore, to give to all these "eschatological" parables an application within the context of the ministry of Jesus. They were intended to enforce His appeal to men to recognize that the Kingdom of God was present in all its momentous consequences, and that by their conduct in the presence of this tremendous crisis they would judge themselves as faithful or unfaithful, wise or foolish. When the crisis had passed, they were adapted by the Church to enforce its appeal to men to prepare for the second and final world-crisis which it believed to be approaching. . . .

The parables of growth, then, are susceptible of a natural interpretation which makes them into a commentary on the actual situation during the ministry of Jesus, in its character as the coming of the Kingdom of God in history. They are not to be taken as implying a long process of development introduced by the ministry of Jesus and to be consummated by His second advent, though the Church later understood them in that sense. As in the teaching of Jesus as a whole, so here, there is no long historical perspective: the *eschaton*, the divinely ordained climax of history, is here.

This exegetical demonstration that Jesus proclaimed only a "realized eschatology" [477] proved very influential both in Anglo-Saxon theological circles and beyond.[478] But the exegetical difficulties that were thrown up by these two extreme solutions of the problem of the early Christian expectation of the End compelled research once again to undertake a basic examination of the problem of the appropriate theological and historical understanding of New Testament eschatology.[479]

It became apparent at the very beginning of this study that the question of what significance the person of Jesus himself had in his eschatological proclamation had to play a decisive role in the solution of this problem. The objection had been raised to R. Bultmann's study of *Jesus* that it was "a book about Jesus without Jesus" (see above, p. 376). **Rudolf Otto,** the Marburg systematic theologian who had become known by his rediscovery of the religious category of the "holy," now opposed to Bultmann's portrait of Jesus one in which the person of the historical Jesus stood at the very center. In an influential book entitled *Reich Gottes und Menschensohn* [*The kingdom of God and the Son of man*] (1934) he emphasized, in latent argument with contemporary New Testament research into Jesus' life and work, notably R. Bultmann's, that Jesus' preaching of the kingdom of God was characterized by a strictly temporal expectation of the End, but that in addition Jesus just as unmistakably proclaimed an anticipation of this future "marvel" in the present, since he was conscious of himself as the manifestation of the inbreaking divine power and the Son of man. Furthermore, Otto seeks to show that Jesus established a connection between the expected Son of man and the Suffering Servant of Second Isaiah (Isa. 40 ff.), a connection in which he saw the fulfillment of his divine calling. But behind this proclamation of Jesus stands the figure of the charismatic Jesus who, because of these God-given capabilities, necessarily belongs together with the kingdom of God.[480]

Fully as his preaching rested upon the late Jewish eschatology, itself borne forward by a swelling apocalyptic, yet it did not move in the direction of continuing the apocalyptic-fantasy. . . .

That the coming of the kingdom does not mean a mere correction of previous existence but the end of all previous and present forms; that the kingdom as a treasure and a costly pearl, that the vision of God which he promises to those who are pure in heart are wholly other goods than earthly goods or values; that they are, indeed, goods of a kingdom of heaven—that has surely been grasped by everyone who has grasped them from the viewpoint of the one leading idea of all Biblical material, i.e. the idea of the holy. . . .

It follows that the preaching of the kingdom is also and of necessity consistently eschatological, and this, of course, means that it includes insistently the temporal opposition between now and then. . . .

Jesus preached: The time is fulfilled. The end is at hand. The kingdom has come near. It is quite near. So near that one is tempted to translate: It is present. At least, one can already trace the atmospheric pressure of that which is ready to break in with mysterious dynamis ["power"]. Fom its futurity it already extends its operation into the present. It is perceptibly near. . . .

In keeping with the apocalyptic doctrine, Jesus reckons . . . on an undefined length of time. . . .

Thus we encounter a peculiar double-sideness, which must appear paradoxical. On the one hand the liveliest feeling of the immediate inbreaking of the supramundane future; on the other hand a message which is completely undisturbed by the former fact in its relation to time, the world, and life, which reckons on duration, on continuance in time and in temporal and world affairs, and is related thereto. This is what we call the irrationality of the genuine and typically eschatological attitude. That this irrationality is of the essence, and is typical of a special attitude, is proved by the circumstance that it is not accidentally found only in Jesus, but recurs in typical form, and may break forth with the same characteristics at different times and in different places. . . .

Whether future or present, whether transcendent or immanent—the chief thing is that the kingdom of heaven is pure *mirum,* pure miracle. . . .

Ordinary things can only be either future or already present. Purely future things cannot sally forth from their future and be operative here and now. Marvels can be both and do both. . . . Thus with Jesus the conception of a purely and strictly future thing passes over into that of something working even now, "in your midst." . . .

It is not Jesus who brings the kingdom—a conception which was completely foreign to Jesus himself; on the contrary, the kingdom brings him with it. Moreover, it was not he but rather God Himself who achieved the first great divine victory over Satan. His own activity lies in, and is carried forward by, the tidal wave of the divine victory. The victory and the actual beginning of the triumph of divine power, he not only deduces from his own activity, but knows of it because he has seen it. . . .

He does not bring the kingdom, but he himself, according to the most certain of his utterances, is in his actions the personal manifestation of the inbreaking divine power.

He knew himself to be a part and an organ of the eschatological order itself, which was pressing in to save. Thereby he was lifted above John and everyone earlier. He is the eschatological saviour. Only thus understood are all his deeds and words seen against their right background and in their true meaning. . . .

A man came . . . who knew and saw that the kingdom of heaven was near, or rather in process of dawning already; that in his own activity it had "come upon you"; and that the conditions of entry into the kingdom of heaven were to confess him and become a personal follower of him. He was supported, not by a general eschatological feeling of power, but by a consciousness of mission which raised him above the prophets, Solomon, and the greatest of those born of woman ["John the Baptist"]. He lived in the ideas of Enoch's apocalyptic tradition. We assert that if there is any such thing in history conceived as a complex of ideas, and if powerful traditions do offer moulds and settle outlines, then such a one not only could, but *must* have known himself as the one destined to be the Son of Man, and at work even now as representative of the Son of Man. This idea was the form which his consciousness of mission necessarily assumed under the conditions of his age. We repeat: His consciousness of mission did not issue from such a previously formed idea, but from the constitution and essence of his person. For the historian this is the essence of a figure and a situation whose uniqueness cannot be explained; but for the eye of faith it was a divine disposition and mission. Under contemporary and historical conditions, however, it necessarily clothed itself in that form. . . .

As the one destined to be Son of Man, Christ knew himself as the one who must be exalted. . . .

He did not contemplate a bodily revivification and resurrection after his death, but that he would depart and be exalted like Enoch, and, from the time when he recognized that "the Son of Man must suffer," he thought of death itself as a direct gateway to exaltation. . . .

Now a new synthesis appeared, of which no one had thought or could think: the synthesis of the Christ with the suffering and dying servant of God from Deutero-Isaiah. . . .

As Son of Man he must suffer. It was part and parcel of the Messianic saving work committed to him. It was redemptive suffering. It was thereby the ultimate conclusion of his consistent eschatology. The saving of the lost for the eschatological order was, as such, and as a whole, the meaning of his person and message. If suffering befell him, it was of a divine necessity; it was the completion of his general Messianic calling, and it fitted into the meaning which his person and message had from the start. . . .

The original tradition describes Christ as a charismatic. We submit that this description is genuine, for in this way and only in this way can we explain the historical consequence, that is, the production of a spirit-led, enthusiastic church. It is genuine, again, because its individual traits harmonize into a unity of the charismatic type. Yet, again, it is genuine because this whole charismatic type harmonizes with, and has the same meaning as, the message of the kingdom of God which is already breaking in, and which has been experienced as dynamis ["power"]. . . .

If our object is to discuss the person of Jesus, we must deal seriously with the exorcistic and charismatic elements in him. His charismatic gift was not an *accidens* ["something accidental"] in him, but was of the essence of his person, and helps to reveal its significance. And only when we understand his person and its meaning is the meaning of his message of the kingdom disclosed. The kingdom for him was the inbreaking saving power of God, and he was not a rabbi but an eschatological redemptive figure, who was an integral part of the eschatological order itself. Charisma and kingdom of God belong together by their very nature and they illuminate one another.

Otto offered a portrait of Jesus in which Jesus' person was portrayed as an instance of a type that can be made intelligible by history-of-religions methods and yet was the central point of a uniquely new proclamation. His book explained Jesus' sense of mission as the result of a combination of different prophetic traditions, and the difficulty of making Jesus' temporally conditioned eschatological proclamation understandable to men of today seemed to have vanished. This portrait of Jesus therefore was warmly welcomed in many quarters,[481] but in just as many it was rejected as historically and theologically untenable.[482] This diversity of judgment revealed at least that research was faced again with the problem of how to interpret Jesus appropriately, that is, in a way that would correspond to historical fact and would answer the question of his ultimate significance. In this connection the most urgent question to be answered was that of the historical and essential relationship of Jesus' person to his message and consequently it was to this question that further research concerned with Jesus returned again and again.[483]

In all the studies to which reference has been made it was presupposed that basically only the Synoptic Gospels could serve as sources for the presentation of Jesus' life and teaching. To be sure, this presupposition was by no means shared by all who engaged in New Testament research after World War I, and its validity continued to be challenged energetically. In this connection the discussion concerning the history-of-religions classification of the Johannine writings (see above, pp. 350 ff.) was combined in a peculiar fashion with the debate about the theological character of the Gospel of John as well as its value as a witness for our knowledge of the historical Jesus. This development is especially apparent in the works of **Friedrich Büchsel**, the conservative New Testament scholar at Rostock. In his study of *Johannes und der hellenistische Synkretismus* [John and Hellenistic syncretism] (1928) he proceeded on the assumption that "the question of the relationship of the Gospel of John and the Johannine letters to Hellenistic syncretism is *the* question of the Johannine writings" and that "the judgment concerning the Gospel and the letters both as a whole and in many details, [turns] on the answer to this question." By an examination of John's central ideas and concepts he tried to demonstrate, therefore, that in their entirety they either develop genuinely Christian ideas or are dependent on Jewish concepts, and he concluded from this that the author, who belonged to Palestinian Judaism, is to be understood as an eyewitness who testifies to the reality of his experience of Jesus, though in the form in which he had later learned to understand it. And in his commentary on the Gospel of John, which appeared a few years later (1934), Büschsel drew the further conclusion that John is much superior to the Synoptists in his knowledge of the historical Jesus and especially in his insight into Jesus' own essential nature.[484]

When the question of the relationship of the Johannine writings to Hellenistic syncretism is clarified, we shall also be in a much better position to answer the question concerning John and Jesus. . . .

For John and his readers the confession of Jesus' messiahship is not merely a matter that belongs to the past, but rather still has importance for the present. It follows, then, that an idea that stems from Judaism, from the Old Testament, an idea neither current among, nor completely intelligible, let alone congenial, to Hellenists lies at the basis of his view of the person and the history of Jesus. It is quite wrong to say that John replaces the fundamental Jewish concept of the confession of Jesus with Hellenistic ideas such as Savior of the world, or Lord, or the like. Hellenism has not affected him or his congregations so deeply as that. In this situation a piety which comes from Judaism has won adherents among Hellenists; here influences from the Hellenistic cultural milieu have not assimilated a piety that came originally from Judaism. . . .

It is superfluous to seek a derivation for the designation of Jesus as the Son of God. . . . The designation . . . goes back to Jesus himself and is simply taken over by John. . . .

The Johannine sayings about the unity and equality of the man Jesus with God must be set in the history of the early Christian estimation of the person of Jesus. It is understandable in this setting, for it developed within it. . . . It is not the effect of Hellenistic syncretism on early Christian faith in Christ which first makes this view of the person of Christ intelligible. It is to be understood entirely in the context of the history of early Christian faith in Jesus.

John is a witness and wishes to be a witness. He is governed by the reality he himself has experienced. Even he who is not willing to accept John's testimony ought not to overlook that fact that he wants to be accepted as a witness, that he wishes to present proof and does present proof for what he says. He who regards what John says about the fellowship of the Son and the Father as a reiteration of mere theories which John has learned approaches his writings from the very outset with a false presupposition. . . .

Knowledge, especially knowledge of God, plays a role in the Johannine writings such as it does nowhere else in the New Testament. Consequently the question arises at once: Does this indicate that John is influenced by gnosticism, i.e., by Hellenistic syncretism? Does he represent basically a Christianity colored by gnosticism? Or is the estimate of knowledge that we find in his writings only the fullest development of what we find earlier in Judaism and elsewhere in early Christianity? . . .

It seems to me that, despite all similarities to gnosticism, all that is peculiar to gnosticism is lacking; for the value attached to knowledge as such is nothing else than the development of what is to be documented in Judaism and Christianity before John. John, who had a special interest in and gift for knowledge, was responsible for the special development of this side of the Jewish inheritance of early Christianity. The desire of the Greeks for revelation may have encouraged this interest of his but can scarcely have been the occasion of it. In all probability its occasion was his special endowment and his great experience as a disciple of Jesus. . . .

The Gospel testifies to the fact that the author is an eyewitness. But the evangelist does not tell his story in such a way as to put himself back consciously and intentionally into the events as they once transpired. Rather, he represents them as he has later learned to understand them. In fact, it is quite basic to his view that it was only the reception of the Spirit after Jesus' death that made it possible for him fully and correctly to understand what he had heard and seen.

It is by no means unlikely that Jesus' ministry extended over several years and was exercised alternately in Galilee and Jerusalem. On the contrary,

Jesus' various visits to festivals in Jerusalem are most probable. So then, when . . . John expressly corrects Mark's portrayal, he demonstrates in any case the superiority of his knowledge of the external framework of the story of Jesus. In any case the Johannine account is not to be understood as a purely literary expansion, exaggeration, or what have you of the synoptic narrative framework. John exhibits an independent and superior knowledge of the facts. . . . The Johannine portrait of Jesus is clearly distinguished in two directions from the Synoptic: the fellowship of Jesus with God as his Father, which in the Synoptics is veiled in mystery, is made far more evident and graphic in John than in the Synoptics, although it is not presented simply; and further: In John, Jesus' fellowship with God is eternal; he came as a person from heaven and possessed the limitless love of God before the foundation of the world. Here the question arises: Are we not to assume that the developed faith in Christ, the corresponding christological dogma of the Church at the end of the first or the beginning of the second century, has colored the picture of the historical Jesus? The answer is this: Obviously John has taken into consideration everything that had been learned after the death of Jesus of his person, his divine sonship, when he drew in his Gospel the picture of Jesus' unique divine sonship. But what he says of the fellowship of the Father and the Son, of the nature of the Son of God, possesses such an inherent power of conviction that it cannot be dismissed as invention, but must be regarded as the historical reality. When he describes Jesus as the One who hears and sees the Father as no one else does, to whom the heaven above is open, who stands in invisible fellowship with God, who is in "heaven"; when he describes the oneness of Jesus and God and the unlimited love of God for Jesus; when he describes this superterrestrial and yet undeniably personal fellowship, this at-oneness in the deepest sense; he does what he is enabled to do as an eyewitness, as the closest confidant, as the especially beloved disciple of Jesus. Those who recorded the tradition of the Church were incapable of that. They mediate to us an impression of the majesty of Jesus by stressing the distance that separates Jesus' nature from ours and by allowing Jesus to appear as the one who towers mysteriously over all men. By revealing the oneness of Jesus with God, which is the very reason for that distance between him and us, John adds the positive complement. What the Synoptists show from without, so to speak, John exhibits from within. What they hint at, he reveals.

Because in its judgment of the history-of-religions and historical setting of John's Gospel this view differed radically from the one to which it was opposed and since from now on this view assumed a place beside the new history-of-religions critical judgment we have been considering in this chapter, as well as the new and just-emerging theological interpretation of John's Gospel, further historical and theological discussion of John's Gospel had to be not only very flexible but also very basic. A further consequence was that the question continued as before to be raised whether and to what extent the Gospel of John can be employed as a witness to the life and work of Jesus and what place must be assigned to John's Gospel historically in the development of the early Christian world of thought and objectively within New Testament theology.[485]

In addition to the complex of questions related to eschatology, there were two others whose treatment in connection with the new orientation of New Testament studies especially engaged the attention of scholars in the twenties, viz., the idea of the Church and the problem of revelation. We saw that at the end of the nineteenth century R. Sohm maintained that the Church for early Christianity was a divine creation, but that this thesis elicited scarcely any support (see above, pp. 214 ff.). In this instance also, as in others we have considered, a change took place after the First World War which had its roots in the general revolt from individualism and the new understanding of community, as well as in the altered theological situation.[486] And once again it was a systematic theologian who provided the impetus to a fresh consideration of church consciousness in primitive Christianity. In a brief essay **Ferdinand Kattenbusch** tried to demonstrate that the consciousness of unity among early Christians, their faith in the primary character of the Church as a whole, had its roots in Jesus; for Jesus had thought of himself as the representative of the holy people that he wished to bring into being among men, and Jesus' association of himself with the Son of man prediction of the book of Daniel (7:13) was the "seedbed" of the idea of the Church. Therefore Kattenbusch wished not only to retain the saying to Peter, "Thou art Peter, and on this rock I will build my church" (Matt. 16:18-19), as a genuine logion of Jesus—a saying that critical research had almost unanimously rejected as inauthentic—but even believed that he could equate Jesus' foundation of the Church with Jesus' last supper with his disciples.[487]

> Without distinguishing in its thinking between community and Church . . . primitive Christianity thought of itself, or felt obliged to think of itself as a unity with its Lord and within itself. . . .
> In their thought of themselves as a Church the Christians of the apostolic age thought of it as a mystery. . . . We must make it clear to ourselves what it means when they looked upon themselves as an object of *faith*. The Church, as God, Christ, and the Holy Spirit, as the forgiveness of sins and the resurrection of the flesh, became to them an article of the symbol of baptism! Accordingly the Christians as Church were to themselves a *religious* entity. . . . Every individual church was aware that it was *one* (not just "in concord") with all others; the local congregation was to itself always the total Church, only the total Church in *concrete* representation, "appearance." . . . *When they were assembled,* Christians had a lively awareness of their autonomy . . . as "the people of God" vis-à-vis every "human" sort of society. But they were not assembled except as *they assembled to celebrate the Eucharist.* . . .
> From the beginning, in accordance with Jesus' interpretation of himself and his *deepest desire,* the "Church" has really been two things, the community of faith and of the Holy Spirit in the hearts of believers, and at the same time a specific congregation of external manifestations and rites.

I believe that I can see that Jesus himself made the following distinction with reference to himself. First and foremost he thought of himself as an *individual* in the form of the "Son of man"; he, *Jesus of Nazareth,* was the one whom Daniel [7:13 ff.] saw carried (up) to God "with the clouds of heaven." . . . The Son of man in Daniel receives from God "dominion and glory and kingdom"; *all peoples* must *serve* him, and his dominion is "an everlasting dominion, which shall not pass away," and his "kingdom" is not to be destroyed. It is clear that the Son of man is the Messiah. However, in his being aware of the drive, the inner compulsion (for that is what it must have been!), to interpret himself as the one whom Daniel "saw," he "meant" to himself, in accordance with what he learned from Daniel about the Son of man, not only what was hidden in himself as an individual, the *personal "Son"* of God, but also the "representative," the one who was called as Lord of a special "people," the *people of the saints of the Most High.* He knew that from now on everything that he lays claim to as Jesus the Son of God, everything he declares to others, does, or allows, must *bring* something *into being* among men, namely this, that they could *apprehend* in him the *Christ,* the Messiah, and that they would be brought face to face with the inward necessity of *acknowledging* him as such in his way of making himself *clearly* apparent to them. In his personal nature he had so to represent himself that he really would become, might claim to be, the type of a "people" of "the saints of the Most High." And as such he had to *form* this people, "create" it among men. . . .

Does all this mean, then, that *the prediction in Daniel* has become *the "seedbed of the idea of the Church"?* Certainly! . . .

But how did the *Church* of the disciples come into being out of the *fellowship* of the disciples, the chosen group of confidants? (The number twelve may have had a symbolic meaning for Jesus, may have been intended by him to *represent* Israel, the people of God.) . . . We have, indeed, *one* passage where Jesus announces his intention to found ("build") a Church, Matt. 16:18. Is this an authentic saying of Jesus? I believe it is. But today it is almost rash to maintain that. . . .

Why should the possibility be excluded that Jesus had it in mind . . . to establish a separate synagogue of his disciples? That was not necessarily a dissociation from the *temple!* Rather (and, indeed, probably) from the synagogue. But what could the "synagogue" still be to his own?! When he was no longer with them! That he "rewards" the "faith" of Peter as he does, that he "honors" the evident plerophory ["full assurance"] of his "confession" with so great a *trust* . . . gives expression to the joy of the occasion. Simon the "rock" is the man of joyous faith that is as full of insight as it is courageous. Jesus does not promise him a place of leadership, a "chairmanship," in any juridical sense. But he expresses the confidence that he will always prove to be the spiritual *support,* the right authority, of the synagogue. . . .

The Last Supper *was the act of the founding of his "Church" as such.* . . . He who regards the saying to Peter about the building of the Church as a genuine logion of Jesus will not find it implausible that Jesus on that evening at the latest did arrange and announce something (as it were in his last will and testament) which "organized" his disciples.

The ideas expressed in the essay on "Der Quellort der Kirchenidee" [The seedbed of the idea of the Church] that Messiah and Church are indissolubly related and the consequent claim that the primitive Christian idea of the Church as a foundation of God goes back to Jesus himself exerted a most profound influence on later research, especially when in a study of "Die Kirche des Urchristentums" [The Church of early Christianity"] (1927) **Karl Ludwig Schmidt** took up and developed the all too complicated ideas that Kattenbusch had formulated. Schmidt adopted Kattenbusch's tracing back of the primitive Christian church consciousness to the message of Jesus, but at the same time took up the question of unity in the primitive Christian thinking about the Church,[488] emphasizing on the one hand the dependence of the Gentile Christian church on the primitive church as the bearer of the tradition about Christ, and on the other the Pauline protest against the overstress on human traits in the primitive community's early Christian conception of the Church. Accordingly the primitive Christian church consciousness was traced back once again to Jesus and the basic importance of faith in the whole Church was once more articulated, but the problem also became unavoidable concerning the unity of New Testament thought in light of the new theologico-historical research into the New Testament thought-world.[489]

From the mass of the Jewish people Jesus had separated a little flock, sharply distinguished from the scribes and ultimately from the whole people, "the hard of heart." . . . Jesus' so-called founding of the Church does not stand or fall with Matt. 16:18, is not an isolated act which the Matthean passage relates, but is to be understood in light of Jesus' total attitude in relation to his people, from among whom, for whom, and against whom he assembled a collegium of twelve as a special synagogue and commissioned it to represent the Church of God. . . . The believing congregation, which Jesus had separated out from the [Jewish] people and which continued to be separate, guaranteed the existence of this peoples' Church in that it laid claim to be the Church of God. . . .

To the extent that in connection with the expression "church" . . . we have opened up a discussion of the Church, we have presupposed the unanimity of primitive Christianity in this matter. But how then is the well-known conflict between Paul and the primitive Palestinian church to be understood? Does it not actually have to do with the proper grasp of what the Church is?

In believing itself to be, and representing itself as the Church of God which had been constituted by the Resurrection occurrences the primitive church in Jerusalem emphatically stressed two things: in the first place, the special competence of the earliest disciples to render a definitive decision on all questions that cropped up regarding the activity in which the Church should be engaged even beyond the limits of Jerusalem; and in the second place, and related to the first, the primacy of Jerusalem. Authoritative personalities and a holy place form the midpoint of the Church. If a Church has been newly established by God through the resurrection of Christ, then it is necessary to assure the existence of this structure by means of quite specific, chosen, living personalities who have received their commission from Christ. . . . On this basis Jerusalem is and remains the core of the Church. Other congregations are only its offshoots. Jerusalem is Christianity's center of authority.

Paul agreed with these claims of the earliest church at Jerusalem, but at the same time waged a vigorous war against the overstress on the personalities (the original apostles as permanent authorities!) and the locale (Jerusalem as the center of authority!). Both the personality issue and the locale issue are uncommonly important to Paul. For without the original apostles and without Jerusalem there is no Church: By means of the original apostles and in Jerusalem the Church was constituted. And that must remain constitutive. But the claim of the earliest disciples is unwarranted that their role as persons and that of Jerusalem as the center impose obligations on others. . . .

Paul's polemic against Judaizers reveals indirectly that his fight with the primitive church was a fight with individuals who had overemphasized the authority of their persons and that of their holy city, that his polemic was decidedly not directed against the "Church" of the earliest disciples but against its rank theocratic outgrowth. . . . While his attack on the Judaizers is uncurbed, he has to be, and wishes to be, cautious and restrained in relation to the primitive Jerusalem church, for he has to and wishes to leave one thing standing that cannot be brushed aside. . . .

If we look at the over-all picture, at what is essential, at what is decisive, we are driven to the conclusion that the primitive Jewish Christian and Gentile Christian churches, including Peter and Paul, had the same view of the Church. The apparent differences cannot obscure the actual agreement. It could scarcely be otherwise, since Peter and Paul underwent the same experience of Christ. . . .

The Church itself was constituted for the duration with Jesus Christ and those who first believed in him. . . . When in Jerusalem people connected with Peter, who had been specially singled out by Jesus, constituted themselves as a group that believed in Jesus as the Messiah and consequently as the Church of God (that is to say, the Old Testament people of God) by reason of its claim, this individual congregation became at once the whole body of the faithful, the Church. And when individual congregations came into being in Hellenistic cities, primarily through links with Paul, connected as they were with Jerusalem and yet conscious of personal, local, and national autonomy, every such individual congregation became at once the representation of the whole Christian community, just like the Jerusalem church. . . . Catholicism appeals to Peter and the primitive church which gathered about Peter as the rock of the Church of God. Protestantism has no right to take from Peter what belongs to him within the framework of the ever-important primitive church, but Protestantism has the right and duty to keep alive Paul's protest against Peter and the primitive church in order that the Church may present itself as the *people of God* and *not* as the *hierarchy of men*.

Following the lead of these preliminary studies, further research into the primitive Christian concept of the Church concerned itself primarily with the basic structure of this church consciousness and its uniformity, and secondarily with the connection of this thought of the Church with the person and message of Jesus.[490] In addition to its consideration of the idea of the Church the new line of inquiry in relation to New Testament theology had especially to turn also to the question of the nature of revelation in primitive Christianity, for it was the very insight into the claim of the New Testament proclamation to be revelation which had led to a change in the approach to the study of the New Testament world of ideas. It is worthy of note in this connection that in an academic address (1927) on the question "Was ist Wahrheit?" [What is truth?] **Hans von Soden,** the church historian and New Testament scholar at Marburg, first of all made an acute and strictly historical analysis of the two conceptions of truth which historically influenced ancient Christianity: the Old Testament, and the Greek understanding of truth. From the fact of the union of these two ideas of truth in our culture and scholarship, determined as they are by Christianity, he then drew the conclusion that truth is really truth only as a reality that unifies and determines life and only within the community. Historical reflection therefore leads to the insight that an understanding of the truth proclaimed in the New Testament is possible only by means of a decision.[491]

In Jesus and Pilate [in the scene in John 18:13 ff.] appear two different concepts of truth, two concepts of truth in relation to reality: that of the Jews and that of the Greeks, that of the Oriental and that of the Greek spirit. Our own history stands under the influence of this twofold concept of truth, the biblical-religious on the one hand, and the Greek-philosophical on the other, under their diversity and their combination. This duality of the Orient and Hellenism, which has become a complex and tensioned unity in Christianity, exercises determinative influence on us intellectually and is seen in all areas of our life. . . .

The chief characteristic of the Hebraic concept of truth is that for it the truth is not just known, said, heard, and in given instances misunderstood, veiled, and denied, as it is with us, but that it is done, that it comes to pass. Furthermore, in this connection it is not a matter of the inference the act would draw from the known facts, but of a completely free action of persons on persons. . . . Truth is that conduct which fulfills a given expectation, a definite claim, which justifies a quiet trust. . . .

Accordingly, what is peculiar to the Hebraic concept of truth on the one hand is its temporal orientation, its specifically historical character. It is always a matter of something that has happened or will happen, not of something that exists by nature, that is and must be so. In this connection and to this extent there would be absolutely no way of distinguishing between reality and truth, except that truth is reality seen as history. Truth is not something that somehow lies under or back of things and that would be found by penetrating into their depths, their inner constitution. On the contrary, truth is what will appear in the future. The opposite to truth would not actually be, so to speak, deception, but essentially disillusionment. . . . What has permanence, existence, a future, is true, and therefore in particular the eternal as the imperishable, the abiding, the ultimate, the final.

Ἀλήθεια ["truth"] designates the actual, the real as something known, inferred, discovered, and therefore it always occurs with verbs of perception—to see, to hear, to experience, to find, to seek—and communication—to say, to proclaim, to write, to show, to attest—but never with to do, since the real fact designated as truth must always already exist before it is known; only knowledge of it, not its existence, can be future. . . . Truth is dialectically in our concept of things, not in the things themselves. . . . What characterizes Greek thought is that what is rightly thought *is* real, and consequently rational thinking becomes the measure of being, the decisive means of knowing what exists. . . .

Accordingly, what is decisive in the Greek concept of truth is that truth is discernment, knowledge, or, more exactly, knowledge of being, of its "what" and its "how." . . . For the Greek the knowledge of being is the measure of the thought of God, while for the Hebrew, being is the reality created by God; for the former God is the totality of nature, while for the latter he is the author of history.

Now, history has combined these two disparate ideas, and to reflect about the combination is no less important than to recognize the difference. In their combination each of the two concepts of truth preserves its own particular distinctiveness, but in addition there are extremely significant exchanges and combinations of their essential traits, their functions. In that great process in intellectual history and in the history of religions whose stages and times we have not yet had illuminated as we might wish, in that process in which Greece and the Orient interpenetrated even in pre-Christian times, in the so-called syncretism a system of thought takes form to which we may give the name science as well as that of religion and whose leading idea is life through knowledge. . . . The life that here is meant is life in the sense of an existence safeguarded against all transitoriness, and the knowledge that here is meant is not a discovery but a revelation; and it has an extremely concrete rather than a general content: namely, the nature of the new, the coming, the future life and the conditions or means of participating in it.

The truth is *one* in economics and in scholarship, in state and in church; it is *one* for body and soul, for Jews and Greeks, for Christians and men in general; for it is life. In the unity in which it stands, however, it is always a combination of nature and history, of fact and act, of something that is demonstrated and something that demands decision, of knowledge and conscience. . . . A right decision presupposes a critical knowledge of real and actual facts but does not follow from such knowledge. It must be made in faith. . . . Truth verges very closely on what today is called pragmatism—it requires courage to recognize this—and yet there is a fine distinction—one must have the conscience to maintain that; for truth is acting, it is history. . . . It is not the general opinion or agreement, the consensus in judgment, that decides concerning truth—people are led into lies like a flock of sheep, but truth is given to individuals; all the same, truth is determined by the community to the extent that truth belongs to it, is known and spoken in its behalf, is serviceable and beneficial to it, becomes effective and fruitful in the community as truth incorporates the individual into the whole rather than isolating him, as it is love and is found by love and is done in love. . . .

Religion should be and can only be truth as personal conviction and decision, and this in fact only in freedom. But at the same time it can only really be truth when it establishes a community, when it assembles and builds; where that is disavowed or ignored, religion is not truth, however fanatical or critical it may be. Here also the conviction of all does not have to be identical, but in its individual manifestations it must be oriented to the community and work towards it. The state of the Church in the end passes judgment on the truth of our religion.

And this is true also of scholarship. The most acute detailed research, objective determination of facts, rigorous professional study, all prepare the way in it for truth which is not revealed to any speculative construction and which mocks all the aberrations of supposed genius. But actually there is no real fact which could stand by itself and be comprehended as it were in transverse section, but each stands in a historical and related context and, whether our scholarship is aware of this and makes us aware of it, determines its truth. . . . For there is no such thing as truth except in relation to life, not apart from it; except as something unifying and responsible.

This investigation of the New Testament claim to be truth, calling for decision and yet employing strictly historical methods, once more exhibits the problem we noted in K. L. Schmidt's study of the New Testament idea of the Church, the problem, namely, of the unity of the New Testament world of thought. To be sure, in H. von Soden's study this problem appears only in the negative form, namely, that the New Testament is taken as a unity within the framework of the Old Testament understanding of truth. But the problem became really acute in view of the appearance shortly thereafter of a discussion by **Rudolf Bultmann** of the *Begriff der Offenbarung im Neuen Testament* [The idea of revelation in the New Testament] (1925). In this essay Bultmann shows that the New Testament clarifies the preunderstanding of revelation possessed by every individual in that it declares revelation to be the annulment of the limitation of human existence, so that what the New Testament says of revelation can be understood only by listening to the New Testament as it speaks.[492]

Why do we ask when we already know what revelation means and when we can encounter in the New Testament with more or less great clarity only one of the possible differentiations of this concept? And without having a concept of revelation there is indeed no possibility at all of asking. . . .

If we are not trying to fit its beliefs into a preconceived scheme of ideas, we interrogate the New Testament obviously in the expectation that the question of the correct understanding of revelation could conceivably be clarified. . . .

We know about revelation because it belongs to our life. . . . When we speak to someone of revelation, we speak to him of his actual life in the belief that revelation belongs to him, just as light and darkness, as love and friendship, belong to him. Only in this sense, then, can a question directed to the New Testament be a genuine question, that is to say, when it anticipates that the questioner here wants to hear something *about* himself—better stated, he wants to hear something said *to* himself. . . .

The fact of the limitation of our life governs our life; we carry our death around with us. But in this way the question concerning revelation qualifies our life; for it arises out of our limitation. And as we can affirm or deny or obscure this, so too we can handle the question of revelation. . . .

Here also we cannot expect the answer in the sense of hoping to discover a belief ready-made in the New Testament which could be fitted into a pre-designed scheme of all possible concepts of man's limitation. Rather, the question is a genuine one only when the questioner wishes to have a radical articulation given to the, as it were, wavering understanding of his limitation. . . . In like manner, also, the answer to the question of how revelation is to be understood in the New Testament cannot be understood merely as information, but only as the New Testament addressing the questioner. The question of revelation is at the same time the question of man's limitation; and an answer to the question of what revelation is can only be heard when the questioner is willing to allow his limitation to be disclosed. . . .

If we ask about the concept of revelation in the New Testament, we shall ask first how man is viewed here in his limitation. And the answer nearest at hand is simple: *Man is limited by death,* the last, the real, enemy. . . .

Revelation can only mean the destruction of death. . . . Revelation can only be the gift of life that overcomes death. . . . But the New Testament not only says that this is what revelation must be, but also that this is what it is. But how? Revelation is an *event* which destroys death, not a teaching that there is no death. But not an event *within* human life, but one that *comes into human life from without.* . . .

All this holds true only under the presupposition of faith, but not of faith as a human attitude, a disposition of the soul, but of faith *in* an event, *in* Jesus Christ, in him who died on our behalf and rose again. . . .

Revelation, then, consists in nothing else than in the fact of Jesus Christ. . . .

To what extent is anything actually revelatory? How is the saving event visible? Not as cosmic event, any more than as inner experience! *It is evident as proclamation, in word.* . . . At the same time that preaching communicates information, it addresses the hearer; it appeals to the hearer's conscience, and he who does not allow himself to be addressed also does not understand what is communicated. . . .

So it becomes fully clear that *revelation is an act of God, an event,* not a supernatural communication of knowledge. Furthermore, that revelation reveals *life;* for it frees men from what is for the present and what belongs to the past and presents him with the future. Likewise that *Christ is the revelation* and that revelation is *the Word;* for these two are one. . . . The love that is directed at *me* . . . cannot be apprehended by historical observation. It is conveyed by the proclamation. To go behind the preached Christ means to misunderstand the preaching; he meets us only in the Word, as the one who is proclaimed, and in him the love of God encounters us. . . .

All that has been said so far is an explication of what is said in the New Testament, or at least seeks to be an explication. If this explication made it clear that it is only to be undertaken on the basis of a preunderstanding and in the readiness to let that preunderstanding be given radical articulation, it must be admitted in closing that all explication remains only in the preunderstanding and that radicalization is only then really effected when what is said in the New Testament is heard in its real meaning. From this it follows, then, that the question concerning the concept of revelation in the New Testament runs into *the claim of the New Testament to be itself the revelation;* that is, the New Testament is able to say what it understands by revelation only by maintaining at the same time that it itself is the revelation. . . . To the question of what the New Testament understands by revelation it answers, then, with the question of whether it itself is listened to as revelation.

In Bultmann's discussion the New Testament appears as a unity. "Any differences among the biblical writings (which Bultmann in other connections is clearly aware of and stresses) are not mentioned; influences from within the history-of-religions are not taken into consideration. . . . There is no concern for genetic understanding, but the substance, and in this respect the New Testament may and must be taken without further ado as a unity." [493] But if we examine this unity more closely we discover that the understanding of revelation in the New Testament which Bultmann expounds is taken almost exclusively from Paul's letters, the Gospel of John, and I John. There is, then, no reference at all to the message of Jesus in the Synoptics; and so the critic who has just been cited, though he declines with M. Kähler (see above, pp. 222 ff.) to go back of the Christ who is preached, nevertheless insists that "the history of Jesus is also an essential component" of the history to which witness is borne in the New Testament preaching.[494] But by this route we are brought face to face with the most difficult problem with which New Testament research saw itself confronted as, in view of the New Testament's claim to be revelation, it proceeded to investigate its world of thought with all the tools of strictly historical method: namely, the problem of the unity of the New Testament message.

In connection with the radical criticism of the New Testament from the history-of-religions perspective this problem became particularly acute in the form of the question concerning the relation of Paul's theology to the proclamation of Jesus (see above, pp. 288 ff.), and it is no accident that after a long interval this question was taken up again in the twenties.[495] But in the meantime the inquiry had been so greatly broadened by further insights from the study of comparative religion, the observations of form criticism, and the discussion of the eschatological problem that the more comprehensive question that now was to be answered was whether behind the variety of the New Testament forms of the proclamation any overriding unity is to be found and what scholarly method must be used if justice is to be done to the demand that both the historical individualities be preserved and the common proclamation be discovered. The scope and difficulty of this central task of New Testament research[496] can be seen most clearly by reference to the book on *The Riddle of the New Testament* (1931) by **Sir Edwyn Hoskyns**, the Cambridge New Testament scholar, which deliberately sets out "to display the critical method at work upon the New Testament documents" and which, in the judgment of the publisher of the German translation, "describes the situation of New Testament research after a

century of historical and critical study in a more complete and impressive fashion" than any other book. According to Hoskyns, the real riddle
of the New Testament is the question: "What was the relation between
Jesus of Nazareth and the Primitive Christian Church?" [497] By reference
to the problems of research into the language, text criticism, synpotic
criticism, the exegesis of Jesus' sayings, and the demonstration of the
central motifs of the great theologians (Paul, the author of the Johannine
writings, and the author of the Letter to the Hebrews), he seeks to
demonstrate that the same fact emerges from a discussion of all these
areas: namely, that the real riddle is the historical character of the man
Jesus, whose life and death were understood even by himself as the fulfillment of the messianic promise of the Old Testament, and that all the
efforts of the evangelists and the theologians of the New Testament only
serve the purpose of making this fact more intelligible. It is therefore
not the faith of the early church which created the messianic interpretation of the ministry of Jesus, but it is the historical reality of Jesus himself which was "the ground of Primitive Christian faith." [498]

> The peculiarity of the language of the New Testament is the result of a new
> Hebraic-Aramaic-Palestinian history, by which the Old Testament Scriptures
> have emerged with a new emphasis. This whole creative process has taken place
> in a particular history which lies behind the Greek-speaking Christians and
> behind the writers of the New Testament books. . . . The actual creative element
> which is at work in the New Testament language is everywhere due to a vigorous
> recognition that the Living God has acted in a particular history, and that
> Christian moral and spiritual experience depends entirely upon that particular
> history. Further, it is also clear that the New Testament language is unintel-
> ligible unless that particular history took place in the heart of Judaism and on
> the background of the Old Testament Scriptures.
> Clearly the writer [of 1 Peter 2:1 ff.] was picturing Christ in terms taken
> from the suffering of the faithful slave of God in the Prophecy of Isaiah. But
> this passage and other parts of the Epistle show that the author quite con-
> sciously sets the Passion of Jesus, not primarily in the context of Christian
> piety, but in the context of the Old Testament Scriptures. A clear problem
> therefore arises. Did this conception of the fulfilment of the Old Testament in
> the concrete history of Jesus of Nazareth cause the author of this Epistle and the
> other New Testament writers both to set down as history details not actually
> true and also to introduce in the process a context foreign to the actual history?
> . . . Is the Jesus of history wholly submerged in the New Testament, or does
> that history rigorously control all our New Testament documents? . . .

Was it that Old Testament aspiration did in fact condition the teaching and
action of Jesus, so that He went to His death consciously in order that the
Scripture might be fulfilled, and ordered His ministry to that end? In other
words, is the particular Marcan ordering an imposition upon the original
history, or the very essence of it? . . . Was it because the religious needs of early
converts, and in particular of Gentile converts, had already distorted the life
of a humane moralist in order that they might have an assurance of salvation

401

and so indulge their longing for eternal life? Or was it because the moral demands of Jesus were occasioned by His peculiar relation to God, and were meaningless apart from this claim, so that the fulfilment of these demands would be the supreme result of His Death and Resurrection? . . .

If therefore one main purpose of the historical criticism of the New Testament is to discover the origin of this peculiar interweaving of the Old Testament with the Life and Death of Jesus of Nazareth, it is imperative that some attempt be made to go behind the Synoptic Gospels as they stand, in order if possible to lay bare the nature of the tradition concerning Jesus before it was handled by the editors and incorporated in their narratives. . . .

The attempt to throw upon the Evangelists the responsibility of having manipulated the earlier tradition in the interests of a remarkable Christology does not survive a rigidly critical examination. The interpretation put upon the Actions and Life and Death of Jesus did not originate in the minds of the men who compiled the gospels in their present form. Their records have a clear and conscious purpose. That is obvious. But they extracted their purpose from the traditions they received: they did not impose it roughly upon a material unable to bear it. . . .

Neither Mark, nor Luke, nor Matthew, is interpreting a mere series of facts: still less are they imposing a Christology upon an undefined human personality. The interpretation is given them in the material which comes to them from various sources, and it is the same interpretation which is being presented to them throughout. The Christological, Old Testament interpretation is lying in the history of Jesus of Nazareth in so far as they know the tradition. . . .

The conclusion which follows from an investigation of the aphorisms found in all strata of the Synoptic material is that they are utterances of the Messiah, Who is inaugurating the Kingdom of God in which the Law of God revealed to the Hebrew people is fulfilled. Further, the Kingdom is inaugurated in humiliation, in the midst of persecution and misunderstanding; and this humiliation is not merely the necessary prelude to the final Kingdom, it is the condition of entry into it.

The aphorisms of Jesus, then, cannot be detached from this Messianic background, and they cannot be detached from the particular happening in Palestine. They are not merely ethical aphorisms: they declared the presence of the Kingdom of God, and are rooted in a peculiar Messianic history. Thus the Aphorisms have to be placed with the Miracles and the Parables. The peculiar Christology penetrates the aphoristic teaching of Jesus as it penetrates the record of His miracles and of His Parables. The Christology lies behind the aphorisms, not ahead of them; this means that at no point is the literary or historical critic able to detect in any stratum of the Synoptic material evidence that a Christological interpretation has been imposed upon an un-Christological history. . . .

The Theologians of the New Testament, then, are not moving in a world of their own ideas. They are moving upon the background of a very particular history, which is itself shot through and through with theological significance. No doubt it is their own spiritual and moral experience which enables them to appreciate the significance of the history and to lay it bare; no doubt also considerable theological development results from their endeavour to extract its meaning; but neither their experience nor their theologizing has created the history which they are handling. . . .

Nowhere in the New Testament are the writers imposing an interpretation upon a history. The history contains the purpose, and is indeed controlled by it. That is to say, the historian is dealing in the end with an historical Figure fully conscious of a task which had to be done, and fully conscious also that the only future which mattered for men and women depended upon the completion of His task. The future order, which it was the purpose of Jesus to bring into being, depended upon what He said and did, and finally upon His death. This conscious purpose gave a clear unity to His words and actions, so that the actions interpret the words and the words the actions. The same purpose which caused the whole material in the tradition to move inexorably towards the Crucifixion, forced the Theologians to concentrate upon His death in their endeavour to expose the meaning of His life. Nor is this purpose, which binds together the Life and the Death, in the least degree unintelligible as it is presented in the New Testament. The purpose of Jesus was to work out in a single human life complete obedience to the will of God—to the uttermost, that is, to death. The three great New Testament Theologians saw this and expressed it quite clearly; indeed, this purpose alone makes sense of the Tradition preserved in the Synoptic Gospels.

This extremely impressive picture, which itself claims to have presented "the solution of the historical problem," [499] gives the impression that the strictly historical examination of the individual documents and levels of tradition of the New Testament establishes a fundamental unity in the New Testament proclamation. But hidden in this is the decisive problem that New Testament research has had to face since first it became aware of the task of how modern man, by using the tools of strictly historical research, is to be enabled to hear what the New Testament has to say. For many historical theses which Hoskyns represents are very vulnerable,[500] and even if his major thesis be accepted, that is, that Jesus' personal claim and reality constitute the historical root of the New Testament proclamation, it cannot be denied that not only the three later theologians of the New Testament but also in equal measure the authors of the Synoptic Gospels have given the earliest message new interpretations influenced by ideas foreign to it which do not in every respect offer the possibility of a unified presentation of the New Testament message of Christ. The unity of the New Testament message, obvious if you accept the dogma of the inspiration of the entire corpus of canonical writings, cannot be presupposed as obvious on the basis of strictly historical research, and for the time being there is no other methodologically unobjectionable procedure than the scholarly analysis of every writing or stratum of tradition by itself. It is not to be doubted, however, that the attempt must be made by New Testament research to show the persistent or variable unity back of the multiplicity of forms once one affirms that to acknowledge the claim of this collection of writings on personal decision is an indispensable presupposition of a *relevant* understanding of the New Testament. Consequently New Testament research since its revitalization in the twenties of this century has had to wrestle again and again with this problem.

Conclusion

From the very outset New Testament research was confronted with the problem of how the indispensable *historical* task of examining the New Testament could be brought into harmony with the distinctive demand of these documents on the reader for a decision in response to the divine message they contain (see above, pp. 69-73). This fundamental problem always accompanied scholarly work on the New Testament, but became acute again after the First World War, and all research since then has been governed by it.[501] It is true, in fact, that, "more than any other special field of historical study, New Testament research has always suffered from a curious inability to be thoroughly historical in method and in aim." And on the premise that during the last one hundred and fifty years New Testament research has been a historical science only "in so far as it has produced scientifically valid results," the same critic adds quite properly: "It has a future only if this fact will at long last be fully recognized and consistently acted upon." [502] There has also, then, been no period in the almost two-century-old history of scholarly research into the New Testament which has been free of the danger of neglecting or even denying this. But just when the historian takes his task in relation to the New Testament with great seriousness he "must state that the New Testament demands what he, as an historian, may not give, a judgement of the highest possible urgency for all men and women." [503] And therefore there has likewise never been a time in the whole history of New Testament research in which this claim on decision has not been voiced and has not demanded the consideration which is its due. In fact, New Testament scholarship fails in its task when the scholar precisely in his capacity as scholar thinks he has to exclude this claim.

This perception does not hold true in every case but results solely from personal encounter—of a kind that is prepared to make decisions —with this wholly unusual objective of scholarly research. Surely New Testament research belongs "to any thoroughly profane service which calls itself historical scholarship." [504] Yet whoever performs this profane work responsibly cannot evade the word of the Johannine Christ: "My teaching is not mine, but his who sent me. If anyone wants to do His will, he will know whether this teaching is from God or whether I speak on my own authority" (John 7:16-17).

NOTES AND APPENDIXES

List of Abbreviations

ADB	*Allgemeine Deutsche Biographie, 1875-1912*
BZAW	*Beihefte zur Zeitschrift für die alttestamentliche Wissenschäft*
CHB	*Cambridge History of the Bible,* Cambridge University Press, 1955
DBS	*Dictionnaire de la Bible, Supplément, 1928*
Eichhorn, *Introduction*	J. G. Eichhorn, *Einleitung in das Neue Testament,* 5 vols., Leipzig, 1804-27
EKL	*Evangelisches Kirchenlexikon, 1956-59*
EvTh	*Evangelische Theologie*
FRLANT	*Forschungen zur Religion und Literatur des Alten und Neuen Testaments*
Hirsch, *Geschichte*	*Geschichte der neueren evangelischen Theologie im Zusammenhang mit den allgemeinen Bewegungen des europäischen Denkens, 1949-54*
HTR	*Harvard Theological Review*
JBL	*Journal of Biblical Literature*
Kraus, *Geschichte*	H. J. Kraus, *Geschichte der historische-kritischen Erforschung des Alten Testaments,* 2nd ed., 1969
Kümmel, *Heilsgeschehen*	W. G. Kümmel, *Heilsgeschehen und Geschichte* (Marburger Theologische Studien 3), Marburg/Lahn, 1965
LThK	*Lexikon für Theologie und Kirche*
Meinhold	P. Meinhold, *Geschichte der kirchlichen Historiographie,* 2 vols., 1967 (Orbis Academicus)
NDB	*Neue deutsche Biographie, 1953 ff.*
N.F.	Neue Folge ["new series"]
Neill, *Interpretation*	Neill, Stephen, *The Interpretation of the New Testament, 1861-1961, 1964*
NTS	*New Testament Studies*
ODCC	*Oxford Dictionary of the Christian Church,* ed., F. L. Cross, 1957
PRE	*Realencyklopädie für protestantische Theologie und Kirche,* 3rd ed., 1896-1913
Quest	Albert Schweitzer, *Geschichte der Leben-Jesu-Forschung*

RB	*Revue Biblique*
RGG	*Die Religion in Geschichte und Gegenwart*, 3rd ed., 1957-1962. References to 1st and 2nd editions are especially noted.
Schultz	*Tendenzen der Theologie im 20. Jahrhundert. Eine Geschichte in Porträts*, edited by H. J. Schultz, 1966
Selbstdarstellungen	*Die Religionswissenschaft der Gegenwart in Selbstdarstellungen*, 5 vols., 1925-27
Study	*The Study of the Bible Today and Tomorrow*, ed., H. R. Willoughby, University of Chicago Press, 1947
ThLZ	*Theologische Literaturzeitung*
ThR	*Theologische Rundschau*
ThStKr	*Theologische Studien und Kritiken*, 1828-1947
ThWBNT	*Theologisches Wörterbuch zum neuen Testament*, ed. G. Kittel and G. Friedrich, 1933, 8 vols. have appeared. The first 6 volumes have been translated into English by G. W. Bromiley as *The Theological Dictionary of the New Testament*, Grand Rapids, Mich., 1964.
ThZ	*Theologische Zeitschrift*
WA	Weimar edition of *Luther's Works* (1521). Eng. tr. (Philadelphia: Fortress Press, 1930)
ZNW	*Zeitschrift für die neutestamentliche Wissenschaft und die Kunde der älteren Kirche*
ZthK	*Zeitschrift für Theologie und Kirche*

Notes

1. That the "Prologues" originated in the Marcionite churches was recognized, independently of each other, by D. de Bruyne, "Prologues bibliques d'origine Marcionite" [Biblical prologues of Marcionite origin], *Revue Bénédictine* 24 (1907), 1 ff., and by P. Corssen, "Zur Überlieferungsgeschichte des Römerbriefes" [On the history of the transmission of the Letter to the Romans], *ZNW*, 10 (1909), 1 ff., 97 ff. The demonstration of this was ultimately achieved by A. von Harnack, *ZNW*, 24 (1925), 204 ff., who also showed the probability of their having been produced in the second century A.D., *ZNW*, 25 (1926), 160 ff. This view of the Marcionite origin of the prologues has not been seriously challenged, in spite of the objections raised by M.-J. Lagrange, *RB*, 35 (1926), 161 ff., and H. J. Frede, *Altlateinische Paulus-Handschriften*, Vetus Latina—Aus der Geschichte der altlateinischen Bibel 4 [Concerning the history of the Old Latin Bible], 1964, pp. 168 ff. Finally, see H. von Campenhausen, *Die Entstehung der christlichen Bibel* [The origin of the Christian Bible], 1968, p. 285. The text of the prologues is here translated according to the edition of E. Preuschen, *Analecta: Kürzere Texte zur Geschichte der Alten Kirche und des Kanons* [Analects (fragments): shorter texts on the history of the ancient church and of the Canon], Vol. II, 2nd ed., 1910, pp. 85 ff.

2. On the rise and dubiousness of this criterion, see W. G. Kümmel, "Notwendigkeit und Grenze des Neutestamentlichen Kanons" [Necessity and limits of the New Testament Canon], *ZThK*, 47 (1950), 277 ff. (= Kümmel, *Heilsgeschen*, pp. 230 ff.) ; E. Flesseman-van Leer, "Prinzipien der Sammlung und Ausscheidung bei der Bildung des Kanons" [Principles of inclusion and exclusion in the formation of the Canon], *ZThK*, 61 (1964), 40 ff.; H. von Campenhausen, (*op. cit.*, n. 1), pp. 294 ff. Bibliography on the history of the canon in Feine-Behm-Kümmel, *Introduction to the New Testament*, 14th ed., Eng. tr. by A. J. Mattill, Jr. (Nashville: Abingdon, 1966), pp. 334 ff.; R. M. Grant, *The Formation of the New Testament*, 1965; and H. von Campenhausen (*op. cit.*, n. 1).

3. Quotations with emendations from the Greek text of Eusebius' *Ecclesiastical History*, 6.25. 11-14, tr. J. E. Oulton, 1957, Loeb Classical Library, Vol. II, pp. 77-78. On the uncertain position of Origen concerning the tradition about the authorship of the New Testament writings, see A. von Harnack, *Der kirchengeschichtliche Ertrag der exegetischen Arbeiten des Origenes*, II [The significance for church history of the exegetical work of Origen, Part 2] in *Texte und Untersuchungen zur altchristlichen Literatur* [Texts and studies in the literature of the ancient church], Vol. 42, pt. 4 (1919), pp. 5 ff.

4. The excerpt from the work of Dionysius, "Concerning the Promises," is preserved in Eusebius, *Ecclesiastical History*, 7. 25 (*op. cit.*, n. 3). Quotations with emendations from Vol. II, pp. 197-207. On the historical motive of Dionysius' utterance concerning the Revelation of John, see J. Leipoldt, *Geschichte des Neutestamentlichen Kanons* [History of the New Testament canon], Vol. I, 1907, pp. 65 ff.

5.　　Jerome, *De viris inlustribus*. Chaps. 1, 2, 4, 5, 9, excerpts tr. according to Jerome and Gennadius, *De viris inlustribus*, ed. C. A. Bernoulli, 1895, pp. 6-13. The silence of Jerome, in the chapter on John, about the rejection of the Revelation of John by Dionysius and others is misleading. Although he knows of the fact of their rejection of it, he does not raise the issue since in the West the canonicity of the Revelation was never challenged. See J. Leipoldt, (*op. cit.*, n. 4), pp. 58-59.

6.　　Evidence in support of this criticism is offered by G. W. Meyer, *Geschichte der Schrifterklärung* [History of the interpretation of Scripture], Vol. I, 1802, pp. 157 ff. (on Valla) and Vol. II, 1803, pp. 263 ff. (on Erasmus). More extensive Catholic criticism of the Vulgate was presented by H. Jedin, *Geschichte des Konzils von Trient* [History of the Council of Trent], Vol. II, p. 54. On the influence of L. Valla on Erasmus, see L. Bouyer, "Erasmus in Relation to the Medieval Biblical Tradition," in *Cambridge History of the Bible*, Vol. II, pp. 494 ff. (Hereafter *CHB*.)

7.　　Cf. J. Leipoldt (*op. cit.*, n. 4), Vol. II, 1908, pp. 14 ff.; 33 ff.; A. Wikenhauser, *Introduction to the New Testament* (New York: 1963), pp. 18-19.

8.　　See the quotation on p. 44, and Erasmus, *De libero arbitrio* [Freedom of the will], ed. J. von Walter, 2nd ed., 1935, p. 3: "I could easily become a skeptic if it were permitted in accordance with the invulnerable authority of the divine Scriptures and of the decrees of the Church, to which I always gladly subject myself, whether what that authority prescribes pleases me or not." I am indebted to E.-W. Kohls for the reference to this quotation.

9.　　On the prior history of the fourth decree of April 8, 1546, see H. Jedin (*op. cit.*, n. 6), pp. 42 ff. The council decided explicitly that only the Canon established by the Council of Florence in 1441 was to be approved without any gradation as to canonical value *pari pietatis affectu* [with the same pious attitude] (see p. 27). Cajetan's doubts about the apostolic authorship of those writings already contested in the ancient church were sharply attacked in the course of the discussion (Council Session of February 15, 1546; the sharpest condemnation of Cajetan is by P. Pachecco; see *Concilium Tridentium* [Council of Trent] edition of Societas Goerresiana, Vol. I, 1901, p. 32, ll. 16-20; cf. also p. 32, n. 1). In the decree of April 8, however, Cajetan's position was only implicitly rejected in the references to "the fourteen letters of the Apostle Paul" and the "one letter of the Apostle James." In this way the discussion of the question of authorship was rendered *de facto* impossible. The present-day Catholic exegetes adopt the position—which is scarcely correct historically—that the council intended to reach no decisions on matters of authorship. See A. Wikenhauser, *Introduction to the New Testament*, 4th ed., 1961, p. 45; and J. Schmid, *Theologische Revue*, 62 (1966), col. 306.

10.　　On Luther's teaching concerning scripture see O. Scheel, *Luthers Stellung zur Heiligen Schrift* [Luther's viewpoint on Holy Scripture], 1902; P. Schempp, *Luthers Stellung zur Heiligen Schrift*, 1929; K. Holl, "Luthers Bedeutung für den Fortschritt der Auslegungskunst" [Luther's significance for the progress of the art of exposition] in *Gesammelte Aufsätze zur Kirchengeschichte* [Collected essays on church history], Vol. I, 2nd and 3rd eds., 1923, pp. 544 ff.; G. Ebeling, *Evangelische Evangelienauslegung* [Protestant exposition of the Gospels], 1942; F. Beisser, *Claritas Scripturae bei M. Luther* [The clarity of Scripture in the thought of Martin Luther], 1966; W. G. Kümmel, "Luther und das Neue Testament" [Luther and the New Testament] in *Reformation und Gegenwart* [Reformation and the present] Marburger Theologische Studien 6 [Marburg theological studies], 1968, pp. 1 ff. The quotations given here and in what follows from Luther's works are from the Weimar Edition (hereafter *WA*): "Grund und ursach aller Artikel D. Marti. Luther, szo durch Romische Bulle unrechtlich vordampt seyn" [Basis and origin of all the articles against Dr. Martin Luther, so unjustly condemned through Romish bulls], (January, 1521), *WA*, VII, p. 317. Eng. tr. by C. M. Jacobs, in *Words of Martin Luther*, Vol. III, p. 16 (Philadelphia: Fortress

Press, 1932) ; "Rede vor dem Reichstag zu Worms" [Address before the assembly in Worms] (April 18, 1521) , according to the translation by Spalatin, *WA*, VII, pp. 876 ff., Eng. tr. by Roger A. Hornsby, in *Luther's Works*. Quotations with emendations are from Vol. XXXII, 1958, pp. 112-13. Schmalkaldisch Article (1538) , *WA*, L, p. 206.

11.   A. Rich, *Die Anfänge der Theologie Huldrych Zwinglis* [The beginnings of the theology of Huldreich Zwingli], 1949, pp. 142, 154 ff. The quotations are from Zwingli's collected works (= *Corpus Reformatorum* 88) , 1905: "Von clarheit und gewüsse oder kraft des worts gottes" [Concerning the clarity and certainty or strength of the Word of God] (1522) , p. 352. Eng. tr. from *Zwingli and Bullinger*. LCC, Vol. XXIV, ed. by G. W. Bromiley. Published in the U.S.A. by The Westminster Press, 1953, p. 67; "Ein predig von der ewigreinen magt Maria. . . ." [A sermon on the immaculate virgin Mary] (1522) , pp. 393-94.

12.   *Assertio omnium articulorum M. Lutheri per Bullam Leonis X. novissimam damnatorum* [Declaration of all the articles of Martin Luther condemned through the papal bull of Leo X], *WA*, VII, p. 97 (tr.) .

13.   E. von Dobschütz, "Vom vierfachen Schriftsinn. Die Geschichte einer Theorie" [On the fourfold sense of Scripture: the history of a theory], *Harnack-Ehrung* [Essays in honor of A. von Harnack], 1921, pp. 1 ff.

14.   "Auf das ubirchristlich, ubirgeystlich und ubirkunstlich Buch Bocks Emszers zu Leypzigk Antwort D.M.L." [Answer to the super-Christian, super-spiritual and super-artificial book of goat Emszer from Leipzig, by D (octor) M (artin) L (uther)] (1521) . *WA*, VII, p. 651; Eng. tr. by A. Steimle in *Works of Martin Luther*, Vol. III, 1930, p. 350; *De servo arbitrio* (= Vom unfreien Willen [Bondage of the will] directed against Erasmus, 1525) , *WA*, XVIII, pp. 700 ff., German tr. by Justus Jonas (M. Luther, *Vom unfreien Willen* after the tr. by J. J., ed. Friedrich Gogarten, 1924) , pp. 177 ff. *WA*, Table Talk, III, no. 5285, from the year 1540.

15.   The prefaces to the September Testament of 1522, according to *WA*, German Bible VII, pp. 344, 384, 404; the opinion concerning James is from Table Talk of the year 1533 according to *WA*, Table Talk, III, no. 3292a; Eng. tr. by Jacobs (*op. cit.*, n. 10) , quotations with emendations are from Vol. III, pp. 476-79, 488-89. Cf. Kümmel, "Luthers Vorreden zum Neuen Testament" [Luther's prefaces to the New Testament] (*op. cit.*, n. 10) , pp. 12 ff.

16.   For the evidence, see J. Leipoldt (*op. cit.*, n. 4) , pp. 79 ff.

17.   The text of the decree of the fourth session on April 8, 1546, "Concerning the Canonical Scriptures" is in C. Mirbt and K. Aland, *Quellen zur Geschichte des Papsttums und des römischen Katholizismus* [Sources for the history of the papacy and of Roman Catholicism], Vol. I, 6th ed., 1967, pp. 591-92, and in the *Enchiridium Biblicum* [Biblical handbook], 4th ed., 1961, pp. 25-26.

18.   On the hermeneutic of Flacius see W. Dilthey, "Das natürliche System der Geisteswissenschaften im 17. Jahrhundert" [The natural system of the humane sciences in the 17th century], *Gesammelte Schriften*, Vol. II, 1914, pp. 115 ff.; K. Holl (*op. cit.*, n. 10) , pp. 578 ff.; G. Moldaenke, *Schriftverständnis und Schriftdeutung im Zeitalter der Reformation* [Scriptural understanding and scriptural interpretation in the age of the Reformation], Part I: Matthias Flacius Illyricus, 1936, pp. 124 ff., 248 ff., 562 ff.

19.   See W. Dilthey, *Die Entstehung der Hermeneutik* [The rise of hermeneutics], *Gesammelte Schriften*, Vol. V, 1924, pp. 317 ff., esp. 324-25.

20. Matthaeus Flacius Illyricus, *Clavis Scripturae seu de sermone sacrarum literarum, plurimas generales regulas continentis, altera pars* [Key to the Scripture, or concerning the language of Holy Scripture, wherein numerous general rules are contained, Part 2]. Leipzig, 1965, col. 2, no. 5; col. 72; col. 25, par. 1.

21. *Ibid.*, cols. 82-83.

22. *Ibid.*, col. 39, par. 1.

23. W. Dilthey (*op. cit.*, n. 18), Vol. II, 1914, p. 121.

24. Flacius (*op. cit.*, n. 20), col. 12, par. 2, no. 17.

25. See G. Kittel, *ThWBNT* [Theological Dictionary of the New Testament], 1933, pp. 350-51, tr. G. W. Bromiley, Vol. I., pp. 347-48.

26. Cf. G. Moldaenke (*op. cit.*, n. 18), pp. 526 ff.; K. A. von Schwartz, "Die theologische Hermeneutik des M. Flacius Illyricus" [The theological hermeneutic of M. Flacius Illyricus], *Lutherjahrbuch*, 1933, pp. 143 ff.

27. Joachim Camerarius, *Commentarius in Novum Foedus: In quo et figurae sermonis, et verborum significatio, et orationis sententia, ad illius Foederis intelligentiam certiorem, tractantur* [Commentary on the New Covenant: in which are treated figures of speech, the meaning of words . . .], Cambridge, 1642. The Introduction is here translated from p. 2.

28. *Ibid.*, note 2 comments on Matt. 3:1; John 3:3; I Peter 3:19.

29. Hugo Grotius, *Annotationes in libros Evangeliorum* [Notes on the Gospel books], Amsterdam, 1641. The annotations here translated are on Matt. 6:13; Luke 16:23; 17:21.

30. Hugo Grotius, *Annotationum in Novum Testamentum* II [Notes on the New Testament, Vol. II], Paris, 1646; *Annotationum . . . pars tertia ac ultima* [Notes . . . part third and last], Paris, 1650. Translated here are the preface to II Thess. (Vol. II, pp. 672-73), the prefaces to II Peter and II John (Vol. III, pp. 38, 103 ff.).

31. See W. Kroll *Geschichte der klassischen Philologie* [History of classical philosophy], 2nd ed., 1919, pp. 92 ff.; A. Gudemann, *Grundriss der Geschichte der klassischen Philologie* [Outline of the history of classical philosophy], 2nd ed., 1909, pp. 190 ff.

32. John Lightfoot, . . . *Horae Hebraicae et Talmudicae in Quattuor Evangelistas . . Post editionem primam in Germania e Museo Jo. Benedicti Carpzovi . . . Altera* [Hebrew and Talmudic hours (studies) on the four Gospels . . .], Leipzig, 1684. The translation here given is from pp. 173-74. Cf. also Stephen Neill, *Interpretation of the New Testament*, pp. 282 ff. (Hereafter Neill, *Interpretation*.)

33. The history of the printed Greek text of the New Testament and of the development of textual criticism are traced by C. R. Gregory, *Textkritik des Neuen Testaments* [Textual criticism of the New Testament], Vol. II, 1902, pp. 921 ff., and by Eberhard Nestle, *Einführung in das griechische Neue Testament* [Introduction to the Greek New Testament], 4th ed., by E. von Dobschütz, 1923, pp. 60 ff.; and by Bruce M. Metzger, *The Text of the New Testament*, (New York: Oxford University Press, 1964), pp. 95 ff.

34. Theodor Zahn, *PRE*, V, p. 263.

35. Richard Simon, *Histoire critique du texte du Nouveau Testament, Où l'on établit la Vérité des Actes sur lesquels la Réligion Chrétienne est fondée* [Critical history of the text of the New Testament, wherein is established the truth of the reports on which the Christian religion is based], Rotterdam, 1689. The translations are from the introduction, p. 6; R. Simon, *Histoire critique du Vieux Testament* [Critical history of the Old Testament], new ed., Rotterdam, 1685. The translation is from the author's Introduction, pp. 7-8.

36.   R. Simon, *Histoire critique des principaux commentateurs du Nouveau Testament, depuis le commençement du Christianisme jusques à nôtre temps* [Critical history of the principal commentators on the New Testament from the beginning of Christianity up to our time], Rotterdam, 1693. The translation is from the Introduction, pp. 6, 8-9; and pp. 707-8, 70.

37.   R. Simon, *Histoire critique des versions du Nouveau Testament, où l'on fait connoître quel a été l'usage de la lecture des Livres Sacrés dans les principales Eglises du monde* [Critical history of the versions of the New Testament in which one comes to know what has been the custom in the reading of the Sacred Books in the principal churches of the world], Rotterdam, 1690, pp. 23 ff.

38.   R. Simon, *Histoire critique du texte* (*op. cit.*, n. 35), pp. 14-15, 22, 114, 118, 120 ff.

39.   The manuscripts which Simon examined were located in the Royal Library—now the Bibliothèque Nationale—or in the private library of J. B. Colbert, both of which are in Paris. The information which he cites at the end of the texts here quoted is from manuscripts which were in London or Cambridge and which he must have quoted from the Polyglot Edition of Walton or the Oxford Edition of the New Testament (1675), both of which he knew. See J. Steinmann (*op. cit.*, n. 40), pp. 117 ff., 268; and Bruce Metzger (*op. cit.*, n. 33), pp. 107-8.

40.   H. Ph. K. Henke, *Allgemeine Geschichte der christlichen Kirche nach der Zeitfolge* [General history of the Christian Church according to chronological order], Vol. IV, 4th ed. 1806, pp. 218 ff.; H. Margival, "L'influence de R. Simon," *Revue d'histoire et littérature religieuses*, 4 (1899), 514 ff.; J. Steinmann, *Richard Simon et les órigines de l'exégèse biblique* [Richard Simon and the origins of biblical exegesis], 1960, pp. 7-8, 341 ff. Cf. P. Auvray, in *LThK*, IX, col. 733: "His [Simon's] failure was a misfortune for catholic exegesis." Bossuet was especially annoyed at Simon for having published his criticism in the vernacular (see Steinmann, pp. 416-17).

41.   *Novum Testamentum Graecum cum lectionibus variantibus . . . studio et labore*, Joannis Millii. *Collectionem Millianam . . . locupletavit*, Ludolphus Kusterus [The Greek New Testament with variant readings, being the fruit of the study and labor of John Mill . . . edited by Ludolph Küster], Amsterdam, 1710, p. 167, par. 1503. The origin of the edition is described by A. Fox, in *John Mill and Richard Bentley*, 1954, pp. 56 ff. On Küster's New Edition, pp. 89 ff.

42.   C. R. Gregory, *PRE* XIII, p. 73. Mill was severely upbraided for having collected more than thirty thousand variants, thereby corrupting the text and undercutting the authority of Scripture. As early as 1709 D. Whitby raised this charge. See Bruce Metzger (*op. cit.*, n. 33) pp. 107-9.

43.   J. A. Bengel, *Novum Testamentum Graecum ita adornatum ut Textus probatarum editionum medullam. Margo variantium lectionum in suas classes distributarum locorumque parallelorum delectum. Apparatus subjunctus criseos sacrae Millianae praesertim compendium, limam, supplementum ac fructum inserviente* [Greek New Testament . . . with variant readings in the margin . . . and apparatus attached . . .], Tübingen, 1734.

44.   Prior to Bengel, the few editions which had ventured to produce a critically altered text had exercised no influence. See on this E. Reuss, *Die Geschichte der heiligen Schriften des Neuen Testaments* [The history of the Holy Scriptures of the New Testament], 6th ed., 1887, pp. 467 ff.

45. J. A. Bengel (*op. cit.*, n. 43), p. 379, sec. 10; p. 385, sec. 26; p. 384, sec. 21; p. 433, sec. 34. The last-named of these rules had already been proposed in another formulation by J. S. Mill. See A. Fox (*op. cit.*, n. 41), pp. 147-48. The frequently used formulation, *difficilior lectio potior* [The more difficult reading is more probably (original)], seems to have been formed by combining several different rules proposed by J. J. Griesbach in the second edition of his text of the New Testament (1796), as E. Bickersteth of the editorial staff of the *Encyclopaedia Britannica* has kindly pointed out to me.

46. See on this E. Nestle, *Marginalien und Materialen* [Marginal notes and materials], Vol. II, pt. 3, 1893, pp. 66 ff.; concerning Bengel's defense against this attack, cf. H. Reiss, *Das Verständnis der Bibel bei J. A. Bengel* [J. A. Bengel's understanding of the Bible], Münster University dissertation in typescript, pp. 68 ff.

47. J. A. Bengel, *Gnomon Novi Testamenti, in quo ex nativa verborum vi simplicitas, profunditas, concinnitas, salubritas sensuum coelestium iudicatur* [Gnomon of the New Testament, in which on the basis of the natural setting of the words, is vindicated the simplicity, the profundity, the elegance and the wholesomeness of the heavenly sense (of Scripture)], Tübingen, 1742, frequently reprinted.

48. P. Wernle, *Der schweizerische Protestantismus in XVIII. Jahrhundert* [Swiss Protestantism in the eighteenth century], Vol. I, 1923, pp. 522 ff.

49. *Novum Testamentum Graecum editionis receptae cum lectionibus variantibus . . . necnon commentario pleniore . . . opera et studio Joannis Jacobi Wetstenii* [The Greek New Testament in the received edition with variant readings . . . not without a full commentary . . . (being) the work and study of John Jacob Wettstein], 2 vols., Amsterdam, 1751/52.

50. In this manner there appeared, for example, the Lukan form of the Lord's Prayer (Luke 11:2-3) as it is recognized today; the additions to John 7:53 ff., Matt. 27:35b, and I John 5:7 were omitted, but in I Tim. 3:16, ὃς ἐφανερώθη ["who was manifested"] was read—all of them as in the present-day critical text. On the other hand, the addition to John 5:4 was not omitted.

51. Wettstein (*op. cit.*, n. 49), Vol. I, p. 1; Vol. II, pp. 875, 876, 878 as here translated.

52. G. V. Lechler, *Geschichte des englischen Deismus* [History of English Deism], 1841; E. Troeltsch, "Der Deismus" [Deism], in *Gesammelte Schriften* [Collected writings], Vol. IV, 1925, pp. 429 ff.; L. Zscharnack, "Englischer Deismus," in *RGG*, I, 2nd ed., cols. 1805 ff.; E. Hirsch, *Geschichte der neueren evangelischen Theologie* [A history of recent Protestant theology], Vol. I, 1949, pp. 271 ff. (Hereafter Hirsch, *Geschichte*.) M. Schmidt, "Englischer Deismus," in *RGG*, II, cols. 59 ff.

53. John Locke, *The Reasonableness of Christianity, as delivered in the Scriptures*, 1695, pp. 30-31, 290-95, 304; John Locke, "An Essay of the Understanding of St. Paul's Epistles, by consulting St. Paul himself," 1705-1707. Quotations from the latter as published in *The Works of John Locke*, 10 vols., 1801. Vol. VIII, 10th ed., Preface, pp. viii, xvi, xxi.

54. John Toland, *Nazarenus: or Jewish, Gentile and Mahometan Christianity*, London, 1718, esp. chaps. 9–14. Cf. G. V. Lechler (*op. cit.*, n. 52), pp. 469 ff.

55. Frequently asserted, for example, in Hirsch, *Geschichte*, Vol. I, p. 323.

56. [Matthew Tindal], *Christianity as Old as the Creation: or the Gospel a Republication of the Religion of Nature*, London, 2nd ed., 1731, pp. 234-35, 237. A German translation by J. L. Schmitt also appeared anonymously under the title *Beweis, dass das Christenthum so alt als die Welt sei, nebst Herrn Jacob Fosters Widerlegung desselben*

[Proof that Christianity is as old as the world, together with Mr. Jacob Foster's contradiction of the same], 1741.

57. Thomas Chubb, *The True Gospel of Jesus Christ, Asserted,* London, 1738, pp. 43-44, 46-47, 142.

58. [Thomas Morgan], *The Moral Philosopher in a Dialogue between Philalethes a Christian Deist and Theophanes a Christian Jew,* London, 2nd ed., 1738; *The Moral Philosopher,* Vol. II, *Being a Farther Vindication of Moral Truth and Reason . . . by Philalethes,* London, 1739; *The Moral Philosopher,* Vol. III, *Superstition and Tyranny inconsistent with Theocracy, by Philalethes,* London, 1740, Vol. I, pp. 80, 377; Letter to Eusebius, p. 25 in the Appendix to Vol. II; III, pp. 188-90.

59. See on the history of the influence of Deism, A. Tholuck, *Vermischte Schriften* [Miscellaneous writings], Vol. II, 1839, pp. 23 ff.; G. V. Lechler (*op. cit.,* n. 52), pp. 444 ff.; E. Troeltsch (*op. cit.,* n. 52), Vol. IV, pp. 468 ff.; P. Wernle (*op. cit.,* n. 48), Vol. I, pp. 472 ff.; M. Schmidt, *RGG,* II, cols. 158-59. In Germany the Halle theologian S. J. Baumgarten, from 1748 on, directed attention to the deistic literature through his abstracts and reports of it. See Hirsch, *Geschichte,* Vol. II, pp. 371-72.

60. *De Sacrae Scripturae interpretandae methodo tractatus bipartitus, In quo Falsae Multorum Interpretum Hypotheses Refelluntur, Veraque Interpretandae Sacrae Scripturae Methodus adstruitur, Auctore* Joanne Alphonso Turretino [A Bipartite tractate concerning the method by which the sacred Scriptures are to be interpreted, in which the false hypotheses of interpretation used by many are refuted, and the true method by which the sacred Scriptures are to be interpreted is presented by Jean Aphonse Turretini], Trajecti Thuviorum, 1728. The translations are from pp. 196, 311 ff., 322-23, 333-34. On the manner of publication of this book, see the information in the *Bibliothèque raisonée des ouvrages des savants de l'Europe,* Vol. I, 1728, pp. 121 ff., according to which the book was published in Dordrecht.

61. W. A. Teller, a younger contemporary of Ernesti, said concerning the *Institutio* after the latter's death, "Quite apart from my own view, it was determined that the draft of the interpretation of the New Testament as Ernesti conceived it should be a wholly classic work of its kind. It should also remain so, as a result of what it even now is through the supplements and information adduced by such a masterhand, and of what one might wish it to become through the progressive growth of insight in subsequent developments." Teller, *Des Herrn Joh. August Ernesti . . . Verdienste um die Theologie und Religion* [The contribution of Mr. J. A. Ernesti to theology and religion], Berlin, 1783, pp. 9-10. The fifth edition of the *Institutio* appeared in 1809.

62. Jo. Augusti Ernesti, *Institutio interpretis Novi Testamenti,* ed. alt. [Advice for the Interpreter of the New Testament, rev. ed.], Leipzig, 1765. The translation is from pp. 11-15 and 87.

63. Semler's teacher, S. J. Baumgarten, had made the deistic literature known in Germany (see n. 59), and Semler had devoted himself to reading and partial translation of this literature (see P. Gastrow, *J. S. Semler,* 1905, pp. 64 ff.; and L. Zscharnack, *Lessing und Semler,* 1905, pp. 30 ff.). Semler wrote prefaces and annotations for H. M. A. Cramer's German translations of R. Simon's treatise on the text and translations of the New Testament (1776-80). Certainly Semler directed his criticism explicitly against the Catholic-dogmatic tendency of Simon's work. See the evidence in G. Hornig's *Die Anfänge der historisch-kritischen Theologie; J. S. Semlers Schriftverständnis . . .* [The beginnings of historical-critical theology: J. S. Semler's understanding of Scripture], 1961, pp. 184 ff. Michaelis himself attributes to his stay in England a decisive influence on his thought (J. G. Eichhorn, in the appendix to J. D. Michaelis' autobiography, 1793, pp. 155, 203-4; L. Salvatorelli in *HTR,* 21 [1929], 272-73). According to Th. Zahn (*PRE,* V, 264), Michaelis based the first edition of his

Einleitung in die göttlichen Schriften des Neuen Bundes [Introduction to the divine Scriptures of the New Covenant], 1750, entirely on Simon.

64. J. G. Eichhorn, *Allgemeine Bibliotek der biblischen Litteratur* [Universal library of biblical literature], Vol. V, 1793, p. 8.

65. *Ibid.,* p. 24.

66. G. Hornig (*op. cit.,* n. 63), pp. 251 ff., cites 218 writings of Semler as having appeared in print.

67. Hirsch, *Geschichte,* Vol. IV, 1952, p. 50. So previously in J. G. Eichhorn; see G. Hornig (*op. cit.,* n. 63), 16, *n.* 17.

68. *D. Joh. Salomo Semlers Abhandlung von freier Untersuchung des Canon* [Dr. J. S. Semler's treatise on free research in the Canon], Vols. I-IV, Halle, 1771-75. On this work see L. Zscharnack, *Lessing und Semler,* 1905, pp. 96 ff.; H. Strathmann, "Die Krisis des Kanons der Kirche," *Theologische Blätter* 20 (1941), 298 ff.; G. Hornig (*op. cit.,* n. 63), pp. 59 ff. H. Scheible, whose new edition for academic instruction is somewhat modernized linguistically (Semler, *Abhandlung* . . . : Texte zur Kirchen- und Theologiegeschichte 5 [Texts for the history of Church and theology], 1967, has reprinted only the basic treatise of the first volume (pp. 1-128). The page numbers in n. 69 refer to quotations from this new edition only from that part of Semler's work.

69. J. S. Semler (*op. cit.,* n. 68), Vol. I., pp. 75, 117, 25-26, 53-54; Vol. II, Preface a, 4 f.; Vol. II, pp. 39-40; Vol. I, 15-16, 19. "Response to the Tübingen defense . . . ," 125 f. (in Scheible [*op. cit.,* n. 68], pp. 60, 85, 28-29, 47, 21-22, 24). On Semler's concept of "moral" in the "ethical-religious" sense, cf. G. Hornig (*op. cit.,* n. 63), pp. 106 ff.

70. *J. S. Semlers Vorbereitung zur theologischen Hermeneutik, zur weiteren Beförderung des Fleisses angehender Gottesgelehrten nebst Antwort auf die Tübingische Vertheidigung der Apocalypsis* [J. S. Semler's preparatory study on theological hermeneutics, for the promotion of diligence among beginning learned divines, together with a reply to the Tübingen defense of the Apocalypse], Halle, 1760, pp. 6-8, 149-50, 160-62.

71. Jo. Sal. Semleri, *Paraphrasis epistolae ad Romanos cum notis translatione vetusta et dissertatione de appendice cap. XV-XVI* [Paraphrase of the Epistle to the Romans, with notes, an ancient translation and a dissertation on the appendix, chaps. 15 and 16], Halle, 1769, pp. 277 ff. Other literary theses of Semler's are enumerated in A. Hilgenfeld, *Der Kanon und die Kritik des Neuen Testaments in ihrer geschichtlichen Ausbildung und Gestaltung* [The Canon and criticism of the New Testament in their historical development and formation], 1863, pp. 115 ff.; and G. Karo, *J. S. Semler,* 1905, pp. 46 ff.

72. J. S. Semler (*op. cit.,* n. 68), Vol. I, pp. 124 ff.; Semler, *Versuch einer freiern theologischen Lehrart* [An Attempt at a freer mode of theological instruction], Halle, 1777, pp. 154 ff.

73. J. S. Semler (*op. cit.,* n. 68), Vol. IV, Preface, b, 8 recto—c, 1 recto.

74. E. Reuss (*op. cit.,* n. 44), p. 644.

75. F. C. Baur, *Theologische Jahrbücher,* 9 (1850), 525.

76. An outstanding review of this is to be found in C. W. F. Walch, *Neue Religions-Geschichte* [New history of religion], pt. 7, 1779, pp. 291. ff.

77. J. S. Semler (*op. cit.*, n. 68), Vol. III, Preface a, 2 verso, Preface c, 4 verso. On Semler's ideas about the divinity of Holy Scripture see G. Hornig (*op. cit.*, n. 63), pp. 73 ff.

78. See Th. Zahn, *PRE*, IV, p. 264.

79. See n. 63. After all, Michaelis is concerned in his first edition with the origin of individual writings of the New Testament and already poses there the question about the "divinity" of individual scriptures in connection with the question about their apostolic authorship. Cf. W. G. Kümmel, " 'Einleitung in das Neue Testament' als theologische Aufgabe," in *EvTh*, 19 (1959), 4 ff. (= Kümmel, *Heilsgeschehen*, pp. 340 ff.)

80. G. W. Meyer, *Geschichte der Schrifterklärung* [The history of the exposition of Scripture], Vol. V, 1809, p. 453.

81. He refers only to the fact that "in very recent times the doctrine of the Canon began to be researched, or rather contested" (J. D. Michaelis, *Introduction*, Vol. I, 4th ed., Göttingen, 1788, p. 91), and he simply asserted that "the collecting of the writings that we now call the New Testament" for the most part took place after the death of the apostles and must be very old, so that for this reason, it is concealed in the dark of unhistorical times" (Vol. I, pp. 277 ff.). So far as I can see, Semler's *Treatise* was not referred to at all in the whole of Michaelis' *Introduction*, even though he had published a review of it (Orientalische und exegetische Bibliotek 3 [Oriental and exegetical library], 1773, pp. 26 ff.). G. W. Meyer (*op. cit.*, n. 80) Vol. V, pp. 373, 450, traces Michaelis' silence about Semler in another connection to "a certain jealousy toward Semler and his contribution to New Testament criticism."

82. J. D. Michaelis (*op. cit.*, n. 81), Vol. I, pp. 13-14, 73, 75-76, 82, 92, 100; Vol. II, pp. 893, 997, 1395, 1400-1401, 1403, 1444, 1515-16.

83. *Ibid.*, Vol. I., p. 81.

84. Hirsch, *Geschichte*, Vol. IV, p. 33. On this problem see the essay mentioned in note 79.

85. Nevertheless, Griesbach did improve in later editions the existing text and the apparatus. See on this G. W. Meyer (*op. cit.*, n. 80), Vol. V, 1809, pp. 227 ff., 273 ff.; and E. Reuss (*op. cit.*, n. 44), 6th ed. 1887, pp. 470-71.

86. See C. R. Gregory, *Textkritik des Neuen Testaments*, Vol. II, 1902, pp. 910-11.

87. G. W. Meyer (*op. cit.*, n. 80), pp. 474 ff.

88. *Synopsis Evangeliorum Matthäi Marci et Lucae una cum iis Joannis pericopis quae omnino cum caeterorum Evangelistarum narrationibus conferendae sunt. Textum recensuit* . . . J. J. Griesbach [Synopsis of the Gospels of Matthew, Mark, and Luke, together with those pericopes in which all the evangelists can be compared as to their narratives. The text edited by J. J. Griesbach], Halle, 1776. The text had already appeared as part of the first edition of Griesbach's Greek New Testament in 1774. The quotation from the Preface to the second edition of 1797 is translated according to the fourth edition of 1822, pp. viii-ix.

89. In this hypothesis Griesbach had a predecessor, obviously unknown to him, in H. Owen, whose *Observations of the Four Gospels* had appeared in 1764 (according to the note of J. G. Eichhorn, *Einleitung in das Neue Testament* (*op. cit.*, n. 96), Vol. I, 1804, p. 375, n. e.

90. J. J. Griesbach . . . *Commentatio qua Marci Evangelium totum e Matthaei et Lucae commentariis decerptum esse monstratur* [Demonstration in which the entire Gospel of Mark is shown to be excerpted from the narratives of Matthew and Luke],

1789/90; reprinted in an expanded form in *Commentationes Theologicae*, ed. J. C. Velthusen, C. Th. Kuinoel, and G. A. Ruperti, Vol. I, 1794, pp. 360 ff. The translated excerpts are from this edition, pp. 417, 434.

91.   G. Chr. Storr, *Über den Zweck der evangelischen Geschichte und der Briefe Johannis* [On the aim of the gospel history and the letters of John], Tübingen, 1786, pp. 274 ff., 287 ff.

92.   G. E. Lessing, "Theses aus der Kirchengeschichte" [Theses from the history of the Church], *Lessings Werke* [Lessing's works], complete edition in twenty-five parts, ed. J. Petersen and W. v. Olshausen; pt. 21, *Theologische Schriften* [Theological writings], Vol. II, ed. L. Zscharnack, pp. 284 ff.; the quotation is from sec. 47.

93.   G. E. Lessing, "New Hypothesis Concerning the Evangelists Considered as merely Human Historians," *Theologische Schriften*, Vol. IV, pp. 120 ff. Eng. tr. by Henry Chadwick, in *Lessing's Theological Writings*, translation with an introduction (London: A. and C. Black, and Palo Alto: Stanford University Press, 1956). Quotations with emendations. Cf. on the historical place of this writing L. Zscharnack (*op. cit.*, n. 92), pp. 15 ff.

94.   *Ibid.* (Eng. tr.), pp. 70, 72-73, 78-79, 80-81.

95.   J. G. Eichhorn, *"Über die drey ersten Evangelien: Einige Beyträge zu ihrer künftigen kritischen Behandlung"* [Concerning the first three Gospels: some contributions to their future critical treatment], from Eichhorn's *Universal Library* (*op. cit.*, n. 64), Vol. V, pp. 759-996; the quotations are from pp. 775 and 967.

96.   J. G. Eichhorn, *Einleitung in das Neue Testament* [Introduction to the New Testament], 5 vols. Leipzig, 1804-27, Vol. I, 1804, pp. 406, 411, 458-59. (Hereafter Eichhorn, *Introduction*.

97.   J. G. Herder, *Christliche Schriften*. [Christian Writings] Second collection: *Vom Erlöser der Menschen. Nach unsern drei ersten Evangelien* [Concerning the Redeemer of men; according to our first three Gospels], 1796. Third collection: *Von Gottes Sohn, der Welt Heiland. Nach Johannes Evangelium. Nebst einer Regel der Zusammenstimmung unserer Evangelien aus ihrer Entstehung and Ordung* [Concerning the Son of God, the Savior of the world; according to the Gospel of John; together with a rule for the agreement of our Gospels based on their origin and order], 1797. Also in Herder's *Collected Works*, ed. B. Suphan, Vol. XIX, 1880, pp. 135 ff., 253 ff.

98.   Herder, *ibid.*, Vol. XIX, p. 416 *n.*

99.   *Ibid.*, Vol. XIX, pp. 196-97, 382, 273 *n.*, 198-99, 209-11, 213-14, 417-18, 391.

100.   Attention was drawn to this by C. H. Weisse, *Die evangelische Geschichte kritisch und philosophisch bearbeitet* [The Gospel history treated critically and philosophically], 2 vols., Leipzig, 1838, Vol. I, p. 10; and A. Hilgenfeld (*op. cit.*, n. 71), pp. 142, 146. F. A. Wolfius, in *Prolegomena ad Homerum*, Vol. I, 1795, represented the viewpoint that the Homeric poems were transmitted orally as individual songs and only in later times were they for the first time put together and written down.

101.   Herder (*op. cit.*, n. 97), Vol. XIX, pp. 239, 242-43, 250.

102.   J. C. L. Gieseler, *Historisch-kritischer Versuch über die Entstehung und die frühesten Schicksale der schriftlichen Evangelien* [An historical-critical essay concerning the formation and the earliest fate of the written Gospels], Leipzig, 1818, pp. 93, 137.

103. F. Schleiermacher, "Über die Schriften des Lukas, ein kritischer Versuch" [Concerning the writings of Luke; a critical essay], 1817. *Sämtliche Werke* [Collected works], Vol. I, pt. 2, 1836, pp. 1 ff.

104. F. Schleiermacher, "Über die Zeugnisse des Papias von unseren ersten beiden Evangelien, 1832" [Concerning the witnesses of Papias for our first two Gospels], (*op. cit.*, n. 103), pp. 361 ff.

105. F. Schleiermacher, "Über den sogenannten ersten Brief des Paulos an den Timotheos. Ein kritisches Sendschreiben an J. C. Gass, 1807." [Concerning the so-called first Letter of Paul to Timothy; a critical communication addressed to J. C. Gass], (*op. cit.*, n. 103), pp. 221 ff. The quotations are from pp. 224 and 318.

106. F. Schleiermacher, *Einleitung ins neue Testament, Aus Schleiermachers handschriftlichem Nachlasse und nachgeschriebenen Vorlesungen . . hrsg. v. G. Wolde* [Introduction to the New Testament, edited by G. Wolde on the basis of Schleiermacher's handwritten literary remains and notes taken from his lectures], (*op. cit.*, n. 103), Vol. I, pt. 8, 1845, pp. 87, 121-22, 194). Schleiermacher doubted also that Paul was the direct author of Ephesians, but he at the same time rejected the position as "rash" that the *three* Pastorals were ungenuine. (p. 172). As early as 1811, Schleiermacher had declared in his "Kurze Darstellung des theologischen Studiums" [Brief presentation of theological study] (critical ed. by H. Scholz, 1910), sec. 110, that it was more important to decide if a book was canonical or not than if it belonged to this or that author, since in either case it could still be canonical.

107. Eichhorn, *Introduction*, Vol. III, pt. 1, 1812, pp. 315 ff.

108. Enumerated by A. Hilgenfeld, "Die Evangelienforschung nach ihrem Verlauf und gegenwärtigen Stand" [Gospel research; process and present state] *Zeitschrift für wissenschaftliche Theologie* 4 (1861), 39-40.

109. [E. F. Vogel], *Der Evangelist Johannes und seine Ausleger von dem jüngsten Gericht* [The Evangelist John and his interpreters before the Last Judgment], Vols. I and II, 1801-4. Vogel emphasized particularly that this could mean "only the most recent judgment, not the last judgment at the end of the world" (Vol. I, p. 40).

110. G. K. Horst, "Über einige Widersprüche in dem Evangelium des Johannis in Absicht auf den Logos, oder has Höhere in Christo" [Concerning some contradictions in the Gospel of John with a view to the Logos or the higher reality in Christ]; *idem* "Läst sich die Echtheit des johannischen Evangeliums aus hinlänglichen Gründen bezweifeln, und welches ist der wahrscheinliche Ursprung dieser Schrift?" [Are there sufficient grounds for doubting the genuineness of the Johannine Gospel, and what is the probable origin of this writing?] *Museum für Religionswissenschaft in ihrem ganzen Umfange* [Museum for religious science in its entire scope], ed. H. Ph. K. Henke, Vol. I, Magdeburg, 1804, pp. 21 ff., 47 ff.

111. H. H. Cludius, *Uransichten des Christenthums nebst Untersuchungen über einige Bücher des neuen Testaments* [Primitive perspectives of Christianity, together with researches concerning a few books of the New Testament], Altona, 1808, pp. 50 ff. A similar opinion was represented by Christoph Friedrich Ammon in 1811, that our Gospel of John is an adaptation of the authentic Johannine Gospel (in *Erlanger Oster-programm, "quo docetur Johannem Evangelii auctorem ab editore huis libri fuisse diversum"* [in which it is demonstrated that the author of the Gospel of John was someone different from the editor of this book]; cf. J. D. Schmidt, *Die theologischen Wandlungen des Christoph Friedrich von Ammon* [The theological shifts of C. F. von Ammon] (Erlangen dissertation, 1953, p. 39). I owe this reference to the kindness of Dr. O. Merk.

112.   C. Th. Bretschneider, *Probabilia de evangelii et epistolarum Joannis, apostoli, indole et origine eruditorum judiciis modeste subjecit* [Probability concerning the mode and origin of the Gospel and of the Letters of the Apostle John, modesty offered for the judgment of the learned], Leipzig, 1820. The quotations are from pp. vii and 113.

113.   "Einige Bemerkungen zu den Aufsätzen des Herrn D. Goldhorn . . . über das Schweigen des Johanneischen Evangelium von dem Seelen-kampf Jesus in Gethsemane; von Bretschneider" ["A few remarks on the essays of Mr. D. Goldhorn concerning the silence of the Johannine Gospel about the struggle of soul of Jesus in Gethsemane, by Bretschneider"], *Magazin für christliche Prediger* [Magazine for Christian preachers], ed. H. G. Tzschirner, Vol. II, no. 2, Hannover and Leipzig, 1824, pp. 153 ff. The quotation is from p. 155. In his autobiography, *Aus meinem Leben* [Out of my life], (Gotha, 1851) Bretschneider declared (pp. 119-20) : "I answered to no one and allowed free course to the judgment of the scholarly world," and accordingly he concealed his publicly uttered agreement with those who rejected his critical thesis!

114.   H. H. Cludius (*op. cit.*, n. 111) , pp. 296 ff.; W. M. L. de Wette, *Lehrbuch der historisch-kritischen Einleitung in die kanonischen Bücher des Neuen Testaments* [Textbook of historical-critical introduction to the canonical books of the New Testament], Berlin, 2nd ed., 1830, pp. 231, 262 ff. In the fifth edition of his Introduction, de Wette designated the Letter to the Ephesians as the "work of an imitator"; later he also came to consider the Pastoral Letters, James and II Peter as not genuine (see R. Smend, *W. M. L. de Wettes Arbeit am Alten und am Neuen Testament* [W. M. L. de Wette's work on the Old and New Testaments], 1958, pp. 156 ff.)

115.   Eichhorn, *Introduction* (*op. cit.*, n. 96) .

116.   *Ibid.*, Vol. IV, p. 25.

117.   *Ibid.*, Vol. IV, pp. 8, 67-68. An even less clear position was adopted by de Wette (*op. cit.*, n. 114) , who offered no history of the Canon at all, but said of all three Pastorals that they ought not to be received historically as Pauline letters, although critical doubt about them did not reach the point of shattering faith in them as genuine, since "in any case there could be no talk of excluding from the Canon these monuments of the apostolic age" (p. 288) . Cf. R. Smend (*op. cit.*, n. 114) , pp. 159 ff., 180 ff.; after 1844 de Wette declared unambiguously that the Pastorals were not genuine; cf. R. Smend, p. 161.

118.   A. C. Lundsteen, *H. S. Reimarus*, 1939, pp. 26 ff.

119.   "Von dem Zwecke Jesu und seiner Jünger" [On the purpose of Jesus and his disciples], pt. 1, secs. 3, 30; pt. 2, sec. 53; (= G. E. Lessing (*op. cit.*, n. 92) , Vol. XXII, pp. 212, 259, 308-9.

120.   A. C. Lundsteen (*op. cit.*, n. 118) , pp. 14-15. D. F. Strauss still speaks only of the "Wolfenbüttler Fragmentist."

121.   J. S. Semler, in an imaginary conversation which appeared as an appendix to his writing, "Beantwortung der Fragmente eines Ungenannten insbesondere vom Zweck Jesu und seiner Jünger" [An answer to the fragments by an unknown person, especially "on the aim of Jesus and his disciples"], Halle, 1779, compared Lessing with a man who discovered a candle burning in a granary and did not extinguish it, but fanned it into flame with straw in order to prevent the fire from breaking out during the night. Semler left open the question about Lessing's true motive in publishing the fragments. On Lessing's position concerning the Fragments, see Lundsteen (*op. cit.*, n. 118) , pp. 149 ff., and W. von Loewenich, *Luther und Lessing* 1960 pp. 9 ff.

122.   D. F. Strauss, *Gesammelte Schriften* [Collected writings], Vol. V, p. 398; A. Schweitzer, *Geschichte der Leben-Jesu-Forschung*, 2nd ed., English tr. *The Quest of the Historical Jesus* (*op. cit.*, n. 161), p. 22. (Hereafter *Quest*.)

123.   P. Wernle, *ThLZ* 31 (1906), 502; A. C. Lundsteen (*op. cit.*, n. 118), pp. 108 ff., 137 ff.

124.   J. S. Semler, (*op. cit.*, n. 121), p. 280.

125.   *Ibid*, Preface, sheet b. p. 1.

126.   Examples given by A. Schweitzer (*op. cit.*, n. 161), pp. 51 ff. The forerunners of H. E. G. Paulus are noted on pp. 27 ff.

127.   Hirsch, *Geschichte*, Vol. V, 1954, p. 28. When Hirsch continues, "He makes no attempt at source or narrative criticism," that is an overstatement. In single instances Paulus had even declared one event to be a "non-fact," such as the guard at the tomb. See H. E. G. Paulus, *Philologisch-kritischer und historischer Kommentar über die drey ersten Evangelien, in welchem der griechische Text, nach einer Recognition der Varianten, Interpunctionen und Abschnitte, durch Einleitungen, Inhaltsanzeigen und ununterbrochene Scholien als Grundlage der Geschichte des Urchristentums synoptisch und chronologisch bearbeit ist* [A philological, critical, and historical commentary on the first three Gospels, in which the Greek text, after the recognition of variants, punctuation and sections, is made to serve through introductions, indications of content and uninterrupted marginal comments, as the basis for a synoptic and chronological history of primitive Christianity], 3 vols., Lübeck, 1800-1802; the quotation is from Vol. III, p. 855. Paulus, *Das Leben Jesu, als Grundlage einer reinen Geschichte des Urchristentums* [The life of Jesus, as the foundation of a purely historical study of primitive Christianity], (4 vols., Heidelberg, 1828), Vol. I, pt. 1; Vol. II, pt. 2. See Vol. I, pt. 2, pp. 260 ff.

128.   H. E. G. Paulus, *Kommentar* (*op. cit.*, n. 127), Vol. I, pp. xii-xiii; *Leben* (*op. cit.*, n. 127), Vol. II, pt. 1, pp. x-xi, xiii-xiv, Vol. I, pt. 1, pp. 362, 364.

129.   *Das Leben Jesu: Vorlesungen an der Universität zu Berlin im Jahre 1832 gehalten von Friedrich Schleiermacher* [The Life of Jesus: lectures presented by F. Schleiermacher at the University of Berlin in the year 1832], ed. K. A. Rütenik on the basis of posthumous notes and the records of those who heard the lectures (= Schleiermacher, *Sämtliche Werke* [Collected works], Vol. VI, pt. 1, p. 1864.) Cf. A. Schweitzer (*op. cit.*, n. 161), pp. 62 ff.; and Hirsch, *Geschichte*, Vol. V., pp. 33 ff.

130.   K. Hase, *Das Leben Jesu: Ein Lehrbuch* [The life of Jesus: a textbook], Leipzig, 1829. The quotations in the text are from pp. iii, 63, 159-60, 5, 107, 87, 113, 12; the following section of the foreword is from pp. vii-ix. In his recollections of youth, which appeared in 1871, Hase justly described his book as "the first purely scientific representation of the new life-of-Jesus science in anticipation of its great stormy future." In 1865 he brought out a new, expanded fifth edition ("Ideale und Irrthümer" [Ideal and error], reprinted in *Gesammelte Werke* [Collected works], Vol. IX, pt. 1, 1890, p. 203. The origin and later development of Hase's Jesus research is described by G. Fuss, in "Die Auffassung des Lebens Jesu bei dem Jenaer Kirchenhistoriker Karl von Hase," pt. 1; Jena Dissertation (typescript), 1955. Reported in *ThLZ*, 84 (1959), 136-37. Fuss shows that at the time of the appearance of the first edition of his *Life of Jesus*, Hase had only heard of Schleiermacher's lectures on this subject, but had not seen them at all (p. 21).

131.   L. Usteri, *Entwicklung des Paulinischen Lehrbegriffes mit Hinsicht auf die übrigen Schriften des Neuen Testamentes. Ein exegetisch-dogmatischer Versuch* [Development of the Pauline doctrine with a view to the other Scriptures of the New Testament: an exegetical-dogmatic essay], Zürich, 1824. The quotations are from pp. v-vi, 2, 5, iii, 57-58, 92, 163. Several less important forerunners of Usteri are commented on by E. Reuss, *Histoire de la théologie chrétienne au siècle apostolique* [A history of Christian theology in the apostolic age], Vol. II, 1852, pp. 10 ff.

132. Only in isolated instances was objection raised about the doubtful genuineness of I Timothy. Usteri (*op. cit.*, n. 131), pp. 60, 149.

133. See E. Reuss (*op. cit.*, n. 131), Vol. II, pp. 280-81.

134. K. Frommann, *Der Johanneische Lehrbegriff in seinem Verhältnisse zur gesamten biblisch-christlichen Lehre* [Johannine teaching in its relation to the whole biblical, Christian doctrine], Leipzig, 1839, pp. 48, 73-74, 82, 505.

135. See the titles in F. C. Baur, *Vorlesungen über Neutestamentliche Theologie* [Lectures on New Testament theology], 1864, p. 3. On the history of the concept, "biblical theology," see G. Ebeling, "The Meaning of 'Biblical Theology,'" in *Word and Faith*, 1963, pp. 79-97, where it is shown that the concept *Theologia Biblica* arose at the beginning of the seventeenth century.

136. G. T. Zachariä, *Biblische Theologie, oder Untersuchung des biblischen Grundes der vornehmsten theologischen Lehren* [Biblical theology, or research into the biblical basis of the major theological teachings], 4 vols., Göttingen and Kiel, 1771-75. Zachariä offers as a definition: "By biblical theology I understand here as a whole, an exact determination of the entire range of theological teachings, with all the doctrinal statements appropriate to them, and the proper understanding of these statements according to biblical concepts, according to their evidential grounding in Holy Scripture" (Vol. I, p. 1). Cf. F. C. Baur (*op. cit.*, n. 135), pp. 4 ff.

137. J. Ph. Gabler, *De iusto discrimine theologiae biblicae et dogmaticae regundisque recte utriusque finibus* [On the proper distinction between biblical and dogmatic theology and the proper determination of the goals of each], Altdorf, 1787; (=Jo. Phil. Gableri Opuscula Academica II, Ulm, 1831, pp. 179 ff.). The quotations are translated from pp. 183-87; 190-93. Cf. R. Smend, Johann Gabler's "Begründung der biblischen Theologie," *EvTh* 22 (1962), 345 ff.; and K. Leder, Universität Altdorf: *Zur Theologie der Aufklärung in Franken* [On the theology of the enlightenment in Franconia], 1965, pp. 284 ff.

138. This evidence was first adduced by Chr. Hartlich and W. Sachs, in *Der Ursprung des Mythosbegriffs in der modernen Bibelwissenschaft* [The origin of the concept of myth in modern study of the Bible], 1952, pp. 11 ff. See H. J. Kraus, *Geschichte der historisch-kritischen Erforschung des Alten Testaments* [History of the historical-critical research in the Old Testament], 2nd ed., 1969, pp. 147 ff. Hereafter Kraus, *Geschichte*.

139. Cf., for example, J. G. Eichhorn, "Über die Engelerscheinungen in der Apostelgeschichte" [Concerning the appearance of the angel in Acts], (*op. cit.*, n. 64), Vol. III, 1790, pp. 381 ff. The quotation is from pp. 396-99. On this fundamental hermeneutical principle of Eichhorn, see O. Kaiser, "Eichhorn und Kant" in *Das Ferne und nahe Wort* [The distant and near Word], Festschrift for L. Rost, 1967, pp. 114 ff.

140. J. Ph. Gabler, "Über den Unterschied zwischen Auslegung und Erklärung erläutert durch die verschiedene Behandlungsart der Versuchungeschichte Jesu" [On the distinction between exposition and explanation, illustrated by the various modes of treatment of the narrative of the temptation of Jesus], *Neuestes theologisches Journal* [Journal of the most recent theology] 6 (1800), 224 ff.; reprinted in J. Ph. Gabler,

Kleinere theologische Schriften (Lesser theological writings], Vol. I, 1831, pp. 201 ff., from which the quotations are drawn, pp. 201-5, 207, 210, 212-13. Gabler, "Ist es erlaubt, in der Bibel, und sogar im N. T. Mythen anzunehmen?" [Is it permitted to suppose that in the Bible and even in the New Testament there are myths?"] *Journal für auserlesene theologische Literatur* [Journal for selected theological literature], 2 (1806), 43 ff., reprinted in *Kleinere . . . Schriften*, Vol. I, pp. 699-706. See further in C. Hartlich and W. Sachs (*op. cit.*, n. 138), pp. 66 ff., 87 ff.

141.   G. L. Bauer, *Hebräische Mythologie des alten und neuen Testaments, mit Parallelen aus der Mythologie anderer Völker, vornehmlich der Griechen und Römer* [Hebrew mythology of the Old and New Testaments, with parallels from the mythology of other peoples, especially the Greeks and Romans], 2 vols., Leipzig, 1802. In his critical examination of the New Testament myths, Bauer proceeds in a by no means consistent manner, in that he asserts of Jesus himself that he "was fully conscious that he was merely using mythical images," while to the apostles, who "were not philosophers of our time" he would not concede such an insight (Vol. I, p. 33).

142.   G. L. Bauer, *Biblische Theologie des Neuen Testaments,* 4 vols., Leipzig, 1800-1802, Vol. I, pp. 6 and iv-v.

143.   *Ibid.,* Vol. I, pp. 254, 124-25; Vol. II, p. 284.

144.   *Ibid.,* Vol. II, pp. 260-61; Vol. I, p. 8.

145.   W. M. L. de Wette, *Lehrbuch der christlichen Dogmatik in ihrer historischen Entwicklung dargestellt. Erster Theil. Die biblische Dogmatik enthaltend, Biblische Dogmatik Alten und Neuen Testaments. Oder kritische Darstellung der Religionslehre des Hebraismus, des Judenthums, und Urchristenthums* [Textbook of Christian dogmatics presented in its historical development, first part, containing the biblical dogmatics of the Old and New Testaments, or a critical presentation of the religious teaching of Hebraism, Judaism, and primitive Christianity], Berlin, 1813, pp. 19-20.

146.   *Ibid.,* pp. 223-24, 211-12, 252. De Wette expressed himself, somewhat skeptically, on the methodological problem concerning the historical Jesus. But at the same time he affirmed that it was not the historical representation but the living Christ who was essential for faith, thereby preparing the way for M. Kähler's posing of the question (see pp. 222 ff). See R. Smend (*op. cit.*, n. 114), pp. 166 ff. Smend also shows (pp. 177 ff.) that de Wette was not basically interested in historical development, and in later editions of his *Biblical Dogmatics* he blended the different groups of the teachings of the apostles into a composite picture.

147.   C. A. Th. Keil, *De historica librorum interpretatione eiusque necessitate* [On the historical interpretation of the (sacred) books and its necessity], Lepzig, 1788; reprinted in C. A. Th. Keil, *Opuscula academica ad Novi Testamenti interpretationem grammatico-historicam . . . pertinentia,* Leipzig, 1821; here translated from pp. 85-88, 98-99; in the same collected volume: *Argumentorum pro historicae interpretationis veritate brevis repetitio eiusque adversus variorum dubitationes vindiciae ultimae* (1815), translation from pp. 383-84.

148.   See on this J. Wach, *Das Verstehen* [Understanding], Vol. II, 1929, pp. 113 ff., 239 ff. On the history of Hermeneutics see further G. Ebeling, "Hermeneutics," in *RGG*, III, col. 245 ff., with bibiography; and J. D. Smart, *The Interpretation of Scripture,* Philadelphia, 1963, pp. 232 ff.

149.   L. J. Rückert, *Commentar über die Briefe Pauli an die Römer* [Commentary on Paul's Letters to the Romans], Leipzig, 1831, pp. viii-x. On this see J. Wach (*op. cit.,* 148), pp. 242 ff.

150.   H. A. W. Meyer, *Das Neue Testament Griechisch nach den besten Hülfsmitteln kritisch revidiert mit einer neuen deutschen Übersetzung und einem kritischen und exegetischen Kommentar* [The Greek New Testament critically reviewed according to the best scholarly aids, with a new German translation and a critical and exegetical commentary] div. 1, pt. 1, xxxi. In the second edition of 1844, Meyer called exposition on the basis of churchly presuppositions "a procedure established prior to its being herein employed." See W. G. Kümmel, "Das Erbe des 19. Jahrhunderts für die neutestamentliche Wissenschaft von heute" [The heritage of the nineteenth century for New Testament study today], in *Deutscher Evangelischer Theologentag 1960: Das Erbe des 19. Jahrhunderts*, ed. W. Schneemelcher, 1960, p. 75. (= Kümmel, *Heilsgeschehen*, pp. 370-71.)

151.   Three years later, however, he extended the acknowledgment of myths to the New Testament as well (see note 141).

152.   G. L. Bauer, *Entwurf einer Hermeneutik des Alten und Neuen Testaments. Zu Vorlesungen* [Sketch of a hermeneutic of the Old and New Testaments: for lectures], Leipzig, 1799, pp. 20, 118, 156, 157-58, 175-76. Cf. Hartlich and Sachs, (*op. cit.*, n. 138), pp. 70 ff.

153.   C. F. Stäudlin, *De interpretatione librorum Novi Testamenti historica non unice vera* [On the historical interpretation of the books of the New Testament, as not containing unique truth], Göttinger Pfingstprogramm, 1807. Translated from p. 5. Also, "Über die blos historische Auslegung der Bücher des Neuen Testaments" [On the purely historical exposition of the books of the New Testament], *Kritisches Journal der neuesten theologischen Literatur* [Critical journal of the most recent theological literature], ed. F. Ammon and L. Bertholdt, Vol. I, pt. 4, 1814, pp. 321 ff.; Vol. II, 1814, pp. 1 ff., 113 ff., the quotations from pp. 17, 23-24, 32, 126-128, 148. See further J. Wach (*op. cit.*, n. 148), Vol. II, pp. 140 ff.

154.   F. Schleiermacher, *Hermeneutik und Kritik mit besonderer Beziehung auf das Neue Testament* [Hermeneutics and criticism with special relation to the New Testament], ed. F. Lücke. (= *Collected Works*, Vol. I, pt. 7, 1838, p. 148). Lücke's edition depends only in part on Schleiermacher's manuscripts and to a larger extent on several sets of lecture notes. The new edition edited by M. Kimmerle, F. D. E. Schleiermacher, *Hermeneutik: Nach den Handschriften neu herausgegeben und eingeleitet* [Hermeneutics: Newly edited according to the manuscript, with a new introduction], Heidelberg, 1959, pt. 2, reproduces only in chronological sequence Schleiermacher's own manuscripts. The quotation from Lücke, p. 148, corresponds to what is according to Kimmerle (p. 162) no more than a marginal comment of Schleiermacher in 1833: "Recapitulation of the relative opposition between the psychological and the technical. The first represents more the emphasis on the origin of thought out of the totality of the living moment." On Schleiermacher's hermeneutics cf. J. Wach (*op. cit.*, n. 148), Vol. I, 1926, pp. 83 ff., pp. 138 ff.; Vol. II, 1929, pp. 37 ff.; W. Trillhaas, "Schleiermachers Predigt und das homiletische Problem," 1933; W. Schultz, "Die Grundlage der Hermeneutik Schleiermachers, ihre Auswirkungen und Grenzen" [The foundation of Schleiermacher's hermeneutics, its effects and limits], *ZThK* 50 (1953), 158 ff.; Kimmerle, *op. cit.*, pp. 14 ff.

155.   F. Schleiermacher, *Hermeneutik* (*op. cit.*, n. 154), pp. 22-23, 27. The quotation from p. 22 corresponds word for word with that of the manuscript reproduced by Kimmerle on p. 85 (see n. 154). The quotation on p. 27 has no exact parallel in Kimmerle's edition, but on the other hand similar thoughts are found, e.g., on p. 159. On these ideas of Schleiermacher, see J. Wach (*op. cit.*, n. 148), Vol. I, p. 123; W. Trillhaas (*op. cit.*, n. 154), p. 143; W. Schultz (*op. cit.*, n. 154), p. 159.

156.   W. Schultz (*op. cit.*, n. 154), p. 162. See also J. Wach (*op. cit.*, n. 148), Vol. II, p. 54. For Schleiermacher, the Bible is "a religious document that we must understand as such." Schleiermacher always defended a universal hermeneutic and interpreted "understanding" as an unending movement. See W. Schultz, "The Unending Movement in the Hermeneutic of Schleiermacher and Its Effect on the Hermeneutical Situation of the Present," *ZThK* 65 (1968), 23 ff.

157. Schleiermacher by no means intended a disinterested objectivity with his rejection of any special hermeneutic for the New Testament, as he showed in his remark in *Kurze Darstellung des theologischen Studiums* [Brief presentation of theological study], 2nd ed. 1830, sec. 147; critical ed. by H. Scholz, 1910: "A continuing occupation with the New Testament canon which was not motivated by one's own interest in Christianity could only be directed against the Canon."

158. F. Lücke, in the preface to his edition of Schleiermacher's *Hermeneutics*, (*op. cit.*, n. 154) p. xv.

159. F. Lücke, *Grundriss der neutestamentlichen Hermeneutik und ihrer Geschichte. Zum Gebrauch für akademische Verlesungen* [Outline of New Testament hermeneutics; for use in academic lectures], Göttingen, 1817, pp. 80-82, 85-87, 89, 168. "Übersicht der zur Hermeneutik, Grammatik, Lexikographie" und Auslegung des Neuen Testament gehörigen Litteratur . . . von Dr. Lücke," [Survey of the literature related to the hermeneutics, grammar, lexicography, and exposition of the New Testament . . . by Dr. Lücke], *ThStKr*, 3 (1830), 420-22. Cf. J. Wach (*op. cit.*, n. 148), Vol. II, pp. 153 ff.

160. D. F. Strauss, *Streitschriften zur Vertheidigung meiner Schrift Über das Leben Jesu und zur Charakteristik der gegenwärtigen Theologie* [Polemical writings in defense of my writing concerning the life of Jesus and concerning the characteristics of present-day theology], Vol. III, *Collected Works*, 1837, pp. 57-61.

161. See the list in A. Schweitzer, *Geschichte der Leben-Jesu-Forschung*. In the English translation by W. Montgomery, *The Quest of the Historical Jesus* (New York: Macmillan, 1948, and London: A. & C. Black, 1910), reprinted with new introduction by Schweitzer, 1954, the discussion of Strauss's opponents is on pp. 97 ff. A supplement to this in Th. Zeigler, *D. F. Strauss*, Vol. I, 1908, p. 207, *n.* 1. On the content of the criticism, see G. Müller, *Identität und Immanenz. Zur Genese der Theologie von D. F. Strauss* [Identity and immanence: on the genesis of Strauss' theology], 1968, pp. 12 ff., and for further bibliography p. 13, *n.* 2. Cf. E. Wolf, "Die Verlegenheit der Theologie. David Strauss und die Bibelkritik" [The dilemma of theology: David Strauss and biblical criticism], in *Libertas Christiana* (Festschrift for F. Delekat on his sixty-fifth birthday), 1957, pp. 219 ff.

162. Th. Ziegler (*op. cit.*, n. 161), p. 197. Similarly, Neill, *Interpretation*, p. 12, "a turning point in the history of the Christian faith."

163. See the comprehensive survey by L. Salvatorelli, *HTR*, 22 (1929), 287-89. That Strauss "never posed the question about a trustworthy kernel in the Gospels" (so G. Backhaus, *Kerygma und Mythos bei David Friedrich Strauss und Rudolf Bultmann*, 1956, p. 13, supported by G. Müller [*op. cit.*, n. 161]. p. 10, is simply not true to the evidence.)

164. D. F. Strauss, *Das Leben Jesu kritisch bearbeitet* [The life of Jesus treated critically], Vol. I, 1835, p. viii; Vol. II, 1836, pp. 686, 736.

165. See the evidence in Hartlich and Sachs (*op. cit.*, n. 138), pp. 121 ff. Already before Strauss, L. Usteri had defined the concept of myth in an exactly similar way, *ThStKr*, 5 (1932), 782-83, to which Strauss himself drew attention in his *Life of Jesus* (Vol. I, pp. 69-70). On Strauss's concept of myth, see G. Backhaus (*op. cit.*, n. 163), pp. 22 ff., and G. Müller (*op. cit.*, n. 161), pp. 192 ff.

166. G. Müller (*op. cit.*, n. 161) showed that Strauss's concept of myth was essentially shaped through the thought of Schelling, which had been communicated to him when he was a schoolboy in Blaubeuren through his teacher F. C. Baur, who was conveying to his pupils through lectures the content of Schelling's work published in 1824-25, *Symbolik und Mythologie oder die Naturreligion des Althertums* [Symbolism and mythology; or the natural religion of antiquity]. Strauss's critcism of the concept of myth used by the "mythical school" corresponds to the purely speculative mythical concept of Schelling and therefore of Baur.

167. D. F. Strauss (*op. cit.*, n. 164), Vol. I, 4th ed., 1840, pp. 90-94.

168. "The greatest peculiarity of the work is that it offers a criticism of the gospel history without any criticism of the Gospels themselves. . . . Just as that separation of historical criticism from the literary criticism is the most one-sided aspect of Strauss's criticism, so it is also the point from which his critical work leads beyond itself." This was the judgment of F. C. Baur as early as 1847 in his *Kritische Untersuchungen über die kanonischen Evangelien* [critical research in the canonical Gospels], p. 41. Baur's further criticism of Strauss is summarized by G. Müller (*op. cit.*, n. 161), pp. 19-20.

169. D. F. Strauss (*op. cit.*, n. 164), Vol. I, pp. 469, 477; Vol. II, p. 373. The following quotations are from Vol. I, pp. iii-vii; 71-72, 74-75; Vol. I, 4th ed., 1840, pp. 107-8; Vol. II, pp. 263, 269, 273, 686.

170. D. F. Strauss (*op. cit.*, n. 164), Vol. I, pp. 470, 473-74, 477, 648-49; Vol. II, pp. 460, 471-72.

171. G. Müller (*op. cit.*, n. 161), pp. 94, 105, 167, 209-10 has shown that neither in his course of study nor in his dissertation (on philosophy) did Strauss ever come into contact with actual exegesis. The elucidation of the prehistory of Strauss's *Life of Jesus* shows further that he "never became or was in the full sense a theologian, but only attempted to utilize his philosophical presuppositions for considering theological questions" (p. 261, and *passim*). That does not alter the fact, however, that Strauss's *Life of Jesus* exerted a decisive influence on theological research in the New Testament.

172. S. F. Wagner, *Geschichtswissenschaft* [Historical science], 1951, pp. 172 ff.; G. P. Gooch, *Geschichte und Geschichtsschreiber im 19. Jahrhundert* [History and historians in the nineteenth century], 1964, pp. 25 ff.; H. Ritter von Srbik, *Geist und Geschichte vom deutschen Humanismus bis zur Gegenwart* [Spirit and history from the time of German humanism down to the present], Vol. I, 3rd ed., 1964, pp. 210 ff. For the influence of Niebuhr on F. C. Baur, see K. Scholder, "Ferdinand Christian Baur als Historiker," *EvTh*, 21 (1961), 436 ff.; W. Geiger, *Spekulation und Kritik. Die Geschichtstheologie Ferd. Christ. Baurs* [Speculation and criticism: the theology of history of F. C. Baur], 1964, p. 175.

173. More exactly in G. Fraedrich, *Ferdinand Christian Baur*, 1909, pp. 13 ff.; E. Pältz, F. C. Baur's "Verhältnis zu Schleiermacher" [Baur's relationship to Schleiermacher], Jena Dissertation, 1954 (typescript), pp. 34 ff.; and G. Müller (*op. cit.*, n. 161) pp. 178 ff.

174. F. C. Baur, *De orationis habita a Stephano Act Cap. VII consilio . . .* [On the intention of the address delivered by Stephen, Acts 7], Weihnachtsprogramm Tübingen 1829, pp. 27-28.

175. J. S. Semler (*op. cit.*, n. 168), Vol. IV Preface, see p. 68. Whether Baur was influenced by this statement of Semler's, as K. Bauer (*RGG*, 2nd ed., I, col. 818) and M. Werner (*Der Protestantische Weg des Glaubens* [The Protestant way of faith],

Vol. I, 1955, pp. 491-92.) assume, cannot be inferred from the essay of Baur mentioned in note 177.

176. F. C. Baur, "Die Einleitung in das Neue Testament als theologische Wissenschaft" [Introduction to the New Testament as a theological science], *Theologische Jahrbücher*, ed. F. C. Baur and E. Zeller, Vol. X, 1851, pp. 294-96.

177. F. C. Baur, "Die Christuspartei in der korinthischen Gemeinde, der Gegensatz des petrinischen und paulinischen Christenthums in der ältesten Kirche, der Apostel Petrus in Rom" [The Christ party in the Corinthian community, the opposition between Petrine and Pauline Christianity in the most ancient church, the apostle Peter in Rome], *Tübinger Zeitschrift für Theologie*, 4 (1831), 61 ff. The quotations are from pp. 83, 107-8, 114, 205-6. The new edition of *Historisch-kritische Untersuchungen zum Neuen Testament* [Historical-critical researches in the New Testament], with an Introduction by Ernst Käsemann, is Volume I of the series, *Ferdinand Christian Baur, Ausgewählte Werke in Einzelausgaben* [F. C. Baur: selected works in individual editions], ed. K. Scholder, 1963, pp. 1 ff., which gives the original page numbers. It is established unambiguously that Baur had recognized the opposition between Petrine and Pauline Christianity, which was so basic for his understanding of Christianity, long before his acquaintance with Hegel. See P. C. Hodgson, *The Formation of Historical Theology: A Study of F. C. Baur* (New York, Harper & Row, 1966), pp. 22, 196, *n.* 175.

178. F. C. Baur, *Die sogenannten Pastoralbriefe des Apostels Paulus aufs neue kritisch untersucht* [The so-called Pastoral Letters of the apostle Paul once more critically examined], Stuttgart and Tübingen, 1835, pp. iii-iv, 69, 143, 93, 4, v, 57.

179. *Ibid.*, pp. 1, 145.

180. W. Geiger (*op. cit.*, n. 172), p. 201. Note 104 contests this conclusion, since Baur expressly declares that we "can add nothing to the Canon, and take nothing away from it." *Theol. Jahrbücher*, Vol. X, 1851, p. 307. But this statement of Baur's shows only that he drew back in the face of the conclusions implied by his criticism of the Canon, asking of historical criticism, in fact, that it decide the theological question of true canonicity. Cf. Baur's arguments, p. 139 ff. Although Baur did not consider pseudonymity to be "falsification" (see the quotations in W. Geiger [*op. cit.*, n. 172], p. 202) that does not change the false link of Baur's between apostolic authorship and canonical authority.

181. K. Barth, *Die protestantische Theologie im 19. Jahrhundert* [Protestant theology in the nineteenth century], 1947, p. 454; similarly, E. Käsemann (*op. cit.*, n. 177), p. xix. Concerning Baur's shift to Hegel, see esp. G. Fraedrich (*op. cit.*, n. 173), p. 93 ff.; E. Pältz (*op. cit.*, n. 173), pp. 78 ff.; H. Liebing, "F. C. Baurs Kritik an Schleiermachers Glaubenslehre," [Baur's criticism of Schleiermacher's 'Christian Doctrine'] *ZThK*, 54 (1957), 226-27; E. Barnikol, "Das ideengeschichtliche Erbe Hegels bei und seit Strauss und Baur im 19, Jahrhundert" [The Hegelian contribution to the history of ideas in the thought of, and since Baur and Strauss in the nineteenth century], *Wissenschaftliche Zeitschrift der Martin-Luther-Universität Halle-Wittenberg, Gesellsch. und Sprachwiss*, Series 10, pt. 1, 1961; P. C. Hodgson (*op. cit.*, n. 177), pp. 20-21, 23-24, 64 ff.; W. Geiger (*op. cit.*, n. 172), pp. 42 ff.

182. F. C. Baur, "Kritische Übersicht über die neuesten, das γλώσσαις λαλεῖν in in der ältesten Kirche betreffenden Untersuchungen" [Critical survey of the most recent research on speaking in tongues in the ancient church] *ThStKr*, 11 (1838), 630, 694: "Who ever gave us warrant for supposing that Mark and Luke use formulae in such a documentary, historical sense that we could retrospectively draw any conclusions from them about the time in which the events under consideration actually first took place (i.e., the speaking in tongues). . . . Since the writing of the First Letter to the Corinthians clearly took place at a significantly earlier date (than did the writing of the Acts) we are not justified to clarify the shorter formula, 'to speak with tongues' by the longer formula, 'to speak with other tongues.' The 'speaking' as reported in Acts—'to speak in strange tongues,' Acts 2:1 ff.—is the natural heightening and expansion of the phrase in the Corinthian Letter."

183.　F. C. Baur, "Über den Ursprung des Episcopats in der Christlichen Kirche" [On the origin of the episcopacy in the Christian Church], *Tübinger Zeitschrift für Theologie,* 3 1838) , 123, 141-43 (reprinted with the original pagination, see n. 177, pp. 321 ff.)

184.　M, Schneckenburger, *Über den Zweck der Apostelgeschichte. Zugleich eine Ergänzung der neueren Commentare* [On the aim of the book of Acts, with a supplement to the more recent commentaries], Bern, 1841. Quotations from pp. 92, 5.

185.　F. C. Baur, *Paulus, der Apostel Jesu Christi. Sein Leben und Wirken, seine Briefe und seine Lehre. Ein Beitrag zu einer kritischen Geschichte des Urchristenthums.* [Paul, the apostle of Jesus Christ: his life and activity, his letters and his teachings: a contribution to a critical history of primitive Christianity], Stuttgart, 1845, pp. 130, 4-5, 105.

186.　In 1834/35 Baur did not yet see the conflict between the representation of the Apostolic Council in Acts and that in the Letter to the Galatians, but became convinced of it through conversations with E. Zeller. The evidence for this is given by E. Barnikol (*op. cit.,* n. 181) , pp. 288, 310-11.

187.　F. C. Baur (*op. cit.,* n. 185) , pp. 247, 449.

188.　*Ibid.,* pp. vi-vii, 510, 520.

189.　K. Barth, (*op. cit.,* n. 181) , p. 456; A. Schweitzer, Geschichte der paulinischen Forschung, 1911; *Paul and His Interpreters,* Eng. tr. by W. Montgomery, (New York: Macmillan, and London: A. & C. Black, 1912) , pp. 15-16.

190.　F. C. Baur, *Kritische Untersuchungen über die kanonischen Evangelien, ihr Verhältnis zueinander, ihren Charakter und Ursprung* [Critical research in the canonical Gospels, their relation to each other, their character and origin], Tübingen, 1847, pp. 316, 386, 73-74, 76, 108, 239. Like Schleiermacher, Baur had originally (1837) viewed the Gospel of John as a historical source of value equal to that of the Synoptics. But by 1838 in a letter to D. F. Strauss, and from 1844 on he adopted the viewpoint that John could not be used as a source for the history of Jesus. See P. C. Hodgson (*op. cit.,* n. 177) , pp. 212-13.

191.　E. Hirsch's attempt (*Geschichte,* Vol. V, 1954, pp. 541-42) to make Baur the founder of modern research in gospel history, even though he had a false opinion about the question of synoptic sources, is untenable.

192.　F. C. Baur (*op. cit.,* n. 190) , p. 604.

193.　F. C. Baur, "Die Einleitung in das Neue Testament als theologische Wissenschaft. Ihr Begriff und ihre Aufgabe, ihr Entwicklungsgang und ihr innerer Organismus" [Introduction to the New Testament as a theological science: its conceptuality and its task, its course of development and its organic unity] in *Theol. Jahrbücher,* Vol. IX, 9, 1850, pp. 466-67, 478.

194.　F. C. Baur, *Das Christenthum und die christliche Kirche der drei ersten Jahrhunderte* [Christianity and the Christian Church of the first three centuries],

Tübingen, 1853, offered no more than a brief representation. *Lectures on New Testament Theology* was published from Baur's lecture notes after his death (Leipzig, 1864). (Hereafter Baur, *Lectures*.)

195. Baur, *Lectures*, pp. 38, 33.

196. *Ibid.*, pp. 283-84.

197. *Ibid.*, pp. 45, 122, 64; *Christenthum* (n. 194), pp. 28-29. Baur expressly declared that "the teaching of Jesus could [not] be considered as the content of the history of dogma." (From *Lehrbuch der christlichen Dogmengeschichte*, 2nd ed., 1858, p. 6, *n.* 2; cited by E. Barnikol, (*op. cit.*, n. 181), p. 313, *n.* 93. A good summary of Baur's presentation of the teaching of Jesus is offered by Hirsch, *Geschichte*, Vol. V, pp. 543 ff. Cf. also W. Geiger (*op. cit.*, n. 172), pp. 87 ff.; P. C. Hodgson (*op. cit.*, n. 177 pp. 114-15, 199, 224 ff.

198. Baur, *Lectures*, pp. 123-24.

199. F. C. Baur, *Die Tübinger Schule und ihre Stellung zur Gegenwart* [The Tubingen school and its position in relation to the present], Tübingen, 2nd ed., 1860, p. 58, *n.*

200. M. A. Landerer, *Zur Dogmatik, Zwei akademische Reden, beigegeben Gedächtnisrede auf F. C. Baur . . .* [On dogmatics: two academic addresses presented as a memorial to F. C. Baur (held in the Aula on Feb. 7, 1861)], Tübingen, 1879, pp. 76-77, where the reference is to Baur's *Christenthum* (*op. cit.*, n. 194), 2nd ed., 1860, p. 45. This second edition is Volume III of the series mentioned in note 177, and reproduces the original pagination. The statement of C. Holsten in *Das Evangelium des Paulus*, Vol. II, 1898, p. xv, that Landerer made this remark "in his address at his colleague's grave" is in error, as Professor Dr. Gehring, the director of the Tübingen University Library, has kindly informed me.

201. E. Zeller, *Die Apostelgeschichte nach ihrem Inhalt und Ursprung kritisch untersucht* [Acts studied critically as to its content and origin], Stuttgart, 1854, pp. 357, 524.

202. A. Schwegler, *Das nachapostolische Zeitalter in den Hauptmomenten seiner Entwicklung* [The postapostolic age in the high points of its development], 2 vols., Tübingen, 1846, Preface (1845); quotations from Vol. I, pp. 13-14, 43, 169, 192.

203. O. Pfleiderer, *Die Entwicklung der protestantischen Theologie in Deutschland seit Kant* [The development of protestant theology in Germany since Kant], 1891, p. 280.

204. A. Schwegler (*op. cit.*, n. 202), Vol. I, p. 148, *n.* In his *Quest of the Historical Jesus* and his *Paul and His Interpreters*, A. Schweitzer overlooked the fact that Schwegler had observed the central role of the near expectation of the parousia for the whole of primitive Christianity (Schwegler, Vol. I., pp. 109-10).

205. Cf. on this H. J. Holtzmann, *Lehrbuch der historisch-kritischen Einleitung in das Neue Testament* [Textbook for historical-critical introduction to the New Testament], 3rd ed., 1892, pp. 169 ff., 176, 178-79.

206. G. V. Lechler, *Das apostolische und das nachapostolische Zeitalter. Mit Rücksicht auf Unterschied und Einheit zwischen Paulus und den Übrigen Aposteln, zwischen Heidenchristen und Judenchristen* [The apostolic and postapostolic age, with a consideration of the distinction and unity between Paul and the other apostles, between Gentile and Jewish Christians], Haarlem, 1851. The work received the prize of the Teylerian Theological Society for 1848.

207. *Novum Testamentum Graece et Latine.* Carolus Lachmannus recensuit, Philippus Buttmanus . . . *Graecae lectionis autoritates apposuit* [New Testament in Greek and Latin, ed. Karl Lachmann; authorities for the readings of the Greek appended by Philip Buttmann], Berlin, 2 vols., 1842-50.

208. "Rechenschaft über seine Ausgabe des Neuen Testaments von Professor Lachmann in Berlin." [An account by Professor Lachmann of Berlin concerning his edition of the New Testament], *ThStKr,* 3 (1830), 817 ff. The quotations are from pp. 817-20, 826. The essay was reprinted in K. Lachmann, *Kleinere Schriften zur klassischen Philologie* [Shorter writings on classical philology], Vol. II, 1876, pp. 250 ff., with notations of the original pagination.

209. Cf. C. R. Gregory (*op. cit.,* n. 33), Vol. II, pp. 966 ff.

210. C. Lachmann (*op. cit.,* n. 207), Vol. I, p. v. Lachmann had already indicated in a philological review 1818 that the most pressing requirement for a text edition was to reproduce the oldest manuscript tradition "without the slightest consideration as to meaning or grammatical rules." K. Lachmann (*op. cit.,* n. 208) p. 2, quoted by T. Timpanaro, *La Genesi del metodo del Lachmann,* 1963, p. 29. In the same work on pp. 37 ff., Timpanaro shows that Lachmann was himself unable to carry through this mechanical way of setting up the textual work, which he called a "recension" and for which he appealed above all to Bengel, "since not only did he have to understand the various textual readings in order to classify them, but also because, after he had excluded certain readings, he was left with a great mass of variants, all of them well-attested, but between which he had to choose on the basis of internal criteria" (p. 42).

211. C. Lachmann (*op. cit.,* n. 208) p. 843.

212. C. Lachmann, *De ordine narrationum in evangeliis synopticis, ThStKr,* 8 (1935), 570 ff. The quotations are from pp. 574, 577. An English translation of the majority of Lachmann's statements may be found in N. H. Palmer, "Lachmann's Argument," *NTS,* 13 (1966/67), 370 ff. In the passage quoted, Lachmann associates himself with Schleiermacher's position that the oldest report of the Gospel of Matthew as having been written by the apostle Matthew—attributed to Papias in Eusebius, *Ecclesiastical History* 3.39.16—in reality refers not to the Gospel of Matthew but to a collection of the words of Jesus that goes back to Matthew (F. D. Schleiermacher, "Über die Zeugnisse des Papias von unsern beiden ersten Evangelien," *ThStKr,* 1932, 735 ff.; also *Collected Works,* Vol. I, pt. 2, 1836, pp. 361 ff.). Lachmann contested the theory that, since the evidence of the order of material in Mark showed the Matthean and Lukan order to be a secondary alteration, one could infer that Matthew and Luke had before them "an exemplar of Mark which they both imitated" (p. 582). He took the position rather that all three Gospels were dependent on the same source, but that Mark best preserved its order, although his further theory that this source was written on the basis of five earlier narrative collections is of no significance. See on the latter H. J. Holtzmann, *Die synoptischen Evangelien,* 1863, p. 26. On the basis of Lachmann's evidence that Mark had preserved the oldest order of the material, the conclusion was later drawn that Mark was itself the source for Matthew and Luke; recently his conclusion has been described as "Lachmann's Fallacy," though Lachmann was not guilty of this. (See B. C. Butler, *The Originality of St. Matthew,* 1951, pp. 62 ff.; W. R. Farmer, "A 'Skeleton' in the Closet' of Gospel Research," *Biblical Research* 6 [1961], 18 ff., and *The Synoptic Problem* [New York: Macmillan, 1964], pp. 16-17, 63 ff.; Palmer, *op. cit.,* p. 370.) Lachmann had, however, prepared the way for this "fallacy" with formulations such as, "I have shown how often and why Matthew departs from the order that Mark has" (p. 579).

213. C. G. Wilke, *Der Urevangelist oder exegetisch kritische Untersuchung über das Verwandtschaftsverhältniss der drei ersten Evangelien* [The original evangelist, or exegetical and critical research concerning the kindred relationship of the first three Gospels], Dresden and Leipzig, 1838. The quotations are from pp. 293, 684. Wilke does not refer to Lachmann, and probably did not even know his work. J. Wellhausen (in *Einleitung in die drei ersten Evangelien* [Introduction to the first three Gospels], 2nd ed., 1911, p. 34) showed that Wilke had achieved his basic position before Lachmann's essay appeared. The agrements of Matthew with Luke, Wilke explained on the basis of Matthew's dependence on Luke (p. 685).

214. C. H. Weisse (*op. cit.*, n. 100). The quotations are from Vol. I, pp. i, v, iii, 594, 282-83, 67-68, 71-73, 82-83.

215. A. Ritschl forms an exception to the cohesiveness of the Tübingen School, as evident in an essay that appeared in 1851, "Über den gegenwärtigen Stand der Kritik der synoptischen Evangelien" [Concerning the present situation in the criticism of the synoptic Gospels], reprinted in his *Collected Essays*, 1893, pp. 25 ff. The essay which appeared only a year after Ritschl, in the first edition of his *Die Entstehung der altkatholischen Kirche*, said that he still considered himself a pupil of F. C. Baur (see p. 162).

216. C. H. Weisse, *Die Evangelienfrage in ihrem gegenwärtigen Stadium* [The question of the Gospels at the present stage], 1856, p. 85.

217. H. J. Holtzmann (*op. cit.*, n. 205), pp. 351 ff., 537.

218. A. Schweitzer (*op. cit.*, n. 161), p. 204.

219. *Ibid.*, pp. 193 ff., 200, 221.

220. H. J. Holtzmann, *Die synoptischen Evangelien. Ihr Ursprung und ihr geschichtlicher Charakter* [The Synoptic Gospels: their origin and historical character], Leipzig, 1863, pp. 482, 1, 52, 75, 437, 455, 458-59, 468, 475-76, 748-79, 485-86.

221. E. Reuss, *Die Geschichte der heiligen Schriften Neuen Testaments* [The History of the Sacred Scriptures of the New Testament], Halle, 1842, p. 41.

222. E. Reuss (*op. cit.*, n. 221), 3rd ed., 1860, pp. 5, 2, 12-13, 124-25, 332-33; E. Reuss, *Histoire de la théologie chrétienne au siècle apostolique*, 2 vols., Strasbourg and Paris, 1852. Translated from Vol. I, pp. 11, 271-73, 287, 292, 306-7; Vol. II, pp. 266-69, 512, 570-71. In the sixth edition of his *Geschichte* (1887), Reuss, in contrast to the third edition, unambiguously rejected the genuineness of all the Catholic Epistles, of the Revelation of John, of I Timothy and of Titus.

223. On this development see O. Ritschl, *Albrecht Ritchls Leben* [Life of A. Ritschl], Vol. I, 1892, pp. 112 ff., 125 ff., 151 ff., 167-68, 271 ff.

224. A. Ritschl, *Die Entstehung der altkatholischen Kirche, Eine kirchen- und dogmengeschichtliche Monographie* [The origin of the ancient Catholic Church; a monograph on the history of the Church and of dogma], Bonn, 2nd ed., pp. 22-23, 46-52, 56-57, 107, 147, 151-52, 271-73; A. Ritschl, "Über geschichtliche Methode in der Erforschung des Urchristenthums," *Jahrbücher für deutsche Theologie*, 6 (1861), 458-59. On the theological grounds for Ritschl's opposition to Baur in the second edition of Ritschl's *Entstehung*, see Ph. Hefner, "Baur vs. Ritschl on Early Christianity," in *Church History*, 31 (1962), 259 ff.

225. C. Weizsäcker, *Untersuchungen über die evangelische Geschichte, ihre Quellen und den Gang ihrer Entwicklung* [Research in the history of the Gospels: their sources and the course of their development], Gotha, 1864, pp. iv-v.

226. F. Loofs, *ThLZ*, 12 (1887), 55. See also Weizsäcker's own account of Baur's method in his chancellor's address on the hundredth birthday of Baur; *F. C. Baur*, Stuttgart, 1892, especially p. 14.

227. C. Weizsäcker, *Das Apostolische Zeitalter der christlichen Kirche* [The apostolic age of the Christian Church], Freiburg, 1886, pp. 175, 172, 329, 16, 24, 381-82, 384-85, 408, 107-8, 112, 151-52, 159, 164, 171-72, 234-35, 535-36.

228. B. Weiss, *Lehrbuch der biblischen Theologie des Neuen Testaments* [Textbook of the biblical theology of the New Testament], Berlin, 1868, pp. 2, 9, 36, 656.

229. B. Weiss, *Lehrbuch der Einleitung in das Neue Testament* [Textbook of introduction to the New Testament], Berlin, 1886, pp. 9, 317.

230. B. Weiss (*op. cit.*, n. 228), p. 51; B. Weiss, *Das Leben Jesu* [Life of Jesus], Vol. II, 1882, p. 267. A. Schweitzer, in his *Quest* (*op. cit.*, n. 161), pp. 216-17, has correctly asserted that Weiss's *Life of Jesus* belongs to the liberal lives of Jesus.

231. See W. F. Howard, *The Romance of New Testament Scholarship* (London: Epworth Press, 1949), p. 68

232. J. B. Lightfoot, *Saint Paul's Epistle to the Galatians*, London, 1865, pp. 307, 311, 359. An essential part of Baur's historical reconstruction—the late date of the shorter Pauline letters which Baur inferred from the lack in them of conflict between Petrine and Pauline Christianity—was undermined by Lightfoot's evidence that I Clement and the genuine Ignatian Letters, which were written in the last decade of the first century A.D., or in the first two decades of the second century, also know nothing of such a conflict. (See Neill, *Interpretation*, pp. 40 ff.)

233. *Die Religionswissenschaft der Gegenwart in Selbstdarstellungen* [Religious scholarship of the present as represented by the scholars themselves], Vol. IV, 1928, p. 171. Hereafter *Selbstdarstellungen*.

234. A. Jülicher, *Einleitung in das Neue Testament* [Introduction to the New Testament], Freiburg and Leipzig, 1894, pp. vi, 3, 12-13, 17, 13, 25, 263, 229-32, 258-59. Eng. tr. by J. P. Ward. Copyright © 1904 by G. P. Putnam's Sons (New York) and Smith, Elder and Co. (London). Quotations with emendations are from pp. vi, 5, 4, 20-21, 39-40, 436-41, 371-74, 285-86.

235. On literary questions, A. Harnack represents in essence the same views as Jülicher, and his frequently misunderstood saying about "moving backward to the tradition" is in direct dependence on Jülicher, who had "already begun to reap the results of the backward-directed insight of the last two decades." (Adolph von Harnack, *Geschichte der altchristlichen Litteratur bis Eusebius*, Vol. II, pt. 1, 1897, p. x.; see on the reaction to this Agnes von Zahn-Harnack, *Adolf von Harnack*, 1936, pp. 258 ff.

236. Agnes v. Zahn-Harnack (*op. cit.*, n. 235), p. 135. As early as his thesis for academic qualification (lit., "habilitation"), Harnack had taken the position that "for the exegesis of Holy Scripture there is no other method than that of grammatical historical method." This quotation is given by A. von Zahn-Harnack (p. 69), though it can no longer be determined what its actual source is, since it does not appear in the published version of the thesis. The trustworthiness of the citation is not to be doubted, however, as I conclude from a kind communication received from Dr. A. von Zahn-Harnack of Tübingen.

237. A. Harnack, *Lehrbuch der Dogmengeschichte* [textbook of the history of dogma], Vol. I, Freiburg, 1886, p. 16.

238. F. Loofs, in A. von Zahn-Harnack (*op. cit.*, n. 235) p. 244.

239. In a personal debate with a critic, Harnack affirmed as his goal "to move across the muddied conceptions of Paul and John back to the Old Testament and to those sayings of the Lord, transmitted in the Synoptics that are genuine." (in A. v. Zahn-Harnack, *op. cit.*, n. 235, p. 142). See also E. Bammel, "Der historische Jesus ein der Theologie Adolf von Harnacks," *Jahrbuch der Evangelische Akademie Tutzing*, 12 (1962/63), 25 ff.

240. A. Harnack, *Das Wesen des Christentums* [What is Christianity?], Leipzig, 1900, p. 82. Eng. tr. by T. B. Saunders. Copyright © 1901 by G. P. Putnam's Sons (New York) and Williams and Norgate (London). New edition with introduction by R. Bultmann (New York: Harper and Row, 1957), p. 51.

241. A. Harnack (*op. cit.*, n. 237), pp. 41, 48-51, 53, 55, 58-59, 63, 66, 93-94; Harnack (*op. cit.*, n. 240), German original. Quotations with emendations are from the Eng. ed., pp. 14-15, 160, 17, 36-37, 56, 58, 60-61, 66-67, 68 ff., 137-38, 154-56. For criticism of *Wesen*, see E. Rolffs, *Christliche Welt*, 15 (1901), 929 ff., 958 ff., 1049 ff., 1073 ff; but see also K. Holl's enthusiastic expression of thanks for the book, through which the reader should "regain the simple sense of the majesty of Christianity." (In K. Holl, *Briefwechsel mit A. Harnack* [Correspondence with A. Harnack], ed. H. Karpp, 1966, pp. 28 ff.)

242. I. Ševčenko, "New Documents on Constantine Tischendorf and the *Codex Sinaiticus,*" *Scriptorium*, 18 (1964), 55 ff., where it is shown on the basis of newly found documents that Tischendorf transacted the transfer of the Sinai manuscript to the Czar in a way by no means honorable.

243. Constantinus Tischendorf, *Novum Testamentum Graece ad antiquissimos testes denuo recensuit, apparatum criticum omni studio perfectum apposuit, commentationem isagogicam praetextuit, Editio octava critica major* [The Greek New Testament edited anew on the basis of the most ancient witnesses, with a complete critical apparatus], 2 vols., Leipzig, 1872. Quotation from Vol. I, p. vii.

244. *The New Testament in the Original Greek,* text revised by B. F. Westcott and F. J. A. Hort, 2 vols., Cambridge and London, 1881. Quotation from Vol. I, p. 541.

245. A more exact report of Westcott and Hort's text-critical fundamentals in A. Rüegg, *Die Neutestamentliche Textkritik seit Lachmann* [New Testament criticism since Lachmann], 1892, pp. 62 ff.; C. R. Gregory (*op. cit.*, n. 33), pp. 917 ff.; B. M. Metzger (*op. cit.*, n. 33), pp. 129 ff.

246. A. Jülicher, *Die Gleichnisreden Jesu* [The parables of Jesus], Vol. I, 2nd ed., 1899; pp. 11, 42, 49, 61, 76, 107, 152, 182, 317. The second volume, which appeared in 1898, offered a detailed "Exposition of the parables of the first three Gospels" which has not been surpassed to the present day.

247. H. Lüdemann, *Die Anthropologie des Apostels Paulus und ihre Stellung innerhalb seiner Heilslehre. Nach den vier Hauptbriefen dargestellt* [The anthropology of the apostle Paul and its place within his doctrine of redemption, based on the four main letters], Kiel, 1872, pp. 12, 38, 125, 144, 151, 161, 171-72, 210-11, 216.

248. H. J. Holtzmann, *Lehrbuch der Neutestamentlichen Theologie* [Textbook of New Testament theology], 2 vols., Freiburg and Leipzig, 1897. Quotations from Vol. 1, pp. 24-25, 285, 346, 351; Vol. II, pp. 3, 15, 199, 208, 203; Vol. I, 341-43; II, 222, 224-25. See the brilliant account of the flaws in Holtzmann's depiction of Paul in A. Schweitzer (*op. cit.*, n. 189), pp. 100-116.

249. H. Cremer, *Biblico-Theological Dictionary of New Testament Greek Idioms,* tr. from the German of the 2nd ed.; 3rd Eng. ed., Edinburgh, 1883, Preface.

250. On the requirement of one's own faith as a presupposition for proper understanding of the New Testament according to Schlatter, see G. Egg, *Adolf Schlatters kritische Position gezeight an seiner Matthäusinterpretation* [A. Schlatter's critical position demonstrated by his interpretation of Matthew], 1968, pp. 55, 64 ff., 107-8.

251. See A. Schlatter's *Rückblick auf seine Lebensarbeit* [Retrospect of his life's work], 1952, pp. 233-34. ("I possessed a unified New Testament.") ; see also K. Holl's impression of Schlatter's *Theology of the New Testament* (1909) in a letter of Holl's to Schlatter in 1909: "You have made clear to me the unity of the thoughtworld of the New Testament in a way entirely different from how I had sensed it up until now" (from the "Letters of K. Holl to A. Schlatter 1897-1925," ed. R. Stupperich, *ZThK*, 64 [1967], 201). On the methodological presuppositions of the entire work of Schlatter, see W. Tebbe, "The Young Schlatter" in *Aus Schlatters Berner Zeit* [From Schlatter's period in Berne], 1952, pp. 64-65, and G. Egg (*op. cit.*, n. 250), pp. 130 ff. (p. 131, n. 4), where evidence is offered for a "chronologically demonstrable decrease of critical judgments about the genuineness of individual New Testament writings."

252. See A. Schlatter, "Self-portrait," in *Selbstdarstellungen*, Vol. I, 1925, p. 19. G. Egg (*op. cit.*, n. 250), pp. 55 ff., 123 ff., shows that Schlatter restricted the history-of-religions analogy with the Palestinian setting still more completely to linguistic factors.

253. A. Schlatter, *Der Glaube im Neuen Testament. Eine Untersuchung zur neutestamentlichen Theologie* [Faith in the New Testament: a study in the New Testament theology], Leiden, 1885 (awarded the Hague Society Prize for the Defense of the Christian Religion), pp. 4-5, 9, 536-37, 126, 229-30, 315-17, 339, 342, 502.

254. H. J. Holtzmann, *Lehrbuch der historisch-kritischen Einleitung in das Neue Testament* [Textbook on the historical-critical introduction to the New Testament], 3rd ed., 1892, pp. 75 ff.

255. Agnes von Zahn-Harnack (*op. cit.*, n. 235), pp. 65, 87. Cf. on the original friendship between Zahn and Harnack the published letters of Harnack, *ThLZ*, 77 (1952), 498 ff.

256. Th. Zahn, *Geschichte des Neutestamentlichen Kanons* [History of the New Testament Canon], Erlangen and Leipzig, Vol. I, pt. 1, 1888; pt. 2, 1889; II. pt. 1, 1890; pt. 2, 1892. The quotations are from Vol. I, pt. 1, pp. 446, 435-36, 83-84, 433-34, 794-96.

257. A. Harnack, *Das Neue Testament um das Jahr 200. Th. Zahn's Geschichte des Neutestamentlichen Kanons (Erster Band, erste Hälfte) geprüft* [The New Testament around the year 200: Zahn's "history of the New Testament canon" (Vol. I, pt. 1) put to the test], Freiburg, 1889, p. 4.

258. F. Overbeck, *Kurze Erklärung der Apostelgeschichte von Dr. W. M. L. de Wette, vierte Auflage bearbeitet und stark erweitert von F. O.* [Short exposition of Acts by Dr. W. M. L. de Wette: 4th ed. revised and greatly expanded by F. O.], Leipzig, 1870, pp. xvi, xviii; F. Overbeck, *Über Entstehung und Recht einer rein kritischen Betrachtung der Neutestamentlichen Schriften in der Theologie, Antrittsvorlesung* *gehalten in der Aula zu Basel am 7. Juni 1870* [On the origin and justification for a purely critical view of the New Testament Scriptures in theology: inaugural address held in the Aula at Basel], Basel, 1871, pp. 3-4, 24, 30, 32-34.

259. F. Overbeck, *Über die Christlichkeit unserer heutigen Theologie, Zweite, um eine Einleitung und ein Nachwort vermehrte Auflage* [On the Christianity of our contemporary theology, second edition enlarged by an Introduction and an epilogue], Leipzig, 1903, pp. 124, 3-4, 26-27, 33, 36, 108-9, 125, 181.

260. F. Overbeck (*op. cit.,* n. 259), p. 163; Overbeck, *Selbstbekenntnisse* [Confessions], 1941, p. 131; see also Overbeck's statement in a letter to A. Jülicher on Nov. 11, 1901: "Before all the world nearly thirty years ago I closed out for myself the ways I see you walking as a theologian; I have never found my way back to that point, nor even yearned to go back, and as for the possibility that I might at any time reach this state of mind, the prospect is continually in the process of vanishing." (In M. Tetz, "A. Jülichers Briefwechsel mit F. Overbeck." [A. Jülicher's correspondence with Franz Overbeck] *Zeitschrift für Kirchengeschichte,* 76, N.F. 14 [1965], 319.)

261. See especially E. Vischer's introduction to his edition of Overbeck's *Confessions* (n. 260).

262. *Christentum und Kultur. Gedanken und Anmerkungen zur modernen Theologie von F. Overbeck* [Christianity and culture: ideas and observations on modern theology by F. Overbeck], edited from Overbeck's literary estate by C. A. Bernoulli, Basel, 1919, pp. 76, 91.

263. F. Overbeck (*op. cit.,* n. 259), p. 86.

264. F. Overbeck, "Über die Anfänge der patristischen Literatur" [On the beginnings of patristic literature], *Historische Zeitschrift,* 48 (1882), 423, 432, 436-37, 443 (reprinted by the Wissenschaftliche Buchgesellschaft, n.d., pp. 12, 23, 28-29, 36-37). On the early history and further development of form-critical approach in the work of Overbeck, see M. Tetz, "Über Formengeschichte in der Kirchengeschichte" [On form criticism in church history], *ThZ,* 17 (1961), 413 ff.

265. A. Hausrath, *Neutestamentliche Zeitgeschichte* [History of New Testament times], 3 vols., Heidelberg, 1868-74. The quotation is from Vol. I, p. ix. Hausrath's eagerness to write a biography of Paul for cultured persons that would place the apostle in the cultural context of his time led him to a penetrating study of the history of New Testament times. See K. Bauer, *A. Hausrath: Leben und Zeit* [Hausrath's life and times], Vol. I, 1933, p. 204.

266. A. Hilgenfeld, *Die jüdische Apokalyptik in ihrer geschichtlichen Entwicklung. Ein Beitrag zur Vorgeschichte des Christenthums nebst einem Anhange über das gnostische System des Basilides* [Jewish apocalyptic in its historical development: a contribution to the early history of Christianity together with an appendix on the gnostic system of Basilides], Jena, 1857, pp. 1, ix, 189. J. M. Schmidt, in *Die jüdische Apokalyptik. Die Geschichte ihrer Erforschung von den Anfängen bis zu den Textfunden von Qumran* [Jewish apocalyptic: the history of its investigations from the beginnings to the discovery of the Qumran texts], 1969, pp. 13-14, 20-21, 64 ff., 98 ff., 119 ff., shows that Hilgenfeld's predecessors in research on noncanonical Jewish apocalyptic as a preparation for Christianity, after all sorts of starts, were F. Lücke and E. Reuss. According to Lücke's information, K. I. Nitzsch was the first to use the expression "apocalyptic" (see Schmidt, pp. 98-99). Hilgenfeld himself described for the first time the whole of Jewish and Christian apocalyptic as "a distinctive historical force" and saw in Jewish apocalyptic "the historical bridge between Old Testament prophecy and Christianity" (Schmidt, pp. 127 ff., esp. 144).

267. E. Schürer, *Lehrbuch der neutestamentlichen Zeitgeschichte* [Textbook on the history of New Testament times], Leipzig, 1874, Vol. III, pp. 506, 513, 510-11. E. Bammel, in his memorial article on the fiftieth anniversary of Schürer's death (in the *Deutsch Pfarrerblatt*, 60 (1960), p. 226) has rightly noted that Schürer "did not face the object (of his research) with undivided sympathy," and thus allowed apocalyptic to retreat inappropriately into the background.

268. R. Seeberg, *PRE*, XXIV, p. 319.

269. For the first time in the second edition of his *Urchristentums* [Primitive Christianity], Vol. I, 1902, pp. 615 ff., Pfleiderer in his discussion of the Gospels introduced a representation of the preaching of Jesus and the faith of the early church in which Jesus is portrayed exclusively as a proclaimer of the *near* reign of God and the primitive church as the creator of faith in Jesus as the Messiah.

270. O. Pfleiderer, *Das Urchristenthum, seine Schriften und Lehre, in geschichtlichem Zusammenhang beschrieben* [Primitive Christianity, its literature and doctrine, described in historical interrelationship], Berlin, 1887, pp. 175, 191, v, 31, 175, 298-99. 301, 303-6, 259 n; 2d ed., 1902, pp. vi-viii. Eng. tr. by W. Montgomery. Copyright © 1906 by G. P. Putnam's Sons (New York) and Williams and Norgate (London). Quotations with emendations are from Vol. I, pp. 463-64, vi-viii.

271. C. F. G. Heinrici, *Das zweite Sendschreiben des Apostels Paulus an die Korinthier* [The Second Letter of Paul the apostle to the Corinthians], Berlin, 1887, pp. 556-57, 573, 576, 582, 594.

272. O. Linton, "Das Problem der Urkirche in der neueren Forschung" [The problem of the primitive church in recent research], *Uppsala Universitets Årsskrift*, 1932, Teologi 2, p. 5, who also indicates the intellectual-historical presuppositions of this "consensus around the year 1880."

273. Predecessors for this viewpoint are mentioned by R. Sohm, *Kirchenrecht* [Church law], Vol. I, 1892, p. 8, *n.* 7, and O. Linton (*op. cit.*, n. 272), pp. 21-22.

274. Edwin Hatch, *The Organization of the Early Christian Churches* (Bampton Lectures for 1880), 3rd ed., London, 1918, pp. 29-31, 38, 59-66, 213. In his authorized translation (from the first edition, Giessen, 1883) A. Harnack introduced miscellaneous additional comments, among which he indicates as Hatch's most important insight the fact that the community organization which later became fixed—bishop, college of presbyters, the diaconate, the people—was a combination of two different organizational patterns: leadership by the presbyters, and an administration through bishops and deacons. On these concrete research results, see Linton (*op. cit.*, n. 272), pp. 31-32.

275. The translation of the Greek text of the "Teaching of the Lord through his Twelve Apostles" is to be found in the editions of *The Apostolic Fathers*, Loeb Classical Library, pp. 303-33. On the date and historical setting, see E. Molland, *RGG*, I, col. 508; P. Th. Camelot, *LThK*, III, pp. 369-70; esp. J. P. Audet, *La Didachè*, 1958.

276. A. Harnack, *Lehre der zwölf Apostel nebst Untersuchungen zur älteren Geschichte der Kirchenverfassung und des Kirchenrechts* [The teaching of the twelve apostles together with research on the older history of church organization and church law], 1884, pp. 103, 110, *n.* 23, with information on sources.

277. R. Sohm, *Kirchenrecht* [Church law], Vol. I: *Die geschichtlichen Grundlagen* [The historical foundations], = Systematisches Handbuch der Deutschen Rechtswissenchaft [Systematic handbook of German legal science], Vol. VIII, Leipzig, 1892, pp. 1, 26. A. Bühler, *Kirche und Staat bei Rudolph Sohm* [Church and state by Rudolph Sohm], 1965, pp. 14-15, shows that Sohm as early as 1886-87 presented the thesis of a law-free church, but in the first volume of his *Kirchenrecht* in 1892, he "for the first time changed from a study of church legal aspects by conceptual-deductive method to a theological-exegetical method" (p. 17).

278.   See Linton (*op cit.*, n. 272), pp. 64 ff., 136-37; and E. Foerster, *R. Sohms Kritik des Kirchenrechts* [R. Sohm's critical study of church law], 1942, pp. 8 ff.

279.   E. Foerster (*op. cit.*, n. 278), pp. 86, 53. Cf. W. Maurer, "Die Auseinandersetzung zwischen Harnack und Sohm und die Begründung eines evangelischen Kirchenrechts" [The debate between Harnack and Sohm and the establishment of a Protestant ecclesiastical law], *Kerygma und Dogma*, 6 (1960), 194 ff.

280.   Quotations from R. Sohm (*op. cit.*, n. 278), pp. 4-6, 8-10, 22, x.

281.   See p. 139 and the summary by W. Weiffenbach, *Der Wiederkunftsgedanke Jesu. Nach den Synoptikern kritisch untersucht und dargestellt* [The idea of the return of Jesus, critically studied and presented according to the Synoptics], 1873, 3 ff.; A. Schweitzer, *Quest* (*op. cit.*, n. 161), pp. 138-39, 204-5, 222 ff.; G. R. Beasley-Murray, *Jesus and the Future* (New York: St. Martins, 1954), pp. 2 ff.

282.   W. Baldensperger, *Das Selbstbewusstsein Jesu im Lichte der messianischen Hoffnungen seiner Zeit* [The self-consciousness of Jesus in light of the messianic hopes of his time], Strassburg, 1888, pp. iv, 85, 80, 108, 139, 96, v, 114.

283.   O. Everling, *Die paulinische Angelologie und Dämonologie. Ein biblisch-theologischer Versuch* [The Pauline angelology and demonology; a biblical-theological essay], Göttingen, 1888, pp. 5, 126, 20, 38.

284.   H. Gunkel, *Die Wirkungen des heiligen Geistes nach der populären Anschauung der apostolischen Zeit und nach der Lehre des Apostles Paulus* [The actions of the Holy Spirit according to the popular view of the apostolic age and according to the apostle Paul], Göttigen, 1888, pp. 63, 107, 34, 25, 52-53, 95, 24. On this work see W. Klatt, *Hermann Gunkel*, 1969, pp. 29 ff.

285.   G. Dalman, *Die Worte Jesu. Mit Berücksichtigung des nachkanonischen jüdischen Schrifttums und der aramäischen Sprache* [The words of Jesus, with a consideration of the postcanonical Jewish scriptures and the Aramaic language], Vol. I., Leipzig, 1898, p. 57. Eng. tr. by D. M. McKay, *The Words of Jesus*, Edinburgh, 1902. Dalman consciously linked up his work with that of Lightfoot, as is evident in his account, "In the Footsteps of John Lightfoot," *Expository Times*, 35 (1923/24), 71 ff.

286.   A. Deissman, in *Selbstdarstellungen*, Vol. I, 1925, p. 53.

287.   A. Deissman, *Light from the Ancient Past. The New Testament and the Newly Discovered Texts from the Hellenistic-Roman World* (= *Licht vom Osten*, Tübingen, 1908). Eng. tr. L. R. M. Strachan. Copyright © by Hodder and Stoughton (London, 1910) and Harper & Row (New York, 1927). A. Deissman, *Bible Studies. Contributions Mostly from Papyri and Inscriptions to the History of the Language, the Literature, and the Religion of Hellenistic Judaism and of Primitive Christianity* (= Bibelstudien. Beiträge, zumeist aus den Papyri und Inschriften, zur Geschichte der Sprache, des Schrifttums und der Religion des hellenistichen Judentums und des Urchristentums, Marburg, 1895). Eng. tr. by A. Grieve (Edinburgh: T. and T. Clark, 1901), pp. 66, 80-81, 3, 6, 9, 35-36, 43-44, 58; A. Deissmann, "Die sprachliche Erforschung der griechischen Bibel, ihr gegenwärtiger Stand und ihre Aufgabe" [Linguistic research in the Greek Bible, its present state and its task], *Vorträge der theologischen Konferenz zu Giessen,* XII, 1898, pp. 10-11.

Neill, *Interpretation*, p. 145, *n. 2*, indicates as characteristic of German scholarship that in the first edition of this present book the name of William Ramsay does not occur, although his archaeological research in Asia Minor he had demonstrated the reliability of numerous items in the book of Acts and the letters of Paul. (A similar charge of neglect of Ramsay was made by W. Gasque, in "Sir William Ramsay and the New Testament," *Studia Evangelica*, V [Texte und Untersuchungen 103], 1968, pp. 277 ff.) But in contrast to Deissmann's adducing of a fund of epigraphic and manuscript material (even so, Neill describes Deissmann as "the incomparable popularizer"!), Ramsay's apologetic analysis of archaeology signifies no methodologically essential advance for New Testament research. Therefore Ramsay is missing from the second edition of this book as well. (On Ramsay, in addition to Neill, pp. 141 ff., see J. Schmid, *LThK*, VIII, col. 986). One can regard this judgment of mine as in error, but it is beside the point to regard this as a characteristic example of German scholarship.

288. K. F. Nösgen, "Das Neue Testament und die pseudepigraphische Literatur," *Theologisches Literaturblatt*, 11 (1890), 457.

289. R. Kübel, review of R. Kabisch *Die Eschatologie des Paulus*, 1893 (see pp. 232 ff.) in *Theologisches Literaturblatt*, 14 (1893), 340.

290. *Theologe und Christ. Erinnerungen und Bekenntnisse von Martin Kähler* [Theologian and Christian: recollections and confessions of Martin Kähler], 1926, p. 185. In accordance with this and without seeing any of the problems, Kähler characterized as the task of exegesis the paraphrastic exposition of the train of thought and the setting forth of the central concepts of the Bible. See C. Seiler, "Die Theologische Entwicklung Martin Kähler's bis 1869" [The theological development of Martin Kähler up to 1869], in *Beiträge zur Förderung christlicher Theologie*, 51 (1966), pp. 65-66.

291. M. Kähler, *Der sogenannte historische Jesus und der geschichtliche biblische Christus*. Vortrag auf der Wuppertaler Pastoralkonferenz, Leipzig, 1892. In the new edition (Theol. Bücherei II, ed. E. Wolf, 1953), pp. 18, 37, 21, 44, 37, 50; further, 16, 24-26, 28-29, 34, 41, 38-39, 41, 44, 71-72, 73-74 [Eng. tr., with an introduction by Carl Braaten, *The So-called Historical Jesus and the Historic Biblical Christ* (Philadelphia: Fortress Press, 1964).

292. See the essay of Julius Schniewind on Martin Kähler in *Nachgelassene Reden und Aufsätze* [Posthumous speeches and essays], 1952, pp. 169, 171; J. Wirsching, *Gott in der Geschichte. Studien zur theologischen Stellung und systematischen Grundlegung der Theologie Martin Kählers* [God in history: studies in the theological position and systematic foundation of Martin Kähler's theology], 1963, pp. 212-13. As early as 1863 in a lecture and always thereafter, especially in his letters, Kähler defended the rightness of criticism and, for example, had explicitly agreed methodologically with L. J. Rückert and E. Reuss (see pp. 110-11, 155 ff.). Cf. C. Seiler (*op. cit.*, n. 290), pp. 80 ff. On the skeptical position of Kähler concerning the question as to how historical facts can be securely ascertained, see O. Zänker, *Grundlinien der Theologie Martin Kahlers* [The basic lines of Kähler's theology], 1914, pp. 72-73; H. Gerdes, "Die durch Martin Kählers Kampf gegen den 'historischen Jesus' ausgelöste Krise in der evangelischen Theologie und ihre Überwindung" [The crisis in Protestant theology triggered by M. Kähler's attack on the 'historical Jesus' and its resolution], *Neue Zeitschrift für Systematische Theologie*, 3 (1961), 177-78.

293. It was for the first time in the "second, completely revised edition" of his book (1900) that J. Weiss took as his premise the depiction of Jesus' preaching as patterned after the Old Testament and Jewish prototypes of the idea of the kingdom of God (pp. 1-35).

294. This is justly denounced by R. Schäfer, "Das Reich Gottes bei Albrecht Ritschl und Johannes Weiss" [The kingdom of God in the thought of A. Ritschl and J. Weiss], *ZThK* 61 (1964), 77. The designation of post–Old Testament Judaism as "late Judaism" arose at the end of the eighteenth century (see on this J. Schmidt, *op. cit.*, n. 266, p. 11) and was generally in use among Christian scholars until the middle of our century, but it is factually in error and accordingly will not be used in this edition. Cf. K. Schubert, *LThK*, IX, cols. 949-50.

295. J. Weiss, *Die Predigt Jesu vom Reiche Gottes* [Jesus' message of the kingdom of God], Göttingen, 1892, pp. 7, 67, 12, 21-22, 24, 30-32, 42-43, 49-50, 60-62, 67. The third edition (ed. by F. Hahn, Göttingen, 1964) reproduces the 2nd edition of 1900 and offers in an appendix excerpts from the first edition. Yet one finds there nearly all the citations here given (with the exception of pp. 30-32) : pp. 291-92, 246, 220, 223, 224, 228-29, 236, 240-42, 246-47. On Weiss's distinction between the biblical and the modern meanings of the kingdom of God, see D. L. Holland, "History, Theology, and the Kingdom of God: A Contribution of Johannes Weiss to Twentieth Century Theology," *Biblical Research*, 13 (1968), 54 ff.

296. W. Bousset, *ThLZ*, 26 (1901), 563, 568; R. Schäfer (*op. cit.*, n. 294), pp. 68 ff. employs an unjustifiably sharp criticism against the exegetical method of J. Weiss.

297. W. Lütgert, *Das Reich Gottes nach den synoptischen Evangelien. Eine Untersuchung zur neutestamentlichen Theologie* [The kingdom of God in the Synoptic Gospels: a study in New Testament theology], Gütersloh, 1895, mentions Weiss not at all and deals extensively with the "present kingdom" and the "hidden kingdom"; G. Schnedermann, *Theol. Lit. Blatt*, 15 (1894), 387-88, declared, "Johannes Weiss has nonetheless not made clear the connection between Jesus and the thought of his people and, furthermore, by introducing the term 'thoroughly' has overstated the element of the eschatological."

298. A. Titius, *Die neutestamentliche Lehre von der Seligkeit und ihre Bedeutung für die Gegenwart* [The New Testament teaching of blessedness and its importance for today], Vol. I, 1895, pp. 4, 12, 17: "The greatest caution is in any case necessary with regard to the idea of the immediate nearness of the end so strongly turned to account by Johannes Weiss." H. H. Wendt, "Das Reich Gottes in der Lehre Jesu," [The kingdom of God in the teaching of Jesus], *Christliche Welt*, 7 (1893), 338 ff., 361 ff., 410 ff., 434 ff.: "On the ground of the perfect father love of God, Jesus infers the certainty of both the otherworldly state of salvation that God will bring about for his own and of the eternal, heavenly nature of this state of salvation" (p. 388); and on p. 413: "If therefore Jesus speaks of the presentness of the kingdom of God, he means that the promised, ideal salvation-situation is already actualizing itself in the present, in him and his disciples, to the extent that they stand in a fellowship with God that is ideal and full of redemption." On p. 435: "Jesus therefore presents us with the idea of a development of the kingdom of God . . . a development out of the present condition to a future that is formed in a wholly different way, out of earthly preparation to heavenly completion." Further evidence of this view in A. Schweitzer (*op. cit.*, n. 161), pp. 249-50.

299. J. Wellhausen, *Israelitische und jüdische Geschichte* [Israelite and Jewish history], 1894, p. 314: "Jesus presents the kingdom of God as the goal of a struggle; it will first be fulfilled in any case through God in the future, but it has already begun in the present. He does not himself merely predict it, but from its transcendence he brings it to pass on the earth; at least he plans its germ. . . . The eschatological conceptions receive a generally human and a superhistorical stamp. Of gnosis and phantasy one finds nothing: what is formulated is only a moral metaphysic, a wholly grave simplicity." A. Harnack (*op. cit.*, n. 240), 54: "Such conceptions as the two kingdoms—of God and Satan—of their conflict and of the final last battle, Jesus simply shares with his contemporaries. The other view, however, that the kingdom of God does not come with outward signs, that it is already there, that was really Jesus' own."

300. P. Wernle, *Die Anfänge unserer Religion* [The beginnings of our religion], Tübingen and Leipzig, 1901, p. 32.

301. E. Ehrhardt, *Der Grundcharakter der Ethik Jesu im Verhältnis zu den messianischen Hoffnungen seines Volkes und zu seinem eigenen Messiabewusstsein* [The basic character of Jesus' ethic in relationship to the messianic hopes of his people and to his own messianic consciousness], Freiburg and Leipzig, 1895, pp. 49, 81, 84.

302. H. Gunkel, *ThLZ*, 18 (1893), 43.

303. W. Bousset, *Jesu Predigt in ihrem Gegensatz zum Judentum. Ein religionsgeschichtlicher Vergleich* [The preaching of Jesus in contrast to Judaism. A religiohistorical comparison], Göttingen, 1892, pp. 6-7, 69-70, 38-39, 44, 49, 64-65, 102-3, 130, 89.

304. R. Kabisch, *Die Eschatologie des Paulus in ihren Zusammenhängen mit dem Gesamtbegriff des Paulinismus* [The eschatology of Paul in its relationships with the total Pauline concepts], Göttingen, 1893, pp. 5, 11-12, 74-75, 134-35, 183, 188, 317

305. In a comprehensive review, W. Wrede (*ThLZ*, 18 [1894], 133) declares that "the picture as drawn is a complete caricature"; R. Kübel, *Theol. Lit. Blatt*, 14 (1893), 399, says: "Apart from his exaggerations, the author is certainly right. But these exaggerations are severe." E. von Dobschütz in "The Eschatology of the Gospels," *The Expositor*, 7 (series IX, 1910), 104, speaks of "onesided archaism."

306. A. Schweitzer, *Das Abendmahl im Zusammenhang mit dem Leben Jesu und der Geschichte des Urchristentums:* First half, "Das Abendmahls-problem auf Grund der wissenschaftlichen Forschung des 19. Jahrhunderts und der historischen Berichte"; Second half, "Das Messianitäts- und Leidensgeheimnis. Eine Skizze des lebens Jesu." [The Lord's Supper in connection with the life of Jesus and the history of primitive Christianity: (1) the problem of the Lord's Supper on the basis of scholarly research of the nineteenth century and the historical accounts; (2) The mystery of messiahship and suffering; a sketch of the life of Jesus], Tübingen and Leipzig, 1901. The second half was translated into English by Walter Lowrie under the title, *The Mystery of the Kingdom of God* (First published in the United States by The Macmillan Company [New York, 1957] and in England by A. C. Black [London, 1914]). Quotations with emendations are from pp. ix-x, 53, 88, 115, 116, 117, 131-32, 157-59 and are used by permission.

307. A. Schweitzer, *Selbstdarstellung*, 1929, pp. 4-5; *Aus meinem Leben und Denken* [Out of my life and thought], 1931, pp. 5-6; W. G. Kummel, "L'eschatologie conséquente d'Albert Schweitzer jugée par ses contemporains," *Revue d'histoire et de philosophie réligieuses*, 37 (1957), 58 ff. (= in German, Kümmel, *Heilsgeschehen*, pp. 328 ff.) ; W. G. Kümmel, "Albert Schweitzer als Jesus- und Paulusforscher," in *Albert Schweitzer als Theologe*, ed. W. G. K. and C. -H. Ratschow, 1966, pp. 9 ff.; K. Scholder, "Albert Schweitzer und Ferdinand Christian Baur," in *A. Schweitzer: Sein Denken und sein Weg* [A. Schweitzer, his thought and way], ed. by H. W. Bähr, 1962, pp. 184 ff., shows how strongly in agreement with F. C. Baur, Schweitzer stands in radical historical questioning and in the central stress on Jesus' ethic in spite of the fact that their respective portrayals of Jesus are so different.

308. G. Hollmann, *ThLZ* 27 (1902), 465 ff. ("The systematician surpasses the historian") ; P. Feine, *Theol. Lit. Blatt*, 24 (1903), 439 ff. With this work "the evidence is brought into the open that eschatology is not the key to an understanding of Jesus"; H. Weinel, *ThR* 5 (1902), 244: "Both the final, the last powerful word, and also the entire construction is false, even though the whole is presented with great self-confidence and high self-consciousness"; F. Spitta, *Streitfragen der Geschichte Jesu* [Controversial issues concerning the historical Jesus], 1907, p. 133: "Thus Schweitzer, with his own contempt for the presupposition of a solid historical study—that is, a careful examination of the sources—constructs a picture of the life of Jesus that hardly any other later carrying forward of the object of this research would link up with." Cf. Schweitzer, *Selbstdarstellung*, p. 14: "At first my sketch of the life of Jesus caused no offense because almost no one noticed it."

309.   A. Schweitzer, *Von Reimarus zu Wrede. Eine Geschichte der Leben-Jesu-Forschung.* [From Reimarus to Wrede: a history of Jesus research], Tübingen, 1906. Translated into English by W. Montgomery as *The Quest of the Historical Jesus* (*op. cit.*, n. 161). Quotations with emendations are from pp. 1, 239-40, 218-19, 221, 237, 396-97, 399, and are used by permission.

310.   R. H. Grützmacher, *Ist das liberale Jesus-Bild modern?* [Is the liberal Jesus modern?], 1907, p. 24; L. Lemme, *Jesu Wissen und Weisheit* [The knowledge and wisdom of Jesus], 1907, pp. 19-20.

311.   K. F. Nösgen, *Theol. Lit. Blatt,* 27 (1906), 511.

312.   See the references in A. Schweitzer (*op. cit.*, n. 161), 2nd ed., pp. 592-93. Cf. the preface by F. C. Burkitt, pp. v-viii.

313.   For example, P. Wernle, *ThLZ*, 31 (1906), 504: "Horrible devastation and violation of the sources, such as we have not experienced in decades." A. Jülicher, *Neue Linien in der Kritik der evangelischen Überlieferung* [New lines in the criticism of the Gospel tradition], 1906, p. 5: "The violation of law and rule of historical research can scarcely be more grossly accomplished."

314.   A. Schweitzer (*op cit.*, n. 189), pp. ix, x, 177, 239-41.

315.   See R. Bultmann, *Deutsche Literaturzeitung*, 2 (3rd Series, 1931), 1153 ff.: "The conception of this book is really a great thing." Martin Dibelius, *Neue Jahrbücher für Wissenschaft und Jugendbildung*, 7, 685 (= *Botschaft und Geschichte, Gesammelte Aufsätze* [Message and history: collected essays], Vol. II, 1956, p. 97): "Schweitzer has in fact posed the decisive question for the discussion." M. Goguel, *Revue d'Histoire et de Philosophie réligieuses*, 11 (1931), 198: "In essence we believe that Schweitzer has portrayed the spirit of Paulinism in a marvelous way."

316.   E. Vischer, *ThR*, 16 (1913), 252: Schweitzer has "really proved neither the justice of his criticism of prior research nor the consistency of his own thesis." H. Windisch, *Zeitschrift für wissenschaftliche Theologie*, 55 (1954), 174: "Paul must indeed be grasped on the basis of his eschatology, but when Paul is to be understood from the standpoint of late Judaism, then he is immediately placed under syncretistic influences and explained on a history-of-religions basis." On the enduring importance of A. Schweitzer's New Testament research, see O. Cullmann, "Albert Schweitzers Auffassung der urchristlichen Reichgotteshoffnung im Lichte der heutigen neutestamentlichen Forschung" [Schweitzer's understanding of the primitive Christian hope of the kingdom of God in the light of present-day New Testament research], *EvTh*, N. F. 20 (1965), 643 ff.

317.   W. Kroll, *Geschichte der klassischen Philologie* [History of classical philology], 2nd ed., 1919, pp. 739 ff.; M. P. Nilsson, *History of Greek Religion*, tr. from Swedish by F. J. Fielden (Oxford: Clarendon Press [1925], 1948), 2nd ed., pp. 263 ff. M. Wegner,

Altertumskunde, 1951, pp. 254 ff.; K. Latte, *Römische Religionsgeschichte* [History of Roman religion], 1960, pp. 11 ff.

318. E. Rohde, *Psyche*, First Installment, Leipzig, 1890. Eng. tr. from the 8th ed. by W. B. Hillis (New York, 1925), pp. 3-42.

319. H. Usener, *Religionsgeschichtliche Untersuchungen I, Das Weihnachtsfest*, Bonn, 1889, pp. 25, 75, 78, 69, 187. In a methodological essay on mythology, Usener later urged that for the study of the history of religion, ethnology, and folklore be drawn together with the study of the forms of religious conceptions. See *Archiv für Religionswissenschaft*, 7 (1904), 6 ff. (= *Vorträge und Aufsätze*, 1907, pp. 39 ff.).

320. A. Dieterich, *Abraxas. Studien zur Religionsgeschichte des spätern Altertums* [Studies in the history of religion in late antiquity], Leipzig, 1891, pp. 3, 84, 61, 117, 153.

321. A. Dieterich, *Eine Mithrasliturgie erläutert* [Commentary on a Mithraic liturgy], Leipzig, 1903, pp. 106, 178.

322. P. Wendland, "Philo und die kynisch-stoische Diatribe," in *Beiträge zur Geschichte der griechischen Philosophie und Religion*, ed. P. Wendland and O. Kern, Berlin, 1895, p. 7.

323. As Wendland observed, J. G. Droysen had coined the term "Hellenism" eighty years earlier and asserted the importance of this epoch as an important "link in the chain of human development." Cf. M. Wegner (*op. cit.*, n. 317), pp. 211 ff.; F. C. Grant, s. v. "Hellenism," *RGG*, Vol. III, cols. 209 ff.

324. P. Wendland, *Die hellenistisch-römische Kultur in ihren Beziehungen zu Judentum und Christentum* [The Hellenistic-Roman culture in its links with Judaism and Christianity], Handbuch zum Neuen Testament, I, 2, Tübingen, 1907, pp. 50, 126, 131, 178-79.

325. F. Cumont, *Textes et monuments figurés relatifs aux mystères de Mithra*, Vol. I, Brussels 1899, pp. 339-41.

326. His biographer expresses this opinion: "Everything leads one to think that he consciously kept his distance from the study of Christianity" (F. Cumont, *Lux perpetua*, 1949, pp. xxi-xxii).

327. F. Cumont, *Oriental Religions in Roman Paganism*, tr. from the Paris ed., 1910, reprint ed., New York: Dover, n.d., p. xii.

328. R. Reitzenstein, *Zwei religionsgeschichtliche Fragen nach ungedruckten griechischen Texte der Strassburger Bibliotek* [Two history-of-religions questions from unpublished Greek texts in the Strassburg library], Strassburg, 1901, pp. 100, 84.

329. R. Reitzenstein, *Poimandres. Studien zur griechisch-ägyptischen und frühchristlicher Literatur*, Leipzig, 1904, pp. 2, v, 81, 244, 248. On Reitzenstein's thesis of the existence of a Hellenistic myth of the god, "Man," see C. Colpe, *Die religionsgeschichtliche Schule. Darstellung und Kritik ihres Bildes vom gnostischen Erlösermythus* [The history-of-religions school: description and critique of its portrayal of the gnostic redeemer myth], *FRLANT*, N. F., 60 (1961), 10 ff.

330. On the origin and history of the history-of-religions school in New Testament study, see W. Bousset, "Die Religionsgeschichte und das Neue Testament," *ThR*, 7 (1904), 265 ff., 311 ff., 353 ff; H. J. Holtzmann, "Neutestamentler und Religionsgeschichtler" [New Testament scholar and historian of religion], *Prot. Monatshefte* 10 (1906), 1 ff.; M. Rade, *RGG*, 1st ed., 1913, IV, cols. 2183 ff.; H. Gressmann, *Albert Eichhorn und die Religionsgeschichtliche Schule*, 1914; O. Eissfeldt, *RGG*, 2nd ed., 1930, IV, cols. 1898 ff.; G. W. Ittel, *Urchristentum und Fremdreligionen im Urteil der Religionsgeschichtlichen Schule* [Primitive Christianity and foreign religions in the view of the history-of-religions school], (Erlangen Dissertation, 1956), containing sketches of the life and work of the major representatives of the history-of-religions school; H. Schlier, *LThK*, Vol. VIII, cols. 1184-85; C. Colpe (*op. cit.*, n. 329). Colpe in *n.* 9 shows that it cannot be established now who coined the name, "history-of-religions school"; it first appears in 1904. Cf. J. Hempel in *RGG*, V, cols. 991 ff.

331. These scholars themselves stress that this entire work is indebted for its being recognized and promulgated to A. Eichhorn (W. Bousset, *ThR*, 7 (1903), p. 313; H. Gunkel, *Schöpfung und Chaos in Urzeit und Endzeit. Eine religionsgeschichtliche Untersuchung über Gen. 1 und Ap. John 12*, Göttingen, 1895, p. vii; H. Gressmann (*op. cit.*, n. 330), pp. 21, 24. Cf. also M. Reischle, *Theologie und Religionsgeschichte*, 1904, pp. 3-4), and in addition, H. Gunkel's statements in a letter to Gressmann on the influence of Eichhorn on Gunkel's posing of the problems (*before* Gresssmann's written pronouncements about Eichhorn, see under n. 330); Gunkel's statements were published by W. Klatt, *Ein Brief von Hermann Gunkel über Albert Eichhorn an Hugo Gressmann* [A letter to Hugo Gressmann from Hermann Gunkel concerning Albert Eichhorn], *ZThK*, 66 (1969), 1 ff. See also W. Klatt (*op. cit.*, n. 284), pp. 20 ff., 52 ff.

332. H. Gunkel (*op. cit.*, n. 331), pp. 207-9, 272-73, 369-71, 397, 391. On the methodological problems in this work, see J. M. Schmidt (*op. cit.*, n. 266), pp. 195 ff., and W. Klatt (*op. cit.*, n. 284), pp. 51 ff.

333. W. Bousset, *Der Antichrist in der Überlieferung des Judentums, des neuen Testaments und der alten Kirche. Ein Beitrag zur Auslegung der Apocalypse* [The anti-Christ in the tradition of Judaism, of the New Testament, and of the ancient church: a contribution to the exposition of the Apocalypse], Göttingen, 1895, pp. 1, 18-19, 5, 10, 93-94; Bousset, *Die Offenbarung Johannis* [The revelation to John], Kritisch-exegetischer Kommentar Series, 16th sec., ed. H. A. W. Meyer, Göttingen, 5th ed., 1896, pp. 143, 163-66. Bousset expressly declared that "through research in Jewish apocalyptic one can reach an essentially deeper understanding of the genesis of the Gospel, to the extent that this is historically achievable," (Neueste Forschungen auf dem Gebiet der religiösen Lituratur des Spätjudentums" [Recent research in the field of the religious literature of late Judaism], *ThR*, 3 (1900), p. 302, cited by J. M. Schmidt (*op. cit.*, n. 266), pp. 203, 243. In spite of his description of Christianity as a "syncretistic religion," H. Gunkel stressed: "Thus we grasp the rationality of history: that the religion of the New Testament arose on the foundation of Israel. Whether modern man wants to hear it or not, 'salvation' has come 'from the Jews.'" ("Das Alte Testament im Lichte der modernen Forschung" [The Old Testament in light of modern research], in *Beiträge zur Weiterentwicklung der christlichen Religion* [Contributions to the advancement of the Christian religion], 1905, p. 62, quoted by W. Klatt (*op. cit.*, n. 284), p. 262. See also pp. 307-8.

334. A. Eichorn, "Das Abendmahl im Neuen Testament," Supplement to *Christliche Welt*, no. 36, Leipzig, 1898, pp. 5, 14, 11, 26, 22, 30-31, 14-15, 28, 30-31.

335. W. Heitmüller *"Im Namen Jesu." Eine sprach- und religionsgeschichtliche Untersuchung zum Neuen Testament, speziell zur altchristlichen Taufe* ["In the Name of Jesus"; a linguistic and religio-historical study in the New Testament, with special interest in baptism in the early church], Göttingen, 1903; the quotations are from pp. 223-24, 239-41, 253-54, 268. W. Heitmüller, *Taufe und Abendmahl bei Paulus. Darstellung und religionsgeschichtliche Beleuchtung* [Baptism and Lord's Supper ac-

cording to Paul. Description and religio-historical illumination], Göttingen, 1903, pp. 14, 25, 35, 51, 54 f.; quotations from pp. 35-38, 51-52.

336. H. Gunkel, *Zum religionsgeschichtlichen Verständnis des Neuen Testaments* [On the religio-historical understanding of the New Testament], Göttingen, 1903, pp. 1, 11, 34-36, 85-86, 87-89, 95. Cf. W. Klatt (*op. cit.*, n. 284), pp. 90 ff.

337. W. Bousset, *Die Religion des Judentums im neutestamentlichen Zeitalter* [The religion of Judaism in New Testament times], Berlin, 1903, pp. 492-93 .

338. W. Bousset, *Die jüdische Apokalyptik, ihre religionsgeschichtliche Herkunft und ihre Bedeutung für das neue Testament* [Jewish Apocalyptic: its religio-historical origin and its importance for the New Testament], Berlin, 1903, pp. 58, 66, 52-53, 55-59, 61-66.

339. W. Bousset, *Hauptprobleme der Gnosis* [Major problems of gnosis], Göttingen, 1907, pp. 350, 54, 260.

340. M. Dibelius, *Die Geisterwelt im Glauben des Paulus* [The world of spirits in the faith of Paul], Göttingen, 1909, pp. 2-5, 93, 202-5; M. Dibelius, *Die urchristliche Überlieferung von Johannes dem Täufer untersucht* [The primitive Christian tradition of John the Baptist analyzed], Göttingen, 1911, pp. iii, 2, 4-6, 137-38.

341. J. Weiss, in *Die Aufgaben der Neutestamentlichen Wissenschaft in der Gegenwart* [The present tasks of New Testament scholarship], Göttingen, 1908, pp. 12-13, had urged that the style of Paul be compared "with those writings which are in so many ways related."

342. R. Bultmann, *Der Stil der paulinischen Predigt und die kynischstoische Diatribe* [The style of the Pauline sermon and the Cynic-Stoic diatribe], Göttingen, 1910, pp. 2-3, 107-9; R. Bultmann, "Das religiöse Moment in der ethischen Unterweisung des Epiktet und das Neue Testament" [The religious impulse in the ethical instruction of Epictetus and the New Testament], *ZNW*, 13 (1912), 180-81, 185-86, 191.

343. R. Reitzenstein, *Die hellenistischen Mysterienreligionen, ihre Grundgedanken und Wirkungen* [The Hellenistic mystery religions: their fundamental ideas and influence], Leipzig and Berlin, 1910, pp. 1, 209-10, 58-60, 53, 55-56.

344. Shortly before the appearance of Bousset's *Kyrios Christos*, W. Heitmüller, in complete independence of Bousset, in an essay, "Zum Problem Paulus und Jesus" (originally in *ZNW*, 13 (1912), 320 ff.; reprinted with the original pagination in *Das Paulusbild in der neueren deutschen Forschung* [The image of Paul in recent German research], ed. K. H. Rengstorf, Wege der Forschung XXIV, 1964), advanced the theory that "the course of development ran: Jesus—the primitive community—Hellenistic Christianity—Paul" (p. 330) and that the designation of Jesus as "Lord" arose, not in the primitive community but in Hellenistic Christianity (p. 334).

345. W. Bousset, *Kyrios Christos. Geschichte des Christusglaubens von den Anfängen des Christentums bis Irenaeus* [The history of Christology from the beginnings of Christainity to Irenaeus], Göttingen, 1913, pp. v, vii, 6, 20, 164, 198, 213, 172, 222, 12, 15-17, 21, 41-43, 47, 91-93, 105, 118-20, 124-25, 129-30, 132-33, 135, 137, 141-42, 145, 148, 164-65, 171-72, 192, 195, 213, 222. The many Greek words in Bousett's original are transliterated, followed by a translation into English.

346. J. Weiss, "Das Problem der Entstehung des Christentums" [The Problem of the Origin of Christianity], *Archiv für Religionswissenschaft*, 16 (1913), 413-515; the quotations are from pp. 425-26, 428, 434-37, 445, 451, 457, 470-71, 480-81, 486, 488, 492. J. Weiss, *Das Urchristentum* [Earliest Christianity], (Edited and expanded at the conclusion, after the death of the author, by R. Knopf), Göttigen, 1914. Eng. tr., *Earliest Christianity: A History of the Period A.D. 30-150*, by F. C. Grant (New York: Harper Torchbooks [1959]). Quotations with emendations are from pp. 174-77, 193, 519-20, 526, 42-43, 650, and are used by permission. Cf. the sharp, unjustified critical attack on Weiss by K. Prumm, on "the prejudice of an immanentist historian," in "Johannes Weiss als Darsteller und religionsgeschichtlicher Erklärer der paulinischen Botschaft" [J. Weiss as portrayer and religio-historical interpreter of the Pauline message], *Biblica*, 40 (1959), 815 ff.

347.   On Wellhausen's withdrawal from the theological faculty in Greifswald and his assumption of an associate professorship in the University of Halle, see A. Jepsen, "Wellhausen in Greifswald," *Festschrift zur 500-Jahr-Feier der Universität Greifswald*, Vol. II, 1956, pp. 51 ff. In the same article appears also Wellhausen's moving letter to the Prussian Minister of Culture, Althoff, concerning this affair, pp. 54-55. Cf. H. J. Kraus, *Geschichte der historisch-kritischen Erforschung des Alten Testaments*, 2nd ed., 1969, p. 256.

348.   J. Wellhausen, *Israelitische und jüdische Geschichte*, Berlin, 1894, pp. 312, 318. See also the quotation in note 299. The view that Jesus used the term "Son of man" of himself only as "man" in the earthly sense has been represented both before and after Wellhausen; see A. Schweitzer (*op. cit.*, n. 161), pp. 276-77; and F. Hahn, *Christologische Hoheitstitel. Ihre Geschichte im früen Christentum*, FRLANT, 83 (1963), 13 ff., 23-24; Eng. tr. by H. Knight and G. Ogg, *The Titles of Jesus in Christology: Their History in Early Christianity* (New York: World Publishing Co., 1969), pp. 15-16.

349.   J. Wellhausen, *Das Evangelium Marci übersetzt und erklärt* [The Gospel of Mark translated and expounded], Berlin, 1903; *Das Evangelium Matthaei übersetzt und erklärt* [The Gospel of Matthew translated and expounded], Berlin, 1904; *Das Evangelium Lucae übersetzt und erklärt* Berlin, 1904. On the development of this view of Wellhausen's, cf. E. Bammel, "Judentum, Christentum und Heidentum: Julius Wellhausen's Briefe an Theodor Mommsen 1881-1902" [Judaism, Christianity, and the Gentile world: J. Wellhausen's correspondence with Th. Mommsen], *Zeitschrift fur Kirchengeschichte*, no. 80, pp. 109, 221 ff.

350.   J. Wellhausen, *Einleitung in die ersten Evangelien* [Introduction to the first three Gospels], Berlin, 1905, pp. 3, 43, 51-52, 94, 97-98, 107, 113-15.

351.   See on this, p. 309.

352.   See the dedication of Wrede's book on the messianic secret; and further, H. Gressmann, *Albert Eichhorn und die Religionsgeschichtliche Schule*, 1914, pp. 5-6; and W. Klatt (*op. cit.*, n. 284), p. 22 (letter from E. Troeltsch).

353.   W. Wrede, *Das Messiasgeheimnis in den Evangelien. Zugleich ein Beitrag zum Verständnis des Markusevangeliums* [The messianic secret in the Gospels: at the same time, a contribution to the understanding of Mark], Göttingen, 1901, pp. vii, vi, 3, 132, 227, 46-47, 65-67, 71, 79-80, 114-15, 129-31, 216-18, 227-29.

354.   A. Schweitzer, *Von Reimarus zu Wrede*, 1906, pp. 327 ff. Cf. Schweitzer (*op. cit*, n. 161), pp. 332 ff. Against the placing together (of Schweitzer and Wrede) in the same camp, see A. Jülicher (*op. cit.*, n. 313), pp. 7-8: "The pairing of Wrede and Schweitzer as twins exists only in the visions of this historicizing poet." See also pp. 239 ff.; and G. Strecker, "William Wrede," *ZThK* 57 (1960), 85, n. 2.

355. H. J. Ebeling, *Das Messiasgeheimnis und die Botschaft des Marcusevangelisten* [The messianic secret and the message of the evangelist Mark], 1939, pp. 13 ff., offers an outstanding history of the criticism of Wrede. The further discussion is described by E. Percy, *Die Botschaft Jesu*, Lunds Universitäts Årsskrift, N.F. Avd. 1, Vol. 49, 1953, pp. 271 ff.; and G. Minette de Tillesse, *Le secret messianique dans l'Évangile de Marc*, 1968, pp. 16 ff.

356. W. Bousset, "Das Messiasgeheimnis in den Evangelien," *ThR* 5 (1902), 350; W. Bousset, *Jesus*, Religionsgeschichtliche Volksbücher 1, 2/3, Tübingen, 1904, pp. 84-85, 98.

357. P. Wernle, *Der Christ und die Sünde bei Paulus* [The Christian and sin according to Paul], Freiburg i. Br. and Leipzig, 1897, p. 121.

358. See P. Wernle in *Selbstdarstellungen*, Vol. V, 1929, p. 11.

359. P. Wernle, *Die Anfänge unserer Religion* [The beginnings of our religion], Tübingen and Leipzig, 1901, pp. 27, 35, 81, 96, 220, 208, 219, 81, 89, 128-30, 153-54, 167, 189-90.

360. M. Brückner, *Die Entstehung der paulinischen Christologie* [The origin of Pauline Christology], Strassburg, 1903. Preface, pp. 29, 32, 96-97, 190-91, 221, 236-37.

361. M. Goguel, *L'apôtre Paul et Jésus-Christ* (licentiate thesis), Paris, 1904, pp. ii, 270-72, 357, 366, 370-71, 378-79.

362. A. Schweitzer (*op. cit.*, n. 189), p. 168.

363. W. Wrede, *Paulus* (Religionsgeschichtliche Volksbücher I, nos. 5/6), Tübingen, 1904, pp. 48, 53-56, 63, 66-68, 84, 86, 92-96, 103-4 (reprinted with the original pagination in the collection mentioned in note 344). Eng. tr. by Edward Lummis, *Paul* (Boston: Beacon Press, [1908]). Quotations with emendations are from pp. 76, 85-86, 88-89, 90, 91, 105-6, 11-12, 113-15, 147, 151, 161, 162-63, 165-67, 177-78, 179-80.

364. A. Loisy, *L'Évangile et l'Eglise*, Paris, 1902. A second, improved edition was published only in a German translation by Joh. Grière-Becker, Munich, 1904: *Evangelium und Kirche*, pp. 26, 34. On the whole, Loisy took a position in this book in opposition to Harnack's *Das Wesen des Christentums?* [What is Christianity?], adopting the eschatological understanding of the announcement of the kingdom of God and the messianic claim of Jesus. This was done in knowledge of, even if not in dependence on, the thought of Johannes Weiss. See pp. 37 ff., 61 ff.; on this see F. Heiler, *A. Loisy*, 1947, pp. 44-45, 53; and D. Hoffmann-Axtheim, "Loisys *L'Évangile et l'Église: Besichtigung eines zeitgenössischen Schlactfeldes* [Inspection of a contemporary battlefield]," *ZThK* 65 (1968), 297: "Loisy needed only to refer to the work of such scholars as Weiss and Wellhausen, which he knew as well as can be conceived."

365. A. Loisy, *Le quatrième Évangile*, Paris, 1903, pp. 139, 55-56, 80, 85, 75, 73-74, 71-73, 130. H. J. Holtzmann, *ThLZ*, 29 (1904), 405, conceded that the commentary signified an "enduring milestone" on the path opened up by F. C. Baur and D. F. Strauss, that it represented a purely scientific motivation and "so high a level of unprejudiced judgment" as had not been achieved by a theologian who remained in a higher sense a Catholic.

366. W. Wrede, "Charakter und Tendenz des Johannessevangeliums," *Sammlung gemeinverständlicher Vorträge und Schriften aus dem Gebiet der Theologie und Religionsgeschichte* 37 [Collection of lectures and writings from the sphere of theology and the history-of-religions for the understanding of parishioners], Tübingen and Leipzig, 1903, pp. 69, 5, 10, 13, 17, 22, 26-28, 39, 29-30.

367. What I here have called "the radically historical approach to the New Testament" is not identical with what one customarily calls "radical criticism of the New Testament." Although Schweitzer compared with Bruno Bauer, Reimarus, the first scholar to dispute the historicity of Jesus and the authenticity of all the Pauline letters, and characterized Bauer's *Kritik der evangelischen Geschichte* [Critique of Gospel history] as "the ablest and most complete collection of difficulties of the Life of Jesus which is anywhere to be found" (*Quest*, p. 159). The denial of the existence of Jesus and of the Pauline origin of all or nearly all of the letters attributed to Paul—first denied by Bauer and then by Dutch, German, French, and Anglo-Saxon scholars at the end of the nineteenth and the beginning of the twentieth centuries— was so arbitrary and ill-founded that one can hardly designate this "radical criticism" as an "important, even an indispensable, episode in the working out of the history of primitive Christianity" (so L. Salvatorelli, "From Locke to Reitzenstein: The Historical Investigation of the Origins of Christianity," *HTR*, 22 [1929], 349). This whole trend in research is therefore not reviewed in the present book. On Bauer, see E. Barnikol, *RGG*, Vol. I, cols. 922 ff. and J. Schmidt, *LThK*, II, cols. 57-58; on radical criticism as a whole, see Schweitzer, *Quest* (*op. cit.*, n. 161), pp. 141 ff., 444 ff., *Paul and His Interpreters*, (*op. cit.*, n. 189), pp. 92 ff.; G. A. van den Bergh van Eysinga, *Die holländische radikale Kritik des N. T.*, 1913; L. Salvatorelli, *op. cit.*, pp. 296-97, 342 ff., 364-65; H. Windisch, "Das Problem der Geschichtlichkeit Jesu," *ThR*, N.F., 1 (1929), 226 ff.; 2 (1930), 270 ff.; J. Schmid, "Christusmythe," *LThK*, II, cols. 1182-83.

368. P. de Lagarde, "Über das Verhältnis des deutschen Staates zu Theologie, Kirche und Religion. Ein Versuch Nicht-Theologen zu orienteren," *Deutsche Schriften*, 5th ed., 1920, p. 74.

369. Cf. H. Gunkel, *Evangelische Freiheit* 20 (1920), 145-46: "At the same time, in the background of the new movement but without any awareness of this movement, there stood the many-sided and enigmatic Lagarde and the profound Duhm, both of them without influence among the mass of students in their own time, but even so, exercising a quiet and enduring effect on individuals." Also, E. von Dobschütz, *Probleme des Apostolischen Zeitalters* [Problems of the apostolic age], 1904, p. 77: "There is a broader stream that has flowed out into New Testament research—may I say it is from Lagarde?"

370. P. de Lagarde (*op. cit.*, n. 368), p. 47.

371. See H. Gressmann, *Albert Eichhorn und die Religionsgeschichtliche Schule*, 1914, p. 8. Eichhorn's qualifying theses are completely reprinted in E. Barnikol, "Albert Eichhorn," *Wiss. Zeitschr d. Martin-Luther-Universität Halle-Wittenberg, Ges.-Sprachw.*, IX, no. 1, 1960, pp. 144-45. Gressmann also gives the information that Eichhorn wanted to edit the Apostolic Fathers along with the New Testament, "in order to make apparent that there is no absolute distinction between the two groups of writings, but only a relative difference." Accordingly, the first proposal for the *Handbook to the New Testament*, which was founded by the representatives of the history-of-religions school, was according to the formulation of its editor, Hans Lietzmann, *Handbook to the New Testament and Its Apocrypha*. Yet the prospectus for the *Handbuch* made no mention of a broadening of the scope of the series; the "supplemental volume" on the Apostolic Fathers appeared only in 1920/23 (according to information kindly provided from the archives of J. C. B. Mohr, publisher, in Tübingen).

372. G. Krüger, *Das Dogma vom Neuen Testament*, Programm Giessen, 1896, pp. 4, 37, 13, 5-6.

373.   W. Wrede, *Über Aufgabe und Methode der sogenannten Neutestamentlichen Theologie* [On the task and methods of the so-called New Testament theology], Göttingen, 1897, pp. 8-12, 34-35, 58-61, 80.

374.   P. Wendland, *Die Urchristlichen Literaturformen* [Literary forms of primitive Christianity], Handbuch zum N. T., I, 3, Tübingen, 1912, pp. 257, 261-62, 267.

375.   H. Weinel, *Biblische Theologie des Neuen Testaments. Die Religion Jesu und des Urchristentums* [Biblical theology of the New Testament: the religion of Jesus and of primitive Christianity], Tübingen, 1911, pp. 2-3, 130, 129, 211, 390, vii.

376.   H. Gunkel, Review of M. Reischle's "Theologie und Religionsgeschichte," in *Deutsche Literaturzeitung*, 25 (1904), 1109.

377.   H. Gunkel, "Was will die 'religionsgeschichtliche' Bewegung?" [What is the purpose of the history-of-religions movement?], *Deutsch-Evangelisch* 5 (1914), 387-88, 386-87, 392. Cf. also Gunkel's statement cited in note 331.

378.   W. Bousset, *ThR*, 7 (1904), 265-66; M. Rade, *RGG*, Vol. IV, 1st ed., 1913, cols. 2190-91; H. Gressmann, (*op. cit.*, n. 371), p. 26; Gunkel, *Ev. Freiheit*, 20 (1920), 146.

379.   J. Wellhausen, *Skizzen und Vorarbeiten* [Sketches and preliminary work], VI, Berlin, 1899, pp. 233-34.

380.   J. Wellhausen, *Einleitung in die drei ersten Evangelien* [Introduction to the first three Gospels], Berlin, 1905, p. 107; that Wellhausen means Schweitzer here is shown by P. Wernle, *ThLZ*, 31 (1906), 505.

381.   A. Harnack, *ThLZ*, 24 (1899), 514.

382.   A. Harnack, *Die Aufgabe der Theologischen Facultäten und die allgemeine Religionsgeschichte: Rede zur Gedächtnisfeier des Stifters der Berliner Universität* [The task of the theological faculties and the universal history of religion: address at the ceremony in memory of the founder of Berlin university], Berlin, 1901, pp. 7, 8, 16, 11.

383.   A. von Harnack, *Lehrbuch der Dogmengeschichte* [Textbook of the history of dogma], Vol. I, 4th ed., 1909, pp. 45-46.

384.   A. Jülicher, "Moderne Meinungsverschiedenheiten über Methode Aufgabe und Ziel der Kirchengeschichte" [Modern differences in understanding of the method, task, and goal of church history], *Marburger Akademische Reden*, V, 1901, pp. 4, 6, 8.

385.   A. Jülicher, *Neue Linien in der Kritik der evangelischen Überlieferung* [New directions in the critical study of the gospel tradition], Giessen, 1906, p. 6; see above, note 313.

386.   A. Jülicher, *Paulus und Jesus*, Religionsgeschichtliche Volksbücher [Popular books in the history of religion], no. 114, Tübingen, 1907, pp. 27-28, 34-35, 56, 62, 68-69, 70-72.

387.   E. von Dobschütz, *Probleme der Apostolischen Zeitalters* [Problems of the apostolic age], Leipzig, 1904, pp. 78, 77-78, 128.

388.   A. Schweitzer (*op. cit.*, n. 189), quotations with emendations are from pp. 206, 214, 215, 228.

389. P. Wernle, "Jesus und Paulus: Antithesen zu Boussets Kyrios Christos," *ZThK*, 25 (1915), 87-88, 90-91.

390. M. Kähler, "Biblische Theologie," *PRE*, III, 1897, pp. 197, 199.

391. M. Reischle, *Theologie und Religionsgeschichte: Fünf Vorlesungen*, Tübingen and Leipzig, 1904, pp. 44, 29, 32, 33, 31, 39, 31-32, 48-50, 60-61.

392. P. Feine, "Das Christentum Jesu und das Christentum der Apostel in ihrer Abgrenzung gegen die Religionsgeschichte" [The Christianity of Jesus and that of the apostles in their delimitation from the history of religion], *Christentum und Zeitgeist* [Christianity and the spirit of the times], I, Stuttgart, 1904, pp. 42-44, 61-62.

393. C. F. G. Heinrici, "Ist das Christentum eine Mysterienreligion?" [Is Christianity a mystery religion?], *Internationale Wochenschrift für Wissenschaft, Kunst und Technik* [International weekly for scholarship, art, and technology], 5 (1911), 424, 429-30.

394. K. Deissner, *Paulus und die Mystik seiner Zeit* [Paul and the mysticism of his age], Leipzig, 1918, pp. 47, 70, 114, 121, 120; 2nd ed., Leipzig and Erlangen, 1921, p. 136; the following quotations from the 1st ed., pp. 66-67, 82, 85; 2nd ed., pp. 133, 139, 146-47.

395. Pointed to correctly by F. Holmström, *Das eschatologische Denken der Gegenwart* [Eschatological thought in the present day], 1935, pp. 179 ff.; H. Stephan and M. Schmidt, *Geschichte der deutschen evangelischen Theologie seit dem deutschen Idealismus*, 2nd ed., 1960, pp. 316 ff., 323 ff. R. Bultmann declared (in a letter of 1926, published by W. Schmithals in *Die Theologie Rudolf Bultmanns*, 1966, p. 9) that "the war has [not] influenced my theology." But that is doubtless not generally the case.

396. E. Fascher, *Vom Verstehen des Neuen Testamentes. Ein Beitrag zur Grundlegung einer zeitgemässen Hermeneutik* [On understanding the New Testament: a contribution to laying the foundation for a contemporary hermeneutic], 1930, pp. 1 ff.; A. M. Hunter, "Interpreting the New Testament 1900-1950," 1951, pp. 124-25; P. Tillich, "Die Geisteslage der Gegenwart. Rückblick und Ausblick" [The spiritual condition of the present-day: retrospect and prospect], (1930), published for the first time in his *Collected Works*, Vol. X, 1968, pp. 108 ff.

397. E. Brunner, *Erlebnis, Erkenntnis und Glaube* [Experience, perception, and faith], 1921, Preface.

398. Hermann von Soden's great edition of the Greek text (1902-13), although it brought together with a previously unknown comprehensiveness the later manuscripts, is not treated here, since he developed an untenable basis for grouping the manuscripts. See on this Eberhard Nestle (*op. cit.*, n. 33), pp. 75-76; F. G. Kenyon, *The Text of the Greek Bible*, rev. ed., 1949, pp. 179-86; B. M. Mertzer (*op. cit.*, n. 33), pp. 139 ff.

399. B. H. Streeter, *The Four Gospels: A Study of Origins Treating of the Manuscript Tradition, Sources, Authorship, and Dates*. London, 1924, p. viii. On the earlier history and wider discussion of this discovery, see F. G. Kenyon (*op. cit.*, n. 398), pp. 176 ff; B. M. Metzger, "The Caesarean Text of the Gospels," *JBL*, 64 (1945), 457 ff.; (=B.M.M., *Chapters in the History of New Testament Textual Criticism*, New Testament Tools and Studies IV [Grand Rapids, Mich.: Eerdmans, 1963], pp. 42 ff.); also Metzger (*op. cit.*, n. 33), pp. 171 ff.

400. The papyrus discoveries are described by W. G. Kümmel, "Textkritik und Textgeschichte des Neuen Testamentes 1914-37," *ThR*, new series, 10, 1938, pp. 292 ff.; F. G. Kenyon–A. W. Adams (*op. cit.*, n. 398), pp. 143 ff.; B. M. Metzger (*op. cit.*, n. 33), pp. 36 ff.; K. Aland, "The Significance of the Papyri for Progress in New Testament Research," in *The Bible in Modern Scholarship*, edited by J. Ph. Hyatt, 1965, pp. 325 ff. Aland, "Das Neue Testament auf Papyrus," in K. Aland's *Studien zur Überlieferung des Neuen Testaments und seines Textes*, Arbeiten zur Neutestamentlichen Textforschung 2, 1967, pp. 51 ff.

401. See K. Grobel, *Formgeschichte und Synoptische Quellenanalyse* [Form criticism and synoptic source analysis], 1937, pp. 24 ff.; L. Vaganay, *Le Problème synoptique*, 1953, pp. 8 ff.

402. B. H. Streeter (*op. cit.*, n. 399), pp. 222, 270.

403. K. L. Schmidt, *Der Rahmen der Geschichte Jesu. Literarkritische Untersuchungen zur ältesten Jesusüberlieferung* [The framework of the story of Jesus: literary-critical studies in the oldest Jesus tradition], Berlin, 1919, p. 317; "Die Stellung der Evangelien in der allgemeinen Literaturgeschichte," [The place of the Gospels in the general history of literature], in *Eucharisterion, Studien zur Religion und Literatur des Alten und Neuen Testaments H. Gunkel zum 60, Geburtstag* [Festschrift for Gunkel on his sixieth birthday], Vol. II, 1923, pp. 76, 124, 127; the following quotations from Schmidt's *Der Rahmen*, pp. v, 1-2, 152, 303, 305.

404. On the background of the history of form-critical research, see E. Fascher, *Die formgeschichtliche Methode*, 1924, pp. 4 ff.; O. Cullmann, "Les récentes études sur la formation de la tradition évangélique," *Revue d'Histoire et de Philosophie religieuses*, 5 (1925), 460 ff.; cf. the hints in Schmidt's essay as mentioned in n. 403. On the many ideas which paved the way for form criticism in the work of A. Seeberg, see K. Weiss, *Urchristentum und Geschichte in der neutestamentlichen Theologie der Jahrhundertwende* [Primitive Christianity and history in New Testament theology at the opening of the twentieth century] and F. Hahn's introduction to the new printing of A. Seeberg's *Der Katechismus der Urchristenheit*, Theol. Bücherei, 26 (1966), vii ff.

405. See M. Dibelius, "Zur Formgeschichte der Evangelien," *ThR*, N.F., 1, 1929, pp. 186-87; K. L. Schmidt, "Die Stellung" (n. 403), pp. 88-89; on Gunkel's literary genre method of investigation, see H. J. Kraus, *Geschichte der historisch-kritischen Erforschung des A. T. von der Reformation bis zur Gegenwart* [History of historical-critical study of the Old Testament from the Reformation to the present], 2nd ed., 1969, pp. 344 ff. The concept, Sitz-im-Leben ("setting in life") appears first in an essay written in 1906, "Die Grundprobleme der israelitischen Literaturgeschichte." [The basic problems of the history of Israelite literature]: "Every ancient literary genre has its place originally in the life of Israel in a completely specific setting" (H. Gunkel, *Reden und Aufsätze*, 1913, p. 33). The term received its final formulation in 1917: "Together with the idea of a literary genre goes the fact that it has a definite 'setting in life'" (*ThR*, 20 [1917], 269).

406. In his linguistic formulation M. Dibelius is following not only F. Overbeck (see p. 204) but especially the classical philologist, Eduard Norden, who gave to his wide-ranging study of the "unknown god" in the Areopagus speech of Paul (Acts 17), *Agnostos Theos* (1913), the subtitle, "Studies in the Form-history of religious addresses." See on this M. Dibelius, *Die Formgeschichte des Evangeliums*, 2nd ed., 1933, pp. 4-5; K. L. Schmidt, *Le Problème du Christianisme primitif*, 1938, pp. 10-11.

407. M. Dibelius, *Die Formgeschichte des Evangeliums*, Tübingen, 1919. Eng. tr. from the 2nd rev. ed. by B. L. Woolf, *From Tradition to Gospel* (New York: Charles Scribner's Sons, 1935). Quotations with emendations are from pp. 3-4, 8, 12-13, 22-23, 24, 26, 69, 70-71, 80, 94, 102, 218, 225, 230, 287, 288, 289-90.

408. R. Bultmann, *Die Geschichte der synoptischen Tradition*, Göttingen, 1921. Eng. tr. by John Marsh, *History of the Synoptic Tradition* (New York: Harper & Row, and Oxford: Blackwell, 1963). Quotations with emendations are from pp. 6, 275, 303, 345-47, 368-69, 370-71, 373-74. Excerpts in brackets are translated by S. M. Gilmour from the first edition.

409. So R. Bultmann himself, in "Zur Frage der Christologie," in *Zwischen den Zeiten* 5, 1927, p. 56, reprinted in *Glauben und Verstehen* 1 (1933), 107; *Geschichte*, 2nd ed., 1931. Eng. tr. (*op. cit.*, n. 408), p. 5.

410. See L. Köhler, *Das formgeschichtliche Problem des Neuen Testaments*, 1927; F. Büchsel, *Die Hauptfragen der Synoptikerkritik*, 1939; P. Benoit, "Reflexions sur la 'formgeschichtliche Methode,'" *RB*, 53 (1946), 481 ff. with bibliography; G. Iber, "Zur Formgeschichte der Evangelien," *ThR*, N.F., 24 (1957-58), 283 ff. Also Neill, *Interpretation*, pp. 237 ff., 258 ff.

411. Only examples are here mentioned; V. Taylor, *The Formation of the Gospel Tradition*, 1933; J. Jeremias, *The Parables of Jesus* (Eng. tr. by S. H. Hooke from the 6th German edition), rev. ed., 1963; O. Cullmann (*op. cit.*, n. 404), pp. 574 ff.; M. Dibelius, *Gospel Criticism and Christology*, Eng. tr. by F. C. Grant (London: Ivor Nicholson & Watson, 1935), pp. 66 ff.; H. Zimmermann, *Neutestamentliche Methodenlehre. Darstellung der historisch-kritischen Methode* [Instruction in New Testament methods; a presentation of the historical-critical method], 1966, pp. 128 ff.

412. See the account by M. Dibelius, "Zur Formgeschichte des Neuen Testaments (ausserhalb der Evangelien)" [On the form criticism of the New Testament outside of the Gospels], *ThR*, N.F., 3 (1931), 207 ff.; H. Zimmermann (*op. cit.*, n. 411), pp. 160 ff., 192 ff.

413. M. Dibelius, "Stilkritisches zur Apostelgeschichte," in *Eucharisterion* (*op. cit.*, n. 403), Vol. II, pp. 27 ff.; in *Studies in the Acts of the Apostles*, pp. 1-25. Cf. E. Haenchen, *Die Apostelgeschichte* (Meyer, Krit.-exeget. Kommentar, III), 14th ed., 1965, pp. 32 ff.

414. See the evidence in E. Esking, *Glaube und Geschichte in der theologischen Exegese Ernst Lohmeyers* [Faith and history in the theological exegesis of Ernst Lohmeyer], 1951, pp. 137 ff., 233 ff.

415. E. Lohmeyer, *Kyrios Jesus. Eine Untersuchung zu Phil. 2:5-11,* (Sitzungsberichte der Heidelberger Akademie der Wissenschaften, phil.-histor. Klasse), 4, Heidelberg, 1927/28, pp. 3-4, 7-8, 13, 43, 12, 16-17, 36, 62-63, 65-67.

416. See pp. 38-39, 218, 196; concerning the other earlier Christian efforts to gain an understanding of early rabbinic Judaism as a means of illuminating the New Testament, see G. F. Moore, "Christian Writers on Judaism," *HTR*, 14 (1921), 197 ff.; G. Kittel, *Die Probleme des palästinischen Spätjudentums und das Urchristentum* [The problems of late Palestinian Judaism and primitive Christianity], 1926, pp. 22 ff.; J. W. Doeve, *Jewish Hermeneutics in the Synoptic Gospels and Acts*, Leiden dissertation, 1953, pp. 5 ff.

417. (Hermann L. Strack and) Paul Billerbeck, *Kommentar zum Neuen Testament aus Talmud und Midrasch*, Vols. I-IV, Munich, 1922-28. Preface to Vol. I. Billerbeck is the sole author of the work; H. L. Strack, the Old Testament scholar from Berlin, only suggested the project and made possible its appearance. See G. Kittel, *Deutsche Literaturzeitung*, new series, 1, 1924, cols. 1224 ff.; J. Jeremias, *ZNW*, 55 (1964), 1-2.

418. G. Kittel, *Sifre zu Deuteronomium*, Stuttgart, 1922. According to the foreword, the translation stemmed from "collegial work stretching over years with Israel J. Kahan." But no further sections appeared.

419. G. Kittel, *Die Probleme des palästinischen Spätjudentums und das Urchristentum* [The problems of late Palestinian Judaism and primitive Christianity], Stuttgart, 1926, pp. 2-4, 71-72, 88, 92-93, 120-21, 124-26, 130-31, 140.

420. J. Schniewind, *Euangelion. Ursprung und erste Gestalt des Begriffs Evangelium* [Euangelion: origin and first form of the concept, gospel], pts. 1 & 2, Gütersloh, 1927 and 1931, pjp. 5, 14, 18, 34, 43, 61-63, 220-21. Publication was never completed of Schniewind's evidence that in the rabbinic movement this idea from Second Isaiah continued to live and that it exercised influence on Jesus from within Palestinian Judaism. But his ideas were turned to account by G. Friedrich, *THWBNT*, 2 (1935), 712-13, 715, 723, 725-26. Cf. with regard to Schniewind's explanation of the genesis of the term "Euangelion," P. Stuhlmacher, "Das paulinische Evangelium. Pt. I, Vorgeschichte," *FRLANT*, 95 (1968), 80 ff.

421. See the superior report by G. Lindeskog, *Die Jesusfrage im neuzeitlichen Judentum. Ein Beitrag zur Geschichte der Leben-Jesu-Forschung* [The Jesus question in recent Judaism: a contribution to the history of the life-of-Jesus research], 1938, continued in the essay, "Jesus als religionsgeschichtliches und religiöses Problem in der modernen jüdischen Theologie," *Judaica* 6 (1950), 190 ff., 241 ff.

422. C. G. Montefiore, *The Synoptic Gospels*, 2 vols., 2nd ed., 1927.

423. C. G. Montefiore, *Rabbinic Literature and Gospel Teachings*, London, 1930, pp. xvi-xvii, 61-62, 68-69, 71, 74, 85, 163, 170, 183, 195-96, 201.

424. E. Lohmeyer, *Die Offenbarung des Johannes* [The revelation of John], Tübingen, 1926, pp. 103, 191-92.

425. R. Reitzenstein, *Das mandäische Buch des Herrn der Grösse* [The Mandaean book of the Lord of greatness], Sitzungsberichte der Heidelberger Akademie der Wissenschaften, phil. -histor. Klasse, 1919, p. 12. Reitzenstein, *Das iranische Erlösungmysterium: Religionsgeschichtliche Untersuchungen* [The Iranian redemption mystery: studies in the history of religion], 1921. See on this L. Salvatorelli, *HTR* 22 (1929), 354 ff., and H. Schlier, "Zur Mandäerfrage" *ThR*, N.F., 5 (1933), 8 ff. Obviously it was through H. Gunkel that Bultmann first was made aware of the importance of the Mandaean writings. See W. Klatt (*op. cit.*, n. 284), p. 82, n. 9.

426. See p. 70 and the reference of H. Schlier (*op. cit.*, n. 425), p. 22, n. 1.

427. M. Lidzbarski, *Das Johannesbuch der Mandäer* [The Mandaean book of John], Giessen, 1915; *Mandäische Liturgien mitgeteilt, übersetzt and erklärt* [Mandaean liturgies communicated, translated and explained], Abhandlungen der Kön. Gesellschaft der Wissenschaft zu Göttingen, phil-histor. Klasse, N.F., XVII, pt. 1, Berlin, 1920; *Ginza, der Schatz oder das grosse Buch der Mandäer* [Ginza, the treasure, or the great book of the Mandaeans], Göttingen and Leipzig, 1925.

428. R. Bultmann, "Der religionsgeschichtliche Hintergrund des Prologs zum Johannesevangelium" in *Eucharisterion*, (*op. cit.*, n. 403), pp. 10-11, 13-14, 17-18, 22-23, 25-26; R. Bultmann, "Die Bedeutung der neu erschlossenen mandäischen und manichäischen Quellen für das Verständnis des Johannesevangeliums," *ZNW*, 24 (1925), pp. 100-104, 139-41, 145-46. Both essays have been reprinted with the original page numbers given in *Exegetics*, 1967, pp. 10 ff., and 55 ff.

429. W. Bauer, *Das Johannesevangelium erklärt* [The Gospel of John expounded], Tübingen, 2nd ed., 1925, pp. 3-4.

430. H. Windisch, *Der Herbräerbrief erklärt* [The Letter to the Hebrews expounded], Tübingen, 2nd ed., 1931, Preface.

431. The attempt of E. Esking (*op. cit.*, n. 414) to explain the strong advance of the Mandaean question in the past twenty years on the ground that it offered the possibility "to interpret the history of the rise of Christianity on a nonliberal but at the same time wholly 'natural' basis" is completely lacking in substantiation.

432. K. Holl, *Urchristentum und Religionsgeschichte* (Studien des apologetischen Seminars X), Gütersloh, 1925; reprinted in K. Holl, *Gesammelte Aufsätze zur Kirchengeschichte*, Vol. II, 1928, pp. 1 ff.; quotations are from this edition: 7-10, 13, 18-19, 25-27. Eng. tr. by N. V. Hope, *The Distinctive Elements in Christianity* (New York: Scribner's, 1937). Criticism of this work is reported and counterattacked by W. Bodenstein, *Die Theologie Karl Holls*, 1968, 15 ff.

433. Cf. A. von Harnack's statement on this work of Holl in the memorial address for Holl in 1926 (in the appendix to the correspondence mentioned in note 241).

434. A. von Harnack, *Die Entstehung der christlichen Theologie und des kirchlichen Dogmas* [The rise of Christian theology and of church dogma], Gotha, 1927, pp. 17, 45-47, 56, 58-59. Eng. tr. by Neill Buchanan [1894], reprinted (New York: Russell & Russell, 1958).

435. M-J. Largrange, "La gnose mandéene et la tradition évangelique" [Mandaean gnosticism and the gospel tradition], *RB*, 37 (1928), 5 ff. Quotations from pp. 24-25, 17.

436. M. Goguel, *Au seuil de l'évangile. Jean-Baptiste* [On the threshhold of the Gospel: John the baptist], Paris, 1928, p. 113.

437. A. Loisy, *Le mandéisme et les origines chrétiennes*, Paris, 1934, pp. 146, 156.

438. H. Lietzmann, *Ein Beitrag zur Mandäerfrage* (Sitzungsberichte der preuissischen Akademie der Wissenschaften, phil.-hist. Klasse, 1930, no. 27), Berlin, 1930, pp. 3, 8, 14-15. (= 596, 601, 607-8); reprinted in his *Kleine Schriften* I, texte und Untersuchungen, No. 67, 1958, pp. 124, 131, 139-40.

439. R. Bultmann, *ThLZ*, 56 (1931), cols. 578-79.

440. See the survey of the literature by H. Schlier, "Zur Mandäerfrage" [On the Mandaean question], *ThR*, N.F., 5 (1933), 1 ff.; 69 ff.; W. Baumgartner, "Zur Mandäerfrage," *Hebrew Union College Annual*, Vol. 23, pt. 1, 1950/51, pp. 41 ff.; also by Baumgartner, "Der heutige Stand der Mandäerfrage" [The present state of Mandaean studies], *ThZ*, 6 (1950). 401 ff.; R. Macuch, "Alter und Heimat des Mandäismus nach neu erschlossenen Quellen," *ThLZ*, 82 (1957), cols. 401 ff.; S. Schulz, "Die Bedeutung neuer Gnosisfunde für die neutestamentliche Wissenschaft" *ThR*, N.F., 26 (1960), 301 ff.; K. Rudolph, *Die Mandäer*, Vol. I, Prolegomena: Das Mandäerproblem, *FRLANT*, 74 (1960); H. -M. Schenke "Das Problem der Beziehung zwischen Judentum und Gnosis," *Kairos*, 7 (1965), 124 ff.

441. The literature, which is too extensive to be surveyed, is indexed in C. Burchard, *Bibliographie zu den Handschriften vom Toten Meer* [Bibliography on the manuscripts from the Dead Sea], Vol. I, 1957, Vol. II, 1965; (*BZAW*, 76 and 89). The most important texts may be found in E. Lohse, *Die Texte aus Qumran, Hebräisch* *und deutsch*, 1964; and J. Maier, *Die Texte vom Toten Meer*, 2 vols., German translation and comments. Eng. tr. by T. H. Gaster, *The Dead Sea Scriptures* (Garden City, N. Y.; Doubleday, 1964), 2nd ed., with introductions and comments. For orientation in the importance of the scrolls for the understanding of the New Testament, *The Scrolls and the New Testament*, ed. K. Stendahl; K. G. Kuhn in *RGG*, V, cols. 751 ff.; H. Braun, *Qumran und das Neue Testament*, 2 vols., 1966; F. M. Cross, *The Ancient Library of Qumran and Modern Biblical Studies* (Garden City, N.Y.: Doubleday [1958], 1961); Matthew Black, *The Scrolls and Christian Origins* (New York: Scribner's, 1961).

442.   See the evidence in O. Cullmann, "Das Rätsel des Johannesevangeliums im Lichte der neuen Handschriftenfunde" [The riddle of the Gospel of John in light of the new manuscript find], in *Vorträge und Aufsätze* [Lectures and essays], 1925-62, 1966, p. 263.

443.   See p. 218 ff; A. Diessman, *Licht vom Osten*, 4th ed., Tübingen, 1923. Eng. tr. by L. R. M. Strachan, *Light from the Ancient East* (London: Hodder and Stoughton, 1923), pp. 401 ff.

444.   E. Preuschen, *Griechisch-Deutsches Wörterbuch zu den Schriften des Neuen Testaments und der übrigen urchristlichen Literatur* [Greek-German dictionary of the New Testament and other early Christian literature], 2nd ed., W. Bauer, ed. Giessen, 1928; from the 3rd ed. (1937) on, the work bears Bauer's name; 5th ed. in 1958. Eng. tr. by W. T. Arndt and F. W. Gingrich from the 4th ed. *Greek-English Lexicon of the New Testament and other Early Christian Literature* (University of Chicago Press, 1957).

445.   See p. 194. Cremer's dictionary also went through numerous editions; after 1911 it was edited by J. Kögel (11th ed. in 1923) who had already begun to draw together new linguistic information. (See M. Dibelius, *Deutsche Lit. Zeitung*, 54 (1933), col. 2453.)

446.   G. Kittel, ed., *Theologisches Wörterbuch zum Neuen Testament*, Vol. I, Stuttgart, 1933, Preface, p. v. Up until 1969, eight volumes had appeared (up to the letter *Y*); the editor since Volume V has been G. Friedrich. The entire work is being translated into English by G. W. Bromiley; six volumes have already appeared, 1964-68.

447.   G. Kittel, *Urchristentum, Spätjudentum, Hellenismus* [Primitive Christianity, late Judaism, and Hellenism], Stuttgart, 1926, pp. 4-5, 13, 16-19.

448.   C. H. Dodd, *Journal of Theological Studies*, 34 (1933), 281.

449.   See n. 395.

450.   For a discussion of "theological exegesis" etc., see E. von Dobschütz, *Vom Auslegen des Neuen Testaments* [On the interpretation of the New Testament], 1927; E. Lerle, *Voraussetzungen der neutestamentlichen Exegese* [Presuppositions of New Testament exegesis], 1951, pp. 23 ff.; E. Esking (*op. cit.*, n. 414), pp. 74 ff.

451.   Cf. J. Rathje, *Die Welt des freien Protestantismus* . . . [The world of free Protestantism], 1952, pp. 170, 172; D. P. Fuller, *Easter Faith and History*, 1965, describes the shock effect that Harnack's statement at the beginning of the First World War made on his pupil, Karl Barth.

452.   K. Barth, *Der Romerbrief* [The letter to the Romans], Bern, 1919, 2nd ed., Munich, 1921, pp. xii-xiii. Reprinted in *Anfänge der dialektischen Theologie* [The

beginnings of the dialectical theology], Vol. I, ed. J. Moltmann, Theol. Bücherei, XVII, 1962, p. 112. Eng. tr. by E. C. Hoskyns, *The Epistle to the Romans* (London: Oxford University Press, 1933), pp. 1 ff.

453. K. Barth (*op. cit.*, n. 452), pp. v-vi; Barth, *Das Wort Gottes und die Theologie*, Gesammelte Vorträge [Collected addresses], Munich, 1924. Reprinted with the exception of p. 28 (see note 452). Eng. tr. by Douglas Horton, *The Word of God and the Word of Man* (Boston: Pilgrim Press, 1928). Quotations with emendations from pp. 43, 60-61, 72-73, used by permission of Harper & Row. See the remarks concerning the deep impression that Barth's *The Word of God* made on American and English theologians, in Neill, *Interpretation,* pp. 202-203.

454. See for example, Ph. Bachman, *Neue Kirchliche Zeitschrift,* 32 (1921), 517 ff.; other reviews of the first and second editions of the *Epistle to the Romans* indexed in M. Strauch, *Die Theologie Karl Barths,* 5th ed., 1933, p. 58.

455. H. Windisch, *ThLZ,* 45 (1900), 200.

456. A. Jülicher, in *Die Christliche Welt,* 34 (1920), 466-68. Reprinted (*op. cit.,* n. 452), pp. 94, 97). Highly typical is the statement of K. Holl in a letter to A. Schlatter of Dec. 27, 1920 (*op. cit.,* n. 251), p. 231: "Surely you have also read Barth's commentary on Romans . . . . My own reaction is that it is nothing other than *Karlstadt* (i.e. the spiritualistic opponent of Luther). One picks out what corresponds to his own perception, his own experience, in one case operating freely with the text, in another case clamping on to the letter of the text, decking it out in the style of Nietzsche . . . and presenting himself at the same time as the man of the future and as a conservative theologian. And in the name of irrationality not giving a hoot about scholarship, logic, etc. I am so grandfatherly that for me seriousness and strictness of thinking always belong to the seriousness of faith."

457. K. Barth (*op. cit.,* n. 452). Quotations with emendations from pp. 2-3, 4, 6-8, 10-11. Barth (*op. cit.,* n. 453). Quotations with emendations from pp. 192-93, 214.

458. See, for example, P. Althaus, *Zeitschrift für systematische Theologie,* 1 (1923), 741 ff.; A. Schlatter, *Die Furche,* 12 (1921/22. Reprinted (*op. cit.,* n. 252), pp. 142 ff.; the quotation here is from p. 230 (= 145): "At the hands of the interpreter, the Letter to the Romans ceases to be a letter to the Romans." On the theological differences between the first and second editions of the *Römerbrief,* see H. U. v. Balthasar, *Karl Barth. Darstellung und Deutung seiner Theologie,* 1951, pp. 71 ff.

459. A. Jülicher, *ThLZ,* 47 (1922), 540, 542. The violation of Paul in Barth's commentary on I Corinthians 15, which appeared in 1924 under the title, *Die Auferstehung der Toten* [The resurrection of the dead] is indicated by the following: P. Althaus, "Paulus und sein neuester Ausleger" [Paul and his most recent interpreter], *Christentum und Wissenschaft,* 1 (1925), 20 ff. and 97 ff., and R. Bultmann, *Theologische Blätter,* 5 (1926), pp. 1 ff. (= *Glauben und Verstehen,* Vol. I, 1933, pp. 38 ff. Eng. tr. by L. P. Smith, *Faith and Understanding* (New York: Harper & Row, 1969), Vol. I, pp. 66-94.

460. R. Bultmann, "Karl Barths *Romerbrief* in zweiter Auflage" [Karl Barth's *Epistle to the Romans,* 2nd ed.], *Christian World,* 36 (1922), 320 ff. Reprinted (*op. cit.,* n. 434), quotations from pp. 372-73 (= 140-42).

461. O. Procksch, "Ziel und Grenze der Exegese" [Goal and limits of exegesis], *Neue kirchliche Zeitschrift,* 36 (1952), 728.

462. A. von Harnack and K. Barth, in *Christian World* 37 (1923), pp. 7-8, 89, 245, 248, 89, 305, 142, 144. Reprinted in K. Barth, *Theologische Fragen und Antworten*

[Theological questions and answers], *Gesammelte Vorträge*, Vol. III, 1957, pp. 7, 9-10, 20, 24, 10, 30-31, 14, 17. On this exchange of letters, see D. Braun, "Der Ort der Theologie. Entwurf für einen Eingang zum Verständnis des Briefwechsels zwischen Adolf v. Harnack und Karl Barth" [The place of theology: sketch of an access to understanding the correspondence between Harnack and Barth], in *Parrhesia* Festschrift for Karl Barth's Eightieth Birthday, 1966, pp. 11 ff.; E. Fascher, "Adolf v. Harnack und Karl Barths Thesenaustausch von 1923" in *Frage und Antwort*, 1968, pp. 201 ff. See in the same essay information on the earlier history of the correspondence. The sharp substantive differences between Harnack and Barth did not separate them as human beings. On this see A. v. Zahn-Harnack (*op. cit.*, n. 235), pp. 529 ff.

463. K. Girgensohn, "Geschichtliche und übergeschichtliche Schriftauslegung," [Historical and suprahistorical interpretation of Scripture], *Allgemeine Evangelisch-lutherische Kirchenzeitung*, 55 (1922), 628, 642, 644, 660; Girgensohn, "Die Grenzgebiete der systematischen Theologie" [The border areas of systematic theology], *Griefswalder Reformgedanken zum theologischen Studium*, Munich (1922), 90-91.

464. See A. Oepke, *Geschichtliche und übergeschichtliche Schriftauslegung*, Gütersloh, 1931, p. 30: "The Word must first be understood in connection with the concrete situation in which it was proclaimed, and on the other hand it must be transferred into the concrete situation of the hearers today." H. Windisch, *Der Sinn der Bergpredigt*, Leipzig, 1929, p. 111. Eng. tr. by S. M. Gilmour, *The Meaning of the Sermon on the Mount*, Philadelphia: 1951, p. 18): "Strict distinction between historical and theological exegesis is therefore our program." On the discussion concerning Girgensohn, see E. Esking (*op. cit.*, n. 414), pp. 88 ff.

465. R. Bultmann, "Das Problem einer theologischen Exegese des Neuen Testaments," *Zwischen den Zeiten* 3, 1925; reprinted in *Anfänge der dialektischen Theologie* II, ed. by T. Miltmann, 1963. English tr. by K. Crim and L. de Gvaziz, *Beginnings of Dialectic Theology*, Vol. I, ed. J. M. Robinson, 1968, pp. 236 ff. Bultmann, "Die Bedeutung der 'Dialektischen Theologie' für die neutestamentliche Wissenschaft?" [The importance of dialectical theology for New Testament scholarship], *Theol. Blätter*, 7 (1928), 63-64, 67. Eng. tr., *Faith and Understanding*, (*op. cit.*, n. 459), pp. 145 ff.; Bultmann, *Jesus*, Berlin, 1926. Eng. tr. by E. H. Lautero and L. P. Smith, *Jesus and the Word* (New York: Charles Scribner's Sons, 1934). Quotations with emendations are from pp. 3-4, 11, 47-48, 51, 54, 55, 211, 217-19.

466. The challenge raised by Bultmann in his address of 1941 on "Neues Testament und Mythologie: Das Problem der Entmythologisierung der neutestamentlichen Verkündigung" [New Testament and mythology: the problem of demythologizing the New Testament message]. To demythologize the New Testament through existentialist interpretation is the fully appropriate continuation of the fundamental methodological principles expressed in his works from 1925 to 1928 mentioned in note 465. That there was a sharp reaction to this program from the side of the churchly public is an indication that his earlier statements had passed unnoticed. The address mentioned and the most important evidence for the discussions that followed are in the collection, *Kergyma and Mythos*, 5 vols., ed. H. W. Bartsch, 1948-55. Comprehensive bibliography in Vol. II. Eng. tr. of vols. I and II by R. H. Fuller, *Kerygma and Myth* (London: S.P.C.K., 1953-1962). Further bibliographies in R. Marlé, *Bultmann und die Interpretation des Neuen Testaments*, 1959, pp. 199 ff., and in G. Bornkamm, "Die Theologie Bultmanns in der neueren Diskussion, *ThR*, N.F., 29 (1963), 33 ff. (= G. B. *Geschichte and Glaube* I, Ges. Aufsätze III, 1968, pp. 173 ff.) Cf. also the superior review of the literature by G. Gloege, *Verkündigung und Forschung* 1956/57 [Preaching and scholarship], 1957, pp. 62 ff. and the comprehensive presentations of W. Schmithals (*op. cit.*, n. 395), pp. 254 ff., and E. M. Good, "The Meaning of Demythologization," in *The Theology of Rudolf Bultmann*, ed. by C. W. Kegley (New York: Harper, 1966), pp. 21 ff.

467. E. Lohmeyer, *ThLZ*, 52 (1927), 438, 433, 437-39.

468. For the first time, the name is mentioned in the essay from the *Theol. Blätter*, 7 (1928), 65 (n. 465). In an earlier letter (1926), however, Bultmann declared: "I found help . . . in phenomenology, into which my colleague and friend, Heidegger, introduced me." (In the correspondence edited by Schmithals [n. 395], p. 18.) Cf. also the autobiographical sketch, included in the Kegley volume (n. 466), p. xxii; and the relation to Heidegger is clearly evident in the essay mentioned in note 471 from *Theol. Blätter* 6 (1927), p. 73.

469. Cf. G. Kuhlmann, "Zum theologischen Problem der Existenz," *ZThK*, new series, 10 (1929), 34-35, 39 ff.; E. Traub, "Heidegger und die Theologie," *Zeitschrift f., system. Theol.* 9 (1932), 724 ff.; E. Fascher, *Vom Verstehen des Neuen Testaments*, 1930, pp. 41 ff. On the fundamental issues, see R. Marlé (*op. cit.*, n. 466), pp. 80 ff., 114 ff.; G. W. Ittel, "Der Einfluss der Philosophie Martin Heideggers auf die Theologie Rudolf Bultmanns" [The influence of the philosophy of Heidegger on the theology of R. Bultmann], in *Kerygma und Dogma*, Vol. II, 1956, pp. 90 ff.; and J. Macquarrie, *An Existentialist Theology: A Comparison of Heidegger and Bultmann* (New York: Macmillan, 1955).

470. E. Lohmeyer, "Vom Begriff der religiösen Gemeinschaft. Eine problemgeschichtliche Untersuchung über die Grundlagen des Christentums" [On the concept of the religious community: a study of the history of the problem concerning the foundations of Christianity], in *Wissenschaftliche Grundfragen. Philosophische Abhandlungen*, ed. R. Hönigswald, Vol. III, Leipzig/Berlin, 1925, pp. 2-3, 16-17, 24, 30, 70; Lohmeyer, *Die Offenbarung des Johannes*, 1926, pp. 191-93.

471. R. Bultmann, "Vom Begriff der religiösen Gemeinschaft," *Theol. Blätter* 6 (1927), 65, 68, 71-73; Bultmann, *ThLZ* 52 (1927), 509-10. That E. Lohmeyer was heavily dependent on the Breslau philosopher, Richard Hönigswald, who was a representative of neo-Kantian idealism, is evident from the quotations in his essay, "Vom Begriff der religiösen Gemeinschaft." On this see E. Esking, (*op. cit.*, n. 414), pp. 122 ff., and *passim*.

472. M. Dibelius, *Geschichtliche und übergeschichtliche Religion im Christentum* [Historical and suprahistorical religion in Christianity], Göttingen, 1925, pp. 15, 44-46, 63, 146, 169-71.

473. With justification, F. Holmström (*op. cit.*, n. 395), pp. 251 ff. shows the impetus given by K. Barth to M. Dibelius' way of posing the problem.

474. R. Bultmann, "Geschichtliche und ubergeschichtliche Religion im Christentum?" [Historical and suprahistorical religion in Christianity?] *Zwischen den Zeiten*, 4 (1926), 385, 392-94, 396, 400 (= *Glauben und Verstehen*, Vol. I. Eng. tr. in *Faith and Understanding* (*op. cit.*, n. 459). Quotations with emendations are from pp. 95 ff.

475. A. Schweitzer's book *The Mysticism of the Apostle Paul*, first appeared in 1930 (see p. 243). Further see F. Buri, *Die Bedeutung dur neutestamentliche Eschatologie für die neuere protestantische Theologie* [The importance of New Testament eschatology for recent Protestant theology], 1935, and M. Werner, *Die Entstehung des christlichen Dogmas problemgeschichtlich dargestellt* [The Origin of Christian dogma presented in terms of the history of its problems], 1941, pp. 81 ff. *The Formation of Christian Dogma* (London: A. & C. Black, Ltd., 1945), pp. 9 ff.

476. C. H. Dodd, "Das Innerweltliche Reich in der Verkündigung Jesu" [The Kingdom within in the preaching of Jesus]. *Theol. Blätter*, 6 (1927) 121-22; C. H. Dodd, *The Parables of the Kingdom* (London: James Nisbet & Co., and New York: Charles Scribner's Sons, 1935). Quotations are from pp. 49-51, 97, 107-9, 174, 193.

477. Instead of the expression which Dodd himself used in *The Parables of the Kingdom*, "realized eschatology," he recommends more recently as less capable of misunderstanding, "inaugurated eschatology" or "sich realisierende Eschatologie," in his *The Interpretation of the Fourth Gospel* (Cambridge University Press, 1953), p. 447.

478. See the particulars in W. G. Kümmel, *Verheissung und Erfüllung* [Promise and fulfillment], 3rd ed., 1956, pp. 11-12, 135 ff. Eng. tr. in *Studies in Biblical Theology*, no. 2ª 'London: T. & T. Clark, 1964), pp. 15-16, 144 ff. Also J. Jeremias, "Eine neue Schau der Zukunftsaussagen Jesu" [A new look at Jesus' sayings about the future], *Theol. Blätter* 20 (1941), 216 ff. From this C. H. Dodd sketched a new, comprehensive perspective on early Christian thought, *The Apostolic Preaching and its Developments* (London: Hodder & Stoughton, 1936), which is more informative concerning the theological presuppositions of this view. See my review in *ThR*, N. F., 14 (1942), 93 ff.

479. Cf. on the further history of this investigation, A. N. Wilder, "The Eschatology of Jesus in Recent Criticism and Interpretation," *Journal of Religion* 28 (1948), 177 ff.; N. Perrin, *The Kingdom of God in the Teaching of Jesus*, New Testament Library (Philadelphia: Westminster, 1963); H. R. Balz, *Methodische Probleme der neutestamentlichen Christologie* [Methodological problems of New Testament Christology], Wissenschaftliche Monographien zum N. T., XXV, 1967, pp. 204 ff.

480. R. Otto, *Reich Gottes und Menschensohn, Ein religionsgeschichtlicher Versuch* [The kingdom of God and Son of man: a religio-historical essay], Munich, 1934. Eng. tr. by F. V. Filson and B. L. Woolf, *The Kingdom of God and the Son of Man* (London: Lutterworth Press, 1938). Quotations with emendations from pp. 47-48, 50-51, 59, 60, 62, 72 73, 103, 104, 213, 237, 246, 247-48, 344, 375.

481. Cf. H. Windisch, *Deutsche Literaturzeitung* 3.F.5 (1934), 1393 ff.; H. Frick, "Wider die Skepsis in der Leben-Jesu-Forschung: R. Ottos Jesus-Buch" [Against skepticism in the life-of-Jesus research: R. Otto's book on Jesus] *ZThK*, N.F., 16 (1935), 1 ff.; M. M. Parvis, "New Testament Criticism in the World-Wars Period," in *The Study of the Bible Today and Tomorrow*, ed. H. R. Willoughby (University of Chicago Press, 1947), p. 64; A. M. Hunter, *Interpreting the New Testament 1900-1950* (Philadelphia: Westminster, 1951), p. 57 ff.

482. Cf. R. Bultmann, *ThR*, N.F., 9 (1937), 1 ff.; M. Dibelius, *Göttingische Gelehrte Anzeigen*, 1935, pp. 209 ff.

483. An adequate presentation of the study of Jesus since Schweitzer's *Quest* is lacking. See the surveys by G. Pfannmüller, *Jesus im Urteil der Jahrhunderte* [Jesus in the judgment of the centuries], 2nd ed., 1939, pp. 363 ff.; C.-H. Ratschow, "Jesusbild der Gegenwart" [The image of Jesus in the present day], *RGG*, III, cols. 655 ff.; W. G. Kümmel, "Jesusforschung seit 1950" [The study of Jesus since 1950] *ThR*, N.F., 31 (1965/66), 15 ff., 289 ff.; above all for the Anglo-Saxon conservative research, see O. Piper, "Das Problem des Lebens Jesu seit Schweitzer" in *Verbum Dei manet in aeternum*, Festgabe für O. Schmitz, 1953, pp. 73 ff. On the present state of the problem, see E. Käsemann, "The Problem of the Historical Jesus," *ZThK* 51 (1954), 125 ff. Eng. tr. in *Essays on New Testament Themes*, Studies in Biblical Theology, 1964, pp. 1-47; Hugh Anderson, *Jesus and Christian Origins*, 1964; J. M. Robinson, *A New Quest of the Historical Jesus*, Studies in Biblical Theology, no. 25 (Napierville, Ill.: A. K. Allenson, 1959), 2nd ed. in German, *Kerygma und Historischer Jesus*, 1967; N. Perrin, *Rediscovering the Teaching of Jesus*, New Testament Library (New York: Harper, 1967); see the review of Perrin by W. G. Kümmel, *Journal of Religion* 49 (1969), 59 ff.

NOTES

484. F. Büchsel, *Johannes und der hellenistische Synkretismus*, Gütersloh, 1928, pp. 7, 9, 17-18, 20-21, 24-26, 43, 75, 79, 111-12; Büchsel, *Das Evangelium des Johannes übersetzt und erklärt* [The Gospel of John translated and expounded], Das Neue Testament Deutsch, Göttingen, 1934, pp. 18-20.

485. On the recent history of the study of John, W. Bauer, "Johannes-evangelium und Johannesbriefe," *ThR*, N.F., 1 (1929), 135 ff.; W. F. Howard, *The Fourth Gospel in Recent Criticism and Debate* (Napierville, Ill.: A. R. Allenson, 1955), 4th ed. revised by C. K. Barrett; Ph.-H. Menoud, *L'Evangile de Jean d'après les recherches récentes*, 2nd ed., 1947, and "Les études johanniques de Bultmann à Barrett," in *L'Évangile de Jean. Études et Problèmes*, Récherches Bibliques III, 1958, pp. 11 ff.; E. Haenchen, "Aus der Literatur zum Johannesevangelium 1929-1956, *ThR*, N.F., 23 (1955), 295 ff.; R. Schnackenburg, *Neutestamentliche Theologie. Der Stand der Forschung* [New Testament theology: the state of research], Bibl. Handbibliothek I; Eng. tr. by David Askew, *New Testament Theology Today* (New York: Herder & Herder, 1963), pp. 171 ff. Schnackenburg, *Das Johannesevangelium*, pt. I, Herder's Theol. Kommentar zum N. T., 1965, pp. 171 ff.

486. Thus correctly O. Linton (*op. cit.*, n. 272), pp. 132 ff.

487. F. Kattenbusch, "Der Quellort der Kirchenidee," *Festgabe für A. v. Harnack*, 1921, pp. 145-46, 170-72, 160, 162, 164-66, 167, 169 *n.*

488. Karl Holl in his discussion of "The concept of the Church in Paul in relation to the Primitive Community," Sitzungsberichte der Preussichen Akademie der Wissenschaften in Berlin, phil.-hist. Klasse, 1921, pp. 920 ff. (reprinted in his collected essays on church history [*op. cit.*, n. 432], pp. 44 ff., and in the collection of essays edited by Rengstorf [*op. cit.*, n. 344], pp. 144 ff.) presented the thesis that the primitive community in Jerusalem had established a legal claim to be the dominant central point of the whole Church, on the basis of the presence within it of eyewitnesses of the Resurrection there, while Paul represented a spiritualized view of the Church, according to which the Church exists everywhere. With this sharp antithesis of concepts of the Church K. L. Schmidt took issue. Cf. on this controversy, W. Bodenstein (*op. cit.*, n. 432), pp. 27 ff.

489. K. L. Schmidt, "Die Kirche des Urchristentums. Eine lexikographische und biblisch-theologische Studie" [The Church of primitive Christianity: a lexicographical and biblical-theological study], in *Festgabe fur A. Deissmann*, Tübingen, 1927, pp. 290-92, 302-4, 309-11, 317-19.

490. See the survey of the literature in O. Linton (*op. cit.*, n. 272), pp. 132 ff.; F. M. Braun, *Neues Licht auf die Kirche. Die Protestantische Kirchendogmatik in ihrer neuesten Entfaltung* [New light on the Church: Protestant Church dogmatic in its recent development], 1946; W. G. Kümmel, *ThR*, N.F., 17 (1948), 123 ff.; bibliography in K. Stendahl, art. on "Kirche" II, in *RGG*, Vol. III, cols. 1296 ff., and in R. Schnackenburg, in *Die Kirche im Neuen Testament*, 1961 (= Eng. tr. by W. J. O'Hara, *The Church in The New Testament* (New York: Herder & Herder, 1962); bibliography on Jesus and the church in W. G. Kümmel, "Jesus und die Anfänge der Kirche," *Studia Theologica* 7, 1953 (= Kümmel, *Heilsgeschehen*, pp. 289 ff.; and A. Vögtle, "Der Einzelne und die Gemeinschaft in der Stufenfolge der Christusoffenbarung" ["The individual and the community in the stages of unfolding of the revelation of Christ], in *Sentire Ecclesiam*, Festschrift for H. Rahner, 1961, pp. 53 ff.

491. H. V. Soden, "Was ist Wahrheit? Vom geschichtlichen Begriff der Wahrheit" [What is truth? On the historical concept of truth], Marburger Akademische Reden XLVI, Marburg, 1927, pp. 10, 13-16, 18-20, 25-27 (= "Urchristentum und Geschichte" in *Gesammelte Aufsätze und Vorträge*, Vol. I, Tübingen, 1951, pp. 6, 9-12, 14-16, 21-23).

459

492. R. Bultmann, *Der Begriff der Offenbarung in Neuen Testament*, Tübingen, 1929, pp. 8-12, 20, 22, 24-26, 30, 40-41, 43-45 (= in *Glauben und Verstehen*, Vol. III, 1960, pp. 1 ff., with indication of the original pagination.) Eng. tr. (*op. cit.*, n. 459).

493. P. Althaus, *ThLZ* 54 (1929), 414.

494. P. Althaus, *ThLZ*, 54 (1929), 417. Althaus rightly points out at this place the influence of Mr. Kähler on Bultmann's stress on the preached Christ. See on this also H. Leipold, *Offenbarung und Geschichte als Problem des Geschehens. Eine Untersuchung zur Theologie Martin Kählers* [Revelation and history as problem of event], 1962, pp. 14 ff., and N. Perrin (*op. cit.*, n. 483), pp. 220-21.

495. The bibliography in W. G. Kümmel, "Jesus und Paulus," *Theol. Blätter* 19 (1940), 209-10 (= Kummel, *Heilsgeschehen*, pp. 81 ff.) and in "Jesus und Paulus," *NTSt* 10 (1963/64), 163 ff. (= Kummel, *Heilsgeschehen*, pp. 439 ff.). More recent discussion in V. P. Furnish, "The Jesus-Paul Debate: From Baur to Bultmann," *Bulletin of the John Rylands Library* 47 (1964/65), 342 ff.; J. Blank, *Paulus und Jesus*, Studien zum Alten und Neuen Testament, Vol. XVIII, 1968.

496. The resolution of this problem was proposed by C. H. Dodd, for example, in *The Present Task in New Testament Studies* (New York: Macmillan, 1936), pp. 31, 35: "The centrifugal movement must be balanced by a centripetal movement which traces back those representations which are better understood in their special character to the unity of the life which originally gave them their form." Cf. also A. N. Wilder, "New Testament Theology in Transition," in *Study* (*op. cit.*, n. 481), pp. 432 ff.; A. M. Hunter, *The Unity of the New Testament* (New York: Macmillan, 1943); B. Reicke, "Einheitlichkeit oder verschiedene 'Lehrbegriffe' in der neutestamentlichen Theologie?" [Unity or differing 'doctrine' in New Testament theology?], *ThZ* 9 (1953), 401 ff.; W. Künneth, "Zur Frage nach der Mitte der Schrift" [On the question of the mid-point of Scripture], *Dank an Paul Althaus*, 1958, pp. 121 ff.; W. G. Kümmel, "Das Problem der 'Mitte des Neuen Testaments'" [The problem of the mid-point of the New Testament], in *L'Évangile hier et aujourd'hui*, Festschrift for Prof. F. J. Leenhardt, 1968, pp. 71 ff.

497. Hoskyns found the approach to this question benefited by Schweitzer, who "showed that in fact it was the Lord who founded Christianity." Quoted from an essay of 1910 by R. J. C. Gutteridge, "Sir Edwyn Hoskyins," *Kerygma und Dogma* 10 (1964), 49.

498. E. C. Hoskyns and F. N. Davey, *The Riddle of the New Testament* (London: Faber & Faber, Ltd., 1931), pp. 11, 14. Although Davey's innate modesty and profound respect for his teacher, Hoskyns, led him to describe his role in this work as only that of amanuensis—he drew an analogy with Papias' portrayal of Mark as the recorder of Peter's memoirs—he has subsequently acknowledged that the writing was wholly his own. He sought the advice and guidance of Hoskyns and the two of them discussed the book chapter by chapter, so that although the ideas of both men are interwoven in the book, it is essentially the work of Davey. The quotations from pp. 45-46, 77-79, 98-99, 101, 159-60, 206-207, 244-45, 249-50 are reprinted by permission of the publisher.

499. Hoskyns and Davey (*op. cit.*, n. 498), p. 259.

500. For example, the position, already encountered in R. Otto, which accepts as of fundamental importance for Jesus the Suffering Servant poems of Second Isaiah, has since his time been frequently represented: J. Jeremias, *ThWBNT*, V, 1954, pp. 709 ff. (Eng. tr., V, 1967, pp. 677-717; O. Cullmann, *The Christology of the New Testament*, Eng. tr. by S. C. Guthrie & C. A. M. Hau (London: SCM Press, 1959), pp. 51-82; W. G. Kümmel, *Promise and Fulfillment* (*op. cit.*, n. 478), pp. 72 ff. and *nn.* 177 and 179, where other scholars are named; more recently, R. H. Fuller, *The Foundations of New Testament Christology* (New York: Scribner's, 1965), pp. 115 ff.; nevertheless, this position has met with considerable objections; R. Bultmann, *ThR*, N.F., 9 (1937), 27 ff.; C. T. Craig, "The identification of Jesus with the Suffering Servant," *Journal of Religion*, 24 (1944), 241 ff.; M. D. Hooker, *Jesus and the Servant: The Influence of the Servant Concept of Deutero-Isaiah in the New Testament*, 1959; F. Hahn (*op. cit.*, n. 348, Eng. tr.), pp. 54 ff. It is in no way demonstrable that all the utterances of Jesus are "demonstrations of the Messiah" (so H. Windisch, *The Meaning of the Sermon on the Mount*, pp. 26 ff.); this thesis cannot be derived from the individual items of the tradition, but only as the consequence of viewing in a single comprehensive fashion all the old Jesus tradition.

501. On the main features of the history of New Testament study over the period of the past twenty years, see the surveys mentioned on page 462: H. J. Cadbury, C. T. Craig, A. M. Hunter, S. E. Johnson, E. Käsemann, W. G. Kümmel (1957), W. Neil, M. M. Parvis, A. Richardson, and A. N. Wilder; the most recent presentations among those named there are R. H. Fuller, W. G. Kümmel (1969), St. Neill, and R. Schnackenburg.

502. P. Schubert, "Urgent Tasks for New Testament Research," in *Study* (*op. cit.*, n. 481), pp. 214, 212.

503. E. C. Hoskyns and F. N. Davey (*op. cit.*, n. 498), p. 263.

504. E. Käsemann, "Neutestamentliche Fragen von Heute," *ZThK*, 54 (1957), 7. Eng. tr. by W. J. Montague, "New Testament Questions of Today," appears as the first essay in a book by the same name (Philadelphia: Fortress Press, 1969), pp. 1-22.

Literature on the History
of New Testament Scholarship

Baur, Ferdinand Christian. ("Concept, History and Divisions of New Testament Theology,") *Vorlesungen über neutestamentliche Theologie* [Lectures on New Testament], ed. F. P. Baur. Leipzig, 1864, pp. 1 ff.

Bultmann, Rudolf. *Theologie des Neuen Testaments.* Tübingen, 1953, pp. 581 ff. (Eng. tr. by Kendrick Grobel, New York, 1955. Vol. II, pp. 241 ff., "The History of Research in New Testament Theology.")

Cadbury, Henry J. "The Present State of New Testament Studies," in *The Haverford Symposium on Archaeology and the Bible.* Haverford, Pa., 1938, pp. 79 ff.

Craig, Clarence T. "Current Trends in New Testament Study." *JBL,* 57 (1938), 359 ff.

Craig. Clarence T. "Biblical Theology and the Rise of Historicism." *JBL,* 62 (1943), 281 ff.

Cullmann, Oscar. "Wandlungen in der neueren Forschungsgeschichte des Urchistentums" [Changing directions in recent historical study of primitive Christianity], in *Discordia concors,* Festschrift for Edgar Bonjour. Basel, 1968, pp. 51 ff.

Cyriaci, G. *Die Darstellung der Gottesverkündigung Jesu in der deutschen theologischen Forschung seit H. J. Holtzmann* [The Presentation of Jesus' Preaching about God in German Theological Study since H. J. Holtzmann]. Jena dissertation in typescript, 1955.

Esking, Erik. *Glaube und Geschichte in der theologischen Exegese Ernst Lohmeyers. Zugleich ein Beitrag zur Geschichte der neutestamentlichen Wissenschaft* [Faith and history in the theological exegesis of Ernst Lohmeyer, at the same time a contribution to the history of New Testament scholarship]. Acta Seminarii Neotestamentici Upsaliensis, XVIII, 1951.

Filson, Floyd V. "The Central Problem Concerning Christian Origin," in *The Study of the Bible Today and Tommorow,* ed. H. R. Willoughby. Chicago, 1947, pp. 329 ff.

Fuller, Reginald H. *The New Testament in Current Study.* New York, 1962.

Hartlich, Christian, and Sachs, Walter. *Der Ursprung des Mythosbergriffs in der modernen Bibelwissenschaft.* [The origin of the concept of myth in modern biblical scholarship]. Schriften der Studiengemeinschaft der evangelischen Akademien, II, Tübingen, 1952.

Heinrici, Georg. "Hermeneutik." *PRE,* VII (1899) , cols. 718 ff.

Hilgenfeld, Adolf. "Die Evangelienforschung nach ihrem Verlauf und gegenwärtigen Stand" [The study of the Gospels: process and present state]. *Zeitschr. f. wissenschaftl. Theol.* 4 (1861) , 1 ff., 137 ff.

Hilgenfeld, Adolf. *Der Kanon und die Kritik des Neuen Testaments in ihrer geschichtlichen Ausbildung und Gestaltung* [Canon and criticism of the New Testament in their historical development and formation]. Halle, 1963.

Hoffmann, Jean G. *Les vies de Jésus et le Jésus de l'histoire* [The lives of Jesus and the Jesus of history]. Acta Seminarii Neotestamentici Upsaliensis XVII, 1947.

Holtzmann, Heinrich Julius. *Lehrbuch der historisch-kritischen Einleitung in das Neue Testament* [Textbook of historical-critical introduction to the New Testament]. Freiburg i: Br., 3rd ed., 1892, pp. 1 ff., "On History and Literature"; pp. 154 ff., "On the Protestant Canon."

Howard, Wilbert Francis. *The Romance of New Testament Scholarship.* — Naperville and London, 1949.

Hübner, Eberhard. *Evangelische Theologie in unserer Zeit* [Protestant theology in our time]. Bremen, 3rd ed., 1969.

Hunter, Archibald M. *Interpreting the New Testament 1900-1950.* London and Philadelphia, 1951.

Johnson, Sherman E. "The Emergence of the Christian Church in the Pre-Catholic Period," in *Study,* pp. 345 ff.

Kähler, Martin, "Biblische Theologie." *PRE,* III, 1897, pp. 192 ff.

Käsemann, Ernst. "Neutestamentliche Fragen von Heute." *ZThK,* 54 (1957) , 1 ff.; in *New Testament Questions of Today,* Philadelphia and London, 1969, — pp. 1-22.

Kümmel, W. G. "Bibelwissenschaft des Neuen Testaments." *RGG,* I, Tübingen, 1957, cols. 1246 ff.

Kümmel, W. G. "Die exegetische Erforschung des Neuen Testaments in diesem Jahrhundert," in *Bilanz der Theologie im 20. Jahrhundert,* ed. H. Vorgrimler and R. van der Gucht, Vol. II. Freiburg i. Br., 1969, pp. 279 ff.

Lampe, G. W. H. "The Exposition and Exegesis of Scripture: To Gregory the Great," *CHB,* II, 1969, pp. 155-56.

Leclercq, Jean. "The Exposition and Exegesis of Scripture: From Gregory the Great to St. Bernard." *CHB* II, pp. 183 ff.

Linton, Olaf. *Das Problem der Urkirche in der neueren Forschung. Eine kritische Darstellung.* [The problem of the primitive church in recent research]. Uppsala Universitets Ärrskrift Teologi, 2, 1932.

Meyer, Arnold. "Bibelwissenschaft: II, Das Neue Testament." *RGG* I, 2nd ed., 1927, cols. 1074 ff.

Meyer, Gottlob Wilhelm. *Geschichte der Schrifterklärung seit der Wiederherstellung der Wissenschaft* [The history of the interpretation of Scripture since the recovery of the sciences]. Five vols., Göttingen, 1802-1809.

Neil, W. "The Criticism and Theological Use of the Bible, 1700-1950." *CHB* I, 1963, pp. 238 ff.

Neill, Stephen. *The Interpretation of the New Testament, 1861-1961.* London, 1964.

Parvis, Merril M. "New Testament Criticism in the World-Wars Period," in *Study*, pp. 52 ff.

Pfleidered, Otto. *Die Entwicklung der protestantischen Theologie in Deutschland seit Kant und in Grossbritannien seit 1825* [The development of Protestant theology in Germany since Kant and in Great Britain since 1825]. Freiburg i. Br., 1891.

Reuss, Eduard. *Die Geschichte der Heiligen Schriften Neuen Testaments.* Braunschweig, 6th ed., 1887, pp. 574 ff.

Richardson, Alan. "The Rise of Modern Biblical Scholarship and Recent Discussion of the Authority of the Bible." *CHB*, 1, 1963, pp. 294 ff.

Salvatorelli, Luigi. "From Locke to Reitzenstein: The Historical Investigation of the Origins of Christianity." *HTR*, 22 (1929), 263 ff.

Schnackenburg, Rudolf. *Neutestamentliche Theologie. Der Stand der Forschung.* Biblische Handbibliothek I, 1963. (Eng. tr., *New Testament Theology Today*, New York, 1965.)

Scholder, Klaus. *Ursprünge und Probleme der Bibelkritik im 17. Jahrhundert* [Origins and problems of the criticism of the Bible in the seventeenth century]. Forschung zur Geschichte u. Lehre de Protestantismus, Series X, Vol. XXXIII, 1966.

Schweitzer, Albert. *Geschichte der Leben-Jesu-Forschung.* 2nd ed., 1913; reprinted at the 6th ed. in 1951. Eng. tr. of the 1st ed. as *The Quest of the Historical Jesus*, 1910.

Schweitzer, Albert. *Geschichte der paulinischen Forschung.* Tübingen, 1911. (Eng. tr. by W. Montgomery as *Paul and His Interpreters*, London, 1912.)

Smart, James D. *The Interpretation of Scripture.* Philadelphia, 1963.

Stephan, Horst. *Geschichte der deutschen evangelischen Theologie seit dem deutschen Idealismus*. 2nd ed. ed. Martin Schmidt, 1960.

Turner, Cuthbert Hamilton. *The Study of the New Testament: 1883 and 1920*. Oxford, 1926.

Wilckens, Ulrich ."Über die Bedeutung historischer Kritik in der Bibellexegese," in *Was heisst Auslegung der Heiligen Schrift?* [What does interpretation of Holy Scripture mean?], W. Joest, F. Mussner, Leo Scheffczyk, Anton Vögtle, Ulrich Wilckens. Regensburg, 1966, pp. 85 ff.

Wilder, Amos N. "New Testament Theology in Transition," in *Study*, pp. 419 ff.

Wilder, Amos N. "Biblical Hermeneutic and American Scholarship," in *Neutestamentliche Studien für Rudolf Bultmann*. Berlin, 1954 and 1957, pp. 24 ff.

Wood, J. D. *The Interpretation of the Bible. A Historical Introduction*. London, 1958.

Zahn, Theodor. "Einleitung in das Neue Testament: I. Geschichte der Diziplin." *PRE*, V, 1898, cols. 261 ff.

Biographical Appendix

Reference articles precede the rest of the bibliography. Completeness in the literature is not attempted; further biographical and bibliographical information is given by J. C. Hurd, Jr., *A Bibliography of New Testament Bibliographies,* New York, 1966, especially pp. 59 ff.: "New Testament Scholars: Biographies and Bibliographies."

The academic titles in use in Germany have no exact equivalents in Britain or America. Until the middle of this century, academically qualified persons were permitted to offer lecture courses at German universities for which they received no pay, except fees paid by the students who wanted to hear them. Accordingly, anyone who lived by this form of quasi-private enterprise was called a Privatdozent. Now the prefix, *privat,* has been dropped. *Dozent* is roughly the same as an instructor in America or a lecturer in Britain. *Extraordinary Professor,* a literal translation of the German or Latin (extra-ordinarius) means in fact a permanent teaching post, but at a lower level than that of the *Ordinary Professor* (ordinarius), which is the highest rank in German faculties. These two ranks approximate respectively that of Associate Professor and Professor in America (and are here so translated), or Senior Lecturer and Professor in Britain.

Baldensperger, Wilhelm
Born December 12, 1856 in Mühlhausen, Alsace. After pastoral service in Alsace and a short period as instructor in Strassburg, he was Professor of New Testament in Giessen from 1892 until the First World War, during which he lectured in Lausanne (Switzerland), returning in 1919 as Professor to the newly reopened University of Strassburg. Died July 30, 1936. Published many works on apocalyptic and the role of apologetics in primitive Christianity. Bibliography and obituary in *Revue d'histoire et de philosophie religieuses,* 16 (1963), pp. 185 ff.

Barth, Karl
Born May 10, 1886 in Basel. In 1909, editorial assistant on the staff of *Christliche Welt,* edited in Marburg by Martin Rade; then in 1910, assistant pastor in Geneva, and in 1911, pastor in Safenwil (Aargau). In 1921, Honorary Professor of Reformed Theology in Göttingen; in 1925, Professor of Systematic Theology in Münster; at Bonn in 1930; dismissed from his post in 1935. Appointed that year as Professor in Basel. Most important representative of the "dialectical theology"; in addition to his *Church Dogmatics* and numerous works

on systematics, wrote commentaries on Romans, I Corinthians, and Philippians. Died December 10, 1968. See G. Gloege, *RGG*, I, cols. 894 ff.; H. Bouillard, *LThK*, II, pp. 5 ff.; W. Matthias, *EKL*, I, cols. 317 ff.; S. Neill, *Interpretation*, pp. 201 ff.; bibliography in *Antwort* [Response], Festschrift on Barth's Seventieth Birthday, 1956, pp. 945 ff.; continuation in *Parrhesia* [Boldness], Festschrift on Barth's Eightieth Birthday, 1966, pp. 709 ff.

Bauer, Georg Lorenz

Born August 14, 1755 in Hiltpolstein, near Nüremburg. Pastor in Nüremburg; in 1788 Professor of Rhetoric, Oriental Languages and Morality at Altdorf; in 1805 Professor of Oriental Languages and Biblical Exegesis at Heidelberg. Died January 12, 1806. In addition to works on biblical mythology and theology, he wrote numerous works on Old Testament. See Erdmann, *ADB*, II, pp. 143 ff.; L. Zscharnack, *RGG*, I, 2nd ed., p. 798; H. Strathmann, *NDB*, I, cols. 637-38; E. Wolf, *RGG*, I, col. 924.

Bauer, Walter

Born August 8, 1877 in Königsberg. Privatdozent in New Testament in Marburg, 1903; in 1913, Associate Professor at Breslau; at Göttingen 1916 until 1919, when he became Professor there. Wrote numerous works on the history of primitive Christianity and the early church; edited an important dictionary of the Greek language of the New Testament and early Christian literature. Died November 17, 1960. See F. W. Gingrich, "The Contribution of Professor Walter Bauer to New Testament Lexicography," *NTS* 9, 1962/63, pp. 3 ff.; E. Fascher, "Walter Bauer als Kommentator," *NTS* 9, pp. 23 ff.; bibliography in *ThLZ*, 77, 1952, cols. 501 ff.; additional bibliography in *ThLZ*, 86, 1961, cols. 315-16.

Baur, Ferdinand Christian

Born June 21, 1792 in Schmiden, near Cannstatt. Received the customary theological training in Blaubeuren, Maulbronn and the Stift (Theological Foundation) at Tübingen. After a period as assistant pastor was for a short time a tutorial assistant (Repetent) in Tübingen; in 1817 became a schoolteacher in Maulbronn, where David Friedrich Strauss was his pupil. In 1826, Professor of Church History and Dogmatics in Tübingen, where he remained until his death on December 2, 1860. Apart from his works on primitive Christianity, he wrote many works on the history of the Church and of dogma, and also on ancient mythology and symbolism. See M. Tetz, *RGG*, I, cols. 935 ff.; H. Mulert, *NDB* V, 1953, pp. 670-71; J. Schmid, *LThK*, II, pp. 72-73; G. Fraedrich, *F. Chr. Baur, der Begründer der Tübinger Schule, als Theologe, Schriftsteller und Charakter* [F. C. Baur, founder of the Tübingen School, as theologian, author, and character], 1909; "F. C. Baur," in W. D. Dilthey, *Gesammelte Schriften* [Collected writings], IV, 1921, pp. 403 ff.; K. Barth, *Die protestantische Theologie im 19. Jahrhundert*, 1947, pp. 450 ff.; Hirsch, *Geschichte der neuren evangelischen Theologie*, Vol. V, pp. 518 ff.; C. Senft, *Wahrhaftigkeit und Wahrheit. Die Theologie des 19. Jahrhunderts zwischen Orthodoxie und Aufklärung* [Truthfulness and truth: nineteenth century theology between orthodoxy and enlightenment], 1956, pp. 47 ff.; H. Liebing, "Historisch-kritische Theologie. Zum 100. Todestag F. C. Baurs" [On the one hundredth anniversary of Baur's death], *ZThK* 57 (1960), 302 ff.; E. Barnikol, *Das ideengeschichtliche Erbe Hegels bei und seit Strauss und Baur im 19. Jahrhundert* [The influence of Hegel on the history of ideas in and since Strauss and Baur in the nineteenth century] (Wissenschaftliche Zeitschrift der Martin-Luther-Universität Halle-Wittenberg, Gesellschafts- und sprachwissenschaftliche Reihe 10:1), 1961; K. Scholder, "F. C. Baur als Historiker," *EvTh*, 21 (1961), 435 ff.; K. Geiger, *Spekulation und Kritik. Die Geschichtstheologie F. C. Baurs* [Speculation and criticism: theology of history of F. C. Baur], 1964; Meinhold, *Geschichte der kirchlichen Historiographie*, Vol. II, pp. 170 ff.; P. C. Hodgson, *The Formation of Historical Theology: A Study of F. C. Baur*, 1966. Bibliography in Geiger and Hodgson.

Bengel, Johann Albrecht

Born June 24, 1687 in Winnenden (Württemberg). Beginning in 1713, a teacher at the Klosterschule (a Protestant preparatory school for theological study) in Denkendorf; in 1741, became provost in Herbrechtingen; and in 1749, a member of the Church Governing Council (Konsistorialrat) in Stuttgart. In addition to his edition of the Greek New Testament and the *Gnomon*, he published school editions of the letters of Cicero and of the church fathers and many writings on biblical chronology. Died November 2, 1752. See Hartmann-Hauck, *PRE* II, pp. 597 ff.; M. Metzger, *RGG* I, cols. 1037-38; H. J. Rothert, *EKL*, I, cols. 389-90; K. Hermann, *NDB*, II, col. 47; Eb. Nestle, "Bengel als Gelehrter" [Bengel as scholar], *Marginalien und Materialen* II, 3, 1893; Hirsch, *Geschichte*, Vol. II, pp. 179 ff.

Billerbeck, Paul

Born April 4, 1853 in Bad Schönfliess in Neumark (Brandenburg). From 1880 to 1889, pastor in Zielenzig; 1889-1915, pastor in Heinersdorf (both in the Ost-Sternberg district). Died December 23, 1932 in Frankfurt a. d. Oder. Wrote, prior to the appearance of his great commentary, numerous works on rabbinic studies. J. Schmid, *LThK*, II, col. 476; J. Jeremias, *Theol. Blätter*, 12 (1933), 33 ff.

Bousset, Wilhelm

Born on September 3, 1865 in Lübeck. In 1889, Privatdozent in Göttingen, and in 1896, Associate Professor of New Testament there; Professor of New Testament in Giessen from 1916 on. Died March 8, 1920. In addition to the fundamental works on the history of religion, relating to both Judaism and early Christianity, he published important works on the textual criticism of the New Testament, on Hellenistic-Jewish and patristic aspects of literary and intellectual history, popular summaries on central New Testament themes, numerous review articles in the *Theologische Rundschau*, founded with Heitmüller. W. Kamlah, *RGG*, I, cols. 1373-74; H. Gunkel, "Gedächtnisrede auf Wilhelm Bousset" [Memorial address], *Evangelische Freiheit* 20 (1920), 141 ff.; R. Reitzenstein, (Nachrichten von der königlichen Gesellschaft der Wissenschaften zu Göttingen; Geschäftliche Mitteilungen), 1920, pp. 84 ff.; incomplete bibliography, *DBS*, I, col. 990.

Bretschneider, Karl Gottlieb

Born February 11, 1776 in Gersdorf (Saxony). In 1804, theological instructor in Wittenberg; from 1807 on, a pastor in Saxony; in 1816, general superintendent in Gotha. Died January 22, 1848. A representative of the rationalistic supernaturalism, he wrote on biblical and dogmatic subjects, prepared a dictionary of the Old Testament, Apocrypha, and the New Testament, and edited the works of Melanchthon and Calvin. See Hagenbach, *PRE*, III, pp. 389 ff.; H. H. Schrey, *NDB*, II, col. 603; K. G. Bretschneider, *Aus meinem Leben* [From my life], an autobiography, Gotha, 1851.

Brückner, Martin

Born June 16, 1868 in Friedensdorf (Lahn). A pastor in 1895; military chaplain in 1899, later chief of army chaplains. In 1922, pastor in Berlin, and after 1922, an instructor there in New Testament. Died January 4, 1931. See A. Meyer, *RGG*, I, 2nd ed., col. 1274.

Büchsel, Friedrich

Born July 2, 1883 in Stücken (Brandenburg). Inspector in the Tholuck-Konvikt (a home for theological students) in Halle in 1909; in 1911, Privat-dozent in New Testament at Halle; in 1917, Professor of New Testament in Rostock. In the turmoil of the occupation after World War II, he was shot on May 5, 1945. Wrote many works on the theology and exegesis of the New Testament, especially on the Johannine writings. See G. Quell, *ThLZ*, 73 (1948), 176 ff.; bibliography in *ThLZ*, 82 (1957), 311 ff.

Bultmann, Rudolf

Born on August 20, 1884 in Wiefelstede in Oldenburg. In 1912, Privatdozent in New Testament at Marburg; 1916, Associate Professor of New Testament in Breslau; in 1920, Professor of New Testament in Giessen, and after 1921 in Marburg. Has written numerous studies on the Gospels, Paul and the Catholic Letters, on theology and the problem of the existentialist interpretation of the New Testament. See E. Fuchs, *RGG*, I, pp. 1511-12; H. Schlier, *LThK*, II, cols. 768-69; H. W. Surkau, *EKL*, I, cols. 616 ff.; Neill, *Interpretation*, pp. 222 ff.; H. Conzelmann, in Schultz, pp. 243 ff.; W. Schmithals, *Die Theologie Rudolf Bultmanns. Eine Einführung* [An introduction to Bultmann's theology], 1966; E. Dinkler, in the introduction to Rudolf Bultmann, *Exegetica. Aufsätze zur Erforschung des Neuen Testaments* [Essays on the study of the New Testament], 1967, pp. ix ff.; *The Theology of Rudolf Bultmann*, ed. by C. W. Kegley, 1966; Bibliography in *Exegetica*, pp. 482 ff.; W. G. Kümmel, "R. Bultmann zum 80. Gebürtstag," *Forschungen und Fortschritte*, 38 (1964), 253 ff.

Cajetan

His real name was Thomas de Vio from Gaëta. Born in 1468 or 1469, a Dominican, active at various Italian universities, and finally at Rome, where he became the superior of his order and Cardinal in 1517; in 1519, became bishop of his native city, Gaëta, and was again in Rome after 1524 until his death in 1534. He wrote on church law and theological discussions, on the interpretation of the Old and New Testaments. His interpretation of "The Letters of Paul and the other Apostles" first appeared in 1932. See Th. Kolde, *PRE*, III, pp. 632-33; R. Bauer, *LThK*, II, pp. 875-76.

Camerarius, Joachim (Kammermeister)

Born April 12, 1500 in Bamberg. A humanist, a pupil and friend of Melanchthon; after a short period of teaching in the gymnasium (preparatory school) in Nüremberg, became in 1535 Professor and reformer at the University of Tübingen, and in 1541, Professor of Greek at Leipzig, where he died on April 4,

1574. His notes on the New Testament first appeared in Leipzig in 1573; *Notatio figurarum sermonis in libris IV evangeliorum, et indicata verborum significatio et orationis sententia, ad illorum scriptorum intelligentiam certiorem* [Indication of the forms of speech in the four Gospels, along with information on the meaning of the words and the intention of the address, for the better understanding of these Scriptures]. See Th. Kolde, *PRE*, III, pp. 687 ff.; F. Lau, *RGG*, I, col, 1602; F. Stählin, *NDB*, III, cols. 104-5, and *Humanismus und Reformation im bürgerlichen Raum. Eine Untersuchung der biographischen Schriften des Joachim Camerarius* [Humanism and reformation in the middle class sphere. A study of the biographical writings of Joachim Camerarius], 1936, pp. 1 ff.

Chubb, Thomas

Born September 29, 1679 in East Harnham, near Salisbury; a glovemaker in Salisbury, where he died, February 8, 1747. On the basis of his knowledge of the English Bible, he published, after a few short works, his major writing (1738): *The True Gospel of Jesus Christ, Asserted.* See L. Zscharnack, *RGG*, I, 2nd ed., col. 1678; D. Carter, *RGG*, I, cols. 1820-21; G. V. Lechler, *Geschichte des englischen Deismus* 1841, pp. 343 ff.; Hirsch, *Geschichte*, Vol. I, pp. 338 ff.

Cludius, Hermann Heimart

Born March 28, 1754 in Hildesheim. From 1777 to 1835, pastor in Hildesheim; also city superintendent after 1788. Died June 23, 1835. Wrote many works on the history and philosophy of religion. See Phil. Meyer, *Die Pastoren der Landeskirchen Hannover und Schaumburg-Lippe seit der Reformation*, Vol. I, 1941, pp. 502, 506. (I owe this reference to the kindness of the Archives of the City of Hildesheim.)

Cremer, Augustus Hermann

Born October 10, 1834 in Unna (Westphalia). From 1859 until 1870, a pastor in Ostönnen (Westphalia), where he prepared his Biblical-Theological Dictionary of New Testament Greek (1st ed., 1866; 9th ed., 1902). In 1870, Professor of Systematic Theology and until 1890, pastor of the Marienkirche in Greifswald. A strong representative of Lutheran biblicism. Besides works in dogmatics and practical theology, wrote *Die paulinische Rechtfertigungslehre* [The Pauline doctrine of justification by faith], 1899. Died on October 4, 1903. See J. Haussleiter, *PRE*, XXIII, pp. 329 ff.; W. Koepp, *RGG*, I, cols. 1881-82; H. H. Schrey, *NDB*, III, col. 409.

Cumont, Franz

Born January 3, 1868 in Alost (Belgium). From 1892 to 1910, instructor in classical philology in Ghent; after 1898, Curator of the Museum in Brussels. Lived in Rome after 1912, traveling on many research and lecture tours. Wrote fundamental works on the relationships of the Near East to Greek and Roman culture, on otherworldly images in antiquity, astrology, etc. Died August 20, 1947 in Woluwé-Saint-Pierre near Brussels. See B. Rigaux, *LThK*, III, pp. 107-8; obituary with bibliography of most important works in Franz Cumont, *Lux Perpetua*, 1949, pp. vii ff.; complete bibliography to 1936 in *Annuaire de l'institut de philologie et d'historie orientales et slaves*, 4 (= Mélanges Franz Cumont, pp. vii ff.

Dalman, Gustav

Born June 9, 1855 in Niesky (Oberlausitz). Attended the gymnasium (preparatory school) of the Brüdergemeinde (Brethren community) in Niesky; studied theology in Gnadenfeld; short period as a teacher in the service of the Brethren community. In 1882, instructor at the theological seminar in Gnadenfeld; in 1887, a teacher at the Institutum Delitzchianum; in 1891 Privatdozent in Old Testament at Leipzig; from 1902 to 1914, Director of the German Evangelical Institute for the Study of Antiquity in the Holy Land, at Jerusalem. After 1925, Professor of Old Testament in Greifswald, and from 1925 on, Director of the Gustav-Dalman Institute for the Study of Palestine. Died at Herrnhut August 8, 1941. Numerous publications on the Aramaic language and on the land of Palestine. See G. Meyer, *NDB*, III, pp. 493-94; autobiographical sketch in *Die Religions-wissenschatf in Selbstdarstellungen*, Vol. IV, 1928, pp. 1 ff.; K. H. Rengstorf, "Gustav Dalmans Bedeutung für die Wissenschaft vom Judentum," [G. Dalman's importance for scholarly study of Judaism], *Wissenschaftliche Zeitschrift der Ernst-Moritz-Arndt Universität Greifswald*, Gesellschafts- und sprachwissenschaftliche Reihe, IV, 1954/55, pp. 373 ff. Bibliography in the same volume, pp. 209 ff.

Deissmann, Adolf

Born November 7, 1866 in Langenscheid (Nassau). Served term as an assistant pastor; in 1892, Privatdozent in New Testament at Marburg; pastor and instructor in the theological seminar at Herborn; in 1897, Professor of New Testament in Heidelberg, and after 1908, in Berlin. Died April 5, 1937. Wrote on Paul and on political and ecumenical questions, in addition to his many works on the linguistic and sociological relationships of primitive Christianity. See H. Strathmann, *NDB*, III, cols. 571-72; autobiographical sketch in *Selbstdarstellungen*, Vol. I, 1925, pp. 43 ff.; H. Lietzmann, *ZNW*, 35 (1936), 299 ff.; W. F. Howard, *The Romance of New Testament Scholarship*, 1949, pp. 117 ff.; G. Harder, *Kirche in der Zeit* 22 (1967), 297 ff.; this essay in memory of Deissmann, together with biographical information and bibliography, in *Zum Gedenken an Adolf Deissmann*, 1967.

Deissner, Kurt

Born April 4, 1888 in Frohse near Magdeburg. In 1915, Privatdozent in New Testament, and in 1919 Associate Professor, in 1920 Professor, all at Greifswald. Wrote many works of criticism against the history-of-religions research. Died Nov. 6, 1942. See R. Hermann, *ThLZ*, 68 (1943), 119-20.

De Wette, Wilhelm Martin Leberecht

Born January 12, 1780 in Ulla (Thuringia). Pupil of Griesbach and Gabler in Jena. Privatdozent in Jena, 1805; Professor of Exegesis at Heidelberg in 1807, and at Berlin in 1810. In 1819, because of a letter he wrote to the mother of the murderer of Kotzebue, he was dismissed, and became a Professor at Basel in 1822. Died June 16, 1849. Wrote on Old and New Testament criticism and exegesis (including a *Kurzgefässtes exegetisches Handbuch* [Compact exegetical handbook] on the entire New Testament!), on dogmatics and practical theology. See G. Frank, *PRE*, XXI, pp. 189 ff.; E. Wolf, *RGG*, II, cols. 158 ff.; J. Schmid, *LThK*, III, col. 315; H. J. Kraus, *Geschichte der historisch-kritischen Erforschung des Alten Testaments*, 2nd ed., 1969, pp. 174 ff.; E. Staehlin, *Dewettiana*.

Forschungen und Texte zu W. M. De Wettes Leben und Werk, 1956; R. Smend, *Wilhelm Martin Leberecht de Wettes Arbeit am Alten und Neuen Testament,* 1958.

Dibelius, Martin

Born September 9, 1883 in Dresden. Privatdozent in New Testament at Berlin in 1910; Professor at Heidelberg after 1915. Died November 11, 1947. Wrote numerous New Testament commentaries and studies on the Gospels, Paul, Acts, and on the literary and religious history of primitive Christianity. W. G. Kümmel, *NDB,* III, col. 632; H. Rusche, *LThK,* III, col. 350; W. G. Kümmel, "Dibelius als Theologe," *ThLZ,* 74 (1949), 129 ff. (=Heilsgeschehen, pp. 193 ff.) ; bibliography in *Bibliographia Dibeliana atque Bultmanniana,* Coniectanea Neotestamentica, VIII, 1944, pp. 1 ff.; Supplement, *ThLZ* 74 (1949), 131, n 1.

Dieterich, Albrecht

Born May 2, 1866 in Hersfeld. After a short period as a teacher in a gymnasium, became Privatdozent (1891), then Associate Professor of Classical Philology at Marburg (1895), and Professor at Giessen (1897) and finally at Heidelberg (1903). Died May 6, 1908. As a student of Usener, he was a leader in the study of the popular stratum of ancient religion, and investigated particularly folk lore and the basic concepts in primitive religions. See P. R. Franke, *NDB,* III, cols. 669-70; R. Wünsch, *Biographisches Jahrbuch für die Altertumswissenschaft* XXXII, 1909, pp. 70 ff., with bibliography.

Dionysius

Born of pagan parents at the end of the second century, a pupil of Origen and the second in succession after Origen as leader of the Alexandrian Catechetical School. From 247/8 to 264/5, Bishop of Alexandria. Chiefly a practical churchman. See O. Bardenhewer, *Geschichte der altkirchlichen Literatur,* II, 2nd ed., 1914, pp. 203 ff.; W. Schneemelcher, *RGG,* II, col. 201.

Dobschütz, Ernst von

Born October 9, 1870 in Halle. In 1893, Privatdozent in New Testament and in 1898, Associate Professor at Jena; in 1904, Professor at Strassburg; in 1910, at Breslau; in 1913, at Halle. Died May 20, 1934. Wrote many works on New Testament textual criticism, exegesis, history and theology of primitive Christianity, and the study of legends. See J. Schmid, *LThK,* III, p. 434; A. Adam, *NDB,* IV, cols. 7-8; autobiographical sketch in *Selbstdarstellung,* IV, 1928, pp. 31 ff., with bibliography; E. Klostermann, "In memoriam Ernst von Dobschütz," *ThStKr,* 106 (1935), 1 ff., with bibliography.

Dodd, Charles Harold

Born April 4, 1884 in Wrexham (North Wales). After studies in classical philology and theology, served as pastor in the Congregational Church, 1912-15; from 1915-30, Professor of New Testament at Mansfield College, Oxford; 1930-35, Professor of Biblical Criticism and Exegesis at the University of Manchester; since 1935, at Cambridge University. Wrote commentaries on Romans and the Letters of John, several works on New Testament theology and ethics, *The Interpretation of the Fourth Gospel* (1953), and *Historical Tradition in the Fourth Gospel* (1963), in addition to numerous essays on philology and theology. See J. Jeremias, *RGG*, II, cols. 214-15; J. A. T. Robinson, in Schultz, *Tendenzen*, pp. 237 ff.; biographical data and bibliography in *The Background of the New Testament and Its Eschatology*, Festschrift for C. H. Dodd, 1956, pp. xi ff.

Eichhorn, Albert

Born October 1, 1856 in Garlstorf near Lüneburg. From 1881-84 in the pastorate; 1886, Privatdozent; 1888, Associate Professor of Church History in Halle; 1901-13, as Associate Professor in Kiel; lived thereafter in Braunschweig. Died September 3, 1926. Because of severe illness, published only a little, but was all the more active as a stimulus to others. See K. Galling, *RGG*, II, cols. 344-45; H. Gressmann, *Albert Eichhorn und die religionsgeschichtliche Schule*, 1914; E. Barnikol, "Albert Eichhorn. Sein 'Lebenslauf,' seine Thesen 1886, seine Abendmahlsthese und seine Leidensbriefe an seinen Schüler Erich Franz nebst seinen Bekenntnissen über Heilige Geschichte und Evangelium, über Orthodoxie und Liberalismus" [A. Eichhorn: the details of his career, his theses (1886), his thesis about the Lord's Supper, and the letters about his suffering written to his student, Erich Franz, together with his confessions concerning sacred history and the Gospel, concerning orthodoxy and liberalism], *Wissenschaftliche Zeitschrift der Martin-Luther-Universität Halle-Wittenberg*, Ges.-Sprach wiss., IX, 1, 1960, pp. 141 ff.

Eichhorn, Johann Gottfried

Born October 16, 1752 in Dörrenzimmern (Hohenlohe). Studied in Göttingen with J. D. Michaelis and the classical philologist, C. G. Heyne. In 1775, Professor of Oriental Languages in Jena; in 1788, Professor of Philosophy in Göttingen. Was the author of numerous oriental studies, of a three-volume introduction to the Old Testament, and of numerous works of secular and literary history, commentaries on the biblical accounts of primeval history and the Apocalypse. Died June 25, 1827. See K. Seigfried, *ADB*, V, pp. 713 ff; E. Bertheau *PRE*, V, pp. 234 ff.; E. Kutsch, *RGG*, II, cols. 345-46; K. Galling, *NDB*, IV, cols. 377-78; Kraus, *Geschichte*, pp. 133 ff.

Erasmus, Desiderius

Born October 28, 1466 or 1469 in Rotterdam. First a monk, then a scholar in Holland and England; after 1521, in Basel and Freiburg. Died on July 12, 1536 in Basel. The first edition of his translation of the New Testament into Latin and of his Greek New Testament appeared in Basel in 1516. Surveys! O. Schottenloher, *RGG*, II, cols. 534 ff.; E. Iserloh, *LThK*, III, cols. 955 ff.; J. Lindboom, *EKL*, I, cols. 1110 ff.

Ernesti, Johann August

Born August 4, 1707 in Tennstädt (Thuringia). In 1734, Rector (principal) of the Thomas School in Leipzig; 1742, Professor of *Litterae Humaniores;* in 1756, Professor of Rhetoric at Leipzig, and after 1759, a member of the theological faculty as well. Died September 11, 1781. Important as a philologist ("the German Cicero") as well as theologian. See G. Heinrici, *PRE*, V, pp. 469 ff.; K. H. Blaschke and F. Lau, *NDB*, IV, cols. 604 f.; W. Philipp, *RGG*, II, cols. 600 f.; Hirsch, *Geschichte*, Vol. IV, pp. 10 ff.

Eusebius

Born about 265 in Palestine. Studied at the school founded in Caesarea by Origen. Forced to flee in connection with the persecution of the Christians. Became Bishop of Caesarea about 313. An enthusiastic adherent of Constantine. Died in 339. Important as historian of the Church and as collector of the whole of church literature down to his time, of which significant excerpts are transmitted in his works. Surveys: H. Rahner, *LThK*, III, cols. 1195 ff.; K. Aland, *RGG*, II, cols. 739 ff.; B. Altaner, *Patrologie*, 5th ed., 1958, pp. 206 ff.; Meinhold, Vol. I, pp. 95 ff.

Everling, Otto

Born March 31, 1864 in Eschweiler near Aachen. Pastor in the Rhineland from 1906-22, Director of the Evangelical Federation and at the same time, a member of the German parliament (Reichstag). From 1923 until its dissolution in 1934, President of the Schutzkartell Deutscher Geistesarbeiter [Protective Trust for German Academicians]. Died on December 27, 1945, while fleeing to the isle of Rügen. (This information provided through the kindness of his son, Professor E. Everling of Berlin.)

Feine, Paul

Born September 9, 1859 in Golmsdorf near Jena. After study of classical philology and theology, became a gymnasium teacher and a private tutor (Hauslehrer); in 1893, Privatdozent in New Testament at Göttingen; in 1894, Professor at Vienna, in 1907, at Breslau, in 1910, at Halle. Died August 8, 1933. Wrote studies on numerous subjects in the field of New Testament, and textbooks on New Testament introduction and theology that passed through many editions. See H. Schlier, *LThK*, IV, col. 63; H. Strathmann, *NDB*, V. col. 61; *Selbstdarstellungen*, Vol. V, 1929, pp. 39 ff., with bibliography.

Flacius, Matthias

Called Illyricus M. Vlacich, born on March 3, 1520 in Albona in Istria (now in Yugoslavia). He wanted to be a monk, but his uncle, a Franciscan, sent him to Luther. After 1541, in Wittenberg; in 1544, converted to evangelical faith, and became Professor of Hebrew. Left Wittenberg in 1549, as an opponent of the Leipzig interim; active in Magdeburg; in 1557, Professor at Jena; on account of his reckless polemics was a perennial subject of persecution in various places. Died on March 11, 1575 in Frankfurt a. M. In addition to innumerable polemical writings, Flacius published fundamental works on church history (*Magdeburger Centurien*, 1559 ff.). In 1567, the *Clavis Scripturae Sacrae* [Key to the Sacred Scriptures] and in 1570 a comprehensive commentary on the New Testament (*Glossa Compendiaria*). See G. Kawerau, *PRE*, VI, pp. 82 ff., G. Moldaenke, *NDB*, V, cols. 220 ff.; Meinhold, Vol. I, pp. 268 ff.

Frommann, Karl

Born on March 28, 1809 in Unterlaubach near Coburg. In 1833, a Privatdozent; in 1837, an Associate Professor at Jena; in 1839, preacher at the German Lutheran Church of St. Peter in St. Petersburg; 1865-68, Honorary Professor at Berlin University, in 1868, General Superintendent and Spiritual Vice-president of the Evangelical-Lutheran Consistory in St. Petersburg. Died at Jena December 5, 1879. See J. Günther, *Lebensskizzen der Professoren der Universität Jena seit 1558-1858*, 1858, pp. 40-41; *Die Sanct Petrigemeinde. Zwei Jahrhunderte evangelischen Gemeindelebens in St. Petersburg*, Vol. I, 1910, pp. 305 ff. (For this reference I am indebted to the kindness of Dr. E. Amburger, formerly of Berlin, now of Giessen.)

Gabler, Johann Philipp

Born June 4, 1753 in Frankfurt a. Main. Studied in Jena with J. G. Eichhorn and Griesbach. In 1780, tutorial assistant in theology at Göttingen; in 1785, taught at the gymnasium in Dortmund; in 1785, Professor of Theology at Altdorf; in 1804, at Jena; after 1912, as Griesbach's successor. Died February 17, 1826. Wrote many essays on the New Testament, church history and the history of dogma in the journals which he edited. Revised Eichhorn's *Urgeschichte*. See Henke, *PRE*, VI, pp. 326-27; E. Kutsch, *NDB* VI, col. 8; E. H. Pältz, *RGG*, II, col. 1185; K. Leder, *Universität Altdorf. Zur Theologie der Aufklärung in Franken* [The University of Altdorf: on the theology of the Enlightenment in Franconia], *Die theologische Fakultät in Altdorf 1750-1809*, 1965, pp. 273 ff.

Giesler, Johann Carl Ludwig

Born March 3, 1792 in Petershagen near Minden. 1817, Assistant Rector in the gymnasium at Minden; in 1818, Director of the gymnasium in Cleve; in 1819, Professor of Theology at Bonn; in 1831, Professor in Göttingen. Died July 8, 1854. His first work was on the Gospels, followed by numerous writings on church history, especially his eight volume textbook of church history (1824 ff.), with rich excerpts from the sources. See N. Bonwetsch, *PRE*, VI, pp. 663-64; E. Wolf, *NDB*, VI, col. 388; Meinhold, Vol. II, pp. 207 ff.

Girgensohn, Karl

Born May 22, 1875 in Carmel on Ösel (in the Baltic). In 1903, Privatdozent in Systematic Theology; in 1907, Associate Professor in Dorpat; in 1919, Professor at Greifswald and 1922 at Leipzig. Died September 20, 1925. Wrote on systematic theology and psychology of religion. See W. Grönbach, *NDB*, VI, col. 410; *Selbstdarstellungen*, Vol. II, 1926, pp. 41 ff., with bibliography.

Goguel, Maurice

Born March 20, 1880 in Paris. Professor of New Testament in the Protestant theological faculty in Paris in 1906; in addition, after 1927 occupied A. Loisy's chair of exegesis in the École Pratique des Hautes Études in Paris. Died April 1, 1955. Wrote comprehensive works on New Testament introduction and on the history of primitive Christianity, in addition to countless essays and reviews, through which he informed French readers concerning the whole scope of New Testament research in German and English. See O. Cullmann, *RGG*, II, col. 1687; also Cullmann in *École Pratique des Hautes Études, Section des Sciences Religieuses, Annuaire* 1955/56, pp. 28 ff.; Ph-H. Menoud, *Verbum Caro* 9, 1955, pp. 1 ff.; Bibliographia Gogueliana in *Coniectanea Neotestamentica* X, 1946, pp. 5 ff.

Griesbach, Johann Jakob

Born January 4, 1745 in Butzbach (Hesse). In Halle, a pupil of Semler; after the conclusion of his studies in Germany, carried on research in Holland, England, and Paris on New Testament manuscripts; in 1771, Privatdozent; in 1773, Associate Professor of Theology in Halle; in 1775, Professor in Jena. Died March 12, 1812. Besides his text-critical work, he published a mildly orthodox dogmatics. See E. Bertheau, *ADB*, IX, 1879, pp. 660 ff.; E. Reuss, *PRE*, VII, pp. 170 ff.; E. Seesmann, *NDB*, VII, cols. 62-63.

Grotius, Hugo (de Groot)

Born April 10, 1583 in Delft. Studied classical philology and jurisprudence. Was at first a lawyer in The Hague; beginning in 1613, in government service. As adherent of the dogmatically liberal politician, Oldenbarnevelt, he was imprisoned when Oldenbarnevelt fell from power in 1619, but escaped in 1621, living first as a freelance scholar, then served in Paris for the Swedish government. Died in Rostock, September 28, 1645, while on a journey. Grotius became best known as the founder of international law and as a historian. His "Notes on the New Testament" appeared between 1641 and 1650 in Paris. See H. C. Rogge, *PRE*, VII, pp. 200 ff.; M. Elze, *RGG*, II, cols. 1885-86; R. Baumer, *LThK*, IV, cols. 1243-44; W. Philipp, *EKL*, I, cols. 1726 ff.; J. Schlüter, *Die Theologie des Hugo Grotius*, 1919, esp. pp. 25 ff.; Hirsch, *Geschichte*, Vol. I, pp. 225 ff.

Gunkel, Hermann

Born May 23, 1862 in Springe (Hannover). In 1888, Privatdozent in Biblical Theology and Exegesis in Göttingen; in 1889, Privatdozent in Old Testament at Halle; in 1895, Associate Professor in Berlin; in 1907, Professor in Giessen, and in 1920 at Halle. Died March 11, 1932. Following the completion of his youthful work in New Testament, became the founder of form-critical and history-of-religions research in the Old Testament. See K. Galling, *RGG*, II, cols. 1908-9; H. Hennequin, *DBS*, III, cols. 1374 ff.; K. v. Rabenau, *NDB*, VII, cols. 322-23; also Rabenau in Schultz, *Tendenzen*, pp. 80 ff.; H. Schmidt, *Theol. Blätter*, II (1932), pp. 97 ff.; Kraus, *Geschichte*, pp. 341 ff.; W. Klatt, *Hermann Gunkel. Zu seiner Theologie der Religionsgeschichte und zur Entstehung der formgeschichtlichen Methode* [Hermann Gunkel: on his theology of the history-of-religions and the rise of the formcritical method], *FRLANT*, 100, 1969; bibliography in *Eucharisterion*, Gunkel Festschrift, II, 1923, pp. 214 ff.

Harnack, Adolf

Born May 7, 1851 in Dorpat. In 1874, Privatdozent; in 1876, Associate Professor of Church History in Leipzig; in 1879, Professor at Giessen; 1886, in Marburg, and in 1888, in Berlin. From 1905 to 1921 he was also Director-General of the Prussian State Library, and beginning in 1911, President of the Kaiser-Wilhelm Society for the Advancement of Science. Died June 10, 1930 in Heidelberg. Wrote in all the areas of church history, but also on New Testament and the history of the Berlin Academy, etc. See Hans v. Soden, *RGG*, II, 2nd ed., cols. 1633 ff.; W. Schneemelcher, *RGG*, III, cols. 77 ff.; H. Liebing, *NDB*, VII, cols. 688 ff.; A. v. Zahn-Harnack, *Adolf von Harnack*, 1936; E. Benz, *Die Ostkirche im Lichte der protestantischen Geschichtsschreibung von der Reformation bis zur Gegenwart* [The Eastern Church in the view of Protestant historians from the Reformation to the present], 1952, pp. 230 ff.; K. Kupisch, *Theologia viatorum* VI, 1954/58, pp. 54 ff.; T. Rendtorff in Schultz: *Tendenzen*, pp. 44 ff.; Meinhold, Vol. II, 263 ff.; bibliography: F. Smend, *A. v. Harnack: Verzeichnis seiner Schriften*, 1927; Supplement, 1931.

Hase, Karl August

Born August 25, 1800 in Niedersteinbach (Saxony). Qualified academically as Instructor in Tübingen (1823) in the philosophical and theological faculty, but after his arrest on account of membership in a student organization (Burschenschaft) and a period as a freelance writer, he requalified in Leipzig in 1828; in 1830, Associate Professor; in 1836, Professor for Theology in Jena. Died January 3, 1890. Hase's major field was church history, but he also wrote in other aspects of theology as well as in other fields. See G. Krüger, *PRE*, VII, pp. 453 ff.; M. Schmidt, *RGG*, III, col. 85; Meinhold, Vol. II, pp. 230 ff.

Hatch, Edwin

Born September 4, 1835 in Derby. After 1859, in different teaching posts in Canada; 1867-85, Vice President of St. Mary's Hall, Oxford, and at the same time (after 1883) a pastor in the vicinity of Oxford and Lecturer in Church History at the University. Died November 10, 1889. Wrote on the constitution of the Church and the Greek influences on the ancient church; was coeditor of a concordance to the Septuagint. See W. Sanday, *The Expositor*, 4th Series, 1, 1890, pp. 93 ff.; E. Preuschen in E. Hatch, *Griechentum und Christentum*, 1892, pp. viii ff. (German tr. of *The Influence of Greek Ideas and Usages upon the Christian Church*, London and Edinburgh, 1891; Neill, *Interpretation*, pp. 137 ff.

Hausrath, Adolf

Born January 13, 1837 in Karlsruhe. After two years as an assistant pastor in Heidelberg and three years in the Karlsruhe Superior Church Council, became Associate Professor of Church History (1867) and Professor (1871) at Heidelberg. Died August 8, 1909. Wrote many works on church history intended for a wide circle of readers; for example, on Paul, Luther, D. F. Strauss, R. Rothe, and in addition, several historical novels. See K. Hesselbacher, *PRE*, XXIII, pp. 623 ff.; E. H. Pältz, *RGG*, III, col. 99; H. J. Holtzmann, *Prot. Monatshefte*, 13 (1909), 369 ff.; K. Bauer, *A. Hausrath. Leben und Zeit* [Hausrath's life and times], I, 1913.

Heinrici, C. F. Georg

Born March 14, 1844 in Karkeln (East Prussia). In 1871, Privatdozent in New Testament at Berlin; in 1873, Associate Professor and in 1874, Professor in Marburg; in 1892, Professor at Leipzig. Died September 29, 1915. Wrote numerous commentaries and discussions on New Testament and patristic problems. See J. Schmid, *LThK*, V, col. 205; W. G. Kümmel, *NDB*, VIII, cols. 434-35; A. Hauck, *Berichte der Gesellschaft der Wissenschaft zu Leipzig, philosophisch-historische Klasse* 67, 1915, pp. 121 ff.; E. v. Dobschütz, in C. F. Heinrici, *Die Hermesmystik und das Neue Testament* [Hermes mysticism and the New Testament], 1918, pp. vii ff., with bibliography.

Heitmüller, Wilhelm

Born on August 3, 1869 in Döteberg (Hannover). In 1902, Privatdozent in New Testament at Göttingen; in 1908, Professor at Marburg; 1920, at Bonn; 1924, at Tübingen. Died January 29, 1926. Wrote on baptism and the Lord's Supper, and a commentary on the Gospel of John in the series, *Schriften des Neuen Testaments . . . für die Gegenwart erklärt*, 1907, 3rd ed., 1918; *Jesus*, 1913 and many essays. With W. Bousset, he was cofounder of the *Theologische Rundschau*. See W. G. Kümmel, *NDB*, VIII, col. 459; R. Bultmann, *Christliche Welt*, 40 (1926), 209 ff.

Herder, Johann Gottfried

Born August 8, 1744 in Mohrungen (East Prussia). Teacher and preacher in Riga from 1764-69, and after a long journey, Court Preacher and member of the church governing council in Bückeburg; in 1776, Chief Pastor, Superior of the Church Council and General Superintendent in Weimar. Died December 18, 1803. Among his theological works, other than instruction for the theological program of study, were books on Jesus, on the Gospels and an exposition of the Apocalypse, and most significantly, works on the Old Testament: *"Alteste Urkunde des Menschengeschlechts* [Oldest documents of the human race], *Vom Geist der ebräischen Poesie* [On the spirit of Hebrew poetry]. See A. Werner, *PRE*, VII, pp. 697 ff.; H. Stephan, *RGG*, II, 2nd ed., cols. 1814 ff.; M. Redeker, *RGG*, III, cols. 235 ff.; M. Schmidt, *EKL*, II, cols. 116-17; A. Schweitzer, *Quest*, pp. 34-37; Hirsch, *Geschichte*, Vol. IV, pp. 207 ff.; E. Benz in *Die Grossen Deutschen* II, 1956, pp. 210 ff.; K. Scholder, "Herder und die Anfänge der historischen Theologie" [Herder and the beginnings of historical theology], *EvTh*, 22 (1962), 425 ff.; Meinhold, Vol. II, pp. 113 ff.

Hilgenfeld, Adolf

Born June 2, 1823 in Stappenbeck near Salzwedel. Privatdozent in New Testament (1847); Associate Professor in Jena (1850); Honorary Professor (1869) and Professor in 1890. Died on January 12, 1907. Critical adherent of the Tübingen School; wrote many studies on the New Testament, its Jewish cultural setting and the extracanonical early Christian literature. See K. Bauer, *RGG*, II, 2nd ed., col. 1891; J. Schmid, *LThK*, V, cols. 348 ff.; F. Nippold, *Zeitschrift für die wissenschaftliche Theologie*, 50 (1908), 158 ff.; J. M. Schmidt, *Die jüdische Apocalyptik*, 1969, pp. 127 ff.

Holl, Karl

Born May 15, 1866 in Tübingen. Tutorial assistant at Tübingen (1891); in 1894, an academic assistant at the Berlin Academy; in 1896, Privatdozent in Church History at Berlin; in 1900, Associate Professor at Tübingen; in 1906, Professor at Berlin. Died May 23, 1926. Wrote many works on the history of the ancient church, of the later Eastern Church, and of Luther. See, A. Jülicher and E. Wolf, *RGG*, III, cols. 432 ff.; H. Jedin, *LThK*, V, col. 444; H. Lietzmann, in K. Holl, *Gesammelte Aufsätze zur Kirchengeschichte*, III, 1928, pp. 568 ff., with bibliography; E. Benz, *Die Ostkirche im Lichte der protestantischen Geschichtsschreibung von der Reformation bis zur Gegenwart* [The Eastern Church in the view of Protestant historians from the Reformation to the present], 1952, pp. 284 ff.; H. Rückert, in Schultz: *Tendenzen*, pp. 102 ff.; H. Karpp, Introduction to *Karl Holl: Briefwechsel mit A. v. Harnack* [Holl's correspondence with A. v. Harnack], 1966, pp. 1 ff., with Harnack's memorial address for Holl on pp. 83 ff.

Holtzmann, Heinrich Julius

Born May 17, 1832 in Karlsruhe. After a period as assistant pastor, became in 1858 a Privatdozent in Heidelberg, where he rose in 1861 to Associate Professor and in 1865 to Professor; from 1874 to 1904, Professor at Strassburg; then lived in retirement at Baden-Baden, where he died August 4, 1910. In addition to his works on the Synoptic Gospels and the theology of the New Testament, he wrote studies of Colossians and Ephesians and the Pastorals, as well as a comprehensive introduction to the New Testament (1885; 3rd ed. in 1892). Published commentaries on the Gospels and Acts; also wrote on practical theology. See E. v. Dobschütz, *PRE*, XXIII, pp. 655 ff.; A. Faux, *DBS*, IV, cols. 112 ff.; E. Dinkler, *RGG*, III, cols. 436 ff.; W. Bauer, *H. J. Holtzmann: Ein Lebensbild* [Life picture of Holtzmann], 1932 (= Bauer's *Aufsätze und kleinere Schriften*, ed. by G. Strecker, 1967, pp. 285 ff.)

Horst, George Konrad

Born June 26, 1767 in Lindheim (South Hesse). From 1796 to 1817, a pastor; after that a freelance writer. Died January 20, 1832. Wrote many works on magic and witchcraft. (This information provided by the kindness of the City Archives of Friedberg in Hesse.)

Hort, Fenton John Anthony

Born April 23, 1828 in Dublin. In 1857, Anglican minister in the vicinity of Cambridge; in 1871 Professor of Theology in Cambridge. Died November 30, 1892. In addition to some essays on the history of the early church, he wrote some commentaries, which were edited after his death. From 1853 on, he worked with Westcott on the edition of the Greek New Testament, which appeared in 1881. See C. R. Gregory, *PRE*, VIII, pp. 368 ff.; *ODCC*, cols. 656-57.

Hoskyns, Sir Edwyn Clement

Born August 9, 1884 at Notting Hill (London). Began pastoral service in the Church of England in 1908; army chaplain in 1915; Fellow in New Testament at Corpus Christi College, Cambridge in 1919. Died June 28, 1937. Strongly influenced by Karl Barth, whose commentary on the Romans he translated. Wrote *The Riddle of the New Testament*, an uncompleted commentary on John, and some smaller works on New Testament theology. See J. O. Cobham, *The Dictionary of National Biography*, Vol. for 1931-40, 1949, pp. 448-49; *ODCC*, cols. 658 ff.

Jerome

Born about 347 in Stridon in Dalmatia. Educated in Rome; at an early age, became an ascetic, lived the greatest part of his life as a hermit in Palestine (Bethlehem) but spent an interim in Rome as the reviser of the Latin translation of the Bible. Died in Palestine in 420. Great collector and linguist, but his dependability and his character are much disputed. His catalog of authors was written in 392. Surveys in P. Th. Camelot, *LThK*, V, cols. 326 ff.; B. Altaner, *Patrologie*, 5th ed., 1958, pp. 354 ff.; on his catalog of authors, Meinhold, Vol. I, pp. 151-52.

Jülicher, Adolf

Born January 26, 1857 in Falkenberg near Berlin. In 1887, a Privatdozent in Berlin; 1888, Professor of Church History and New Testament in Marburg, where he remained until retirement in 1923. Died August 3, 1938. Along with his *Introduction* and *Parables,* he wrote several studies of church history and an important edition of the Old Latin version of the Gospels. See E. Fascher, *RGG*, III, col. 1008; N. van Bohemen, *DBS*, IV, cols. 1414 ff.; *Selbstdarstellungen*, Vol. IV, 1928, pp. 159 ff., with bibliography; Hans v. Soden, "Akademische Gedächtnisvorlesung für Adolf *Jülicher*," [Memorial lecture for Jülicher], *Theol. Blätter*, 18 (1939), 1 ff.

Kabisch, Richard

Born May 21, 1868 in Kemnitz near Greifswald. After a brief period as a candidate, during which he was a schoolteacher, he was engaged in teacher education in various places. From 1910-14, served on the governmental and school councils in Düsseldorf, then briefly in Bromberg. Killed as an army volunteer in Flanders, October 10, 1914. Besides his initial theological writings, he published on religious and general pedagogy. See O. Eberhard, *Pädagogisches Lexikon*, II, 1929, pp. 1195 ff.; W. Iannasch, *RGG*, III, col. 1081.

Kähler, Martin

Born January 6, 1835 in Neuhausen near Königsberg. In 1860, Privatdozent in New Testament at Halle; in 1864, Associate Professor in New Testament and Systematic Theology at Bonn; in 1867, held the same post at Halle, but at the same time Inspector of the Silesian Students' Home; in 1879, Professor of New Testament and Systematic Theology at Halle. Died in Halle September 9, 1912. Wrote many works on dogmatics, New Testament paraphrases and essays on various subjects. See R. Hermann, *RGG*, III, cols. 1081 ff.; W. Klaas, *EKL*, II, 503-4; *Theologe und Christ. Erinnerungen und Bekenntnisse von Martin Kähler* [Theologian and Christian: recollections and confessions of Martin Kähler], 1926, with bibliography; B. Lohse in Schultz, *Tendenzen*, pp. 19 ff.

Kattenbusch, Ferdinand

Born October 3, 1851 in Kettwig on the Ruhr. Tutorial assistant in Göttingen; in 1873, Privatdozent for Historical Theology; in Tübingen in 1876; in 1878 Professor of Systematic Theology in Giessen; in 1903 at Göttingen; in 1906 at Halle. Died December 28, 1935. Pupil of A. Ritschl. Wrote numerous works in Luther studies, on denominational history, on the history of the apostolic confession of faith, and on systematic theology, but only a few individual essays on the New Testament. See E. Schott, *RGG*, III, col. 1228; *Selbstdarstellungen*, Vol. V, 1929, pp. 85 ff.; O. Ritschl, "F. Kattenbusch als Persönlichkeit, Forscher und Denker" [F. Kattenbusch as personality, scholar, and thinker], *ThStKr*, 107 (1936), 289 ff.

Keil, Karl August Gottlieb

Born April 23, 1754 in Grossenhain (Saxony). In 1781, a Privatdozent; in 1785, an Associate Professor of philosophy, in 1787, Associate Professor of theology, and in 1792, Professor of theology—all in Leipzig. Died April 22, 1818. Published many exegetical discussions and represented the grammatico-historical views of his teachers, Ernesti and Morus. See W. Schmidt, *PRE*, X, pp. 196-97; H. Doering, *Die gelehrte Theologie Deutschlands im 18. and 19. Jahrhundert* [Scholarly theology of Germany in the eighteenth and nineteenth centuries], Vol. II, 1832, pp. 70 ff.

Kittel, Gerhard

Born September 23, 1888 in Breslau. In 1913, a Privatdozent in New Testament at Kiel; in 1917, at Leipzig; in 1921, Associate Professor at Leipzig, and in the same year, Professor at Greifswald; 1926, Professor at Tübingen. In 1945, he was removed from his post. Died August 11, 1948. Wrote several works on late Judaism and early Christianity; founded the *Theological Dictionary of the New Testament*. See O. Michel, *RGG*, III, col. 1626; G. Friedrich, *ThLZ*,

74 (1949), 171-72. (bibliography in cols. 172 ff.); O. Michel, "Das wissenschaftliche Vermächtnis G. Kittels" [Kittel's scholarly legacy], *Deutsches Pfarrerblatt*, 58 (1958), 415 ff.

Krüger, Gustav

Born June 29, 1862 in Bremen. In 1886, a Privatdozent; in 1889, Associate Professor; in 1891, Professor of Church History at Giessen. Died March 3, 1940. Many works on all periods of church history. See E. Beyreuther, *RGG*, IV, cols. 82-83; H. Mulert, *Christl. Welt*, 54 (1940), 155 ff.; Meinhold, Vol. II, pp. 342 ff.

Lachmann, Karl

Born March 4, 1793 in Braunschweig. Studied theology briefly, then classical philology; in 1816, Privatdozent in Berlin; in 1818, Associate Professor of German and Classical Philology in Königsberg; in 1825, Associate Professor in Berlin, and Professor after 1827. Died March 13, 1851. Significant as editor of classical and middle-high-German texts, especially for analysis of metre and discovery of interpolations. See W. Scherer, *ADB*, XVII, 1883, pp. 471 ff.; M. Hertz, *Karl Lachmann*, 1851; F. X. Pölzl, *Über Karl Lachmann, Begründer der neuen Ära der neutestamentlichen Textkritik* [Karl Lachmann: founder of a new era in New Testament textual criticism], Rektoratsrede, Vienna, 1889; A. Rüegg, *Die neutestamentliche Textkritik seit Lachmann*, 1892, pp. 8 ff.

Lagarde, Paul de

Real name, P. Bötticher; in 1854, took the name of his great aunt, Ernestine de Lagarde. Born November 2, 1827 in Berlin. After the study of theology and oriental languages and a break with the orthodox Lutheranism in which he was reared, became a Privatdozent in Oriental Studies at Halle (1851); in 1854, taught at a gymnasium in Berlin; given leave for scholarly work in 1866-68; in 1869, Professor of Oriental Languages at Göttingen. Died December 22, 1891. Wrote over seventy works, among them numerous text editions in various languages, especially biblical texts and materials for a critical edition of the Greek Old Testament. Beyond this, he wrote theological-political tractates, which he published as a collection, *Deutsche Schriften*. See E. Littmann, *RGG, III*, 2nd ed., cols. 1452-53; W. Holsten, *RGG*, IV, cols. 200-201; J. Schmid, *LThK*, VI, cols. 730-31; A. Rahlfs, "Paul de Lagardes wissenschaftliches Lebenswerk in Rahmen einer Geschichte seines Lebens dargestellt" [P. Lagarde's scholarly life work presented in the framework of a history of his life] (= *Mitteilungen des Septuaginta-Unternehmens der Gesellschaft der Wissenschaften zu Göttingen,* IV:1, 1928]; H. Hermelink, *Das Christentum in der Menschheitsgeschichte von der Französischen Revolution bis zur Gegenwart* [Christianity in the history of humanity from the French Revolution to the present], Vol. III, 1955, pp. 463 ff.; H. Karpp, "Lagardes Kritik an Kirche und Theologie," *ZThK*, 49 (1952), 367 ff.

Lagrange, Marie-Joseph

Born March 7, 1855 in Bourg-en-Bresse (France). First a lawyer, then entered the Dominican order in 1879, went with his order into Spanish exile, where in 1883 he was ordained as a priest. From 1884 on, he continued his theological and orientalistic studies in Toulouse and Vienna. In 1890, he founded in Jerusalem a school for Palestinian biblical research, L'École Pratique d'études bibliques; edited the *Révue Biblique* (1892) and (1903) began the great series of commentaries, *Études Bibliques,* of which he wrote seven volumes chiefly on the New Testament. Besides this, he wrote innumerable books, essays, and reviews on Old and New Testament exegesis, the history of Semitic and Hellenistic religions. Died March 10, 1938. See P. Benoit, *LThK,* VI, col. 731; L. H. Vincent, *DBS,* V. cols. 231 ff.; F. M. Braun, *L'oeuvre de Père Lagrange. Étude et bibliographie,* 1943. R. de Vaux, "Le Père Lagrange," in R. de Vaux, *Bible et Orient,* 1967, pp. 9 ff.; *Le Père Lagrange au service de la Bible. Souvenirs personnels,* 1967.

Lechler, Gotthard Viktor

Born April 18, 1811 in Kloster Reichenbach near Freudenstadt (Black Forest). Passed through preparatory seminar and the Stift at Tübingen. After a short term as Assistant Pastor, was tutorial assistant in Blaubeuren and then in Tübingen. After a period as a student in England, published an important history of English Deism. After several more years as a pastor in Württemberg, became (1858) pastor of the Thomas Church in Leipzig and Professor of Church History and Church law there. Died December 26, 1888. Wrote many works on church history. See Th. Ficker, *PRE,* XI, pp. 336-37.

Lessing, Gotthold Ephraim

Born January 22, 1729 in Kamenz (Oberlausitz in Saxony). After changing occupations and places of residence, a playwright in Hamburg (1767), a librarian in Wolfenbüttel (1770). *Fragments by an Unknown Person* (actually by H. S. Reimarus) was edited by Lessing, beginning in 1774; his work on the Gospels was written in 1778, but did not appear until after his death, when his brother published it. Died February 15, 1781. See E. Bertheau, *PRE,* XI, pp. 406 ff.; O. Mann, *RGG,* IV, cols. 327 ff.; H. Beintker, *EKL,* II, cols. 1078 ff.; L. Zscharnack, *Lessing und Semler,* 1905, pp. 3 ff., 140 ff.

Lidzbarski, Mark

Born January 7, 1868 in Plock (Russia-Poland) as son of orthodox Jewish parents. Fled in 1882 to Germany. In 1896, Privatdozent in Semitic Languages at Kiel; in 1907, Professor at Greifswald and in 1917 at Göttingen. Died November 12, 1918. In addition to his translations of the Mandaean texts, wrote many works on Semitic epigraphy and philology. See A. Spitaler, *LThK,* VI, col. 1031; W. Bauer, *Nachrichten von der Gesellschaft der Wissenschaften zu Göttingen, Geschäftliche Mitteilungen 1928/29,* 1929, pp. 71 ff.

Lietzmann, Hans

Born March 2, 1875 in Düsseldorf. After study of theology and classical philology, became Privatdozent in Church History at Bonn; in 1908, Professor at Jena, and at Berlin in 1924, where he succeeded Harnack. Died June 25, 1942 in Locarno. Wrote a comprehensive account and many individual studies on the history of the early church; edited the *Handbuch zum Neuen Testament,* collections of ancient sources, and after 1920, the *Zeitschrift für die Neutestamentliche Wissenschaft und Kunde der älteren Kirche.* See W. Eltester, *RGG,* IV, cols. 375-76; *Selbstdarstellung,* Vol. II, 1926, pp. 77 ff. (= Kleine Schriften, III, Texte und Untersuchungen, 74, pp. 331 ff.); H. Bornkamm, *ZNW,* 41 (1942), 1 ff., with bibliography; Meinhold, Vol. II, pp. 393 ff.

Lightfoot, John

Born March 29, 1602 in Stoke upon Trent (Staffordshire). Pastor of Anglican Churches in various places, and in addition, Vice-Chancellor of Cambridge University (after 1654). Died December 5, 1675 in Ely. His scholarly activity was purely private. Along with works on the chronology and the harmonization of the Old and New Testaments, he published his *Horae Hebraicae et Talmudicae* on the Gospels, Acts, Romans, and I Corinthians (1658/78). See G. Dalman, *PRE*, XI, pp. 486-87; M. Schmidt, *RGG*, IV, col. 376.

Lightfoot, Joseph Barber

Born April 13, 1828 in Liverpool. In 1861, Professor of Theology at Cambridge; in 1879, Bishop of Durham. Died December 21, 1889. Wrote important commentaries on Galatians, Philippians, Colossians, and Philemon and on the Apostolic Fathers. See C. R. Gregory, *PRE*, XI, pp. 487 ff.; *ODCC*, col. 809; M. Schmidt, *RGG*, IV, col. 376; W. F. Howard, *The Romance of New Testament Scholarship*, 1949, pp. 55 ff.; Neill, *Interpretation*, pp. 33 ff.

Locke, John

Born August 29, 1632 in Wrington (Somerset). Part of the time in government service and in exile. On his return to England in 1688, a freelance writer. Died October 28, 1704, in Oates near London. Chief philosophical work, *Essay on Human Understanding* (1609). See L. Zscharnack, *RGG*, III, 2nd ed., cols. 1704-5; D. Heinrich, *RGG*, IV, cols. 425-26; Hirsch, *Geschichte*, Vol. I, p. 282.

Lohmeyer, Ernst

Born July 8, 1890 in Dorsten (Westphalia). In 1918, Privatdozent in New Testament at Heidelberg; in 1920, Associate Professor and in 1921, Professor at Breslau; in 1936, at Greifswald. Executed by the Russians in September, 1946. Wrote commentaries on the history and theology of early Christianity. See W. Schmauch, *RGG*, IV, cols. 440-41; O. Cullmann, "Memorial for Ernst Lohmeyer," *ThLZ*, 7 (1951, cols. 158 ff. (= O. Cullmann, *Vorträge und Aufsätze 1925-1962*, 1966, pp. 663 ff.); E. Esking, *Glaube und Geschichte in der theologischen Exegese Ernst Lohmeyers. Zugleich ein Beitrag zur Geschichte der neutestamentlichen Interpretation* [Faith and history in the theological exegesis of E. Lohmeyer: a contribution to the history of New Testament interpretation], 1951; bibliography in *In Memoriam Ernst Lohmeyer*, 1951, pp. 368 ff.

Loisy, Alfred

Born February 28, 1857 in Ambrières (Haute Marne). After ordination and various teaching posts, became Professor of Biblical Exegesis at the Catholic Institute in Paris (1890); removed from his post in 1893 because of his views on biblical criticism; from 1893-99, a teacher of religion in Neuilly; from 1901-1904, a Privatdozent in the École Pratique des Hautes Études in Paris; excommunicated in 1908. In 1909, Professor of the History of Religion in the Collège de France and after 1927 also in the École des Hautes Études. Died June 1, 1940. Wrote many works on biblical criticism, history of religions, and philosophy of religion, among them comprehensive commentaries on the Gospels and Acts. See J. Bonsirven, *DBS*, V, cols. 530 ff.; O. Schroeder, *LThK*, VI, col. 1134; F. Heiler, *Der Vater des katholischen Modernismus Alfred Loisy*, 1947, with bibliography; also Heiler in Schultz, *Tendenzen*, pp. 62 ff.; A. Houtin and F.

Sartiaux, *Alfred Loisy. Sa vie, son oeuvre. Manuscript annoté et publié avec une bibliographie Loisy et un Index Bio-Bibliographique* [Loisy: life and work], 1960.

Lücke, Gottfried Christian Friedrich

Born September 24, 1791 in Egeln near Magdeburg. After a period as tutorial assistant in Göttingen, became a pupil of Schleiermacher in Berlin; in 1818, Professor of Theology in Bonn, where he also lectured on New Testament and church history; after 1827, at Göttingen, where he taught New Testament and systematic theology. Died February 14, 1854. Published commentaries on the Gospel and letters of John, on the Apocalypse and numerous exegetical and dogmatic works. See Sander, *PRE*, XI, pp. 674 ff.; E. H. Pältz, *RGG*, IV, col. 470.

Lüdemann, Hermann

Born September 15, 1842 in Kiel. In 1872, Privatdozent at Kiel; in 1884, Professor first in Historical, then in Systematic Theology in Berne. Died October 12, 1933. Wrote many works on systematics, including a comprehensive *Dogmatics* (1924-26). See M (ax) H (aller), *Totenschau zum Jahrgang 1934 des Schweizerischen Pfarrerkalendars* [Roll of the dead for the year 1934, calendar for Swiss pastors], pp. 23 ff. (Brought to my attention through the kindness of W. Michaelis.)

Luther, Martin

Born November 10, 1483 in Eisleben; died at the same place on February 18, 1546. In 1505, a monk in Erfurt; beginning in 1513, Professor at Wittenberg. Survey by H. Bornkamm and G. Ebeling, *RRG*, IV, cols. 480 ff.

Marcion

Son of the Bishop of Sinope in Asia Minor; by calling, a shipper. As early as his going to Rome, was rejected by the Christians on account of his repudiation of the Old Testament and his doctrine of the two godheads; about 144, in Rome, he was excluded from the Church and founded his own church, which endured for centuries. Died about 160. Survey by H. Kraft—G. Klein, *RGG*, IV, cols. 740 ff. Basic is A. von Harnack, *Marcion*, 2nd ed., 1924.

Meyer, Heinrich August Wilhelm

Born January 10, 1800 in Gotha. After theological study in Jena, was for a short time a teacher and then a pastor in churches in Thuringia and Hannover; after 1841, member of the Church governing Council in Hannover. Died June 13, 1873. Beginning in 1829, his commentary began to appear, of which he brought out the text and translation of the whole New Testament, and commentaries on the Gospels, Acts, the Letters from Romans to Philemon (up to 1847) and then new editions. See F. Düsterdieck, *PRE*, XIII, pp. 39 ff.; O. Michel, *RGG*, IV, col. 928.

Michaelis, Johann David

Born February 27, 1717 at Halle, son of the orientalist. Chr. Ben. Michaelis. After studies at Halle and a stay in England, became in 1745 a Privatdozent; in 1746, Professor of Oriental Languages at Göttingen. Died August 22, 1791. Published multivolume translations of the Old and New Testaments, a six-volume description of the "Mosaic Law" and numerous and archaeological works for the illumination of the Bible; also some dogmatic writings. See R. Kittel, *PRE*, XIII, pp. 54 ff.; E. Kutsch, *RGG*, IV, cols. 934-35; *J. D. Michaelis' . . . Lebensbeschreibung von ihm selbst abgefasst mit Anmerkungen von Hassenkamp*, Rinteln und Leipzig 1793 [J. D. Michaelis' autobiography with notes from Hassenkamp]; contains also obituaries, among them that by J. G. Eichhorn, and an index of Michaelis' Writings; Kraus, *Geschichte*, pp. 97 ff.

Mill, John

Born 1645 in Hardendale, Westmoreland. Studied at Oxford; occupied various Anglican pastoral positions; also active from time to time at Oxford. Died June 23, 1707. Took over from John Fell (1677/78), the Bishop of Oxford, the task of editing the Greek text of the New Testament, which first appeared shortly before his death. See C. R. Gregory, *PRE*, XIII, p. 73; A. Fox, *John Mill and Richard Bentley: A Study of the Textual Criticism of the New Testament 1675-1729*, 1954; on the historical place of Mill's edition of the New Testament, see G. W. Meyer, *Geschichte der Exegese* IV, 1805, pp. 161 ff., 295 ff.

Montefiore, Claude Joseph Goldsmid

Born June 6, 1858 in London. From 1895-1921, President of the Anglo-Jewish Association; after 1926, President of the World Association for Liberal Judaism. Died July 9, 1938 in London. Wrote a two-volume commentary on the Synoptic Gospels, and numerous other works on the Jewish understanding of Jesus and Paul, and liberal Judaism. From 1888-1918, editor of the *Jewish Quarterly Review*. See P. Goodman, *Universal Jewish Encyclopedia*, VII, 1942, cols. 642-43; H. Danby, *Dictionary of National Biography*, vol. for 1931-1940, 1949, 624-25; F. C. Burkitt, "C. Montefiore, an Appreciation," in *Speculum Religionis, Being Essays and Studies in Religion and Literature Presented to C. G. Montefiore, 1929*, with bibliography; L. H. Silberman, Prolegomena to the Reprint of Montefiore's *The Synoptic Gospels*, I, 1968, pp. 3 ff.; F. C. Schwartz, "Claude Montefiore on Law and Tradition," *Jewish Quarterly Review*, N. S., 55, 1964/65, pp. 23 ff.; N. Bentwich, *C. M. and His Tutor in Rabbinics*, 6th Montefiore Memorial Lecture, 1966.

Morgan, Thomas

Date and place of birth unknown (1680?). At first, preacher to a dissident congregation; then expelled because of his acknowledgment of his Arianism; then a Quaker physician in Bristol and a writer in London. Died January 17, 1743. The first volume of his work, *The Moral Philosopher*, appeared in 1737; volumes two and three appeared in 1739 and 1740, under the pseudonym "Philalethes" [Lover of truth], in London. The name of the author was first disclosed in 1741 in a polemical writing against Morgan. See L. Zscharnack, *RGG*, IV, 2nd ed., cols. 216-17; H. Hohlwein, *RGG*, IV, cols. 1135-36; G. W. Lechler, *Geschichte des englischen Deismus*, 1841, pp. 370 ff.; Hirsch, *Geschichte*, Vol. I, pp. 331 ff.

Origen

Born probably in 185 of Christian parents in Alexandria. At first was an elementary teacher and a theological writer; about 230/31, journeyed to Caesarea in Palestine, where he was ordained as priest. For this he was put out of the Church by his bishop in Alexandria; founded his own school in Caesarea. Died in Palestine, probably in connection with the torturing of martyrs about 254.

The first great theologian of the Church, a textual critic, an exegete, a dogmatician; because of his speculative theology and his rejection of the ultimate condemnation of the wicked, he was very soon attacked and in the sixth century was denounced as a heretic. Survey: F. H. Kettler, *RGG*, IV, cols. 1692 ff.; H. v. Campenhausen, in *The Fathers of the Greek Church*, 1959, pp. 40-56.

Otto, Rudolf

Born September 25, 1869 in Peine. Privatdozent in 1897; in 1904, Associate Professor of Systematic Theology at Göttingen; in 1914, Professor at Breslau; in 1917, at Marburg. Died March 6, 1937. Wrote many works on the history-of-religions and dogmatics. Chief work: *Das Heilige*, translated into English as *The Idea of the Holy*. See G. Wünsch, *RGG*, IV. cols. 1749-50; B. Thum, *LThK*, VII, col. 1309; H. Frick, Memorial address in *Rudolf-Otto-Gedächtnisfeier der Theologischehn Fakultät der Philipps-Universität*, 1938, pp. 11 ff.; bibliography in H. W. Schütte, *Religion und Christentum in der Theologie Rudolph Ottos*, 1969, pp. 142 ff.

Overbeck, Franz

Born November 16, 1837 in Petersburg. In 1864 Privatdozent in New Testament Exegesis at Jena; in 1870, Associate Professor of New Testament and Early Church History at Basel; in 1871, Professor there. Died June 26, 1905. Revised de Wette's commentary on Acts in dependence on the Tübingen School; wrote several essays on the early church and the history of the Canon. Studies in the Gospel of John appeared posthumously. See E. Vischer, *PRE*, XXIV, pp. 295 ff.; Ph. Vielhauer, *RGG*, IV, cols. 1750 ff.; W. Philipp, *EKL*, II, cols. 1785-86. W. Nigg, *Franz Overbeck*, 1931; *Selbstbekenntnisse* [Confessions], ed. E. Vischer, 1941; Ph. Vielhauer, "Franz Overbeck und die neutestamentliche Wissenschaft," *EvTh*, 10 (1950-51), 193 ff. (= Ph. Vielhauer, *Aufsätze zum N. T.*, 1965, pp. 235 ff.); H. Hermelink, *Das Christentum in der Menschheitsgeschichte von der französischen Revolution bis zur Gegenwart*, III, 1955, pp. 459 ff.

Paulus, Heinrich Eberhard Gottlob

Born September 1, 1761 in Leonberg. Attended the Stift at Tübingen; after period of student journeys and as assistant pastor, Professor of Oriental Languages at Jena in 1789; in 1793 Professor of Theology there; in 1803 Professor of Theology at Würzburg; after failure there, member of district and school councils in Bamberg, Nüremberg, and Ansbach; in 1811, Professor of Theology at Heidelberg. Died August 10, 1851. Wrote many Old Testament commentaries, in addition to his commentaries on the Gospels and his *Life of Jesus*. Edited Spinoza and Schelling. See P. Tschackert, *PRE*, XV, pp. 90 ff.; H. Hohlwein, *RGG*, V, col. 192.

Pfleiderer, Otto

Born September 1, 1839 in Stetten (Württemberg). After a period as assistant pastor, in 1864, Privatdozent in Tübingen; in 1868 pastor in Heilbronn; in 1870, supervising pastor in Jena; in 1871, Professor of Practical Theology in Jena; in 1875, Professor of Systematic Theology in Berlin. Died July 18, 1908. Chief works in the New Testament field are *Der Paulinismus* (1873) and *Das Urchristentum* (1887), translated as *Primitive Christianity* (1906) ; in the field of systematics, *Die Religion, ihr Wesen und ihre Geschichte* [Religion: its essence and its history], 1869. See R. Seeburg, *PRE* XXIV, pp. 316 ff.; E. Schott, *RGG*, V, cols. 312-13; Hirsch, *Geschichte*, Vol. V, pp. 562 ff.

Reimarus, Hermann Samuel

Born December 22, 1694 in Hamburg. In 1723, Rector in Wismar; in 1728, teacher of oriental languages at the gymnasium in Hamburg. Died March 1, 1768. In 1754, published *Die vornehmsten Wahrheiten der natürlichen Religion* [The most distinctive truths of natural religion] and other deistic and physico-theological works. *Apologie oder Schutzschrift für die vernünftigen Verehrer Gottes* [Apology or defensive writing in behalf of the reasonable worshipers of God] was kept from publication by Reimarus, and first appeared after his death when Lessing, with the family's knowledge, published seven sections as *Fragmente eines Ungenannten* [Fragments by an unknown author]. 1774-78. See H. Hohlwein, *RGG*, V, cols. 937 ff.; D. F. Strauss, *H. S. Reimarus und seine Schutzschrift für die vernünftigen Verehrer Gottes*, 1862 (reprinted in *Gessammelte Schriften* of D. F. Strauss, Vol. V, 1877, pp. 229 ff.) ; A. Schweitzer, *Quest*, pp. 13-14; A. Chr. Lundsteen, *H. S. Reimarus und die Anfänge der Leben-Jesu-Forschung*, 1939; Hirsch, *Geschichte*, Vol. IV, pp. 144 ff.; W. Philipp, *Das Werden der Aufklärung in theologiegeschichtlicher Sicht* [The genesis of the Enlightenment in theological-historical perspective], 1957, pp. 21, 33-34, 40, 109, 207-8.

Reischle, Max

Born June 18, 1858 in Vienna. After the customary Swabian theological training, became a tutorial assistant, Tübingen; a teacher of religion in Stuttgart (1888) ; in 1892, Professor of Practical Theology at Giessen; in 1895, Professor of Systematic Theology at Göttingen; in 1897, at Halle. Died December 11, 1905. Wrote extensively on philosophy of religion and dogmatics. Th. Häring, *PRE*, XX, pp. 384 ff.; Th. Häring and Max Loofs, in Max Reischle, *Aufsätze und Vorträge*, 1960, pp. vii ff.; with bibliography.

Reitzenstein, Richard

Born April 2, 1861 at Breslau. After the study of theology and classical philology and a long stay in Italy, became Privatdozent in Classical Philology at Breslau (1888) ; in 1889, Associate Professor in Rostock; in 1892, Professor at Giessen; in 1893, at Strassburg; in 1811, at Freiburg i. Br.; in 1914, at Göttin~~~ Died March 23, 1931. Published many works on Latin poets and the history of Hellenistic religions, especially on mysticism in late antiquity and its connections with Iranian mythology. See C. Colpe, *RGG*, V, col. 951; M. Pohlenz, *Nachrichten der Gesellschaft der Wissenschaften zu Göttingen, Geschäftliche Mitteilungen 1930/31*, pp. 66 ff.; bibliography in *Festschrift Richard Reitzenstein . . . dargebracht*, 1931, pp. 160 ff.

Reuss, Eduard

Born July 18, 1804 in Strassburg. In 1832, Privatdozent in the Protestant Seminar in Strassburg, and Professor of New Testament there in 1834; in 1838, also Professor in the Strassburg theological faculty; in 1864, Professor of Old Testament. Died April 15, 1891. In addition to his New Testament research, he was the first to champion a late date for Old Testament law; he did research on the printed text of the Greek New Testament and was coeditor of the great edition of Calvin. See P. Lobstein, *PRE*, XVI, pp. 691 ff.; G. Anrich, *ADB*, LV, cols. 579 ff.; E. Kutsch, *RGG*, V, col. 1076.

Ritschl, Albrecht Benjamin

Born March 25, 1822 in Berlin. After concluding his theological studies resided in Tübingen, where he was an adherent of the school of Baur, became a Privatdozent at Bonn in 1846; in 1852, Associate Professor of New Testament and Systematic Theology; in 1859, Professor at Bonn; in 1864, Professor of Systematic Theology at Göttingen. Died March 20, 1889. Chief work: *Die christliche Lehre von der Rechtfertigung und Versöhnung* [The Christian doctrine of justification and reconciliation], 1870-74.
See O. Ritschl, *PRE*, XVII, pp. 22 ff.; E. Schott, *RGG*, V, pp. 1114 ff.; H. Hermelink, *Das Christentum in der Menschheitsgeschichte von der französischen Revolution bis zur Gegenwart*, III, 1955, pp. 217 ff.

Rohde, Erwin

Born October 9, 1845 in Hamburg. In 1870, Privatdozent; in 1872, Associate Professor of Classical Philology at Kiel; in 1876, a Professor at Jena; in 1878, at Tübingen; in 1886, at Leipzig; finally, in Heidelberg. Died January 11, 1898. Besides *Psyche,* wrote on various aspects of classical philology, especially on the Greek romance; close friend of Nietzsche. See F. Scholl, *ADB*, LIII, pp. 426 ff.; M. Wegner, *Altertumskunde*, 1951, pp. 266 ff.

Rückert, Leopold Immanuel

Born February 1, 1797 in Grosshennersdorf near Herrnhut (Saxony). At first a prviate teacher; in 1819, a deacon in Grosshennersdof; in 1825, a teacher in the gymnasium in Zittau, where he wrote commentaries on the letters of Paul and edited Plato for use in schools. In 1844, Professor of Theology at Jena. Wrote several dogmatic works from the standpoint of critical rationalism. Died April 4, 1871. See G. Frank, *PRE*, XVII, pp. 186 ff.

Schlatter, Adolf

Born August 16, 1852 at St. Gallen. At first a pastor in the Thurgau; in 1880, Privatdozent in History of Dogma and New Testament; in 1888, Associate Professor of New Testament and Systematic Theology at Berne; in 1888, Professor of New Testament in Greifswald; in 1893, Professor of Systematic Theology in Berlin; after 1898, Professor of New Testament and Systematic Theology at Tübingen. Died June 19, 1938. See U. Luck, *RGG*, V, cols. 1420-21; H. Schlier, *LThK*, IX, col. 410; W. Tebbe, *EKL*, III, cols. 799 ff.; *Selbstdarstellung*, Vol. I, 1925, pp. 145 ff.; *A. Schlatters Rückblick auf seine Lebensarbeit* [Retrospect on his life's work], zu seinem hundertsten Geburtstag herausgegeben von Th. Schlatter, 1952; *Aus Adolf Schlatters Berner Zeit*, including W. Michaelis, "A. Schlatter und die evangelisch-theologische Fakultät in Bern," and W. Tebbe, "Der junge Schlatter"; K. H. Rengstorf, in Schultz, *Tendenzen*, pp. 56 ff.; G. Egg, *Adolf Schlatters kritische Position gezeigt an seiner Matthäusinterpretation*, 1968; U. Luck, introduction to Adolf Schlatter, *Zur Theologie des Neuen Testaments und zur Dogmatik*, Theol. Bücherei XLI, 1969, pp. 7 ff.; bibliography in R. Brezger, *Das Schrifttum von Prof. D. A. Schlatter*, 1938.

Schleiermacher, Friedrich Daniel Ernst

Born November 21, 1768 in Breslau. After education in the Pedagogium of the Brethren community in Niesky and the Brethren seminar in Barby, studied theology in Halle; in 1796, preacher in the Charité in Berlin; in 1802, court preacher in Stolp; in 1804, Associate Professor of Theology at Halle; after 1809 in Berlin, first as freelance scholar, then as preacher at the Trinity Church and beginning in 1810, as Professor of Theology in the newly founded University of Berlin, where he lectured in almost all the theological disciplines. Died February 12, 1834. In the field of New Testament, he published only the critical studies on I Timothy and the Synoptics; after his death, his lectures on New Testament introduction were edited and published on the basis of notes and rough drafts. See O. Kirn, *PRE*, XVII, pp. 587 ff.; R. Hermann, *RGG*, V, col. 1422 ff.; H. -G. Fritzsche, *EKL*, III, cols. 801 ff.; P. Meinhold, *LThK*, IX, cols. 413 ff.; Meinhold, Vol. II, pp. 134 ff.; on Schleiermacher as a New Testament scholar, see A. Hilgenfeld, *Der Kanon und die Kritik des Neuen Testaments* . . . 1863, pp. 147 ff.

Schmidt, Karl Ludwig
Born February 5, 1891 at Frankfurt a. M. In 1918, Privatdozent in New Testament in Berlin; in 1921, Professor at Giessen; in 1925, at Jena; 1929, at Bonn, where he was dismissed from his post in 1933. He entered the pastorate in Switzerland, and became Professor of New Testament at Basel in 1935. Died January 10, 1956. Wrote numerous works on form criticism, lexicography, and the theology of the New Testament. From 1922-37, edited *Theologische Blätter*, and from 1945-53, was chief editor of the *Theologische Zeitschrift*, published in Basel. See J. Schmid, *LThK*, IX, col. 434; O. Cullmann, *ThZ*, 12 (1956), 1 ff. (= Cullmann, *Vorträge und Aufsätze 1926-1962*, pp. 675 ff.); Ph. Veilhauer *150 Jahre Rheinische Friedrich-Wilhelms-Universität zu Bonn 1818-1968*, 1968, pp. 190 ff.

Schneckenburger, Matthias
Born January 17, 1804 in Thalheim near Tuttlingen. Passed through the customary study program of the Württemberg Theological Seminar and the Stift at Tübingen; tutorial assistant at Tübingen in 1827; in 1831, in the pastorate; after 1834, Professor of Systematic Theology at Berne. Died June 3, 1848. Lectured on church history, systematic theology, and New Testament. Wrote extensively on New Testament and systematics. See Hundeshagen, *PRE*, XVII, pp. 666 ff.; K. Scholder, *RGG*, V, col. 1464.

Schniewind, Julius
Born May 28, 1883 in Elberfeld. In 1914, a Privatdozent in New Testament; in 1921, Associate Professor at Halle; in 1927, Professor at Greifswald; in 1929, at Königsberg; transferred to Kiel in 1935, and in 1936, to Halle, where he was dismissed in 1937. Restored to academic office in 1945, at the same time Ecclesiastical Provost at Halle and Merseburg. Died September 7, 1948. Wrote many works and commentaries on the Synoptic Gospels and on New Testament theology. See G. Delling, *RGG*, V, col. 1467-68; E. Schweizer, *EKL*, III, col. 821; H. W. Bartsch, *Monatsschrift für Pastoraltheologie*, 38, 1948/49, pp. 59 ff.; O. Michel, *EvTh*, 8 (1948/49), 337 ff.; H. J. Kraus in Schultz, *Tendenzen*, pp. 219 ff., and in *Julius Schniewind. Charisma der Theologie*, 1965, with bibliography.

Schürer, Emil
Born May 2, 1844 in Augsburg. In 1869, Privatdozent in New Testament at Leipzig; in 1879, Professor at Giessen; in 1890, at Kiel; in 1895, at Göttingen.

Died April 30, 1910. In addition to his *Geschichte des jüdischen Volkes* (4th ed. in 3 vols., 1901/09; Eng. tr. of the 2nd ed., London, 1891), founded and with a brief interruption edited the *Theologische Literaturzeitung*. See A. Titius, *PRE*, XXIV, pp. 460 ff; E. Bammel, *RGG*, V. col. 1550, and "Emil Schürer, der Begründer der Wissenschaft vom Spätjudentum" [Schürer, the founder of the scholarly study of late Judaism], *Deutsches Pfarrerblatt*, 60 (1960), 225-26.

Schwegler, Friedrich Karl Albert

Born February 10, 1819 in Michelbach near Schwäbisch-Hall. Went through the preparatory seminary and Stift in Tübingen. After a student tour, became Privatdozent in Philosophy and Philology at Tübingen. Since he was denied a post as tutorial assistant on the basis of his work on Montanism and a history of postapostolic times in two volumes (1846), he shifted to Roman history; in 1848, Associate Professor of Roman Literature at Tübingen. Died January 6, 1857. Wrote a history of philosophy and an uncompleted Roman history in 3 volumes. See W. Teuffel, *ADB*, XXXIII, pp. 327-28; I. Ludolphy, *RGG*, V, col. 1605; E. Zeller, *Vorträge und Abhandlungen* II, 1877, pp. 329 ff.

Schweitzer, Albert

Born January 14, 1875 at Kaysersberg (Alsace). After a term as assistant pastor in Strassburg, became a Privatdozent in New Testament and Director of the Thomasstift in Strassburg; at the same time studied medicine, was active as an organist, wrote on the philosophy of Kant and the music of J. S. Bach. Beginning in 1913, with some interruptions, he was a missionary doctor in Lambaréné (West Africa); during this time he wrote on the philosophy of culture, on the history of religions, and *Die Mystik des Apostels Paulus* (1930; Eng. tr. by W. Montgomery, *The Mysticism of Paul the Apostle*, New York, 1931). Died September 4, 1965 at Lambaréné. See R. Grabs, *RGG*, V, col. 1607-8; K. Stürmer, *EKL*, III, cols. 881 ff.; A. Schweitzer, *Selbstdarstellung* [Self-portrait], 1929, and *Aus meinem Leben und Denken* [Out of my life and thought], 1930 (Eng. tr., New York, 1933); W. Bremi, in Schultz: *Tendenzen*, pp. 145 ff.; *Albert Schweitzer, Sein Denken und Weg*, ed. H. W. Bähr, 1962; Neill, *Interpretation*, pp. 191 ff.; W. G. Kümmel and C.-H. Ratschow, *Albert Schweitzer als Theologe*, 1966.

Semler, Johann Salomo

Born December 18, 1725 at Saalfeld. Studied at Halle; was for a short time a teacher at the gymnasium in Coburg and Professor of History and Latin Poetry at Altdorf; then from 1752 until the end of his life, he was Professor of Theology at Halle. Lectured and published numerous works in all areas of theology. He was the actual father of the new critical theology, the "Neology," but without being consistent. At the end of his life he defended the religious edict of Wöllner in 1788, but he did not surrender his own free-thinking convictions. See C. Mirbt, *PRE*, XVIII, pp. 203 ff.; H. Hohlwein, *RGG*, V, cols. 1696-97; W. Philipp, *EKL*, III, cols. 933 ff.; J. G. Eichhorn, *Allgemeine Bibliothek der biblischen Literatur* V, 1793, pp. 1-202 (critical obituary with index of writings); P. Gastrow, *J. S. Semler in seiner Bedeutung für die Theologie mit besonderer Berücksichtigung seines Streites mit G. E. Lessing* [Semler in his significance for theology, with special consideration of his conflict with Lessing], 1905; G. Karo, H. Hoffmann, *Die Theologie Semlers*, 1905; L. Zscharnack, *Lessing und Semler*, 1905; Hirsch, *Geschichte*, Vol. IV, pp. 48-49; H. J. Kraus, *Geschichte der his-*

torisch-kritischen Erforschung des Alten Testaments, 2nd ed., 1969, 103 ff.; G. Hornig, *Die Anfänge der historisch-kritischen Theologie. J. S. Semler's Schriftverständnis und seine Stellung zu Luther* [The beginnings of historical-critical theology: Semler's understanding of Scripture and his position in relation to Luther], 1961; Meinhold, Vol. II, pp. 39 ff.

Simon, Richard

Born May 13, 1638 in Dieppe. Entered an oratory and became a priest. When he published his *Critical History of the Old Testament* in 1678, the book was proscribed by Bossuet, and Simon was expelled from the order. He lived thereafter in various places, for a long time in Paris. Died in Dieppe April 11, 1712. In addition to his four critical histories of the Old and New Testaments, he wrote a new French translation of the New Testament and works on church history and lore, as well as numerous polemical writings. See E. Reuss and Eb. Nestle, *PRE*, XVIII, pp. 361 ff.; P. Auvray, *LThK*, IX, cols. 773-74; H. Margival, "R. Simon et la critique biblique au XVIII° siècle: 10. Les travaux de R. Simon sur le Nouveau Testament," *Revue d'histoire et de littérature religieuses*, 4, 1899, pp. 193 ff.; J. Steinmann, *R. Simon et les origines de l'exégèse biblique*, 1960; Kraus, *Geschichte*, pp. 65 ff.

Soden, Hans Freiherr von

Born November 4, 1881 in Dresden. In 1910, Privatdozent in Church History at Berlin; 1918, Associate Professor at Breslau, in 1924, Professor of Early Church History and New Testament at Marburg; after 1933, leader of the Confessing Church in Kurhesse-Waldeck. Died October 2, 1945. Wrote works on textual criticism, on New Testament theology, and on church order, especially essays, which have been collected under the title *Urchristentum und Geschichte*, Vols. I and II, 1951 and 1956. See E. Dinkler, *RGG*, VI, col. 114; R. Bultmann, Foreword to *Urchristentum und Geschichte* I, 1951, pp. v ff.; H. v. Campenhausen, *Kirche in der Zeit*, 11 (1956), 233-34.

Sohm, Rudolph

Born October 29, 1841 in Rostock. In 1866, Privatdozent for law; in 1870, Professor at Göttingen and then in Freiburg; in Strassburg (1872) and Leipzig (1887). Died May 16, 1917. In addition to his works on church law, wrote important studies on the history of German and Roman law. See Grundmann, *RGG*, VI, cols. 116-17; D. Stoodt, *EKL*, III, cols. 990 ff.; *R. Sohms Kritik des Kirchenrechts zur 100sten Wiederkehr seines Geburtstages am 29. Oktober 1941* untersucht von E. Foerster, 1942; H. Fehr, *Zeitschrift der Savigny-Stiftung für Rechtsgeschichte*, germanistische Abteilung 38 (1917), 59 ff.; Meinhold, Vol. II, pp. 288 ff.; A. Bühler, *Kirche und Staat bei Rudolph Sohm* (Basler Studien z. hist. u. syst. Theologie VI), 1965.

Stäudlin, Carl Friedrich

Born July 25, 1761 in Stuttgart. Attended the Tübingen Stift. Was a private teacher and traveled for a few years; in 1790, Professor of Theology at Göttingen. Died July 5, 1826. Lectured and wrote on all the theological areas; represented a rational belief in revelation. See E. H. Pältz, *RGG*, VI, cols. 326-27; H. Doering, *Die gelehrte Theologie Deutschlands im 18. und 19. Jahrhundert* IV, 1835, pp. 287 ff.; Wagenmann, *PRE*, XVIII, pp. 741 ff.

Storr, Gottlob Christian

Born September 10, 1746 in Stuttgart. After service in the Church and scholarly journeys to other lands, in 1775, Professor of Philosophy at Tübingen; in 1777, Professor of Theology there; in 1797, court preacher in Stuttgart. Died January 17, 1805. Founder of the biblical supernaturalism of the older Tübingen School. Author of a dogmatics introduced with state support. See M. A. Landerer, *PRE*, XX, pp. 149 ff.; G. Hornig, *RGG*, VI, col. 391.

Strauss, David Friedrich

Born January 27, 1808 in Ludwigsburg. After the usual philosophical and theological education in the seminar at Blaubeuren and the Tübingen Stift—in both places his teacher was F. C. Baur—he became an assistant pastor and then a teacher in Maulbronn; during a long stay in Berlin (1831-32), he became acquainted with Schleiermacher's lectures on the life of Jesus; from 1832-35, tutorial assistant at the Stift in Tübingen, where he lectured on philosophy, interpreting Hegel in a monistic sense, and worked out his *Life of Jesus*, which appeared in 1835-36. But before the second volume appeared he was transferred to the post of professorial deputy at Ludwigsburg and then moved to Stuttgart, where he published his *Streitschriften zur Verteidigung meiner Schrift über das Leben Jesu und zur Charakteristik der gegenwärtigen Theologie* [Controversy-writings in defense of my book on the life of Jesus and on the characteristics of present-day theology], 1837; in 1839, called to Zürich as Professor of Theology, but as a result of the opposition of the conservative Christians there, Strauss was placed on pension before he was inaugurated as Professor; from then on, he lived as a freelance writer in Stuttgart, Heilbronn, Darmstadt, and Ludwigsburg, where he died on February 8, 1874. Other major works: *Die christliche Glaubenslehre* [Christian doctrine], 1840-41; *Ulrich von Hutten*, 1858; *Leben Jesu für das deutsche Volk* [Life of Jesus for the German people], 1861; *Der alte und der neue Glaube*, 1872. See Th. Ziegler, *PRE*, XIX, pp. 76 ff.; E. Schott, *RGG*, VI, cols. 416-17; F. Mussner, *LThK*, IX, cols. 1108-09; A. Schweitzer, *Quest*, pp. 68-120; Th. Ziegler, *D. F. Strauss*, 2 vols., 1908; *Die Universität Zürich 1833-1933 und ihre Vorläufer*, 1938, pp. 380 ff.; K. Barth, *Protestant Thought from Rousseau to Ritschl*, 1959, pp. 362-89; Hirsch, *Geschichte*, Vol. V, pp. 492 ff.; G. Müller, *Identität und Immanenz. Zur Genese der Theologie von D. F. Strauss*, 1968.

Streeter, Burnet Hillman

Born November 17, 1874 in Croydon. In 1899, Dean of Pembroke College; in 1905, Fellow of Queen's College in Oxford. Died September 10, 1937. Major work, *The Four Gospels;* also *The Primitive Church* (1929), and numerous works intended for educated laymen to assist their understanding of Christianity. See J. Schmid, *LThK*, IX, cols. 1110-11; J. C. Hardwick, *Expository Times*, 49 (1937/38), 249 ff.; L. W. Grensted, *Dictionary of National Biography (1931-1940)*, 1949, pp. 836 ff.

Tindal, Matthew

Born 1657 in Beer-Ferris (Devonshire). Jurist; at the age of 22 Fellow of All Souls in Oxford; later Senior Fellow of this college and then Senior of the entire university. For a long time a Catholic, then an adherent of the liberal, antichurch politics. At the age of seventy-three, he published anonymously his major work, *Christianity as Old as the Creation*. Died August 16, 1733. See

M. Schmidt, *RGG*, VI, col. 904; G. V. Lechler, *Geschichte des englischen Deismus*, 1841, pp. 326-27; Hirsch, *Geschichte*, Vol. I, pp. 325 ff.

Tischendorf, Constantin

Born January 18, 1815 at Lengenfeld in Vogtland (Saxony). In 1839, a Privatdozent; in 1845, Associate Professor; in 1859, Professor of Theology at Leipzig. Over many years, went on scholarly journeys. Died December 7, 1874. Published many manuscripts and manuscript fragments, about twenty-four editions of the Greek New Testament, and many editions of the Greek Old Testament, of the Apocrypha, etc. See C. Bertheau, *PRE*, XIX, pp. 788 ff.; W. Schrage, *RGG*, VI, cols. 904-5; K. Junack, "Constantin Tischendorf in seiner Bedeutung für die neutestamentliche Textkritik," *Das Altertum*, 2 (1956), 48 ff.; bibliography in Tischendorf, *Novum Testamentum Graece III, Prolegomena scripsit*, C. R. Gregory, 1884, pp. 7 ff.

Toland, John

Born September 9, 1670 at Redcastle (Ireland). Converted to Protestantism and studied in England and Holland; in 1696 appeared his best-known work, *Christianity not Mysterious*, which in Ireland was publicly burned. From then on, his life was filled with polemics and defense, as well as with journeys and further deistic publications and political activity. Died March 11, 1722 in London. See L. Zscharnack, *RGG*, V, 2nd ed., cols. 1210-11; M. Schmidt, *RGG*, VI, col. 931; G. V. Lechler, *Geschichte des englischen Deismus*, 1841, pp. 180 ff.; Hirsch, *Geschichte*, Vol. I, pp. 295 ff.

Turretini, Jean Alphonse

Born 1671 at Geneva. Studied there and in Holland. In 1693, a pastor; in 1697, Professor of Church History at Geneva. Died May 1, 1737. Led the battle against the compulsory confession and for a union between the Lutherans and the Reformed. See R. Pfister, *RGG*, VI, cols. 1089-90; E. Choisy, *PRE*, XX, pp. 166 ff.; P. Wernle, *Der schweizerische Protestantismus im 18. Jahrhundert I*, 1923, pp. 494 ff.; P.-F. Geisendorf, *L'Université de Genève 1559-1959*, 1959, pp. 137 ff.

Usener, Hermann

Born October 23, 1834 in Weilburg. After a short period as a gymnasium teacher, became Associate Professor of Classical Philology in Berne (1861); Professor at Greifswald (1863); in 1866, at Bonn. Died October 21, 1905. Represented a strongly historical approach to philology, and was a leading scholar in the field of comparative religions and the history of the early church. See A. Dieterich, *Archiv f. Religionswissenschaft*, 8 (1905), pp. i ff.; L. Deubner, *Biographisches Jahrbuch für die Altertumswissenschaft*, 31 (1908), pp. 53 ff.; M. Wegner, *Altertumskunde*, 1951, pp. 254 ff.

Usteri, Leonhard

Born October 22, 1799 in Zürich. Studied there and in Berlin; from 1823 on, gave private lectures on the Pauline letters in Zürich, out of which grew his presentation of Pauline doctrine; in 1824, Professor and Director of the gymnasium in Berne. Died September 18, 1833. Writings include editions of classical texts and New Testament treatises—among others, a defense of the genuineness of the Gospel of John. See Güder, *PRE*, XX, pp. 368 ff.

Valla, Laurentius

Born 1407 in Rome, Italian humanist. As a result of his attacks on Christian ethics and church Latin, spent long years of traveling about; then was in the service of King Alfonso V of Aragon, under whose protection he challenged the genuineness of the "Donations of Constantine" and exercised critical judgments on the trustworthiness of the text of the Latin Vulgate; after 1447, was a writer under papal patronage in Rome. Died 1457. His comparison of the Vulgate with the original Greek text of the New Testament, written in 1444, was first edited and published by Erasmus in 1505, with the title, *In latinam Novi Testamenti interpretationem ex collatione graecorum exemplarium adnotationes.* See J. Wagenmann, *PRE*, XX, pp. 422 ff.; J. Leuschner, *RGG*, VI, cols. 1227-28; F. Zoepfl, *LThK*, X, cols. 606-7.

Vogel, Erhard Friedrich

Born November 17, 1750 in Bayreuth. Pastor in Rehau and Arzberg; after 1803, superintendent at Wunsiedel (Franconia). Died May 2, 1823. Wrote numerous treatises of various kinds. Although his work, *Der Evangelist Johannes und seine Ausleger vor dem jüngsten Gericht* [John the Evangelist and his interpreters before the Last Judgment], appeared anonymously in 1801, by 1803 its authorship was already known: J. G. Meusel, *Das gelehrte Teutschland* X (1803), 773. See M. Simon, *Bayreuthisches Pfarrerbuch*, 1930, p. 347 (this reference through the kindness of the City Library of Bayreuth).

Weinel, Heinrich

Born April 29, 1874 in Vonhausen (Hesse). In 1899, Privatdozent in New Testament at Berlin; in 1900, at Bonn; in 1904, Associate Professor and in 1907, Professor of New Testament at Jena, where he took over the Chair of Systematics in 1925. Died September 29, 1936. Wrote voluminously on the history and theology of primitive Christianity from the history-of-religions standpoint, on present-day questions, and other matters of a general nature. See A. Meyer, *RGG*, V, 2nd ed., col. 1798.

Weiss, Bernhard

Born June 20, 1827 in Königsberg. In 1852, Privatdozent; in 1897, Associate Professor of New Testament in Königsberg; in 1863, Professor at Kiel; after 1876, at Berlin, where he died on Jan. 14, 1918. Besides his textbooks on New Testament introduction and theology, he wrote many volumes of the new editions of the Meyer Commentary and individual works on literary and text-critical matters. See H. O. Metzger, *RGG*, VI, col. 1582; Bibliography and biography in W. Scheffen, ed. *Zum Gedächtnis von D. Dr. B. Weiss* [Memorial for B. Weiss], 1918; A. Deissmann, *Theol. Blätter*, 6 (1927), cols. 241 ff.

Weiss, Johannes

Son of Bernhard Weiss, born December 13, 1863 in Kiel. In 1888, Privatdozent in New Testament; in 1890, Associate Professor at Göttingen; in 1895, Professor at Marburg; in 1908, at Heidelberg. Died August 24, 1914. Wrote many commentaries and studies over the whole range of New Testament, concluding with *Das Urchristentum*, 1917 (incomplete). See J. Schmid, *LThK*, X, cols. 1007-8; F. C. Burkitt, "Johannes Weiss: in memoriam" *HTR*, 8 (1915), 291 ff.; R. Bultmann, "Johannes Weiss zum Gedächtnis," *Theol. Blätter*, 18 (1939), 242 ff.

Weisse, Christian Hermann

Born August 10, 1801 in Leipzig. In 1823, Privatdozent in Philosophy; from 1828-37, Associate Professor in Leipzig; after an interruption, again a Privatdozent (1841) ; Associate (1844) and Professor of Philosophy (1845) at Leipzig; after 1852, he also lectured in the theologcial faculty. Died September 19, 1866. As representative of late idealism, he wrote extensively in Philosophy and theology. See L. B. Puntel, *LThK*, X, col. 1010; Heinze, *ADB*, XLI, pp. 590 ff.; K. Leese, *Philosophie und Theologie im Spätidealismus*, 1929, pp. 10 ff.

Weizsäcker, Carl

Born December 11, 1822 in Öhringen, Württemberg. Attended preparatory seminar and the Stift at Tübingen; in 1847, Privatdozent at Tübingen; after some years as pastor in Billingbach and Stuttgart; in 1861 became F. C. Baur's successor as Professor of Church History at Tübingen; after 1890, Chancellor of the university. Died August 13, 1899. Major works are *Das Apostolische Zeitalter* [The apostolic age], *Untersuchungen über die evangelische Geschichte* [Studies in gospel history], 1864, and his translation of the New Testament, which began to appear in 1875. Also, he wrote many essays and articles on church history and dogmatics for reference works. See H. J. Holtzmann, *PRE*, XXI, pp. 76 ff.; A. Jülicher, *ADB*, LX, pp. 27 ff.; H. -O. Metzger, *RGG*, VI, col. 1593.

Wellhausen, Julius

Born May 17, 1844 in Hameln. After his theological study, became first a private teacher; then began study of oriental languages and the history of Israel under the Old Testament scholar H. Ewald, one of the "Göttingen Seven"; in 1872, Professor of Old Testament at Greifswald where on account of the controversy which arose through his publication of his History of Israel, he resigned in 1882, as a theological professor and went to Halle as Associate Professor of Semitic languages; in 1885, Professor of Semitic languages at Marburg; at Göttingen in 1892. Died January 7, 1918. His work was epoch-making as an Old Testament source critic, and as student of the history and religion of Israel, of Arabic paganism, and of Islam. In the field of New Testament, he published commentaries in the Gospels, his *Einleitung in die drei ersten Evangelien*, his analyses of the Fourth Gospel, of Acts, and of the Revelation of John. See O. Eissfeldt, *RGG*, VI, col. 1594 ff.; C. v. Gablenz, *EKL*, III, cols. 1775-76; E. Schwartz, *Nachrichten der Königlichen Gesellschaft der Wissenschaften zu Göttingen, Geschäftliche Mitteilungen* 1918, pp. 43 ff.; Kraus, *Geschichte*, pp. 255 ff.; L. Perlitt in Schultz, *Tendenzen*, pp. 32 ff.; R. Smend, Foreword to J. Wellhausen, *Grundrisse zum Alten Testament* [Outlines of the Old Testament], Bücherei XXVII, 1965, pp. 5 ff.; bibliography in *Studien zur semitischen Philologie und Religionsgeschichte*, Festschrift on Wellhausen's Seventieth Birthday, 1914, pp. 353 ff.

Wendland, Paul

Born August 17, 1864 son of a pastor in Hohestein (East Prussia) . After his period of study of classical philology and theology, became a gymnasium teacher in Berlin; while there, coeditor of the critical edition of Philo (with Cohn) ; in 1902, Professor of Classical Philology at Kiel; in 1906, at Breslau; in 1909, at Göttingen. Died September 10, 1915. Published extensively on the cultural history of Hellenism and on Philo research. See M. Pohlenz, *Neue Jahrbücher für das klassische Altertum*, 19 (1916), 57 ff.

Wernle, Paul

Born May 1, 1872 in Zürich. During his theological study at Göttingen was influenced by the founders of the history-of-religions school, without being wholly tied to that view. In 1897, a Privatdozent in New Testament at Basel; in 1900, became Associate Professor of Church History and the History of Dogma at Basel. Died after years of severe illness on April 10, 1939. Up until 1904, he wrote several New Testament works: *Der Christ und die Sünde bei Paulus* [The Christian and sin according to Paul], *Die synoptische Frage* [The synoptic question], *Die Anfänge unserer Religion* [The beginnings of our religion], and in 1916, he published *Jesus.* Later he published many works on the history of the Church and of dogma (*Glaube der Reformatoren* [The faith of the Reformers], *Der schweizerische Protestantismus im 18. Jahrhundert*, *Einführung ins theologische Studium*, etc.). See P. W. Scheele, *LThK*, X, col. 1057; *Selbstdarstellungen*, Vol. V, 1929, pp. 207 ff.

Westcott, Brooke Foss

Born January 12, 1825 in Birmingham. In 1852, taught preparatory school at Harrow; in 1868, Canon of Peterborough; in 1870, Professor of Theology at Cambridge; in 1884, Canon of Westminster; in 1890, succeeded J. B. Lightfoot as Bishop of Durham. Died January 27, 1901. Published many commentaries, and books on the Gospels, on the history of the Canon, and on dogmatics; from 1853 until 1881, he worked with Hort on their edition of the Greek New Testament, which appeared in the latter year. See C. R. Gregory, *PRE*, XXI, pp. 152 ff.; *ODCC*, cols. 1448-49; C. K. Barrett, *Westcott as Commentator*, 1959; Neill, *Interpretation*, pp. 91 ff.

Wettstein, Johann Jakob

Born March 5, 1693 in Basel. Studied philosophy and theology there; while on a student tour and as preacher to a Swiss regiment in England and Holland (1714-17) he studied many manuscripts of the New Testament; beginning in 1717, an Assistant Pastor in Basel, during which time he prepared his edition of the New Testament; in 1730, he was dismissed in connection with a struggle against the church's confession; from then on, he was in Amsterdam as Professor in the College of the Remonstrants. After forty years of preparation, his edition of the New Testament appeared in 1750/51. Died March 9, 1754. See E. Bertheau, *PRE*, XXI, pp. 198 ff.; O. Riecker, *EKL*, III, col. 1800; H. -O. Metzger, *RGG*, VI, col. 1671; P. Wernle, *Der schweizerische Protestantismus im 18. Jh.*, Vol. I, 1923, pp. 525-26; C. L. Hulbert-Powell, *John James Wettstein. 1693-1754. An Account of his Life, Work and some of his Contemporaries*, 1938, with bibliography.

Wilke, Christian Gottlob

Born May 13, 1786 in Badrina near Delitzsch (Saxony). At first, a military chaplain; then in 1821, a pastor at Hermannsdorf in the Erz Mountains; after his dismissal, he lived in Dresden (1837) as a freelance writer; in 1846, he converted to the Roman Church, and then moved to Würzburg. Died on November 11, 1854. Besides his work on the Gospels, he published a frequently reprinted New Testament dictionary and studies of New Testament rhetoric and hermeneutics. See Lauchert, *ADB*, XLIII, pp. 235-36; J. Schmid, *LThK*, X, col. 1158; H. Mulert, "Zur Lebensgeschichte Chr. G. Wilkes," *ThStKr*, 90 (1917), 198 ff.

Windisch, Hans

Born April 25, 1881 in Leipzig. In 1908, Privatdozent in New Testament at Leipzig; in 1914, Professor at Leiden; in 1929, at Kiel; in 1935, at Halle. Died November 8, 1935. Wrote extensively on interpretation, history-of-religions, and the history of dogma in relation to the New Testament and the primitive church. See J. Schmid, *LThK*, X, col. 1179; G. Delling, *ThLZ*, 81 (1956), 499 (col. 500 ff. for bibliography); E. Beijer, "H. Windisch und seine Bedeutung für die neutestamentliche Wissenschaft" [Windisch's importance for New Testament scholarship], *ZNW* 48 (1957), 22 ff.; K. Prümm, "Zur Früh- und Spätform der religionsgeschichtlichen Christusdeutung von H. Windisch" [On the early and late forms of the "history-of-religion" mode of interpretation of Christ in the thought of Windisch], *Biblica*, 42 (1961), 391 ff.; 43 (1962), 22 ff.

Wrede, William

Born May 10, 1859 in Bücken (Hannover). After being occupied as teacher and inspector in the theological Stift at Göttingen, became a pastor (1887); in 1891, Privatdozent in New Testament at Göttingen; in 1893, an Associate Professor in Breslau; in 1895, Professor. Died November 23, 1906. Major publications, *Das Messiasgeheimnis in den Evangelien* and *Paulus*; in addition, shorter works on Thessalonians, Hebrews, and the Gospel of John. See A. Jülicher, *PRE*, XXI, pp. 506 ff.; J. Schmid, *LThK*, X, col. 1244; A, Wrede, in W. Wrede, *Vorträge und Studien*, 1907, pp. iii ff.; W. Bousset, Foreword to the second Edition of *Paulus*, 1907, 3 ff.; G. Strecker, "William Wrede," *ZThK*, 57 (1960), 67 ff., with bibliography.

Zachariae, Gotthilf Traugott

Born November 17, 1729 at Tauchardt (Thuringia). In 1775, Rector of the *Ratsschule* in Stettin; in 1760, Professor of Theology at Bützow (Mecklenburg); in 1765, at Göttingen; in 1775, at Kiel. Died February 8, 1777. Besides his *Biblical Theology*, he wrote only paraphrases of biblical books and some essays. See H. Hoffmann, *PRE*, XXI, pp. 587 ff.

Zahn, Theodor

Born October 10, 1838 in Moers (Rheinland). In 1861, a teacher in the gymnasium in Neustrelitz; in 1865, tutorial assistant; in 1871, Associate Professor of New Testament at Göttingen; in 1877, Professor at Kiel; in 1878, at Erlangen; in 1888, at Leipzig; from 1892 on, once more in Erlangen. Died March 15, 1933. Wrote an introduction to the New Testament (1897-/99, 3rd ed. 1905), nine volumes of commentary series of which he was editor, and numerous works on the history of the ancient church and the Canon. See A. Meyer, *RGG*, V, 2nd ed., cols. 2070-71; H. -O. Metzger, *RGG*, VI, col. 1865; *Selbstdarstellungen*, Vol. I, 1925, pp. 221 ff., with bibliography.

Zeller, Eduard

Born January 22, 1914 at Kleinbottwar near Marbach (Württemberg). Attended the seminar in Maulbronn, where D. F. Strauss was for a few years his teacher, and the Tübingen Stift, where he studied especially with F. C. Baur. After a short period as an assistant pastor and as a schoolteacher, he became

(1839) a tutorial assistant, a Privatdozent (1840) in Theology at Tübingen. In 1847, Professor of Theology at Berne; 1849, he was called to the theological faculty at Marburg, but at the instigation of Vilmar, was installed in the philosophical faculty. In 1862, Professor of Philosophy at Heidelberg; in 1872, at Berlin. Died September 13, 1908 in Stuttgart. Famous as historian of Greek philosophy. See G. Patzig, *RGG*, VI, 1892; Th. Ziegler, *Biographisches Jahrbuch und deutscher Nekrolog*, XIII, 1910, pp. 47 ff.

Zwingli, Huldrych
Born January 1, 1484 in Wildhaus (Toggenburg). In 1506, priest in Glarus; in 1516, at Einsiedeln; beginning in 1519, chief priest at the cathedral in Zürich; reformer of the church in Zürich. Killed as a military chaplain on the battlefield near Kappel, October 11, 1531. Survey: F. Blanke and G. W. Locher, *RGG*, VI, cols. 1952 ff.

Index of Names

Index of Subjects

505